EDUCATING THE CONSUMER-CITIZEN

A History of the Marriage of Schools, Advertising, and Media

Sociocultural, Political, and Historical Studies in Education
Joel Spring, Editor

EDUCATING THE CONSUMER-CITIZEN

A History of the Marriage of Schools, Advertising, and Media

Joel Spring
New School University

LEA LAWRENCE ERLBAUM ASSOCIATES, PUBLISHERS
2003   Mahwah, New Jersey   London

Lawrence Erlbaum Associates, Inc., Publishers
10 Industrial Avenue
Mahwah, New Jersey 07430

Cover design by Kathryn Houghtaling Lacey

Library of Congress Cataloging-in-Publication Data

Spring, Joel H.
 Educating the consumer-citizen : a history of the marriage of schools, advertising,
and media /   Joel Spring
   p.   cm. — (Sociocultural, political, and historical studies in education)
 ISBN 0-8058-4273-X (c : alk. paper) — ISBN 0-8058-4274-8 (pbk. : alk. paper)
  1. Consumer behavior—United States—History. 2. Consumer education—United
States—History. 5. Advertising—United States—History. 4. Mass media—United
States—History. I. Title. II. Series.

HF5415.33.U6 S67   2002
306.3—dc21   2002192790
                                                                  CIP

Books published by Lawrence Erlbaum Associates are printed on acid-free paper,
and their bindings are chosen for strength and durability.

Printed in the United States of America
10 9 8 7 6 5 4 3 2 1

Contents

Preface

Consumerism is the dominant American ideology of the 21st century. "Shop 'til you drop" is the clarion call of our age. The triumph of consumerism was made possible by the related actions of schools, advertising, and media. This book illustrates the history of that joint endeavor to create a consumerist ideology and ensure its central place in American life. Like any history, this story is not a straight line from one time period to another. There was no master plan or conspiracy. However, through the twists, turns, and contradictions of life, consumerism now rules the American economic system and society.

I begin this history in chapter 1 by defining *consumerist ideology* and *consumer-citizen* and discussing their 19th-century origins in schools, children's literature, commercialization of American cities, advertising, newspapers, and development of department stores. In chapter 2, I examine the development of the home economics profession and its impact on the education of women as consumers and the creation of an American cuisine typified by Jell-O and Wonder Bread in home economics courses, school cafeterias, hospitals, and the food industry. The new professions of advertising and home economics created public images of the new woman as a consumer. In chapter 3, I discuss the crisis in White male identity in the late 19th and early 20th centuries and its resolution in male identification with professional sports, high school sports, cowboy images, and advertising images of the clean-shaven businessman. In this chapter, I also trace how a teenage consumer market was created when the high school became a mass institution and attempted to control male sexuality through sports, sex education courses, and ritualized dating practices.

Inherent in consumerist ideology is the dictate that commercial leisure, such as movies, radio, and TV, should spur people to consume more, work harder, and live moral lives. In chapter 4, I explore the interrelationship and conflicts that arose between educators and movie executives with the simultaneous growth of the movie industry and the high school in the early 20th century. Movies competed with school instruction and contributed to the sexual revolution among youth as movie houses became centers of ritualized teenage dating and movie stars provided lavish consumer images. By the 1930s, this tension was complicated when radio revolutionized consumerism by integrating advertising and entertainment. In the 1930s, educators worried that commercial radio would decrease their control over national culture, use advertising to manipulate student minds, and teach violence.

An important advance in consumerist ideology was the attempt to create a spontaneous association in the public mind among consumption, democracy, free enterprise, and Americanism. In chapter 5, I discuss the effort by business groups, patriotic organizations, advertisers, and educators to create these associations through public relations methods, censorship of textbooks and comic books, and the purging of so-called *radical teachers*. In the 1950s, schools, TV, and the advertising profession played leading roles in creating an image of the ideal American home and housewife based on the consumption of endless new products. This consumer image became central to America's anticommunist ideology of the 1950s.

The consumer image of the early 1950s was primarily of White Americans. In chapter 6, I discuss how the civil rights movement endeavored to integrate previously excluded groups into the consumer society. Targeting textbooks, school curricula, media, and advertising companies, civil rights groups attempted to erase negative images of cultural minorities and replace them with positive images. The result was the racial integration of the consumer market. Also women's groups demanded image changes in textbooks, school curricula, media, and advertising. The result was a changed image of women in the consumer market. In the 1960s, *Sesame Street* revolutionized children's TV by combining education and entertainment with efforts to teach racial tolerance and prepare children for school. *Sesame Street* also taught consumerism to preschool children by marketing product spinoffs in the form of dolls, games, videos, and books. *Sesame Street* epitomizes the marriage of schools, advertising, and media in creating an integrated consumer market.

In chapter 7, I conclude the book by demonstrating how the evolution of the marriage of schools, advertising, and media has resulted in the 21st-century consumer society. Advertising is now present in schools, and schools specifically teach consumerism in Family and Consumer Science courses. Global teenage culture is unified by consumerism. Teenage identity centers on brand names and icons. The combination of education, advertising, and entertainment in textbooks, media, and theme parks educates children into consumerist ideology. Symbolic of this marriage is the involvement of fast-food franchises such as McDonald's, Pizza Hut, KFC, Taco Bell, and Burger King in education and entertainment. Fast-food education represents the fruition of American cuisine as initiated by 19th- and 20th-century home economists, integration of schools into the consumer market, and the advertising dream of combining education, entertainment, and shopping.

ACKNOWLEDGMENTS

My daughter, Dawn Spring, drew my attention to consumerism while she was writing a film script on the appearance of middle-class female shoplifters after the first department stores opened in the 19th century. The film script was her master's degree project in Media Studies at the New School. Our conversations led me to examine the burgeoning literature on the history, impact, and ideology of consumerism in contemporary society. I explored the topic by examining the history of advertising, the economic justifications for consumerism, and the role of media in my New School courses on The History and Dissemination of Ideas and Culture and Transnationalism. In these classes, we concluded that America's contribution to world culture was consumerism, advertising, Hollywood movies, mass media, and processed, packaged, and fast foods.

During these investigations, I found a close relationship between schools and the development of consumerism in U.S. society that paralleled the work I did in a previous book, *Images of American Life: A History of Ideological Management in Schools, Movies, Radio, and Television*. Here I explored the mutually influential relationships among professional educators, school officials, and the development of the movie and broadcasting industries. *Images of American Life* is now out of print, and I have used some of the material on educators and media, as well as textbooks from that book, in this current work on consumerism.

Again I would like to thank my daughter, Dawn, for her suggestion to explore the history of consumerism and our many conversations on the topic. I would also like to thank Lawrence Erlbaum Associates' external reviewers, Debra Merskin, University of Oregon, and William Pinar, Louisiana State University, for their helpful comments and suggestions. I would like to thank my wife and editor, Naomi Silverman, for teaching me how to write and for her editorial insights. Also I would like to thank Naomi for all the fun times we have had shopping.

Horace Mann Meets the Wizard of Oz

PART ONE: INTRODUCTION
AND OVERVIEW OF THE BOOK

"A survey of American school children finds that 96 percent could identify Ronald McDonald. The only fictional character with a higher degree of recognition was Santa Claus. . . . The Golden Arches are now more widely recognized than the Christian cross," Eric Schlooser reported in *Fast Food Nation*.[1] On arriving in the United States from Bangladesh at the age of 8, Dewan Kazi knew two English words: *hello* and *Coca-Cola*.[2] The Golden Arches, Ronald McDonald, and Coca-Cola symbolize the worldwide spread of the icons of consumerism.

The prelude to a mass consumer society began in the early 19th-century society when schools, newspapers, national postal service, and advertising created a common culture among Americans mainly of European descent. Before discussing these origins of mass consumer society, I would like to explain the basic premises of this book and outline the historical argument that is presented about how the marriage of schools, advertising, and media contributed to the development of a consumer society. I also explain the ideology of *consumerism* and the meaning of *consumer-citizen*.

A premise of this book is that consumerism is the dominant ideology of the United States and the driving force of the global economy. Mass-consumer culture integrates consumerism into all aspects of life from birth to death, including, but not limited to, education, leisure time activities, the popular arts, the home, travel, and personal imagination. Mass-consumer culture captures the fantasy world of people with brand names and fashions

1

that promise personal transformation, the vicarious thrill of imagining the glamorous lives of media celebrities, the promise of escape from hard work through packaged travel and cruises to an envisioned paradise, and the idea that in America everyone has an equal opportunity to consume. When I ask current American college students how they would introduce an immigrant to American culture, the response without exception is, "I would take them to the mall!"

The most important aspect of mass-consumer culture is the ideology of *consumerism.* This ideology was articulated in the late 19th and early 20th centuries with the appearance of industrial and agricultural abundance. As articulated by the turn-of-the-century economist Simon Patten, consumerism reconciled the Puritan virtue of hard work with the abundance of consumer goods. From the Puritan standpoint, the danger of abundant goods was more leisure time and possible moral decay. This fear was expressed in the folk saying, "Idle hands . . . [are the] devil's tools."[3] In Simon Patten's 1907 book, *The New Basis of Civilization,* he argued that the consumption of new products and leisure-time activities would spur people to work harder. In Patten's words, "The new morality does not consist in saving, but in expanding consumption."[4] Patten explained, "In the course of consumption . . . the new wants become complex . . . [as a result the] worker steadily and cheerfully chooses the deprivations of this week . . . they advance onto a period of restraint and morality, Puritan in essence. . . . Their investment in to-morrow's goods enables society to increase its output and to broaden its productive areas."[5]

The professionalization and expansion of advertising in the late 19th and early 20th centuries was a key contribution of the United States to the creation of a mass-consumer culture. Advertising prompted desires for new products; it convinced consumers that existing products were unfashionable and, therefore, obsolete; it made brand names into playthings in personal fantasies. The advertising profession transformed the capitalist model of buyers making rational choices in a free market into a consumerist model where the buyer was driven by irrational emotions associated with particular brand names and/or products.

In chapter 2, I explore one major theme of this book: While advertising professionalized, home economists were advocating reforms of American diets and families by introducing home economics courses in schools, starting school cafeterias, and linking greater freedom for women from household drudgery through processed and packaged foods. Jell-O epitomized the new American cuisine as it became a staple in school cafeterias, hospital kitchens, and family cooking. I pick up this thread of the story in chapter 7, when I discuss how, by the 1950s, McDonald's, Burger King, Taco Bell, and other fast-food franchises had joined with prepared and processed food manufacturers to define American cuisine and provide the American family with a quick meal. Today these fast-food franchises have not only entered school cafeterias, but also sponsor their own educational programs. Burger King Academies and Pizza Hut's BOOKIT! reading program typify what I call fast-food education and the marriage of schools, advertising, and media.

A second major theme is how, in the first half of the 20th century, schools and advertising joined radio and TV in educating workers and consumers. This theme is discussed in chapter 4. Movies were an important form of commodified leisure that captured the fantasy world of workers and helped them escape the drudgery of the office and shop floor. Simon Patten had predicted that people would work harder to consume leisure products. "Their [workers'] zest for amusement," Simon wrote, "urges them to submit to the discipline of work, and the habits formed for the sake of gratifying their tastes make the regular life necessary in industry easier and more pleasant."[6]

Educators worried about the potential threat of movies to the school's efforts to regulate national morality and culture. In the 1920s, a major concern existed about the effect of movies on the morality of youth. The development of radio resulted in a public debate in the 1930s about whether schools or media should control national culture. Commercial media eventually gave advertisers a new means of shaping a consumer society. By the late 1960s, with the development of *Sesame Street*, media were fully recognized by school people as the third educator. *Sesame Street* and other children's TV programs taught children the art of consumption through the marketing of program-related dolls, toys, and games.

A third major theme of this book is the importance of the emergence of a teenage market that served to prepare future consumers. This is addressed in chapter 5, where I show how this teen market was a result of the high school becoming a mass institution in the 1930s and 1940s. The term *teenager* was coined in the 1940s to identify the high school cohort group as a particular consumer market. The founding of *Seventeen* magazine in the 1940s played a major role in defining the teenage market for advertisers. By the 21st century, marketers were referring to a *global teen market*. This market developed in the same period of the 1940s and 1950s when the advertising and public relations industries were creating a popular image of the American way of life symbolized by a suburban family with a stay-at-home housewife who consumed vast amounts of new products. In the 1950s, this consumer model of the American way of life was used as propaganda against the Soviet Union.

A fourth major theme in this book, which I focus on in chapters 2, 3, and 6, is how the marriage of education, advertising, and media was affected by issues of gender identity and racism. In chapter 2, I discuss the interplay between late 19th- and early 20th-century concerns about female identity, home economics, packaged and process foods, schools, and advertising.

The changes in this interplay—particularly among female identity, schools, and advertising—is continued in later chapters. In chapter 3, I discuss the interrelations among male identity, school sports, and advertising. I continue the discussion of these interconnections through later chapters. In chapter 6, I focus on efforts by civil rights leaders in the 1950s and 1960s to provide positive images of all Americans in school textbooks, advertising, and media. These changes transformed earlier textbook and advertising images that are discussed in earlier chapters of the book. In part, I argue, the civil rights movement attempted to achieve equal participation in the consumer market for all Americans.

In the concluding chapter 7, I pull together the various themes to show how the historical evolution of schools, advertising, and media is now manifested in commercial advertising in schools; in the transformation of home economics into Family and Consumer Sciences; in the development of themed environments, such as Disneyland, that function as educators; and in the marriage of schools, advertising, and media in the fast-food industry.

Consumer-Citizen and Ideology

Before examining the early 19th-century roots of a mass-consumer society, it is necessary to provide some brief definitions of what I mean by *consumer-citizen* and *consumer ideology*. These brief definitions take on more meaning in the context of the total book. By *consumer-citizen*, I mean a person who accepts any political situation as long as there is an abundance of consumer goods. I refer to this as "Sonya's choice." As I discuss in chapter 2, Sonya Vrunsky, a character in Anzia Yezierska's 1923 novel, *Salome of the Tenements*, exclaims, "Talk about democracy. . . . All I want is to be able to wear silk stockings and Paris hats the same as Mrs. Astorbilt, and then it wouldn't bother me if we have Bolshevism or Capitalism, or if the democrats or the republicans win."[7] In the 1950s, a consumer-citizen is a person who supports the American way of life against Soviet communism and is a *responsible* consumer. In this context, responsible consumers buy what they can afford within their limits of credit card debt. In contrast to the 19th-century Protestant ethic, with its emphasis on saving, avoiding debt, and simple living, the consumer-citizen's goal is spending, maximizing their use of credit, and consuming as much as possible. Shopping becomes a patriotic act that demonstrates the superiority of the American way of life over other political and economic systems. The anthem of the consumer-citizen is "Shop 'til you drop." Seemingly apolitical, the consumer-citizen is wedded to the ideology of consumerism.

Sonya's choice does embrace consumerist ideology. Understanding of an ideology requires a knowledge of how its various individual ideas were assembled. No ideology appears fully formed on the world's stage. Consumerist ideology emerges in the 20th century as a mixture of earlier ideas about the value of work, the accumulation of wealth, and equality as equality of opportunity. In addition, there is an acceptance of progress as economic growth, the development of new products, and consumer spending.

Consumerism is strikingly different from other ideologies that place an emphasis on either social harmony or an abandonment of worldly concerns. Many religions value the denial of materialistic desires. Different branches of Islam, Hinduism, Buddhism, and Christianity reject the way of life represented by the consumer seeking personal transformation through the buying of goods. Confucianism emphasizes the importance of social harmony over individual pursuit of wealth. Today fundamentalist Islamic governments, such as in Iran and Afghanistan, are attempting to protect their populations from what they consider to be degenerate Western consumerism.[8]

The following is a list of the basic ideas that form the ideology of consumerism. When I use the term *consumerism* throughout this book, I refer to this ideology. This book explains how these ideas become mutually supporting and influence human actions. For example, three essential ideas of consumerism—work ethic, equality of opportunity, and savings—are present in the early 19th century. In the 20th century, these three ideas take on new meaning within the context of consumerism. The utilization of the work ethic provides the means to purchase goods that promise personal transformation. Equality of opportunity takes on a slightly added meaning to that of just having an equal chance to get ahead in society. It comes to mean an equality of opportunity to consume. The 19th-century emphasis on the virtue of saving is in the 20th century used to justify consumer credit plans as forced savings. As a form of forced savings, people have immediate access to new products while still being required to pay their credit bills.

Consumer purchases and credit motivate and discipline the workforce. Consider the interrelationship among the work ethic, equality of opportunity, and consumer credit. Equality of opportunity gives everyone an equal chance to work hard to purchase goods. Consumer credit allows immediate use of goods by providing a forced savings plan to cover the cost of the goods. Purchasers must then work hard to pay off the debt accrued through consumer credit. Both the desire to purchase goods and the necessity of paying off consumer debt causes the purchaser to work harder.

Basic Ideas of Consumerist Ideology

1. Work is a virtue and it keeps people from an indolent life that could result in vice and crime.

2. Equality means equality of opportunity to pursue wealth and consume.

3. Accumulation of material goods is evidence of personal merit.

4. The rich are rich because of good character and the poor are poor because they lack virtue.

5. The major financial goal of society should be economic growth and the continual production of new goods.

6. Consumers and producers should be united in efforts to maximize the production and consumption of goods.

7. People will want to work hard so they can consume an endless stream of new products and new forms of commodified leisure.

8. Differences in ability to consume (or income) is a social virtue because it motivates people to work harder.

9. Advertising is good because it motivates people to work harder to consume products.

10. The consumer is irrational and can be manipulated in his or her purchases.

11. The consumption of products will transform one's life.

12. Consumer credit is forced savings allowing for the immediate consumption of products.

Early American Puritanism provides many of the consumerist ideas that turned the United States into a nation driven by work and consumption. However, it is not within the scope of this book to detail the history of Puritan thought. It should be noted, however, that scholars such as Jackson Lears link the history of advertising with early Puritan fear that in the Americas the abundance of goods and opportunities for pleasure would destroy the work ethic. In reference to the effect of Puritan thought on recent industrial development, Lears wrote, "The process of accumulation [of property] had to be kept moving forward, energized by the restless desire for purchase rather than the pleasures of possession. In the modern culture of abundance ... desire ... is curiously dematerialized."[9]

I think that Lears and other scholars are correct in emphasizing the Puritan quality of American thought. Later in this chapter, I discuss how Puritanism was contained in 19th-century textbooks and Sunday School literature. Puritanism is a continuing influence on U.S. culture. Throughout this book, I refer to its impact on the development of schools, advertising, and media. Having introduced the book's basic structure and providing a brief definition of consumerism and consumer-citizen, I expand on the meaning of mass consumer society by examining its early roots in the 19th century.

PART TWO: PRELUDE TO A CONSUMER SOCIETY

There were certain developments in post-Revolutionary society that set the stage for the mass-consumer society that developed in the 20th century. First, the interaction with Native Americans made White Americans conscious of the differences between societies based on manufacturing and consumption and those based on minimal wants and needs. Second, the origins of a mass society can be found in the shared experience of advertising, newspapers, telegraph, postal service, and schools. These provided a shared body of experience, knowledge, and icons that created common bonds among people, mostly those of European descent, across the nation. Third, early 20th-century leaders of school reform, home economics, advertising, and advocates of censorship of the early movie industry were mainly White Anglo-Saxon Protestants who were exposed to the same or similar texts in public schools and in Sunday schools creating a certain unity of values.

The early interactions between the U.S. government and Native Americans exemplified the use of consumer desires as a prod to hard work and reactions against consumerism. The example was important because anti-consumerism groups in the 20th and 21st centuries romanticized Native American values in their searches for alternative economic and social organizations. In the early years of the new Republic, the U.S. government attempted to integrate Native Americans into Anglo-Saxon culture through exposure to manufactured products. Foreshadowing later arguments that consumerism motivated people to work hard, President Thomas Jefferson, after assuming office in 1801, argued that government trading posts selling manufactured goods would attract Native Americans to a cash economy. Wanting to buy manufactured goods, Jefferson reasoned, Native Americans would sell their lands and use the money to buy manufactured goods from trading posts. The acceptance of a cash economy, Jefferson reasoned, would cause Native Americans to abandon hunting for farming. "When a man has enclosed and improved his farm," Jefferson wrote in reference to the trading post policy, "builds a good house on it and raised plentiful stocks of animals, he will wish when he dies that these things shall go to his wife and children, who he loves more than he does his other relations, and for whom *he will work with pleasure during his life*" (italics added).[10]

Many Euro-Americans believed that the major flaw in Native American cultures was the lack of value placed on hard work and the accumulation of material goods. Missionary work among Native Americans was often direct at instilling a work ethic. Typical of most White settlers and missionaries, the Moravians believed that a major problem was the lack of a work ethic among Native Americans. Before teaching reading and writing, the Moravians organized model farms where Indian students were put to work from sunrise to sunset. Moravian missionary John Gambold wrote, "that where the Indians are not cured from their idleness, which is admired in their nations and deeply ingrained in their nature, things must remain precarious for Christianity."[11]

The failure of the trading post system to change Native American values prompted the U.S. Congress to pass the Civilization Act of 1819. This legislation sent missionaries into Indian lands to convert tribes to Christianity, farming, and hard work. Although many members of Southern tribes were converted and took up farming, this did not result in large-scale land sales. Consequently, President Andrew Jackson in his first annual message to Congress in December 1829 declared the Civilization Act of 1819 a failure and called for the forced removal of the Southern tribes from their lands to Indian Territory (later Oklahoma).[12]

While Euro-Americans struggled to convert Native Americans to Christianity and hard work, the great Shawnee leader Tecumseh attempted to unite Western and Southern tribes against the U.S. government. Given the size of these tribes, tribal unification might have resulted in the defeat of the U.S. government and a major change in the course of American history. Tecumseh's failure in 1811 to persuade Southern tribes to join his confederacy and the destruction of his army at the Battle of Tippecanoe doomed efforts to create a united front against U.S. aggression.[13]

Tecumseh hoped to keep the materialistic White culture from infecting Native American cultures. His brother, Tenskwatwa, also known as the Prophet, served as the movement's ideological leader. Echoes of Tenskwatwa's message later appeared in the 20th and 21st centuries as anti-consumerist groups sentimentalized Native American values. The Prophet argued that the White cash economy and desire to accumulate material goods had resulted in the destruction of forest animals and, consequently, Native American's traditional hunting cultures. As recorded by one of his disciples, the Prophet delivered the Great Spirit's message: "My children, you complain that the animals of the forest are few and scattered: How shall it be otherwise? You destroy them yourselves for their skins only [to be sold to Whites]. . . . You must kill no more animals than are necessary to feed and clothe you. . . ."[14]

Preparing a Consumer Public: Schools and Equality of Opportunity

In the 1830s, while President Jackson was removing Southern Indians because of unwillingness to relinquish their lands, a spreading common school system was inculcating children with the values of hard work, amassing wealth, and equality of opportunity. The concept of equality of opportunity resolved the contradiction that faced early White American leaders between the existence of inequality and the claim that America was the land of equality. The idea of equality of opportunity emerged from the equalitarian rhetoric of the U.S. Declaration of Independence and the pronouncements of Revolutionary leaders. In *The Pursuit of Equality in American History*, historian J. R. Pole wrote, "The Declaration of Independence proclaimed a universalist egalitarian rhetoric as the standard of a highly differentiated social order."[15] In fact, Revolutionary society was socially and legally unequal by gender, race, and wealth. As Pole indicated, it "was almost believed, women were by *nature* different from men."[16] Most, if not all, slave holders did not believe Blacks were equal to Whites, and most Whites did not accept equality with Native Americans. In addition, full citizenship rights were only given to men with property. As Pole pointed out, the resolution of the contradiction between rhetoric of equality and existence of inequality was to define equality as equality of opportunity.

After the American Revolution, equality of opportunity meant that every free White man had an equal chance to work hard to accumulate property. In the late 18th century, ownership of property was required to exercise full citizenship rights through the right to vote. Noah Webster, the so-called Schoolmaster of America, creator of the American language, and author of spelling books used in schools throughout the 19th century, argued in 1793 that equality in the United States meant, "here every man finds employment, and the road is open for the poorest citizen to amass wealth by labor and economy, and by his talent and virtue to raise himself to the highest offices of the State."[17] Webster hoped that his version of the American language and ideology as represented in his spelling books would create a unified American culture.

Webster's influence in creating a common culture and popularizing the idea of equality of opportunity is difficult to measure. We do know that his textbooks were a success. Both his salesmanship and the content of his textbooks proved successful. One and a half million copies of the speller had been sold by 1801, 20 million by 1829, and 75 million by 1875. The speller became a model used by other spelling book authors. Its extreme popularity was demonstrated by the publication in 1863 of a Civil War edition in the South that was adapted "to the youth of the Southern Confederacy."[18]

The work ethic also played a role in the acceptance of the doctrine of equality of opportunity. As J. R. Pole indicated, there was a general acceptance in the early 19th century among American leaders that "God intended indolence to lead to poverty and want."[19] Poverty indicated a failure of character. This meant that character could be measured by the willingness of people to work hard to accumulate wealth. From this perspective, those who achieved wealth had good character and those in poverty had poor character.

Therefore, the doctrine of equality of opportunity gave a chance to everyone to gain wealth and prove, through work, that they were moral and of good character. In the late 19th century, a Massachusetts speaker declared to a society of mechanics, "Every man stands on his own merits. . . . The fact that he may become a capitalist, is a spur to exertion to the very newsboy in our streets."[20]

Common school advocates, particularly Horace Mann, the so-called *father of the public school system*, declared that schools should be the central social institution for ensuring equality of opportunity. In *Pillars of the Republic*, one of the best discussions of the foundations of U.S. public schools, Carl Kaestle argued that public school advocates wanted to protect and ensure the domination of Anglo-Saxon Protestant culture. The virtue of property and the availability of economic opportunity in the United States, according to Kaestle, were to be taught in public schools. Kaestle wrote, "property was to be respected because it taught virtue. Everyone should be taught to desire property and to respect property."[21]

Eventually the schoolhouse became a public icon symbolizing equality of opportunity. In this context, public schools helped establish the foundations of a mass-consumer culture. School attendance promised everyone an equal chance to consume property, and it linked school success with good character and good character with accumulation of property. Failure in school supposedly limited the possibility of economic success. Linking school failure with poverty and low income, the school could perpetuate the idea that poverty was often a sign of failed character. The formula for schooling was this: If you worked hard in school and worked hard after graduation (a sign of good character), you would be blessed with high income and the ability to consume vast quantities of material goods.

Children Read About Wealth and Its Uses

Most late 19th-century Protestant White children were exposed to similar textbooks and children's literature distributed by Sunday Schools. Considered together, textbooks and Sunday school literature taught similar values regarding work, wealth, and salvation. Later in the early 20th century, these values were frequently reflected in professional work employing primarily Anglo-Saxon Protestants, such as advertising, social work, and education. In *Advertising the American Dream*, Roland Marchand analyzed the backgrounds of the architects of American advertising. He found that the overwhelming majority were White, Northern European, Protestant, male, and Ivy League graduates.[22] Also it was primarily those of Protestant background who restructured public schools to meet what they perceived to be the needs of the urban-industrial society that blossomed at the end of the 19th century.[23] It was mainly Protestant religious groups and Protestant social reformers who led the campaigns to close urban taverns, dance halls, and movie theaters.[24] It was also the influence of these values on rising industrial abundance that helped form a consumerist ideology.

Textbooks and Sunday School literature dealt with themes that shaped the direction of American consumer society. Important themes in this literature were differences in wealth and the temptations of urban life. Worries about the evil of urban life directly affected the expansion of the school as a social welfare institution and the efforts to impose censorship on movies. The reading material also dealt with shopping and the ostentatious display of wealth. Finally, this children's literature reflected the tension between Christian pastoralism and industrial destruction of the environment.

An examination of the most popular textbooks of the mid- and late 19th century, the *McGuffey Readers*, will provide insight into the shared information and ideas of those (primarily White Protestant children) who attended public schools. Children's literature in the 19th century came mainly from religious societies, and it was distributed through Sunday Schools to Protestant children. The *McGuffey Readers*, first published between 1836 and 1838, contained a primer, a speller, and four readers. Sales figures for the series indicate their popularity. Between 1836 and 1920, approximately 122 million copies were sold.[25] By the 1830s, the American Sunday School Union and the American Tract Society were publishing over 12 million children's books, tracts, pamphlets, hymn books, devotional books, journals, magazines, and newspapers. In 1832, 75% of Sunday Schools had children's libraries. The Sunday School Union's book approval committee was composed of representatives from the following Protestant dominations: Baptist, Methodist, Congregationalist, Episcopal, Presbyterian, Lutheran, and Reformed Dutch. Surrounded by public school textbooks and Sunday School books, Protestant children were receiving similar ideas and information.[26]

The issue of economic inequality appeared frequently in *McGuffey Readers* and Sunday School books. The existence of economic inequality was presented as a blessing that allowed people to gain salvation. Wealth was presented as both a blessing from God and a sign of a virtuous character, and as a burden that could lead to moral failure. Similarly, poverty could be a sign of failed character and an ungodly life, but it could also provide the suffering needed to achieve salvation. It was religious faith that determined the ultimate value of wealth or poverty. Wealth was a sign of industrious character, but not necessarily a sign of salvation. Without salvation, the rich could quickly become indolent and sink into a life of luxurious dissipations. Without salvation, the poor could become criminals or succumb to alcoholism. Despite these similar possibilities, the poor were presented as better off because their sufferings helped them achieve salvation.

In *Making the American Mind: Social and Moral Ideas in the McGuffey Readers*, Richard Mosier argued that the economic philosophy of the Readers was premised on the Calvinistic concept that wealth is an outward sign of inner salvation. In other words, the accumulation of material goods is a sign of a virtuous character. This economic argument allowed for an acceptance of a society divided by wealth. Wealth was a sign of God's blessing, and poverty was a sign of God's disapproval. Within this economic argument, for the poor to gain wealth they had to be godly and industrious, and for the rich to continue receiving the blessings of God they had to use their wealth in a godly fashion. Mosier argued that the *McGuffey Readers* taught that, "Those who are wealthy are reminded that they are so by the grace of God, and that this grace and concession implies a responsibility toward the poor. . . . Many are the lessons that praise the charitable activities of the merchant, and many are those that show the kindness of the rich to the poor."[27]

The conflicting attitudes about the rich and poor were highlighted in two successive stories in the 1843 edition of McGuffey's *Newly Revised Eclectic Second Reader*: "The Rich Boy" and "The Poor Boy." In the first story, the rich boy learned "that God gives a great deal of money to some persons, in order that they may assist those who are poor." The rich boy was also presented as a model of virtue who cared for the poor. He proclaimed, "If I were a man, and had plenty of money, I think no person who lived near me should be very poor."[28] The poor boy was also presented as virtuous. He was industrious, helpful, moral, and eager to learn. However, the story makes a clear distinction between poor boys who were good and those who were bad. In the story, the poor boy hurried home from his lessons to help his parents. On the way, the reader was told, "he often sees naughty boys in the streets, who fight, and steal, and do many bad things; and he hears them swear, and call names, and tell lies; but he does not like to be with them, for fear they should make him as bad as they are; and lest anybody who sees him with them, should think that he too is naughty." Unlike the rich boy wanting to help the poor, the poor boy dreamt of earning his own living. The poor boy liked his food of bread and bacon and did not envy the rich little boys and girls "riding on pretty horses, or in coaches." At the end of the story, the poor boy stated his acceptance of his social position: "I have often been told, and I have read, that it is God who makes some poor, and others rich;—that the rich have many troubles which we know nothing of; and that the poor, if they are but good, may be very happy: indeed, I think that when I am good, nobody can be happier than I am."[29]

Although virtue was often associated with gaining of wealth, it was poverty and suffering that provided the easiest route to salvation. This idea was clearly presented in two Sunday School books, *The Factory Boy, or, the Child of Providence* and *I Wish I Was Poor*. In *The Factory Boy*, the main character's father is described as "industrious, frugal, and prudent. His industry enabled him to make money; his frugality prevented him from wasting it in unnecessary indulgences. . . . A merciful Providence blessed his business, so that he was able not only to meet his necessary expenses, but gradually to accumulate money."[30]

Yet the problem for the father, and later the son, Alfred Stitson, was the absence of religious conversion despite the presence of virtue and regular church attendance. After the father's death, the mother lost the family's property to swindlers and they sunk into dire poverty. The mother fell ill and Alfred experienced a world of suffering. On the brink of starvation, the author commented, "we shall soon see that God does not err in his ways and that our greatest trials are designed for our good."[31]

The family's suffering provides an opportunity to gain something the father had lacked, which was religious salvation. Alfred's salvation saved the family from poverty. The lesson was that poverty was a blessing because it provided the opportunity for the virtuous to find God. After Alfred's salvation experience, the author declared, "Again he [Alfred] thought of his early afflictions, and of all the temporal circumstances in the history of his family. He now felt most grateful for them, as the means which finally led them to the knowledge and experience of religion."[32]

A similar scenario was presented in the Sunday School tract, *I Wish I Was Poor*. The story opens with Lucy Lee, who was confined to her home because of illness. Lucy complained, "Yes, I do wish I was poor; then Christians would talk to me about dying; they always do talk to poor people."[33] She felt neglected because, from her perspective, evangelical efforts were primarily directed at saving the poor. Then Aunt Lawrence arrived, who was described by a household servant as "so rich." On hearing of the visit, Lucy moaned, "I'm so tired of seeing rich people."[34] Yet Aunt Lawrence turns out to be a different type of rich person—she was a saved Christian. Aunt Lawrence provided a grateful Lucy with religious instruction that led to Lucy's salvation.

As the story closed, Lucy and Aunt Lawrence discussed the relationship between economic status and religious salvation. Lucy, of course, wanted to know why it is easier to be saved if you were poor. Quoting the Biblical statement, "It is easier for a camel to go through the eye of a needle than for a rich man to enter into the kingdom of heaven." Lucy wondered, "How can any rich people be saved? It does seem as if I should be a great deal more certain that I and all our family would go to heaven, if we were poor."[35]

In response, Aunt Lawrence asked, "Are all poor people good?" and "Are all rich people wicked?"[36] After Lucy admitted that good and evil exist in all economic groups, Aunt Lawrence explained the problem, "the minds of wealthy men and women are so taken up with the things of this world, that they neglect the greater good. And their children often have [more] temptations than the children of the poor."[37] As for the poor, their advantage was suffering, which helped bring about salvation. Lucy was saved because her illness opened her heart to religion. Aunt Lawrence explained, "God sent upon me, as he has upon you, a long sickness; he compelled me to take the time to think; and when my humbled heart sought him, I trust for Jesus's sake he freely forgave all my former pride and ingratitude. Was he not kind to afflict me?"[38]

Similar to the rich boy in the *McGuffey Reader*, Lucy learned that wealth was a blessing if used to help others. Aunt Lawrence justified the concentration of wealth with this argument:

> Wealth, rightly enjoyed and rightly used, is a great blessing to its possessor and to the world. The poor cannot be relieved, benevolent institutions of different kinds cannot be carried on, even the gospel cannot be preached in our own and foreign lands, without money. So you see, if God keeps the heart from loving it, money is of great worth.[39]

This justification of wealth eventually has to be adapted to a consumerist ideology that glorifies the purchase of goods. In the framework of these stories, wealth was a blessing when it was used to benefit the needy. Wealth was not a blessing when it led to the ostentatious display of goods. In a Sunday School Union publication, *Common Sights in Town & Country*, Farmer Jones accumulated wealth because "Industry and economy, under the blessing of God, will secure for the farmer an abundance of the good things of this life."[40] Once a year, he traveled to the city to purchase goods not available in a country store. In the city, Farmer Jones acted in a fashion quite contrary to later consumerism: "What he buys, however, he buys for use and not for show. He looks upon money as one of God's gifts, and tries to use it in a way that will be pleasing to the Giver."[41]

In summary, these stories provided a justification for inequality and equality of opportunity within the framework of 19th-century Protestantism. Inequality of wealth was not only inevitable, but provided opportunities for religious awakening and benevolence. The suffering of the poor opened the door to possible religious conversion. Religion combined with industry and virtuous actions provided the poor with the opportunity to climb the economic ladder. The suffering of the poor also provided the rich with an opportunity to use their wealth in a benevolent and Godly manner. Without the poor, the rich would have no one to save. Yet the failure to practice virtuous behaviors and achieve religious conversion led the poor down the path of drink and crime. Without religion, the rich were tempted by their wealth to squander their time and money on the purchase of ostentatious goods.

19th-Century Protestantism and the Environment

One later criticism of mass-consumer society was the destruction of the environment and the depletion of natural resources. Nineteenth-century children's literature provided contrasting views that could be used to either support protection of the environment or justify its exploitation. Many children's stories spoke highly of the beauty of nature as a blessing from God.

In *The Factory Boy*, the narrator reflected on the importance of nature in making humans aware of God's glory: "Nature is the goodly work of God, and like a glass, reflects back the smiles of His countenance. When we can escape away from the noise and wickedness of men, to where God's works alone surround us, how serene do our thoughts become, and how pleasant is it then to feel that there is a God who made all things."[42] The narrator worried that the growth of the surrounding city "has injured much this lovely scenery; the hills about the basin have been much dug away."[43]

In contrast to this Christian pastoralism was the argument that the earth was created by God for humans to exploit. An example is the Sunday School story, "The Coal-Cart." The story opened with the Biblical statement, "All that is in the earth is thine."[44] This Biblical line was followed by the statement, "It is but a few years since Anthracite or Stone-Coal was used for fuel. Now hundreds or thousands of tons are taken from the bowels of the earth every year, and consumed in grates, furnaces, steamboats, factories, etc."[45] This exploitation of the earth was then given another religious twist in the final lines about the driver of the coal cart: "We hope he is kind to his hard-working horse, faithful to the interests of his employers, not given to strong drink, and above all, one who fears God and keeps his commandments."[46]

Throughout the 20th and 21st centuries, there would be a continuing tension between the exploitation of the earth and the desire to preserve nature. Many anticonsumerist movements, such as the Green Party, combined environmental with consumer concerns. This tension existed in the children's literature of the 19th century with exploitation of the environment and was justified by the belief that God created Earth for the use of humans and that the act of exploitation was all right if it was performed by Christians.

Protestantism and Urban Leisure

Important for later development of movies and other forms of commodified leisure were stories that illustrated the potentially degrading temptations of city life. As I describe later, Protestant social reformers in the late 19th and early 20th centuries worried that dance halls, movies, bars, amusement parks, and other forms of working-class and immigrant urban leisure might destroy the moral fiber of the nation. Among other things, these concerns shaped the course of movie history in the United States.

The 1847 Sunday School book, *Frank Harper; or, the Country-Boy in Town*, illustrated these early concerns with urban living. After graduating from elementary school, Frank Harper left his farm in New Jersey to work in a store in New York City. Frank exhibited the industrious virtues that could lead to financial success, but he lacked religious salvation. Knowing little about city life, Frank's father consulted with the local tavern keeper about lodging for the young boy. Consequently, Frank's city lodgings proved less than reputable. Two of his fellow roommates tempted him into going to the Bowery theater. At the theater, Frank discovered that "he was among bad men and bad women. He saw and heard things that night which made him sure that it was wicked place."[47] Frank's city life also surrounded him with the enticing sights of store windows and taverns.

The lengthy narrative about Frank's city adventures took him from temptation to salvation. He was befriended by a Christian man, joins a Sunday School, and receives religious salvation from a minister. His country virtues combined with conversion saved him from city sins and ensured his financial success. In contrast, his original theater companions succumbed to city vices and ended up in jail.

The childhoods of the pioneers of advertising, the educational leaders who adapted the school system to the labor needs of mass production, and the moral leaders who demanded censorship of movies and purity in other forms of commodified leisure were surrounded in their childhood by this public school and Sunday School literature. They had to ignore or adapt the information and ideas from this literature to conditions of a mainly urban-industrial society that appeared to be producing more than could be consumed. They also worried about the temptations of mass media. Also some of these future leaders were surrounded by city reading and read newspapers.

Creating a Consumer Public: Advertising and Newspapers

"To a significant extent," David M. Henkin argued in *City Reading*, a study of signs, newspapers, and money in early 19th-century New York City,

> city reading helped to lay the social foundations for what would emerge by the end of the century as a consumer society—a society in which the mere capacity to spend money secured membership, though often on glaringly unequal terms and under increasingly impersonal and potentially alienating conditions.[48]

By *city reading*, Henkin referred to the proliferation of shop signs, trade bills, sandwich boards, banners, and newspaper vendors that characterized America's urban spaces.

Henkin maintained that because of the lack of street signs, and in many cases uncertainty about street names, people tended to identify public space in early urban America by signs hanging on buildings. Indicating the difference between European and American cities, foreign visitors frequently commented on how their city walks and fulfillment of personal desires were guided by commercial signs. Urban dwellers thought about their spacial locations by the location of signs on commercial establishments. For instance, people often identified the location of their homes by nearby businesses rather than by street names.

Buildings were designed to display advertising and reproduce well in illustrated newspaper ads. This meant that an urban dweller's sense of public space was identified closely with commercial advertising. Henkin's book contains photos from the mid-19th century that illustrate the cacophony of signs that dominated the urban landscape. One 1865 photo of New York City's Lower Hudson Street showed 3 three-story buildings displaying 13 commercial signs and what appears to be two posted handbills and one sandwich board. The signs indicated businesses that provided printing services, drugs, carpentry, house and sign painting, "oil'd clothing," shirts, drawers, "over-alls, and horse, cart & truck covers."[49]

In addition to building signs, the city walker was confronted with a wide range of temporary and mobile signs. Posters advertising goods, services, and entertainment were plastered across the city landscape. These temporary signs would eventually be covered by other posters. Mobile advertising signs adorned horse-drawn trams. People wearing sandwich boards advertising goods and services crowded sidewalks. Trade bills and cards were shoved into pedestrian's hands.

Eventually advertisers competed with each other for public attention. Leading the way was America's premier impresario and advertising genius P. T. Barnum, who, after opening the American Museum in 1841, covered New York with handbills and posters advertising a dwarf named General Tom Thumb and 161-year-old Joice Heth. Also Barnum used advertising to create mass interest in the 1850 New York concerts of Swedish opera singer Jenny Lind. Barnum's success in promoting Lind as a celebrity foreshadowed the celebrity and media star promotions of the 20th and 21st centuries.

Barnum was credited with introducing an advertising style of "spectacular discourse . . . where every item of publicity worked to create new items."[50] A typical Barnum ad contained eye-catching titles in a variety of type sizes, such as "A Mammoth Fat Woman" or "Noah Orr, The American Giant." Under the bold titles was more information in smaller type, such as "Miss Rosina D. Richardson, Weighing 660 lbs" and "Eight Feet three inches in Height." In some cases, even smaller type was used to give more details about the attraction, such as "unequaled in stature."[51] After being captured by a spectacular title, the reader's eye had to adjust to absorb new bits of information in smaller type. In this manner, the reader's eye was tempted into reading each item of the ad. In his 1869 autobiography, Barnum explained his methods in selling museum attendance to the public. "I fell in with the world's way; and if my 'puffing' was more persistent, my advertising more audacious, my posters more glaring, my pictures more exaggerated . . . it was [because] . . . I had . . . more energy, far more ingenuity."[52]

Later professional advertisers called Barnum a charlatan and tried to distance themselves from his tradition. In his cultural history of advertising,
Jackson Lears stated,

> Seeking to deny their [advertisers] origins, most protested too much. On
> the hundredth anniversary of Barnum's birth, 1910, *Printer's Ink* [an adver-
> tising journal] disavowed the prophet. To celebrate his "advertising ability,"
> the magazine charged, would be like doctors celebrating a quack as their
> godfather.[53]

Despite the denial by later advertisers that they were following in Barnum's
tradition, most current historians recognized the connection. In her history
of advertising, Juliann Sivulka contended, "New York showman P.T.
Barnum (1810–1891) set out to attract public attention and ended up as
the first advertising genius."[54]

It seems clear that commercial signs, posters, sandwich boards, handbills, and trading cards set the stage for America's pioneering role in professional advertising. City reading created a sense of public connections based
on commerce and consumption. Henkin demonstrated how city reading
spilled over into the world of political culture as political announcements
joined commercial signs. Consequently, Henkin's conclusion on the effect
of city reading goes beyond the creation of a mass-consumer society. He
wondered,

> How significantly this impersonal urban print public has contributed to the
> historical processes yielding a society dependent on mass consumption, a dis-
> engaged electorate, a largely nondeliberative political culture, or a narrow
> popular understanding of the public good is difficult to measure.[55]

Of course city reading required literacy, and public schools were increasing literacy rates by the reading of common textbooks that instilled the idea
that virtue could be measured by the material gains of hard work. Surrounded by advertising signs, the urban school student learned the material rewards of a good education. Within this urban context, it was not hard
to translate equality of opportunity and hard work into an equal chance to
consume.

Newspapers, Post Office, Telegraph, and Advertising

The sharing of common news about local and world events was important
in creating a mass culture. The advertising accompanying the news was an
essential step in creating a mass-consumer culture. By the 20th and 21st
centuries, consumer news—that is, information about new products and
price trends—became an accepted part of local and world news. The line

between advertising and political news, and between consumption and social news, was increasingly blurred from the 19th to the 21st centuries.

The development of the newspaper as a mass consumer product paralleled the expansion of public school systems. A major factor was the U.S. Post Office's goal of ensuring a wide geographical distribution of newspapers. The U.S. Post Office Act of 1792 created a national postal system. European postal systems primarily existed to send official messages and collect revenue. In contrast, the U.S. postal system, in the words of Benjamin Rush, existed to disseminate "knowledge of every kind . . . through every part of the United States."[56] The result was the rapid spread of post offices as local communities petitioned for postal services. Between 1790 and 1840, the number of post offices per person improved from 1 for every 43,084 to 1 for every 1,087.[57]

Similar to the later goal of the common school system, an objective of the 1792 Post Office was to create a common culture by setting low rates for newspapers to encourage their national distribution. This allowed newspaper publishers in remote areas to draw on news provided by other papers. The result was a rapid sharing of political information among literate and primarily White residents. Between the 1830s and 1840s, railroads increased the speed of mail delivery. The result, according to Headrick, was that "the numbers of newspapers sent through the mail increased from half a million in 1790 (one for every five inhabitants) to thirty-nine million in 1840, or 2.7 newspapers per capita. . . . *The postal system became largely a newspaper delivery service*" (italics added).[58]

A contributing factor to the rapid increase in newspapers was the advent of the penny newspaper in the 1830s while the common school system spread. Prior to the 1830s, newspapers were relatively expensive. In 1830, New York City's 11 newspapers had a circulation of about 25,000 a day at a price ranging around six cents. Then in 1833, penny newspapers were introduced, and newspaper circulation climbed dramatically with the three leading penny newspapers reaching a circulation of 44,000 a day in 1835. Aided by technological advances in printing, newspapers became a mass commodity.[59]

The development of the telegraph increased the sharing of information. The telegraph and the establishment of the Associated Press news service in 1848 resulted in similar news stories appearing around the country. As a news organization, the Associated Press distributed news over the telegraph to local newspapers so that the newspaper reader in a small town was reading the same news as the reader in an urban area. They all shared the same news articles. By the 1880s and 1890s, syndicated features and comics appeared in newspapers.[60]

The importance of the newspaper in creating a mass culture cannot be overemphasized. Richard Ohmann argued, "That was the first time Americans had available in the format of the newspaper a homogeneous national experience of the news, of opinion, of household advice, and of entertainment."[61] In part, this mass culture included an imagined community. Having greater information about the world, the newspaper reader could imagine and think about geographical places they would probably never visit. "The newspaper," Henkin wrote, "replaced spatial communities with imagined ones, unsettling geographical boundaries and nullifying physical distances."[62]

The celebrity was created by newspapers and advertising. P.T. Barnum's sponsorship of Jenny Lind's performances sent her name into every community in the country. When Hungarian nationalist Lajos Kossuth visited New York in 1851, newspapers were filled with his daily activities and speeches. His visit resulted in look-a-like commodities, such as Kossuth boots, cigars, and hats. As a celebrity created by newspapers, Kossuth, similar to media celebrities of the 21st century, became a national fashion statement.[63]

Newspapers contributed to the rise of nationalism in the 19th century through the creation of an imagined community and by playing on patriotic feelings in news stories. Cherokee leaders recognized the contribution of newspapers to nationalism by publishing the first bilingual Native American newspaper, *Cherokee Phoenix*, on February 21, 1828. The columns were written in English and a Cherokee character system invented by Sequoia. The newspaper helped unite the Cherokees against the encroachments of the U.S. government through the dissemination of news and Cherokee laws.[64]

With the advent of penny newspapers in the 1830s, news quickly became a commodity. Newspapers competed with each other by displaying the most dramatic headlines. In urban centers, newsboys cried out headlines to gain sales. News dealers became part of the urban scene with their stands displaying front pages designed to attract the eyes of potential buyers. The front-page layouts became advertisements for the newspapers. Headlines that screamed terror or lurid events tempted passing readers to buy them.

Newspapers not only sold news, but they also sold advertising. The more copies a newspaper sold, the more its publisher could charge advertisers. By the 1840s, newspapers depended on advertising revenue to earn profits. "We lose money on our circulation by itself considered," Horace Greeley wrote in an 1841 *Tribune* editorial, "but with 20,000 subscribers we can command such advertising and such prices for its as will render our enterprise a remunerating one."[65] Cheap newspapers could only be sustained through advertising revenues.

The sale of news was linked to the sale of advertising. News became a commodity to sell other commodities. Newspaper layouts had to achieve a balance between attracting readers and seducing them to examine the advertisements. Henkin argued that newspaper layouts blurred the distinction between advertising and news. He contended, "To begin with, the very juxtaposition of items on the same newspaper pages tended to deny (or at least suppress) their differences."[66]

Many of the early newspaper ads featured patent medicines. Professional advertising agencies and advertisers would later distance themselves from the patent medicine tradition. For instance, the *Ladies Home Journal,* which depended on advertising revenue for its existence, banned patent medicine ads from its pages in 1892. The editor of the magazine, Edward Bok, wrote, "There is no evil in America to-day so great as this accursed passion for self-doctoring."[67]

Despite this later reaction to patent medicine, many of these medicines were eventually sold for different purposes or as homeopathic cures. They also represent the influence of Native American medicine on the American homeopathic tradition. For instance, Coca-Cola and Pepsi-Cola were originally sold as patent medicines for the brain and stomach, respectively. An 1892 ad for Coca-Cola proclaimed, "The Ideal Brain Tonic . . . For Headache and Exhaustion." Featured in the ads were testimonials from druggists. In contrast, a 1900 Coca-Cola ad only stated, "Delicious and Refreshing—Drink Coca-Cola—At Soda Fountains and Carbonated Bottles 5¢." There were no testimonials from druggists in these later ads, but these were endorsements from celebrities such as a large illustration of actress Helda Clark holding a glass of Coca-Cola. This transition from patent medicine to soda was marked by the increasing importance of the celebrity and the link between celebrity life and the advertising of products.[68]

A striking feature of early patent medicine ads were their promises of personal transformation. Consider the promise of Dr. Townsend's Sarsaparilla, which was sold as the "Wonder and Blessing of the Age." The ad stated, "To those who have lost their muscular energy by the effects of medicine or indiscretion committed in youth, or excessive indulgence of the passions . . . [that have] brought on . . . want of ambition . . . premature decay and decline . . . can be entirely restored by this pleasant remedy."[69] When I first read this ad, I thought of recent ads for sports utility vehicles that displayed the car on top of a mountain surrounded by wilderness. The promise of these recent ads is that the buyers' environment will be magically transformed from the drab cement of the city or blandness of suburbia into pristine beauty of the wilds with the purchase of the vehicle.

While the ad for Dr. Townsend's Sarsaparilla promised personal renewal, ads for Dr. Swayne's Compound Syrup of Wild Cherry and Morse's Compound syrup of Yellow Dock Root identified specific maladies. In addition, these patent medicines reflect the influence of Native American medical treatments. The claims of these 1850s' ads parallel those in John Lust's *The Herb Book* published in 1974 and reprinted 20 times by 1987.

The 1850s' ad for Wild Cherry states it would cure "coughs, colds, asthma, influenza, bronchitis. . . ."[70] Lust's book claimed, "Its [wild cherry] effectiveness was attributed to a sedative action on the respiratory nerves."[71] Lust listed uses by Native Americans including treatment for diarrhea and lung problems. The 1850s' ad for yellow dock root stated that it was a blood purifier and helped with skin problems. Lust's book also listed yellow dock root as a blood purifier and aid in curing skin problems. Lust wrote, "American Indians applied crushed yellow dock leaves to boils and pulverized roots to cuts."[72]

With the commitment of the postal service to the spread of newspapers, patent medicine ads appeared around the country. For those reading newspapers, there was a sharing of product information. Regardless of whether it was believed, this shared information included a claim that the purchase of products could result in personal transformation. This became an important advertising claim in the 20th and 21st centuries. Newspapers, while blurring the distinction between news and ads, turned news into a product to be sold like any other product. In addition, news became a form of entertainment used to sell other products through its ads. These trends would be important as consumerism took shape at the end of the 19th century.

The Wizard of Oz and the Architecture of Desiring

Another important 19th-century development that set a trend that later produced Disneyland and other themed consumer architecture was the department store. The department store turned urban strolling into window shopping. A pioneer designer of department store show windows was L. Frank Baum, who was also an author of children's books including *The Wonderful Wizard of Oz*. Both show windows and *The Wonderful Wizard of Oz* captured the consumer's fantasy world as both shopping and leisure time activities. Born in 1856, Baum grew up in a wealthy family in upstate New York, and during his youth he worked in theater and as a traveling salesman. With his experience in theater and merchandising, Baum eventually became an advisor on store displays to Chicago businesses. In 1898, he founded the National Association of Window Trimmers, and in 1899, he published a monthly journal called *The Show Window*.[73] In Baum's words, *The Show Window* taught window designers to "arouse in the observer the cupidity and longing to possess the goods."[74]

The use of the department store windows to arouse consumer desires should be understood in the context of architectural history.[75] Eventually the trend in designing buildings to attract consumers would lead to the distinctive architectural designs embodied in fast-food restaurants, shopping malls, and Disneyland-like theme parks. Traditionally, architectural designs were used to attract people and represent the building's functions. For instance, churches and temples were designed to attract worshipers and represent religious activity. When seeing a themed religious structure, most people understand the nature of the activity that took place within its confines. The same thing was true of schoolhouses. Of course some architectural designs were more powerful than others in attracting people. The beauty of European medieval cathedrals attracted and invited attendance of both the worshiper and nonworshiper as represented today by their popularity as tourist sites.

The architectural goal of themed consumption palaces was to attract consumers—this means the transformation of public space into planned consumer spaces. Open-air markets and enclosed arcades were traditional forms of consumer environments. In modern times, the first consumption palaces were department stores, with the first being Paris' Bon Marche, which opened in 1869. Department store buildings were designed to entice shoppers into their interiors. They were designed to stimulate consumer desires through the display of goods in exterior windows. Referring to the show windows that lined the exterior ground floors of his department store buildings in New York and Philadelphia, John Wanamaker wrote in 1916, "Our minds are full of windows. . . . Show windows are eyes to meet eyes."[76] Through the eyes of store windows, people were to be pulled into the interior space of consumer goods.

In the early stages, window shopping was encouraged by professional window gazers hired by department stores. People were taught to linger before store windows and energize their consumer desires. The use of plate glass allowed a clear view into the interior. In *The Show Window*, Baum, like the Wizard of Oz, recommended the use of a variety of theatrical methods to attract window shoppers, including revolving electrical displays. He was not interested in the quality of the goods, but how they looked in a display arrangement. If goods were properly displayed, he argued, "the show window will sell them like hot cakes, even though [they] are old enough to have gray whiskers."[77] As show window expert Frederick Kiesler stated, the goal was to "break down the barriers separating customers and merchandise."[78]

Mannequins enhanced the seductive qualities of window displays. Traditionally, only headless mannequins—without head, arms, or feet—were used as dress forms. According to historian William Leach, mannequins as complete human forms appeared around 1912 in displays of ready-to-wear clothes.[79] Eventually mannequins were built with movable parts so they could be made to assume different poses. According to one retailer, mannequins made it possible to "create an atmosphere of reality that aroused enthusiasm and acted in an autosuggestive manner."[80]

Female mannequins wearing only underwear stimulated sexual desires. Even the novelist John Dos Passos referred to the sexual arousing effect of "girls' underwear in store windows" in his novel, *1919*. Some underwear displays caused crowds to gather in front of store windows. In Spokane, Washington, police had to disperse a crowd gathered in front of a shop that displayed women's underwear. One man was arrested for refusing to leave the display window.[81]

The interiors of department stores were turned into palaces of consumption and made shopping a leisure time activity. Goods were displayed in plate glass counters that allowed consumers to be entertained as they strolled up and down aisles gazing at the cornucopia of merchandise. Prior to department stores, goods were sold in stores specializing in one area of merchandising. In these earlier stores, little effort was made to provoke consumer desires. Goods were kept behind counters, and shoppers asked clerks to put merchandise on the counter for examination.

In department stores, quick-selling items were kept far from entrance doors so that shoppers would be forced to reach them by walking through displays of luxury items. Each floor and department was organized in the same manner. Escalators were introduced in the early 20th century, which allowed the easy movement of shoppers to upper floors. Prior to escalators, many shoppers avoided the upper floors because of the crowding and perceived inconvenience of elevators. One merchandiser in 1912 claimed that its store's five escalators allowed for placing "the staple, year-round 'sellers' on the second and third floors, relieving the congestion of departments on the main floor."[82]

Departments stores made shopping a social activity. Cafeterias, lunch rooms, fountains, and coffee bars added to the social quality of department store shopping. Friends, particularly women, arranged to meet in department stores for lunch, and after eating they would continue to socialize as they wandered through the store's aisles gazing at the array of goods. They could attend the store's fashion show or demonstrations of housewares. Holidays, which by the end of the 20th century became another excuse for shopping, were celebrated with lavish displays designed to entertain and stimulate a desire to buy a holiday present.

Themed store interiors added to the grandeur of the shopping experience. Mirrors placed on elevator doors, walls, and pillars reflected merchandise back and forth across the expanses of each floor. Stopping to look at their images, shoppers found themselves starring at mirrors that combined their images with that of surrounding merchandise. Looking at their reflections, consumers could imagine themselves wearing or using the merchandise. Walking around the store, shoppers' images were constantly merged into images of consumer goods. Some department stores went to extreme lengths to entertain the shopper with the beauty of their interiors. The most renowned design was the iridescent glass-mosaic dome completed by Louis Tiffany for Chicago's Marshall Field department store. Supposedly the dome with its illusion of reaching up into a heavenly domain was to cast a mystical aura over the goods below.[83] Under this dome shopping was like going to church.

As department stores were themed to attract buyers, amusement parks were themed to attract consumers of commodified leisure. In fact, Fred Thompson, the pioneer builder of Coney Island theme parks and New York's theatrical extravaganza, the Hippodrome, linked his designs to the new department stores. Thompson's Luna Park, which opened in Coney Island in 1903, was the first theme park.[84] His biographer, Woody Register, argued that Thompson wanted to liberate theatrical entertainment from traditional concepts in the same manner that department stores liberated retailing from small stores. Register wrote, "The concept of the department store provided Thompson with an organizational model as well as a class setting and democratic vocabulary of public service to his theater."[85] While department stores turned shopping into a combination of social event and leisure time activity, Thompson wanted theme parks to be a commodified form of play that was social and fun. He proclaimed, "The trouble with this present age is too much work and too little play."[86] His Coney Island extravaganza, Luna Park, set the pattern for all future theme parks. Calling Luna Park "the Biggest Playground on Earth," Thompson's completed project included human cannonballs, marriage ceremonies in hot-air balloons, a floor show with 800 dancers, and a trip to the moon complete with moving scenery and a moon landing surrounded by midgets.[87]

Thompson believed that commodified fun was the answer to the drudgery and boredom of industrial and corporate work. As Register stated, "Thompson ultimately exploited it [the desire for fun] by applying his industrial patrimony to produce a marketable and fantastic form of rebellion against the diminishing rewards of work in an industrializing corporate society."[88] The very forms of Thompson's architecture provided an avenue of escape into a world of fantasy. Visitors to Luna Park paid their 10-cent entrance fee at five hand-carved Roman chariots posted at the entrance. The spectacular use of 200,000 incandescent lights caused it to be called "Electric City by the Sea." Inside the park, there were constructed illusions, similar to later ones created by Disney, of famous places. The spatial dimensions at Thompson's New York City Hippodrome were designed to impart a sense of awe and wonderment to the audience while they waited for performances enhanced by mechanical stage sets and lights.[89]

The difference between Thompson and Walt Disney's later vision of theme park entertainment was the audience. Thompson's world was geared for adults, with Luna Park offering child-care services so parents would be free to roam. Disney's parks were created for families and projected images of domestic morality. The closest to Disney's later moral world was Coney Island's Dreamland amusement center. Dreamland provided customers with educational exhibits of the Fall of Pompeii and exhibits claiming to show real life in Japan, Switzerland, and Venice. Moralizing themes were included in the biggest exhibit, which was "The Creation and the End of the Earth." The "End of the Earth" extravaganza showed people being thrown into hell for vanity, kissing before marriage, stealing, and drinking. The End of the Earth represented a Protestant vision of the future if urban America did not change its behavior.[90]

Conclusion: Development of a Consumer Society

The information and ideas disseminated in the 19th century through schools, textbooks, children's literature, city reading, and newspapers set the stage for the development of a consumer-oriented society. Department stores established a pattern of architecture intended to stimulate consumer desires. The public school became an icon for equality of opportunity and provided a resolution for the contradiction between the rhetoric of equality and the reality of existing inequalities. In America, equality was most often associated with an equal chance to accumulate property. Textbooks and children's literature presented inequality in wealth as an opportunity for the rich to gain salvation by serving the poor and for the poor to gain salvation through personal suffering. Inequality provided a test of individual character in the land of opportunity. In other words, equality of opportunity to gain wealth provided a chance for testing personal virtue and character.

The work ethic as a sign of virtuous character was represented in textbooks, schools, and children's literature. In the late 19th and early 20th centuries, fears that industrial advances would create too much leisure time resulted in arguments that the work ethic could be sustained by increasing desires to consume. Belief in the importance of the work ethic remained a strong fixture in American life. By the 21st century, Americans held the honor of working more hours than any other industrial nation. In fact, the number of hours worked increased from the 20th to the 21st centuries. According to Jeff Johnson, economist for the International Labor Organization, "The average American worked 1,978 hours in 2000, compared with 1,942 hours in 1990."[91] Americans worked almost an additional 40-hour week. Johnson emphasized, "The increase in the number of hours worked within the United States runs counter to the trend in other industrialized nations where we see declining annual hours worked."[92] Also the "compassionate conservativism" of President George W. Bush emphasized the work ethic along with the value of inequality for the promotion of morality among the rich and poor.[93]

There were other tensions resulting from industrial and economic abundance. Some Protestants felt threatened by the cultural values of Catholic and Jewish immigrants in pursuit of wealth that entered the United States in the late 19th and early 20th centuries. Although these newer immigrants embraced the products of industrial abundance, some traditional Protestants felt torn between the values of simple living and the necessity of buying new industrial products to maintain the economy. Also Protestant values of thrift and saving conflicted with the increasing use of consumer credit. The exploitation of natural resources as a result of industrial expansion created a tension between the belief that nature was an expression of the beauty of God and that God intended humans to exploit nature.

Finally, by the end of the 19th century, advertising signs, handbills, posters, department store windows, and other forms of city reading presented the urban dweller with a steady display of manufactured goods. As newspapers turned news into a commodity, the distinction between news and advertising was blurred. The public that shared the values embedded in schools, children's literature, city reading, and newspapers was ripe for a world where virtue and work were tied to consumption.

Chapter 2

Liberation With Jell-O
and Wonder Bread:
Educating the New Woman

At the turn of the 19th and 20th centuries, new public images of women and consumerism were introduced by advertisers and home economists working in schools, the food industry, and other public institutions. Home economists envisioned the education of a new woman who, skilled in scientific household management, would be freed from domestic drudgery to participate in the general improvement of society. As part of this goal, home economists developed a distinctive American cuisine through instruction in public schools, setting standards and training cooks for school cafeterias and hospitals, and in their advocacy of using prepared and packaged foods in the home. Professional advertisers considered themselves engaged in mass education and central to the success of an economy dependent on consumer purchases. Home economists and advertisers had differing concepts of the public. The home economist imagined a rational and scientifically thinking public, whereas the advertiser thought of the masses as being driven by irrational desires. There were also important racial divisions as African Americans developed their own consumer markets and advertised using themes of racial pride. In contrast, Euro-American advertising agencies used African-American images to portray servitude to Whites.

THE CONSUMER WOMAN AND BRAND NAMES

In the late 19th and early 20th centuries, industrialization sharpened division of labor between men and women. The public image of domestic relations became that of the wage-earning husband as producer and the housewife as consumer.[1] As Susan Strasser argued, consumer wives took on more of the household tasks as husbands defined their work roles in industrial and corporate organizations. In the primarily rural settings of the past, husbands actively participated in household work by engaging in such tasks as carrying water, chopping and carrying wood for the stove, and cleaning poultry, wild game, and livestock while wives worked as producers maintaining vegetable gardens, storing food, and making clothes.[2] Discussions of masculinity resulting from increasing urbanization and employment in bureaucratic organizations centered on the loss of what Theodore Roosevelt called the *strenuous life*. In this framework, men were to recapture their masculinity by participating in sports, weekend and vacation hiking and camping, and fishing and hunting. Although fishing and hunting were no longer required to maintain the household food supply, they were considered necessary for retaining masculine attributes.[3]

The focus of this chapter is on the public discussion of the domestic and consumer role of women as household tasks shifted from production to consumption. During this period, women's roles as producers of household goods were being replaced by the availability of ready-to-wear clothing, factory-made bread, packaged and canned foods, and processed foods. Leading the discussion about the new domestic role of women as consumers were home economics experts. Schools played an important part in attempts to redefine the role of women. In addition, producers of food and household goods, advertisers, and the burgeoning cosmetics and ready-to-wear industries tried to shape the image and consumer patterns of housewives and wage-earning women.

Underlying all the forces shaping women's roles were tensions between the increasing abundance of goods, traditional Protestant culture, and new immigrants arriving from Southern and Eastern Europe. These cultural tensions were sometimes reduced by claims that democracy was being enhanced by a new consumer society that allowed equal opportunities to buy new products and fashions. Ready-to-wear clothing made it possible for the average person to engage in rapid fashion changes that, in the past, had only been available to those who could afford to buy tailored clothing. Home economists, as I discuss, believed they were promoting a democratic household by teaching a single standard of cooking and domestic management to all students.

The new consumer woman emerged as brand names flooded the market. After the passage of the 1870 federal trademark law, manufacturers were able to protect their trademarks by registering them with the federal government. One of the first registered was the "Underwood devil," a product image used on canned meats manufactured by the William Underwood and Company. This was followed by noted brand images such as Quaker Oats Man (1877), Michelin Man (1895), Aunt Jemima (1905),

Morton Salt Girl (1911), Betty Crocker (1921), Jolly Green Giant (1926), and Ronald McDonald (1966).[4] By 1917, a study in the *Journal of Applied Psychology* reported that 1 in 300 men could name one brand of pen, watch, and soap. By the 1920s, Susan Strasser reported that Chicago grocers said that more than three quarters of their customers asked for baked beans by brand name and that Campbell's soups were the best sellers.[5] By the 1920s, America was well on the road to a world dominated by brand- and designer-named clothing, appliances, cars, foods, restaurants, leisure-time activities, toys, recreational commodities, cosmetics, and health care products. Brand and designer names promised a predictable world of uniform goods.

Brand names established new ways to cook and think about food. What eventually distinguished the American way of eating were foods from cans, boxes, packages wrapped in wax paper, and, eventually, plastic containers and frozen food. Branding and packaging invaded the restaurant trade with the 1921 opening of the White Castle chain, which was later replaced in popularity by McDonald's. Like the manufacturers of processed foods, White Castle promised a predictable eating experience. An early advertisement claimed, "When you sit in a White Castle remember that you are one of thousands; you are sitting on the same kind of stool; you are being served on the same kind of counter; the coffee you drink is made in accordance with a certain formula."[6]

The transformation of American eating habits was an important factor in the growth of the advertising industry. Many of the early ad agencies depended on accounts from food manufacturers along with producers of soap, soft drinks, and new technologies. Few, if any, of the early food ads stressed the pleasure of taste. Ads sounded like the advice that home economists would give school children as they posted nutrition charts in classrooms without any suggestion that eating could be fun. Early advertising neglected pleasure in the same way that home economists neglected enjoyment as they planned meals for school cafeterias and hospitals.

Exemplifying the issue of food tastes was the discovery that Italian immigrants in Chicago were staying away from hospitals because of hospital food. Horrified, home economists tried to adjust their menus by making a few harmless concessions to immigrant tastes during the initial parts of the hospital stay. Later it was hoped by food planners that the immigrant could be weaned from their traditional foods to the solid and healthy fare of the hospital kitchen. It was suggested that, "Perhaps the treatment of an Italian during this period of change should be studied much as the treatment of an inebriate being won from his strong drink is studied."[7] A similar attempt to change the eating habits of immigrant children occurred in school cafeterias.

TEACHING CONSUMER IDEOLOGY: HOME
ECONOMICS

Home economists supported consumerism because it promised to liberate women from the drudgery of household tasks, particularly cooking. Through the purchase of prepared foods and new cleaning technologies, housewives, home economists hoped, would have more time available to further their education and engage in efforts to improve society. Home economists imagined the new woman as highly educated and dedicated to social improvement projects. Early home economists were career scientists who, unable to find employment in existing scientific fields, created departments of domestic science in universities.

After its professional birth in the 1890s, the spread of home economics courses to public schools and colleges was ensured by the 1917 Smith–Hughes Act of 1917. This federal legislation provided support for home economics teachers in public schools to prepare girls for the occupation of homemaker. In turn, this required the hiring of home economic instructors on college campuses to train teachers. These college and university instructors also trained cooks for hospitals, school cafeterias, and other institutional settings. Home economists also expanded their careers by becoming researchers in food technology at private companies and universities and consultants to private industry for product development and sales. The vocational emphasis of the Smith–Hughes Act tended to compromise the role of home economists as scientists. Historian Rima Apple concluded, "In the early twentieth century, women who wanted to pursue careers in scientific research were frequently counseled to study home economics. . . . As home economics units became increasingly involved with teacher training for public school instruction . . . [this] lessened the perceived significance of the scientific aspects of home economics."[8]

In *Perfection Salad: Women and Cooking at the Turn of the Century*, Laura Shapiro credited home economists with the development of a distinctive American cuisine. She argued that, during the latter part of the 19th century, home economists "made American cooking American, transforming a nation of honest appetites into an obedient market for instant mashed potatoes."[9] Reflecting on the Puritanical quality of the teachings and writings of early home economists, Shapiro wrote, "But to enjoy food, to develop a sense for flavors, or to acknowledge that eating could be a pleasure in itself had virtually no part in any course, lecture, or magazine article."[10]

Home economists helped develop and sell the new American diet of prepackaged foods. In public school and college classes, they taught how to prepare the new American diet, how to handle fashion trends and consumer credit, and how to manage household budgets. As researchers, they did pioneer work in food technology that resulted in the development of new food products and made possible the proliferation of fast-food chains. They helped manufacturers develop and sell new gadgetry for the home, such as refrigerators, vacuum cleaners, and washing machines.[11] They helped make school and hospital cafeteria food healthy, inexpensive, and bland.[12] Through the school cafeteria, they hoped to persuade immigrant children to abandon the diet of their parents for the new American cuisine.

Home economists hoped that domestic science would protect the family unit against the worst aspects of urbanization and industrialization. As a profession, it focused on the adaptation of home life to new developments in science and technology. The 1909 announcement of the founding of the American Home Economics Association gave as its goal "the improvement of living conditions in the home, the institutional household, and the community."[13]

As a profession, home economics evolved from an annual series of conferences held at Lake Placid, New York, beginning in 1899 under the leadership of Ellen Richards. Richards, the founder of the American Home Economics Association and the first woman to receive a degree from the Massachusetts Institute of Technology (MIT), brought together a faith in the ability of science to improve human existence, a desire to improve women's education, and a belief that the home was the central institution for reforming society. Reflecting these concerns, after graduating from MIT in 1873, Richards convinced the institution to establish a Woman's Laboratory in 1876. In 1883, Ellen Richards became the first female instructor at MIT as the separate women's laboratory was torn down and women joined men as students at the institution. Richards taught courses on sanitary and household chemistry that focused on cooking and cleaning.[14] In 1887, Richards conducted a study of municipal sewage treatment systems and developed the first water purity standards.[15]

The new American diet resulted, in part, from Richards' research at MIT and her work with the New England Kitchen and the Boston School of Housekeeping. Richards and others at the New England Kitchen and the Boston School of Housekeeping believed that improper diet and household management were undermining society. "Is it not pitiful, this army of incompetent wives," declared domestic scientist M. V. Shailer in an 1898 issue of *New England Kitchen Magazine*, "whose lack of all knowledge of domestic science is directly and indirectly the means of filling our prisons, asylums, reformatories and saloons."[16] This feeling echoed earlier claims by Juliet Corson, the superintendent of the New York Cooking School. Written In 1877, Corson's booklet, *Fifteen Cent Dinners for Workingmen's Families*, claimed, "The laborer who leaves home in the early morning, after an ill-cooked breakfast, and carries in his basket soggy bread and tough meat for his luncheon, is apt to return at night tired and cross, not unfrequently he tries, *en route*, to cure his discomfort at a neighboring saloon."[17]

Placing society's ills at the doorstep of the home, domestic scientists saw a cure through nutritional food, sanitary cooking, budgeting, and household cleanliness. Nutritionally balanced food, it was believed, would provide the energy for hard work and resistance to the temptations of the tavern. Wholesome food served in the home and school cafeteria would stimulate the student to study and protect them from illness. Hospital patients would recover more quickly as a result of scientifically planned menus and food. Sanitary cooking and household cleanliness would protect everyone from sickness. Protected from illness and energized by nutritional foods, it was believed, workers would be less likely to miss work and more likely to retain their jobs. According to the calculations of home economists, these circumstances would reduce unemployment, crime, and alcoholism. For the same reasons, students would be able to complete their studies and find good jobs. Also proper management of the household budget would keep families from falling into poverty. Workers would be less likely to strike if their wives could make existing wages satisfactory through proper budgeting. This belief in the ability of home economics to reform society was summed up in 1902 by Marion Talbot at the fourth annual meeting of the Lake Placid Conference on Home Economics. These conferences foreshadowed the establishment of the American Home Economics Association. Talbot stated, "the obligations of home life are not by any means limited to its own four walls, that home economics must always be regarded in light of its relation to the general social system, that men and women are alike concerned in understanding the processes, activities, obligations and opportunities which make the home and family effective parts of the social fabric."[18]

Along with saving society, home economics was to liberate women from household drudgery and make them active participants in shaping society. Ellen Richards worried that "the industrial world is ruled by science that all the things with which we surround ourselves are now manufactured upon scientific principles, and, alas! women are ignorant of those principles."[19] The study of science and home economics would, Richards hoped, make housekeeping into a profession. A 1890 editorial in the *New England Kitchen Magazine* proclaimed, "We need to exalt the profession of home making to see that it is as dignified and requires as much intelligence as other professions."[20] Science and technology would be the key to eliminating household drudgery. As Ellen Richards explained, "The woman who boils potatoes year after year, with no thought of the how or why, is a drudge, but the cook who can compute the calories of heat which a potato of given weight will yield, is no drudge."[21]

Portending the future marketing of packaged and frozen dinners, Ellen Richards helped found the New England Kitchen in 1890. The founders hoped to improve the lives of working and poor people by providing already prepared sanitary and economical food that would have consistent flavor and texture. Richards envisioned a neighborhood establishment that would prepare and sell food. The establishment would be educational because buyers could observe the sanitary conditions and cooking methods. Also, cooked under scientific conditions, buyers would learn to expect the food to always taste the same.

Richards' dream of standardizing American eating habits was made possible by the work of Fannie Farmer and the Boston Cooking School. The Boston Cooking School opened in 1879; by the 1890s, it was training cooks for public school cafeterias using a curriculum that included Psychology, Physiology and Hygiene, Bacteriology, Foods, Laundry Work, the Chemistry of Soap, Bluing, and Starch, and Cookery Applied to Public School Work. Fannie Farmer joined the Boston Cooking School in 1888. Legend has it that standardized measurements were born when Marcia Shaw asked Fannie Farmer what it meant to measure out "butter the size of an egg" and "a pinch of salt."[22] In 1896, Fannie Farmer's *The Boston Cooking-School Cook Book* was published and quickly became a national best seller. A major innovation in Farmer's book was the use of leveled measurements, which gained her the epithet of the "Mother of Level Measurements." Embodying American approaches to scientific cooking, Fannie Farmer wrote, "A cupful is measured level. A tablespoonful is measured level. A teaspoonful is measured level."[23]

Ellen Richards' dreams of prepackaged and standardized meals spread across the country. Jane Addams sent a settlement worker from Chicago to learn Richard's methods and created a similar kitchen at Hull House. Another kitchen opened in Providence, and Richards was invited to create a New England Kitchen at the 1893 Chicago World's Fair. The exhibit was lined with food charts, menus, diagrams, and consumerist mottoes such as, "Wherefore do you spend money for that which is not bread, and your labor for that which satisfieth not?"[24]

After the World's Fair, the New England Kitchen focused its efforts on selling prepared foods to Boston's nine public high schools and office workers. In 1895, Richards helped create a model program in Boston's public school cafeterias. Prior to 1895, janitors in Boston schools were responsible for the lunch program. Using new theories on nutrition, sanitation, and food preparation, Richards and her cooking colleagues introduced the new American diet to Boston school children.[25] These efforts set the stage for trained domestic scientists to take over school cafeterias to ensure that students received healthy and sanitary foods. The other focus was on hospital food. Richards declared that "no better school of diet could be found than an intelligently managed hospital."[26]

In both schools and hospitals, cafeterias served the double function of supplying nutritional food and changing people's diets. Of primary concern were changing the diets of immigrants from Southern and Eastern Europe. Home economists believed that immigrants were harmed by foods that required long periods of digestion. American scientific cooks were guided by a 1820s' timetable created by an American army surgeon who studied a young man with a hole in his stomach caused by a hunting accident. The surgeon suspended food on a string in the man's stomach to determine the speed of digestion. According to this experiment, pork turned out to be the most difficult to digest, whereas clear broth and rice were the easiest.[27]

Concern about rates of digestion had a limiting effect on the role of spices in cooking. Fears about the overuse of spices reinforced already negative attitudes of home economists regarding immigrant food. In *The Chemistry of Cooking and Cleaning*, Ellen Richards argued that spices did have a role in stimulating digestive juices, but warned against heavy seasonings because they might wear out the digestive tract. In her words, spices should be, "Just enough to accomplish the purpose. . . ."[28] Based on concerns about digestion, menus were created that balanced the digestive aspects of one food against another. For instance, it was proposed that the first serving should include easily digestible items such as oysters and white fish, which would prepare the gastric juices for the more difficult meat dishes. The result were recipes and menus noted for their blandness and lack of sensitivity to taste.

The development of this new American diet was directly linked to an image of the new woman. As home economists invaded school and hospital cafeterias with their gospel of scientific cookery, they saw the possibility of freeing the American woman from home cooking and making it possible for her to extend her education. Ellen Richards believed that prepared foods, like those served by the New England Kitchen, would increase women's freedom.

In addition, the new American diet was associated with the so-called *democratization of domesticity*. Home economist believed the school cafeteria and home economics courses would unite students from differing social class backgrounds under a single standard of domesticity. In both the school cafeteria and food preparation classes, students were to develop similar tastes. Girls from lower class backgrounds were to be brought up to the same standard of cooking and cleaning as upper class girls, whereas upper class girls were to learn the arts normally practiced by their household help. The belief in democratic leveling was exemplified by a statement of a New York public school's supervisor of cooking's comment—that the female student "is wonderfully interested in the bacteria of the dishcloth, and the ice box, and the garbage pail, and when she becomes mistress of a home these things will receive her attention as well as the parlor, library, and music room."[29] Home economists hoped that standardized cooking and shared attitudes about housework and sanitation would open the door to a more democratic society.

PREPARED FOOD AND WOMEN'S EDUCATION

By freeing women from cooking chores, home economists believed, the new woman would have more time for education and civic reform. Also as a result of the social involvement and education of the new woman, the quality of civic life would improve, and the cultural level of homes and husbands would be elevated. In fact, the 1897 meeting of the Woman's Suffrage Association featured a keynote speech on the value of domestic science to the women's movement.[30] As educated women, home economists wanted other women to receive the benefits of an extended schooling. Prepared food, it was believed, would mean freedom from cooking and liberation of women along with supplying the family with a sanitary, nutritious, and balanced diet. In choosing the path of prepared food, the housewife shifted her emphasis from producer to consumer.

Ellen Richards projected this liberating role for prepared food in a 1900 article entitled, "Housekeeping in the Twentieth Century." In her dream home where the purchase of cheap mass-produced furniture allowed more money for intellectual pleasures, the pantry was filled with a large stock of prepared foods—mainly canned foods and bakery products. Richards' dream pantry was based on the reality of a growing industry for canned foods. As early as the 1820s, William Underwood sold meats packed in bottles, and in 1856 Gail Borden patented a method for condensing milk and preserving it with sugar. By the 1870s, the technology for canning meats was perfected. In the 1870s, H. J. Heinz sold crocked pickles, horseradish, and sauerkraut, and a decade later the company expanded its product list to include cooked macaroni products and vegetables. In the 1880s, the Franco-American Company began to distribute canned meals. In 1897, Campbell's introduced canned soups after the development of a method for condensing the product. According to Ruth Cowan, "By the turn of the century [19th to 20th], canned goods were a standard feature of the American diet . . . [including] processed foods of all kinds—packed dry cereals, pancake mixes, crackers and cookies machine-wrapped in paper containers, canned hams, and bottled corned beef."[31]

In Richards' ideal home, a pneumatic tube connected to the pantry speeded canned and packaged food to the kitchen where the wife simply heated up the meal. In addition, the meal would be accompanied by store-bought bread. Besides being unsanitary, home economists believed that home-made bread and other bakery goods required an inordinate amount of preparation time and therefore housewives should rely on factory-pro-duced bread products. Richards dismissed the issue of taste with the com-ment, "I grant that each family has a weakness for the flavor produced by its own kitchen bacteria, but that is a prejudice due to lack of education."[32] People would stop worrying about taste, she argued, when they fully real-ized the benefits of the superior cleanliness and consistency of factory kitchens and bakeries. In a 1900 book, *The Cost of Living as Modified by Sani-tary Science*, Richards provided another version of her vision of the com-modified housework. "Housekeeping," she explained, "no longer means washing dishes, scrubbing floors, making soap and candles; it means spend-ing a given amount of money for a great variety of ready-prepared articles and so using commodities as to produce the greatest satisfaction and the best possible mental, moral, and physical results."[33]

The so-called philosopher of home economics, Caroline Hunt delin-eated the role of women as consumers. Her interest in science and social reform paralleled those of Ellen Richards. Born in Chicago in 1865, Hunt entered Northwestern University in 1881 and, after interrupting her stud-ies to teach high school, graduated in 1888. Teaching high school for sev-eral more years, she again returned to Northwestern University to study chemistry. While at Northwestern, she lived with Jane Addams at Hull House and engaged in studies of newly arrived immigrants, including *The Italians in Chicago: A Social and Economic Study* (1897) and *Dietary Studies in Chicago* (1898). In 1896, she was hired to teach Domestic Economy and operate the cafeteria at Chicago's Lewis Institute. Then in 1903, she was hired by the University of Wisconsin to organize and head the School of Domestic Science.[34]

While at Lewis Institute, Hunt equated women's freedom with a change in household roles from producer to consumer. Women would have more free time for education, she argued, if they bought factory-made products rather than producing them in the home. For instance, a housewife could be a producer of soap or a consumer of factory-made soap. "The woman who today makes her own soap instead of taking advantage of machinery for its production," she wrote, "enslaves herself to ignorance by limiting her time for study. The woman who shall insist upon carrying the home-making methods of today into the tomorrow will fail to lay hold of the possible quota of freedom which the future has in store for her."[35]

Throughout her writings, she highlighted the importance of the transi-tion of the household tasks from that of production to consumption. For Hunt, this transition was part of the larger process of industrialization and job specialization. Comparing the past to existing conditions in a paper she read at the 1904 Lake Placid Conference on Home Economics, Hunt ar-gued, "The home has delegated to the school not only the technical but also the general education of the child; to the factory the manufacture of clothing, of furniture, and of house furnishings."[36] Although the responsibilities of the household were changing, she contended, they still played an important role in society. Households were still responsible for raising the child to school age and teaching morality. Plus, Hunt added, homes were responsible for education about beauty and what she called "rational sociability."

According to Hunt, rational sociability was an important aspect of the consumer's education. From her perspective, the consumer had a social responsibility to influence producers regarding their treatment of workers and the sanitary production of food products. In her discussion of higher education at the 1906 Lake Placid Conference, she argued that "home economics, if considered as primarily a training for intelligent consumption, should be introduced into the college education."[37] She defined *intelligent consumption* as demonstrating a concern for the general welfare of society. "The wise consumer," she told the Conference, "has in mind not only his own advantage, but the welfare of those who make, transport and care for the commodities he uses."[38] From this perspective, the consumer must be educated into an awareness of workers' conditions. This added a social reform aspect to the role of consumption. "He [the wise consumer] thinks of himself as responsible, not only for the happiness and well being, but also for the continued efficiency and social usefulness of the producer. He hopes that by his own use of wealth he may so direct human energy as to educate the worker and to increase the world's resources."[39]

Arguing that home economics should be introduced into the college curriculum "primarily [as] a training for intelligent consumption," Hunt listed the need for food, shelter, clothing, cleanliness, and beauty as the focus of this study.[40] Although food courses were well defined, she argued, instruction on the satisfaction of the other needs had to be expanded. In a telling statement of her vision of the future role of women, Hunt argued, "There is . . . an important way, other than thru [sic] purchase of food, in which women control a large amount of human energy, and that is thru [sic] buying and using what may be called art products including clothing and house furnishing. We feel, I am sure, that the college should give students an intelligent attitude with reference to the responsibilities arising from their consumption of these products."[41]

Hunt envisioned college-educated women finding time to engage in social reform movements by consuming rather than producing household goods. In other words, women would be freed to engage in *municipal housekeeping*. Released from household chores, women could apply their education, particularly from home economics, to protecting the household from deleterious industrial and social practices. She called this "Woman's Public Work For the Home."[42] At the 1907 Lake Placid Conference, she argued that when women forced by their responsibility for the family welfare into a fight for a public milk supply of assured purity, and are unsuccessful in the fight, we may take this as an indication that young women now in college should be taught to seek and to overcome the difficulties which lie in the way of the present accomplishment of this much needed reform.[43]

Hunt related freedom from food preparation to the rise of democratic thought and an emphasis on freedom for the individual. Under democracy, she contended, individual freedom meant enhanced opportunities for women rather than absence of restraints. Freedom for women, Hunt argued, required passing "over to public enterprise the work of food preparation and the responsibility for the care of houses, thus releasing in woman's life energy for individualization."[44]

Richards and Hunt's hopes seemed to be realized with the rapid spread of home economics courses in public schools and colleges. According to Barbara Ehrenreich and Deirdre English, 20% of high schools offered courses by 1916–1917, and the number of college students enrolled in courses increased from 213 in 1905 to 17,778 in 1916. Most of those enrolled in college courses were preparing to be home economics teachers.[45]

Richards wanted training in home economics to begin in elementary school. Along with Alice Norton, she prepared a widely used curriculum, which began:

Ideals and Standards of Living

13. Historic Development of the Family
    a. The darkest ages of history
    b. The beginnings of human society
    c. The psychology of races—expression of the home ideal in races other than the Anglo-Saxon
    d. Early social life of the Anglo-Saxon people
        i. The home life of the Anglo-Saxon vs. the communistic family system.[46]

Besides teaching domestic science, this curriculum was designed to Americanize immigrant children to Anglo-Saxon standards. In this context, domestic science leaders saw their efforts as an evolution in Anglo-Saxon culture. In the first grade, children were to compare their homes "with that of lower animals and primitive peoples." By the third grade, they were to build and decorate model homes.[47] The impact of these courses on non-Anglo-Saxon cultures continued after World War II. Elinor Polansky, a second-generation Russian–Jewish immigrant, reported about her 1949 home economics classes in a Bronx junior high school:

What came across was this idea that your home environment was no good and you had to make it different. For example, we learned that the only right way to cook was to make everything separately . . . that was the good, wholesome way. Things all mixed together, like stews, that was considered peasant food. I would never have admitted to my teacher that my family ate its food mixed together. There was something repulsive about food touching. The string beans weren't supposed to touch the mashed potatoes and so forth. . . . Only later did I realize that I hate that kind of cooking. But then I can remember even asking my mother to buy plates with separations in them.[48]

WONDER BREAD AND JELL-O: HOME ECONOMICS, THE NEW WOMAN, AND SOCIAL REFORM

The evolution from home-made to factory-made bread exemplifies the variety of forces shaping the new consumerism. From the perspective of home economist, the purchase of factory-made bread freed the housewife from the time required to mix, knead, and bake bread at home. Also factory-made bread prepared under proper supervision ensured sanitary conditions and standardization. Following this line of reasoning, the consumption of factory-made bread contributed to a healthy diet while freeing the homemaker to engage in municipal housekeeping. In turn, municipal housekeeping ensured that the bread factory would provide adequate wages and working conditions for its employees, maintained sanitary conditions for bread production, and baked a uniform and nutritional product.

Caroline Hunt preached the gospel of factory bread and social reform at the Ninth Annual Lake Placid Conference. She argued that women wasted a great deal of energy on home-made bread. 'If they spent half that time in the effort," she contended,

> to agree upon a standard for good bread and in the insistence that the baker's product must come up to that standard, they would not now . . . depend on the use of a kind of bread which in no way comes up to their ideals as to quality, and which is frequently sold and delivered without proper protection from dirty hands, from dust and from flies.[49]

The separate packaging of each loaf of bread ensured the sanitary condition of the product. Following the same line of reasoning, the prepackaging of all food products would make food distribution even more sanitary.

What happens if the husband does not like prepackaged factory-made bread? According to Hunt, the husband was compensated by having an educated wife. Using an example of a wife taking a course on Dante's writings rather than staying home and baking, Hunt claimed, "if he [the] husband considers the advantages of eating . . . his baker's bread flavored with drippings of information concerning the great poet and his times, he may conclude that baker's bread with Dante sauce is more to him than homemade bread."[50]

Although home economists believed these prepared products liberated women for political and social action, advertisements often conveyed a different message. This was particularly true of ads in women's magazines, such as the *Ladies Home Journal, The Delineator,* and *Good Housekeeping,* which, according to historian Ellen Garvey, had "a special and often more self-conscious role in the construction of the woman reader as consumer."[51] Similar to newspapers, advertisements became the largest source of revenue for magazines. Edward Bok, editor of the *Ladies Home Journal* from 1889 to 1919, tried to develop the image of women as stay-at-home consumers as opposed to the home economics' image of the consumer woman fighting for social improvement. Garvey argued that, although Bok and other male editors of women's magazines tried to play down the idea of the politically and socially active women in their columns and stories, the advertisements appearing in the magazines often stressed the new woman. However, these magazine ads, Garvey contended, used

> feminist and quasi-feminist catch phrases and slogans [that] patronizingly trivialized a serious quest for political power into a choice of trimmings and appliances, and suggested, along with anti-suffrage propaganda, that a woman's effect on the home sphere was so powerful that it exceeded and made unnecessary any power she sought in the larger world.[52]

The difference between the vision of home economists and what was often conveyed by ads was exemplified by a 1930s cartoon-style ad for Wonder Bread that showed in the top panel the face of a distressed wife looking up into the eyes of a stern-faced husband with the couple surrounded by the headline "People Whispered." In the next smaller panel, the wife was shown on the phone saying, "But, Dick, you're *always* eating in town! Please come home!" Near her was a woman whispering to another woman, "I *told* you so." In the next panel, the wife announces the husband is coming home and invites both of the other women to stay. One woman excuses herself and the other agrees to stay. In the next panel, the wife complains that her bread was stale, and her guest responds by offering to buy bread that never got stale. In the following panels, the guest presents the wife with a loaf of Wonder Bread, the husband returns home and loves the Wonder Bread. In the next to last panel marked "Next Day," the husband turns down an office invitation for lunch with the statement, "Can't . . . I'm reporting home for a real meal."[53]

In the ad, the home economist vision of female liberation was replaced by a servile wife struggling to maintain her marriage by serving the best prepackaged food. However, the ad did support the home economists contention that good food would keep husbands from straying from family life. The final panel illustrated the gulf between the feminist and advertising images of the housewife. Across the top of the final panel was written, "Hurry *Your* Husband Home!" Below this headline was, "Smart women know that *meals* are an important part of *every* husband's life! That's why wives by thousands serve Wonder Bread. It's made of the *finest* ingredients. Slo-baked. Makes *every* meal *worth* hurrying home for!"[54]

Wonder Bread and Jell-O became signature dishes of the new American cuisine. Wonder Bread, with its soft, white, and mushy texture, and supposedly easy-to-digest contents, quickly replaced the hard-crusted breads of European tradition. Invented in 1897, Jell-O transformed an aristocratic European dish, as declared in an ad featuring George Washington, into "America's Most Famous Dessert."[55] Jell-O signaled the beginning of American instant foods, which only required adding water and stirring. In her history of Jell-O, Carolyn Wyman opened the introductory chapter:

> COCA-COLA MAY SELL BETTER.
> APPLE PIE MAY SEEM MORE TRADITIONAL.
> BUT THE TRUE TWENTIETH-CENTURY AMERICAN
> FOOD WAS CERTAINLY
> JELL-O GELATIN.[56]

Wyman continued, "Jell-O more closely resembles such high-tech marvels of the '50s and '60s as Cool Whip and Cheez Whiz . . . Jell-O was, in fact, one of America's first processed foods. As such it was a model for all the bland, sweet, cheap convenient foods we now eat."[57]

Although home economists loved Jell-O, immigrants arriving at Ellis Island in the early 20th century refused to eat it. One Ellis Island detainee stated, "because they didn't like the . . . wobbly texture." Aboard a ship bound for the United States, one German immigrant was frightened by her introduction to American cuisine. Served as the first dinner course, she wrote, "It was a square piece of Jell-O and as the ship was moving the Jell-O was wiggling. And they told us we could eat this Jell-O. I was really frightened by this piece of orange Jell-O."[58]

In contrast, home economists hailed Jell-O as an essential dish in the new American cuisine and made it a frequently served dish in school and hospital cafeterias. Domestic scientists loved Jell-O because it democratized the American diet while providing a digestible dish. Originally, gelatin foods were primarily served at the tables of the wealthy because of the difficulty of preparation. It required the laborious efforts of servants to produce a good gelatin dish. Preparation required the cleaning of calves' feet and extraction of fat between the claws. The calves' feet were then boiled and, after cooling, residual fat was skimmed off. The feet were boiled again with the addition of egg whites and shells to pick up the impurities. After straining through a cloth, spices and sugar were added, and the mixture was placed in a mold and packed in ice. Similar to Jell-O molds of the 20th and 21st centuries, the original gelatin molds came in elaborate shapes and designs.[59]

Democratization of gelatin dishes occurred in 1893 after home economist Sarah Tyson Rorer of the Philadelphia Cooking School asked the Knox Company to develop an instant gelatin. Responding to the request, Knox introduced an instant gelatin with the descriptive label, "Sparkling Granulated Calves Foot Gelatine."[60] Almost immediately, home economists jumped on the gelatin bandwagon as a vehicle for making salads along with desserts. They recommended blending granulated gelatin with whipped cream, grated cheese, or mayonnaise and to harden dishes such as chicken salad. Gelatin was proclaimed an ideal mold for layers of fruit. The crowning touch to the American gelatin salad appeared shortly after the beginning of the 20th century. Perfection Salad, as it has been called, used gelatin to hold together a mixture of finely chopped raw cabbage, celery, and red peppers. Making gelatin dishes became a common part of the public school home economics courses.[61]

Jell-O, and later Crisco, opened corporate doors for domestic scientists to work as recipe writers and publicity agents for process foods. As publicity agents, they promised that the new processed foods would liberate women. As a preflavored gelatin, Jell-O further reduced the skills and time required for cooking. Domestic scientist Marion Harland helped advertise Jell-O with assurance that, "Even the woman who cannot cook need have no difficulty in devising a new desert every day if she is supplied with Jell-O and common sense."[62] As an example, Harland suggested mixing prunes into lemon Jell-O. A Jell-O ad featured a statement by the principal of Fanny Farmer's School of Cookery, "Jell-O is an up-to-minute food designed to meet the needs of the modern housekeeper whose problem is to save time, energy, and money in doing her daily tasks."[63] Philadelphia Cooking School instructor Sarah Tyson Rorer offered her opinion of the healthfulness of Jell-O in the advertising booklet, *What Six Famous Cooks Say of Jell-O*: "Elaborate desserts, such as boiled and baked puddings and dyspepsia-producing pies, have given place to the more attractive and healthful desserts made from Jell-O." In the tradition of domestic scientists, Rorer also proclaimed the liberating effects of Jell-O: "Why should any woman stand for hours over a hot fire mixing compounds to make people ill, when in two minutes, with an expense of ten cents, she can produce such attractive, delicious desserts."[64]

Procter & Gamble used the same method to market Crisco. A vegetable shortening, Crisco was a product of 5 years of secret experimentation prior to its marketing in 1911. One of the reasons for its development was to ensure Procter & Gamble's domination of the cotton seed oil market, which it also used in its soap products. Its rivals for control of this market were Armour and Company and the N. K. Fairbank Company, which sold cooking fats mixed with lard. Procter & Gamble's goal was an all vegetable solid fat. Crisco was an entirely new product that required changing the traditional use of animal fats, particularly lard and butter, in cooking.[65]

The company hired the editor of the Boston Cooking School Magazine, Janet McKenzie Hill, to write the first Crisco cookbook. She invented another signature dish of the new American cuisine—the Crisco white sauce composed of two melted tablespoons of Crisco, two tablespoons of flour, and one cup of milk. About this invention, food historian Laura Shapiro wrote, "With the Crisco white sauce, scientific cookery arrived at a food substance from which virtually everything had been stripped except a certain number of nutrients and the color white. Only a cuisine molded by technology could prosper on such developments, and it prospered."[66]

Besides establishing a market for processed foods, Crisco helped sell the idea of packaged goods. Traditionally, lard and butter were sold in bulk from containers. Following the pattern of home economists, Crisco ads stressed the sanitary and scientific qualities of the product. One of the first full-page ads appearing in a 1912 issue of the *Ladies Home Journal* proclaimed, "Crisco is never sold in bulk, but is put up in immaculate packages, perfectly protected from dust and store odors. No hands touch it. . . ."[67] The ad contained photos of fried fish, a cake, cookies, and a large pile of Crisco shortening on a plate. The headline declared, "An Absolutely New Product," followed by the subtitles, "A Scientific Discovery Which Will Affect Every Kitchen in America" and "Crisco—Better than butter for cooking."[68]

MAKING UP THE MODERN WOMAN

As domestic scientists were attempting to achieve their vision of the modern woman, the cosmetics industry was creating another image of the modern woman. Cosmetic ads provided models for how to look and act like a so-called *new woman*. This new woman was envisioned as independent, outspoken, and sexually assertive. The female leaders of the cosmetic industry were independent business women defining their roles in the new corporate world. However, their model of the sexually assertive and independent woman was often in conflict with the sanitized model of independent reformer presented by home economists.

As chronicled by Kathy Peiss in her wonderfully titled book, *Hope in a Jar: The Making of America's Beauty Culture*, cosmetic ads were the most blatant sellers of sexuality and promises of personal transformation.[69] Prior to the

20th century, Peiss argued, cosmetic products were primarily sold to keep the skin free of blemishes and maintain a clear and clean appearance. The face was considered a reflection of inward purity. Heavy use of paintlike cosmetics was associated with prostitution. In the early 20th century, the use of cosmetics changed with the marketing of make-up products by Estee Lauder, C. J. Walker, Helena Rubinstein, Elizabeth Arden, and Max Factor.

The leading women in the cosmetic industry—Max Factor got his start as a make-up artist for Hollywood films—promoted cosmetics as an industry open to women that would result in increasing women's power by enhancing their independence and sexuality. "The cosmetic business is interesting among modern industries in its opportunities for women," Helena Rubinstein argued. "Here they have found a field that is their own province—working for women with women, and giving that which only women can give—intimate understanding of feminine needs and feminine desires."[70] By 1930, beauty writer Nell Vinick was able to declare that cosmetics were "merely symbols of the social revolution that has gone on; the spiritual and mental forces that women have used to break away from conventions and to forward the cause of women's freedom."[71]

Although Elizabeth Arden did support women's suffrage, her political activity did not match that of Helena Rubinstein and C. J. Walker. Helena Rubinstein was a life-long supporter of women's equal rights, and C. J Walker, a pioneer developer of African-American cosmetics, supported equal rights for both women and African Americans. Walker promoted the use of cosmetics as a matter of racial pride. African-American women, she felt, should look good and project a positive social image. Using saleswomen, Walker hoped to create a new career route for African-American women. One of her salespeople claimed that she had enabled "hundreds of colored women to make an honest and profitable living."[72] Walker gave financial support and time to industrial education, recreational programs, and charitable giving to African Americans. She was active in the National Equal Rights League and the International League of Darker Peoples.[73]

The image of independent and politically active women sometimes appeared in advertisements. Leading women in advertising sometimes went out of their way to include their own political views in ads for cosmetics. The 20th century's largest advertising firm, J. Walter Thompson, had a separate Women's Editorial Department. In the early 1920s, members of the department cheered when they heard that Alva Belmont, a wealthy suffragist and feminist, agreed to endorse Pond's Cold Cream for a $1,000 donation to a feminist cause.[74] The resulting 1924 ad showed a small picture of her library at the top and a small picture of two bottles of Pond's creams at the bottom. The ad was entitled, "An Interview with Mrs. O.H.P. Belmont on the care of the skin." The opening quote from Mrs. Belmont quickly established that using Pond's creams increases a woman's chance for influence and success. "A woman who neglects her personal appearance loses half her influence. The wise care of one's body constructs the frame encircling our mentality, the ability of which ensures the success of one's life. I advise a daily use of Pond's Two Creams."[75] In the ad, Mrs. Belmont commented to the interviewer, "I suppose you want me to tell you what I think is the relation between a woman's success and her personal appearance. . . . It is vital. That is just as true for the woman at home or in business as for those who are socially prominent. . . . Don't you know how often the woman with an unattractive face fails in the most reasonable undertaking."[76]

A 1928 advertisement for Armand face powder portrayed eight different versions of the modern woman from sexual powerhouse to energetic club type:

1. Cleopatra Type—Masculine hearts pound when she goes by
2. Godiva Type—Anglo-Saxon, blond, winsome, and how!
3. Sonya Type—Dark and mysterious, she has a way with her
4. Cherie Type—She brings the boulevards of Paris to America
5. Sheba Type—Dark-brown and a queenly air
6. Lorelei Type—Blond and aggressive, she "gets her man"
7. Mona Lisa Type—Light-brown hair and a devastating smile
8. Collen Type—She has more pep than a jazz band.[77]

The modern political woman was emphasized in Listerine tooth paste ads in the 1920s. One ad showed a sultry-looking woman standing in a dimly lit room. Just below her in large type was: "When lovely women vote."[78] In smaller type, the ad claimed, "To thousands of women of this type—charming, educated, well-to-do, prominent in the social and civic life of her city, we put this question: What tooth paste do you use? To our delight, the majority answered Listerine Tooth Paste."[79]

Ads produced by African-American-owned companies emphasized the new African-American woman and enhancement of racial pride. A 1925 ad for C. J. Walker cosmetics showed a group of women attending an opera performance. Next to the drawing of the opera house interior was a photo of C. J. Walker. Below the photo and drawing was the declaration in large type, "Glorifying Our Womanhood." The text of the ad stated, "No greater force is working to glorify the womanhood of our Race than Madam C. J. Walker's Wonderful Hair and Skin Preparations. . . . We tell you, Madam C. J. Walker through her preparation, if for no other reason, remains yet, the greatest benefactress of our race."[80]

Advertisements directed at African-American consumers did provoke a great deal of criticism. Cosmetic ads were the richest source of revenue for magazines and newspapers published for the African-American community.[81] Some critics suggested that these ads promoted a White standard of beauty as exemplified by the following: "New 3-way Skin discovery Gives You WHITE SKIN OVERNIGHT"; "At last! The lighter complexion that increases beauty and . . . Makes Skin So Light Would Hardly Know She is Colored"; and "MAKE YOUR HAIR STRAIGHT AND BEAUTIFUL."[82] However, there were differences between the ads produced by White- and African-American-owned companies. White companies tended to portray the hair of African Americans as *ugly*, *kinky*, and *unruly*, whereas African-American companies simply marketed their hair products as promoting healthy hair and skin.[83]

The commodification of the woman's body created an advertising image of the new woman who was independent, aggressive, and sexually alive. In the 20th century, advertising portrayed make-up, soaps, underarm deodorants, mouthwashes, toilet paper, and body odor treatments as sources of social freedom. Although ads played on personal fears and anxieties, they also promised greater social freedom for women through the consumption of products. The purchase and use of products promised the new woman freedom from embarrassment and rejection. Through consumption of the right items, every woman was promised sexuality, independence, and assertiveness.

PLACING THE PRODUCT IN THE WOMAN'S MIND

Dominated by Protestants who grew up with the McGuffey readers and Sunday school literature, the advertising agencies that blossomed at the turn of the 20th century tried to distance themselves from earlier patent medicine ads, P.T. Barnum methods, and other forms of city reading.[84] Richard Ohmann argued that manufacturers poured money into these new advertising agencies to match industrial output with consumption. By the end of the 19th century, the crisis was no longer production, but consumption. People needed to buy more goods to keep the wheels of industry rolling. Not only did gross national product increase from $9.1 billion in 1873 to $29.6 billion in 1896 (figures in 1929 dollars), but, more important, output per person hour or productivity increased by 64% between 1869 and 1899. Increased productivity meant cheaper goods. Also new types of goods appeared on the market. In 1860, ready-to-wear men's clothing was practically nonexistent, but by 1890 ready-to-wear made up 90% of the market.[85]

Through advertising a new relationship was established between the owner and worker. In Ohmann's words, "They [manufacturers and advertisers] would urge workers—first those of the middle class, then all workers—to bring more and more commodities into homes, and to share in the vision of the good life conducted through the use and display of these products."[86] Between 1890 and 1904, advertising expenditures grew at the impressive rate of 128%.[87] In summary, the primary drive in building the advertising industry was the increased industrial output of old and new products.[88]

How did these early advertisers deal with abundance? After spending hours examining early advertisements, I was struck by the fact that few suggested the purchase of a product would result in some form of indulgent pleasure. An exception was Coca-Cola's claim to be "Delicious and Refreshing."[89] One of the earliest brand images was the Quaker Oats' man who first appeared in an 1888 ad to sell packaged oatmeal. Prior to packaging, people bought their oats directly from grocery store bins without any brand markings. There were few hints on packages or in ads that eating oatmeal was tasty and pleasing. The kindly figure of an elderly Quaker man appeared in the first ad with the promise that, "One pound of Quaker Oats makes as much bone and muscle as three pounds of beef . . . [they] supply what brains and bodies require."[90] Other food and beverage ads through the 1920s, as far as I can determine, emphasized the home economist's goals of purity, health, and good digestion. An early Schlitz beer ad compared "Poor Beer vs. Pure Beer" without any mention of taste or, heaven forbid, the pleasurable mental state caused by alcohol. The ad sold Schlitz beer as healthier than poor beer. The ad stated in making the comparison, "One is good, and good for you; the other is harmful." After comparing the differences in production, the ad asked, "Don't you prefer a pure beer, a good beer, a healthful beer, when it costs no more than the common?"[91] An early ad by the Quaker Oats Company for Puffed Wheat, Puffed Rice, and Corn Puffs mentioned one time that they had a "fascinating taste." Otherwise the emphasis was on digestion. The text might have been written by a professional home economist: "The purpose in Puffed Grains—Puffed Wheat or Puffed Rice—is to make digestion easy and complete. Digestion usually consumes much energy, because food cells are not broken." The ad continued with an explanation of how the puffing process made grains "wholly digestible without any tax on the stomach."[92] A famous 1925 Lucky Strike cigarettes' ad, which was designed to entice women into smoking, failed to mention anything about taste or the pleasure of nicotine racing through the nervous system. The ad proclaimed, "To Keep a slender figure, No one can deny, Reach for a Lucky instead of a sweet."[93]

The Lucky Strike ad highlighted another way consumption was separated from the pleasure of using a product. In *Fables of Abundance: A Cultural History of Advertising in America,* Jackson Lears argued that in "national advertisements . . . designed by . . . educated Anglo-Saxon professionals, pleasure was subordinated to a larger agenda of personal efficiency."[94] Food, tobacco, and beer ads promised health or slimness. Personal efficiency was linked to personal transformation. In the Lucky Strike ad, an attractive woman in a low-cut gown with puckered lips and half-closed eyes looks into an empty distance. The ad suggests that by smoking Lucky Strikes a woman will be transformed into the woman in the ad.

The goal of advertisers, according to Lears, was to awaken consumer desires while keeping them within the boundaries of Protestant propriety and market needs. Lears claimed, "advertisements did more than stir up desire, they also sought to manage it—to stabilize the sorcery of the marketplace by containing dreams of personal transformation within the broader rhetoric of control."[95] The combination of tapping into desire along with the stress on personal efficiency was exemplified by a 1916 Quaker Oats ad that read, "Mark the lovers of Quaker Oats. . . . They believe in keeping young. For oats create vitality. They feed the fires of youth. They are vim-producing, spirit-giving. . . . Lovers of life eat them liberally. Lovers of languor don't."[96] Throughout the ad were illusions of sexual desire through words such as *lovers* and *fires of youth*. The ad promised personal efficiency through greater *vitality* and *keeping young*.

SERVING WHITES: AFRICAN AMERICANS AND NATIVE AMERICANS

Advertising targeted at Euro-Americans used African-American images to give respectability to products. These images were in sharp contrast to advertisements directed at the African-American community. As mentioned previously, the ad for C. J. Walker cosmetics showed African-American women attending an opera. In contrast, ads for Euro-American audiences showed African Americans as smiling servants and cooks. The ads implied that a product was used by a family that could afford the use of African-American servants. Two of the most famous African-American icons were Aunt Jemima, who was used for a pancake mix, and Chef Rastus for Cream of Wheat Cereal. Besides being a pancake icon, Aunt Jemima, in the person of Nancy Greene, traveled around the country cooking pancakes at fairs with the advertising slogan: "I's in town, honey."[97] A 1897 ad for Cream of Wheat showed a poorly dressed and elderly African-American man staring at a billboard illustration of the smiling face of Chef Rastus. The billboard simply stated, "Cream of Wheat for Your Breakfast." The elderly African-American man proudly said, "AH RECKON AS HOW HE'S DE BES' KNOWN MAN IN DE WORL'."[98]

In contrast to African Americans, there were no ads directed to Native American consumers. While African Americans were forming a consumer market, Native Americans continued to be marginalized and considered outside the mainstream of Euro-American culture. In his study of the depiction of Native Americans in advertising, Jeffery Steele concluded, "African-Americans, wearing familiar [European-style] clothing are often depicted

indoors in domestic or vocational scenes, whereas American Indians are almost always shown outdoors in traditional, native attire (for example, moc-
casins, leggings, and headdresses)."[99] Images of exotically dressed Native
Americans were used to sell Hiawatha canned corn, Cherokee coal, Red
Warrior axes, and Savage rifles. Even to this day an Indian chief adorns cans
of Calumet baking powder, and packages of Land O'Lakes butter shows a
kneeling Indian maiden.

THE IRRATIONAL CONSUMER

Early advertising agencies dipped into psychological theory to design advertisements to direct human emotions to consumer purchases. Ads attempting to manipulate human emotions appeared around 1908 when Stanley
Resor was hired by J. Walter Thompson, the largest and most financially
successful advertising agency of the 20th century.[100] Originally, Resor was
hired to head the Cincinnati branch of J. Walter Thompson. In turn, he
hired as a copywriter his future wife, Helen Lansdowne, who became the
first major female advertising executive. Cincinnati was the location of
Procter & Gamble, which became one of the world's largest manufacturers.
Resor's branch was the first outside advertising agency to be hired by Procter & Gamble. Helen Lansdowne played the major role in the Procter &
Gamble ad campaigns, adding what she called "the feminine point of
view."[101] Her first Procter & Gamble ads were for the 1911 introduction of
Crisco and later Yuban coffee, Lux soap flakes, and Cutex nail polish. In
1916, Stanley Resor bought out J. Walter Thompson and assumed the presi-
dency of the firm. In 1917, he married Helen Lansdowne and they both became the driving forces in the firm.[102]

Resor believed that "Advertising, after all, is educational work, mass education."[103] While attending Yale, Resor said he was influenced by William
Graham Sumner's lectures on how the irrational desires of hunger, vanity,
fear, and sexuality determined human action. Whereas traditional economics posited a rational consumer making choices in a market of goods, Sumner's analysis of human motivation posited consumer choices as resulting
from basic instincts rather than rational choice.

In the early 20th century, both advertising and public relations operated
on the view that the public was primarily driven by irrational emotions. By
the 1920s, theories of irrational crowd behavior dominated advertising and
public relations views of the public. For instance, Ivy Lee, one of the founders of public relations, told a newspaper reporter in 1921 that, "Publicity is
essentially a matter of mass psychology. We must remember that people are
guided more by sentiment than by mind."[104] In the same year, he told an audience at Columbia's School of Journalism that, "You must study human

emotions and all the factors that move people, that persuade men in any line of human activity. Psychology, mob psychology, is one of the important factors that underlay this whole business."[105] In general, social psychologists who were influential in advertising and public relations emphasized the irrationality of the public mind. Historian Stuart Even wrote, "For publicists of the 1920s, however, irrationality had become the habitual filter through which human nature, in its most general terms, was understood."[106]

In playing on human emotions, advertising tended to accent social fears as opposed to pleasure as reflected in the work of famed child psychologist John Watson. In 1920, Resor hired John Watson and made him a vice president in the firm in 1924. Watson reinforced Resor's belief in the role of basic instincts in consumer decisions. The difference was that Watson believed that these instincts could be controlled. Referring to the human as an "organic machine," he explained to his advertising colleagues, "To get hold of your consumer or better, to make your consumer react, it is only necessary to confront him with either fundamental or conditioned emotional stimuli."[107] Besides controlling emotions to direct consumer choices, he believed that it could also be used to spur "the individual to reach a higher level of achievement."[108]

Watson exemplified how so-called *scientific methods* could be used to achieve traditional Protestant goals. He believed that emotional controls could stimulate the drive for achievement and the motivation to work. Watson translated the work ethic into the scientific jargon of psychology. He argued that the manipulation of emotions could cause a person to eliminate "his errors, work longer hours, and plan his work in a more systematic manner."[109] Watson's biographer concluded, "For Watson, then, the application of emotional controls could have the effect of increasing efficiency, order, and, of most importance for an industrial society, individual productivity."[110]

Fundamental to Watson's psychological theory of control were fear, rage, and love. Watson's actual experiments attempted behavioral control of infants' emotions. In his famous "Little Albert" experiments, he elicited fear from an infant by pounding a hammer on an iron bar while presenting the child with stuffed animals. The goal was to condition the infant to fear animals. It was these emotional controls that were to be translated into advertising copy.

At J. Walter Thompson, Watson dismissed the idea of advertising a product by its actual ingredients or components. For instance, cars, he argued, all contain the same basic components of engines, wheels, and other mechanical parts. Therefore, constantly changing designs and styles should be the basis for selling cars. This argument fit into an important part of the developing ideology of consumerism. Making a product obsolescent could be achieved by changing its style rather than through the deterioration or wearing out of the product. For Watson, it was important to create emotional conditioning for the design or style of a product.

Changes in design and style were planned to keep consumers in a state of dissatisfaction so they would continue to buy. Actual buyer satisfaction would defeat the purpose of consumerism, which was to keep factories busy and the economy rolling. The realization of happiness through the purchase of a product—something that many ads seemed to promise—would be destructive to the economy. In the 1920s, the director of research at General Motors said, "The whole object of research is to keep everyone reasonably dissatisfied with what he has in order to keep the factory busy making new things."[111]

Under Watson's guidance, and with the participation and approval of Stanley and Helen Resor, ads were consciously directed at emotions rather than at the content of the product. Cigarette ads presented smoking as sexual, contributing to enhanced attractiveness, independence, and self-fulfillment. Toothpaste ads emphasized sex appeal as opposed to personal hygiene. Many ads were erotic. These ads promised, as Lears noted, personal transformation.

Helen Lansdowne (later Helen Resor) used sex appeal in the 1911 Woodbury's Facial Soap ad. How much of this ad reflected discussions with her future husband and at the time agency head, Stanley Resor, would be difficult to determine. However, the ad certainly mirrored the lessons Stanley Resor had learned from William Graham Sumner that humans act from irrational desires connected with hunger, vanity, fear, and sexuality. The ad depicted a couple with the woman clutching a bouquet of flowers while the man ardently kissed her hand. In large type, the ad proclaimed, "A skin you love to touch" and in smaller type warned, "A skin of this kind is as rare because so few people understand the skin and its needs. They neglect it, and then use some powerful remedy. . . . Woodbury's Facial Soap re-supplies what is exhausted from the Skin. . . . Use it [Woodbury] regularly, not sporadically, and gradually the texture of your skin changes. . . ."[112] Here was sexual allure combined with the promise of personal transformation. Cleaning, the essential purpose of soap, is not mentioned. The ad portrays the objective of purchasing the soap to be creating skin that men will love to kiss and, consequently, turning the user into a sexual magnet. The purchaser buys an advertising dream of sexual transformation rather than a simple cake of cleansing soap.

Social fears played a role in J. Walter Thompson's ads for the first underarm deodorant, Odorno. Originally, Odorno was developed by a Cincinnati doctor to control perspiration during surgery. His daughter hit on the idea of selling it to women. The Odorno ad appeared in 1919, 2 years after Resor and Lansdowne's marriage and 1 year before Watson's arrival at the ad firm. The Odorno ad showed a man and woman embracing with the caption, "There isn't a girl who can't have the irresistible, appealing loveliness of perfect daintiness."[113] Filled with text the ad introduced readers to a new product. The ad alluded to sexuality and fear of social embarrassment. The ad opened, "A woman's arm! Poets have sung of it, great artists have painted its beauty. It should be the daintiest, sweetest thing in the world." The ad quickly went from the picture of the couple's embrace and the po-etry of women's arms to the warning, "There's an old offender in this quest for perfect daintiness—an offender of which we ourselves may be ever so unconscious, but which is just as truly present. . . . For it is a psychological fact that persons troubled with perspiration odor seldom can detect it themselves." Unlike the Woodbury ad, personal transformation is replaced with protection against a natural bodily function that might reduce one's sexual appeal. Fear and sexuality were combined.

These types of ads were given scientific legitimation after Watson joined the firm and conducted a study that found that smokers with particular brand preferences could not actually distinguish between brands in a blind-folded test. The result, according to Watson, proved that consumer choice was not based on reason but on emotions. In an ad for Pepco toothpaste, Watson showed a seductive woman smoking a cigarette. The cigarette was associated with independence and assertiveness for women. The ad sug-gested that is was all right to smoke as long as one used Pepco toothpaste. In the words of Watson's biographer,

> the advertising copy subtly raised the fear that one's attractiveness might be diminished by the effects of smoking on the breath and teeth. Toothpaste was promoted, not as contributing to health and hygiene, but as a means of heightening the sexual attraction of the user. Consumers were not merely buying toothpaste—they were buying "sex appeal." In this sense, commodities themselves became eroticized.[114]

The methods used by the J. Walter Thompson agency were used by other firms. An ad campaign by the Williams & Cunningham agency for the first mouth wash, Listerine, showed a tearful woman clutching a handkerchief while kneeling before what was apparently a marriage hope chest. Com-bining social fear, sexuality, and personal transformation, the large type of the ad introduced the catchphrase, "Often a bridesmaid but never a bride." The smaller type read, "Edna's case was really pathetic one. Like every woman, her primary ambition was to marry. . . . That's the insidious thing about halitosis (unpleasant breath). You, yourself, rarely know when you have it. And even your closest friends won't tell you."[115] The use of Listerine promised personal transformation into a sexual object attractive to men.

Ads flooded magazines, newspapers, and outdoor displays with brand names associated with relief from social anxieties and personal emotions.

Soaps promised protection against body odors and blackheads. An ad for Lifebuoy soap was entitled, "Why I cried after the party." In cartoon fashion was presented "The B. O. Experience 321." In the first frame of the cartoon, a woman lamented, "I knew I was the best dancer in the hall, but after the first few dances, the men drifted away. Like every party it ended in tears for me." Later, her best friend told her that the problem was body odor or B.O. She then bathed with Lifebuoy soap and her life was magically transformed: "Lifebuoy has been an 'open sesame' into life for me. My dance program is always full. Do you wonder I am deeply grateful."[116]

Probably the most explicit play on personal fears were Scot Tissue ads, which promised to protect against Acids, Mercury, and Arsenic supposedly found in other brands. An accompanying picture showed an attentive nurse looking at a bed-ridden child with the warning, "Be careful Mother!"[117] Mothers were asked to worry about rectal disease caused by the rubbing of harsh tissues. In this manner, the advertising industry played on personal and social fears, sexuality, and promises of personal transformation to sell consumerism to the American public and eventually the global community.

In the early 20th century, advertising images of women as consumers were in sharp contrast with those envisioned by home economists. In public schools, colleges, and in industry, home economists were imagining consumption as a vehicle for liberating women from the home. Advertising images portrayed women as wracked by emotional fears that could only be quieted by the consumption of the right product. However, in both instances, women were imagined as the consumer and the man as the producer.

WOMEN'S FASHIONS AS ARTIFICIAL OBSOLESCENCE

Fashion, central to the ready-to-wear industry, became a driving force in consumerism. Prior to the rapid growth of the ready-to-wear clothing industry in the early 20th century, the middle class and poor could only afford a limited number of garments. Only the rich could spend hours at dressmakers and clothiers being fitted. The middle class and poor spent time refurbishing worn clothing and buying from second-hand shops. The purchase of sewing machines in the latter half of the 19th century made it possible for middle-class families to expand their wardrobes. However, few poor people could afford to purchase a sewing machine.[118]

Changes in fashion spurred desires to buy new products. Fashion became a form of built-in obsolescence that eventually spread to other products, such as automobiles and home products. For immigrants, ready-to-wear fashions represented the promise of American life. In *A Perfect Fit: Clothes, Character, and the Promise of America*, Jenna Joselit wrote, "For . . .

countless immigrant women . . . ready-to-wear was not only a source of personal pleasure; ready-to-wear symbolized America—its abundance and flexibility its choices and resources. Ready-to-wear, proclaimed *Vogue*, aptly capturing its essence, was 'as American as turning on—and having—hot-water'."[119]

The ready to wear industry pioneered a system of consumption based on planned obsolescence. By changing the design of a product and advertising these changes, industries put the consumer in a constant state of dissatisfaction. Satisfaction over the purchase of new shoes or dresses was short-lived if the clothing and shoe industry suddenly advertised a new fashion trend. A perfectly good pair of shoes might suddenly be put aside for new styles. The early ideologue of consumerism, Simon Patten, argued that consumer dissatisfaction was key to economic growth. He contended, "It is not the increase of goods for consumption that raises the standard of life . . . [but] the rapidity with which [the consumer] tires of any one pleasure. To have a high standard of life means to enjoy a pleasure intensely and to tire of it quickly."[120]

Schools and home economists played an important role in promoting obsolescence through changing fashions. In her history of the clothing industry, Joselit commented, "Home economists were equally didactic in their use of the fashion show, hoping to transform high school students into surefooted consumers by teaching them 'buymanship'."[121] During the 1920s, home economists promoted the idea of high school fashion shows that used live models and music. The goal, from the standpoint of home economists, was for the high school to prepare girls for the modern role of consumer. Also home economics teachers claimed fashion shows helped students improve their postures.

Fashion changes sparked a public debate. Joselit argued that the growing ready-to-wear industry in the early 20th century caused, "A broad swath of Americans, from self-styled aesthetes to certified domestic scientists . . . to [worry] about the social and moral consequences of a nation now at liberty to change its clothes—and its image—at will."[122] Before World War I, critics in popular magazines called the use of fashion to control the public mind a new form of tyranny that caused addictive consumer tendencies comparable to opium or alcohol.

Working in high schools and youth clubs, home economists in the 1920s tried to turn fashion-conscious shoppers into wise consumers. High school and 4-H club members engaged in clothing contests where they modeled clothing before panels of teachers. Prizes were given for the most economical and sensible clothing. Working with the U.S. Department of Agriculture, home economists published and distributed a series of score cards to teach students how to evaluate their clothing purchases. On the score card, 30 points were given for "general appearance," 20 points each for "suitability" and "economic factors," and 10 points each for "health aspects" and "social influence."[123]

In addition, public schools promoted fashion as Americanization for immigrants and as a means of social uplift for minority populations. An educator at Cleveland's Technical High School taught that "good taste in dress" transformed immigrants, minorities, and the poor into "efficient thinkers and workers, homemakers and good citizens."[124] New York's Hebrew Technical School promoted proper dress as part of their broader educational program. The New Jersey Manual Training and Industrial School, which served African-American youth, learned that "people dress in order to make a picture and that to make a beautiful picture the correct colors must be combined in the right proportion."[125] While criticizing the dress of African-American students at Fisk University, civil rights leader W. E. B Du Bois argued that proper dress would help the African-American community.[126]

Fashions, similar to the new American cuisine, promised democratization of consumption. With inexpensive, ready-to-wear clothing, all people could participate in changes in fashion. In the 19th century, social class distinctions were obvious between those who could or could not afford to have their clothes made by professional tailors. Later in the 20th century, the mass appeal of blue jeans blurred social class distinctions in dress. However, designer names and logos began to identify the cost of clothing. Social class distinctions in fashion shopping were clearly established in the latter part of the 20th century when the Gap Corporation created a three-tier hierarchy of clothing stores—namely, Old Navy, Gap, and Banana Republic. This model of consumer markets was borrowed from the automobile industry, which turned fashion into artificial obsolescence and made cars into symbols of their owner's social class.

EQUALITY OF OPPORTUNITY AND CONSUMPTION

Along with changing their fashions, consumers were to use education to change jobs and status. Public schools continued as an icon for equality of opportunity. Nineteenth-century Protestantism often interpreted equality of opportunity as the acquisition of wealth while continuing to uphold the values of thrift and simple living. With 20th-century consumerism, equality of opportunity was more closely tied to spending and the acquisition of products. The translation of equality of opportunity into consumerism was most visible in the buying of cars. Leaders of the auto industry consciously tied financial success to the ownership of a particular model of car. Driving on city streets and highways, cars were an outward symbol of the financial success of the owner. In addition, the industry held out the promise that everyone had an equal opportunity to move up or down the scale of success through the purchase of a particular model, such as from Chevrolet to Cadillac.

Before creating a conscious scale of financial success through car models, the industry wrestled with the idea of artificial obsolescence. Fighting consumerist trends, the opening of Henry Ford's assembly line in 1913 was dedicated to the production of a durable and inexpensive automobile. Reflecting traditional Protestant values, Ford's commitment was to a simply designed car in one color. By the 1920s, Ford's black Model T was forced to compete with the trend of using changing fashions to increase sales.

During the 1920s, General Motors introduced the idea of preplanned artificial obsolescence through annual changes in technology and model designs. The campaign for annual models was led by Charles Kettering, who believed the mission of company research was to consciously keep the auto consumer in a state of dissatisfaction. General Motor's Chevrolet, Ford's major competitor, went through styling changes to overtake Ford's Model T in sales in 1927. In the same year, Alfred Sloan, president of General Motors, adopted the principle of the yearly model change as the principle method for selling all cars. Faced with the competition from Chevrolet, Ford finally capitulated to artificial obsolescence in 1927 with the production of the Model A.[127]

General Motors pioneered the idea of using social class or status as a means to sell a car. They wanted automobile models to be outward symbols of income and not simply a machine to travel from one point to another. General Motors offered symbols of income status beginning with the humble Chevrolet and moving up the line to Pontiac, Oldsmobile, Buick, and Cadillac. This income slope created the possibility of selling cars to people who were simply in search of status. A person might be tempted to sink a disproportionate amount of their income into buying a Cadillac to achieve a public symbol of affluence.[128]

Advertising became the means for relating products with social class and changing fashions. Considered one of the most celebrated ads in advertising history, Theodore MacManus pioneered the association of status symbols with particular products and models in his 1914 ad for Cadillac. "The Penalty of Leadership," the ad proclaimed in large type, while in smaller type the copy opened, "In every field of human endeavor, he that is first must perpetually live in the white light of publicity. Whether the leadership be vested in a man or in a manufactured product, emulation and envy are ever at work."[129] A 1926 ad promised the status symbol of a Cadillac in a choice of "50 Body Styles and types" and "500 Color Combinations."[130]

While the automobile industry became noted for creating artificial obsolescence, the practice was taken up by other industries. For instance, Elgin Watch Company's ads asked, "Was your present watch in style when *Uncle Tom's Cabin* came to town?" Elgin ads cautioned that watches were

an "index to . . . business and social standing." Standard Plumbing Fix-
tures warned that "bathrooms have aged more in the past year than in all
the twenty before." Radio ads suggested that older models "would look
funny now." During the 1920s, noted home economist, Christine Frederick, found that the typical American was quickly changing homes "because they seemed obsolescent to this family so rapidly moving up on the
social scale."[131]

Artificial obsolescence ensured that ownership of a product could never
be completely satisfying to the consumer. Ads might promise that purchasing a particular brand would provide for personal transformation, but
there would always be the disquieting knowledge that some other brand or
model might indicate a superior social class or status. Keeping the consumer in a constant state of dissatisfaction added to the stressful nature of
consumer society. Now the consumer was made anxious about the outward
signs of their social class along with the social fears generated by advertising. The flow of brand images in the public mind created fear of body and
mouth odors along with the shame of driving a lowly Ford or Chevrolet.
With artificial obsolescence and advertising that related products to income, consumerism defined *equality of opportunity* as the ability to move up
and down a slope of income and ability to consume products.

CONCLUSION: THE PURITAN AND THE IMMIGRANT

Anzia Yezierska's 1923 novel *Salome of the Tenements* illustrates the conflict
among consumerism, traditional Protestant values, and newly arrived immigrants. By the 1920s, public schools, magazines, and newspapers were inun-
dating the public with consumer values, fashion changes, and brand icons.
The novel's main character, Sonya Vrunsky, exemplified the educated and
independent women who were growing up in the mix of Protestant and immigrant cultures of the early 20th century. In many ways, she was the type of
new woman that home economists were aiming for as they taught and
worked in public schools, colleges, and the food industry.

In contrast to Sonya, the novel's main male character, John Manning,
tried to imbue new immigrants with traditional Protestant values of simple
living and hard work. Manning was a composite character drawn from the
author's real-life knowledge of John Dewey, the philosopher, educator, and
social reformer, and Graham Stokes, the millionaire socialist and philan-
thropist.[132] In fact, the novel was written a few years after the author refused
to have sex with John Dewey.

John Manning, supposedly reflecting the passionless character of John
Dewey, wrote to the passionate Sonya, a poor Jewish immigrant living in the
teeming ghetto of the Lower East Side, "Identify yourself with your work.

Work is the only thing real. The only thing that counts. The only thing that lasts."[133]

The tensions between John and Sonya dramatize the interactions between the Protestant elite and immigrants over a world filled with an abundance of goods and new forms of leisure. Sonya embraces the new possibilities for consumption and regards consumerism as being more important than existing political ideologies. Referring to the growth of the fashion industry, Sonya made her famous statement of choice, "Talk about democracy. . . . All I want is to be able to wear silk stockings and Paris hats the same as Mrs. Astorbilt, and then it wouldn't bother me if we have Bolshevism or Capitalism, or if the democrats or the republicans win."[134]

Protestant reformers and educators feared that the morality of the nation would be undermined by the movie theaters and dance halls popping up in immigrant neighborhoods. Throughout *Salome of the Tenements,* the author highlighted the divide between the stiff morality of the Anglo-Saxon Protestant and the passionate morality of the new immigrants. The author was probably made acutely aware of this divide while attending Columbia's Teachers College and, at the same time, working as a laundress. At Teachers College, she met John Dewey, who in 1917 offered to help her publish some early writings. Her contact with Dewey, other educators at Teachers College, and social reformers working in tenement areas left her with bitter feelings about Protestant Anglo-Saxons. To her they were ice people incapable of experiencing pleasure. In the novel, a Jewish newspaper writer tells Sonya, "The Anglo-Saxon coldness, it's centuries of solid ice that all the suns of the sky can't melt. Nobody can tell what that frozen iciness is, except those that got to live with it."[135] John and Sonya symbolize the struggle between the two cultures. The author describes,

> Sonya and Manning . . . were the oriental and the Anglo-Saxon trying to find a common language. The over-emotional Ghetto struggling for its breath in the thin air of Puritan restraint. An East Side savage forced suddenly into the strait-jacket of American civilization. Sonya was like the dynamite bomb and Manning the walls of tradition constantly menaced by threatening explosions.[136]

The clash between cultures appeared in attitudes about material goods. It was the Sunday School ethic of unostentatious living and buying only necessities versus fashion and buying for pleasure. Dressed in the latest fashion, Sonya meets John in a ghetto tea room where he is bewildered by the loud noise and activity. The author describes his reaction, "Her [Sonya's] abandon, her nakedness staggered him, and John Manning, the product of generations of Puritans, retreated into his shell."[137] After Sonya declares that she was "the ache of unvoiced dreams, the clamor of suppressed desires," John responds, "I am a Puritan whose fathers were afraid to trust experience. We are bound by our possessions of property, knowledge and tradition."[138] At another point in the novel, John pronounces his love for the poor's simplicity. Sonya responds, "You like the working-girl in her working dress. . . . You like her with the natural sweat and toil on her face—no make-up—not artifice to veil the grim lines of poverty?"[139] The reference to make-up reflected the growing association of cosmetic use with the liberated woman. Reminiscent of the glorification of poverty and hard work in 19th-century children's literature, John answers, "Exactly. . . . Poverty and toil are beautiful crowns of the spirit and need no setting off."[140] Later, in an act of Puritan philanthropy, John proclaimed, "The service I feel myself called upon to render the East Side is to teach the gospel of the Simple Life."[141]

In *Salome of the Tenements,* John wanted working women to avoid the fashions of ready-to-wear clothes by returning to the practice of making their own clothes. He asked Sonya to teach the "working-girl . . . to avoid, vulgar styles and showing her how beautiful it is to be simple."[142] When Sonya replied, "But they buy those gaudy styles because they're cheap and ready-made," John exclaimed, "We want to get them away from that. We want to teach them how to make their own clothes."[143]

As embodied in John, Protestant morality required a world freed from the temptation of worldly goods. The social expert, the new guardian of morality, was to control any consumption that might lead to degradation. John proudly explained to Sonya how he was using social experts to help immigrants. "The words 'social experts,' 'scientific,' 'plane of reason,' " the novel's narrator commented, "were like icy winds over her [Sonya's] enthusiasm."[144] Shortly after John's comments on social experts, Sonya concealed herself behind a pillar in a lecture room where a social expert complained about finding a woman cooking chicken after being given rations of corn-meal, rice, and macaroni. Sonya dashed from the room thinking, "So it's a crime to eat chicken if you get charity. . . . Worthy poor—those who are content with cornmeal!"[145]

For Sonya, representing the new immigrants, the promise of America was access to consumer goods. Arriving from mainly peasant villages in Southern and Eastern Europe, immigrants were surrounded by advertisements promising personal transformation and relief from social anxieties. Consumer goods and brand icons promised stability in the rapidly changing world of the immigrant. Ads targeting African-American consumers promised race pride and uplift. For many African Americans, clothes and cosmetics became part of a broader dream of achieving equal rights and equality of opportunity. Reflecting the tensions in public racial images, ads targeted for the Euro-American market continued to show African Americans in service to Whites and marginalized Native Americans as the exotic other.

Underlying these tensions was the debate over a rational versus irrational public. Regarding this debate, Stuart Ewen argued,

> At one end there was the Progressive democratic faith, which assumed that people were essentially rational beings, that could be most effectively persuaded by a . . . factual, logically framed argument. At the other end was the perspective . . . that human nature was essentially irrational and . . . that "opinion" was most efficiently shaped by scientifically informed subliminal appeals to unconscious urges and instinctual drives.[146]

By emphasizing fashion and status models, industry and advertisers treated the public as if it were irrational. The goal was to keep the consumer in a constant state of dissatisfaction. Hoping for social transformation through consumption, the buyer was often disappointed. When confronted with more prestigious models of the same product that they owned, consumers were made to feel dissatisfied. Consumerism depended on the constant desire to buy more rather than achieving satisfaction. In this climate, the public school promise of equality of opportunity offered the unattainable goal of achieving consumer satisfaction by earning more money and buying more products. The American dream became a nightmare about working hard to attain the unattainable goal of consumer satisfaction.

Chapter 3

Cowboys and Jocks:
Visions of Manliness

In the first half of the 20th century, the dominant public image of White men was sports-minded, patriotic, and patron of women as domestic consumers. Men sought their identities in leisure time activities, particularly sports. Commodified forms of leisure were male consumer activities, which included buying tickets to sporting events and equipment for golf, fishing, hunting, and other outdoor activities. Of course men participated in major decisions regarding domestic consumption. Also ads presented car purchases as joint decisions. However, men interested in fashions, particularly clothing fashions, were considered effeminate. In contrast to the 19th century, 20th-century educators and image makers drew a sharper line between homo- and heterosexuality.

Sports and other leisure time activities were to provide the new male with a means of sexual control, particularly control of adolescent sexuality. Despite the emphasis on controlling sexuality, advertising used male and female imagery to imbue consumer items with the promise of sexual fulfillment. In this particular context, consumerism became another form of sexual activity. Ironically, the Puritan effort to control sexuality resulted in making consumer items objects of sexual desire. In schools, popular magazines, and ads, the new White man was strictly heterosexual, athletically oriented, muscular, and someone separated from the supposedly more emotional world of women.

Patriotism was important to both consumerism and male identity. By the 1930s, the ideology of consumerism was related to something called the *American way of life*, which promised a high standard of living as measured by the consumption of the increased output of industrialism. Threatened by communism as an alternative to American consumerism, schools, the press, and media bombarded the public with patriotic messages. The patriotism of the 1920s was different from earlier forms. The new patriotism was a form of economic nationalism that considered the threat to America to come from alternative economic systems. In direct contact with the American Legion, the public schools linked this form of patriotism to the image of the new White male.

THE CRISIS IN MALE IDENTITY

In part, the image of the new White man that appeared at the turn of the 19th and early 20th centuries was a reaction to the image of the new woman. Some White men were outraged that women scientists, physicians, and voters were displacing manhood with womanhood. Gail Bederman claimed, "Yet the new woman did 'displace manhood with womanhood' if only because her successes undermined the assumption that education, professional status, and political power required a male body. The woman's movement thus increased the pressure on middle-class men to reformulate manhood."[1] Typical of the satirical press about the new woman, an 1897 illustration showed a woman warning her husband as he took over laundry and child-care duties, "Don't Get the Clothes Too Blue!"[2] Even as early as 1869, there were expressions of male fears that women wanted to reverse roles. A Currier and Ives lithograph showed a woman entering a carriage driven by another woman while men are depicted doing child care and the laundry.[3]

Also as Bederman indicated, White males felt a loss of independence as they increasingly worked in corporations and factories. Before the Civil War, 88% of Americans were self-employed.[4] Between 1870 and 1910, the number of self-employed White middle-class men declined from 67% to 37%.[5] As a result of work in corporate structures, doctors declared that the newly discovered disease of neurasthenia caused by excessive brain work was spreading rapidly among professional and businessman.[6] Some people advocated rigorous physical activities such as body building, sports, hiking, camping, hunting, and fishing as a cure for neurasthenia. Theodore Roosevelt, a national symbol for the new manhood, declared that the continuation of American civilization depended on men practicing, as his 1899 speech was entitled, "The Strenuous Life."[7]

In public schools, organized athletics and gym were to develop the new man. In fact, the growing educational importance of athletics and gym for boys paralleled the inclusion of home economics courses in public schools. In this context, public schools were given an important role in educating the new man and woman. Besides invigorating the body as protection against the lethargy of modern living, athletics, gym, and outdoor activities were to teach self-control of sexuality. Fearing that modern living and entertainment, particularly movies, would unleash sexual drives that would undermine civilization, educators contended that organized sports and school activities could channel sexual drives into social service activities.[8]

As consumers, according to Mark Swiencicki, between 1880 and 1930 men spent twice as much as women on leisure time activities, which amounted to about 30% of a family's disposable income.[9] The consumption of leisure time activities supports Bederman's contention that, "The growth of a consumer culture encouraged many middle-class men . . . to find identity in leisure instead of in work."[10] By the 21st century, I would contend, the TV viewing and discussion of sports, such as football, basketball, and baseball, would occupy a large amount of the time for white- and blue-collar workers.

Differences in spending between men and women on personal grooming items highlight the distinctions in personal identity. The men found their identity in leisure time activities, whereas women found it in cosmetics and clothing fashions. According to Swiencicki's figures for 1890, men spent only 30% of the total dollars spent on perfumery and cosmetics.[11] However, these figures do not diminish the importance of the male market for personal grooming items such as shavers, shaving creams, hair lotions, cologne, and skin conditioners.

With regard to clothing, men's interest in fashions reflected a growing trend to define the new masculinity in heterosexual terms. In her history of clothing, Jenna Joselit argued, "From their vantage point [men in the early 20th century], not only was it dumb to pay attention to what one wore, it was foppish or effeminate. . . . American men did not concern themselves too much with clothing lest they be thought 'pansies'."[12] The feeling that a focus on fashion threatened male images reflected the role of schools and advertising in nurturing a public image of heterosexuality as the *normal* form of sexual relations. As George Chauncey argued, "the hetero–homosexual binarism, the sexual regime now hegemonic in American culture, is a stunningly recent creation."[13] Prior to the middle of the 20th century, abnormality was primarily associated with men who acted effeminate and not with sexual relations between men. Men who acted according to the socially ascribed characteristics of being male while also engaging in sexual activities were considered normal. Chauncey contended that, "Only in the 1930s, 1940s, and 1950s did the now-conventional division of men into 'homosexuals' and heterosexuals,' based on the sex of their sexual partners, replace the division of men into 'fairies' [effeminate men] and 'normal men' on the basis of their imaginary gender status as the hegemonic way of understanding sexuality."[14] In both the proper dating practices taught in schools and the depictions of couples in advertising, heterosexuality was made the norm.

Advertising created gender images that contrasted the emotional consumer and dependent female with the self-controlled, athletic, and outdoor male. The cowboy came to symbolize the lost masculinity of the modern White male. Theodore Roosevelt, born and bred in New York City, tried to affirm his masculinity by buying a Western ranch and donning the garb of the cattleman and hunter. The statue outside the Roosevelt Memorial rotunda at the American Museum of Natural History in New York City bears testimony to this self-created image. Roosevelt sits snugly in a saddle in full cowboy attire with Indians standing alongside the horse.[15] This image was re-created in the 1950s in America's most famous icon of masculinity, the Marlboro Man, who was depicted consuming Marlboro cigarettes while riding horses, corralling cattle, and hanging out by the campfire.[16] Earlier this symbol of masculinity appeared in a 1913 Cream of Wheat ad with a depiction of a cowboy with a holstered revolver on horseback placing a letter in a wooden mailbox mounted on a tall post. The mailbox was marked "Cream of Wheat," and the ad's caption read, "Where the mail goes Cream of Wheat goes."[17]

Also there was a racial component to the depiction of the new man as protector of civilization. The statue outside the American Museum of Natural History depicts the masculine image of Roosevelt on horseback towering above a Native American on foot. The Indian clings to Roosevelt's saddle bag with his nose just below Roosevelt's holstered revolver. Roosevelt's White manliness is presented in sharp contrast to the subdued and conquered Native American. It is this White manliness that was supposed to lead the savage into civilization. In the late 19th and early 20th centuries, as Gail Bederman stated, "In a variety of venues and contexts, white Americans contrasted civilized white men with savage dark-skinned men, depicting the former as paragons of *manly* virtue."[18]

There was also a social class component to male identity. In the early 20th century, advertising primarily presented images of businessmen dressed in suits and ties even while lounging at home. It was these denizens of the modern corporation that needed to protect their manly identity. Corporate life, it was believed, was weakening male bodies. However, not all men in the early 20th century were businessmen who wore suits at home. Many could not afford to own a suit. By the end of the economic boom period of the 1920s, there still existed "35 to 40 percent of the non-farm population" living in poverty.[19] According to Susan Porter, only about a third of working class families owned automobiles while barely half the households had flush toilets.[20]

Among low-income males, male identity was defined in a variety of ways. For some men, union activity, including strikes and political actions, exemplified an independent and manly life. Some men established their identity by rejecting marriage and family obligations. They were *real men* who were not going to be tied down by a wife and children. Others rebelled against the industrial discipline of the factory and refused to be tied down by a job. Similar to their businessmen counterparts, these men believed that factory life was stealing their manhood. Yet rather than working and seeking their male identity in leisure time activities, these working class men simply rejected a life of steady work becoming drifters and hoboes. Many working class men maintained their sense of independence and manliness by retaining part of their wages for personal spending on smoking, drinking, and gambling.[21]

Although I do not have any statistics available, I would hypothesize that many factory workers continued to maintain their manliness, like their businessmen counterparts, by spending weekends hunting and fishing. Later, with the advent of TV, men would spend many weekend hours watching sports. Manliness could be achieved through sports as a participant or spectator. The consumption of sports became the greatest venue for maintaining a sense of manliness.

SPERMATIC POLITICAL ECONOMY AND PATRIOTISM

Advocacy of male sexual control accompanied the new patriotic efforts to defeat alternative economic systems. Puritan fear of uncontrolled male sexuality infused activities supporting the new male image, including college and high school sports, sex education courses, school clubs, and high school dating and dancing. *Self-control* was often the word used to indicate the channeling of sexual desire into other activities. Self-control was also associated with what was the male adolescent vice of masturbation. Fear of masturbation and sexual excess in marriage was based on what M. E. Melody and Linda Peterson called "spermatic political economy."[22] There was a popular belief in the late 19th century that loss of semen, through masturbation or other sexual activity, weakened the male physically and mentally. It was even suggested that loss of sperm led to feeble-mindedness and criminality. John Harvey Kellogg, producer of Kellogg cereals and operator of the Battle Creek Sanitarium, popularized the idea of seminal control in *Plain Facts about Sexual Life* (1877) with authoritative statements such as, "The seminal fluid is the most highly vitalized of all the fluids of the body, and its rapid production is at the expense of a most exhaustive effort on the part of the vital forces, is well attested by all physiologists."[23] Marital excesses and masturbation, Kellogg told his popular readership, resulted in a man finding "manhood lost, his body a wreck, and death staring him in the face."[24] Summarizing Henry Hanchett's *Sexual Health: A Plain and Practical Guide for the People on All Matters Concerning the Organs of Reproduction in Both Sexes and All Ages* (1887) in the language of political economy, Melody and

Peterson wrote, "Sex exhausts men, it saps their vitality. Semen is an 'expensive' fluid for the body to produce and so spending decisions must be made carefully."[25]

Spermatic political economy was basic to preservation of the male amid the temptations of modern urban life. Men had to find outlets for their sexual desires that did not result in the loss of sperm. Adding a note of romanticism to the protection of sperm loss, it was argued that sexual desire could be redirected to fighting for social and political ideals. Communing with nature through hiking, hunting, and fishing along with participation in sports would save the body and mind of the male from the deleterious loss of sperm and, at the same time, educate the male to service the country. In this sense, patriotic war became sexualized.

A good example of this new male image is the Theodore Roosevelt rotunda at the American Museum of Natural History. Roosevelt was considered one of the strongest advocates of the late 19th and 20th centuries for educating youth in manhood to overcome the debilitating effects of modern life.[26] Michael Kimmel wrote, "America's self-proclaimed and self-constructed 'real man,' Roosevelt was, as he proclaimed a completely Self-Made Man."[27] Both Roosevelt and his father worked actively to promote and expand the work of the Museum as part of their belief in the importance of contact with nature in maintaining masculine values. In the *Winning of the West*, written in four volumes in the 1880s and 1890s, Roosevelt presents the Indian wars as a test for White American males that established their superiority over Indians. It was the actual fighting that demonstrated, according to Roosevelt, the virile and heroic qualities of White males. In this sense, a willingness to fight and die in battle was the ultimate test of manhood.[28]

These masculine and patriotic values were embodied in the cowboy image on the statue of Roosevelt and the Indian outside the Roosevelt Rotunda and in Roosevelt's words etched on the interior walls. Roosevelt's linkage of nature to masculinity and war are found in the wall etching entitled "Nature," "Youth," "Manhood," and the "State." In Roosevelt's world, these four topics were interdependent. The strenuous life experienced in "Nature" was essential for the proper education of "Youth" for "Manhood." "Manhood" was essential for maintaining the civilized "State."

As president, Roosevelt put into practice—through the establishment of national parks and forests—his belief that preservation of nature was essential to maintaining White American manhood and, consequently, American ideals. In his personal life, although somewhat frail and asthmatic, Roosevelt tramped around the United States and the world exploring and hunting. The continued existence of places for men to experience the strenuous life through camping, hiking, hunting, and fishing, he believed, would ensure the continued manliness of the urban male. His statement on

"Nature" intertwines the hardy life with the conservation of resources and destiny of the nation. The romanticization of nature is eventually linked in the inscriptions of the patriotic ideal of fighting for the state. The inscription on nature reads,

Nature

There is a delight in the hardy life of the open
There are no words that can tell the hidden spirit of the wilderness that can reveal its mystery its melancholy and its charm
The nation behaves well if it treats the natural resources as assets which it must turn over to the next generation increased;
and not impaired in value Conservation means development as much as it does protection.[29]

Roosevelt's inscription on "Youth" was obviously intended for male youth. From his perspective, it was obviously manly men who were the most important beneficiaries of nature and central to the preservation of the nation. Also the statement reflected his own emphasis on sports and games while he was a student at Harvard. He believed boxing at Harvard contributed to the development of his own manliness. Games, bravery, manliness, gentleness, and character were all linked to the success of the nation.

Youth

I want to see you game boys
I want to see you brave and manly and I also want to see you gentle and tender
Be practical as well as generous in your ideals
Keep your eyes on the stars and keep your feet on the ground
Courage, hard work, self-mastery, and intelligent effort are all essential to successful life
Character in the long run is the decisive factor in the life of an individual and of nations alike.[30]

Roosevelt believed daring, courage, endurance, and ideals were essential features of manliness. Courage was a willingness to die for one's ideals. This willingness to pursue death for an ideal was a result of the training received in youth.

Manhood

A man's usefulness depends upon his living up to his ideals insofar as he can
It is hard to fail but it is worse never to have tried to succeed
All daring and courage all iron endurance of misfortune make for a finer nobler type of manhood

Only those are fit to live who do not fear to die and none are fit to die who
have shrunk from the joy of life and the duty of life.

The inscription on "The State" completes the link among preservation
of nature, education of youth, manliness, sports, war, and nationalism. In
fact, Roosevelt classified war as the "noblest sport the world affords." As I
discuss, the introduction of athletics in American high schools was considered preparation for citizenship and nationalism. From Roosevelt's perspective, and that of many of his generation, manliness meant the courage
to die for ideals and the state.

The State

Ours is a government of liberty by through and under the law
A great democracy must be progressive or it will soon cease to be great or a de-
mocracy
Aggressive fighting for the right is the noblest sport the world affords
In popular government results worth while can only be achieved by men who
combine worthy ideals with practical good sense
If I must choose between righteousness and peace
I choose righteousness.[31]

The Roosevelt rotunda embodies the educational ideals of masculinity at
the beginning of the consumer age. These ideals were embodied in educational changes, which stressed athletics and extracurricular activities in
high schools as preparation for manhood and patriotism. They also paralleled the ideas of psychologist and educators.

THE SPERMATIC POLITICAL ECONOMY OF HIGH
SCHOOL SPORTS

Male consumption of tickets to sporting events, sporting equipment, and
the following of sporting events through the media were affirmed by theories of masculinity and spermatic political economy. Becoming a mass institution by the 1930s, the high school became a training ground for male pre-
occupation with sports. Crucial to the development of modern high school
life was the work of psychologist G. Stanley Hall. Like others, Hall was influenced by ideas on spermatic political economy. In his classic work *Adolescence* (1904), Hall made a direct link between the control of male sexuality
and the maintenance of modern civilization. For Hall, girls needed to preserve their sexual energies for reproduction.[32] In contrast, men needed to
channel their sexuality into service to others and the nation. Manliness and
civilization required self-control of sexual drives. Hall proposed that sports,

organizations (such as the YMCA, Boy Scouts), and schools were crucial in channeling male sexuality into social service. Hall wrote, "The whole future of life depends on how the new powers [of adolescence] now given suddenly and in profusion are husbanded." Hall believed the control of sexuality was necessary for society to evolve to its modern stage. He wrote, "The whole future of life depends on how the new powers [of adolescence] now given suddenly and in profusion are husbanded." According to Hall's theory of recapitulation, each stage of individual development paralleled a stage of social evolution. Childhood—the years between 4 and 8—corresponded to a cultural epoch when hunting and fishing were the main activities of humanity. From 11 to 12, according to Hall, the child recapitulated the life of savagery. During puberty, the new flood of passions developed the social person: "The social instincts undergo sudden unfoldment and the new life of love awakens."[33]

Bederman argued, "like many of his contemporaries, [Hall] feared overcivilization was endangering American manhood. As a nationally recognized expert on pedagogy, he believed it was his responsibility to make sure American boys received a virile education that avoided overcivilized effeminacy."[34] Hall believed that a virile education, which meant the channeling of adolescent sexual drives into manly social activities, would be the panacea for most social problems: "womb, cradle, nursery, home, family, relatives, school, church and state are only a series of larger cradles or placenta, as the soul . . . builds itself larger missions, the only test and virtue of which is their service in bringing the youth to ever fuller maturity."[35]

The popular press and Hall's psychology created an image of adolescence as a romantic stage of life during which the developing sexual-social drives could lead the adolescent to either a life of decadence or a life of social service. The romantic and poetic impulses of youth, it was believed, could be captured and directed toward socially useful projects such as helping the poor, the community, or the nation. Boy Scouts, the YMCA, and other youth organizations were justified by their ability to channel the sexual-social drives of youth.

Organized sports was considered a key element in dissipating and controlling youthful sexuality. Historian Michael Kimmel captioned this change, "Restoring Masculinity by Remaking the Body." Kimmel summarized the sports movement, "Turn-of-the-century [19th to 20th] America went 'sports crazy,' as thousands of men sought to combat the enervating effects of their urban white-collar working lives with manly physiques, health regimens, and participation in sports."[36] A 1900 book ad in the leading body building magazine, *Physical Culture*, demonstrated the connection being made between sexual control and athletic activity. Entitled *Manhood Wrecked and Rescued*, the book ad promised to save men from sexual weakness and resulting self-destruction by making them "strong manly men, instead of physical and social wrecks."[37] The ad's outlined chapter summaries captured the belief that sexual activity destroyed manliness and that athletics could protect the body from sexual dissipation: "Chapter IV—A Youthful Wreck: Masturbation . . . Prevalence of this solitary vice . . . Loss of semen is loss of blood-Results of its expenditure—Seminal Emissions—Effects on the nervous system . . . Where masturbation and marital excess do their deadly work." The final three chapters of the book were devoted to "The Rescue," with an explanatory emphasis on the relationship between nervous function and muscular power. The book was sold along with a year's subscription to *Physical Culture* and a copy of Bernarr Macfadden's booklet on *Physical Training*.[38] The naked and sculpted muscular body of Bernarr Macfadden was displayed on the cover of his book, *The Virile Powers of Superb Manhood*.[39]

A 1922 poster entitled "The Sex Impulse and Achievement" of the American Social Hygiene Association captured the same belief in the relationship between athletic activity and sexual control. The poster showed a group of young men running hurdles. The caption under the picture read:

> The sex instinct in a boy or man makes
> him want to act, dare, possess, strive.
> When controlled and directed, it gives
> ENERGY, ENDURANCE,
> FITNESS.[40]

Educators expanded the public school's social activities to protect adolescent sexuality from the temptations of modernity. The 1911 report of the National Education Association's (NEA)—at the time the most influential education organization—Committee on a System of Teaching Morals stated that adolescence is "the time of life when passion is born which must be restrained and guided aright or it consumes soul and body. It is the time when social interests are dominant and when social ideals are formed."[41] The report proposed teaching morals in high school through cooperative social activities, student government, and a curriculum dealing with the relationship between the individual and society. In *The High-School Age* (1914), Irving King, professor of Education at the University of Iowa, argued that a high school education must provide the adolescent with opportunity for social service because, at the age of 16, "youth emerges from the somewhat animal-like crassness of the pubertal years and begins to think of his social relationships, his duties and the rights and wrongs of acts."[42] Reflecting a belief that education could lead youth to accept social ideals, he continued, "Every youth is . . . an incipient reformer, a missionary, impatient with what seem to him the pettiness and the obtuseness of the adult world about him." The same sentiment was echoed by Michael V. O'Shea, professor of Education at the University of Wisconsin, in *Trend of the Teens*, published in 1920. According to O'Shea, the "reformer . . . realizes that if he would get his cause adopted he must appeal to youth. . . . Youth longs for a new order of things."[43]

To a major extent, concerns about male sexuality influenced the development of the modern American high school with its trappings of organized athletics, pep rallies, cheerleaders, and extracurricular activities. The modern high school that emerged in the 1920s was quite different from the classically oriented school of the 19th century. Under the influence of new sexual concepts of youth, the National Education Association organized a commission in 1913 whose report eventually established the basic framework for the modern high school. This group, the Commission on the Reorganization of Secondary Education, issued its final report in 1918 as the now famous *Cardinal Principles of Secondary Education.*

According to the Cardinal Principles, high school athletics and extracurricular activities would channel adolescent sexuality into socially useful activities. Social cooperation, the report stated, was necessary for a modern democracy, and it could be developed through "participation of pupils in common activities . . . such as athletic games, social activities, and the government of the school."[44] Athletics was considered a key method in channeling adolescent sexuality into cooperative social activity. It taught youth how to cooperate and work with a team. This argument was one reason for the rapid growth of football in the public schools. As a team game, football fostered the coordination and cooperation needed in a corporate organization. A Seattle high school principal told the National Education Association in 1915, "In the boy's mind, the football team is not only an aggregation of individuals organized to play, but a social instrument with common needs, working along common lines, and embodying a common purpose."[45]

Comparisons to war and corporate life made sports into a metaphor for modern life. Likening competitive sports to war persisted from the 1890s into the 21st century. At the turn of the 19th to 20th centuries, the father of modern football, Walter Camp, claimed there was a "remarkable and interesting likeness between the theories which under lie great battles and the miniature contests of the gridiron."[46] The competition of the playing fields was equated to the competition of capitalism. However, that competition, as in sports, needed to be contained within the organization needs of corporate life. Writing in *Outlook*, Cunningham LaPlace argued that team competition taught students the "subordination of the unit to the total, the habit of working with his fellows, of touching elbows."[47] Theodore Roosevelt made a direct comparison between life and team sports: "In life, as in foot-ball game, the principle to follow is: Hit the line hard; don't foul and don't shirk but hit the line hard . . . [sports are] a means of preparation for the responsibilities of life . . . [and teach] qualities useful in any profession."[48] As a church-going man observed in the 1920s, "Life is a football game, with the men fighting it out on the gridiron, while the minister is up in the grandstand, explaining the game to the ladies."[49]

SEX EDUCATION

Ironically, despite the efforts of educators and moral reformers, adolescent sexuality seemed to be heightened with the development of the high school as a mass institution. By bringing together all adolescents, the high school made possible a teenage culture that focused on the rituals of dating, sex and, eventually, a teenage consumer market. Athletics was only one part of the high school program designed to control adolescent sexuality. Another was sex education.

The addition of sex education to the school curriculum was a logical step in attempts to control adolescent sexuality. One goal of the American Social Hygiene Association, organized in 1905, was to get sex education into the schools. Influenced by the social hygiene movement, the NEA endorsed sex education courses for the schools.[50] In 1926, the NEA's Committee on Character Education recommended sex education as a means to combat the decline of the family and regulating sexual impulses for the good of society. Its report gave the purpose of human life as: "The creation of one's own home and family, involving first the choice and winning of, or being won by, one's mate." Sex education was to prepare youth to fulfill this purpose. "The recent activities," the report states, "in sexual and social hygiene are in the nature of forerunners to this work."[51]

The type of sex education advocated by the NEA was modeled on the work of a member of the NEA's Character Education Committee, Thomas Galloway. Galloway was Associate Director of the American Social Hygiene Association Department of Educational Measures and the author of its official training manual, *Sex and Social Health: A Manual for the Study of Social Hygiene*. He was also author of a number of other books, including *The Sex Factor in Human Life* and *Biology of Sex*.

Galloway's preface to the official sex education training manual, *Sex and Social Health*, suggested using it to guide community discussions, as a textbook for parent–teacher groups and teacher training programs, and as a reference book.[52] The stated premise of the manual was that "reproductive processes and the associated sexual impulses are not individual but social privileges and phenomena."[53] Paralleling the psychological theories of G. Stanley Hall, the manual argued that sexual energies should not be repressed, but should be channeled into socially constructive activities. In making this argument, the manual emphasized the necessity of controlling male sexuality because men were considered the pursuers in sexual relations. In fact, the manual stated that, "Defense and chivalry in males are probably correlated with this tendency of pursuit, biologically."[54]

Also similar to Hall, the manual considered the control of male sexuality as the key to maintaining civilization and modern democracy. Using the concept of redirected sexual energy, the manual described the sexual underpinnings of democracy. It asserted that sexual drives contributed to the development of social and unselfish motives, which made possible a cooperative society. Using a social definition of democracy, the manual contended that a cooperative spirit, growing out of sexual energy directed toward the good of society, was the basis for a modern democracy: "Clearly this sense of the worth of social sacrifice and democracy, which is so largely the gift of the sex and reproductive processes, can in turn be applied most effectively to the guidance of sex impulses themselves."[55]

The manual contended that sexual energy permeated all social activities, and the goal of sex education was to direct this energy into socially constructive activities. The manual rejected the idea of repressing because it could result in the breakdown of character and the molding of submissive and obedient children.

The manual made a sharp distinction between male and female sexuality. Male sexuality was portrayed as aggressive and requiring more control. Male assertiveness was related to localized sexual energy in the "generative organs," whereas female sexuality was less localized and less intense. The combination of biological factors and social repression resulted, according to the manual, in women being more "capable of control [of sexual drives], of suppression, and of refinement into more intellectual and aesthetic forms than ... most men." The role of women was to restrain the sexual drives of men. The manual argued that proper feminine qualities included "purity as a social obligation, a restraining rather than an inciting attitude toward the male, and a sense of obligation for conserving and 'mothering' life."[56]

The purpose of both sex and marriage was reproduction. In the words of the manual, sex control is necessary for "proper home functioning, which includes the comfort and happiness of all, maximum development of the mates, proper child production, and effective personal and social education of children." Sexual intercourse outside of marriage should be avoided because of its potential threat to the stability of the family. The manual stated that physical "intercourse ... without the social sanction of formal marriage ..., wholly ignores the interest of society in all questions of sex and reproduction."[57]

For these reasons, the manual stated, sexual abstinence, except among married couples, was necessary for the good of society. The manual informed the reader, "If abstinence is desirable or necessary, it is primarily because of the effects of sex behavior on the home, on the emotional qualities in the individual upon which the success of the home is based, and on the larger society which depends on the home and on personal character."[58] The manual made a similar argument when it warned that sexual intercourse outside the institution of marriage not only weakened the family structure, but caused diseased and defective individuals, prostitution, and the shame of an illegitimate pregnancy. Premised on the idea that sexual intercourse was a social privilege, the goal of sex education, as stated in this American Social Hygiene Association manual, was to educate people so they would have sexual intercourse only within the confines of marriage. Interestingly, the manual urged teaching about venereal diseases because "they make an appeal to fear."[59] Regarding adolescent sexual energy, the manual called for draining the energy away from sexual thoughts and activities to constructive interests: "If young people are given many wholesome, attractive enterprises which strongly appeal to them personally during the whole of childhood and adolescence, there is much less likelihood that they will be drawn into sexual or other errors and excesses."[60]

HIGH SCHOOL DANCES AND DATING:
CREATING A NEW CONSUMER MARKET

By the 1930s, capstone of high school activities was the senior prom. The senior prom symbolized the shift of youth activities from relatively unsupervised dance halls to the controlled environment of the school. The prom experience was also a consumer experience with the unending requirements of grooming and dressing. The prom culminated the high school's dating and dancing rituals. Educators considered high school dating rituals as a prelude to marriage and the foundation for a consumer family.

High schools sponsored dances because moral reformers and educators worried that the wrong dancing in the wrong place threatened youthful morality. This worry persisted from the 1890s through the flapper age of the 1920s, the swing period of the 1930s and 1940s, and, of course, the blossoming of rock and roll in the 1950s. The "dance craze," as Kathy Peiss called it in *Cheap Amusements*, resulted in the opening by 1910 of over 500 public dance halls in New York City and 100 dancing academies instructing over 100,000 students. A 1912 survey found that the vast majority of those attending urban dance halls were between the ages of 13 and 20.[61] A major part of this group would eventually find their dancing activities relocated from the dance hall to the school gym.

One can imagine the horror of Protestant reformers and educators when faced with dancing with full body contact and various forms of shimmying. In the 19th century, the waltz was considered scandalous despite the requirement of 4 inches of separation between partners and that eyes be directed over the partner's shoulders. In contrast, youth in dance halls engaged in what was called *tough dancing*, which included the slow rag, lovers' two-step, and turkey trot.[62] Kathy Peiss described, "Tough dancing not only permitted physical contact, it celebrated it. Indeed, the essence of the tough dance was its suggestion of sexual intercourse. As one dance investigator noted obliquely, 'What particularly distinguishes this dance is the motion of the pelvic portions of the body, bearing in mind its origins [i.e., in houses of prostitution]'."[63]

Reformers and educators not only worried about dance styles, but also the environment of the dance halls. The Committee of Fourteen, a Protestant reform agency concerned with urban vice, sent its investigators into the commercial dance halls of the 1910s. One shocked investigator reported, "I saw one of the women smoking cigarettes, most of the younger couples were hugging and kissing . . . they were all singing and carrying on, they kept running around the room and acted like a mob of lunatics let loose."[64]

Amusement parks posed another challenge for reformers and educators. In the 1890s, dance pavilions on piers and beaches were the most popular places on Coney Island. One investigator described, "thousands of girls who are seized with such madness for dancing that they spend every night in the dance halls and picnic parks."[65] Another observer commented at the different types of dance halls, "in the most fashionable there is a good deal of promiscuous intercourse, flirting and picking up of acquaintances, but the dancing itself is usually proper and conventional; in the Bohemian, behavior is free and pronouncedly bad forms of dancing are seen."[66]

As a result of the dance hall atmosphere, the Women's Branch of the Brooklyn Mission in 1901 campaigned against immorality and prostitution at Coney Island. In 1912, the West End Improvement League of Coney Island joined the crusade. Reverend Mortenson of the Society of Inner Mission and Rescue complained about bawdy dance halls, movie pictures, and rowdyism on the beach. Over time commodified sexuality replaced dance halls. Penny machines were introduced to measure kisses. The Tunnel of Love and the Canals of Venice provided opportunities for couples to embrace. The Steeplechase Park built in 1897 provided rides, such as the Barrel of Love, the Dew Drop parachute ride, and compressed air jets to lift women's skirts.[67]

As commercial enterprises created new leisure time activities, other youth recreation was offered in chaperoned community centers and clubs. Efforts were made to limit the sale of alcohol. The New York public Recreation Commission suggested having older women chaperone younger ones at dance halls and movies. Under pressure from community organizations, some movie houses set aside special seats for single women. To lure youth away from dance halls, settlement houses provided social activities, including regulated and chaperoned dances.[68]

In 1902, John Dewey proclaimed before the NEA that the public schools should become the new social centers. Dewey wanted to provide an alternative social world to the dance halls and saloons. However, Dewey's concept of the social center went one step beyond protecting the working class from immorality. He saw it as a method to keep people working harder in a world of mass production. In contrast to the consumer-oriented approach of Patten, Dewey emphasized the social meaning of work. He told the NEA meeting that the school as a social center, "must interpret to [the worker] the intellectual and social meaning of the work in which he is engaged; that is must reveal its relations to the life and work of the world."[69]

Prior to Dewey's speech, schools and parks were opening social centers. In 1897, New York City organized its after school activities into social centers. The Chicago park system created social centers in their field houses and provided for adult clubs and choral groups. Public schools in Milwaukee opened their doors to evening adult programs. In 1913, the Russell Sage foundation reported that almost half of the school superintendents they contacted reported the creation of school social centers. Schools were built to accommodate evening activities, including chaperoned dances. In 1912, the president of the Western Municipal League of Boston wrote regarding social centers, "it is our endeavor to make our city a true home for the people, it is not enough that we should merely make it a house. . . . We must ensure that there shall be within it recreation, enjoyment, and happiness for all."[70]

High school activities created a shared experience for youth. In *From Front Porch to Back Seat: Courtship in Twentieth-Century America*, Beth Bailey argued that the high school standardized youth culture in the United States. A common youth culture was spread by radio and magazines. Beginning in 1935, this national White youth culture was confirmed by surveys conducted by the American Institute of Public Opinion. Bailey concluded, "From about the late 1930s on, many young people knew to the percentage point what their peers throughout the country thought and did. They knew what was normal."[71]

High school activities provided an alternative to the commodified pleasures of the dance halls, amusement parks, and movies. In the process, high school activities became a new form of consumerism involving the purchase of athletic equipment, club materials, and special clothing such as lettermen's jackets. The school prom represented the coming together of consumerism and the attempts to control the sexuality of youth.

Leading up to the prom were ritualized dating behaviors that emerged from the high school culture of the 1920s and 1930s. High school textbooks and marriage manuals helped create a formalized dating ritual that involved both control of youthful sexuality and selection of a mate for marriage. Dating involved an economic and sexual exchange. In "Rate Your Date: Young Women and the Commodification of Depression Era Courtship," Mary McComb wrote, "Generally, men were expected to pay for their date's entertainment, transportation, and meals. Women were expected to repay men with varying levels of sexual favors, usually a chaste kiss good night."[72]

While young men paid for the date, young girls bought dresses, shoes, and makeup. In purchasing these products, young women commodified the process of selecting a husband. McComb contended, "Women not only rewarded men with sexual favors, but young females in the 1930s and early 1940s fashioned themselves into commodified beings who existed in a heterosexual marketplace of exchange."[73] The commodification of marriage selection through ritualized high school dating was spelled out in Frances Strain's 1939 marriage text, *Love at the Threshold: A Book on Dating, Romance, and Marriage.* Strain advised, "Besides being fun, single dating defines a person and brings out his or her capacity. . . . It's like selling—you must be alert to the other person's responses. An appropriate turn of the phrase, and everything is won. Too much high pressure, perhaps, and everything is lost."[74]

High school marriage texts and manuals built sexual boundaries around dating. According to McComb, every book during this period dealt with the issue of petting, which meant anything from hand holding to sexual acts short of actual penetration. All the books warned against promiscuous petting. High school girls were cautioned that heavy petting would lead to a decline of their dating value in the marketplace. Women were given the task of ensuring that petting did not go too far. They were warned that boys tended to sit around and talk about their sexual exploits. The worst thing that could happen to a girl was to become an object of locker room discussions. Girls were told to achieve a balance between being known as an "icicle" or a "hot number."[75]

The high point of the high school dating ritual was the prom. In *Prom Night: Youth, Schools, and Popular Culture,* Amy Best argued that as a growing number of youth attended high school, "School clubs, school dances, and student government increasingly became a significant part of the kids' lives."[76] Proms became widespread in the 1930s when the high school became a mass institution. They were considered a poor or middle-class version of the debutante ball, which instructed youth in proper dating and mating rituals. Amy Best contended, "Proms were historically tied to a schooling project used to govern the uncontrollable youth. By enlisting you to participate in middle-class rituals like the prom, schools were able to advance a program that reigned in student's emerging and increasingly public sexualities."[77]

Proms opened new vistas for consumerism, particularly female consumerism. Shopping for the right dress became an important part of the prom ritual along with the purchase of makeup, shoes, lingerie, handbags, and jewelry. Among teenage girls, there were countless discussions about what to buy and how to fix one's makeup and hair.[78] Eventually prom-oriented magazines appeared, such as *Your Prom* and *Teen Prom*, to guide both prom manners and consumerism. These magazines surveyed readers with consumer-oriented questions such as, "How many stores will you visit when shopping for a prom dress?" and "Would you be interested in looking at gowns like these for other special occasions such as homecoming?"[79]

Protestant reformers and educators changed the direction of the commodification of youth's leisure time from commercial dance halls to attendance at high school dances and proms. These efforts did not end the commercialization of youth's leisure time activity or their sexual activity. The end result, as exemplified by the prom, was to create a controlled consumer market. The emergence of the high school as a mass institution created a common experience for youth across the nation. This common experience inevitably created a common culture related to the high school experience.

By bringing teenagers together, the high school formed a teenage consumer group that was noted by the publication of the first issue of *Seventeen* magazine in 1944. The magazine's editors, reflecting the development of the high school, assumed the existence of a teenage market. Their goal was to shape teenage female spending patterns. Estelle Ellis, the promotional director of *Seventeen*, stated, "Of course the emphasis was on consumption—the buying power of this age group."[80] Articles in *Seventeen* preached the importance of education in politics and world affairs along with proper consumption.

In summary, the high school's institutionalization of youth, extracurricular activities, athletics, home economics, sex education and marriage courses, dances, and the prom helped establish gender roles. The high school male's image was that of the muscular athlete who, while keeping up with his studies, found his identity in leisure time activities. Too much focus on scholarship or the arts without active participation in the world of jocks opened the door to charges of being a pansy or queer. Male youth bought sexual favors on dates by assuming the role of paying for transportation, food, and dinners. Girls prepared themselves for future consumption by focusing on clothes and makeup. Similar to the male image, girls were to do well in school while projecting an image of primarily worrying about boys and consumption.

PATRIOTISM AND ECONOMIC NATIONALISM

The new male image included a patriotic scorn for economic alternatives to consumerism, particularly communism. The new man was imagined as sports minded, rugged, sexually controlled, and loyal to consumer capitalism and his nation. Patriotic exercises, history and social studies courses, and character education were to dedicate men, particularly future businessmen, to corporate spirit and "100% Americanism." Referring to the image of the businessman of the 1920s, the report of the 1926 Committee on Character Education of the NEA declared, "This is why 'live wires' and 'go-getters' are such heroes to the bulk of the people; in and of itself all this is quite legitimate, and indeed moral."[81] The object of character education was to form live-wires and go-getters for the expanding corporate world of business. Besides defining gender roles, the high school world of football, basketball, cheerleaders, student government, assemblies, clubs, and rallies promoted school spirit, which was considered the underpinning of the corporate male personality.

School and corporate spirit were accompanied by a spirit of Americanism. Leading the Americanism campaign in public schools was the American Legion. Topping the list of resolutions at the American Legion's first convention in 1919 was a resolution against "Bolshevism, I.W.W., radicalism . . . [and] all anti-Americanism tendencies, activities, and propaganda." Targeting its Americanism campaign at the public schools, the American Legion eventually joined arms with the NEA in a campaign for citizenship education.[82]

While the public schools were educating their version of the 100% American businessman, the newly founded public relations industry was issuing probusiness editorials and articles for inclusion in newspapers and magazines. According to the leading distributor of these probusiness materials, the purpose was to reduce "the volume of legislation that interferes with business and industry . . . to discourage radicalism by labor organizations" and to "campaign against any socialistic propaganda of whatever nature."[83]

Reflecting the same goal as the probusiness public relations campaign, the U.S. Commissioner of Education, John Tigert, declared in 1921 his "determination to crush out of the schools communism, bolshevism, socialism, and all persons who did not recognize the sanctity of private property and 'the right of genius to its just rewards'."[84] Teachers and administrators were called on to purge schools of all subversive ideas. Writing in the 1930s, historian Howard Beales expressed his belief that the reason a War Facts Test was given to New York high school teachers in 1919, which asked about Russian communism and the sources for such information, was to identify teachers with radical views.[85] In another study by Beales published in 1941, he ranked the relative influence of various organizations interested in purging schools of subversive ideas. "On the whole," he wrote, "the American Legion seems to be the most important. Next come benefactors of the school, the D.A.R., the Chamber of Commerce, and 'other patriotic organizations,' including in the South the United Daughters of the Confederacy."[86]

In 1921, the NEA formed a permanent Committee on Character Education to work in cooperation with the American School Citizenship League and the NEA Committee on the Teaching of Democracy.[87] In 1926, the Committee on Character Education issued its report, which was reprinted and distributed as a bulletin of the U.S. Bureau of Education.[88] The report stressed the importance of cooperation and group activity by claiming, "The most profoundly moral lives are those in which the I is most completely merged into the We." The integration of the I into the We, the report argued, would result "in achievement, success, life-career. This is an impressive phase of moral development and furnishes a powerful motive for conduct."[89] The businessman's achievements, according to the report, would motivate the school boy. In discussing the motivational power of dreams of a successful career, the report stated, "It [success] has powerful appeal to 'man on the street,' who loves to hear about 'doing big things,' and probably dreams more or less about doing big things himself." The report claimed that the public worships successful people who are live-wires and go-getters.[90]

The involvement of the American Legion in high school education and its connection with the NEA strengthened efforts to educate a patriotic go-getter and spark-plug businessman. In March 1919, the American Legion started in Paris at a meeting called by Theodore Roosevelt, Jr. to organize a World War I veterans' organization. The organizing members worried that U.S. military personnel were being exposed to radical economic ideas that would aid the spread of Bolshevist ideas. William Gellerman concluded in his study of the American Legion's involvement in education, "Ex-soldiers were restless. Bolshevism had triumphed in Russia. American leaders both at home and abroad were worried. They were afraid that ex-servicemen might organize along Bolshevistic lines, and exercise such power as to threaten the status quo in America. The American Legion was organized to prevent any such catastrophe."[91]

The organizational structure of the American Legion maximized opportunities for influencing both local and national educational policy. Whereas membership was attached to local American Legion posts, policymaking was centralized. Legion leaders wanted to present a united front. The membership of the American Legion during the 1920s grew from 845,146 in 1920 to 1,153,909 in 1931. By 1923, the Legion had established 11,129 local posts.[92] Within this organizational structure, the Legion's National Americanism Commission dictated its Americanism campaign to local posts.

In the official version of the organization's history as told by Russell Cook, National Director of the Legion's Americanism Commission to delegates at the 1934 NEA convention,

> The members of the American Legion were rudely awakened to the necessity of more general education while serving the flag of our country on the battlefields of the World War. At no other period in our national history has the importance of education been more pronounced than during the war when members of the Legion experienced a handicap which a lack of schooling placed upon comrades.[93]

The inability to read orders, he claimed, caused deaths among the troops. Voicing concern about the problem of illiteracy among the foreign-born, he recounted how the Americanism Commission had originally sought the NEA's help "in establishing an annual program in which the American people might dedicate themselves each year to the ideal of self-government based upon an enlightened citizenry. Out of that thought was born American Education Week." Reminding the NEA of the Legion's dedication to the education of the foreign-born, he told the delegates, we "realized that aliens in this country must have help in fitting themselves to accept the responsibilities of American citizenship and in understanding and solving the problems of everyday life in America."[94]

The American Legion influenced students through political censorship of teachers and textbooks and by supporting patriotic exercises. These activities were controlled by the Legion's Americanism Commission. The Commission was formed at the Legion's first convention in 1919. The founding resolution stated, "the establishment of a National Americanism Commission of the American Legion to realize in the United States the basic ideal of this Legion of 100% Americanism through the planning, establishment and conduct of a continuous, constructive educational system. . . ."[95]

The resolution listed the following goals in the promotion of 100% Americanism:

1. combat all anti-American tendencies, activities and propaganda;
2. work for the education of immigrants, prospective American citizens and alien residents in the principles of Americanism;
3. inculcate the ideals of Americanism in the citizen population, particularly the basic American principle that the interests of all the people are above those of any special interest or any so-called class or section of the people;

4. spread throughout the people of the nation information as to the real nature and principles of American government;
5. foster the teaching of Americanism in all schools.[96]

As part of its Americanism campaign, local Legion members were urged
to weed out subversives from local school systems. The 1921 Legion convention passed a resolution calling for state laws to cancel certificates of teachers
"found guilty of disloyalty to the government." In addition, Legion members
were asked to volunteer the names of subversive teachers to local school
boards. In 1919, the National Americanism Commission warned that, "We
have those who believe that the red, white and blue presided over by the eagle shall be replaced by the red flag with the black vulture of disloyalty and international unrest perched upon its staff. Through the schools and through
the churches the radicals are now seeking to put across their policies."[97]

In 1921, the National Americanism Commission joined with the NEA to
sponsor American Education Week. Henry J. Ryan, Chair of the Joint Advisory Committee of the NEA and the American Legion, and National Director of the Americanism Commission for 1921–1922, explained to the delegates of the 1921 NEA convention the reasons for the Legion's interest in
supporting an American Education Week. "America is God's last chance to
save the world," he told the delegates. "We can save it only by giving to every
boy and girl in America an equal opportunity for education . . . opportunity
to learn of that government . . . so that . . . they will be able to say, 'We
learned to love our country at school'."[98]

In 1925, the American Bar Association and the Daughters of the American Revolution (DAR) also joined in sponsoring American Education Week.
In that year, one day of Education Week was called Equal Opportunity Day,
devoted to making "Democracy safe for the world through universal education."[99] The DAR participated in American Education Week because "reverence for the nation's founders and interest in schools fit in with our conservation of the values of the past, and the constructive growth of the future."[100]

During American Education Week, educators and representatives from
local Legion posts, DAR chapters, and the American Bar Association coop-
erated in sponsoring a series of activities supporting the public school and
projects for education in Americanism. In 1925, American Education Week
emphasized instruction on the U.S. Constitution and the building of patriotism. In 1926, each day in American Education Week was designated by
descriptive titles such as, "For God and Country Day," "Constitutional
Rights Day," "Patriotism Day," "Equal Opportunity Day," "Know Your
School Day," and "Community Day."[101]

The Legion tried to shape students' political ideologies by sponsoring essays around patriotic and antiradical themes. In 1923, the assigned topic in
the contest was, "Why America should prohibit immigration for five years";

in 1924, it was, "Why Communism is a menace to Americanism." The Americanism Commission argued that their school awards were an "effective antidote for the teachings of those groups opposed to the patriotic principles embraced by the American Legion." In addition to these activities, local Legion posts promoted flag education and the saying of the Pledge of Allegiance in local public schools.[102]

In the 1920s and 1930s, the American Legion, the D.A.R., the Women's Christian Temperance Union, and religious organizations monitored the content of public school textbooks. In the 1930s, Howard Beales recorded the feelings of an author of American history texts regarding the impact of these organizations: "In trying to guard against criticism and opposition, authors are driven to sins of omission and commission." After describing how he added material of little importance to his history texts and deleted other material because of pressure from outside advocacy groups, such as the American Legion, the textbook author told Beales, "And, if any author tells you he is not influenced by such pressure, that he tells 'the truth, the whole truth and nothing but the truth' as far as he knows it, don't you believe him. He is a conscious or unconscious liar."[103] Also textbooks conformed to state laws requiring an education for patriotic citizenship. For instance, the Lusk Laws passed by the New York State legislature in 1918 prohibited any statements in textbooks fostering disloyalty to the United States. The law established a state commission to examine books in "civics, economics, English, history, language and literature for the purpose of determining whether such textbooks contain any matter or statements of any kind which are seditious in character, [or] disloyal to the United States." A 1923 Wisconsin law prohibited any textbook "which falsifies the facts regarding the war of independence, or the war of 1812, or which defames our nation's founders or misrepresents the ideals and causes for which they struggled and sacrificed, or which contains propaganda favorable to any foreign government." An Oregon law banned any textbook that "speaks slightingly of the founders of the republic, or the men who preserved the union, or which belittles or under values their work."[104] In *Civic Attitudes in American Schools* (1930), Bessie Louise Pierce concluded that, "Most makers of courses of study are united in their belief that the main aim of instruction in American history is the development of a vivid conception of American nationality and a high sense of patriotism and civic religion."[105]

THE CLEAN-SHAVEN BUSINESSMAN: ADVERTISING IMAGES OF THE NEW MAN

The high school's ideal of the sports-minded, patriotic businessman was duplicated in advertising images. In general, ads most often portrayed generic businessmen who were either admiring the consumption of women, stoically using or modeling a product, or acting as an expert. Regarding early 20th-century ads, Roland Marchand summarized, "Men appeared almost as frequently as women, but often in nondescript, standardized parts as husbands or as businessmen at work . . . men rarely assumed decorative poses or exaggerated bodily proportions. Their hands exemplified the contrast between the functional grasp of the male and the ethereal gesture of the female."[106] Advertising agents avoided any suggestion of effeminacy in the male image. Ads implied that the competitive world of business made men *true men*, and agencies "worried that the attempt to pretty him up for the collar ads and the nightclub scenes would sissify and weaken man's image, tailoring it too much to feminine tastes."[107]

Some traditional Protestant advertising men linked images of the businessman with theology. Advertising executive Bruce Barton popularized the idea that businessmen represented a form of muscular Christianity. In *The Man Nobody Knows*, Barton's best selling 1925 book—it outsold F. Scott Fitzgerald's *The Great Gatsby*—Jesus Christ was portrayed as the exemplary business and advertising man.[108] Barton's muscular, Christian business and advertising man could be seen in various forms in magazine and newspaper advertisements in the early 20th century.

Bruce Barton wrote his tract on business, advertising, and muscular Christianity while heading the firm Batten, Barton, Durstine & Osborn (BBDO). Born in 1886, Barton's father was a Protestant minister who rode a church circuit through rural Tennessee. After working on magazines, he was attracted to advertising during World War I while writing fundraising copy for the Salvation Army, YMCA, YWCA, and other nonprofit organizations. In 1919, he joined Alex Osborne and Roy Durstine in opening an advertising agency that, in the early 1920s, landed important accounts such as General Electric, General Motors, Dunlop tire, and Lever Brothers. Throughout the 20th century, the agency remained in the top 10 of advertising companies as measured by earnings.[109]

Barton's muscular Christ exemplified the division taking place between the effeminate world of the fairy and pansy and the new man. Barton's Christ was tough and lived in the tradition of Theodore Roosevelt's "the strenuous life." In a chapter entitled "The Outdoor Man," Barton described Christ driving the money changers out of the temple: "As his right arm rose and fell, striking its blows with that little whip, the sleeve dropped back to reveal muscles hard as iron. No one who watched him in action had any doubt that he was fully capable of taking care of himself."[110] Barton claimed that Christ's muscularity was a result of 30 years of carpentry. Unfortunately, from Barton's perspective, the Bible never provided any details about Christ's physical condition. Barton complained that, as a result, many of the paintings of Christ depicted a "frail man, under-muscled, with a soft face—a woman's face covered by a beard."[111] Barton's portrayal of traditional representations of Christ sounded very much like the 1920s' descriptions of the fairy or pansy. To prove Christ's manly and rugged being, Barton cited four characteristics. The first was that health "flowed out of him to create health in others." The other three characteristics clearly outlined the image of the new man:

1. The appeal of his personality to women—weakness does not appeal to them.
2. His lifetime of outdoor living
3. The steel-like hardness of his nerves[112]

This manly Christ became, as one of Barton's chapters is entitled, "The Founder of Modern Business." What did Christ discover that made Christianity a great business? "You will hear that discovery," Barton wrote, "proclaimed in every sales convention as something distinctly modern and up to date. It is emblazoned in the advertising pages of every magazine."[113] Referring to an advertisement for the *greatest* car company in the world, which I assume was General Motors because it was his company's account, he claimed the key to success was good service, a willingness to understand the life of the lowly worker, and extra effort. Christ's life represented these qualities, and modern businessmen, as muscular Christians, needed to learn the same lessons. Barton listed Jesus Christ's winning business methods:

1. Whoever will be great must render great service.
2. Whoever will bind himself at the top must be willing to lose himself at the bottom.
3. The big rewards come to those who travel the second, undemanded mile.[114]

Of course from Barton's perspective, Christ was able to sell his religion because of good advertising methods. These advertising methods involved service to others. Barton imagined the following advertising headlines:

PALSIED MAN HEALED
JESUS OF NAZARETH CLAIMS RIGHT TO FORGIVE SINS
PROMINENT SCRIBES OBJECT
***
DEFENDS PUBLICANS AND SINNERS
JESUS OF NAZARETH WELCOMES THEM AT LUNCH
***
JESUS OF NAZARETH WILL DENOUNCE
THE SCRIBES AND PHARISEES IN THE
CENTRAL SYNAGOGUE

TO-NIGHT AT EIGHT O'CLOCK
SPECIAL MUSIC[115]

The image of the new man and muscular Christian appeared in advertising copy as what Marchand called the *generic businessman*. Along with BBDO, almost all ads presented men dressed in suits even while relaxing at home. The bodies under these suits appeared muscular. All of the male faces were clean shaven with chiseled features. None of the male faces was similar to those Barton disdained in paintings of Christ, such as "like a woman's face covered by a beard." In ads for women's products, men were often shadow figures admiring some aspect of the featured woman.

Being clean shaven became a mark of the new man. Although mustaches lingered on, beards disappeared from images of the new man. Clean shaven became the norm for White males. In fact, the clean-shaven male became a symbol for patriotic Americans as I discovered in the 1960s when, in my youthful rebellion, I grew a beard. Despite countless centuries of men wearing beards, including the portrayal of religious figures with beards, the beard became the sign of radicalism in the America of the 1960s. Without even opening my mouth to spout a political doctrine, people would immediately associate my beard with anti-Viet Nam war protests. A clean-shaven American male was associated with patriotism, acceptance of the American way of life, and morality. Just as the suit became the uniform for the corporate male, a clean-shaven male became the corporate standard for grooming.

In a 1913 ad for the Arrow Collar Man, three *manly* men wearing ties are shown, with one seated holding a cane, another holding a tennis racquet, and the third holding a leash connected to the studded collar of a bull dog. Looking distinguished, the man with the cane sported a small mustache, whereas the others were clean-shaven outdoors men.[116] In Helen Resor's famous ad for Woodbury's Facial Soap, a clean-shaven and suited man is shown kissing the hand of the featured woman with the caption, "A skin you love to touch." The man was shown behind the woman, and his upper body is only partially visible.[117]

The introduction of the Gillette Safety Razor in 1905 quickly linked the marketing of a brand-named product with the image of the new man, particularly the clean-shaven new man. The new disposable safety razor threatened the traditional masculine social life of the barbershop where many middle-class men went to be shaved. However, within the context of the new corporate life, the safety razor promised greater independence for men to manage their own grooming. Similar to home economists who wanted to save the family from unsanitary cooking conditions, King Gillette, the inventor of the safety razor, promised to save men from the unsanitary conditions of the barber shop. In a 1907 ad, King Gillette claimed, "When you use my razor you are exempt from the dangers that men often encounter who allow their faces to come in contact with brush, soap and barbershop accessories used on other people."[118]

Gillette ads actually taught men how to be clean shaven under any conditions. A series of ads in 1910 demonstrated how to shave to sailors, outdoorsmen, railroad travelers, and others who could not go to a barbershop. One 1910 ad used fear of sexual rejection to send home the message that men could always be clean shaven under any conditions: "A bridegroom on the Canadian Pacific acquired a three-days' growth of beard. Despair was written on his face. A kindly gentleman loaned him a Gillette— and received the united thanks of two fond hearts."[119] The accompanying illustration denoted the racism implied in this male image. On the left of the illustration, the distressed young man was shown talking to the older man. On the right, the young man was shown shaving. Bridging these illustrated sections was an African-American porter shown holding the hat and cane of the older man. The early Gillette ads also emphasized that men who could remain clean shaven represented progress. The previously discussed ad urged readers, "Be progressive. Keep Gillette on your home washstand— take it with you when you travel. . . . Life is brighter when a clean face is an every morning habit."[120]

It seemed inevitable that this new tool for the new man would eventually be linked to sports, particularly from the standpoint of advocates of the new manliness like Theodore Roosevelt, the real man's sport of boxing. With the advent of radio, American minds would be haunted, including this author's mind, with the following jingle:

Gillette Razor Blades

Announcer: *Look sharp!*
Sound: Prizefight bell
Announcer: *Feel sharp!*
Sound: Prizefight bell
Announcer: *Be sharp!*
Sound: Prizefight bell
Announcer: *Use Gillette Blue Blades . . . with the sharpest edges ever honed.*[121]

The new man and new woman confronted each other in a 1927 ad for S.O.S. cleaner. This ad encompassed many of the aspects of the new gender images, including the supportive role of the home economics expert, the generic businessman, and the consuming wife. A fully suited man with a tie was shown sitting on a couch with his legs crossed looking doubtfully at his standing wife. He is clean shaven and appears muscular under his clothing. The wife, with short hair and wearing a flapper dress, juts her chin out defiantly at the husband as she exclaimed, "You think I'm a flapper but I can keep house." Below this scene was a small, round photo of the domestic science expert Mary Dale Anthony, who was described in the ad as "Adviser on kitchen and household cleaning problems to thousands of women." Anthony informed the reader, "Leave it to the modern girl to speak her mind . . . alert and eager to learn . . . looking for new time-savers. Girls today want more leisure, and they get it by using short-cuts."[122] In this ad, the strong and silent man remained the authority in the house, whereas consumer wife claimed greater freedom through consumption.

Two of BBDO's ads for General Motors featured similar clean-shaven men in suits. One 1925 ad was for the General Motors Acceptance Corporation, which pioneered the installment buying of General Motor's cars. In the ad, a woman was seated at a salesman's desk with the salesman—clean shaven in suit and tie—explaining the installment plan. Her husband, also clean shaven in suit and tie, is standing and listening. His standing position demonstrates his authority over his seated wife. However, as symbolic of the new woman, the wife was participating in the purchase of the car.[123] In another 1925 ad for General Motor's Chevrolet, there was a similar scene, except in this case the husband was seated. The wife's hands were poised expressively in the air while the husband had one hand clinched and the other firmly placed on the desk.[124] In both cases, the salesman was providing the service that Bruce Barton believed was the key to Jesus Christ's success as a businessman.

THE COWBOY IMAGE

Schools and advertising upheld the image of the ideal or normal as being a clean-shaven White businessman dressed in a suit who was sports-minded, patriotic, energetic, and rugged in appearance with his personal identity formed through leisure time activities. However, another image was that of the cowboy. For Theodore Roosevelt, the cowboy symbolized the American manliness that was lost with the passing of the frontier and the rise of urban and corporate America. After World War II, this cowboy image was reflected from the screen by John Wayne whose characters embodied patriotic masculinity.[125] It also found its place in the icon of the Marlboro Man.

Removed from the dusty plains of cattle ranching, the modern day version of the cowboy was the jock. Clean shaven and manly, the modern jock was primarily a spectator who most often listened or watched sporting events on radio or TV. With a mind filled with sports statistics, the corporate man could safely commune with fellow males without engaging in the potentially explosive topic of politics. Indeed, the modern corporate man in suit and tie could compare the competitive world of business with the competition of the sports field. Also sports were somehow patriotic, with each game starting with the playing of the national anthem. Besides spectatorship, the new male could find leisure time relaxation in a round of golf, fishing, or hunting. Fulfilling the dreams of Theodore Roosevelt, a man could take his family camping in a national forest or park and relive the frontier experience of cooking over an open fire.

This was the gendered world that many American men of the 20th century encountered in public schools, advertising, and media. Of course there were exceptions. Rebels showed their disdain for this image by wearing long hair, beards, beads, and tie-dyed shirts and pants, and by displaying pierced noses, ears, and tongues. Sometimes these alternative images of masculinity represented a scorn of the patriotic values associated with the sports-loving and clean-shaven *real male.* Alternative clothing and facial hair possibly indicated a variety of dissenting positions, including left-wing politics, anticonsumerism, anti-Americanism, and antisports.

CONCLUSION: RUDOLPH VALENTINO AND THE EROTICIZATION OF AMERICAN SOCIETY

Ironically, the efforts of Puritan leaders and advertising agencies infused sexuality into American institutions and consumer items. The high school was transformed from a purely academic institution to one responsible for controlling the sexual life of teenagers. As a result of athletics, cheerleading, dances, dating, clubs, and marriage and sex education courses, the high school, in fact, became a center of adolescent sexuality. The folklore of the teenage girl giving up her virginity on prom night illustrated the eroticization of the institution. The climax of academic studies was accompanied by the consummation of a relationship between high school lovers.

Sexual themes of denial and fulfillment used to sell products also eroticized those products. The Gillette safety razor became an object for heightening sexual pleasure when it received the "united thanks of two fond hearts" by allowing the honeymooner to shave off a 3-day beard. Underarm deodorant, mouth wash, tooth paste, Wonder Bread, cleaning products, cosmetics, and a host of other products were advertised as either protecting a romantic relationship or ensuring the attentions of a new lover.

As a result, the promise of consumption was often sexual fulfillment. The promise of a high school education was an income that opened the door to consumerism. A goal of schooling was providing equality of opportunity to earn money and consume. Therefore, indirectly, education promised a fulfillment of sexual desires by providing an income that could purchase products advertised to enhance sexuality or gain a sexual partner. Consequently, both the social and academic life of the modern high school promised sexual fulfillment.

Of course the eroticization of American society was complicated by the racial and heterosexual nature of the new man. As a host of historians have argued, the most important being Gail Bederman, Michael Kimmel, and William Pinar, the new male image included a vision of the White male bringing civilization to the rest of the world.[126] This image suggested that African-American men were not real men and therefore should submit to the civilizing effect of White men. In part, the lynching and castration of African-American men in the late 19th and early 20th centuries for supposed sexual impositions on White women were based on the assumptions by White men that African-American men could not practice spermatic political economy. Unlike the new White man, African-American men, in the minds of most Whites, could not control their sexual passions. Consequently, it was the duty of White men, according to this reasoning, to restrain African-American men's lustful nature by public displays of violence. The same attitudes existed toward Indian men as exemplified by the statue of the proud practitioner of spermatic political economy, Theodore Roosevelt, seated on his horse above the conquered Indian as a symbol of the civilizing effects of White men on Indian men.

The violent actions against African-American men occurred while advertising images placed them in subservient positions to Whites. In the Gillette ad, the African-American train porter holds the White man's coat as the older White man ensures the continued sexual activities of the honeymooners by teaching the young man to use a safety razor. This implies that the proper role of the African-American man was to help the White man fulfill his civilized and officially sanctioned sexual acts.

The movie star, Rudolph Valentino, I believe best represented the complex sexual and racial image of the new man and the eroticization of American society. As a public figure, Valentino was a 1920s sex symbol for many White female moviegoers while being despised by most White males. Over 100,000 mostly female mourners visited his open coffin after his premature death in 1926 at the age of 31. The cult of Valentino continued years after his death and included a mysterious Woman in Black bearing roses who annually visited his crypt.

Although Valentino's movie career began in 1918 with small parts, his fame and female following began with the release of *The Sheik* in 1921. His biographer Alexander Walker contended that the female attracted to Valentino's performance was "the liberated 'New Woman' of the 1920s who wore her skirts shorter and her hair bobbed, who smoked, danced, drank from her beau's hip flask and took up every fad or craze of a novelty era." Also, according to Walker, Valentino's portrayal of the Sheik appealed to traditional women who wanted the thrill of uninvited seduction.[127]

In contrast to the image of the new man, Valentino's *character* was the barbarian who, although manly and rugged, was possessed by uncontrolled sexuality. The movie fantasy portrayed a man who seduced women after kidnapping them. It was a rape fantasy without a rape. In the movie, the Sheik kidnapped Lady Diana Mayo and brought her to his tent. "Why have you brought me here?" she asked. "Are you not woman enough to know?" he responded.[128] A militant feminist, Lady Diana was humiliated by the Sheik until she agreed to trade her riding pants for a skirt and lost her militant attitudes. In the seduction scene, Lady Diana proclaimed, "I am not afraid with your arms around me, Ahmed, my desert love, MY SHEIK."[129] With these lines, the independent woman succumbed to the preying nature of the barbarian.

The film encompasses many important issues regarding race and the image of the new man. First, the Sheik turned out not to be a barbarian, but the abandoned child of a Scottish nobleman, the Earl of Glencarryl. This resolved the potential racial problem in the 1920s of a non-White man seducing a White woman. It also resolved the social class issue with both partners coming from upper class backgrounds.

However, the fantasy image of the seductive and sexual Sheik did not match the ideal public image of the sexually restraint White man transmitting civilization around the world. This clash in images might have been a reason that many male moviegoers despised the seductive screen image of Valentino. A male writer in the 1922 issue of *Photoplay* wrote, "I hate Valentino! All men hate Valentino. . . . I hate him because he's the great lover of the screen; I hate him because he's an embezzler of hearts. . . . I hate him because he's too good looking."[130] Male moviegoers considered on-screen seductive approaches to women as effeminate despite that the Sheik and most other roles played by Valentino presented a muscular and adventuresome male. There is certainly nothing necessarily effeminate about kidnapping women for the purpose of seduction.

The conflict between the screen image of Valentino and the public image of the new man was explained by his biographer Alexander Walker: "The truth was that Valentino had made lovemaking into too onerous and time-consuming a task for American males to emulate. He had shown the Latin trait of infinite consideration in his courtship which requires an equivalent amount of time, patience, and vanity. It wasn't the American ideal, at least it wasn't the American *male* ideal."[131]

Valentino's public displays of athleticism were attempts to overcome charges of effeminacy made by the press. Similar to Theodore Roosevelt, Valentino chose boxing as proof of his masculinity. Frequently, after public comment that he appeared effeminate in his screen role as a lover, he would give public demonstrations of boxing. In one photo made for public consumption, the famous boxer Jack Dempsey was shown referring to a fight between Valentino and an unnamed opponent.[132] In addition, he distributed photographs of his muscular body and his exercise routine.

However, no matter how many boxing demonstrations, his screen presence was still considered effeminate by many men. Advertising images
that came close to Valentino's screen image were just shadowy figures in
ads for women's cosmetics and personal care items. In contrast, most
other advertising images of clean-shaven generic businessmen did not
show the passionate gestures and sexuality that Valentino displayed on the
screen.

Ironically, from the perspective of the future, it was Valentino's seductive
and emotional qualities that made American White men uneasy. Valentino's screen image did not practice spermatic political economy. His
screen characters shared themselves with many women, and they focused
attention on sexual relationships rather than channeling sexuality into
sports, adventure, and civilization building. On the screen, Valentino was
not the sexless cowboy riding across the plains to fight Indians. Ironically,
many men thought of Valentino as being a *fairy* or *pansy*.

Valentino's personal issue with masculinity was as complicated as his
screen image. There was a difference, of course, between the fantasy life of
the screen and the real life of the actors. As movies impacted the world of
personal fantasies, moviegoers became more and more interested in the
lives of their off-screen heros and heroines. In many ways, moviegoers
wanted the fantasy of the screen to be replicated in movie actors' lives. Consequently, the movies developed two fantasy worlds. One was on screen and
the other was in the supposed glamorous lives of movie stars.

Off-screen, Rudolph Valentino seemed confused about his own masculinity. As George Chauncey argued in his history *Gay New York*, the public
image of manliness in the early 20th century made sharp distinctions between heterosexuality and homosexuality, with heterosexuality presented
as the norm. You were either gay or straight. There was no room in this
male image for bisexuality. Valentino's life suggested that he was not sexually attracted to women or, as his biographer suggested, Valentino might
have been impotent.[133] In real life, Valentino did not have raging love affairs with a multitude of women. He was divorced from his first wife after
she locked him out of their bedroom on their wedding night. No reason for
this action was ever provided, but the marriage was not consummated. His
second marriage was to a lesbian who supposedly exercised domineering
powers over his personal and professional life. Most of his personal companions were young men.

Whether gay, bisexual, or impotent, Valentino wrestled with the image
of the new male. Just before his death, an editorial in the Chicago *Tribune*
accused him of debauching "American manhood by the 'unmasculine' image he had popularized."[134] He was so angered by the editorial that he immediately organized for newspaper reporters a boxing match with a spar-
ring partner. Alexander Walker suggested that the incident might have

contributed to his early death by aggravating a gastric ulcer that, along with a ruptured appendix, caused his death.[135]

Valentino's lavish public funeral was the first time a movie star's death was given as much attention as that of a president or other major public figure. The debate about Valentino's masculinity on and off the screen highlighted inherent problems of the new male image. Heterosexuality, manliness, sports-mindedness, sexual control, and patriotism embodied in a clean-shaven businessman in a suit was the dominant image of manhood in the 1920s.

Valentino and other movie stars also stimulated consumption fantasies. Movie stars were portrayed as living lavish lives filled with expensive clothes, homes, cars, travel, parties, and sporting activities. Movie fans and aspirant actors could imagine living a celebrity's glamorous life of personal intrigue and drama and, most important, access to limitless consumer goods. In the 1920s, males were considered effeminate if they were interested in shopping and Valentino. This changed by the 1940s and 1950s, as I discuss in chapter 6, when *Esquire* and *Playboy* magazines made the Valentino image of the male lover and shopping acceptable to heterosexual men.

Chapter 4

Commodification of Leisure and Cultural Control: Schools, Movies, and Radio

There were sharp differences between the owners of commercial media and advocates of leisure time activities that would provide moral uplift, enhancement of workers' endurance, and motivation to work harder to consume more recreational products. The problem for the latter group was that commercial movies and radio were driven by the profit motive to maximize their audiences. Media owners discovered that dramatic portrayal of sex and violence ensured the sale of their products. Educators and moral leaders were horrified when they discovered that these new cultural tools were creating a sexual revolution and possibly inciting violent acts. The compromise in this struggle was an emphasis on *family values* in commodified forms of leisure that eventually found expression in the building of Disneyland in the 1950s.

The moral and economic arguments for commodified leisure were discussed by economist Simon Patten in a series of 1907 lectures before the Charity Organization Society of the City of New York. Patten warned, in the same tone as 19th-century Sunday School books, that "Drinking and the new sedative pleasures of smoking and saloon card-games are the vices of a faulty economic system, and an unintelligent attempt to enrich an impoverished, alien situation."[1] The "impoverished" and "alien situation," according to Patten, was urban life, which separated the worker from the invigorating and rejuvenating influence of rural life. Most urban activities, Patten argued, "are irrational and extravagant, for they sate appetite and deaden acute pain without *renewing force or directing vigor toward the day's work* (italics added)."[2] The central question, according to Patten, was: "How shall activity be made pleasurable again, and how shall society utilize the working-man's latent vitality in order to increase his industrial efficiency and give to him the rewards of energies, now ineffective, within his body and mind?"[3]

Patten suggested activities that were both reinvigorating and created a motivation to work. He called on educators and social reformers to influence leisure time activities. Of great importance, he argued, was the ability of commodified leisure to cause people to work harder. In Patten's words, entertainment "is to fix the spurs that prick to work. A circus, a national holiday, a camp meeting, arouse country people sharply and suddenly to a need of ready money. Coney Island attracts the city man as soon as he has achieved a bare subsistence."[4]

Advocating the investment by educators and philanthropists in "people's theaters," he argued that the spur to work harder should be combined with moral lessons. In this context, Patten made one of the strongest statements for the role of commodified leisure in a consumer society: "Their zest [the workers'] for amusement urges them to submit to the discipline of work, and the habits formed for the sake of gratifying their tastes make the regular life necessary in industry easier and more pleasant."[5] However, Patten's prescription for leisure time activities had to be reconciled with traditional Protestant morality. This issue was aggravated by the desire by producers of commodified leisure to enlarge their audiences by offering, from the standpoint of traditional Protestantism, immoral entertainment.

While agreeing with Patten, many educators worried that movies, and later radio, threatened the school's control of national culture and morality. In the early 19th century, common school leaders argued that the schools could unite the population by teaching a common set of moral and political principles and through the mutual contact of students. This role was continued when schools adopted Americanization programs for late 19th-century immigrants. Americanization efforts included home economists who tried to standardize American cooking and change immigrant diets. The same commitment to ensuring a common national culture occurred with the swirling new social world of the high school student.

Profit-seeking movie companies challenged the sexual codes that high schools were teaching in sex and marriage courses and in school activities. Seeking to expand their audiences, early movie makers discovered that sex sold tickets. As University of Chicago sociologist Harold Blumer reported in the 1920s, after reading student journals about going to the movies, "They [the journals] force upon one the realization that motion pictures provide, as many have termed it, 'liberal education in the art of loving'."[6]

Radio provided a similar challenge. There was general agreement that the power of broadcasting to enter homes fundamentally effected American culture. Consequently, school people wanted government and educator controlled broadcasting. In the end, commercial interests won, ensuring an increasing role for advertising in promoting consumerism. Radio and TV helped sell consumerism to the American public.

Movies and radio were part of the revolution in leisure time activities. In the late 19th and early 20th centuries, the majority of leisure activities shifted from family, church, and community gatherings to activities requiring the purchase of recreational products and admission tickets to events and establishments, such as movies, professional athletic games, commercial dance halls, and amusement parks. This shift was a result of urbanization, declining hours of work, and new technologies, including movies, radio, and TV. Industrialization and urbanization created a clear separation between work and leisure activities. Workers left the factory seeking evening and holiday entertainment. In the early 20th century, young and single workers went to movies, dance halls, and saloons. These workers confronted a conflict between a media industry promising escape from the tedium of work and educators and moral reformers demanding that media should provide moral instruction.

MOVIES: PROFIT VERSUS MORAL INSTRUCTION

Similar to newspapers, movies increased the public sharing of a common experience. People meeting from different parts of the country, and eventually the world, could relate through a common movie experience. Movie posters joined other city reading and sparked complaints about sensationalism similar to the earlier ads of P.T. Barnum. John Collier, a cofounder of the National Board of Review or, as it was sometimes called, the National Board of Censorship, complained, "Why I saw the Passion Play in moving pictures recently advertised by a poster showing the elopement of a modern couple in evening dress over a garden wall."[7]

Opening first in immigrant and working class neighborhoods, social reformers believed movies and movie theaters were undermining public morality. It was estimated that, prior to 1910, three fourths of the moviegoers crowding nickelodeons and small store-front theaters were working class. In New York City, nickelodeons increased from 50 in 1900 to 400 by 1908, and daily attendance reached 200,000.[8] Typical of moralistic reactions to nickelodeons was the 1911 Chicago Vice Commission's warning: "Investigations by individuals interested in the welfare of children have pointed out many instances where children have been influenced by the conditions surrounding some of these shows. Vicious men and boys mix with the crowd . . . and take liberties with very young girls." Examples were a nickelodeon owner who assaulted 14 young girls, and a 76-year-old man who enticed young girls to attend movies. The Chicago Vice Commission reported the statement of an unnamed movie critic: "I think the nickel theater is a recruiting station for vice. In the first place from the type of pictures often shown there; in the second place from the association."[9]

Some feared that movies would cause working class and immigrant audiences to engage in acts of civil disobedience. Films that prompted concern included *The Candidate* (1907), in which workers threw dirt at an affluent politician after a speech and he was later beaten by his discontented wife. In *Down with Women* (1907), an upper class male declared women incompetent and condemned women's suffrage. Later in the movie, he encountered women in a variety of occupations, from musician to lawyer to taxi and truck driver. Eventually, he was saved by one woman and defended in court by another. Greedy landlords were condemned in *The Eviction* (1907), and workers in labor-management struggles were treated sympathetically in films like *The Iconoclast* (1910).[10] Bankers and factory owners were frequently criticized in early silent films.[11]

By the 1930s, pro-working class and anti-upper class themes disappeared from most U.S. films. According to film historian Terry Christensen, "One movie maker, however, remained sympathetic with workers, immigrants, and the downtrodden in general as they struggled to withstand the pressures of an urban, industrial society. He was, of course, Charlie Chaplin."[12]

Fears of moral decay, social unrest, and the strengthening of class consciousness prompted demands for censorship. There were two approaches to the issue of censorship. Some people wanted to remove scenes from movies, whereas others wanted to turn movies into another form of moral education. In addition, there was a debate about whether the government should take an active role in censorship or whether censorship should exercised by the movie industry.

Advocates of government censorship wanted removal of scenes and words that might teach audiences how to commit crimes, cause them to participate in some form of social disturbance, contribute to immorality, or promote sexual promiscuity. However, those advocating self-censorship wanted films to teach moral lessons. They wanted movie scripts changed at the time of production so that explicit moral lessons could be taught to audiences.

The first censorship laws requiring police review and licensing of movies were passed by the City of Chicago in 1907. In 1909, the law was challenged when Chicago police refused to license *The James Boys* and *Night Riders*. The Illinois Supreme Court accepted the police's argument that censorship of films was necessary to maintain social order. In the words of the Court, the two films "represent nothing but malicious mischief, arson, and murder. They are both immoral, and their exhibition would necessarily be attended with evil effects upon youthful spectators."[13]

Most government-operated censorship boards reviewed films and then decided whether to license them for distribution. Obviously the film indus-

try resented the process of government censorship because it delayed distribution and created the possibility that each municipality or state would require different standards. Delays and constant editing increased costs. In
the 1920s, Will Hays, as president of the Motion Picture Producers and Directors Association (MPPDA), argued against government censorship on
the grounds that there was lack of agreement on standards. This was exemplified by state laws prohibiting the showing of a woman smoking a cigarette. According to Hays, these laws "might eliminate any scene of a social
gathering happening in another state." In another instance, a lawyer on
one censorship board would not allow any scenes that depicted lawyers as
unethical or crooked. In another example, Hays wrote, "Scenes of strike riots were ordered eliminated from news reels in one state at the same time
newspapers were using photographs of the exact incidents recorded in the
films."[14]

In 1915, the U.S. Supreme Court reaffirmed the necessity of government
censorship for maintaining social order. The case involved the Mutual Film
Corporation's complaint that Ohio required all films to be submitted to a
state censorship board, which resulted in delayed distribution. The lawyers
for the company argued that censorship before distribution was a violation
of the Free Speech Clause of the First Amendment. In a decision that was
not overturned until the 1950s, the U.S. Supreme Court ruled that, "We immediately feel that the argument is wrong or strained which extends the
guarantee of free speech to the multitudinous shows which are advertised
on the billboards of our cities and towns, and which regards them as em-
blems of public safety." In the words of the Court, movies represented a potential threat to public safety: "Their [the movies'] power of amusement,
and it may be, education, the audiences they assemble, not of women
alone, but together, not only adults only but of children, make them the
more insidious in corruption by pretense of worth. . . ."[15]

Comparing state censorship to public schools, Ellis Oberholtzer, Secretary of the Pennsylvania State Board of Motion Picture Censors, argued in
1921,

> The efforts which are made to convert the unlikeliest of young human beings
> at school into useful citizens are many. From the care of their teeth and the
> public feeding of them . . . to the purely education processes. . . . I for one fail
> to see, therefore, how by any fair system of reasoning we can be held to be
> without some duty to inquire into the course of the film man with his 15,000
> or more picture houses . . . at the door of each inhabitant.[16]

Similar to the public schools' role in protecting morality, he believed the
government should censor movies by removing any scenes that might result
in lawlessness and the moral decay of the citizenry. As an advocate of gov-

ernment censorship, Oberholtzer rejected the use of movies to consciously teach morality. He quoted from a British Board of Film Censors report:

> It is said for such films that they serve to warn the public against the dangers of the abuse of drugs, but the Board decided that there being no reason to suppose that this habit was prevalent in this country . . . , the evils of arousing curiosity in the minds of those to who it was a novel idea far outweighed the possible good that might accrue by warning the small minority who indulged in the practice.

Declared Oberholtzer, "I am, therefore, not to be beguiled by the protestations of such a picture man. I have met him and he resembles a teacher less than any one I have ever seen."[17]

Schools, Oberholtzer declared, should remain the central government agency for teaching morality. Rejecting movies as a source of moral lessons, he stated, "It is clear that a theater is not a proper place for the inculcation of such lessons, or the theater man a proper person to bear such delicate messages to the young. We have the church, the school, the home and our social organizations. . . ."[18]

In contrast to government censorship, advocates of self-regulation wanted films to teach audiences moral and social lessons. They criticized government censorship because it only removed negative scenes without controlling the general theme of a film. Through self-regulation, movies could become another form of public education. The strongest champion of this approach was John Collier of the National Board of Review. The National Board of Review was organized after New York City police, under orders from the mayor and chief of police, closed 550 movie houses on Christmas in 1908 for violating Sunday closing laws as part of a larger crusade against vice. In reaction to police actions, theater owners organized the National Board of Review hoping that self-censorship would stop future vice raids. Officially organized in March 1909, the Board received financial support from the film industry, which hoped that Board approval would ensure a movie's nationwide acceptance and, consequently, avoid problems with government censors. Board members wanted movie reform, like schools and settlement houses, to improve urban life. The majority of members of the executive committee of the National Board of Review were wealthy Protestant males, including Andrew Carnegie, Samuel Gompers, presidents of major universities, and "representatives from the Federal Council of Churches, the YMCA, the New York School Board, the Society for the Prevention of Crime headed by the most powerful vice crusader in the city, the Rev. Charles Parkhurst, and the moralistic Postal Inspector, Anthony Comstock."[19]

The Board's guiding principles were presented by Collier in a magazine series in *The Survey*. As Collier explained, the Board's censorship code stressed the importance of always teaching morality by showing good winning out over evil. "The results of the crime [as depicted in a movie]," the Board's code stated, "should be in the long run disastrous to the criminal so that the impression is that crime will inevitably find one out. The result [punishment] should always take a reasonable proportion of the film." The code stressed the importance of teaching that the government was the protector of public morality. "As a general rule," the code stated, "it is preferable to have retribution come through the hands of authorized officers of the law, rather than through revenge or other unlawful or extra-legal means." In keeping with the Protestant leadership's concern about sexual morality, code standards would "not allow the extended display of personal allurements, the exposure of alleged physical charms and passionate, protracted embraces," and it also disapproved "the showing of men turning lightly from woman to woman or women turning lightly from man to man in intimate sexual relationships."[20]

From John Collier's perspective, government censorship would impede the potential of movies as a form of public education. "The challenge of the old and the institution of the new," Collier wrote, "are a responsibility of the drama, no less than is the inculcation of accepted virtues. . . ."[21] The heavy hand of government censorship, Collier insisted, undermined art's social role by applying absolute standards. "Until censorship can discriminate, can limit the audience, can prescribe the destination of the censored product," he wrote, "it is nothing but a bludgeon-like imposition, by some element [government censors] momentarily in power of its prejudices on the mass of the people." As an example, Collier used a movie scene showing a boy torturing a cat. Although the board prohibited depiction of brutality, these scenes were approved because they were "essential in a plot dealing with the relation of defective mentality to juvenile crime. The boy who is here shown torturing a cat is later restored by medical treatment to normality."[22]

As government officials and reformers grappled with the potential impact of movies on the public mind, school people worried about competing with movies for student attention and adapting films for use in the classroom. The early reaction of both reformers and educators set the stage for the movie industry's adoption of self-censorship codes in the 1930s. Self-censorship codes became standard for most forms of commodified leisure.

EDUCATORS AND MOVIES:
COMPETITION OR CONSUMER ITEM

Movies were both a threat to educators and a new consumer item to be used in classroom instruction. Some educators worried that movies would replace schools in controlling culture and morals. "In less than twenty years, the motion picture business has secured a hold on the minds of people," declared Peter Olesen, school superintendent from Cloquet, Minnesota, before the 1914 NEA meeting. Olesen claimed the influence of movies was "almost equal to that of the school and the daily press." Olesen warned that movies might actually possess a stronger hold on the mind of the child than did the schools. "I believe," he observed, "that one reason why it is hard to interest some children in school today is that their minds have been filled and their imagination thrilled with too vivid motion pictures, and, when these children come to school, they are disappointed because the teacher cannot make the subject as interesting as a motion-picture show."[23]

At the same NEA meeting, movies industry officials announced their entry into school markets. Alfred Saunders, manager of Colonial Picture Corporation's Education Department, gave a promotional speech entitled, "Motion Pictures as an Aid to Education." One of the first movie industry representatives to speak to the NEA, Saunders wanted to sell films to public schools. After reviewing available movie projectors and films suitable for schools, he claimed that, "every school that is equipped with a projecting machine may cover the cost of it by allowing the parents to attend exhibitions in the evening."[24]

In response, some educators contended that movies would enhance classroom instruction. David Snedden, Commissioner of Education for Massachusetts and a pioneer in industrial education, argued that movies could present real-life images for classroom instruction. Snedden realized that the "cheapening and vulgarizing of the motion picture, schools and other educational agencies have been loath to attach to it the importance which it deserves."[25] Yet, he stressed, pressure from the education world on the movie industry could result in films that were of instructional value. Snedden's position was echoed by Nathaniel Graham, school superintendent from South Omaha, Nebraska, who contented, "We all believe that encouragement by this body of educators will result in motion pictures being made available for every department of school work. Who can tell in how short a time motion pictures will be as great an accessory to education as is the printed text?"[26]

The debate over competition for the minds of students and the use of movies as educational aids continued into the 1920s and 1930s. Similar to government officials and Protestant social reformers, however, educators remained uneasy about this new form of commodified leisure.

MARKETS, FINANCING, AND THE CONTENT OF MOVIES

The social tensions caused by the advent of movies were similar to the cultural clashes between Protestants and Jewish immigrants portrayed by Yezierska in *Salome of the Tenements*. Looked down on by established American wealth, the film industry became an outlet for the entrepreneurial skills of recently arrived immigrants and their children. Working their way out of the tenements of New York, Boston, and other American cities, Neal Gabler, in *An Empire of Their Own: How the Jews Invented Hollywood*, chronicled the lives of Jewish immigrants and their children who founded the major movie studios and produced films that shaped the consciousness of Americans.[27] Protestant reformers and educators perceived the movie industry as corrupt because of immigrant domination. Typical of the feelings of the Protestant leadership was Henry Ford's complaint in a 1921 issue of the *Dearborn Independent* that, "As soon as the Jews gained control of the 'movies,' we had a movie problem, the consequences of which are not yet visible. It is the genius of that race to create problems of a moral character in whatever business they achieve a majority."[28]

Concerned about their ability to market movies to middle-class Protestant families and raise money to finance their expanding industry, immigrant movie makers decided to create an industry organization headed by a prominent Protestant political leader. This desire was increased with the public scandals of movie stars. In 1920, the nude body of screen star Olive Thomas was found on the floor of a Paris hotel, her death due to an apparent drug overdose. Shortly afterward, comedian Fatty Arbuckle was accused of the rape and murder of starlet Virginia Rappe at a party in San Francisco. In the same year, after director William Desmond was murdered, it was discovered he had been leading a double life under two names and had two wives and two sets of children.[29]

In response to the general attitude of the Protestant establishment toward the movie industry and the scandals, movie makers took their cue from another form of commodified leisure—the baseball industry—by organizing the MPPDA in 1922. After being plagued with numerous bribery scandals in the 1910s, the baseball owners hired Judge Kenesaw Mountain Landis to act as a czar over the industry. Landis was given the task of *cleaning up* baseball and improving its moral image. Using this model, Louis Selznick assumed leadership in organizing the MPPDA. Selznick was a Ukrainian Jew who, in 1912, after immigrating to Pittsburgh and entering the jewelry business, became a partner in the recently organized Universal Pictures.[30]

Searching for someone to head the MPPDA who would please Protestant leaders, studio owners selected William Harrison Hays, an elder of the Presbyterian church from Indiana and former National Chairman of the Republican Party. Protestant, midwestern-born, and politically well connected, Hays was an ideal public relations leader for the industry. The MPPDA was an organization created to help immigrant entrepreneurs function in a Protestant environment that was hostile to both immigrants and Jews.

The growing concentration of the movie industry made it possible for the Hays Office, as it was called, to exercise a *dictatorship of virtue* over the content of American films. In the 1920s, the Big Eight film companies that formed the MPPDA made 90% of American films, whereas in 1912, 60 firms had been in operation in the United States. The Big Eight included Paramount, 20th Century Fox, Loews (M-G-M), Universal, Warner Brothers, Columbia, United Artists, and Radio-Keith-Orpheum (RKO).[31]

In the 1920s, movies became the largest portion of the recreation budget for average American families. Large cities averaged one movie seat for every five to seven people in their population. Furthermore, the composition of movie audiences changed during the 1920s. In 1912, 25% of the movie audiences were clerical workers and 5% were from the business classes, whereas in the 1920s included increasing numbers from the middle class.[32]

As movies became the major form of commodified leisure, reformers and educators demanded greater control over the information and ideas contained in movies. The Hays office responded by organizing a public relations office, a public information department, and a title registration bureau. Hays used the public relations department to establish ties with groups critical of films. At the first meeting of the MPPDA in June 1922, Hays appointed Protestant reformer Lee Hanmer of the Russell Sage Foundation to chair the Committee on Public Relations, which included representatives from the Camp Fire Girls, the Boy Scouts, the General Federation of Women's Clubs, the International Federation of Catholic Alumnae, the Young Men's Christian Association, and the National Education Association.[33]

The Hays Office was concerned about calls for government censorship. Protestant evangelical groups often laced their attacks on movies with statements about the low morality of immigrants. Sounding anti-Semitic, Protestant evangelist Billy Sunday campaigned in 1921 for laws that would close movie theaters on Sunday. He preached that, "No foreign bunch can come over here and tell us how we ought to observe the Lord's Day. The United States at heart is a God-fearing and a God-loving nation and most of our laxity on this point I lay at the door of those elements which are a part of our population, but are not assimilated."[34] In 1920, the Reverend Wilbur Crafts crusaded for Sunday closing legislation at the federal level with the claim that movies, despite their production in the United States, were causing a Europeanization of America.[35]

There were also claims that movies caused public violence and race riots. The years immediately following World War I were punctuated with a number of public bombings. In addition, major race riots occurred in northern cities. Fearful of race riots and social disorder, government codes restricted racial themes and the portrayal of criminal acts. In his study of censorship laws, Richard Randall found that most laws prohibited movie scenes containing obscenity, indecency, and immorality. In addition, many laws banned scenes that would promote racial, religious, or class prejudice. Reflecting the concern that movies taught people how to commit criminal acts, many censorship codes called for removal of scenes that involved "incitement to crime," "portrayal of criminal behavior," and "disturbance of the peace."[36] *The Nation* magazine reported that, in 1921, the Kansas State Board of Review banned from movies all scenes of race riots in Tulsa, Oklahoma, although newspapers carried front-page pictures. The Kansas board also prohibited any mention of the Ku Klux Klan. These actions were taken against newsreels. The words "Probe of murders laid to Klan" were censored from newsreels in Ohio, according to *The Nation*.[37] Consequently, censorship laws inhibited the production of movies dealing with social issues.

Between the enactment of the first municipal censorship law in Chicago in 1907 and the 1930s, a wave of municipal and state censorship laws spread across the country. Between 1922 and 1927, 48 bills on movie censorship were introduced into state legislatures, and prior to the 1950s there existed at various times 90 municipal censorship boards. The most important municipal boards were located in Chicago, Detroit, Memphis, Atlanta, and Boston.[38]

World War I disrupted the European movie industry leaving U.S. companies in a dominant role in global markets. By 1919, over 90% of the films shown in Europe and virtually all films shown in Latin America were made in the United States. Foreign distribution caused American movie makers to avoid portraying any foreign nation in a negative manner for fear that the film would be banned from that country. The desire to protect foreign markets played a major role in the self-censorship standards adopted by the movie industry in the late 1920s and 1930s. Standards banned negative portrayal of foreign governments or the people of foreign nations.[39]

EDUCATORS, YOUTH, AND THE MOVIES

Educators claimed that movies were harming American youth. In response, Will Hays appeared before the NEA in July 1922 within 6 months of assuming leadership of the MPPDA. Hays pledged acceptance of the challenge of the American mother to provide worthy entertainment for American youth.[40] Hays' appearance did little to ease educators' apprehensions. A 1923 editorial in *The Elementary School Journal* complained that after Hays' speech little effort was made to involve educators directly in the movie industry. The writer complained the movie industry only wanted educators to preview and publish a list of approved movies and help develop a market for classroom films. Noting that "the motion picture has come to be one of the most important sources of influence over the public mind," the writer argued that it "behooves everyone who is interested in the creation of sound attitudes among people at large and especially among pupils to study the problems which motion pictures have created."[41]

The NEA created a special committee to work with the MPPDA. This committee received direct financial support from the MPPDA. The committee was chaired by a leading educational psychologist, Charles Judd of the University of Chicago. Its membership included public school representatives from around the country. The MPPDA financed a meeting in New York between members of the committee and representatives of the movie producers. In addition, the MPPDA provided $5,000 for the committee to investigate the use of films for classroom instruction.[42]

The NEA committee's report regarded schools as a new market for films. As a result, the NEA created a Department of Visual Instruction to study the classroom use of movies. The MPPDA, hoping to extend the commercial life of films, asked educators to review old movies for classroom instruction. The movie industry hoped this would extend the commercial live of films. The MPPDA sponsored committees of teachers to select portions of old films that could be used in classrooms.[43]

Building on this cooperation, Colonel Jason S. Joy, MPPDA's Director of Public Relations, told the delegates to the 1927 NEA annual meeting, "The motion picture today is catering to the American family." As part of this effort, he stated, "the industry has been concerned for some time now in finding out exactly what the effect of pictures is—on behavior, as an educator, and as a force for good." Joy cited a Columbia University study of audiences in 12 different New York City theaters. The study found that on average only 8% of movie audiences were under the age of 17 and school-age children attended movie houses on the average 1.15 times per week. Based on these figures, Joy concluded movies had little effect on children. More important, Joy claimed movies had educational and moral value. Ten of the most popular movies selected by children in the study included *Beau Geste, Ben Hur,* and *The Scarlet Letter.*[44]

Dismissing claims that movies had a negative effect on children, Joy outlined what the movie industry was doing to make movies more attractive to educators and families, such as making films of literary classics. Joy told the NEA, "This growing intimacy between the motion picture and the book has met with general although not universal approval. There have been those who feared that many people would 'take their reading out in looking'."[45] However, he argued in reference to a report by the New Jersey Library Association, movies stimulated greater interest in reading the classics and historical novels. In addition, classics made into movies became more accessible to the general population. "Books on the shelves of libraries," he told the NEA, "make it possible for men to attain a certain amount of knowledge and information by hard work and application. But the moving picture, presented as an amusement, will in a few years make it impossible for any average man or woman to remain ignorant."[46]

Despite the MPPDA's claim that movies had educational value, educators continued to complain about the detrimental effects of movies on children. For many educators, the harmful effects of movies were proved by the results of a series of research findings commonly referred to as the *Payne Studies*. The public uproar caused by the publishing of this research contributed to the movie industry's decision to enforce a self-censorship code.[47]

The Payne studies were organized in 1928 under the leadership of W. W. Charters, Director of the Bureau of Educational Research at Ohio State University. Twelve studies were completed and published under the sponsorship of The Payne Fund. In addition, Charters wrote a summary volume in 1933. The research was carried out by a formidable array of social scientists and educators and published in a series of volumes by the Macmillan Company.[48]

Reprinted seven times between 1933 and 1935, James Forman's (1933) *Our Movie-Made Children* popularized the Payne studies' findings and created general public concern about the effects of movies on children and youth.[49] The public was shocked by the finding that movies had a detrimental effect on the health of children by disturbing sleep patterns. Working with the Bureau of Juvenile Research in Columbus, Ohio, researchers in a state institution wired children's beds to measure restlessness during sleep. The children were divided into different groups. One group drank coffee at 8:30 p.m. Another group underwent sleep deprivation by being kept up until midnight and then awakened early in the morning. (This part of the experiment ended after complaints by matrons of the institution.) A third set was taken to the movies prior to going to bed. Researchers found that movie attendance caused as much disturbance during sleep as drinking two cups of coffee at 8:30 p.m. "We can conclude" the report stated, "from our results that seeing some films does induce a disturbance of relaxed, recuperative sleep in children to a degree which, if indulged in with sufficient frequency, can be detrimental to normal health and growth."[50] The results of this study led Charters to warn, "Thus it appears that movies selected unwisely and indulged in intemperately will have a detrimental effect upon the health of children."[51]

Another finding was that children retained information from movies over long periods of time. A group of second and third graders remembered, at the end of 6 weeks, 90% of what they remembered from a movie on the day they saw it. Researchers also concluded that movies had a significant effect on the conduct and attitudes of children. One study compared the behavior of children who attended movies four to five times a week with those from similar economic and social backgrounds who went to movies twice a month. Those who frequently attended movies, compared with those who attended infrequently, had lower deportment grades in school, did more poorly on school subjects, and were rated lower in reputation by their teachers. A study of children living in congested areas of New York City found similar results. The researchers concluded from the statistics gathered in the study "that for this population there is a positive relationship between truancy and delinquency and frequent movie attendance."[52]

The studies confirmed the increasing role of movies in leisure time activities. As part of the Payne Studies, 55,000 children in 44 communities in Ohio were surveyed regarding movie attendance. It was found that children between the ages of 5 and 8 attended movies an average of 0.42 times a week, and for 8- to 19-year-old children the average was 0.99. The study determined that the average boy between the ages of 8 and 19 attended 57 pictures a year, whereas the average girl attended 46 movies. The specter of weekly movie attendance by youth heightened fears about the effects of movies.

The studies confirmed the belief that movies increased promiscuity and crime rates. In *Our Movie-Made Children*, Forman concluded, "A number of adolescent and youthful criminals give circumstantial accounts of their path to, and arrival at, criminality, and, rightly or wrongly, but very positively, they blame the movies for their downfall." Forman reported that girl inmates in an institution for sex delinquents attributed "to the movies a leading place in stimulating cravings for an easy life, for luxury, for cabarets, road-houses and wild parties, for having men make love to them and, ultimately, for their particular delinquency."[53]

MOVIES AND THE SEXUAL REVOLUTION

Was the 1920s' sexual revolution caused by movies, eroticized ads, new sex manuals, high schools, or changing concepts of women? There was a definite shift in the sexual behavior among youth. Despite structuring high schools around principles of spermatic political economy, youth engaged in more sexual activities. In *Intimate Affairs: A History of Sexuality*, John D'Emilio and Estelle Freedman concluded, "Sexual innovation played a key role in this new [1920s] world of youth. Particularly in coeducational institutions, heterosocial mixing became the norm. Young men and women mixed casually in classes, extracurricular activities, and social spaces, with a great deal of freedom from adult supervision."[54] Statistics showed an increase in sexual activity. In a 1939 survey of college-educated women, only 26% of the respondents born between 1890 and 1900 reported engaging in premarital sex, compared with 69% of those born after 1913.[55] The Kinsey studies of the early 1950s showed a steady increase in the number of women achieving orgasm in marriage beginning with the cohort born in the first part of the 20th century. Kinsey found that more than a third of the women born before 1900 remained clothed during sex, in contrast to 8% of those born during the 1920s.[56]

While high school sex education courses were preaching abstinence from sex until marriage, warning of venereal diseases, and avoiding any discussion of sexual techniques to enhance sexual pleasure, popular sexual manuals were appearing that undermined the concept of spermatic political economy and promoted the idea of female orgasm. In addition, Margaret Sanger was advocating birth control to free women from feminine slavery. In *The Pivot of Civilization* (1922), Sanger argued that birth control would raise economic standards for the poor by reducing the number of children in a family and allowing women more free time for self-development. She contented that birth control would allow women to achieve sexual pleasure, and, consequently, the sexual joy of partners would help achieve an "earthly paradise."[57] In *Happiness in Marriage* (1926), Sanger extolled the importance of sexual rapture and rejected the idea that sexual intercourse depleted bodily strength. Instead, she argued that sexual intercourse revitalized the body.[58] The best-selling marriage manual of the 1920s, Joseph Collins' *A Doctor Looks at Love and Live*, rejected earlier concerns about masturbation and declared it a healthy activity. He hoped for a future with less restrictive morality. Other books of the period carried the same message along with suggested techniques for improving love making, including oral sex.[59]

Many educators were convinced that movies were causing the sexual revolution. One Payne study focused on the relationship between changes in sexual behavior and movies. The study asked 1,800 high school and college students, office employees, and factory workers to keep journals on the effect of movies on their lives. A male college sophomore recounted, "She would make me go with her to see [a movie] . . . and then when we returned home she made me make love with her as she had seen the other two on the screen." Another college male wrote, "The technique of making love to a girl received considerable of my attention, and it was directly through the movies that I learned to kiss a girl on her ears, neck, and cheeks, as well as on the mouth." A statement in the journal of a female high school sophomore was typical of those found in other journal by girls her age: "I have learned quite a bit about love-making from the movies."[60] The author of the study, Herbert Blumer, concluded that movies were taking over the fantasy world of youth. He claimed that 66% of 458 journals written by high school students provided evidence that movies were linked to sexual daydreaming.

Another Payne study concluded that aggressive female sexual behavior portrayed in movies did not conform to the public values of the 1920s. To compare public values with those in movies, Charles Peters, professor of Education at Pennsylvania State College, divided the population into 14 categories ranging from middle-aged college professors to western Pennsylvania miners and their wives and children. Each group rated movie scenes according to whether they thought the content was above or below standards of public morality and political attitudes. They were asked to judge movie scenes according to (a) democratic attitudes and practices, (b) treatment of children by parents, (c) kissing and caressing, and (d) aggressiveness of a girl in lovemaking.[61]

Only the fourth movie portrayal, "aggressiveness of a girl in lovemaking," was rated as below general moral standards. "Treatment of children by parents" and "democratic attitudes and practices" in movies were rated by all categories as above the average standards of society. "Kissing and caressing" movie scenes were found to parallel general moral standards.

All studies seemed to confirm fears that movies were undermining public morality. The Catholic Church's Legion of Decency joined the fray by ordering parishioners to avoid immoral movies. Organized in 1933, its founding recommendation included the strong words, "The pest hole that infects the entire country with its obscene and lascivious moving pictures must be cleansed and disinfected: The multitudinous agencies that are employed in disseminating pornographic literature must be suppressed."[62] The Legion of Decency, with the support of the Catholic hierarchy, asked Catholics to sign a pledge that they would "remain away from all motion pictures except those which do not offend decency and Christian morals."[63] The pledge opened with a call for unity in protesting the threat to youth, country, home life, and religion, and it included a promise to boycott objectionable magazines and books. The signer of the pledge promised to condemn movies that were promoting a "sex mania in our land" and to "do all that I can to arouse public opinion against the portrayal of vice as a normal condition of affairs, and against depicting criminals of any class as heroes and heroines, presenting their filthy philosophy of life as something acceptable to men and women."[64]

MAKING MOVIES SAFE

Despite the moral criticism, large attendance attested to the popular appeal of movies. The movie studios were supplying a product that the public was buying. Yet faced with prospect of government censorship, the movie industry wanted to sell movies and placate those calling for censorship. Will Hays tried to achieve this balance after a storm of religious protest over the 1923 best-selling novel adapted to the screen as *West of the Water Tower*, which dealt with illegitimacy and a dissolute clergyman. Hays convinced members of the MPPDA to allow his office to review all books and plays that might interest movie producers.[65]

Fearing additional government censorship, the MPPDA established a mechanism for self-censorship. In 1927, the Hays Office adopted a list of

Don'ts and Be Carefuls. In 1930, this list was replaced by a more extensive "Code to Govern the Making of Talking, Synchronized and Silent Pictures." The 1930 code was enforced by a 1934 agreement among members of the MPPDA that all movies prior to their release had to be approved by a new office of Production Code Administration.

A writer of the movie code, Martin Quigley, argued in *Decency in Motion Pictures* that films were a form of public education that should establish ideals in the minds of audiences. He rejected that art should be allowed to freely develop.[66] The code's text stated that films appealed to the masses and, therefore, were different from other forms of art. Similar to public schools, everyone was exposed to the movies. The code distinguished between art forms appealing to particular social classes and those with mass appeal. Movies, the code stated, attracted "every class—immature, developed, undeveloped, law abiding, criminal." The ease of distribution allowed movies to reach "places unpenetrated by other forms of art." Consequently, the code's writers argued, "it is difficult to produce films intended for only certain classes of people . . . the exhibitor's theaters are built for the masses, for the cultivated and the rude, the mature and the immature, the self-respecting and the criminal. Films, unlike books and music, can with difficulty be confined to certain selected groups. . . . Psychologically, the larger the audience, the lower the moral mass resistance to suggestion."[67]

The code's authors recognized movies as a new form of public education that might replace the school's control over national culture and morality. The code echoed Patten's earlier arguments that commodified leisure should promote the well-being of workers. The code's text differentiated between the morally uplifting qualities of baseball and golf and the degrading qualities of cockfights and bullfighting. The code stated, "correct entertainment raises the whole standard of the nation, Wrong entertainment lowers the whole living conditions and moral ideas of a race."[68]

The code's self-censorship standards can be divided into: (a) religious, (b) moral, (c) offensive to certain individuals, (d) criminal, and (e) political. The guidelines for religious content in movies dealt with situations that might offend organized religious groups. Moral guidelines were concerned with the portrayal of good and evil and specific sexual situations. The standards for content "offensive to certain individuals" referred to scenes that might spark racial tensions or might be objectionable to some people or organized groups. Guidelines for criminal scenes emphasized the importance of showing crime as objectionable and ensured that scenes did not teach the audience how to commit crimes. The political restrictions of the code dealt with attitudes toward the law, the justice system, the U.S. political system, and foreign countries.

The following divides the 1927 code into the prior categories.[69]

Don'ts and Be Carefuls (1927)
Shall Not Appear in Movies

A. Religious
   1. Pointed profanity . . . this includes the words *God, Lord, Jesus, Christ*
   2. Ridicule of the clergy

B. Moral
   1. Children's sex organs
   2. Any licentious or suggestive nudity
   3. Any inference of sex perversion
   4. White Slavery
   5. Sex hygiene and venereal diseases
   6. The sale of women or a woman selling her virtue
   7. First-night scenes
   8. Man and woman in bed together
   9. Deliberate seduction of girls
   10. The institution of marriage
   11. Excessive or lustful kissing

C. Offensive to Certain Individuals
   1. Miscegenation (sex relations between the White and African-American races)
   2. Scenes of actual childbirth
   3. Brutality and possible gruesomeness
   4. Actual hangings or electrocutions as legal punishment for crime
   5. Apparent cruelty to children and animals
   6. Branding of people and animals
   7. Surgical operations

D. Criminal
   1. Illegal traffic in drugs
   2. Sympathy for criminals
   3. Use of firearms
   4. Theft, robbery, safe cracking, and dynamiting of trains, mines, buildings, and so on (having in mind the effect that a too-detailed description of these may have on the moron)
   5. Technique of committing murder by whatever method
   6. Methods of smuggling
   7. Rape or attempted rape

E. Political
   1. Willful offense to any nation, race, or creed
   2. Use of the flag

3. International relations (avoiding picturizing in an unfavorable light another country's religion, history, institutions, prominent people, and citizenry)
4. Attitude toward public characters and institutions
5. Sedition
6. Titles or scenes having to do with the law enforcement or law-enforcing officers

The 1930 code expanded on the 1927 code by emphasizing the importance of showing the triumph of good over evil. Its first general principle stated, "No picture shall be produced which will lower the moral standards of those who see it. Hence the sympathy of the audience shall never be thrown to the side of crime. wrong-doing, evil or sin." Good people were always to be rewarded. In this movie-made world, cowboys in white hats always beat the bandits in black hats. The code stated that movies must avoid scenes where "evil is made to appear attractive or alluring and good is made to appear unattractive."[70] Distinguishing between sympathy for a crime or sin as opposed to sympathy for the plight of a sinner, the code warned against the sympathy of the audience being directed toward behavior that would generally be considered a crime or sin.

Supporting the religious vision of good struggling against evil, the second general principle of the 1930 code stated, "Correct standards of life, subject only to the requirements of drama and entertainment, shall be presented." In the code, "If motion pictures consistently hold up for admiration high types of characters and present stories that will affect lives for the better, they can become the most powerful natural force for the improvement of mankind."

The third general principle promoted positive images of laws and governments. It stated, "Law, natural or human, shall not be ridiculed, nor shall sympathy be created for its violation." *Natural laws* were defined as the principles of justice dictated by a person's conscience. The code specified that audience support should always be created for government laws and warned against movies that were sympathetic to the commission of crime and did not favor the law. In addition, according to the code, "The courts of the land should not be presented as unjust." Although individual court officials might be portrayed in movies as unjust, the code warns that "the court system of the country must not suffer as a result of this presentation."

Hollywood's movie code made movies into another form of public education. It provided a means for turning the most consumed leisure time product into moral and political lessons. Standing before the 1939 meeting of the NEA, Will Hays accurately claimed, "That educators and motion picture producers have certain specialized and mutual interests in the motion picture as a purveyor of ideas and motivator of activities even the layman has come to realize." Hays contended that the movie code had established an enduring truce between educators and the movie industry. The movie code, he stated, required that in films, "crime, wrongdoing, evil, or sin shall not be made attractive; that correct standards of life shall be presented; that law, natural or human, shall not be ridiculed, or sympathy created for its violation." It was the standards of this code, Hays maintained, that made it possible to bring together the world of the movies and the schools as purveyors of ideas.[71]

The movie code represented one resolution of the tension between the public's desire for commodified forms of leisure and the desire by educators and Puritan reformers to make leisure time activities supportive of an efficient industrial and moral society. The advent of radio sparked another conflict over cultural and moral control.

THE TRIUMPH OF ADVERTISING: COMMERCIAL RADIO

The triumph of commercial radio, and eventually commercial TV, over government or educator-operated media, created a close link between advertising and entertainment. In general, movies were free of ads except for ads about coming movies and in later years the practice of product placement in films. With commercial radio and TV, listeners and viewers wanting to be entertained had to accept constant interruptions from commercials. To compete for listener and viewer attention, ads had to be as entertaining as the media programming. Eventually ads and entertainment would merge in the form of programs devoted to selling products. As described in chapter 7, Walt Disney pioneered this method on TV by devoting full-length programs to the Disneyland theme park and to the making of Disney movies. Commercial media assisted in the integration of consumerism into all aspects of American life.

Educators realized the importance of commercial media to shaping American culture. How could the school compete with a media that could enter every home with continuous entertainment? In addition, educators worried about the domination of business values as advertising became more potent with catchy jingles to haunt the public mind, such as "I'm Chiquita Banana and I've come to say . . ." and "Halo, everybody, Halo/Halo is the shampoo that glorifies your hair."[72] Initially, the struggle was over educator versus commercial control of the air waves. After educators lost that battle, the struggle was over the content of advertising-driven radio programs.

Reflecting the debate over the commercialization of radio, the August 1933 headline on the theatrical trade journal *Variety* announced: "BRITISH

VS. AMERICAN Radio Slant, Debate Theme in 40,000 Schools."[73] The pro-industry *Variety* considered the debate theme part of an antiradio propaganda campaign being waged by educators, religious groups, and nonprofit organizations against commercial broadcasting. *Variety* used *antiradio* when referring to opponents of commercial radio who wanted the federal government to license more educational and nonprofit radio stations. Antiradio groups worried that profits were determining radio programming and that, consequently, commercial radio was destroying American national culture.

The central issue in the high school debates was whether radio should be privately owned and financially supported by advertising or, like the British system, operated by the government and supported by taxation. Commercial radio networks worried that with an estimated attendance of 100 persons at each debate, as many as 4 million people might hear the question being discussed. "Many, perhaps most," *Variety* lamented, "of these people have been unaware of the existence of the question."[74]

While educators worried that the crass commercialization of privately operated radio would subvert American culture, the radio industry claimed that commercial programming fostered a democratic culture by allowing listeners to vote for the type of culture they wanted by turning the radio knob to their favorite programs. Operated as a business, industry leaders argued, commercial radio responded to the choices made by listeners. What educators wanted, they argued, was to impose a culture on the population. In opposition, private broadcasters claimed, commercial radio reflected listeners' choices and, consequently, was fostering the development of a truly democratic culture.

The debate between educators and commercial radio interests reached a peak in the early 1930s. By then commercial radio networks dominated the airwaves. However, they operated under a constant fear that government action might take away their newly established dominion. They were particularly concerned about educators who, in addition to voicing concerns about the decline of national culture, were fighting mad over their recent loss of radio licenses resulting from government favoritism toward commercial radio. The Radio Act of 1927 created the Federal Radio Commission (FRC), which in 1928 adopted a new allocation plan favoring stations with more financial resources, the most expensive equipment, and the most varied programming. This decision favored commercial broadcasters. By 1937, the number of radio licenses held by educational institutions declined from 202 to 38.[75]

Commercial networks worried about a vocal coalition of educators, religious organizations, and other interested groups that were demanding 25% of all broadcasting licenses be given to nonprofit institutions. Leading this movement was the National Committee on Education by Radio. Formed in 1930, the Committee was funded by the Payne Foundation and had representatives from 11 major national educational organizations, including the National Education Association, the National Catholic Education Association, the American Council on Education, the National Association of State Universities, and the National Council of State Superintendents of Education.[76]

Advertising was a central concern of the National Committee on Education by Radio. When the Committee met in May 1934, Jerome Davis, a faculty member at the Yale Divinity School, complained about the cultural values disseminated by radio advertising: "Children are told that when they drink Cocomalt they are cooperating with Buck Rogers and heroine Wilma. . . . I am not questioning the quality of Cocomalt, but the outrageous ethics and educational effects of this advertising on the child mind." Davis contended that programs planned "for the younger generation on an educational instead of a profit basis, the dramatic adventures of historical figures in American life—those who have really contributed something to the welfare of the nation and the world—could be told."[77]

Joy Elmer Morgan, chair of the Committee, echoed Davis' sentiments: "You will discover that the advertising agency is taking the place of the mother, the father, the teacher, the pastor, the priest, in determining the attitudes of children."[78] Based on a pursuit of profits, she argued, radio entertainment was destroying positive cultural values: "America today is operating on a momentum which was acquired in the days before radio. It is operating on a momentum which the people acquired before the motion picture began teaching crime and gambling and the cheap and flippant attitude toward the verities of life." Morgan worried about the effect on the United States of a generation raised on commercial media. "No one knows what will happen," she warned, "when this country comes into the hands of those who have been exposed to the propaganda of the money changers and to the debasing material which they have broadcast into the lives of the people."[79]

In response, commercial broadcasters launched a campaign to prove the educational worth of commercial radio. At the 1934 NEA's annual meeting, Merlin H. Aylesworth, president of the National Broadcasting Corporation (NBC), spoke on "Radio As a Means of Public Enlightenment." Aylesworth contended that radio had joined the church, home, and school as a source of public enlightenment. Using questionable numbers, Aylesworth claimed that 50% of network radio was educational.[80] At the 1934 FCC hearings, William Paley, president of Columbia Broadcasting System (CBS), defended commercial radio in a talk entitled, "Radio As a Cultural Force." Driven by market forces, Paley argued, commercial radio responded to listeners' desires. Commercial radio had to win and hold audiences. Also radio had to appeal to a mass audience. In contrast, newspapers could be written for special audiences, whereas radio required universal appeal. Consequently, Paley maintained, radio programs appealed to the emotions and self-interest of listeners as well as their intellect.

Regarding the control of mass culture, Paley declared that a democratic culture required control by the audience. Commercial radio was democratic because it was based on listener selection. "We cannot assuredly," Paley argued, "calmly broadcast programs we think people ought to listen to . . . and then go on happily unconcerned as to whether they listen or not."[81] Paley criticized educational radio for being based on aristocratic assumptions. Quoting from an article he wrote for the *Annals of the American Academy of Political and Social Sciences,* Paley contended that an aristocratic concept of education emphasized learning for learning's sake. In his words, "Experience has taught us that one of the quickest ways to bore the American audience is to deal with art for art's sake, or to deify culture and education because they are worthy gods."[82] Commercial radio, he claimed, was part of a democratic culture and that scholars who thought the goal of education should be learning for learning's sake would be shocked that "we even went so far as to classify a broadcast of the World's Fair opening as an educational program."[83]

Paley considered direct experience of events a form of democratic learning. Paley claimed that CBS devoted 2,207 hours to educational programming during the first 9 months of 1934. Using the same reasoning, NBC argued that "Amos 'n' Andy" was educational and had the actors perform a comedy routine before the FCC as an example.[84] Paley named CBS's "American School of the Air" and "Church of the Air" as educational radio programs. Paley went on to argue that, for "radio's democratic audience," history should be presented as a living experience and science should not be discussed as abstract theory, but "as an answer to the daily needs of man in his struggle with his environment."[85]

In summary, Paley defended commercial radio by invoking the idea of the marketplace and free choice, and claiming that radio would ensure the worthy use of leisure time. "It is worth repeating here," Paley concluded his presentation to the FCC,

> we conceive of education by radio not in the narrow classical sense, but in the broadest humanitarian meaning. Nor, in our democratic society, is culture merely a matter of learning the difference between Bach and Beethoven . . . but it is equally a knowledge of how to rear a family in health and happiness— or to spend leisure wisely and well.[86]

Paley and educators agreed that radio was an educational force in developing a national culture. Where they differed was over the control and form of this new means of mass education. Both groups wanted control over radio programming. Educators on the National Committee on Education by Radio believed that intellectual leaders should determine what was good or best for the education of the general public. However, leaders in the radio industry justified their control by claiming that, if education over radio were to be effective, it had to be packaged as entertainment that appealed to the masses. One issue not stressed by the radio industry was that programming also had to appeal to the sponsor. Would the advertising sponsors determine the content of radio?

CONSUMERISM, CRIME, AND VIOLENCE ON CHILDREN'S RADIO

Ads on children's radio programs provided fertile ground for training future consumers. Having lost the battle over advertising-driven media, educators and some public members turned their attention to the content of children's radio. Violent radio programming was increasingly being used to capture the listener's interest. Advertising revenues depended on the size of the radio audience. Local radio stations reacted to the complaints of educators and parents. For instance, in December 1934, Thomas Rishworth, director of radio station KSTP in St. Paul, Minnesota, asked the local Parent–Teachers Association (PTA) to stop their glib criticism of children's radio programs and offer constructive advice. He was tired of hearing complaints that radio broadcasts disturbed children with tales of blood and gore, causing them to toss and turn in their sleep, and making them miss meals when their favorite programs were on the air.[87] Within a week, representatives of the PTA, Boy Scouts, and other community organizations met with Rishworth. At the meeting, John Donahue, a probation officer in St. Paul, warned that radio programs like "Jack Armstrong" caused law-breaking tendencies among the communities' children by the portrayal of likeable villains.[88] The meeting ended with a call for boycotts of advertisers and strict censorship of radio listening by parents. *Variety* reporters were surprised by the vehemence of the reaction. *Variety's* original story gave the impression that Rishworth would easily handle the critics of children's radio. After critics announced a boycott of advertisers, a *Variety* article entitled "Air Reformers After Coin" claimed that critics in St. Paul wanted to make money by peddling their own scripts to commercial sponsors.[89]

Rishworth's meeting exemplified the protests against children's radio that began shortly after the NBC broadcast on April 6, 1931, of the first children's radio serial "Little Orphan Annie." Serialized adult mystery drama began in 1929 with "True Detective Mysteries." The most popular of the mysteries, "The Shadow," appeared in the same year as "Little Orphan Annie." Children could listen to both the evening mystery programs and late afternoon children's programming: CBS broadcast "Buck Rogers in the Twenty-fifth Century" in 1932; in 1933, the "Lone Ranger" and "Jack Armstrong, the All-American Boy" made their debuts. By 1938, the most popular children's serials included the previously mentioned programs plus "Dick Tracy," "Don Winslow of the Navy," "Terry and the Pirates," and "Tom Mix."[90]

Historian Raymond Stedman argued, "The agitated fantasy of 'Buck Rogers' must have been at the heart of many of those articles expressing worry about radio's effect on young minds."[91] In the daily fantasy series, Buck Rogers battled fleets of spaceships, missiles, death rays, and other futuristic weapons to save the universe from destruction. In contrast, "Tom Mix" provoked little apprehension in parents. "Tom Mix" was a classic cowboy drama of the 1930s with the good cowboy Tom Mix always defeating the evil cowboy. The epigram of "Tom Mix" was, "Lawbreakers always lose. Straight shooters always win. It pays to shoot straight!" The sponsor, Ralston Cereals, tried to win parental support by placing promotional advertising in *Parents Magazine*.[92] Even programs emphasizing the conquest of evil were considered disturbing to children. In the first episode of the "Lone Ranger," the hero was restored to health by his faithful Indian companion after being shot in an ambush that left his five companions dead. "The Shadow" opened with the chilling question: "Who knows what evil lurks in the hearts of men? The Shadow knows."[93]

Parents Magazine led public complaints about radio violence. A 1933 editorial was accompanied by a cartoon of a frightened young girl listening to a radio broadcasting, "Scram! Don't Shoot! Kidnapped! They're Going To Kill Me! Help! Murder! Bang! Bang! Kill Him! Police!" The editorial urged parents to write sponsors protesting the quality of the children's program.[94]

Parental complaints about children's radio were voiced at meetings of PTAs and women's clubs. In February 1933, the Central Council of the PTA of Rochester, New York, issued a public warning that radio broadcast "crime ideas harmful to the moral fibre of children and the bloodcurdling situations tend to excite youngsters in a manner to interfere with their sleep."[95] The PTA sent protests to local stations with hints of a boycott of advertisers. A few months later, the California State PTA issued a list of *bad* radio programs and called for unofficial censorship of programs broadcast between 5 p.m. and 8 p.m—the prime hours for children to listen to radio. The California PTA expressed concern about "all programs emphasizing killing, robbing, impossible or dangerous situations."[96]

The National Council of Women, representing 28 national women's organizations, joined the public outcry against radio by organizing the Women's National Radio Committee headed by Mrs. Harold V. Milligan. The organization's concern was sparked by a study conducted by the Woman's Club in the wealthy Westchester County, New York, community of Scarsdale.[97] In 1933, protests erupted in Scarsdale against children's radio after a committee of Scarsdale women met at Teachers College, Columbia University and rated 40 children's programs. They found only five programs that were suitable. The rest were condemned for keeping "children in emotional suspense and [for] excit[ing] them so they can't sleep." The committee publicly objected to mystery thrillers because "children don't just hear it and forget it, but they carry the story in their mind from day to day, or week to week."[98] To provide an alternative to existing children's programs, the Scarsdale Woman's Club wrote an unsuccessful radio serial entitled "Westchester Cowboys."[99]

Mrs. Harold Milligan laced her attack against children's radio with strong feminist language. In a 1935 letter to *Variety*, she described the Committee as a coordinated effort by women to register their complaints against radio, which in her words was "man-made" and "man-regulated."[100] The following year at a national radio conference she declared, "Women vote, and they have influence on public opinion, yet big business does very little to indicate its willingness to earn the respect of millions of women who are serious about the one problem—children's programs on the radio."[101] Also at issue was advertising. Milligan charged advertisers with exploiting children as consumers. Urging parents to counter the work of advertisers, she reported, "Some parents have met the 'box-top' problem by suggesting that if the child wants the prize offered for sending in a certain number of box tops, he pay for the package out of his own allowance."[102]

The Women's National Radio Committee gave awards for good children's radio. Some went to programs that could not find commercial sponsorship, such as CBS's historical program "Wilderness Road." Some member organizations of the National Council of Women sponsored radio programs. The American Legion Auxiliary sponsored a radio dramatization of James Truslow Adams' *The Epic of America* and offered prizes for the best children's essay on "What the 'Epic of America' Has Taught Me About the Future of America."[103]

NBC responded to criticism by announcing in February 1933 that it would "blue pencil" radio scripts with criminal themes to keep children from mimicking unlawful actions.[104] *Variety* announced that August, "Commercials are yielding to the agitation of PTA associations."[105] The Jello's advertising agency shifted sponsorship from horror programs to a radio version of *The Wizard of Oz*. Members of other advertising agencies expressed surprise that protests had not started sooner because horror was overdone on radio. Radio networks mounted a public relations campaign as noted in this *Variety* headline: "Radio Wants Clubwoman Good Will: Offer Transmitters to Gals with Messages." The CBS Chicago affiliate, WBBM, offered free air time to local women's clubs, the DAR, and PTAs.[106]

In 1935, the FCC responded to complaints from PTAs and women's clubs. *Variety* described, "Deluged with bleats from educators and parents, Commish [FCC Chairman] is agreed that if broadcasters do not move on their own to cook up more satisfactory entertainment for children, the government must apply the whip." Pressure came from the White House and Congress to do something about "Goose-Pimple Kid Shows." *Variety* claimed, "Kids' programs of blood-and-thunder type appear doomed under new drive."[107]

By May 1935, the FCC radio cleanup was in full swing. Its efforts extended beyond children's radio. Admitting that it could not directly censor radio, the FCC let radio stations know that it was concerned about the following types of programming and advertising:

1. lotteries
2. fortune tellers
3. racing tips
4. blood and thunder kids' programs
5. birth control compounds
6. fat-removing compounds

MAKING COMMODIFIED LEISURE SAFE
FOR AMERICANS

In 1935, CBS announced a self-censorship code.[108] NBC reacted to CBS's announcement by claiming it had adopted a similar code in 1934.[109] However, NBC did not pull together its broadcasting standards into a single booklet for public distribution until 1939. Prior to 1939, NBC distributed broadcast standards in personal letters to advertisers.[110]

President Paley broadcast the CBS codes over the Columbia network on May 14, 1935. Paley reminded listeners that radio permeated the lives of most Americans. "You hear the voices of Columbia," Paley said, "for many hours each day. These voices are familiar in your home, perhaps in your workshop, and even in your automobile and the restaurants and theaters you visit." Paley described the close relationship between listeners and radio: "These voices are frequently more familiar comrades than some of your closest personal friends." After painting a picture of the intimate and personal relationship between the listener and the broadcaster, Paley went on to describe the general outlines of the new broadcasting code.[111]

CBS Reference Library files indicate that the self-censorship code was part of a well-orchestrated public relations campaign. The code was immediately distributed to important public leaders, and their responses were carefully collected and used in public relations announcements. The code was distributed with an announcement that CBS was employing Professor Arthur Jersild of Columbia University Teachers College as a consulting psychologist for children's programming.

Appropriately, Professor Jersild's major area of research was children's fears. In a book coauthored with another child psychologist, Frances Holmes, Jersild wrote, "The use of fear-inspiring materials in books, radio programs, and moving pictures designed for children might, no doubt, be controlled to some degree by rigid censorship." He continued, this type of censorship might protect some individuals at the expense of others. Therefore, he felt parents of susceptible children should exercise control over their movie going and radio listening.[112]

Of central importance for the future of children's radio programs was the code's emphasis on providing children with moral and social heroes. The code recognized the importance of hero worship in a child's life. "Superman," "The Lone Ranger," and "Tom Mix" exemplified the heroic model recommended in the CBS code. Like the movie code, the CBS code also emphasized the importance of not teaching children antisocial behavior by presenting crime and criminals in a positive light. In addition, the code tried to answer complaints from women's clubs about the quality of advertising on children's programs.

The code recognized that CBS "does have an editorial responsibility to the community, in the interpretation of public wish and sentiment, which cannot be waived."[113] Using this justification, the code identified themes and dramatic treatments that would be excluded from children's programs:

1. The exalting, as modern heroes, of gangsters, criminals, and racketeers will not be allowed.
2. Disrespect for either parental or other proper authority must not be glorified or encouraged.
3. Cruelty, greed, and selfishness must not be presented as worthy motivations.
4. Programs that arouse harmful nervous reactions in the child must not be presented.
5. Conceit, smugness, or an unwarranted sense of superiority over others less fortunate may not be presented.
6. Recklessness and abandon must not be falsely identified with a healthy spirit of adventure.
7. Unfair exploitation of others for personal gain must not be made praiseworthy.

8. Dishonesty and deceit are not to be made appealing or attractive to the child.[114]

Indicating the future of children's radio, the code made hero worship a central theme. For children of elementary school age, programs were to provide entertainment of a moral nature. The code noted that children's literature provided "heroes worthy of the child's ready impulse to hero worship, and of his imitative urge to pattern himself after the hero model." Literature of this sort, the code claimed, "succeeds in inspiring the child to socially useful and laudable ideals such as generosity, industry, kindness and respect for authority. . . . It serves, in effect, as a useful adjunct to that education which the growing and impressionable child is absorbing during every moment of its waking day."[115]

Released in 1939, the NBC code banned advertisements dealing with speculative finances, personal hygiene, weight-reducing agents, fortune tellers, professions, cemeteries, alcoholic beverages, and firearms.[116] Children's programs were to stress law and order, adult authority, good morals, and clean living. Like the CBS code, heroes were to play a role in shaping children's morality. The NBC code stated, "The hero or heroine and other sympathetic characters must be portrayed as intelligent and morally courageous . . . and disrespect for law must be avoided as traits in any character that may be presented in the light of a hero to the child listener."[117] In addition, programs were to emphasize mutual respect, fair play, and honorable behavior. Adventure programs were prohibited from using themes of kidnapping, torture, extreme violence, horror, superstition, and "morbid suspense."[118]

By the end of the 1930s, those attending movies and listening to the radio received the same message about the triumph of good over evil. In the case of radio, moral messages were being conveyed through the adventures of superheroes. The moral and political message of radio in the second half of the 1930s was the ultimate triumph of good, the importance of obedience to the law, and patriotism.

CONCLUSION: CONTROLLING COMMODIFIED LEISURE

In the first half of the 20th century, movies and radio, using self-censorship codes, achieved Simon Patten's objective of creating forms of commodified leisure that would spur consumption while maintaining traditional Protestant morality. It was commercial radio, and later TV, that played the major role in driving a consumer economy by tying entertainment directly to ads. Through radio and TV, Americans learned to accept a commercialized fantasy world where products were inseparable from entertainment.

Of course media would later change, and the self-censorship codes would be modified as the Protestant hegemony was challenged. More sex, violence, and social criticism would appear on movie screens and radio and TV programs. However, these changes did not stop the spread of advertising and consumer values into almost all aspects of American life. Certainly, the most important aspect of commercial media was its training of the public to accept advertising and consumer values as part of the American way of life.

Chapter 5

The American Way and the Manufacturing of Consent

Schools, advertising, commercial media, and public relations campaigns created a spontaneous association between consumption and the American way of life. By the 1950s, the fantasy world of most Americans was filled with consumer objects. A 1959 *Saturday Evening Post* magazine cover showed a young couple sitting under a tree gazing into a night sky illuminated by a full moon. Floating among a host of stars was their dream world consisting of a house, swimming pool, two cars, pets, two children, power drill, refrigerator, washer and dryer, stove, toaster, electric coffee pot, waffle maker, iron, TV, sound system, and vacuum cleaner. The cover's artist, Constantin Alajalov, had originally planned to have the couple staring at castles floating in the air. Yet, capturing the spirit of America, he replaced castles with consumer items.[1]

Beginning in the 1930s, the newly founded public relations profession was enlisted in a campaign to create an automatic association in people's minds among Americanism, free enterprise, and consumption. In the 1920s, the famous political theorist Walter Lippmann characterized this process as an attempt to "manufacture consent."[2] In the 1980s, this phrase was again made popular by Noam Chomsky's critical study of the control of public opinion, *Manufacturing Consent: The Political Economy of the Mass Media.*[3] Whereas Chomsky was critical of attempts to manufacture consent, Lippmann and public relations experts considered it essential for a democratic society.

The term *public opinion* had a specific meaning for public relations professionals. The term was popularized by Walter Lippmann's (1922) book

Public Opinion.[4] In this context, opinion referred to attitudes about the world that were *not* products of rational deliberation. Public opinion was considered an irrational force. In the writings of Lippmann and public relations experts of the 1920s and 1930s, public opinion was created by pictures, words, and symbols. Public opinions set the stage for experiencing and interpreting the world. Experience was filtered through preexisting opinion. In Lippmann's words, "For the most part we do not first see, and then define. We define first and then see. . . . We imagine things before we experience them. And these preconceptions . . . govern deeply the whole process of perception."[5] Therefore, the control of public opinion referred to the preparation of the public mind to interpret events in a distinct manner.

American business, working with public relations experts, tried to infuse into public opinion the "American way of life" and the "American dream" as preconceptions about the good life and the United States. To help mold public opinion, public relations experts used advertising, schools, and media. This chapter traces efforts to create a spontaneous association in the public mind among Americanism, free enterprise, and consumerism. I begin by discussing the rise of the public relations industry and its efforts to create a positive image of American business in the public mind and to link consumption to personal fulfillment and the good life.

SELLING THE "AMERICAN WAY" IN SCHOOLS AND ON BILLBOARDS

Launched in 1936, the American Way public relations campaign was designed to counter the growth of radical and antibusiness attitudes during the 1930s' depression years. Business' efforts to introject particular economic ideas into the school curricula paralleled the Americanism campaign of the American Legion. The National Association of Manufacturers (NAM) spearheaded business' public relations efforts. A 1936 internal NAM memo contended that public opinion was not based on rational discourse. The memo stated, "Public sentiment is everything—with it nothing can fail; without it nothing can succeed. . . . Right now Joe Doakes—the average man—is a highly confused individual."[6] The memo went on to argue that Joe Doakes should be resold the advantages of a competitive economy. The next year, the NAM began a national campaign placing billboards in every U.S. community over 2,500 declaring either "World's Highest Standard of Living—There's no way like the American Way" or "World's Highest Wages—There's no way like the American Way."[7]

An early American Way advertisement captured the meaning of the campaign:

WHAT IS YOUR AMERICA ALL ABOUT?
Our American plan of living is simple.
Its ideal—that works—is the greatest good for the greatest number.
You . . . are part owner of the United States, Inc. . . .
Our American plan of living is pleasant.
Our American plan of living is the world's envy.
No nation, or group lives as well as we do.[8]

Also in 1937, the National Industrial Council, the newly formed public relations arm of the NAM, issued a diagram for a "Suggested Community Program to Create Better Understanding of Local Industry." The diagram depicted a local public relations committee composed of manufacturers, merchants, civic clubs, churches, bar associations, and educators. Conspicuously absent from this committee were labor union representatives. According to the diagram, the local committee was to hire a publicity director to spread the probusiness message.

The diagram clearly connected the segments of the community to be used for controlling public opinion. This schema corresponded to what founder of the public relations profession Edward Bernays called "the wires which control the public mind"[9] The diagram showed wires leading from the publicity director to schools, newspapers, radio, civic speakers, clubs, open house meetings for workers in factories, and theaters. These wires to the public mind, Bernays suggested, resulted in "regimenting the public mind."[10]

Already feeling the influence of local American Legion officials, the NAM suggested that publicity directors introduce probusiness ideas into schools through the medium of printed materials for school libraries and classrooms by sparking an interest in studying local industries and using movies and slides. In 1937, Lewis H. Brown, president of the Johns–Manville Corporation, declared, "We must with moving pictures and other educational material carry into the schools of the generation of tomorrow an interesting story of the part that science and industry have played in creating a more abundant life for those who are fortunate to live in this great country of ours."[11] He warned that teachers knew more about Karl Marx than the inner workings of local factories.

By the time the NAM focused on schools, the public relations profession had adopted a number of techniques for controlling public opinion. Visualizations and symbols were considered a method for galvanizing public opinion without generating debate. The use of trusted leaders was a means of building public confidence for an idea or product. For example, Bernays' recommended that bacon be sold by having a physician testify as to its health benefits. Also Bernays argued that a public relations campaign should be directed toward a person's desires and emotions rather than reason. The symbol could be used to evoke positive emotions.

To avoid public debate, public relations relied on emotional rather that rational persuasion. For instance, the NAM placed ads in practically every community in the United States. The billboards offered only slogans. True to the principles of visualization and appealing to emotions, the billboards proclaimed "World's Highest Standard of Living" and showed a happy White family of four riding in a car. Through the car's front windshield was a smiling clean-shaven father wearing a suit and tie next to his grinning wife. In the rear seat were equally happy children. Hanging out the window was a white dog. Next to the car was the slogan, "There's no way like the American Way." Billboards proclaiming "World's Highest Wages" showed an aproned White mother standing in a doorway looking out at her clean-shaven husband dressed in a suit, tie, and hat tossing their blond-haired daughter into the sky.[12] There were no suggestions as to why the "American Way" provided the "World's Highest Standard of Living" and the "World's Highest Wages."

In the schools, the NAM conducted a public relations campaign to create in the public mind an interrelation and inseparability between free enterprise and democracy. On the surface, these two ideas were distinct. Free enterprise, of course, was an economic doctrine, whereas democracy was a political principle. Many European countries practiced varying forms of democratic socialism. In other words, a democratic government might have a socialized economy. A totalitarian government might allow for free enterprise. Believing that emotions rather than reason controlled public opinion, the 1939 NAM public relations committee declared as its task to "link free enterprise in the public consciousness with free speech, free press and free religion as integral parts of democracy."[13]

With the goals of creating positive reactions to American business and an involuntary connection in the public mind between free enterprise and democracy, corporations and the NAM flooded classrooms with printed material and movies. The NAM distributed to schools a series of booklets entitled *You and Industry*, which were designed to connect readers' positive emotions to the American industrial system. In 1937, the NAM began distributing to 70,000 schools a newsweekly, *Young America*, which contained articles such as "The Business of America's People Is Selling," "Building Better Americans," and a "Your Local Bank."[14] A 10-minute film, *America Marching On*, was distributed to schools with the message, "America marching upward and onward to higher standards of living, greater income for her people, and more leisure to enjoy the good things of life as the greatest industrial system the world has ever seen began to develop."[15]

PROPAGANDA AND FREE SPEECH IN SCHOOLS

As the NAM was targeting its public relations at schools, some educators were telling students that propaganda was not a problem in a democratic society because of the freedom to debate different subjects. Contrary to the public relations view of an irrational crowd, these educators were operating on the assumption that the U.S. public was capable and willing to engage in rational political discourse. In the early 1930s, educators showed interest in protecting free speech as they worried about the increased role of propaganda in forming public opinion. "The present age might well be called the age of propaganda," wrote the Commission on Character Education for the 1932 yearbook, *Character Education*, of the Department of Superintendence of the NEA. "With the development of the press, the cinema, and the radio, instruments have been forged through which ideas, attitudes, and philosophies may be quickly impressed upon vast populations," continued the Commission. "And in every society there are powerful minority groups struggling for the control of these instruments and bent on conserving or grasping special privileges of all kinds."[16]

Concerned about citizen education, the Educational Policies Commission conducted a survey of school instruction September 1939 and January 1940. The Educational Policies Commission was a joint venture started in 1935 by the NEA and the American Association of School Administrators to improve education for democratic citizenship. The survey, *Learning the Ways of Democracy: A Case Book in Civic Education*, provided snapshots of the actual ideas and values that a large sample of American high schools were trying to disseminate to their students at the outbreak of World War II. The survey found that high schools emphasized the study of public opinion as protection against the propaganda of totalitarian governments.

The survey found that many social studies classes were investigating issues related to public relations methods and government propaganda. For instance, a ninth-grade unit on public opinion in the Cleveland public schools focused on free speech and the censorship of newspapers, radio, and movies. Students studied "The Struggle for Personal and Political Liberty."[17] Twelfth-grade classes in Rochester, New York, discussed, "What serious questions exist in American democracy today concerning public opinion?" In reference to the repressive measures used during the Red Scare of the 1920s, students were asked, "What is a 'red scare'? Look up the Lusk Laws 1921 in New York State."[18] A study guide for the eighth grade in Schenectady, New York, stressed the importance of using actual concrete information in forming opinions. According to the guide, "in a democracy where free speech and free press are so highly prized, this is very important." The guide called for a study of newspapers, magazines, books, radio, and motion pictures as agencies "which aid in opinion expression and formation."[19]

Study guides included sections dealing with threats to freedom of speech. The high school study guide for Rochester, New York, contained a unit that opened with the question, "What serious problems exist in American democracy today concerning public opinion?" The guide listed the following topics:

current threats to civil and political liberty;
academic freedom and discussion of public problems in the classroom;
extension of procedures of scientific thought to public and personal problems.[20]

Commission members were pleased by the discussion of controversial issues
and wrote, "Freedom of discussion of controversial subjects is more than a
right. . . . If citizens do not have this right, they are unable to make intelligent decisions, and control passes into the hands of those individuals who
are adroit enough to attain positions of power and influence."[21]

While the free speech issues were debated in classrooms, the American
Legion continued to work with the NEA to weed out so-called *subversives*
from schools. At their 1935 annual convention, the American Legion
passed a resolution against "the advocacy in America of Nazism, Fascism,
Communism, or any other isms that are contrary to the fundamental principles of democracy, as established under the Constitution of the United
States." Local branches of the Legion's Americanism Commission were ordered to give close attention to possible subversive activities in their communities.[22]

The Legion continued advocating the firing of disloyal teachers and demanded that teachers take loyalty oaths. The Legion considered any opposition to loyalty oaths as the work of subversive elements in American society. In 1935, the Americanism Commission reported that eight states
passed legislation requiring loyalty oaths of teachers. Other reports indicated that by 1935, 20 states required teachers' loyalty oaths. In the same
year, Congress passed an appropriation bill containing a rider forbidding
the payment of salary to any teacher spreading communism doctrines. The
rider kicked off a storm of protest lasting until 1937, when President Roosevelt got the act repealed.[23]

PROTECTING ADVERTISING AND LINKING FREE
ENTERPRISE TO DEMOCRACY

Criticism of textbooks and educators by the American Legion, and business
and advertising organizations typified efforts to ensure that the schools
taught the American way of life. These groups were particularly concerned
with educators who were identified with the doctrines of social reconstructionism. Social reconstructionism originated with a speech given by
George Counts, a professor at Columbia University Teachers College, at the
1932 annual meeting of the Progressive Education Society. Originally
called "Dare Progressive Education Be Progressive?", the speech was distributed in pamphlet form with the controversial title of "Dare the Schools

Build a New Social Order?" Counts criticized capitalism for being "cruel and inhuman" and "wasteful and inefficient." He argued that the development of modern urban-industrial society made obsolete concepts of competition and rugged individualism. A new economic system, he argued, would free people from poverty. Counts urged teachers to assume leadership in the reconstruction of society. Counts stated, "If democracy is to survive, it must seek a new economic foundation. . . . Natural resources and all important forms of capital will have to be collectively owned."[24]

Counts supported democracy and rejected communism and totalitarianism. The problem was that he attacked free enterprise when business was implanting the seed that democracy could only survive with free enterprise. In 1934, Russell Cook, Director of the National Americanism Commission, warned delegates to the 1934 NEA convention, "In the last few years there has grown up a movement in which too many of our teachers are creating ideas in the schoolroom for what is called a new social order." Referring to social reconstructionists, Cook told the convention, "The American Legion is opposed to that movement. We say that it is not the mission of the teacher to lead the child into believing we should have a new social order. . . ."[25]

Some textbooks were criticized for containing social reconstructionist ideas such as Harold Rugg's textbook series. Augustin Rudd, who campaigned to get Harold Rugg's textbooks off the market, blamed the supposed deterioration of public schools and their infiltration by subversives on progressive education. In 1940, Rudd was made chairperson of the newly organized Guardians of American Education. The organization's goal was to defeat "left-wing . . . educational leadership . . . [which is trying to replace] our American way of life . . . [with] a 'new social order' based on the principles of collectivism and socialism."[26] Particularly distressing to Rudd were statements in the social reconstructionist journal, *The Social Frontier,* calling for economic planning and presenting society as a collective organization. Rudd objected to a lead editorial that argued, "For the American people the age of individualism in economy is closing and the age of collectivism is opening. Here is the central and dominating reality in the present epoch. . . ." To Rudd and other members of patriotic organizations, social reconstructionism was a subversive plot to undermine American capitalism. Rudd was particularly upset by an April 1935 issue of the *Social Frontier,* which proclaimed: "The end of free enterprise as a principle of economic and social organization adequate to this country is at hand."[27]

In sharp contrast to NAM's public relations efforts, Harold Rugg's social studies series emphasized collective action and planning. In the 1920s, the series began as pamphlets integrating the teaching of history, economics, and sociology to junior high school students. Between 1927 and 1931, Rugg pulled together the pamphlets into six 600-page books for senior and junior high school students. Published by Ginn and Company from 1933 to

1936, the series was expanded to include Grades 3 through 6. At the peak of their popularity in 1938, the series sold 289,000 copies. Rugg estimated that, during the 1930s, the books were used in over 5,000 schools by several million school children. After public attacks on the books, annual sales plummeted to 21,000 copies.[28]

A series' goal was educating children to assume intelligent control of their institutions and environment. The books did not advocate communism or socialism, but they did argue that intelligence should be applied to planning the economy and operating public institutions. U.S. history was presented as the transformation of an individualistic agrarian society to a collective industrial society. Rugg's message was that modern urban and industrial society required cooperative planning. In the modern world, corporations, factories, public institutions, and urban living all depended on cooperative behavior. In addition, the complexity of modern life required cooperative planning to achieve economic and social goals.

Rugg's ninth-grade textbook, *Citizenship and Civic Affairs*, claimed the "American Spirit" evolved from individualism to cooperation.[29] Rejecting the premise that free enterprise and Americanism were synonymous, Rugg's series brought on the wrath of patriotic organizations and individuals. A typical reaction were the words of a large middle-aged woman at a 1940s' public hearing on the textbook series: "I am here, not thinking that I was going to be at all, but I am and I want to say just a few words. Righteousness, good government, good homes and God—most of all, Christ—is on trial today." Although she admitted not reading any of the Rugg books, she proclaimed, "You can't take the youth of our land and give them this awful stuff and have them come out safe and sound for God and Righteousness." At another meeting, according to Rugg, a twenty-year-old youth leapt into the air waving his arms and shouting, "If you let these books go in and if what I've heard is true, it'll damn the souls of the men, women and children of our state."[30]

The business community's reaction to Rugg's books was orchestrated by B.C. Forbes, financial writer and founder of *Forbes Magazine*, through editorials distributed nationally in Hearst-owned newspapers. In a 1939 articles, Forbes called Rugg's books, "viciously un-American. . . . [Rugg] distorts facts to convince the oncoming generation that America's private-enterprise system is wholly inferior and nefarious." In words that must have made the textbook industry shudder, Forbes wrote, "I plan to insist that this anti-American educator's textbooks be cast out. . . . I would not want my own children contaminated by conversion to Communism."[31] In his syndicated Hearst newspaper column, Forbes asked the question every week during the war years: "Are too many educators poisoning the minds of the younger generation with prejudiced, distorted, unfair teachings regarding the American system of economy and dazzling them with overly-rosy pictures of conditions in totalitarian countries?"[32]

RUGG AND CONSUMERISM

Lessons on evaluating advertising were a unique feature of Rugg's books. The advertising industry was concerned because the lessons prepared public opinion to be skeptical of advertising claims. The Advertising Federation of America, the public relations arm of the industry, distributed pamphlets entitled, "Facts You Should Know About Anti-Advertising Propaganda in School Textbooks." The pamphlets criticized the Rugg books for turning students against advertising.

Both the Rugg books and the reaction of the Advertising Federation of America typified the consumerist concerns of the 1930s. During the depression years, consumer organizations tried to educate the public about false advertising claims and shoddy consumer products. Highlighting the anti-advertising crusade was the 1931 publication of *Ballyhoo* magazine featuring satirical comments on ads and advertising, including the Ten Commandments of Advertising: "10. Thou shalt covet thy neighbor's car and his radio and his silverware and his refrigerator."[33] This surprisingly successful magazine was followed by books criticizing the wastefulness of American consumerism, including F. J. Schlink's *100,000,000 Guinea Pigs* (1933) and James Rorty's *Our Master's Voice* (1934).[34] In 1929, the Consumer Research organization was founded, which in the early 1930s spawned the establishment of the Consumers Union.

It was in this anti-advertising climate that the Advertising Federation of America worried about the Rugg books. In 1939, the Federation declared that critics of advertising were "those who prefer collectivism and regimentation by political force."[35] The Advertising Federation claimed that communism was the basis for anti-advertising attitudes and the development of the Consumer Union. During this period, the House Committee on Un-American Activities held hearings that linked consumer rights efforts to communism. The Consumer Union survived by focusing on product testing and publishing the *Consumer Report.*[36]

The Advertising Federation's anti-Rugg pamphlet objected to an opening section in Rugg's series on advertising because it bred distrust of widely advertised products. The section opened:

Two men were discussing the merits of a nationally advertised brand of oil.

"I know it must be good," said one. "A million dollars' worth of it is sold each year. You see advertisements of that oil everywhere."

The other shook his head. "I don't care how much of it is sold," he said. "I left a drop of it on a copper plate overnight and the drop turned green. It is corrosive and I don't dare to use it on my machine."[37]

In April 1940, the president of the Advertising Federation sent a letter to major advertisers that opened: "Advertised products are untrustworthy!

That is the lesson taught to the children in 4,200 school systems by a social science textbook of Professor Harold Rugg of Teachers College, Columbia University."[38]

The American Legion joined ranks with the Advertising Federation with a 1940 pamphlet, originally published in the *American Legion Magazine*, by O.K. Armstrong entitled, "Treason in the Textbooks." In the pamphlet, a cartoon depicts Rugg as a devil putting colored glasses over children's eyes. The caption on the picture stated, "The 'Frontier Thinkers' are trying to sell our youth the idea that the American way of life has failed." The Legion article and pamphlet also listed several other books and *Scholastic Magazine* as being subversive.[39]

As head of the Guardians of American Education, Augustin Rudd believed Rugg's textbooks would undermine American institutions. Formed in 1940, the Guardians of American Education wanted to preserve American traditions. The association urged parents to: "Examine your child's textbooks, Demand to see the teacher's guides. . . . Look for subversive material in . . . books or courses." Regarding Rugg's series, Rudd wrote, "He [Rugg] was one of the principal architects of the ideological structure known as the 'new social order'." From his faculty position at Columbia University Teachers College, Rudd stated, "His propaganda and doctrines were spread throughout the United States. He also exercised a strong influence . . . through his Teachers' Guides, which interpreted his economic, political and social philosophies to thousands of classroom teachers using his social science courses."[40]

There was a dramatic reaction to these public criticisms. In September 1940, *Time Magazine* reported that members of the Binghamton, New York school board called for public burning of Rugg's textbooks. The article reported, "But last fortnight Rugg book burnings began to blaze afresh in the small-town, American Legion belt. In rapid succession, the school boards of Mountain Lakes and Wayne Township, New Jersey, banished Rugg texts that had been used by their pupils for nearly 10 years. Explained Wayne Township's Board Member Ronald Gall: "In my opinion, the books are un-American but not anti-American. . . ."[41]

Particularly dramatic were events in Bradner, Ohio, where the community divided over the issue of teaching communism in the schools. According to a Cleveland newspaper account of the events, "The rural Red hunt . . . has resulted in: explosion of a dynamite charge and the burning of a fiery cross in front of the home of . . . [the] school board president. The explosions and cross burning were accompanied by the spectacle of school board members shoving books into the school furnace."[42]

Rugg's publishers, Ginn and Company, sent him on a national tour to defend the series. At public hearing in Philadelphia, a participant pointed his finger at Rugg and shouted, "There sits the ringmaster of the fifth col-

umnists in America financed by the Russian government. I want you people
to look at him."[43] Rugg felt frustrated at public meetings by the open admission by critics that they had never read any of his books. Person after person
at these hearings, Rugg wrote, would begin their statements with the
phrase: "1 haven't read the books, but. . . ." The phrase would be followed
with comments such as, "He's from Columbia, and that's enough"; "I have
heard of the author, and no good about him"; and "my brother says the
schools and colleges are filled with Communists."[44]

The demise of the Rugg books demonstrated the power of public relations campaigns to associate in the public mind anything critical of the
United States' economic and political system with un-Americanism and
communism. Similar to the automatic association between democracy and
free enterprise achieved by the NAM's public relations efforts, part of the
public now instinctively associated progressive education with un-Americanism, communism, and socialism. This pattern of public opinion continued after World War II as anticommunism became a standard for evaluating school textbooks and curricula.

EDUCATING THE CONSUMER-CITIZEN

War time dampens dissent and criticism. World War II provided an opportunity for public relations efforts in schools to sell business' message under
the flag of patriotism. The key element of this message, similar to the billboards planted around the country by NAM, was that the American economic system provided the highest *economic* standard of living. This standard of living was measured by the ability to consume. The Secretary of
NEA's Educational Policies Commission, William Carr, declared in a March
1941 article in the *Nation's Business* that public schools would cooperate
with business in teaching "Americanism," "economic literacy," and "personal economics" while preparing "youth for personal work." Economic literacy meant teaching about the economic system of the United States,
whereas personal economics meant the education of the consumer.
Linking consumption, Americanism, and business, Carr wrote, schools
have "provided a highly literate and educated population . . . constituting
the world's greatest consuming markets."[45]

Consumer education was promoted in schools by local Chambers of
Commerce. Their efforts matched the NAM's plan for using schools to foster positive public opinion about American business. According to Carr,
360 local Chambers of Commerce were helping local schools promote an
understanding of the American economic system. Combined with citizenship education, these programs were intended to create an instinctive association of business with patriotic Americanism. Also Chambers of Com-

merce helped local schools mount consumer education programs or, as it was called, *efficiency in personal economics.* These consumer courses emphasized the management of personal buying power. Schools were training people to be good buyers.

In 1942, the NAM took its public relations campaign directly to the National Education Association. Declaring a "new era of understanding" between business and the schools, Walter Fuller, Chairman of the NAM's Board of Directors and President of Curtis Publishing, proclaimed at the 1942 NEA meeting, "Just as the first responsibility of industry today is to produce the weapons of war . . . so the responsibility of education is to make available an increasing manpower, especially to meet the needs for skilled men and women."[46] This new understanding resulted from a series of joint conferences between the NAM and the NEA.

Also the federal government launched a massive program to push the public schools in the direction of serving industry. In 1941, the Office of Education organized a defense vocational training program enrolling 1 million women and men. By 1942, the numbers had increased to 3 million. The U.S. Commissioner of Education hoped the close relationship established between education and employment would be carried over into peacetime. In a speech to the 1943 NEA convention, he told delegates, "Probably the most basic lesson we are learning in the schools in wartime is that boys and girls gain educationally from contact with the real world of work."[47] The four major contributions of the schools, according to Commissioner Studebaker, were citizenship training, vocational education, training for community service, and building national unity.

THE WAR OF ECONOMIC SYSTEMS

After World War II, the American Way became a major theme in the cold war between the United States and the Soviet Union. The cold war was portrayed as a clash between free enterprise and communist economic systems under the banner of American and Soviet nationalism. The winner in this battle would be the system that produced the most consumer goods. In schools, censorship of textbooks and the weeding out of so-called *subversive* teachers centered on economic issues. For those on the political right, subversives were supporters of government intervention in the economy, whereas true Americans supported free enterprise. Also the teenage consumer market rapidly expanded after World War II. Teens were learning at an early age how to be good consumers. Many affluent teens were growing up in new suburban developments where the shopping mall was becoming the center of consumer desires.

The famous 1959 "kitchen debate" between Vice President Richard Nixon and Soviet Premier Nikita Khrushchev at the American Exhibition in

Moscow provided a public lesson in economic differences. Looking at an American kitchen in a model of a six-bedroom ranch house, Nixon explained to Khrushchev the advantages of the U.S. economic system and the meaning of American freedom: "To us, diversity, the right to choose . . . is the most important thing. We don't have one decision made at the top by one government official. . . . We have many different manufacturers and many different kinds of washing machines so that the housewives have a choice. . . ."[48] As Historian Elaine Tyler May argued, both leaders lumped the consumer race with the arms race and space race. It was a test of the superiority of their economies. Khrushchev claimed that his nation would reach the American standard of living in 6 years.[49]

Imbued with the idea that the American Way meant increased consumption through free enterprise, the cold war was to be won through the purchasing of goods for the home. The early 20th-century image of the consumer wife and earner husband now played itself out in the tensions of the cold war. As May wrote, "Although they may have been unwitting soldiers, women who marched off to the nation's shopping centers to equip their new homes joined the ranks of American cold warriors."[50]

In schools, censorship efforts reinforced the equation of Americanism with free enterprise economics. After helping to drive the Rugg books off the market, the Guardians of American Education distributed American Legion articles on communist subversion directly to public schools. They also continued their campaign to associate progressive education with communism and un-Americanism by distributing an article by Kitty Jones entitled, "How 'Progressive' Is Your School?" The article restated claims that progressive and critical education undermined Americanism and free enterprise.[51]

Ironically, it was a 1952 workshop at Columbia's Teachers College that convinced Kitty Jones that progressive education and the professors at Teachers College were destroying the American way of life. After examining her local school district in Tenafly, New Jersey, she charged that progressive education caused illiteracy and juvenile delinquency. She claimed that nine textbooks used by the Tenably system "favor[ed] the Welfare State and Socialism . . . follow [ed] the Communist line, and . . . [were] written by Communist sympathizers and . . . members." Although the school system eventually rejected her charges, the episode propelled Jones into the national spotlight and created an audience for her 1956 book, *Progressive Education Is REDucation*, coauthored with Robert Olivier. The book contained descriptive chapter titles such as "Making Little Socialists."[52]

America's Future, Inc., located in New Rochelle, New York, was a distributor of Jones' book and articles. During the 1950s, America's Future combed textbooks for evidence of subversion. According to historian Mary Anne Raywid, America's Future was one of four organizations created to maintain the tax-exempt status of the Committee for Constitutional Government. The others were America's Future, the Free Enterprise Foundation, Fighters for Freedom, and the original Committee for Constitutional Government. According to Raywid, the goals of all four organizations were characterized in the following platform of Fighters for Freedom:

> Pitilessly expose Communism . . . and stop the march to fascism or socialism.
> Restore the American incentives to work, own, and save.
> Protect every individual's right to work where he will. . . .
> Safeguard our system of free, untrammeled, competitive markets.
> Stop using taxpayers' money to compete against private enterprise.[53]

Visiting America's Future's offices in 1961 and 1962, two newspaper reporters, Jack Nelson and Gene Roberts, were told by the president, Rudolf Scott, that the organization was trying to force publishers to make changes by documenting supposed errors. The main concern was textbook coverage of economic liberalism. "The whole thing of liberalism in the textbooks," Scott told the reporters, "has been an evolution, taking place over the past decade or two. But we are going to change that."[54]

Using committees of educators and business people, America's Future reviewed textbooks with an eye for liberalism and left-wing philosophies. Typical of these reviews was one by Hans Sennholz, Chairman of the Department of Economics at Grove City College in Grove City, Pennsylvania. Sennholz complained that an economics text, *American Capitalism*, made "no mention . . . of the minimum wage legislation that keeps millions of Americans unemployed, or ever-rising unemployment compensation that destroys the incentive to work."[55] In his reviews, Russell Kirk, a professor of political science at Long Island University, objected to textbooks mentioning what he called the *god-term* democracy. He warned that a "besetting vice of democracies is their tendency to submerge the individual in the mass; aristocratic republics are far more concerned for individuals."[56]

The quarterly newsletter, *Educational Reviewer*, inundated publishers with accusations, such as the charge that Frank Magruder's high school text, *American Government*, attacked the free enterprise system and presented a view of democracy that led "straight from Rousseau, through Marx, to totalitarianism." National radio commentator Fulton Lewis, Jr., used portions of the review on a coast-to-coast broadcast with the comment, "That's the book that has been in use in high schools all over the nation, possibly by your youngster." Attacks on the textbook occurred throughout the country; the book was eventually banned in Richland, Washington; Houston, Texas; Little Rock, Arkansas; Lafayette, Indiana; and the entire state of Georgia.[57]

The American Textbook Publishers Institute tried to defend their products in a 1950s' pamphlet, *Textbooks Are Indispensable*. However, this pam-

phlet suggested that publishers "avoid statements that might prove offensive to economic, religious, racial or social groups, or any civic, fraternal,
patriotic or philanthropic societies in the whole United States."[58] A unique
part of this warning was its reference to an economic group, which of
course could be organized labor or business. The general climate for textbooks was summarized in 1960 by the Deputy superintendent of the District
of Columbia school system, Lawson Cantrell: "We try to make sure that the
books we select are not objectionable to anyone."[59]

CIVIC CONSUMERISM: THE NEW TEENAGE CULTURE

"Civic consumerism" was Kelly Schrum's description of the editorial message
for teenagers in *Seventeen* magazine in the late 1940s and early 1950s.[60] Scrum
defined *civic consumerism* as "combining one's democratic role as active citizen with one's duty as a responsible and active consumer."[61] During the late
1940s and 1950s, she argued, "Voting and democracy, as well as pride in
America and the right to buy goods, were common themes through this period, a reflection of both lingering war rhetoric and the beginning of the
Cold War."[62] Corresponding to earlier concerns with controlling adolescent
sexuality through high school activities, advertisers hoped to channel teenage sexuality into consumerism. Ads for girls displayed clothing and other
products that would enhance their dating potential. Boys directed their consumer sexuality at cars with the hope that the *hot car* or *hot rod*, a term with interesting sexual overtones, would result in the hot date.

The post-World War II era witnessed the appearance of the affluent high
school student. The 1930s' teenage culture, spawned by the mass institutionalization of youth in high school, lacked spending power. Between 1900 and
1940, the percentage in high school of those between 14 and 17 years of
age increased from 11% to 80%.[63] After World War II, spending patterns
changed as symbolized by the publication *Seventeen* magazine with its slogan,
"Teena means business." Similar to their mothers, teenage girls were a primary target for marketers. The word *teenager*, according to Kelly Schrum, was
invented by marketers. At first marketers experimented with *teenster* and
Petiteen; then *teenager* was popularized during the 1940s to mean a group defined by high school attendance. In a crass commercial effort, *Seventeen* magazine advertised the potential teenage market with slogans such as, "When is
a girl worth $11,690,499."[64] Sounding like an illusion to prostitution, the slo-
gan referred to the amount of money spent on teenage ads.

Was a national teenage culture a result of advertising? Certainly advertising provided national models for White teenagers to emulate. African-
American, Native American, and Mexican-American youth were not subjects of these early ad campaigns. One can imagine teenagers fantasying

about themselves looking like the youth in national ads. The ads provided models of dress and lifestyles. Also they carried messages about teenage sexuality.

Consider a 1950's Seven-Up ad that played on the concept of *going steady*. In the 1950s, dating rituals of teenagers included going steady, which was similar to a preengagement rite. The boy gave the girl an ankle bracelet, varsity jacket, or other consumer adornment to indicate that they would date only each other or, in the language of the times, they were going *steady*. Violation of the going steady agreement could result in a pseudodivorce. The going steady process mirrored the marriage and divorce practices of adults.

In the Seven-Up ad, a neatly dressed White teenage couple holding Seven-Up bottles are standing next to a jukebox. Above them the ad proclaimed, "It's great to 'go steady' with this COOL, CLEAN, TASTE!" Playing again on the theme of the couple's relationship, the text of the ad declared, "Here's the drink that's fun to be with-it has such a *sparkling personality*. . . . For a really 'cool' date . . . make yours 7-Up."[65] Other ads played directly to female sexuality. A 1945 *Seventeen* perfume ad embodied sexuality in the brand name, illustration, and text. The ad for Vigny's "Beau Catcher" perfume shows a young girl in a wind-blown and revealing skirt holding a string that is wrapped around a "Beau Catcher Date Book." Two other strings are tied to the product icon and a bottle of perfume. The ad's text states, "Vigny's Beau Catcher Perfume fills your date book. It's the saucy scent that won't take 'no' for an answer."[66]

A national White teenage culture was created through the common high school experience and national advertising. *Seventeen* magazine sold advertising on the basis that teenagers shared a common public mind. Magazine copy claimed, "Teena is a copycat—what a break for you. . . . She and her teen-mates speak the same language . . . wear the same clothes . . . use the same brand of lipstick."[67] The magazine included in their proclamation of a national teenage market a message that youth were responsible citizens. In other words, teenagers were responsible consumer-citizens.

Adolescent sexuality was central to teen ads and public concerns. Ironically, the high school heightened teenage sexuality by putting them within close proximity of each other. Advertising added to this concentrated sexuality by playing on themes of dating and relationships. *Seventeen* tried to balance this blatant sexuality with advice that discouraged heavy necking and petting. It also stressed the importance of political involvement, patriotism, and maintaining knowledge of current events. Scrum concluded that the general message was for teenage girls to practice civic consumerism.

Of course advertising placed sexuality at the center of teenage life by following its long tradition of playing to feelings of personal inadequacy. Similar to the fears implanted in adult women in the 1920s, teenagers were confronted with the possibility of being dateless because of body odors, bad breath, and unfashionable hair styles and clothing. The purchase of deodorants, mouth washes, cosmetics, hair products, and fashionable clothing promised the necessary sexual appeal.

The teenager was a cold warrior in training. Dating was to lead to marriage, the purchase of a home, and all of its necessary appliances. One could imagine the teenage girl and boy standing next to Nixon as he explained the advantages of American home appliances to Khrushchev. Swept up in the spirit of patriotism, this chaste and consumer-oriented teenage couple would marry and demonstrate the advantages of the American economic system.

THE AMERICAN WAY: TV AND COMIC BOOK CODES

In the 1950s, teenagers and children were the first generation raised on TV ads. While TV ads stimulated consumption, programs supported the American Way. In 1951, the TV industry's organization, the National Association of Broadcasters (NAB), adopted a self-censorship code. The code was in response to pressures similar to those that affected radio in the 1930s. Both the PTA and *Parents Magazine* wanted to "get rid of tele-violence." At the time of code's adoption, programming included a long list of gore and mystery shows such as, "Lights Out," "Suspense," "Danger," "The Clock," "The Web," "Tales of the Black Cat," and "Man Against Crime." The 1951 code was adopted because, in the words of the NAB, "[of the] threat of government censorship."[68]

Similar to earlier movie and radio codes, the 1951 TV code emphasized the importance of creating a public image of a moral world where crime was always punished and the law and police were given respect. Under the code, marriage was to be respected and illicit sex was not to be presented as commendable. Drunkenness and narcotic use were only to be depicted as vicious habits. Horror for its own sake and lewdness were forbidden. No words were to be used that might offend any race, color, creed, or nationality except to combat racial prejudice. The Code emphasized the need for "respect for the special needs of children, for community responsibility, for the advancement of education and culture, for the acceptability of the program materials chosen, for decency and decorum in production, and for propriety in advertising."[69]

In addition, advertisers imposed codes that supported the American Way and free enterprise. For instance, Procter & Gamble, the major sponsor of soap operas, required that their programs supported patriotism and never tarnished the image of government agents and members of the U.S. armed forces. If a character in a program attacked "some basic conception of the

American way of life," then a rebuttal "must be completely and convincingly made someplace in the same broadcast." In addition, the image of business was to be protected. A Procter & Gamble memo stated,

> There will be no material on any of our programs which could in any way further the concept of business as cold, ruthless, and lacking all sentiment or spiritual motivation. If a businessman is cast in the role of villain, it must be made clear that he is not typical but is as much despised by his fellow business men as he is by other members of society."[70]

Also advertisers worried about sponsoring any program that might be considered communist or an attack on the American way of life. Of particular concern were criticisms from the American Legion, which in 1948, through its Americanism Commission, started a newsletter, *Summary of Trends and Developments Exposing the Communist Conspiracy.* The newsletter told readers to "organize a letter-writing group of six to ten relatives and friends to make the sentiments of Americans heard on the important issues of the day. Phone, telegraph, or write to radio and television sponsors employing entertainers with known [Communist] front records." The newsletter stated in bold type: "DON'T LET THE SPONSORS PASS THE BUCK BACK TO YOU BY DEMANDING 'PROOF' OF COMMUNIST FRONTING BY SOME CHARACTER ABOUT WHOM YOU HAVE COMPLAINED. YOU DON'T HAVE TO PROVE ANYTHING. . . . YOU SIMPLY DO NOT LIKE SO-AND-SO ON THEIR PROGRAMS."[71]

Local Legion posts joined a supermarket campaign to convince sponsors not to employ entertainers listed in the book, *Red Channels: The Report of Communist Influence in Radio and Television.* The book's introduction warned that "Cominform and the Communist Party USA now rely more on radio and TV than on the press and motion pictures as 'belts' to transmit pro-Sovietism to the American public." Issued in 1950, the book was produced by the American Business Consultants, publishers of *Counterattack, the Newsletter of Facts to Combat Communism. Counterattack* started in 1947 by three former agents of the Federal Bureau of Investigation. Besides warning of a communist conspiracy, the newsletter listed names found in articles in the communist newspaper, *The Daily Worker.*[72]

In 1951, a supermarket campaign began when a reader of *Red Channels* and *Counterattack,* Eleanor Buchanan of Syracuse, New York, enlisted her father, Laurence Johnson, who owned four supermarkets, to work with the local American Legion Post. In one letter to the Legionnaires, Buchanan wrote, "Dad and I were pleased that you agree manufacturers can be persuaded to remove Communist sympathizers from their advertising programs on radio and television. As you gentlemen pointed out in our meeting last Friday, the task is too great for me alone. I am grateful for your aid."[73]

Besides owning four supermarkets, Laurance Johnson was an official in the National Association of Supermarkets. This created the impression that he could influence stores around the country and, because of the cooperation of the local Legion post, he had power in the national organization of the American Legion as well. Consequently, the sponsor, Amm-i-dent Toothpaste, took his action seriously when he protested the use of actors listed in *Counterattack* in the TV drama they sponsored, "Danger." Johnson wrote Amm-i-dent's manufacturer about plans to create two displays in his supermarkets. One display would be for Amm-i-dent's competitor Chlorodent Toothpaste. The sign on this display would thank Chlorodent for sponsoring programs with pro-American artists. The other display would be for Amm-i-dent, with a sign, to be written by the company, explaining why the sponsor selected subversives as actors. A copy of the letter was sent to CBS. This and later letters sent sponsors and broadcasters scurrying to review copies of *Red Channels*. Thank-you notes were sent to Johnson from TV sponsors including Borden Milk Company, Kraft Foods, and General Ice Cream Corporation. The Red Scare sent a pall of fear over the broadcast industry.[74]

Maintaining family values was part of CBS' censorship efforts. A divorce situation in "The Seeking Heart" for October 9, 1954, was brought into line with the networks standard that "divorce is never treated casually or justifiably."[75] The following were present to the Senate Subcommittee as examples of lines remove from scripts for moral considerations.

Do you remember the first time you made love to me?
And I think about all the wicked things I have done, and about you and me.
She swears she'll be discreet. She doesn't know the meaning of the word.[76]

NBC executives also claimed to present images of an ideal family life to the American public. Joseph Hefferman, vice president of NBC, told the Senate Subcommittee that NBC's children's shows were designed "to convey the commonly accepted moral, social, and ethical ideals characteristic of American life; to reflect respect for parents, good morals, and honorable behavior; to foster healthy personality development; and to provide opportunities for cultural growth as well as entertainment."[77]

Comic books were also enlisted in efforts to maintain family values and the American Way. Unlike the Sunday School books of the 19th century, comic books were filled with violence and sexuality. One critic went so far as to call comic books "the marijuana of the nursery." These criticisms eventually led to the comic book industry adopting a self-censorship code similar to the early movie and radio codes. The parallels between industry regulation of comic books and those occurring in the movies and broadcasting were pointed out in a 1954 article in *Christian Century*: "Like movie magnates and radio station operators before them, 24 of the 27 leading publishers of these often lurid picture-pulps [comic books] are trying to still cries for censorship by promising to censor themselves."[78]

Some American leaders thought comic books were a direct threat to the American way of life. After their development in the 1930s, comic books became a major part of the American publishing industry. In 1940, there were 150 comic book titles generating an annual revenue of $20 million. By 1950, there were 300 comic book titles, with annual revenues of $41 million. Between 1950 and 1953, the number of titles jumped to over 650, and revenues leaped to $90 million a year.[79]

What set off the hue and cry about this new form of children's literature was the appearance of crime and horror comics between 1945 and 1954. Unlike TV executives, comic book publishers defended the use of crime and gore. In 1954, when the Senate Subcommittee on Juvenile Delinquency opened hearings on comic books, Senator Estes Kefauver confronted William Gaines, president of the Entertaining Comics Group, with a cover of one of his company's comic books, *Shock Suspense Stories*, depicting an ax-wielding man holding the severed head of a blonde woman. Gaines responded by saying that the cover would only be in bad taste if the head were held "a little high so the neck would show with the blood dripping from it." Kefauver shot back, "You've got blood dripping from the mouth."[80]

In fact, horror and crime comic books of the early 1950s depicted criminal acts, maimed and tortured individuals, and suggestive sexual scenes. At the New York City hearings of the Senate Subcommittee on Juvenile Delinquency, a variety of comic books were introduced to illustrate possible harmful effects on children. In one example, "Bottoms Up," from *Story Comics*, an alcoholic father was responsible for the accidental death of his son while obtaining liquor from a bootlegger. The mother is shown taking revenge in the final four panels of the story by proceeding to kill and hack her spouse to pieces with an ax. The first panel shows her swinging the ax and burying its blade in her husband's skull. Blood spurts from the open wound, and the husband is shown with an expression of agony. . . . She then cuts his body into smaller pieces and disposes of it by placing the various pieces in the bottles of liquor her husband had purchased. She then returns the liquor to the bootlegger and obtains a refund. Another example provided by the subcommittee was from "Frisco Mary" from *Ace Comics*. One scene in this story showed Mary standing over a police officer pouring machine gun bullets into his back while other gang members urge her to stop shooting and flee. In "With Knife in Hand" from *Atlas Comics*, a young surgeon ruins his career by being forced by the spendthrift habits of his wife to treat criminals. In the final scenes of this story, a criminal brings in his wounded girlfriend to be treated by the doctor. The doctor discovers that the girl is his own wife. The next panel shows the doctor committing suicide by plunging a scalpel into his own abdomen. His wife, gasping for help, dies on the operating table for lack of medical attention. The last scene shows her staring into space, arms dangling over the sides of the operating table. The doctor is sprawled on the floor, his hand still clutching the knife handle protruding from his bloody abdomen. There is a leer on his face and he is winking at the reader, displaying satisfaction at having wrought revenge on his unfaithful spouse. One comic book was described as ending with the victim "lying dead on the bed with a gaping hole in his chest, a rib protruding, blood flowing over the bed onto the floor, his face fixed in a death mask as he stares at the reader."[81]

Following the pattern of movies and broadcasting, the comic book industry needed a profamily code. Wanting to avoid continued community protest and the threat of censorship laws, comic book publishers organized to create and impose their own standards. Their first attempt was the 1948 formation of the Association of Comics Magazine Publishers and its adoption of a six-point code. A seal was to be attached to comic books to indicate conformity to the code. Like other codes, there was an emphasis on issues involving sex, crime, language, the family, and attacks on religious and racial groups. This early code proved ineffective, with only 12 of the 34 major publishers of comic books belonging to the comic book association. With increased pressure from government and private organizations, a new organization, Comics Magazine Association of America, was formed in 1954 with a membership of 28 of the then 31 major publishers of comic books. This association appointed New York City magistrate Charles Murphy to enforce a comic book code. The words *horror* and *terror* were not allowed in titles. Crime comics were to be screened to exclude methods of committing crimes. No sympathy was to be given for criminals, and nothing should "create disrespect for established authority." In addition, the code banned "profanity, obscenity, smut, vulgarity, ridicule of racial or religious groups."[82]

In keeping with the belief that the sanctity of family was necessary for protection of the American way of life and to prevent juvenile delinquency, the code ensured protection of the sanctity of marriage and the value of the home. In addition, "divorce was not to be shown as desirable."[83] Beginning in 1955, a seal was placed on the front of comics as proof that these values were being protected. It was estimated that the code was enforced on 75% of the estimated 60 million comic books published each month in the United States.[84] Dell Comics, one of the three publishers that did not belong to the Comics Magazine Association of America and publisher of approximately 20% of the comic books in the United States, did not join the association because it already had its own code of ethics. In any case, Dell primarily published comics based on adventure stories and Walt Disney characters. It was known in the trade as having a *wholesome approach.* One of the other nonmembers was Classics Illustrated, which adapted classic novels, such as Charles Dickens' *Oliver Twist,* to a comic book format. William Gaines, the originator of horror comics and another nonmember, announced that he would cease publishing all horror and terror magazines. Thus, comic books joined in the media chorus protecting the American way of life.[85]

TEXTBOOKS AND THE CONSUMER FAMILY

Idealized images of American women and men were part of the American way of life. The ideal American female and male were ardent patriots protecting traditional American values. In general, the idealized 1950s' American woman sought her identity in the home through the upbringing of children and the consumption of home products. Reflecting lingering Puritanical fears that consumption would lead to hedonism, according to May, "Family centered spending reassured Americans that affluence would strengthen the American way of life. The goods purchased by middle-class consumers, like a modern refrigerator or a house in the suburbs, were intended to foster traditional values."[86]

The idealized male sought his identity in his job and family life. The male earned the money to be used to buy products that protected traditional values. His realm of consumption usually included automobiles and products used to maintain the interior and exterior of the home. His province was the yard, garage, and home workshop. Reflecting the traditional sense that outdoors was male territory, he was usually given the responsibility for outdoor barbequing.

These gender roles were represented in school textbooks read by all children regardless of their geographical location or race. In 1954, Frank Tannenbaum published a survey of 10 years of primers and first-, second-, and third-grade reading texts entitled "Family Living in Textbook Town." Tannenbaum noted that all the texts depicted the same type of suburban neighborhood with

> rows of brightly polished little cottages, fronted by neatly manicured lawns, all suggesting an atmosphere of order and cheerfulness. In this sunny neighborhood setting, children have lots of room for out-of-doors play, and families are able to enjoy their living space with the kind of "elbowroom" that is not possible in the more thickly populated cities. The reader gets to know these

picturesque surroundings quite intimately, for much of the action in the stories takes place there.[87]

Textbooks portrayed fathers with their favorite easy chairs and workshops and mothers in well-equipped kitchens. The father was usually slim and handsome, often depicted arriving home from work dressed in a neat suit in the family car. Only when making minor home repairs was the father shown in work clothes. The mother had no occupation outside of housework, devoting her time to caring for her family. She was usually young, attractive, and well dressed. The only time she was seen outside of the house was shopping and on family recreation trips.

Children in Textbook Town were all happy and well adjusted. They spent their time playing and doing minor chores with their parents. They were well behaved and never fought with their siblings or parents. In Tannenbaum's words, "Nothing is ever allowed to interfere seriously with the spirit of joy, security, and cooperativeness that dominates family living in Textbook Town."[88] Everyone in Textbook Town was White. No people of color or with distinctive ethnic characteristics lived in Textbook Town, and no one in Textbook Town was poor.

THE MALE WARRIOR PROTECTS THE AMERICAN WAY

Males could escape from Textbook Town through media-created images of the cowboy and war hero. For women, the only media escapes were through the life of glamorous actresses, insanity, or adopting the role of male delinquents. As Wini Breines stated in her study of female delinquents of the 1950s, "Middle-class white girls who rejected dominant values had little choice but to utilize and adapt male versions of rebellion and disaffection. . . . There were few female models."[89]

The screen image of John Wayne provided men with an escape from the humdrum corporate and suburban life. On the screen, Wayne fought for the American Way and values. For White adults and boys, John Wayne represented the ideal of rugged American masculinity in the tradition of Theodore Roosevelt. Even as late as 1995, 16 years after his death, he was still ranked as America's favorite movie star by a Harris Poll.[90] Wayne's movie career encompassed the 1930s' movie code, Hollywood's active World War II cooperation with the government, and the purge of so-called *communists* after the War. During the 1930s, Wayne rose to stardom as primarily an actor in cowboy movies. In these movies, he portrayed the independent and tough cowboy who fought to protect traditional values.[91] During World War II, the U.S. Government's Office of War Information worked actively with the movie studios to produce propaganda films that would stimulate the war effort, boost morale, and fire up a sense of patriotism.[92] Wayne contributed to this effort by starring in important war films, including *Flying Tigers* (1942), *The Fighting Seabees* (1943), and *Back to Bataan* (1945). His portrayal of patriotic war heroes continued after the end of the conflict with *Sands of Iwo Jima* (1949) and *Flying Leathernecks* (1951). He also made the first war movie about Viet Nam called *The Green Berets* (1968). As a sign of his personal patriotism, Wayne struggled to find a studio that would make the movie because of the controversy surrounding the war. Regarding *The Green Berets*, Wayne stated, "I want to show the folks back home just what they're [U.S. troops in Viet Nam] up against out there, their heroism against tremendous odds."[93]

Wayne's screen images of cowboy and patriotic warrior were often mistaken for reality. His biographer, Ronald Doris, reported the following incident that occurred shortly after World War II: "You know," a woman said to screenwriter Edmund Hartmann, "our most decorated soldier is John Wayne." "I think you're wrong," Hartmann replied. "Wayne was never in the army. He never fired a gun in earnest in his life. John Wayne never shot anybody who didn't get up and go for coffee afterwards."[94] After the destruction of the World Trade Center on September 11, 2002, I was surprised to find a life-size cardboard replica of John Wayne wearing a cowboy outfit and holding a rifle among the flowers and memorial signs for the tragedy's victims in Union Square Park in New York City. Across his chest someone had pasted a sign reading, "God Bless America."

During and after World War II, John Wayne joined others in trying to purge communists from the movie industry. In 1944, he worked with Ayn Rand, Walt Disney, Cecil B. DeMille, and Gary Cooper to form the Motion Picture Alliance for the Preservation of American Ideals. The Alliance declared, "In our special field of motion pictures, we resent the growing impression that this industry is made up of, and dominated by, Communists, radicals and crackpots." The organization gave its promise to the American people "to fight, with every means at our organized command, any effort of any group or individual to divert the loyalty of the screen from the free America that gave it birth."[95]

Writer Ayn Rand wrote the organization's movie code to ensure that movies protected the American way of life. The code included the precepts:

Don't *Smear* the Free Enterprise System
Don't Glorify the Collective
Don't Glorify Failure
Don't Smear Success
Don't Smear Industrialists

It is the moral (no, not just political but moral) duty of every decent man in the motion picture industry to throw into the ashcan where it belongs, every story that smears industrialists as such.[96]

Wayne also associated himself with the American Legion's efforts to purge un-Americanism from movies, schools, and TV. At a 1951 Legion convention, General MacArthur declared to Wayne, despite that Wayne had never served in the armed forces, "You represent the American serviceman better than the American serviceman himself."[97]

John Wayne's screen image was the direct opposite of that of the corporate-suburban family man. However, both images protected against communism and supported American values. The suburban man gave up his individualism to corporate life, whereas John Wayne stood for individualism and independence. "All I'm for," Wayne claimed, "is the liberty of the individual."[98] Yet the corporate man protected the American Way by maintaining the family and providing the income to consume. John Wayne's importance was his role in the fantasy life of Americans and not the reality of his being. Actress Maureen O'Hara said to a congressional subcommittee shortly before Wayne's death, "To the people of the world John Wayne is the United States of America."[99] Commenting on Wayne's role in public fantasies, screenwriter Huggins said, "People actually thought of Wayne as a great hero and, of course, John Wayne was just an actor. He was never in any armed service, never saw a war, never even saw a gun fired that actually had lead in it. . . . It says something about the confusion in the American people between reality and myth."[100]

The John Wayne image found its way into advertising as the Marlboro Man. The story of the Marlboro Man highlights the appeal of the cowboy in 20th century. In the 1920s, Marlboro cigarettes were marketed to women with a red paper beauty tip to conceal lipstick. In the 1950s, it was decided to change marketing strategies and sell the product to men. The Marlboro Man appeared in 1955 dressed in a cowboy outfit sitting on a horse or relaxing by a campfire. All it required was a change in gender image to sell the cigarette to men. As advertising historian Juliann Sivulka wrote, "Cowboys symbolized the most masculine type of man, and . . . [the] ads evoked memorable imagery of real men in a man's world. The campaign became one of the all-time greats in advertising history."[101]

Fantasies about John Wayne and the Marlboro Man's independence and action-filled life might have psychologically relieved the reality of suburban man's dependence on corporate life and completing the mundane tasks of lawn mowing and car washing. In the arena of patriotism, the internalization of the American myths of the cowboy and battlefield added potency to an anticommunism being fought on the front lines of consumerism.

Washing their cars in their suburban driveways, the organization man could envision charging into battle to protect the American way of life.

TRAPPED IN TEXTBOOK AND CONSUMER TOWN: WOMEN AND THE LACK OF INDEPENDENT MEDIA IMAGES

For White women, the screen offered escape into the fantasy images of the ultimate consumer, the Hollywood star. Otherwise the screen was dominated by women treated as sex objects or insane. Women of the 1950s disliked Marilyn Monroe, the era's major sex symbol. This attitude would change in later years. In *From Reverence to Rape: The Treatment of Women in the Movies*, Molly Haskell wrote, "Women, particularly, have become contrite over their previous hostility to Monroe, canonizing her as a martyr to male chauvinism, which in most ways she was."[102]

According to Haskell, men rarely played the role of an actor in movies, whereas women often performed in actress roles. As Haskell suggested, there were two major movie roles for women that paralleled how they might be forced to act in normal life—namely, prostitution and role-playing. The actress role on screen allowed female viewers to image living the life of a glamorous movie star. Haskell wrote, "The actress legend took various forms: the mystique of the actress, the myth of the movie star, the mystique of the actress versus the myth of the movie star."[103] There were a few alternatives to the glamorized sex object and actress role, but nothing that matched the power of the John Wayne image for men. Haskell argued that Grace Kelly and Audrey Hepburn provided screen models for the independent woman: "They never swallowed their pride, exploited their sexuality, or made fools of themselves over men."[104]

Lacking female fantasy role models, female rebels frequently modeled themselves after male media images. Wini Breines found that many women who rejected the life of Textbook Town identified with the male characters in Jack Kerouac's novel, *On the Road*, although they were macho and sexist.[105] On the screen, young women were attracted to Marlon Brando in *The Wild One* and James Dean in *Rebel without a Cause*. Breines argued, "Widespread interest in Dean, Elvis [Presley], the Beats, and young men from the 'other side of the tracks' suggests an attraction to a life that was 'dramatic, unpredictable, possibly dangerous,' the antithesis of white middle-class life in postwar America."[106]

Television reinforced the female roles represented in Textbook Town. Daytime TV, which was programmed for the housewife, intentionally educated women about consumption for the suburban home. When the major networks began daytime broadcasting in the early 1950s, their first project was teaching the housewife how to watch TV while working. For instance, a 1955 NBC ad showed a housewife wearing an apron and holding a feather duster exclaiming, "Where did the morning go?" Surrounding her were TV screens with scenes from NBC's daytime TV programming. The ad's text read, "Time for lunch already? Where did the morning go? The chores are done, the house is tidy . . . but it hasn't *seemed* like a terribly tiring morning." Her morning was portrayed as opening with family breakfast while watching the "Today Show." After breakfast she tidied up while her daughter watched the "Ding Dong School." Then she rested while watching the soap opera serial "Way of the World" and began ironing during the "Sheila Graham Show." The rest of the morning, as depicted in the ad, followed this combination of work and TV.[107]

Some of the programming followed a magazine format that integrated "housework, consumerism, and TV entertainment."[108] In these programs, entertainment was surrounded with advice on shopping and products along with fashion and cleaning tips. Lynn Spigel quoted a production handbook: "The theory is that the housewife will be more likely to take time from her household duties if she feels that her television viewing will make her housekeeping more efficient and help her provide more gracious living for her family."[109]

Plus there were products the woman consumer could buy to make TV viewing more efficient, including snack trays, TV trays, and TV frozen dinners. Dishwashers were advertised as freeing the housewife from the kitchen to join the family before the TV. A 1950 Hotpoint ad showed a housewife washing dishes while in the next room the rest of the family was watching TV. In large print, the ad pleaded, "PLEASE . . . LET YOUR WIFE COME INTO THE LIVING ROOM!" This was followed in smaller type with: "Don't let dirty dishes make your wife a kitchen exile!" In the lower right-hand corner of the ad was a dishwasher with the statement, "No martyr banished to kitchen, she never misses television programs. Lunch, dinner dishes are in an electric dishwasher."[110]

Media provided the housewife few role models for escaping from Textbook Town. The male could dream of being a cowboy or warrior and the woman could imagine escaping into the glamor of Hollywood or latching onto a rebellious male who could free her from her mundane world. Consumption fantasies left her trapped in Textbook Town with men who dreamt of being warriors in defense of the American Way.

CONCLUSION: THE AMERICAN WAY

I really enjoyed writing this chapter because I could pull together similar public images that were emerging from schools and media as a result of consumerism and anticommunism. Most striking were those excluded from this public image—namely, non-Whites, gays, lesbians, and those rejecting the life of Textbook Town. Of course media did present images of beatniks, delinquents, the insane, and the criminal, but these were always constructed as deviant to the American way of life and Textbook Town.

An important development during this period was the growing awareness by private groups of the importance of controlling public opinion, particularly controlling the filters or preconceptions used to interpret world events. This development was highlighted by the NAM's use of public relations in the American Way campaign to create in the public mind an immediate association among democracy, free enterprise, consumerism, and Americanism. Anticommunist groups aided this effort by attempting to eradicate from media and schools anything that might question the value of free enterprise.

The other important event was the interrelationship among schools, advertising, and media in creating a national teenager culture. Advertising would continue to play a role in defining images of differing parts of the public. Because African Americans, Latinos, Asians, gays, and lesbians were recognized as important consumers, advertisers and media would increasingly gear ads and programs to these groups. The result was an interrelationship between group images projected by ads and media and self-identification. Of course this would not be a one-way road. There would be a constant feedback, as there was with teen culture, between the group, as measured by market research and consumer spending, and media and advertisers. This feedback was not static. Often it would be hard to tell whether a public group dressed according to ad and media campaigns or whether ad and media campaigns reflected the dress of the group.

The importance of the general public image continued despite the development of specific images for particular publics, such as teens, older people, African Americans, and so on. The American Way images of democracy, free enterprise, suburbia, and consumption existed side by side with a national teen culture. Although White teens developed their own national cultural, clothing, and media styles, there was still an effort by schools and media to connect teen minds to a more general public mind that valued the American Way.

The problem was that the American Way image did not include all Americans. The poor, composed of Whites, African Americans, Native Americans, and Asian Americans, were not full participants in consumerism. Their images were not in Textbook Town or reflected in national advertising. In part, the great civil rights movement of the 1950s and 1960s reflected a desire to join the consumerist culture. I am not discounting the major political victories of the civil rights movement, such as the end of segregation and the achievement of voting rights. However, I would argue that the civil rights movement's economic goals were primarily to gain full participation of all groups in consumerist culture.

In the next chapter, I discuss the implication of the civil rights movement for consumerism and the American Way. In addition, the civil rights movement occurred as major changes were occurring in marketing, creation of consumer desires, and food processing—namely, the development of shopping malls, the expansion of fast-food chains, the building of Disneyland, and the establishment of Wal-Mart, which is now the world leader in retailing.

Chapter 6

Participating in the American Dream

A goal of the civil rights movement was inclusion of all people's images in textbooks, advertising, and media as equal participants in the American dream. African Americans, Native Americans, Mexican Americans, Asian Americans, women, and people with disabilities hoped that the struggle for equal social and political rights would also result in the projection of positive images of them in textbooks, media, and advertising. Also the civil rights movement's pursuit of equality of opportunity promised a chance for all to participate in consumerism. The women's movement wanted to replace the image of Textbook Town's housewife with one emphasizing women's career options and personal freedoms. Inevitably, these goals were integrated into advertising copy to expand consumerism to all groups.

THE COLORING OF TEXTBOOK TOWN

A 1964 California State Department of Education report on "The Negro in American History Textbooks" declared that "[Ralph Ellison's novel, *Invisible Man*] demonstrates whites frequently do not 'see' Negroes. But Negroes are Americans. . . . They need to be 'seen' in textbooks."[1] The report was issued by a distinguished panel of University of California historians headed by Kenneth Stampp. The panel had been organized in 1963 by the Berkeley, California, chapter of the Congress on Racial Equality (CORE) to analyze American history textbooks adopted for use in Grades 5 and 8 and two textbooks used in the state's high schools. The panel's report was important because the California State Board of Education selected textbooks that were adopted by local state school systems. Given the large number of sales involved, the textbook industry was attuned to the desires of the California State Board of Education. The State Board of Education distributed the report to interested groups, including textbook publishers, and in 1966 it played an important role in the deliberations of the U.S. House of Representatives' investigation of the treatment of minority groups in textbooks, which reprinted it in its proceedings.[2] Intensifying discussions about racial images in textbooks was the news that New York City's African-American elementary school students were drawing White faces when asked to complete self-portraits.[3]

CORE's panel of academic historians found almost total neglect of African-American history. One textbook failed to mention African Americans. One did not refer to slavery during the colonial period, whereas others did not discuss anything about African Americans after the Civil War. The report complained, "The greatest defect in the textbooks we have examined is the virtual omission of the Negro."[4] The panel criticized the unrealistic treatment of the relationships between Whites and African Americans. When discussed at all in the textbooks, interracial contacts were portrayed as harmonious. The history of racial violence was seldom mentioned in textbooks. "In their blandness and amoral optimism," the panel's analysis concluded, "these books deny the obvious deprivations suffered by Negroes. In several places they go further, implying approval for the repression of Negroes or patronizing them as being unqualified for life in a free society."[5] The report recommended full treatment of African-American history. The historians on the panel suggested that books begin with the early importation and treatment of slaves and conclude with the recent history of the civil rights movement. The report also urged, the "Gains that have been made should be described realistically and not as an ode to the inevitable justice and progress of the democratic system."[6]

The National Association for the Advancement of Colored People (NAACP) and the editors of *Ebony Magazine* were also concerned about textbooks. Since the NAACP's demonstrations against the movie *Birth of a Nation* in 1915, the organization had paid vigilant attention to public images of African Americans. In 1966, the organization issued a guide to integrated textbooks that stated, "in the crucial effort to guarantee to all our children, white and black, a curriculum that makes sense in a multi-racial society, such a listing is long overdue."[7] After studying textbooks for 5 years, senior editor of *Ebony*, Lerone Bennett, concluded that, "The use of textbooks filled with half-truths, evasions and distortions is disastrous to both white and black Americans . . . [and] white oriented textbooks tend to inoculate white Americans with the virus of racism. . . ." Bennett called on the federal government to provide the resources and power to solve the textbook problem.[8]

Bennett warned, in testimony before the 1966 House Subcommittee investigating textbooks' racial and cultural content, that "segregated textbooks . . . are as dangerous to the internal peace of America as segregated schools and residential areas." In fact, he argued that if all schools and neighborhoods were immediately integrated without integrating textbooks, then all schools and neighborhoods would soon become segregated again. Bennett found it ironic that the largest race riots had occurred in Chicago, which was originally founded by African-American Jean Baptiste Pointe Du Sable. "And it seems to me," he declared, "that a solution to our current crisis depends to a great extent on the opening of our minds and our textbooks to all the Du Sables and the excluded range of American life and culture that they personified."[9]

Publishers expressed their concerns about racial integration of textbooks through their trade association the American Textbook Publishers Institute (ATPI), which represented 110 publishers of textbooks and other educational materials. The organization scheduled a 1965 joint conference with the Urban League to determine "the needs of the Negro child and the kinds of materials which would help him relate to the total American society."[10] The executive director of the National Urban League, Whitney Young, Jr., told the meeting, "You publishers want the respect of generations born and generations yet unborn. We live together as brothers, or we die together as fools." Another member of the Urban League, Edwin Berry, insisted that publishers do more than just integrate textbooks with pictures of differing ethnic groups. He argued, they should also provide a realistic view of society by including "tall people, short people, fat and slim people, people with glasses, balding men and pregnant women."[11]

Meeting in 1965 with the Great Cities Research Council, the ATPI agreed to collect urban—by this time, *urban* was a code word for poor and non-White students—educational materials in cooperation with the U.S. Office of Education. The ATPI organized itself as a clearinghouse for new research on urban education. To further aid the objectives of publishers, the joint conference arranged visits by teams of publishers to meet with educators in member school systems. Also before congressional investigators, ATPI's McCaffrey described how publishers were being pressured by local school systems to produce multiracial textbooks: "I think 2 or 3 years ago a number of principal cities in the country passed resolutions in their boards of education that it was the policy of these cities to purchase only books that had a fair representation of minorities."[12]

Publishers claimed federal money made it possible to produce multiracial texts. A senior vice-president of McGraw-Hill, Robert W. Locke, told the House Subcommittee, "Purchases of new textbooks and other instructional materials have risen sharply this year because of ESEA, and part of the gap has been closed between what should be done for schoolchildren and what is being done." In fact, Locke indicated that federal money was the most important element in the expansion of the textbook publishing industry in the early 1960s; he told the subcommittee: "My guess is that something like 30 or 40 percent of our increase in sales this year at the elementary and secondary level will be a result of . . . [federal] funds."[13] Publishers sought more federal funds when ATPI and Scott, Foresman & Co.'s president, Darrel Peterson, told the House Subcommittee, "I would like to offer strong endorsement for the Government's efforts to improve the quantity and quality of educational materials available to students in our schools. . . . These Federal investments in libraries and instructional materials in general are eminently worthwhile."[14]

Responding to federal actions, McGraw-Hill published texts depicting multiethnic urban settings. In 1965, the company issued the *Skyline* reading series for Grades 2 through 4, which contained stories about people living in multiethnic cities. For example, one story, "The Hidden Lookout," was about Rosita's search for a place of her own in a city with millions of people. Eventually she builds a box house on an apartment roof. The *Skyline* series was only one of several related series published by McGraw-Hill in 1965. That year it also published a series called *Americans All,* with specific titles on "The American Negro," "Our Oriental Americans," "Our Citizens From the Caribbean," and "Latin Americans of the Southwest." In 1965, the company published a high school textbook focusing on civil liberties, *Heritage of Liberty.*[15]

However, publishers were accused of shady practices by publishing special editions for the Southern market. Harcourt, Brace & World, Inc. issued textbook editions that were free of multiracial pictures. In 1965, Southern states approved sight-unseen new editions of the company's elementary school grammar and composition texts. Southern school districts complained about books containing illustrations of White and African-American children playing together. Harcourt's vice-president, Cameron S. Moseley, explained to the House Subcommittee, "There was an unofficial, implied threat to cancel all our contracts." Consequently, the company printed a special edition that deintegrated the illustrations by showing only White children.[16]

In a similar situation, in 1965 Scott, Foresman published three new multiethnic series in reading, health, and social studies. "These books," the company's president Peterson stated, "which are multiethnic in character, present all kinds of children in natural situations and, where appropriate, contribute to the positive imagery of the diversified composition of American society."[17] However, Scott, Foresman continued printing its 1962 all-White edition of the reading series. When questioned about the all-White series, Peterson claimed that the company was not producing a series just for the South because both series were being sold throughout the country.

All school districts in the country had a choice between the multiethnic and all-White versions. The increased cost of publishing two editions, he explained, was balanced by the bigger volume of business.[18]

Illustrations were the major difference between the all-White and multiethnic editions. In describing its new urban social studies program, the executive vice-president of Holt, Rinehart & Winston, Ross Sackett, emphasized that, "Dramatic photographs capture the interaction between individuals and groups in an actual multicultural, multiracial community."[19] Publishers described books by the number of multiracial illustrations. For example, Craig Senft, president of Silver Burdett Co., proudly described a new first-grade textbook, *Families and Their Needs*, as identifying "facts that determine just how the needs of families from a variety of physical environments and cultures are met. It so happens that of the 54 photographs illustrating some aspect of American families, 18 show minority group families or individuals." He emphasized, "We intentionally chose photographs that included minority groups to show as many ethnic and socioeconomic strains as were needed to portray the differences that give our society its variety and richness."[20]

The process of adding African Americans to pictures was sometimes referred to as giving textbook characters a *sunburn*. There were several techniques involved in this process. One created integrated drawings by using different mechanical color separations or simply two colors. Simple black and white line drawings showed ethnically vague features that could be filled in by the reader's imagination. Photographs of integrated groups were frequently used in popular settings such as stores, playgrounds, neighborhood streets, and homes. Relying on changes in illustrations, textbook publishers could claim integration of a wide variety of texts, including those in science and mathematics. McGraw-Hill's representative Locke considered their elementary school science program, "Experiences in Science," as integrated because, in his words to the House Subcommittee, "we have taken great care to include minority-group children in the illustrations."[21] He also included an arithmetic filmstrip because its frames included both White and non-White groups.

In the new Textbook Town, multiracial images resided in a world of social harmony. In textbook scenes, African Americans and Whites worked and played together despite continued discrimination and racial violence in society. No longer invisible in textbooks, African Americans were catapulted to a world of equality and racial harmony. Integrated textbook stories also conveyed a message of racial harmony. Although illustrations were the easiest and most popular method for publishers to integrate textbooks, multiracial and multiethnic stories were placed in readers. "Galumph," the opening story of Houghton-Mifflin's second-grade reader, was about a cat who divided its time among an African-American child, an Italian baker, a

Hispanic girl, and a sick White child. Another story, "Traffic Policeman," was about a White child cooperating with an African-American policeman. "A Penny for a Jack Rabbit" was the unlikely tale—given the racial tension and housing discrimination in the society at that time—of suburban African-American and White children playing together at a party.[22]

Therefore, the setting and population of Textbook Town changed without disturbing the basic message of harmony and happiness. Political pressures and government funding added an urban dimension and a multiracial and multiethnic population to Textbook Town. Textbook Town now included apartment buildings as well as suburban bungalows, where happy groups of multiracial children played together. History textbooks contained sections on slavery and the civil rights movement. Yet an integrated Textbook Town still seemed out of touch with the reality of racial violence and discrimination.

BEAUTY IN THE PUBLIC MIND

In the 1950s, Black Power advocates condemned the use of skin whiteners and hair straighteners because they reflected beauty standards of the White community. Traditionally, ads for these hair and skin lotions were the richest source of advertising for the African-American press.[23] Black pride was part of a general movement, which also included Indians and Chicanos, to embrace beauty standards based on racial self-esteem. Among these groups, traditional dress, jewelry, and hair styles became a symbol of rebellion against White images in textbooks, ads, and media. African-American pride championed natural beauty fashioned by Afro hair styles and acceptance of natural skin color. The result was a decline in the use of traditional African-American hair and cosmetic products. A study of ads in *Ebony* magazine between 1949 and 1972 found a rapid decline in ads for hair straighteners and skin whiteners and the appearance of ads for Afro hairstyles.[24]

This beauty trend resulted in the growth of new African-American-owned cosmetic companies. In 1965, the Flori Roberts Company began marketing African-American cosmetic products originally developed for African-American models. This was followed by Fashion Fair Cosmetics, which was a product line marketed by *Ebony*. In 1973, Johnson Products became the first African-American-owned company to be listed on a major stock exchange as a result of its wildly popular Afro-Sheen products.[25]

A new magazine, *Essence*, promoted products and new beauty standards to African-American women. Clarence Smith, *Essence*'s publisher, defined his marketing strategy as an outgrowth of the rebellion against dominant White images. Smith wrote, "They [marketers] don't see how much Black women are competing with White women to prove they are as good or better. Since childhood they have been inundated with media images of beauty as the White woman."[26] Marketing strategies, Smith contended, should be cast in the framework of African-American pride. He wrote, "They [black women] want to be as attractive as possible and show the Black man that her beauty is fine. Marketers should see that she is overcompensating in buying products to dispel negative stereotypes."[27]

Robert E. Weems, Jr., noted that the revolution in African-American female identity was not accompanied by the same loyalty to African-American businesses as had existed in the past. Eventually, as they recognized the spending power of the African-American community, White-owned businesses controlled the African-American cosmetic market. In 1991, the Maybelline Company introduced Shades of You cosmetics for African-American women. At the time its major competitor in the general cosmetic's market was Cover Girl. Industry consultant Allan Motus said Maybelline's introduction of Shades of You was a smart move: "Instead of going eyeball to eyeball with Cover Girl, they can go for a specific segment for incremental market share."[28] Also in 1991, Estee Lauder began marketing Prescriptives for All Skins with 100 makeup shades. The product line attracted 50,000 African-American buyers in its first year.[29]

Ironically, the Black pride movement integrated African Americans into the general consumer market while undermining traditional African-American businesses. For some African Americans, the civil rights movement meant equal opportunity to pursue the American dream within the framework of a specific racial identity. Freedom to consume did not mean having to take on a White identity. For many African Americans, equality of educational opportunity and equality of opportunity meant an equal chance to earn and consume.

INTEGRATING CONSUMER MARKETS: AFRICAN-AMERICAN SPORT STARS REPLACE WHITE COWBOYS

The recognition by White-owned companies of an African-American consumer market prompted changes in the traditional use of degrading racial images in ads, and it provided an opportunity for the establishment of African-American-owned ad agencies. Prior to the influence of the civil rights movement, African-American ad images were usually as cooks and butlers to White families, such as Aunt Jemima, Cream of Wheat's Chef Rustus, and Hiram Walker's butler. Clearly these images were not going to sell products to the African-American community.

Vince Culler's was the first African-American-owned ad agency when it opened in Chicago in 1956. At first Culler did ads for African-American-owned companies such Johnson Products. Culler's ads were successful in promoting Johnson's Afro-Sheen products. A 1960s ad by Culler's agency for Afro-Sheen showed the heads of African-American men and women sporting Afro hair styles. Reflecting the emphasis on Black pride and rejection of attempts to look White, the ad proclaimed that these were "People who wear the natural as a proud symbol of beautiful blackness."[30] Culler's agency eventually garnered non-African-American owned company accounts such as Kellogg and Pizza Hut.[31]

An important advertising goal was creating images that would synthesize or integrate the consumer market. By this I mean the creation of ad images designed to appeal to all racial audiences. This step, I would argue, established a certain level of interracial camaraderie about consumer products. According to Bernice Kanner, the author of *New York* magazine's column "On Madison Avenue," one of the best 100 all-time TV ads showed African-American football player Mean Joe Greene drinking a bottle of Coca-Cola. The first thing to note about the ad was that, by the 1970s, the football player had replaced the cowboy as the primary macho image. The vice-president of marketing for Coca-Cola, Bill Van, commented about the ad, in the words of Bernice Kanner, "Just as Marlboro owned macho cowboys, Coca-Cola thought it could own the world of smiling Americans . . . Coke spots featured product as hero, causing the smile."[32]

Made in 1979 by the McCann–Erickson Worldwide agency, the ad opened with Mean Joe Green limping down a stadium tunnel appearing battered from a big game. A little boy admiringly told the player, "I just want you to know, I think you're the best." After the unsmiling player grunted an unfriendly response, the boy offered his Coke. As Mean Joe Green lifted the bottle to his lips, music and lyrics proclaimed, "A Coke and a smile, makes me feel good, makes me feel nice." Revived by the drink, the player smiled and thanked the boy by tossing him his dirty jersey. After the boy shouted, "Wow! Thanks Mean Joe!", a voice-over proclaimed, "Have a Coke and a smile. Coke adds life."[33]

Another example of synthesizing or integrating the consumer market was Pepsi-Cola's ad for the macho symbol of Americanism—the Super Bowl. This 1990 TV ad by the Batten, Barton, Durstine & Osborne featured African-American singer Ray Charles who, in the opening scene, was rehearsing "You Know When Its Right."

> You know when you feel it, baby.
> You hold it. You hear it. You taste it. It's right.
> Diet Pepsi.[34]

The scene shifts to a performance with dancing chorus girls and Ray Charles singing praises to Pepsi-Cola. The final line by Charles was: "You know when it's right. You know when you taste it!" followed by a voice-over, "You got the right one, baby, Uh, Huh, Diet Pepsi."[35]

Another example of the effort to synthesize or integrate the consumer market was a 1993 ad for McDonald's—the same desire to integrate the consumer market. The ad was clearly designed to appeal to White and African-American consumers who might envision eating together at McDonald's. The ad included basketball player Michael Jordan who would eventually become a worldwide consumer symbol for Nike shoes. Also included was White basketball player Larry Bird. Produced by the Leo Burnett agency, the ad was called "Showdown Combo" and portrayed Bird and Jordan competing for a Big Mac and bag of fries. Making impossible shots, the final scene shows them on top of Chicago's John Hancock building trying a shot that would be "off the expressway, over the river, off the billboard, through the window, off the wall . . . nothin' but net. . . ." The voice-over concluded, "McDonald's. What you want is what you get . . . and, The ball goes in, nothin' but net."[36]

The importance of Michael Jordan as a global consumer symbol cannot be overstated. In her market survey of global teens, Elissa Moses found that the icon for the Chicago Bulls' basketball team was the 10th most widely recognized brand name in the world. In her words, "Michael Jordan's superstar status elevated the Bulls, in tenth place, higher than the NBA [National Basketball Association], which came in thirteenth."[37] The recognition of both the Bulls' icon and the NBA resulted from a global media effort by the NBA. Moses argued that Nike's use of Jordan in ads made the Nike icon the fourth most recognized among global teens. In her words, Jordan "embodies the essence of far-reaching greatness that is synonymous with the athletic footwear's 'Just Do It' positioning. Utilizing the world wide recognition and admiration of Michael Jordan leverages a core unifier for the brand's growth and continued success."[38]

Advertising columnist for the *Village Voice*, Leslie Savan, argued that White males were attracted to Nike's African-American advertising images out of a desire to be hip. In reference to the concept of "aspiring white Negroes," she wrote, that it could be used as a "label for the whiter hipsters who . . . strive to imitate black male athletes (Nike says 87 percent of its domestic athletic shoes are sold to whites), sneakers tease all men with the possibility of making hipless out of nothingness."[39] Does being hip also mean incorporating fantasizes of African-American male sexuality?

The transformation of America's macho symbol from the White cowboy to the African-American sports star confirms both the integration of the consumer market and the strange perversions of American images. Nineteenth-century White males would not accept an African-American sports star as an image of ideal masculinity. In *Manliness and Civilization*, Gail Bederman described the reaction of White men to African-American boxer Jack Johnson winning the heavyweight boxing championship in 1908. Similar to the emotions that spurred the lynching of African-American men to protect White womanhood, White men reacted as if the triumph of Johnson was a threat to White masculinity. Recognizing this reaction, Johnson made his penis look larger under his boxing trunks by wrapping it in cloth before stepping into the ring. He also found companionship with White women. The question in White men's minds at the time was, according to Bederman, "Did Johnson's success with white women prove him a superior specimen of manhood?"[40] At the time, White men turned to the macho image of Theodore Roosevelt as cowboy and hunter conquering the primitive Indian and demonstrating to Africans his supposed superiority at hunting.

In the later part of the 20th century, as the cowboy image of manhood disappeared from media, the African-American sports star became the new White model of masculinity. One wonders whether this change resulted from White men capitulating to their fantasizes of superior African-American masculinity and sexual prowess. Rather than being threatened by the myth of African-American male superiority, White men now wanted to embody it in their own beings. This could now be done by buying consumer products. Nike ads promised buyers that they could be like Michael Jordan.

MAKING SHOPPING MASCULINE

A dilemma in men's marketing was the early 20th-century public image of women as consumers and men as producers. Men interested in shopping and fashion were considered effeminate. *Esquire* and *Playboy* magazines remedied this situation by combining ads targeted to males with erotic images of women. Supposedly the objectification of women's bodies provided an aura of masculinity to the accompanying shopping ads. By tying sex directly to consumption, the magazines literally wanted to teach men to love shopping.

Esquire pioneered eroticized male consumption. First published in 1933, the core concept of the magazine was articulated by its editor Arnold Gingrich:

> It is our belief, in offering *Esquire* to the American male, that we are only getting around at last to a job that should have been done a long time ago. . . . The general magazines, in the mad scramble to increase the woman readership that seems to be so highly prized by national advertisers, have bent over backwards in catering . . . to the feminine audience.[41]

The founders believed a magazine targeted to the right male demographics would attract national advertisers. Also in the words of historian Kenon Breazeale, "*Esquire's* founders were fearful that their magazine's interest in apparel, food, decor, and so on might make it appear to be targeted at homosexuals."[42]

Designed for upper middle-class males, columns included advice to men on food, drink, gardening, and etiquette. All columns followed an editorial formula supporting the idea that males were actually better than women at cooking, mixing drinks, gardening, and hosting parties. One result was the magazine's success in attracting ads from the beer, wine, and liquor industries. Also the magazine garnered a large number of ads for men's apparel.

To avoid being seen as a magazine for homosexuals, the magazine featured eroticized female images. However, this had to be done in a manner that did not appear pornographic and offend upper middle-class readers. This was accomplished with pinups and centerfolds of illustrations by George Petty, which became known as "Petty Girls." Petty Girls were White women with erotically proportioned large breasts, long slender legs, and small waists and buttocks. In a similar fashion, *Esquire's* covers were noted in the industry for linking "heterosexual social life . . . [with] female anatomy."[43] *Esquire's* cartoons focused on erotic themes with unsuspecting nude women being chanced on by plumbers, burglars, firefighters, and window washers. The favorite, according to Breazeale, was the artist and nude female model where the artist is more interested in leering than painting.[44] Cartoons additionally featured two female types. The gold digger was willing to sell sex, whereas the African-American domestic freely gave it away.

First published in 1953, *Playboy* elaborated on *Esquire's* techniques by incorporating serious fiction and nonfiction with centerfolds, pinups, and advice on cooking, mixing drinks, and male etiquette. Based on *Esquire's* history, Breazeale rejected the often repeated crediting of *Playboy* "with first organizing and exploiting consuming masculine ideological work."[45] After the 1970s, *Playboy* would be accused of exploiting women's bodies for the purpose of stimulating male consumer desires. However, by this time, advertisers were freely targeting male consumers. *Esquire* and *Playboy* paved the way for including men in the advertised consumer's market.

Esquire and *Playboy* provided an alternative fantasy world to that of the cowboy and warrior. Certainly less violent, the *Playboy* man could fantasize mixing drinks for a beautiful woman in a luxury urban apartment, or he could dream of gliding into a nightclub dressed in the height of fashion with a Petty Girl on his arm. He could imagine sipping champagne while soaking in a hot tub filled with nude women. For the suburban male washing his car, there was now the option of escaping through images of the macho cowboy, the warrior, or the debonair womanizer and consumer.

LIBERATING THE TEXTBOOK TOWN HOUSEWIFE
FOR MORE CONSUMPTION

As the color and setting changed in Textbook Town, women's textbook images changed from being a dependent housewife to include personal freedom outside the home. In its 1966 founding statement, the National Organization for Women (NOW) emphasized that public schools were "the key to effective participation in today's economy . . . [and they should educate women] to her full potential of human ability."[46] The organization engaged in a variety of tactics to change women's education ranging from equal treatment in sports programs to eliminating bias in college admissions. Working actively for the passage of Title IX of the 1972 Higher Education Act, NOW could claim an important role in ensuring equal treatment for women in vocational education, athletic programs, textbooks, and the curriculum. The 1976 Educational Equity Act authorized development of a nonsexist curricula for the public schools. Also in the 1970s, the National Women's History Project pressured publishers to include more women's history in public school textbooks.[47]

Besides changes in public school textbooks that resulted in depicting women in a variety of occupations, schools encouraged women's sports and gender-integrated vocational courses. Media responded with movies and TV programs depicting women as professionals, workers, living as independent singles, and divorced. The public images found in the 1950s' Textbook Town became a thing of the past.

New feminist images were used by the advertising industry. Maidenform bra ads showing political buttons on women's chests resulted in double-digit sales increases. The buttons proclaimed, "No Means No," "My Body My Choice," and "Right to Life." The accompanying ad line read, "Isn't it great when a woman's mind gets as much support as her body?"[48] Nike increased its sales to women by 40% in the 1990s with ads designed to make women feel empowered.[49] In contrast to 1920s ads that promised women weight reduction by smoking, Virginia Slims' cigarette ads of the 1970s declared, "You've Come a Long Way, Baby!"[50]

Products originally marketed with dependent and submissive female images were now targeted to independent women. For instance, a 1988 ad for Revlon's Charlie perfume showed the back of a woman and man dressed in business clothes with both carrying briefcases. The woman's hand was shown patting the man's buttock with the caption reading, "She's Very Charlie."[51] In the 1930s, Tampax pioneered independent women's ads by showing a woman diving off a swimming board with the caption, "In 1936, Tampax invented a little something for women who had things to do."[52] In 1990, Tampax ads associated the product with female political activism as represented by environmentalism. The ad featured the Helen Reddy song "I am Woman" with the line, "I am woman, hear me roar, in numbers too big to ignore." The ad opened with newsreel clips of WWII's Women's Air Force. The ad moved to a 1990s scene emphasizing that Tampax was biodegradable. In it a young woman romped in a field of green as a voice-over proclaimed, "We thought you'd feel good knowing that more women trust their bodies to the tampon that's very, very kind to the earth."[53]

The 1950s housewife was reborn in the 1990s as *Good Housekeeping* maga-zine's "The New Traditionalist," which was described as a "reaffirmation of family values unmatched in recent history."[54] The ad language supporting the concept emphasized the ever-present word *choice*. Regarding the issue of work versus staying home, Carl Casselman, creative director of Jordan, McGrath, Case & Taylor, said, "We're saying they have a choice."[55] Suppos-edly the Yankelovich market research firm discovered the New Traditional-ist and described it as a combination of family values of the 1940s and 1950s and personal choice values of the 1960s and 1970s.[56] In ads, personal choice meant consumer choice.

The real meaning of the new educational feminism for advertising and consumerism was exemplified by Parker Pen's 1974 TV ad "Finishing School." Listed by Kanner as one of the top 100 TV ads, the ad opened in a British finishing school where obviously wealthy students were being pre-pared for a final lesson on "how to spend Daddy's lovely money." The teacher commanded, "Checkbooks open, girls. Pens at the ready." When a student pulled out an unacceptable pen, the teacher warned her that she should not shop with a poor quality pen. The teacher gave the girl a Parker Pen in white rolled gold and declared that it was easy to write a check while shopping with "a pen with style, a pen with elan. A Parker lady in white rolled gold. Words just seem to roll from its tip. Signatures just flow with a flourish. Now, then, altogether girls."[57] In this manner, the educational re-forms promising greater independence for women merged in the advertis-ing world with the consumer market.

MOVIES AND THE RACIAL INTEGRATION
OF CAPITALISM

It was the movie industry that actually pioneered the idea of integrating previously excluded racial groups into the general consumer economy. Corresponding with the efforts of the American Way campaign to gain access for probusiness messages in the media, Eric Johnston, president of the U.S. Chamber, replaced Will Hays, who resigned in 1945, as head of the Motion Picture Producers and Distributors of America. Johnston quickly changed the name of the organization to the Motion Picture As-sociation of America. Previous to this appointed, Johnston had pro-claimed that "All Americans are capitalist."[58]

Eric Johnston believed that integration of all racial groups into the American consumer market was necessary for the United States to gain eco-nomic superiority over the Soviet Union. Johnston brought to Hollywood an economic vision formed during his years as businessman and president of the U.S. Chamber of Commerce. Born in 1896 in Spokane, Washington,

Johnston organized a successful electrical supply company in Spokane and became active in local civic affairs. In 1931, he became president of the Spokane Chamber of Commerce and in 1942 president of the U.S. Chamber of Commerce. His economic views were explained in his 1944 book, *America Unlimited: The Case for a People's Capitalism.*

Similar to the American Way public relations campaign, Johnston advocated greater cooperation between local Chambers of Commerce and school systems to ensure that educational programs served the needs of American business. Johnston believed economic prosperity required some collaboration between business and government. Johnston wrote, "Americans will accept collective action through their government but only to achieve purposes which cannot be achieved by private capital."[59]

Ending racism was part of Johnston's economic agenda. A member of the NAACP, he proclaimed racism a destructive economic force because it kept businesses from adequately using human resources because they could not hire the best workers. In the book's conclusion, he used the image of blending metals to describe the importance of developing racial and cultural tolerance in American society. He wrote, "It is thus with the American, who fuses in his blood and his spirit the virtues and vitalities of many races, creeds, and cultures-giving us an amalgam that is new, unique, and immeasurably strong. That is why tolerance is necessarily and rightly a supreme American characteristic." Johnston claimed it was only "crackpots and psychopaths . . . who teach race hatreds."[60]

In a 1945 speech to the Writers' War Board, Johnston tied the theme of intolerance to the management of public opinion. Linking prejudice and intolerance to the quality of the American economy, he called on the gathered writers and their colleagues in the movies, theater, radio, and the press to use their influence to fight racism. "You are the people with direct access to the mind," he told the writers, "and what is more important, to the heart and emotions of the American people." He urged them to work cooperatively to eliminate racism. "Surely," he told the writers, "the businessman and the artist share responsibility in eradicating the myth of group or class superiority." Again he stressed the importance of eliminating intolerance for economic development: "Wherever we erect barriers on the grounds of race and religion, or of occupational or professional status, we hamper the fullest expansion of our economic society. Intolerance is destructive. Prejudice produces no wealth. Discrimination is a fool's economy."[61]

During Johnston's early years in Hollywood, major studios were willing to explore racial themes. Two important films produced by Darryl Zanuck, *Gentleman's Agreement (1947)* and *Pinky (1949),* dealt with the issue of prejudice. *Pinky* created a stir in Southern states in its portrayal of a White-skinned but partly African-American nurse who traveled from the North to Mississippi.

Another movie, *Lost Boundaries*, was banned in Memphis, Tennessee, because it dealt with "social equality between whites and Negroes in a way that we do not have in the South."[62] The movie portrayed the problems of an African-American physician who passes as White. In *1949*, the Supreme Court of Tennessee upheld the right of the Memphis censorship board to ban the movie *Curley* because it showed, according to the chair of the censorship board, "little negroes [mixed with whites in a classroom], as the South does not permit negroes in white schools nor recognize social equality between the races even in children."[63] Eric Johnston reacted to the Curley decision with the vow that the MPA "intends to meet the issue of political censorship head-on in the highest court."[64]

It was the U.S. Supreme Court's ruling on *Pinky* that finally resolved the issue of municipal and state censorship boards prohibiting the showing of films dealing with racial issues. In 1952, the U.S. Supreme Court overturned the conviction of a Texas theater owner for showing *Pinky*. The *Pinky* case limited the ability of Southern censors to ban movies containing racial themes. The decision dealt with the denial by the censors in Marshall, Texas, to license a showing of *Pinky* because the film was "of such character to be prejudicial to the best interests of the people of said City." The theater owner ignored the ban and was convicted of violating the local censorship law. The U.S. Supreme Court dismissed the conviction as a violation of the First Amendment. This court decision supported Johnston's hopes of achieving racially integrated capitalism with movies that dealt realistically with racial issues.[65]

ADDING COLOR TO TV

It was not just a matter of racial inclusion. It was also a matter of racial stereotypes. This was the major issue over the representation of people of color on TV. For instance, when "Amos 'n' Andy" made its debut on CBS in 1951 with an all African-American cast, the NAACP immediately campaigned to get it off the air. CBS founder William Paley recalled, "Five days after the first broadcast, the National Association for the Advancement of Colored People denounced the show as insulting to blacks. The television show, under attack by black leaders for its entire life, left the network after two seasons."[66] The protest, according to Historian Thomas Cripps, came from the African-American middle class because they worried that the program left audiences with the impression that all African Americans were ignorant and rowdy. According to Cripps, the African-American community was divided over the program. African-American actors saw the program opening doors to employment, whereas other African Americans enjoyed the program and questioned the charge of racism. The sponsor of the program, Blatz Beer, released a poll showing that 77% of African-American New Yorkers liked the program.[67]

Ebony's editors and the NAACP, according to Cripps, led "the black middle class in challeng[ing] what they took to be a parody of their historical struggle for social mobility in a hostile society."[68] In fact, the NAACP was not successful in convincing all African Americans that the show was their enemy. Cripps concluded that Blatz withdrew its sponsorship for a more prestigious show, the "Four Star Playhouse," and not because of the objections of the NAACP.[69] In the light of Cripps' argument, it would be difficult to claim a major victory for the NAACP, but one could assume that the organization's protest played some role in Blatz's decision to end its sponsorship.

Television advertisers and programmers were caught between potential objections from civil rights groups representing non-White racial groups and racist White viewers. As civil rights activities increased in the 1950s, many advertisers refused to sponsor programs that might give the impression of supporting civil rights. One of the first victims of these fears was a 1957–1958 miniseries on the Civil War called "The Gray Ghost." The series presented a romantic portrayal of Confederate Colonel John Singleton Mosby and his band of raiders. It premiered in September 1957 when the civil rights confrontations occurred at Central High School in Little Rock, Arkansas. Fearing entanglement in civil rights issues, advertisers withdrew support from the program. Another source of problems were TV broadcasts of movies. In 1957, many Southern stations refused to air the African-American musical *Cabin in the Sky*. Broadcasts of the movies *Go, Man, Go*, about the Harlem Globetrotters, and *The Jackie Robinson Story* met with Southern resistance. In the early 1960s, Monitor South was organized to coordinate the denial network programming involving racial themes and social equality.[70]

Networks tried to balance these conflicting pressures by, as NBC named its policy in the 1950s, *integration without identification*. This meant the avoidance of racial themes on TV, but the use of African-American actors in minor parts. In 1957, an NBC official stated: "It is so easy, really, in casting for sympathetically portrayed roles to hire actors whose racial derivation is apparent . . . I hope you have noticed here and there everything from taxidrivers to newspapermen, from doctors to social workers, played by competent Negro actors or actors of other racial minority derivation."[71]

These slight gains did not appease civil rights organizations. Under continued criticism, CBS announced in 1962 a policy of "no discrimination because of race, creed, religion, or national origin." In 1963, the American Federation of Television and Radio Artists issued a declaration of nonbias. Yet these pronouncements seemed to have little effect on the actual images in TV programming. A survey in 1963 found that a New York City viewer on an average evening would see three African Americans, only one of these for longer than 1 minute. An editorial in the *Daily Defender* on June 11, 1963, complained that "the TV industry as a whole is still perpetuating a picture of lily-white America on video in keeping with the 'boob tube' concept."[72]

The pressure of political events forced a revolution in African-American TV images. The 1963 March on Washington set the stage for a number of TV documentaries. ABC produced a five-part series, "Crucial Summer," presenting African Americans in a heroic struggle to overcome segregation and prejudice. Featured on the series were Roy Wilkins and Martin Luther King, Jr. An NBC special, "The American Revolution of '63," devoted 5½ hours over 5 weeks to examining the civil rights movement.[73]

A 1966 U.S. Court of Appeals' decision forced Southern TV stations to show programs with racial themes. The case involved TV station WLBT in Jackson, Mississippi. The first complaints against the station were made in 1955 to the Federal Communications Commission (FCC) when a network program on race relations featuring the General Counsel of the NAACP was cut off and replaced by a sign flashing "Sorry, Cable Trouble." Complaints were again lodged in 1957 for the broadcast of a program urging racial segregation, and the subsequent refusals by the station to broadcast opposing viewpoints. Similar charges regarding the presentation of only one viewpoint were filed in 1962 after the outbreak of civil rights demonstrations at the University of Mississippi.[74]

The U.S. Court of Appeals considered the case after the FCC granted a 1-year license renewal over petitioners' protests. The Court's ruling made it possible for organized groups to directly influence the broadcasting industry. Five years after the decision, the journal *Broadcasting* summarized the impact of the decision:

> The case did more than establish the right of the public to participate in a station's license renewal hearing. It did even more than encourage minority groups around the country to assert themselves in broadcast matters at a time when unrest was growing and blacks were becoming more activist. It provided practical lessons in how pressure could be brought, in how the broadcast establishment could be challenged.[75]

Greater public participation made it easier to challenge images disseminated by TV. Media advocacy groups were formed representing African Americans, women, homosexuals, and others. The TV industry now confronted a variety of organizations concerned about the image of their constituents on TV.

Besides the NAACP and CORE, groups such as NOW set up special media task forces. In 1970, NOW announced its intention to change "the derogatory, demeaning and stereotyped images of women presented by broadcast programming and advertising."[76] Other groups organized to protect their TV images, including the National Black Media Coalition, the Italian-American League to Combat Defamation, the German-American Anti-Defamation League, the Polish-American Guardian Society, the Tribal Indian Land Rights Association, and the Gay Media Task Force. Tom Kersey, an ABC vice-president, estimated at the time that "any challenge to a station would be an enormous threat. [And] one of our stations was worth between $35 and $40 million."[77]

The result was an interplay between the desires of advocacy groups to manage TV images and the needs of the TV industry to control the power of the advocacy groups. In *Target: Prime Time: Advocacy Groups and the Struggle over Entertainment Television,* Kathryn Montgomery traced the history of strategies developed by the networks for controlling advocacy groups. For instance, Mexican Americans protested TV characters showing Mexican Americans as meek and hat in hand. The advocacy group Justicia demanded TV networks put aside $10 million for shows portraying Chicano characters in a positive manner. In 1971, Justicia launched challenges to all California TV licenses. Justicia was joined by the Mexican-American Anti-Defamation Committee, the League of United Latino Citizens, and the National Latino Media Coalition to drive two well-known Mexican-American characters off the TV screen. One was the "Frito Bandito" used in commercials for Frito Corn Chips. The cartoon character was charged with creating a racist image of Mexican Americans as sneaky thieves. Another was "Jose Jimenez," who, it was charged, created the image of Mexican Americans being happy go lucky and not very bright. In response, ABC began hiring technical consultants from advocacy groups. ABC invited leaders from Justicia to review scripts containing Mexican-American characters. This policy did not stop criticism of networks' failure to include Mexican-American characters in programs. In addition, advocacy groups were invited to prescreen programs, and networks began to hire minorities into their departments of standards and practices.[78]

Which group represented a particular community? For instance, should Mexican Americans be represented by Justicia or the Mexican-American Anti-Defamation Committee? This question was answered by the one-voice concept, where a network identified a single organization to represent a whole group. Of course TV networks worked with the most moderate organizations. In the case of Mexican Americans, the networks finally decided to work closely with the Nosotros, an advocacy group for Latino actors, rather than more politically active groups. Summarizing the evolution of network management of advocacy groups, Montgomery concluded that advocacy groups "would encounter a team of experts within the networks, equipped with a sophisticated set of skills and strategies designed to minimize disruption and maximize friendly, cooperative relationships."[79]

According to Montgomery, gay activists groups were the most effective in changing network policies. One reason was the large number of gays employed by the industry. Many of these insiders supplied information to outside organizations. For instance, a script for an upcoming episode of "Marcus Welby, M.D." was smuggled out of ABC in 1973 and given to the Gay Activist Alliance (GAA). In the episode, Marcus Welby advises a married man concerned about his homosexual tendencies that he would not fail as a husband and father if he suppressed his gay tendencies. The smuggled script caused angry members of the GAA to descend on network offices. Afterward networks consulted regularly with gay activists about any scripts dealing with homosexuality.[80]

An integrated TV market occurred with the program "All in the Family." The genius of the program was its appeal to both White racist and non-White groups. The main character was the racist and bigoted Archie Bunker. Norman Lear, the program's producer, consciously sought to fight racism and bigotry by having Archie use words such as *spades, spics, spooks, schwartzes, coons, coloreds,* and *chinks.* The program broke all the traditional TV taboos by dealing with issues such as homosexuality, race, female equality, and birth control. A spin-off program, "Maude," caused a storm of protest the following year when it dealt with the issue of abortion. *Time* magazine noted in 1972 that in the wake of "All in the Family" there were 20 new series dealing with controversial themes.[81]

Although "All in the Family" dealt with White racism, the majority of TV shows presented non-White characters as assimilated into White culture or as unrealistic cultural images. During what media historian J. Fred MacDonald called "The Golden Age of Blacks in Television: The Late 1960s," there were over two dozen programs featuring African Americans as leading characters. In addition, there were 19 TV series with supporting African-American characters. Programs with leading roles played by African Americans ranged from "I Spy" and "Mission Impossible" to "The Bill Cosby Show" and "The Young Lawyers." MacDonald contended that "I Spy" had the greatest effect. The show was the first network dramatic series to feature an African-American actor, Bill Cosby. Cosby's character projected a new image of African Americans to White TV audiences. He was equal to White characters in his encounters with foreign spies, women, government leaders, and criminals. In an early episode, he committed the revolutionary act, at least for TV, of kissing a Japanese woman. Cosby's character broke the unspoken TV taboo against showing African Americans kissing and demonstrating affection.[82]

Television images were integrated without any major changes in content. Cosby's part on "I Spy" could have been played by a White without any noticeable change in the character. Certainly, Cosby was not playing a part that would have required an African American. No major African-American themes or issues were raised by the program. In fact, "The Bill Cosby Show," which by the 1990s was the most popular program on TV, featured an African-American family that could have been easily interchanged with any White upper middle-class family.

The major complaints about TV programs featuring African Americans was their depiction, or lack of depiction, of African-American culture. After reviewing the history of African-American sitcoms in the 20th century, Angela Nelson wrote, "Black sitcoms are not 'Black' in that they exhibit an African American world view or a Black philosophy of life. Rather, they are 'Black' because the performers are Black and their characters are supposedly dealing with their sitcom situations from a 'Black' perspective."[83] She argued that the TV shows "Julia" and "The Bill Cosby Show" in the late 1960s presented African-American characters as fully integrated into White culture. In the 1970s, TV introduced a form of assimilated hybrid minstrelsy or coon characters in the programs "The Jeffersons" and "Sanford and Son." In the 1980s and 1990s, the most popular African-American TV show was Bill Cosby's "The Cosby Show." Although it avoided *coon characters*, the program portrayed the life of an upper middle-class African-American family that was fully assimilated into White culture.[84]

The transformation of Native American characters was the most unrealistic integration of positive non-White images. Traditionally, Indians in movies and TV programs were portrayed, except for those who were subservient to Whites such as Tonto in "The Lone Ranger" radio and TV series, as blood-thirsty savages fighting against the expansion of the noble White settlers and cowboys into the West. After the civil rights movement, Native American images were pacified and portrayed as protectors of nature and the environment. Suddenly Native American rituals became popular spiritual events rather than pagan affronts to Christianity. The romanticization of Native American life, like the portrayal of African Americans assimilated into White culture, provided images that were unrealistic and characterized Indians as the exotic other.[85]

This transition in Native American images was exemplified by an ad selected by Kanner as one of the top 100. Research found that the ad was the most recognized in the 1970s. Entitled "Keep America Beautiful: Crying Indian," the 1970 TV ad opened with Cherokee Iron Eyes Cody paddling a canoe past smokestacks onto a littered beach. A voice-over complained, "Some people have a deep, abiding respect for the beauty that was once this country. And some people don't." Then an unfinished fast-food meal was tossed from a passing car landing at Cody's feet. The announcer concluded, "People start pollution; people can stop it."[86]

Highlighting the transition in Native American images was that fact that Iron Eyes Cody originally acted in many cowboy movies opposite John Wayne. The ad was paid for by Keep America Beautiful advocacy group and, according to Kanner, "it has amassed 24 billion-plus household impressions, more than any other single TV spot—both commercial and public—in the history of television. Research showed that during the 1970s, 94 percent of viewers recognized the ad."[87] The ad campaign's printed posters showed Cody's head and braids with an overlaid title "Pollution: It's a crying Shame."[88]

Civil rights, advocacy groups, and market research changed TV programming. There appeared positive TV images, and sometimes overromanticized images, of all racial groups. Watching TV, all groups could now feel part of the American dream. Of particular importance were TV ads that brought all people together in the same consumer market.

THE UNDERCLASS AND BIG BIRD: THE GROWTH OF
A COMMON MEDIA AND CONSUMER EXPERIENCE

Originally "Sesame Street" was targeted at underclass children, but it eventually became a common media and consumer experience for many American children. It exemplified the integration of Textbook Town by showing children engaged in interracial and intercultural play, singing, and acting. As in Textbook Town, people were generally happy in "Sesame Street."

"Sesame Street" was and is important as a common cultural experience that created common cultural icons in the public mind such as Big Bird, Bert and Ernie, Oscar the Grouch, and Elmo. Most college students raised in the United States respond "yes" when I ask, "Did you learn the alphabet and numbers while watching 'Sesame Street'." Besides being a common educational experience, the program became a common consumer experience with brand-name product spin-offs including dolls, videos, and games.

Intended as an educational program for underclass children, "Sesame Street" was inspired by a belief that TV could be both an educator and a social reformer. The program was first shown in 1969 when race riots were occurring across the country. Originally it was thought of as an educational tool that would break the cycle of poverty. The program was created by the Children's Television Workshop with funding from the Carnegie Corporation and the Ford Foundation. The development of educational children's TV programs was considered necessary, in the words of one federal official, Lee Loevinger, because commercial TV was "the literature of the illiterate; the culture of the lowbrow; the wealth of the poor; the privilege of the underprivileged; the exclusive club of the excluded masses . . . a golden goose that lays scrambled eggs."[89]

In the 1960s, there was strong criticism of the 1950s' image of the housewife using TV as a babysitter, particularly in low-income families. Television was considered a source of intellectual pap for the masses. In the 1960s, Arthur Schlesinger, Jr., historian and advisor to Senator Adlai Stevenson and President John F. Kennedy, worried that TV was breeding disrespect for intellectuals and destroying the quality of American life. "I cannot repress my feelings," he wrote, "that in the main, television has been a great bust." He urged government to improve the quality of TV "because there seems no other way to rescue television from the downward spiral of competitive debasement."[90] Child-care advocate Dr. Benjamin Spock wrote President Kennedy that instead of TV instilling virtue in the citizen, "there is the constant search for the commonest level of taste in passive entertainment . . . used, in turn, to sell goods, in a manner which breeds insincerity and cynicism, and which appeals always to more gratification."[91] Writing in the *Saturday Review*, critic Robert Lewis Shayon expressed disgust at a *1958* episode of "Leave It to Beaver" where the main character was upset at a school IQ text that accidentally classified him as a genius. Beaver was portrayed as shunning the title of *genius*. For Shayon, this was another example of TV appealing to the masses by deprecating the intellect.[92]

The Carnegie Corporation, a major funder of "Sesame Street," sponsored the Carnegie Commission on Educational Television, which issued reports criticizing children's TV. The president of the Carnegie Corporation, Alan Pifer, was concerned with both poverty and the quality of TV. He believed the Carnegie Corporation should support "four basic principles: the right to a job for anyone who needs to or wants to work; equal opportunity and fair rewards for everyone in all sectors of employment; development and utilization of the abilities of every citizen; and maximum flexibility for each person in the organization of his or her own pattern of life."[93] Reflecting in 1982 on the activities of the Carnegie Corporation, Pifer wrote that without programs of social justice and welfare,

> there lies nothing but increasing hardship for ever-growing numbers, a mounting possibility of severe social unrest, and the consequent development among the upper classes and the business community of fear for the survival of our capitalist economic system. Just as we built the general welfare state in the 1930s and expanded it in the 1960s as a safety valve for the easing of social tension, so will we do it again in the 1980s. Any other path is simply too risky.[94]

In the minds of all those involved in "Sesame Street," TV was the third educational institution along with the family and public schools. Also there was the hope that TV would be a better educator than the public schools and save the entire educational system. This utopian vision included the time-honored belief from the 19th century that education could end poverty by preparing students for equal participation in competition for jobs— or in other words, equality of opportunity. In 1967, the Carnegie Corporation's Commission on Educational Television recommended that TV be used for the promotion of social justice and education. In reference to the educational potential of TV, the Commission's report stated, "Important as this can be for adults, the informal educational potential of Public Television is greatest of all for children."[95] The Commission suggested that TV focus on preparing preschool children for formal education. "Public Television programs," the report stated, "should give great attention to the informal educational needs of preschool children, particularly to interest and help children whose intellectual and cultural preparation might otherwise be less than adequate."[96]

Lloyd Morrisett played a leading role in "Sesame Street's" creation. He believed TV could be a substitute for the national shortage of kindergarten and nursery schools. Believing preschool education was important for the cognitive development of children, he worried that preschool programs "would slowly, if at all, reach many of the children who needed them, particularly underprivileged children for whom preschool facilities might not be available."[97] The answer to this problem, he felt, lay in the ability of TV to reach enormous numbers of preschool children. As Morrisett conceptualized the project, TV could be a partner with public schools in the general education of children. It would be the third educator. "The real answer to problems of early education," Morrisett wrote, "is for the total culture of childhood, including television as an important element, to work in harmony with the family and later the school."[98]

In 1968, the Children's Television Workshop was organized, and on November 10, 1969, the first production of "Sesame Street" was broadcast. The chief advisor and chairman to the Board of Advisors was Gerald Lesser, Bigelow Professor of Education and Developmental Psychology at Harvard. Lesser was the guiding hand in developing educational goals for "Sesame Street." Unlike many others, Lesser felt education was limited in its role in solving the world's problems. He wrote that, "Educators cannot remedy the injustices to minorities in our society or create new life styles or new communities to replace deteriorating ones. Yet they sometimes act as if they think they can." This attitude tempered the original focus on helping children of the poor.[99] Although Lesser saw a limited educational role in social reform, he did believe that something drastic should be done about educational problems in the United States. Writing about the $50 billion that was spent on a "massive educational superstructure which holds captive over fifty million children," he complained, "we are failing to educate our children, either disastrously or to a degree no worse than the failures of other social and political institutions, is almost beyond dispute."[100]

Lesser hoped TV would rescue the entire educational system from failure. He believed TV instruction could be superior to public school instruction. Public schooling, he maintained, depended on control of the student by others, public humiliation, and the continuous threat of failure. Television contained none of these elements. In front of the TV, Lesser argued, the child learned without fear of a teacher and threats of humiliation. The TV set could not punish the child. In addition, the child could control the learning process by controlling the TV set. Therefore, Lesser believed that TV was an ideal educator because it was not punitive and provided a shelter from the emotional stress of society. "We may regret the conditions in our society that make sanctuaries necessary and must guard against a child's permanent retreat into them," Lesser wrote, "but sanctuaries are needed, and television is one of the few shelters children have."[101]

Lesser believed TV was a superior teacher because it could be entertaining. He argued that traditional educators separated entertainment from education. In fact, many believed that entertainment would contaminate education. Lesser referred to this as a *lunatic* view of education and thought TV was an ideal vehicle for educating through entertainment.

Besides lauding the potential educational value of TV, Lesser was impressed by the statistics on TV viewing. Using calculations made in 1967, Lesser estimated that in homes with preschool children the TV was on 54 hours per week. On the average, a high school graduate spent 12,000 hours in school and 15,000 hours watching TV. In fact, the high school graduate spent more time watching TV than was spent at any other activity.

The use of TV as an educator seemed to contradict charges that TV viewing was a passive and mind-numbing experiencing. Lesser argued that a great deal of learning takes place through modeling. Children do not need to interact to learn, according to Lesser; they can model themselves after TV characters. In fact, modeling fit Lesser's concept of a nonpunitive form of education. "The child," Lesser wrote, "imitates the model without being induced or compelled to do so. . . . By watching televised models, children learn both socially desirable and undesirable behaviors."[102] Television, Lesser argued, could provide models that demonstrated acceptable behaviors.

In addition to modeling behavior, Lesser believed TV could create myths to guide children's actions. In Lesser's words, TV could provide "a vision of the world as it might be." These myths were created by the presentation of what Lesser called *simple goodness*. He believed that children did not learn from preaching. Considering TV's role in presenting life's tensions and deprivations, Lesser reasoned, "Surely it can create others that help them toward a more humane vision of life."[103]

The decision was made to present urban life as "a vision of the world as it might be" and not reality. "Sesame Street" joined Textbook Town in presenting scenes of a harmonious world. Lesser believed that little could be gained in showing to the child living in an urban ghetto the harsh realities of life. As program planning evolved, there was a drift toward presenting the sweeter side of life. In giving only the positive side, they realized that they might be accused of presenting a sugar-coated world. This approach was by a program designed to show children how an urban bus driver and passengers acted on a trip around the city. "Now, we all know that a bus driver is often not our best example of someone who is courteous and civil," Lesser wrote. "But on the 'Sesame Street' bus trip, the driver responds to his passengers' hellos and thank-yous, tells a child who cannot locate his money, 'That's all right, you can pay me tomorrow,' and upon seeing a young woman running after his bus just as it has left the curb, actually stops to let her on." Lesser referred to this as an "outrageous misrepresentation" of most urban transportation systems, but he justified it as presenting a model of behavior that would guide children to a better world. Lesser maintained, "We wanted to show the child what the world is like when people treat each other with decency and consideration. Our act of faith . . . was that young children will learn such attitudes if we take the trouble to show them some examples, even if we stretch familiar reality a bit in order to do so."[104]

Given the desire to present a model of an idealized world, "Sesame Street" was harmoniously and racially integrated. Like the new Textbook Town of the 1960s, this presentation sugar-coated the harsh realities of racial conflict in American society. A criticism that Lesser recognized was that the program taught "minority-group children to accept quietly middle class America's corrupt demands to subjugate themselves."[105]

Although doubting the ability of educational TV to end poverty, Lesser did believe TV was the key to reforming the educational system. He wanted to create a program for all children. In Lesser's words, "To succeed, a national television series must attract as large a national audience as possible, including children from all social classes and cultural groups and from all geographic regions."[106] The decision to seek a national audience resulted in "Sesame Street" becoming a common cultural experience. Yet this also created a fear that the program might increase the educational gap between poor and rich children. Lesser wrote, "We hoped that poor children would learn as much and that the gap would not be widened, despite the fact that almost all comparisons of educational progress show middle-class children proceeding more rapidly."[107] The solution he offered was to make the series appealing to low-income children and to encourage viewing in low-income families. Although Lesser felt negatively about public schooling, he argued that the only realistic goal was to emphasize an education that would prepare children to enter school. This approach tied the program directly to the needs of formal schooling.

Preparing children for school and helping low-income children determined the basic shape of "Sesame Street." The staff believed that low-income parents wanted their children to achieve in the basic subjects of reading, writing, and arithmetic. The major complaint of these parents, the staff understood, was the failure of the school to teach these subjects. Therefore, the staff concluded that the program should focus on preparation for learning these subjects in school. According to Lesser, teaching the alphabet was the most controversial decision on preparation for school. This created "howls of repugnance . . . over . . . use of the new technology to teach what appears to be an arbitrary and useless skill."[108] Yet, it was argued that the alphabet was essential for early reading. What TV could accomplish was to make memorizing the alphabet a form of entertainment.

During its early years, "Sesame Street" scored a major success in reaching low-income children. During its first year, almost 50% of the potential preschool audience was estimated to have watched the program, including children in day care and other prekindergarten programs serving poor children. The program was watched by 91% of the at-home children in low-income Bedford-Stuyvesant and Harlem sections of New York City. Eighty-eight percent of low-income families interviewed in Chicago tuned their sets to "Sesame Street."[109]

Similar to advertising efforts to convince housewives to watch daytime TV and use it as a babysitter, advertising campaigns were used to attract viewers to "Sesame Street." This advertising effort included "Sesame Street" clubs, door-to-door solicitation of viewers, a *Sesame Street Magazine*, and announcements in libraries, schools, and community organizations. In Chicago, 120 mothers in low-income areas conducted "Sesame Street" viewing sessions. A similar project was conducted in the Mexican-American section of Los Angeles. The Children's Television Workshop ran a Neighborhood Youth Corps Project that involved adolescents from poor families in teaching preschool children and focused on viewing "Sesame Street." During the first year, 240 adolescents worked in viewing centers with 1,500 children. The following year, the numbers increased to 1,200 adolescents helping 15,000 low-income children of the poor in 13 different cities. By 1972, there were 10,000 tutors helping 100,000 preschool children in viewing centers.[110]

Even in the 21st century, "Sesame Street" was marketed as an educational package for caregivers, including preschool programs, babysitters, and parents. On its 2002 Web site, Big Bird was shown standing next to a range of caregivers with the message, "Just like you, part of our work is to find new ways to reach and teach children . . . we want to meet the needs of our 2- and 4-year-old viewers by appealing to the way they think, learn, and explore."[111] In keeping with its idealized world, the Web site announced four new programs designed to help children cope with the September 11, 2002, destruction of the World Trade Center. "The season's premiere episode," the Web site stated, "features a group of heroes from Ground Zero. New York City firefighters arrive on Sesame Street after Alan extinguishes a fire at Hooper's Store. Elmo is frightened at first, but feels much safer after spending time with the firefighters, who take him—and viewers—on a tour of a working firehouse."[111]

Also by the 21st century, the program had created a new consumer market. Elmo, Ernie, Bert, Big Bird, and the Cookie Monster became national icons to sell brand-named products. As icons associated with an educational TV program, they could give brand-named products an aura of educational value.

As caregivers seated their charges in front of the TV to watch "Sesame Street," the were preparing preschoolers for product recognition of toys manufactured by Mattel, Fisher-Price, and Arco. Elmo served as a product figure for Mattel's *Elmo's Dance and Learn Game*, whereas other "Sesame Street" figures were used to sell their puzzles *Puzzle* and *Puzzle: "What's Wrong with this Picture."* Arco toys offered *Sesame Street Games: Electronic Cookie Monster's Kitchen Game* and *Elmo's Count & Pop Balloon Game*. These were only a few of the games and puzzles offered with "Sesame Street" icons, others included *Cookie Monster Wood Board, Sesame Street 24-piece, Big Bird Wood Board,* and *Ernie Wood Board.*[112]

The games and puzzles might be educational, but it would be a stretch of the imagination to label as educational the top-selling "Sesame Street" products. In May 2002, the Amazon Web site listed as the top-selling "Sesame Street" spin-offs an Elmo doll called *Let's Pretend Elmo* and in second place the *Talk With Elmo Cell Phone*. The third and fourth places were occupied by the Fisher-Price's *Sesame Street 11" Baby Tickle Me Big Bird Doll* and *Rock 'N Roll Elmo* (an Elmo doll holding a guitar).[113]

I recognize that commercial children's TV is more exploitive than "Sesame Street." However, "Sesame Street" is packaged as an educational program and promoted for use in day-care centers, preschool programs, and home care. It also has a reputation for promoting cultural and racial harmony and positive gender role models for girls and boys. Also it deals with issues affecting children from low-income families.

"Sesame Street" serves as a good example of the marriage of education, advertising, and consumerism in creating common cultural and consumer knowledge among America's children. "Sesame Street" teaches consumerism by creating brand loyalty or, in this case, loyalty to brand icons. The benign atmosphere created by the educational aspects of the program act as a soft sell. Both children and parents learn to trust characters such as Elmo and Big Bird as they entertain, teach, and provide models of good behavior and a happy world. Those exposed to "Sesame Street" recognize Fisher-Price, Mattel, and Arco toys using "Sesame Street" icons or figures. The trust in the "Sesame Street" figure is transferred from the program to the toy. In this manner, generations of preschoolers learn to trust and shop for familiar brands.

CONCLUSION: ALL PEOPLE CAN CONSUME

An important accomplishment of the civil rights movement was an integration of the consumer market. Positive, if sometimes distorted, images of non-White groups now appeared in textbooks, advertising, movies, and TV. The 1950s suburban-housewife image was replaced with a multitasking woman who could make a choice among being a housewife, an independent-living careerist, or married with a job. The struggle for consumer equality reached preschool children through "Sesame Street." In all cases, equality often meant equality of opportunity to consume.

Consumerism was able to absorb social justice issues and turn them into marketing opportunities. The next stage in consumerism's triumph over the public mind was the themed environment. Beginning with Disneyland and McDonald's in the 1950s, theming quickly spilled over into public spaces with naming rights for sports stadiums, parks, and other public sites being sold to the highest bidders. Every place, including schools, became a marketing opportunity. Consumerism found every opportunity to slip into the public mind as brand loyalty offered certainty in a rapidly changing world.

Chapter 7

Sonya's Choice:
Fast-Food Education

Repeating Sonya's declaration in *Salome of the Tenements*, "Talk about democracy. . . . All I want is to be able to wear silk stockings and Paris hats the same as Mrs. Astorbilt, and then it wouldn't bother me if we have Bolshevism or Capitalism, or if the democrats or the republicans win."[1] To describe is not to criticize. Sonya's choice seems to fulfill the wishes of large numbers of the world's population. Many rush to the integrated life of production, schools, advertising, media, and commodified leisure. Brand loyalty is global and provides a level of certainty in a transient and fluid global society. People relate through the brands they wear, drive, and eat. The world's consumer economy fulfills Simon Patten's vision of consumption spurring humans to work harder for increased production and consumption. People seek entry into national economies that promise greater access to goods resulting in migrations that uproot families and result in cultural conflicts. For many, the modern consumer society is desirable.

This book's goal is to describe the history of the interrelationship among schools, advertising, and media in the evolution of U.S. consumer society. Of primary concern is understanding how future citizens—namely, children—learn to be consumer-citizens. "Sesame Street" exemplifies the marriage of preschool education and media in consumer training and sustains the goal of TV executives in the 1950s of using daytime TV as a babysitter. There are, of course, earlier examples of media and babysitting, such as in the 1930s when students spent after-school hours listening to advertising jingles accompanying their favorite radio programs. Schools remain important sites for consumer education, with advertising invading school buildings, students wearing clothes sporting designer logo, and corporate mate-

182

rials being used in classroom instruction. The early 20th-century dream of women escaping the drudgery of cooking is now realized in the plentiful availability of processed foods and in quick trips to fast-food franchises that also serve as an entertainment spot for children. Commodified entertainment, theme parks, and fast-food establishments seduce children into buying product spin-offs from movies and TV programs.

In this concluding chapter, I examine the education of consumer-citizens in schools and in desiring communities such as theme parks and fast-food establishments. All of these sites in some manner bring together education, advertising, and media in the promotion of a consumerist ideology.

EDUCATING FOR CONSUMPTION

Education is now a form of consumerism. College education is marketed through paid advertising. Textbooks are peddled to local school districts and state departments of education. The importance of the prom declined during the anticonsumerism period of the 1970s, but was reborn in the 1990s as an important element in graduating a full-fledge shopper.[2] Even standardized testing is a consumer item with organizations such as the Educational Testing Service buying advertising space to proclaim that Americans "are united-by race, ethnicity, age, income level, and political persuasion—in the belief that increased resources [for education] and increased accountability [testing] go together."[3] Appearing in the *New York Times*, and possibly other newspapers, the ad was a response to the impression created by newspaper headlines "that," according to the president of Educational Testing Service, Kurt Landgraf, "Americans are sick and tired of standardized tests in schools."[4] In the ad, Landgraf tries to assure readers that these protests are the actions of marginal groups.

Schools are consumer sites. Alex Molnar, author of the best-selling book, *Giving Kids the Business: The Commercialization of America's Schools* and head of the University of Wisconsin's Center for the Analysis of Commercialism in Education, details the extremes that companies, such as Coca-Cola and Pepsi-Cola, use to advertise and sell their products in schools.[5] On September 14, 2000, the U.S. General Accounting Office released a report on the commercialization of U.S. schools. The report stated,

> In-school marketing has become a growing industry. Some marketing professionals are increasingly targeting children in schools, companies are becoming known for their success in negotiating contracts between school districts and beverage companies, and both educators and corporate managers are attending conferences to learn how to increase revenue from in-school marketing for their schools and companies.[6]

The General Accounting Office found the following:

1. About 25% of the nation's middle and high schools now show Channel One, a broadcast of news features and commercials.
2. Two hundred school districts signed exclusive contracts with soft-drink companies to sell their beverages in schools.
3. Students using computers in classrooms are being offered incentives to enter personal data—names, addresses, information on personal habits—which is then sold to advertisers.[7]

Other examples abound including, as I discuss later, the involvement of the fast-food industry in education. In "Education and Commercialization: Raising Awareness and Making Wise Decisions," Lynn Schrum provides other instances of advertising in schools:

1. Eli Lilly representatives discuss Prozac to high school students in Washington, DC.
2. Procter & Gamble sponsors oral hygiene classes in elementary school in return for distributing samples of Crest.
3. National Soft Drink Association provides a poster entitled, "Soft Drinks and Nutrition."
4. M&M candy company declares nutritional value in their products.
5. McGraw-Hill's math book, *Mathematics: Applications and Connections*, currently in use by sixth-, seventh-, and eight-grade students in at least 16 states, inserts products such as Barbie dolls, Big Macs, and Oreo cookies right into math problems. For example, "Will is saving his allowance to buy a pair of Nike shoes that cost $68.25. If Will earns $3.25 per week, how many weeks will Will need to save?"[8]

TEXTBOOKS: ENVIRONMENTALISM
AS THE NEW ENEMY

Since the disappearance of Russian communism in the 1990s, the primary enemy of consumerism has become environmentalism. A threat to consumerism is seen in calls for reduction of air pollution; increased mileage standards for cars; criticisms of the mass production of sports utility vehicles (SUVS); demands for more stringent controls on pesticides and herbicides; restrictions on the use of snowmobiles, jet skis, all-terrain vehicles, and motor bikes in public parks and recreational sites; reductions in the use of packaging material for consumer items; protests against the building of mega-discount stores; and protection of green spaces in urban and suburban development. For supporters of consumerism, these demands are a threat to the American way of life.

At the 2002 hearings of the Texas State Board of Education, science textbooks were condemned for saying that there was a scientific consensus that the earth's climate was changing because of global warming. This claim was labeled as "anti-technology," "anti-Christian," and "anti-American."[9] Textbook approval by the Texas Board was important because it was only one of two states, the other being California, in which approval occurred at the state level. The Board rejected Jane L. Person's *Environmental Science: How the World Works and Your Place in It* because of statements such as, "Destruction of the tropical rain forest could affect weather over the entire planet" and "Most experts on global warming feel that immediate action should be taken to curb global warming."[10] To gain acceptance by the Texas Board, the statements were changed to: "Tropical rain forest ecosystems impact weather over the entire planet" and "In the past, the earth has been much warmer than it is now, and fossils of sea creatures show us that the sea level was much higher than it is today. So does it really matter if the world gets warmer?"[11]

In 2001, the Texas Board singled out for censorship Daniel Chiras' *Environmental Science: Creating a Sustainable Future.* The book opened with phrases such as, "Things can't go on as they have been," "We must change our ways," "throwaway mentality," and "obsession with growth." The Board attacked the text for using the "oft-used falsehood that over 100 million Americans are breathing unhealthy air."[12]

One text that did win approval was financed by a consortium of mining companies. Entitled *Global Science: Energy, Resources, Environment,* the book was praised before the Texas Board by Duggan Flanakin, formerly of the U.S. Bureau of Mines and currently a member of the Texas Policy Foundation. The book was also commended by Ms. Shore, chair of the Texas Board and co-owner of TEC Well Service. TEC is a producer of gas and oil and repairs and deepens oil wells. From Ms. Shore's perspective, the oil and gas industries "always get a raw deal" in environmental science textbooks.[13] Although environmental science courses threatened rampant consumerism, home economics courses embraced consumerism under the new name Family and Consumer Sciences.

CONSUMER EDUCATION

Floating candles in a hotel's pool to symbolize the new spirit of home economics, organizational leaders adopted the 1993 "Scottsdale Initiative" and changed the field's name to "Family and Consumer Sciences." The term *consumer* in the new name "was viewed not as a subject matter or content area but as recognition that individuals are both family members and consumers."[14] The Scottsdale Initiative officially recognized students as consumers to be trained for future consumption. Translated into middle and high school Family and Consumer Sciences courses, the outcome goal for students was: "Functioning effectively as providers and consumers of goods and services."[15] Besides being a site for advertising and marketing, schools were now engaged in the specific task of teaching consumerism and careers in consumer industries.

The historic role of home economics courses was transformed from teaching women to be scientific producers of food and clothing in the home to preparation for almost complete reliance on consumer products and for work in the food and textile industries. Of course home economics courses had always taught how to be a good shopper through household management of the budget. What was different was the abandonment of home production for complete reliance on the consumption of products. Despite this change, some patterns remained the same. For instance, fashion shows and learning to shop wisely for ready-to-wear clothes were regular features of 1920s' home economics courses. In the 1990s, this instruction continued under the title "Apparel Shopping on the Web."[16]

In 1994, the American Home Economics Association officially changed its name to the American Association of Family and Consumer Sciences. The core values of the newly named organization included preserving the family as the fundamental social unit, supporting diversity and human rights, and protecting the environment. Regarding consumerism, the core values included:

- holistic, interdisciplinary, integrative, and preventive perspectives in addressing the issues of individuals and families as consumers.
- both global and community perspectives when addressing issues of individuals and families as consumers.[17]

In addition, organizational goals included leadership in "impacting the development, delivery and evaluation of consumer goods and services."[18]

The professional organization for middle and secondary school teachers changed its name in 1995 from the Home Economics Education Association to Family and Consumer Sciences Education Association. This newly named organization issued national standards for Family and Consumer Sciences courses.[19] Unlike the early days when home economics courses focused on teaching cooking, sewing, and household management to girls, the new national standards were directed at teaching both females and males about career, family, and consumer roles. In the new standards, cooking classes were replaced with the study of "careers in food production and services" and "careers in food science dietetics, and nutrition." In the early

20th century, the goals of cooking classes for young women were to Americanize immigrants, reform home diets, and turn the housewives into scientific workers. These new standards were geared toward training workers for production of processed and packaged foods. Unlike early sewing instruction, the new standards were strictly geared to careers in the ready-to-wear and related industries or, in the word of the national standards, "careers in textiles and apparels." Whereas early home economics courses sometimes focused on family leisure time activities, the new standards focused on commodified forms of leisure by introducing students to "careers in hospitality, tourism, and recreation." Finally, household management became a study of "careers in housing, interiors, and furnishing."[20]

Changing instruction from how to do something in the home, such as sewing and cooking, to information on possible careers in food and textile production conveys the consumer message that households should rely on prepared food and ready-to-wear clothing. In addition, informing students about careers in tourism and recreation prepares students to think about leisure time activities as a consumer commodity. Consumer science standards reinforce these attitudes. For instance, under the national standard for "Consumer and Family Resources," the goal is: "Demonstrate management of individual and family resources including food, clothing, shelter, health care, recreation, and transportation."[21] This goal simply means learning to budget for the purchase of these items through reasonable use of consumer credit.

There is a critical edge to these national standards. Ideally, courses are not limited to teaching how to shop and use credit. Students are also to be taught the "relationship of the environment to family and consumer resources" and "support consumer rights and responsibilities."[22] Taken to its critical limits, the implementation of these goals would teach students about the potential detrimental effect of consumerism through environmental pollution and the depletion of natural resources. In addition, education about consumer rights could result in consumer activists concerned about the quality and safety of products. In either case, the goal is to educate a responsible consumer-citizen.

The commitment of these new Family and Consumer Sciences to consumerism is highlighted in the national standards' goal: "Analyze interrelationship between the economic system and consumer actions."[23] This represents the triumph of Simon Patten's economic views. It suggests that the economy should be examined from the standpoint of consumer actions, such as consumer confidence and spending. For instance, students learn why retailers and economists worry about holiday purchases, future consumer spending, and measures of consumer confidence. This view of the economy supports public attitudes that measure the success of a Christmas season by consumer spending.

The national standards also reinforce the importance of consumerism in students' minds by informing them of "careers in consumer services." The term *consumer services* suggests activities directly supporting a consumer-based economy. Students are to "Demonstrate skills needed for product development, testing, and presentation."[24] Also under consumer services is "developing a long-term financial management plan." Reflecting the critical edge in Family and Consumer Sciences courses, consumer services also includes analyzing "consumer advocacy" and "resource consumption for conservation and waste management practices."

While schools are teaching consumerism through conveying the message that education is a form of consumption, in-school ads, and consumerism-oriented courses, the school's most important contribution is creating a peer group of teens who relate through brand names and consumerism-oriented activities. The next section examines how the teen cohort of shoppers is now a global phenomenon.

SCHOOLING CREATES A GLOBAL TEEN MARKET

Mass secondary education created a teenage culture discovered by advertisers in the 1940s and 1950s and incarnated in the pages of *Seventeen* magazine. That teen culture is now a global market. Calling them the "new world teens," market researcher Elissa Moses argued, "Teens who speak different languages all speak the same language of global brand consumption. . . . Teens love brands. . . . Brands are passports to global culture." Asking teens worldwide to identify 75 brand icons, she found the five most popular, in order, were Coca-Cola, Sony, Adidas, Nike, and Kodak.[25]

"Unabashed consumerism" is the number one unifier of global teen culture according to Elissa Moses' advertising study, *The $100 Billion Allowance: Accessing the Global Teen Market.* In the upbeat language of advertising, she wrote, "In an age of abundance for much of the world's growing middle class, teens see consumer products as one of the limitless joys of life." Moses' background in marketing provided her with important background knowledge for the survey. Her clients have been The Coca-Cola Company, Calvin Klein, MTV, General Motors, Levi Strauss, Nike, Burger King, Kodak, and the National Basketball Association. Marketers have found the study useful in selling to teens. "Insights from *The $100 Billion Allowance,*" the president of Royal Philips Electronics, Car Boonstra, claimed, "have already helped Philips better connect to global youth."[26] Representing an icon of global teen jeans, Levi Strauss' Presence and Publicity Director, Ray Edmondson, hailed the study for providing "clever tips and very clear steps to help any marketer find the way through to the hearts and minds of today's youth population."[27] The Worldwide Director of Brand Futures Group,

Marian Salzman says, "the best job I've ever seen of breaking down, bite by bite, a look at teen culture in a range of countries and across a range of industries. A bible for anyone doing business targeting global youth."[28] Despite these claims, it is important to note that the Teen World Survey was limited to lower middle and upper middle-class youth and that only two African nations were presented—South Africa and Nigeria. Although the poorest of the poor were not included in the survey, one wonders if their dreams also include consumption of the world's brand-name products.

The existence of a global teen market suggests that most countries have, through schooling and other institutionalized arrangements, separated youth as a distinct cohort group from children and adults. By indirectly creating a segregated cohort group, secondary schools have allowed for specific marketing techniques to be directed at the global adolescent. Moses suggested that there is a relationship between the unstable period of adolescence and brand affiliation. Brands promise a reliable and standard product. They provide an anchor in an uncertain world of adolescence. Faced with an array of products, a brand name provides guidance. The purchase of Coca-Cola, the world's most recognized brand, in any country promises the consumer the same standardized taste. In addition, Moses' study demonstrates that youth culture, particularly youth consumer culture, varies according to local traditions and economic circumstances. Yes, there is a global teen market, but it is not the same in every nation. Yes, youth consumer groups are transnational. With the rapid movement of the world's population, youth consumers born in one nation might find themselves coming of age in another nation.

Other unifiers of global youth culture sometimes reinforce consumerism. These other unifiers include desires for new technology, entertainment, endless experience, mobility, sports participation and observation, respect for global icons, "humanism," "hope," and "self-navigation."[29] Interest in technology primarily involves the endless purchase of upgraded computers, portable compact disk and tape players, video games, digital cameras, high-definition TV sets, and cell phones. Entertainment is commodified through recordings and videos and world music tours. The search for new experiences and mobility are aided by cheap airline, rail, and bus tickets, which send hordes of backpacking youth across the global landscape. The role of sports in unifying youth is spurred by massive ad campaigns and media. For instance, the American-invented game of basketball is now an international sport because, in part, of the global advertising efforts of the National Basketball League.[30] Of course respect for brand icons is a form of *unabashed consumerism* that unifies youth.

In Moses' study, world teens are divided into six main categories. There are the "Resigned" who believe their futures are decided and that it is futile to engage in any political debate or to keep abreast with the unfolding of human events. In Moses' words, "The resigned have very low expectations for their futures. At an early age, they perceive that their lot in the world has already been determined . . . the resigned are alienated from society and very pessimistic about their chances for economic success."[31] They drop out of secondary schools or scrape by with minimal effort. College is clearly not a destination for this group. They are not interested in political participation.

The marketing segment, "World Savers," are identified closely with participation in political dialogues about alternatives to the good life and, at the same time, are considered avid consumers. "Whether the goal is to combat racism," Moses' summary of the survey data states, "rain forest, or curtail warming, the world saver are marching at the forefront, trying to effect some positive change."[32] Again it should be emphasized that these politically active youth are important world consumers. The marketing strategy for this group contains a cynical edge with the suggestion that a "marketer can piggyback a promotion with a worthwhile cause, and have world savers respond positively to that message."[33]

Targeting "World Savers" results in the commodification of social justice, which is an interesting addition to Simon Patten's earlier pronouncements on consumerism. Recognizing that World Savers are avid consumers, Benetton, the Italian clothing manufacturer, has advertised its clothes with accompanying themes of racial harmony and social justice. For instance, during the late 20th-century civil war in Bosnia, Benetton ads entitled "The Known Soldier" showed "blood-soaked T-shirt and the pants of a Croatian soldier."[34] Another ad showed two handcuffed men, a priest kissing a nun, and an arm tattooed "HIV positive."[35] Turning social and environmental causes into marketing opportunities demonstrates the power of the profit motive to envelop all aspects of life. Nothing can escape the grasp of branding and consumerism.

Along with the "Resigned," the other four teenage groups seem little interested in engaging in rational public discourse about political and economic issues. However, they definitely have strong consumer interests. The "Thrills-and-Chills" are described as "devil-may-care, trying to become independent hedonist . . . who love to buy stuff . . . and . . . do not mind paying the price for expensive items."[36] Coming from middle-class and affluent homes, this group is an important target for marketers. With intellects that are relatively empty of political and social concerns, they can fill their minds with brand icons. Moses wrote, "Spending and shopping are normal activities, and they develop loyalties to those brands that speak their languages."[37]

"Bootstrappers" could almost be described as "Thrills and Chills" wannabes wanting to work hard to achieve affluence and purchasing power. "Bootstrappers," according to Moses, "are young yuppies in training." Similar to the thrills-and-chills crowd, this group fills its minds with brand icons and loyalties as opposed to political and economic interests. "Bootstrappers," the world teen survey concludes, "are . . . on the lookout for goods and services that will help them get ahead . . . [they] stay plugged into the world of media and culture for insights that will give them a competitive edge."[38] Similar to the "Bootstrappers," "Quiet Achievers" work hard for success. The major distinction between the two groups is the degree of conformity. Quiet Achievers are conformists who avoid any type of political or social rebellion and remain tightly linked to their families. Consequently, they are more often followers of political and social rules rather than desiring to make the rules. Although politically inactive, they are active consumers who are concerned with investigating the quality and benefits of a product. "Upholders" are also described as conformists interested in following the rules. In contrast to "Quiet Achievers," this group is not focused on academic and economic success. "Upholders," Moses stated, "do not want to set the world on fire, nor are they into controversy." In the minds of this groups, sports statistics and the names of teams and players often crowd out political and economic issues. Like the other groups, this group is interested in consumption. They want products for their "risk-free quality, value, and reliability."[39]

The classification of global youth into these six categories seems reasonable as long as it is recognized that these groups overlap and that any individual might be a blend of several group characteristics. Moses pointed out that the "Resigned" sometimes act like the "Thrills and Chills" group, but without the same amount of money to spend. Yet I am skeptical of the accuracy of the study's statistical measures. However, they do provide an interesting bases for discussion about the percentage of youth engaged in different forms of consumerism. The following is the study's report on the global distribution of these youth groups. Again, it must be emphasized that most of Africa and the poorest of the poor in other countries are excluded from this survey.

Percentage Distribution of Global Youth Groups

Segment of Global Youth	Percentage Distribution Worldwide
Thrills and Chills	18
Upholders	16
Quiet Achievers	15
Resigned	14
Bootstrappers	14
World Savers	12
Unclassified	11

Source: Adapted from Elissa Moses, *The $100 Billion Allowance: Accessing the Global Teen Market* (New York: John Wiley & Sons, Inc. 2000), p. 82.

For those hoping for a politically active youth, the 12% figure for World Savers must be disappointing. Moses evaluated these figures according to national conditions. She wrote, "This analysis sheds light on why teens in Amsterdam pierce body parts, why youth in Brazil are worried about AIDS, why Japanese you are approaching the edge of rebellion, and why U.S. teens seem so motivated to achieve."[40] According to her study, youth groups are clustered around certain nations.

Segment of Global Youth	Countries with High Concentrations of Segment
Thrills and Chills	Germany, England, Lithuania, Greece, South Africa, Netherlands, United States, Australia
Upholders	Vietnam, Indonesia, Taiwan, China, Italy, Peru, Venezuela, Puerto Rico
Quiet Achievers	Thailand, China, Hong Kong, Ukraine
Resigned	Denmark, Sweden, Korea, Japan, Norway, Germany, Belgium, Netherlands
Bootstrappers	Nigeria, Mexico, United States, India, Chile, Puerto Rico, Australia
World Savers	Hungary, Philippines, Venezuela, Brazil, Spain, Colombia, Belgium, Argentina, Russia, Singapore

Source: Adapted from Elissa Moses, *The $100 Billion Allowance: Accessing the Global Teen Market* (New York: John Wiley & Sons, Inc. 2000), p. 82.

It is important to note that the two world leaders in consumerism—Japan and the United States—lack a high percentage of World Savers. In Japan, only 4% of the teen population is identified as World Savers, whereas the majority are either "Resigned" (38%) or "Thrills and Chills" (24%). Sixty percent of Japanese youth love shopping, compared with 42% worldwide.[41] In the United States, only 9% of the teen population is identified as World Savers, whereas the majority are either "Thrills and Chills" (28%) or "Bootstrappers" (26%).[42]

Have the majority of Japanese and U.S. youth made Sonya's choice? Except for the "World Savers" and "Resigned," global teens are fulfilling Simon Patten's dream that consumerism spur people to work harder. Even with the "World Savers," marketers are trying to commodify movements for social justice. The "Resigned" seemed destined to be nourished by fast-food and alienating music. This is not a pretty picture for those interested in rational public discourse on issues of social justice.

Although schools have created a teen cohort group linked by patterns of consumption, children are being seduced by new palaces of consumption interconnected to media and schooling. Media and architecture merge in theme parks and fast-food establishments designed to lure the child and the entire family.

THE SEDUCTION OF CHILDHOOD

Children are often seduced into consumerism by architecturally themed amusement parks and restaurants linked to media and product spin-offs. This phenomenon is an outgrowth of several trends, including 19th-century consumer-oriented architectural designs, advertising directed at children, the growth of media empires, and the inclusion of educational concepts in commercial enterprises. Regarding architectural designs, chapter 1 discussed architectural designs intended to arouse consumer desires and symbolize forms of consumption. Primarily directed at adults, these consumer themes were embodied in department stores and Coney Island theme parks. In the 1950s, this architectural style was broadened to include children and families with the founding of Disneyland and McDonald's. Coney Island was planned as a commodified respite from the tedium of corporate and industrial, while Disneyland included the same goal along with the preservation an imagined set of traditional values associated with the American family. McDonald's embodied the early home economist's dream of inexpensive fast food that could free the housewife from household slavery. Like Disneyland, McDonald's Golden Arches theme was to represent a haven for family values. These themed architectural forms intended to attract consumers and act as brand icons became familiar parts of the American landscape.

These themed environments were rooted in early advertising efforts to teach children how to consume. In 1904, the advertising manager of the *Atlantic Monthly* wrote that the far-sighted advertiser begins with the female child so that the brand name follows her "to school, thrusts its self upon her as she travels, and all unconsciously engraves it self upon her memory." The result is that when the child grows up and goes on her first shopping trip as a wife: "She orders Pears' Soap, White Label Soup, Pearline, Walter Baker's Cocoa, and Knox's Gelatine, because she knows and remembers the names, and does not realize that she has chosen in every instance an article made familiar to her, perhaps, by advertising only."[43] Advertising competitions were a popular technique for interesting children in brand names. In 1911, Colgate toothpaste launched a contest in a children's magazine that offered monetary prizes for writing the best ad copy. The ads instructed participants: "Just imagine that you're writing a short letter to one of your schoolmates telling how important it is to take proper care of the teeth and how [Colgate] Ribbon Dental Cream is not only the best cleansers but besides is so delicious in flavor that its use is a real treat. . . . And remember, the more you believe it the easier it will be to write it and the better the advertisement."[44] In a 1904 ad in *McClure's* magazine, an 8-year-old boy sits on the floor surrounded by opened magazines. Looking at this mother, he tells her, "Mamma, you know magazines are very useful. They tell you what you want, and where to get it."[45]

Product spin-offs turn children into demanding consumers and serve as marketing tools for media giants such as the Disney Corporation. Early ads utilized cartoon figures marketed to children as dolls. Through these dolls, which were also sources of revenue, children gained brand loyalty. In the early 20th century, Jell-O ads utilized cute little Kewpie figures that were nude infant shapes with pointed hairdos that performed tasks beyond their years. Kewpies appeared on Jell-O packages and Jell-O recipe books. One early recipe book showed a little girl pouring hot water into a container of Jell-O while one Kewpie pointed at the Jell-O box and another held up a Jell-O mold. Campbell Soup ads used Campbell Kids' characters in a similar fashion. Both Kewpies and Campbell Kids were marketed as dolls for children's play.[46]

It was the business genius of Walt Disney's brother Roy that led to product spin-offs of media characters. The Disney Corporation's first product spin-off was Mickey Mouse. Walt Disney created the Mickey Mouse character in 1928 and in the same year produced three animated Mickey Mouse cartoons including the sound cartoon, *Steamboat Willie*.[47] After the opening of *Steamboat Willie*, Walt Disney recalled, "Right after Mickey Mouse hit, I was in New York and we needed money. A fellow kept hanging around the hotel with three hundred dollars cash waving at me, and I finally signed a deal to put Mickey Mouse on these big cheap [writing] tablet type things. It was the first deal ever signed."[48] Roy Disney decided to copywrite the Mickey Mouse character and sell products using Mickey's characters and those of other Disney's cartoon figures. In 1930, Roy began a campaign to adorn products with these figures and signed a contract with George Borgfeldt to make toys and other objects using Mickey and Minnie Mouse.[49]

The marketing of these products were tied to Disney movies, syndicated newspaper comic strips, and newly formed Mickey Mouse Clubs. Roy Disney explained the company's merchandising techniques:

> Mickey Mouse [newspaper cartoon strip] is now being handled . . . through King Features syndicate, who are rapidly placing the strip in many leading newspapers . . . Borgfeldt & Co. of New York have taken the world rights to manufacture toys and novelties . . . Villa Moret, Inc. . . . are publishing the Mickey Mouse song, used in the pictures. . . . Also in connection with our pictures we have launched a campaign for the formation of Micky Mouse Clubs in theaters where the cartoons are shown. . . . The idea is meeting with astonishing success.[50]

In 1932, the Disney brothers realized that there was a two-way relationship between the promotion of Disney movies and the earnings from merchandise bearing Disney logos. Walt was contacted by an advertising man who convinced him the Mickey could be promoted through merchandising. The Disney brothers agreed and a first spin-off was the now famous collector's item, the Mickey Mouse watch. Lionel Toys, which was having difficulty selling model trains during the Depression, joined the promotion effort. Regarding Lionel Toys, Walt recalled, "During the Depression, it was just bad for the toy business. They made this little windup Mickey Mouse that ran around a track. It was a big item. It sold everywhere."[51]

With the advent of TV, Mickey Mouse Clubs became an important part of marketing strategy for movies, products, and theme parks. On October 3, 1955, shortly after the opening of the Disneyland theme park, "The Mickey Mouse Club" children's TV program premiered on ABC. The most famous merchandise sold through the show was a cap with mouse ears. Children around the country would don their mouse ear caps to sing the programs opening song, which began "M-I-C-K-E-Y M-O-U-S-E, Mickey Mouse." "The Mickey Mouse Club" program proved a bonanza for other Disney products. Constantly plugged through the first programs were Disneyland and two recent Disney movies *20,000 Leagues Under the Sea* and *Lady and the Tramp*. It was believed that both were box office successes because of the plugs they received on the TV program.[52]

In the same year as the premier of the "Mickey Mouse Club," Disney launched another TV series called "Disneyland." The first 90-minute show was devoted to the Disneyland theme park. This marked the beginning of the TV infomercial where an entire program was devoted to information about a product. Many subsequent programs were about Disney movies, including one about the making of *20,000 Leagues Under the Sea*. A program devoted to Davy Crockett tied a Disney movie to Disneyland and a variety of product spin-offs. Davy Crockett was linked to the Disneyland attraction Frontierland. In addition, Disney studios released the movie, *Davy Crockett, King of the Wild Frontier*. The movie's theme song proved a hit among children and Disney-licensed products bearing Crockett's name, including coonskin hats, soaps, lamps, dolls, and a host of other children's products.[53]

When Disneyland opened on July 17, 1955, it had received publicity through Disney's TV infomercial and the "Mickey Mouse Club." Every child who donned the mouse-ear cap or wore Crockett's coonskin hat knew about Disneyland. Its success spawned a new generation of theme parks designed to organize and sell leisure time activities to families. Other theme parks included Dolly Parton's Appalachian family park Dollywood, the beer producer Anheuser-Busch's Busch Gardens, the Hershey Corporation's Hershey Park, the Auto World Theme Park in Flint, Michigan, and United Studios. The number of theme parks increased almost daily. By 2002, the Six Flags Corporation was operating 28 theme parks, including Six Flags Over Georgia, Six Flags Kentucky Kingdom, Six Flags AstroWorld, Six Flags Marine World, and Six Flags Wild Waves/Enchanted Village. Similar to Disney, Six Flags Corporation operated overseas theme parks in Holland, Belgium, Germany, France, Spain, and Mexico. The Six Flags Corporation offered this exciting description of its German Movie World theme park created in cooperation with Warner Bros. Movie studios:

> Warner Bros. Movie World Germany is Europe's unique movie and entertainment park located near Dusseldorf. The magical world of Hollywood becomes reality. Five themed areas offer an exciting variety of more than 40 attractions, shows and rides, each of them based on famous Warner Bros. films and successful German productions, that guarantee an unforgettable day. This year, Warner Bros. Movie World presents Eraser - The Ride, a new roller coaster based thematically on the 1996 action film, "The Eraser - The Ride". Eraser - The Ride is a suspended looping coaster making 85 km/h one of the most exhilarating experiences in Europe. Warner Bros. Movie World Germany is open April through October.[54]

In addition, Disneyland Paris and Tokyo represented the exporting of the theme park concept.

In contrast to Fred Thompson's plans for Luna Park in Coney Island, Walt Disney made clear that his goal was clean middle-class fun for the entire family. While riding around the Disneyland construction site, Walt Disney commented to his biographer Bob Thomas, "Disneyland isn't designed just for children. . . . I believe the right kind of entertainment can appeal to all persons, young or old. I want Disneyland to be a place where parents can bring their children—or come by themselves and still have a good time."[55] On another occasion, Disney commented,

> We gotta charge people to get in. If we don't, we'll get all kinds of drunks and molesters; they'll be grabbing girls in the dark. You'll get a better class of people if you charge them to enter. . . . One of the things I hated about carnivals and piers was all the crap that was everywhere. You're stepping on chewing gum and ice cream cones. I think people want clean amusement parks.[56]

The Disneyland model, adopted by other theme park franchises, promised fenced-in security against the world's brutality. First, there was the process of self-selection through the admission charge. In 2002, admission tickets for Disneyland were $43 for those over 9 years old, $33 for children 3 to 9, and free for those under 3.[57] The cost was even higher for out-of-town travelers. According to Disney's online reservation site in 2002, a complete two-night package for two adults and two children in a standard view room at Disney's Grand Californian Hotel with a "Resort Magic Package," and "4-day Ultimate Park Hopper Ticket" was $1,152.90.[58] Air fare or costs for other forms of travel and food made this an expensive family trip. Cost, as Disney planned, kept out the riffraff, whereas tight security controlled the crowds within. One could argue that the combination of security measures and enclosed space made Disneyland into a model for a totalitarian state of pleasure.

With his background in movie production, Disney planned the park as an integrated experience flowing through scenes beginning with the Town Square and leading down Main Street to Fantasyland, Frontierland, Adventureland, and Tomorrowland. Unlike other amusement parks that had several entrances to ease congestion, Disney insisted on only one entrance to ensure a standardized experience. He wanted the Town Square to set the mood, similar to the opening of a movie, with visitors being greeted by brass bands, balloons, flowers, a fire wagon, a horse-drawn trolley, and surreys. Looking from Town Square down Main Street, visitors could see Sleeping Beauty's Castle.[59]

Walt Disney called the view of the Castle a *wienie,* which acted as a lure to draw visitors down Main Street. The use of the term *wienie* suggests all sorts of Freudian interpretations. According to his biographer, Disney frequently used wienie to refer to something that would seduce viewers into following the lines of a movie plot. Again Freudian interpretations are possible because the main wienies at Disneyland were Snow White's Castle and the towering Rocket in Tomorrowland. From this perspective, Disney's planning did have an eroticized dimension. However, Disney borrowed the term *wienie* from dog trainers who used frankfurters to induce dogs to perform tricks.[60]

Disneyland's Main Street was designed to evoke memories of small-town America, similar to the world in which Disney grew up in Marceline, Missouri, when things were simpler than the complex metropolitan world of Los Angeles that surrounded Disneyland. Walt Disney even had his father's name and business displayed on Disneyland's Main Street: "Elias Disney, Contractor, Est. 1895." Other parts of Disneyland were related to America's past and present. Frontierland offered a distorted view of the U.S. government's expansion into the West and the conquest of Native Americans and Mexicans. Adventureland, with its ersatz African jungle experience, suggested the inferiority of Africans and it was related to U.S. and European imperialism around the globe. The cold war's technological and military race between the United States and the Soviet Union was symbolized by the towering space rocket in Tomorrowland. Of course Fantasyland represented American domination of movies and TV and the cluttering of global minds with images of Disney characters.

Disneyland is a worldwide model for themed and commodified leisure. No sophisticated level of interpretation is required to explain brilliance of the Disneyland plan. The Disney Web site, *http://disneyland.disney.go.com,* describes the genius of the park's intermixture of consumption, fantasy, leisure, and nostalgia. Despite the entrance fee, there is still money to be spent inside. Consider how nostalgia and shopping are described on Disney's Web site for Main Street, U.S.A.: "Walt Disney once said, 'I love the nostalgic myself. I hope we never lose some of the things of the past.' So he created Main Street, U.S.A. to make sure we could always embrace those wonderful feelings of days gone by. From the decor in the old-time speciality shops to the music in Central Plaza to the taste of the ice cream sundaes, Main Street is pure Americana."[61] On Main Street, shoppers can find themed snack shops and stores, such as the Candy Palace with "mouth watering caramel apples, fudge, and other yummy delicacies [made] before your eyes"; and the China Closet with "Disney-themed china pieces"; along with the New Century Jewelry, the Mad Hatter, the New Century Times Pieces, the Silhouette Studio, and the Penny Arcade. This is a truly brilliant plan where you charge people to enter a street lined with other opportunities to spend money.

Other parts of Disneyland offer a similar combination of entertainment, shopping, and dining experiences. Disney's Web site describes Adventureland as "the perfect playground—whether you're cruising through the African jungles, avoiding poison darts and snakes while searching for ancient artifacts, or *simply sampling the topical faire in the village shops*" (italics added).[62] The themed stores include Tropical Imports, South Seas Traders, and Indiana Jones Adventure Outpost. The Bengal Barbecue offers kebabs of beef, chicken, and vegetables; the Indy Fruit Cart offers fresh fruit and bottled water; and the Tike Juice Bar provides a "pineapple lover's dream."[63]

With "western-themed shows, shops and eateries . . . [which] celebrate the spirit and strength of the American pioneer," Frontierland provides the Western shopping experience at Pioneer Mercantile, Westward Ho Trading Company, and Bonanza Outfitters and the Western eating experience at Rancho del Zocalo, River Belle Terrace, and Golden Horseshoe Stage. Fantasyland, "where dreams really do come true," offers Tinker Bell Toy Shoppe along with six other shopping opportunities. Diners can partake of Mousekemeals at the Pinocchio-themed Village Haus or hot dogs and pizzas at Troubadour Treats. Tomorrowland, billed as "a tribute to the power of the human mind," offers four shopping opportunities with Autopia Winner's Circle and Star Trader at the top of the list. Themed eating experiences include Redd Rockett's Pizza Port with "Starfire Chicken Pizza, Celestial Caesar Salad, and Mars-inara Pasta," and Club Buzz-Lightyear's Above the Rest with an "out-of-this-world food menu."[64]

Compared to early department stores, Disneyland is a major advance in consumerism. Departments stores sparked consumer desires through displays of merchandise and environments that turned shopping into a leisure time activity. Department stores did not earn money by charging an entrance fee. In department stores, shoppers could receive a day's worth of entertainment without spending any money. During their shopping adventure, consumers could leave the store and eat at some nearby restaurant.

Disney's brilliant ensemble of entertainment and consumer products is replicated at Dolly Parton's Dollywood near Knoxville, Tennessee. Mark Gottdiener wrote, "The park features folksy, down home, country attractions pumped up by marketing and promotional techniques perfected by the Disney Corporation, including Disney-style regulation of customers— 'no litter, no alcohol, no bare feet on young'uns'."[65] When the park opened in 1986, the focus was Appalachian culture and Dolly Parton's rise from rural poverty to global fame. Eventually Dollywood became known for performances by country bands. The result is a theme park that emphasizes a combination of Appalachian mountain culture and country music. These themes appear in the park's amusement rides, craft demonstrations and museums, restaurants, and stores.

Similar to Disneyland, Dollywood represents a new form of merchandising that combines the model of Coney Island theme parks with the department store sales techniques advocated by L. Frank Baum in *The Show Window*. In fusing consumerism with commodified leisure, Disneyland and Dollywood borrow the smoke and mirror methods used by the Wizard of Oz in the Emerald City. At Dollywood, themed restaurants offer various forms of country cooking. Aunt Granny's, the park's first restaurant, advertises food cooked according to Dolly Parton's country recipes. Country fare is also offered at Grannie Ogle's Ham'n Beans located in Dollywood's "Craftsman's Valley."[66] Among Dollywood's many themed stores in Lid'l Dolly's Handcrafted Children's Dresses. The shop's Web site tempts buyers with a photo of a little girl in a hand-made dress called "Easter Bunny Town." The store also offers the Original Southern Belle's dress, which is described as "Grandma's favorite."[67]

Dollywood's Mission Statement is: "Create Memories Worth Repeating." Both Disneyland and Dollywood play with human memories and imagination. Both parks draw on historical memories based in fantasy rather than reality. Few visitors have actually experienced an early 20th-century main street or Appalachian mountain living. However, history books, movies, songs, and other media have implanted feelings and images of these places in people's minds. Walking down Disneyland's Main Street evokes feelings and memories that are learned rather than experienced. A similar response occurs when visiting the Dollywood Craft Preservation School or Dollywood Crafts. Through media, people learn to associate feelings of peace, security, and happy times with mythical pasts. However, the actual experience of Appalachia's past might include exploitation in coal mines, poverty, malnutrition, and lung disease. At Disneyland, the visitor can leave Main Street for Frontierland where nostalgic feelings of the winning of the West seem to contradict the actual Western experience of the expansion of slavery into Texas, the government-sponsored slaughter of buffalo, and the genocide and genital mutilation of Native Americans.

MEMORIES AND CRITICAL HISTORY

In *The Mouse that Roared: Disney and the End of Innocence*, Henry Giroux criticizes Disney for removing any critical elements from its portrayal of history.[68] Similar to proposals by early advocates of the Public Relations, Disney enterprises fabricates memories to add to the enchantment of the consumer experience. There is no room for critical history when it is used to sell products. At Disneyland, Frontierland's Rancho del Zocalo ties the consumption of food to nostalgic memories of happy Mexican cowboy's strumming guitars. Diners are not reminded of Mexico's attempts at the Alamo to keep Americans from extending slavery into Texas or the U.S. government's unprovoked conquest of Mexico's Northern Territories. Diners at Rancho Del Zocalo are not treated to the memory taught to Mexico City residents at the entrance to Chapultepec Park where a large memorial honors the three children killed by U.S. Marines during the 1846 invasion. Nor are diners at Dollywood's Grannie Ogle's Ham'n Beans reminded of the thin-boned emaciation of country people. Nor are shoppers at Lid'l Dolly's Handcrafted Children's Dresses reminded that in the past the store's clothing could only be afforded by the families that owned and managed Appalachia's coal mines.

Just as historical memories can be used to merchandise food and other products, education can be integrated into themed environments and marketing. In chapter 6, "Sesame Street" exemplified a strong relationship between education and consumerism. When Florida's Disney World opened, Walt Disney focused on the educational experience provided at its Epcot Center. Celebration, the Disney corporation's attempt to create model U.S. communities, involved the company directly in the operation of a school system. To inflate their images of being child- and family-friendly, fast-food chains directly support educational programs. In all these cases, education serves as a medium for selling other products.

In 1996, the Walt Disney Company signed a marketing agreement with the king of fast-food restaurants, McDonald's. The global agreement allows Disney to market its films at McDonald's restaurants while giving McDonald's rights to use Disney videos and characters to sell its products.[69] For instance, in 2002, McDonald's so-called Happy Meal was sold with characters from Disney's film, *The Many Adventures of Winnie the Pooh*. This mutual marketing of a movie and food involved toys representing six Winnie the Pooh characters and advertised as "Pooh and Friends! Toys that Bend!" At the same time, McDonald's was offering teachers and public schools a "Black History" curriculum.[70]

FAST-FOOD EDUCATION

Fast-food franchises are a continuation of the American cuisine developed in the 1890s when home economists embraced Jell-O and packaged and prepared foods and attempted to standardize American tastes in school cafeterias and hospital kitchens. Most franchises were born in the 1950s when the automobile and suburban living created a mobile population looking for a quick meal. To a certain extent, fast food realized home economist Ellen Richard's dream of community kitchens and conveyance food that freed women from cooking.

Fast food's involvement in education was a logical outgrowth of efforts, similar to those of Disney, to project an impression of being friendly and clean places for children and families to eat. Also educational involvement served as a public relations method to create a positive community image. Beginning shortly before the opening of Disneyland, themed fast-food designs and logos served to identify their establishments to passing motorists and attract children and families. For instance, McDonald's, founded in 1953, changed the "M" representing the name McDonald into the Golden Arches symbol, which is now recognized around the world. In 1960, a Washington, DC, McDonald's sponsored the children's TV program "Bozo's Circus," and Bozo appeared at the restaurant attracting large crowds. When the TV program was canceled, an ad agency created a new clown called Ronald McDonald.[71] Adding to the kid-friendly image created by Ronald McDonald was the introduction of indoor play areas for children. With its own line of children's videos, McDonald's has wedded advertising and entertainment in one video starring Ronald McDonald, *The Wacky Adventures of Ronald McDonald*.[72] In the early 21st century, it was estimated that at least once a month 90% of U.S. children between 3 and 9 visit a McDonald's.[73]

McDonald's Black History curriculum confirms Henry Giroux's contention that media—in this case, a fast-food chain—strips history of its critical element. McDonald's Black History curriculum includes a list of "Little Known Black History Facts." These facts contain little or no mention of the history of slavery, lynching, race riots, Jim Crow laws, or violent White reaction to the civil rights movement. The following is a list of the first five Black History Facts provided in the curriculum. Each of these facts is followed by an explanation. I am only presenting the boldly printed first lines of the facts as examples of uncritical historical material.

1. Issac Murphy: The First Jockey to win the Kentucky Derby Three Times

2. The Black Lifesavers: A Band of Unsung Heroes on Pea Island, North Carolina
3. The Red Ball Express: Legendary Operation That Provided Vital Supplies to the Front Lines During World War II
4. William Cooper Nell: The First African American to Hold a Federal Position
5. Alexander Lucius Twilight: The First African American to Graduate From an American College[74]

Critical historical questions are absent from the eight-page teacher guide accompanying the facts list. The listed sources for McDonald's teacher guide are from major professional organizations, including the National Council for the Social Studies, the National Council of Teachers of English, and the International Reading Association. The guide is divided into three columns entitled "Objective," "Curriculum Connections," and "Standards." The first of two objectives, which reflects the racial uplift quality of the facts list, is: "Students will discuss the importance of being the 'first' to accomplish something. . . ." and "Students will discuss the importance of leadership. . . ." The last objective could raise critical issues: "Students will discuss the many obstacles that African Americans (and others) must overcome. . . ."[75] The objectives page is followed by a "Welcome Teachers" page, which opens, "McDonald's is pleased to bring you 'Little Known Black History Facts.' The following lessons rely on simple memorization skills without any critical questions. For instance, there is a list of questions requiring memorization, such as 'Who became the first African American to publish a novel?' "[76]

Similar to McDonald's birth in the 1950s' suburban-car age, McDonald's rival Burger King was founded in Daytona, Florida, in 1953 by Keith Cramer after he visited and studied the newly opened McDonald's in California.[77] Like McDonald's, Burger King uses themed architecture including playgrounds. Also Burger King exploits media connections such as a 2002 marketing agreement with Dreamworks film studio to distribute by Virtual Vision Scopes for the studio's showing of *Spirit: Stallion of the Cimarron.* In another media connection, Burger King has an agreement with the Nickelodeon TV network to cooperate in reviewing and showing TV videos submitted by children.[78]

Burger King goes beyond McDonald's educational and community efforts by operating Burger King Academies and is involved in welfare reform. Jumping on the charter school bandwagon, Burger King in cooperation with Communities in Schools, Inc. (CIS) has opened 24 CIS/Burger King Academies across the nation for students facing problems of "poor school attendance, illiteracy, teen pregnancy, drug and alcohol abuse, school violence, and lack of self-esteem."[79] The Burger King Academies, serving as both advertising for the franchise and public relations, work with local service groups, public schools, and universities. Local Burger King franchises also establish partnerships with local school systems to provide mentors and tutors, and they team up with local newspapers to sell newspapers with part of the proceeds going to Burger King Academies.[80] Bearing the appellation Burger King Scholars, needy students can attend college or postsecondary vocational schools with scholarships from the Burger King/ Lahore Foundation's North American Scholarship Program, which in 2001 provided $1,082,000 in awards.[81]

In his 1997 State of the Union address, President Bill Clinton named Burger King as one of five companies working with the federal government on welfare reform. Obviously serving its own needs for low-paid workers, Burger King Corporation was a founding member of the Welfare to Work Partnership. By December 2001, the franchise had hired 35,000 former welfare recipients. For Burger King there was a clear advantage in hiring from welfare roles. Not only did it ensure low-paid workers, but it provided a more stable workforce. According to the Burger King Corporation, "The industry employee turnover rate for quick service restaurants is approximately 300%. Burger King employees hired off public assistance roles have 45% higher retention rates than the turnover rate for all other employees in the industry."[82] Burger King has effectively used media ties, Burger King Academies and Scholarships, and government welfare programs for advertising, building community relations, and providing more reliable and low-cost workers.

The company most involved in education is YUM Brands corporation, which over the years acquired Taco Bell, A&W, KFC, Long John Silver's, and Pizza Hut. When YUM Brands acquired A&W and Long John Silver's in 2002, the company proudly announced that, "The acquisition allows us to accelerate our multi branding strategy and . . . to be expanded international leaders . . . in chicken, pizza, Mexican and seafood." The company's motto is, "Our passion is to put YUM on our customer's faces all over the world."[83] YUM Brands is now a leader in the construction and operation of themed environments. For instance, in 1922, the A&W logo was created by Roy Allen and Frank Wright to represent their two last names. Opening in Lodi, California, the men constructed an outdoor stand that looked like a root beer barrel. In 1923, A&W developed the first car-hop service initiating the spread of drive-in restaurants. Later restaurants relied on the logo rather than the barrel design for name recognition.[84] Opening in 1968, Long John Silver's new "exteriors," as described by the company, sported "a stronger retail identity with bolder colors, accent stripes, illuminated canopies on drive-thrus, and a new roof design."[85]

Three of the five YUM franchises—Taco Bell, Pizza Hut, and KFC—are directly involved in educational activities. In 1999, for the first time, all three franchises were linked to a media event when they gained exclusive rights as global restaurant partners for Star Wars Episode I.[86] Taco Bell's educational projects overshadow those of McDonald's. Taco Bell began the same year and in the same town as McDonald's when Glen Bell opened the Bell Taco stand in San Bernardino, California. Bell experimented with food processing and developed a processed method for producing tacos. The name changed to Taco Bell, and it adopted the logo of the ringing mission bell.[87]

As sponsor of the Discovery Science Center in Santa Ana, California, Taco Bell provides science programs aligned to the requirements of California State Science Content Standards. One program is "Dynamic Earth" program while another is "Astronomy—Avoiding Misconceptions." Both programs are free and done in cooperation with NASA. Also free are science exhibits and a three-dimensional theater with science shows. In cooperation with the Bank of America, the Discovery Center provides a free open house to teachers along with free field trips for students.[88] Taco Bell Foundation, in partnership with Boys & Girls Clubs of America, operates TEENSupreme programs throughout the United States and on worldwide military installations. According to the official statement of Taco Bell, the programs are "designed to develop leadership skills, values, and a voice among our nation's youth to prepare them to become successful adults and productive leaders." To build a public awareness of their sponsorship of TEENSupreme, Taco Bell has in-store canisters so that patrons can make donations to support the program.[89]

In 1988, President Ronald Reagan awarded Pizza Hut's president, Art Gunter, a Private Initiative Citation for its educational program BOOK IT![90] The first Pizza Hut opened in 1958 in Wichita, Kansas, and its first franchise opened in Topeka the following year. In 1965, its first TV commercial featured the musical jingle, "Putt-Putt to Pizza Hut." In 1967, it gained global recognition for baking the world's largest pizza (6 feet in diameter). In 1975, it promoted itself through product placement by being featured in the movie *The Bad News Bears*.[91] In 1982, it linked itself to the movie *ET* by distributing ET glasses at its franchises.

Pizza Hut's BOOK IT! national reading incentive program began in 1984 with an enrollment of 200,000 elementary school students across the nation. By the 1998–1999 school year, 22 million children in 895,000 classrooms were enrolled. The program serves as a public relations project, as advertising gimmick, and indirectly sells extra pizzas to parents of student winners. As advertisers suggested in the early 20th century, it is important to implant brand names in children to establish adult preferences. Under the program, children who achieve their monthly reading goals are rewarded with a Personal Pan Pizza and a button from the manager of the local Pizza Hut restaurant. Achieving 6-month goals earns an All-Star Medallion at a local Pizza Hut restaurant. In 1998, the BOOK IT! BEGINNERS PROGRAM started for preschool and kindergarten students with a monthly Personal Pan Pizza award. In 1999, this beginners program was active in 20,000 kindergarten classrooms and day-care centers around the country.[92]

BOOK IT is a win–win program. Children, particularly preschoolers and kindergartners, are usually escorted by their parents to the local Pizza Hut restaurant. Do the parents simply sit and watch their child eat a Personal Pan Pizza or do they also buy the child a drink and pizzas and drinks for themselves? It is possible that the parents might spend more than the cost of the award. In fact, Pizza Hut might actually make money by giving the award while implanting their brand name in the child's mind. In addition, Pizza Hut gets free help for their advertising campaign from the local school system. Principals and teachers enroll the students in the program, and teachers set monthly goals, verify completion of reading assignments, and mark wall charts to monitor children's progress toward their Personal Pan Pizza.

YUM Brands' Kentucky Fried Chicken (KFC) franchises focus on early childhood education. The original KFC started in 1930 when Harland Sanders began cooking and serving food at his service station in Corbin, Kentucky. Developing his Kentucky Fried Chicken recipe using a "secret blend" of 11 herbs and spices, he moved from his service station to a restaurant across the street. In 1935, Kentucky's governor, Ruby Laffoon, officially named Harland Sanders a "Kentucky Colonel" for his contribution to the state's cuisine. In the early 1950s, the new interstate highway system doomed his restaurant as travelers bypassed Corbin. In 1952, he decided to franchise his chicken recipe by traveling from restaurant to restaurant across the nation offering samples and franchises. By 1964, there were 600 KFC franchises. Similar to other fast-food outlets, KFC used theme architecture with Colonel Sanders serving as its logo. In fact, many KFC franchises placed likenesses of the Colonel sitting on a bench outside their restaurants.[93]

KFC has entered education in a big way. While Burger King Academies serve high school students, KFC has entered the day-care business for infants and preschool children. On August 4, 2001, the nation's first Colonel's Kids Child Care Center opened in Columbus Junction, Iowa, with the center initially offering for children 2 weeks to 12 years old infant care, day care, crisis care, before and after-school care, and summer recreational programs.[94] The company's program is called *The Colonel's Kids Charity*. In the promotion piece the company asks, "Did you know more than 29 million children have no place to go while their parents work?"[95] KFC defines the child-care crisis in the following words.

There is a child-care crisis in the United States. Every state reports shortages in child care. Consider this:

- Nearly two thirds of parents (65%) juggle multiple child-care arrangements.
- More than 15 million people work during nontraditional hours and are in need of child care.
- Nine out of 10 adults agree that finding affordable quality child care is difficult for most American families.

It is fitting to end this brief review of fast-food education with KFC's support of day-care centers. It could be suggested that the need for Colonel's Kids Child Care Centers and Burger King Academies for troubled adolescents is a product of the mobile and frantic family life that made fast food successful. Contrary to the 1950's myth of the traditional family, the harried lives of two wage earner households creates dependence on fast food. It is a distortion of home economist Ellen Richard's dream of saving time from cooking so that women could have more freedom. Would she have approved of a quick and cheap family dinner at McDonald's or Burger King so that the kids could use the franchise's playgrounds?

Interestingly, the evolution of American cuisine has mapped out a whole set of public spaces beyond the school cafeteria and hospital kitchen. The cuisine created a marriage among education, advertising, and media. Obviously fast-food franchises' connection to media and education is a form of advertising and is used to build a public image of being family friendly. The range of fast-food educational projects is amazing when one considers they include a Black History curriculum, college scholarships, cooperative reading programs with public schools, a science center using state educational standards, science programs, day-care centers, teenage programs, and charter schools. In and out of school, children and teenagers consume American cuisine as food and brand names.

CONCLUSION: GETTING COCA-COLA
INTO THE CLASSROOM

This chapter and book conclude with the now famous 1997 story of the overzealous efforts of Colorado Springs School District administrator John Bushey to have students consume more Coca-Cola. The tale provides an important view of historical change. As the reader may recall from chapter 1, Coca-Cola was created in the 19th century as brain tonic for the weary businessman. In the late 1890s, it was transformed and sold as a general beverage and advertised as simply "Delicious and Refreshing." Advertising and marketing eventually made Coca-Cola the most recognized brand symbol among global youth. At the same time that Coca-Cola was being repackaged, the school cafeteria was born with the promise of providing students with a healthy American cuisine. Jell-O made it into the school cafeteria, but not Coca-Cola. However, by the early 21st century, fast food and so-called *junk food* were becoming standard school items, with Taco Bell, Pizza Hut, and McDonald's supplying school cafeterias.

John Bushey's deal with Coca-Cola to increase school consumption of their products was, in part, a result of a defined teenage market created in the 1930s and 1940s as an outcome of mass secondary education. By the 1990s, advertisers were interested in placing ads in high schools to capture the market. Dan DeRose's DD Marketing pioneered the effort after DeRose, as athletic director at the University of Southern Colorado, was able to raise $250,000 in corporate sponsorship for his sports teams. His first deal after organizing DD Marketing was negotiating a $3.4 million partnership between Dr. Pepper and Grapevine–Colleyville school district in Texas. Dr. Pepper's advertising campaign within the school district included placing ads on school rooftops to be seen by passengers flying in and out of the Dallas–Fort Worth Airport. One of his other accomplishments was opening in the Derby, Kansas, school district a Pepsi GeneratioNext Resource Center.[96]

It seems fitting that school sports as a symbol of masculinity and as the 1920s' solution for channeling adolescent male sexuality would become a target of advertising agencies. In Pueblo, Colorado, DD Marketing worked out an agreement between the school district and Burger King to provide for ads throughout the school, including stadium banners and an ad over the stadium's public-address system. Corporate sponsorship of new high school scoreboards bearing the corporate name or logo became common.[97]

Bushey's push for increased soft drink sales was part of a Coca-Cola marketing plan to increase consumption by children and teenagers.[98] Bushey's school district signed an agreement with the company to sell 21,000 cases of Coke products. Bushey's administrative memo urged principals to increase sales of Coke products by allowing students to drink them in classrooms. He suggested placing Coke machines closer to classrooms for easier access. Bushey went on to become principal of the high school in Disney's planned community Celebration.[99]

Not only is the distinctiveness of American cuisine represented by Taco Bell in the school cafeteria and Coca-Cola in the classroom, but also America's marriage of education, advertising, and media. The wedding of these three resulted from efforts to redefine femininity and masculinity in the corporate age, reform the American family, control American youth, resolve the conflict between the schools and media over the control of national culture, sell the American way of life as a product of consumerism and capitalism, use media and schools as part of national defense in the cold war, create efficiency in food production, and maintain consumerism. The ideology of consumerism makes increased production dependent on increased consumption. Within this framework, increased consumption requires motivating consumer desires through advertising. Advertising becomes the driving force of the economy. Every space, including public spaces, becomes an advertising opportunity. The promise of increased levels of schooling is not greater happiness, but increased levels of consumption. Equality of opportunity means equality of opportunity to consume. Schools are now training grounds for consumer-citizens. America's cuisine, advertising, and media are its most important contributions to world culture.

Notes

CHAPTER 1

1. Eric Schlooser, *Fast Food Nation: The Dark Side of the All-American Meal* (Boston: Houghton Mifflin Company, 2001), p. 4.

2. Matthew Purdy, "A Chance to Live, and Then Describe, Her Own American Dream," *New York Times on the Web* (24 June 2001).

3. The dilemmas presented to Americans by industrial and agricultural abundance are explored by Jackson Lears in *Fables of Abundance: A Cultural History of Advertising in America* (New York: Basic Books, 1994).

4. Simon N. Patten, *The New Basis of Civilization* (Cambridge: Harvard University Press, 1968), p. 215.

5. Ibid., p. 141.

6. Patten, p. 137.

7. Anzia Yezierska, *Salome of the Tenements* (Urbana: University of Illinois Press, 1995), p. 27.

8. My review of these civilizational differences can be found in Joel Spring, *Globalization and Educational Rights: An Intercivilizational Analysis* (Mahwah, New Jersey: Lawrence Erlbaum Associates, 2001).

9. Lears, p. 20.

10. Thomas Jefferson, "To the Chiefs of the Cherokee Nation. Washington, January 10, 1806," in *The Life and Selected Writings of Thomas Jefferson,* edited by Adrienne Koch and William Peden (New York: The Modern Library, 1944), p. 578.

11. William G. McLoughlin, *Cherokees and Missionaries 1789–1839* (New Haven: Yale University Press, 1984), p. 61.

12. "President Jackson on Indian Removal, December 8, 1829" in Francis Paul Prucha, ed., *Documents of United States Indian Policy, Second Edition* (Lincoln: University of Nebraska Press, 1990), pp. 47–48.

13. See John Sugde, *Tecumseh: A Life* (New York: Henry Holt & Company, 1998).

14. Ibid., pp. 118–119.

15. J. R. Pole, *The Pursuit of Equality in American History* (Berkeley: University of California Press, 1993), p. 37.

16. Ibid., p. 37.

17. Ibid., p. 151.

18. Harry Warfel, *Noah Webster: Schoolmaster to America* (New York: Macmillan, 1936), pp. 71–75.

19. Pole, p. 138.

20. Ibid., p. 152.

21. Carl F. Kaestle, *Pillars of the Republic: Common Schools and American Society 1780–1860* (New York: Hill & Wang, 1983), p. 90.

22. Roland Marchand, *Advertising the American Dream: Making Way for Modernity 1920–1940* (Berkeley: University of California Press, 1985), pp. 32–38.

23. See David Tyack and Elisabeth Hansot, *Managers of Virtue: Public School Leadership in America 1820–1980* (New York: Basic Books, 1990).

24. Footnote Protestant reformers.

25. Richard Mosier, *Making the American Mind: Social and Moral Ideas in the McGuffey Readers* (New York: Russell & Russell, 1965), pp. 167–170; Harvey C. Minnich, *William Holmes McGuffey and His Readers* (New York: American Book Company, 1936), pp. 30–89.

26. Stephen Rachman, "Shaping the Values of Youth: Sunday School Books in the 19th Century America, *http://memory.loc.gov/ammem/award99/miemhtml/svyhome.html*, pp. 11–12. This essay accompanies the digitization of 19th-century Sunday School books as part of the Library of Congress' National Digital Library Program. I will be using material from this collection in my discussion of the content of Sunday School books. The digitized books are accompanied by the following statement: "This collection presents 163 Sunday school books published in America between 1815 and 1865, drawn from the collections of Michigan State University Libraries and the Clarke Historical Library at Central Michigan University Libraries. They document the culture of religious instruction of youth in America during the Antebellum era. They also illustrate a number of thematic divisions that preoccupied 19th century America, including sacred and secular, natural and divine, civilized and savage, rural and industrial, adult and child. Among the topics featured are history, holidays, slavery, African Americans, Native Americans, travel and missionary accounts, death and dying, poverty, temperance, immigrants, and advice.

27. Mosier, p. 161.

28. William H. McGuffey, *McGuffey's Newly Revised Eclectic Second Reader* (Cincinnati: Winthrop B. Smith, 1843), pp. 47–48.

29. Ibid., pp. 48–50.

30. By A. Lady, *The Factory Boy, or The Child of Providence* (Philadelphia: American Baptist Publication Society, 1839), pp. 8–9 (numbering is based on digitalized version, see endnote 44).

31. Ibid, p. 23.

32. Ibid., p. 49.

33. E. M. Sheldon, *"I Wish I Was Poor"* (New York: American Tract Society, 1864), pp. 1–2.

34. Ibid., p. 3.

35. Ibid., p. 10.

36. Ibid., pp. 10–11.

37. Ibid., p. 12.

38. Ibid., p. 13.

39. Ibid., p. 13.

40. Author Unknown, "A Ride to the City," *Common Sights in Town & Country. Delineated & Described for Young Children* (Philadelphia: American Sunday-School Union, 18-?), p. 2.

41. Ibid., p. 2.

42. By a Lady, *The Factory Boy*, p. 6.

43. Ibid., p. 6.

44. "The Coal Cart" in *Common Sights in Town & Country* . . . , p. 4.

45. Ibid., p. 4.

46. Ibid., p. 4.

47. Author Unknown, *Frank Harper, or, The Country-Boy in Town* (Philadelphia: American Sunday-School Union, 1847), p. 6.

48. David M. Henkin, *City Reading: Written Words and Public Spaces in Antebellum New York* (New York: Columbia University Press, 1998), p. 12.

49. Ibid., p. 50.

50. Ibid., p. 81.

51. Ibid., p. 84.

52. Quoted in Jackson Lears, *Fables of Abundance: A Cultural History of Advertising America* (New York: Basic Books, 1994), p. 267.

53. Ibid., p. 213.

54. Sivulka, p. 31.

55. Henkin, p. 176.

56. As quoted in Headrick, p. 190.

57. Ibid., p. 190.

58. Ibid., p. 191.

59. Henkin, pp. 105–108.

60. Richard Ohmann, *Selling Culture: Magazines, Markets, and Class at the Turn of the Century* (New York: Verso, 1996), p. 21.

61. Ibid., p. 21.

62. Henkin, p. 103.

63. Ibid., p. 127.

64. See Ralph Henry Gabriel, *Elias Boudinot: Cherokee & His America* (Norman: University of Oklahoma Press, 1941), pp. 108–109 and Grant Foreman, *Sequoyah* (Norman: University of Oklahoma Press, 1938).

65. Quoted in Henkin, p. 115.

66. Ibid., p 117.

67. Stephen Fox, *The Mirror Makers: A History of American Advertising and Its Creators* (Urbana: University of Illinois Press, 1997), p. 65.

68. These ads are reproduced in Sivulka, pp. 76–77.

69. Reproduced in Henkin, p. 120.

70. Ibid.

71. John Lust, *The Herb Book* (New York: Bantam Books, 1974), p. 476.

72. Ibid., pp. 411–412.

73. William Leach, *Land of Desire: Merchants, Power, and the Rise of a New American Culture* (New York: Vintage Books, 1993), pp. 55–60.

74. Quoted by Leach, p. 60.

75. I am relying on Gottdiener, *The Theming of America* . . . , for developing this conceptual framework regarding themed environments.

76. Quoted by William Leach in *Land of Desire: Merchants, Power, and the Rise of a New American Culture* (New York: Vintage Books, 1993), p. 39.

77. Quoted by Leach, p. 60.

78. Quoted by Leach, p. 62.

79. Ibid., p. 64.

80. Quoted in Ibid., p. 65.

81. Ibid., p. 66.

82. Quoted in Ibid., p. 74.

83. Leach's description, p. 77.

84. Woody Register, *Coney Island: Fred Thompson and the Rise of American Amusements* (New York: Oxford University Press, 2001), p. 93.

85. Ibid., p. 151.

86. Ibid., p. 15.

87. Register, pp. 95–99.

88. Register, p. 25.

89. Ibid., pp. 92–93, 152–153.

90. Kathy Peiss, *Cheap Amusements: Working Women and Leisure in Turn-of-the Century New York* (Philadelphia: Temple University Press, 1986), pp. 131–132.

91. Associated Press, "U.N. Study: Americans Work More," *New York Times on the Web*, *www.nytimes.com* (1 September 2001) SEP 01, 2001.

92. Ibid.

93. The statement on compassionate conservativism that influenced President George W. Bush is Marvin Olasky's *Renewing American Compassion: How Compassion for the Needy Can Turn Ordinary Citizens Into Heroes* (Washington, DC: Regenery Publishing, Inc., 1996).

CHAPTER 2

1. For a summary statement of historical interpretations of this transition in domestic roles see, Steven Lubar, "Men/Women/Production/Consumption," in *His and Hers: Gender, Consumption, and Technology* edited by Roger Horowitz and Arwen Mohun (Charlottesville: University Press of Virginia, 1998), pp. 7–37.

2. Susan Strasser, *Never Done: A History of American Housework* (New York: Henry Holt & Company, 1982).

3. See Gail Bederman, *Manliness & Civilization: A Cultural History of Gender and Race in the United States 1880–1917* (Chicago: University of Chicago Press, 1995) and Michael Kimmel, *Manhood in America: A Cultural History* (New York: The Free Press, 1996).

4. Sivulka, p. 64.

5. Susan Strasser, *Satisfaction Guaranteed: The Making of the American Mass Market* (Washington, DC: Smithsonian Institution Press, 1989), p. 52.

6. Quoted from a 1932 advertising brochure by Gary Cross in *An All-Consuming Century: Why Commercialism Won in Modern America* (New York: Columbia University Press, 2000), p. 32.

7. Shapiro, p. 152.

8. Rima D. Apple, "Liberal Arts or Vocational Training? Home Economics Education for Girls," in *Rethinking Home Economics: Women and the History of a Profession* edited by Sarah Stage and Virginia B. Vincenti (Ithaca: Cornell University Press, 1997), p. 85.

9. Laura Shapiro, *Perfection Salad: Women and Cooking at the Turn of the Century* (New York: Random House, 2001), p. 4.

10. Ibid., p. 68.

11. See Carolyn M. Goldstein, "Part of the Package: Home Economists in the Consumer Product Industries, 1920–1940," pp. 271–291; " 'Where Mrs. Homemaker Is Never Forgotten': Lucy Maltby and Home Economics at Corning Glass Works, 1929–1965," pp. 163–181; and "Agents of Modernity: Home Economists and Rural Electrification, 1925–1950," pp. 237–252 in *Rethinking Home Economics. . . .* Also, James C. Williams, "Getting Housewives the Electric Message: Gender and the Energy Marketing in the Early Twentieth Century," *His and Hers . . . ,* pp. 95–114.

12. See Lynn Nyhart, "Home Economists in the Hospital, 1900–1930," *Rethinking Home Economics . . . ,* pp. 125–144.

13. Announcement quoted by Sarah Stage in "Ellen Richards and the Social Significance of the Home Economics Movement" in *Rethinking Home Economics . . . ,* p. 17.

14. Ibid., pp. 21–23.

15. Virginia B. Vicenti, "Chronology of Events and Movements Which Have Defined and Shaped Home Economics," in *Rethinking Home Economics . . . ,* p. 322.

16. Quoted in Shapiro, p. 34.

17. Ibid., p. 130.

18. Quoted by Stage, p. 28.

19. Quoted in Shapiro, p. 38.

20. Ibid., p. 39.

21. Ibid., p. 40.

22. Ibid., p. 103.

23. Ibid., p. 109.

24. Ibid., pp. 147–148.

25. Vincenti, p. 322.

26. Shapiro, p. 152.

27. Ibid., pp. 75–76.

28. Ibid., p. 76.

29. Ibid., p. 136.

30. Barbara Ehrenreich and Deirdre English's *For Her Own Good: 150 Years of the Experts' Advice to Women* (New York: Anchor Books, 1978), p. 165.

31. Ruth Schwartz Cowan, *More Work for Mother: The Ironies of Household Technology from the Open Hearth to the Microwave* (New York: Basic Books, 1983), p. 73.

32. Shapiro, p. 161.

33. Quoted in Andrew Heinze, "Jewish Women and the Making of an American Home," in *The Gender and Consumer Culture Reader* edited by Jennifer Scanlon (New York: New York University Press, 2000), p. 22.

34. Marjorie East, "The Life of Caroline Hunt, 1865–1927," in *Caroline Hunt: Philosopher for Home Economics* edited by Marjorie East (College Park: Division of Occupational and Vocational Studies, College of Education, Pennsylvania State University, 2001), pp. 1–33.

35. Caroline Hunt, "Revaluations," *Ibid.,* p. 56.

36. Caroline Hunt, "Home Economics at the University of Wisconsin, A Housekeeper Conference, From the Sixth Lake Placid Conference on Home Economics, 1904, *Ibid.*, p. 71.

37. Caroline Hunt, "Higher Education: Symposium, Eighth Lake Placid Conference on Home Economics, 1906," *Ibid.*, p. 77.

38. Ibid., p. 76.

39. Ibid., p. 76.

40. Ibid., p. 77.

41. Ibid., p. 78.

42. Caroline Hunt, "Woman's Public Work for the Home, Ninth Lake Placid Conference on Home Economics, 1907" in East, pp. 86–92.

43. Ibid., p. 87.

44. Caroline Hunt, "Homes for the Greatest Number," *The Chautauquan* (October 1902) in East, p. 105.

45. Ehrenreich and English, p. 164.

46. Ibid., p. 176.

47. Ibid., p. 176.

48. Quoted in Ibid., p. 177.

49. Caroline Hunt, "Homes for the Greatest Number," p. 90.

50. Caroline Hunt, "More Life for Man," in East, p. 111.

51. Ellen Gruber Garvey, *The Adman in the Parlor: Magazines and the Gendering of Consumer Culture, 1880s to 1910s* (New York: Oxford University Press, 1996), p. 150.

52. Ibid., p. 155.

53. Ad is reproduced in Marchand, p. 113.

54. Ibid.

55. Reproduced in Carolyn Wyman, *Jell-O: A Biography* (New York: Harcourt, Inc., 2001), p. ix.

56. Ibid.

57. Ibid.

58. As quoted in Ibid., p. 21.

59. This process is described in Ibid., p. 1.

60. Ibid., p. 3 and Shapiro, p. 93.

61. Shapiro, p. 94.

62. Wyman, p. 22.

63. Ibid., p. 23.

64. Ibid., p. 23.

65. See Strasser, *Satisfaction Guaranteed* . . . , pp. 3–5.

66. Shapiro, p. 204.

67. Shapiro, p. 203.

68. Strasser, *Satisfaction Guaranteed* . . . , p. 4.

69. Kathy Peiss, *Hope in a Jar: The Making of America's Beauty Culture* (New York: Henry Holt & Company, 1998).

70. Quote by Peiss, p. 95.

71. Ibid., p. 135.

72. Ibid., p. 91.

73. Ibid., pp. 90–94.

74. Jennifer Scanlon, "Advertising Women: The J. Walter Thompson Company Women's Editorial Department," in *The Gender and Consumer Culture Reader* . . . , p. 218.

75. This ad is reproduced in Peiss, p. 138.

76. Ibid.

77. Reproduced in Ibid., p. 146.

78. Reproduced in Marchand, p. 187.

79. Ibid.

80. Reproduced in Peiss, p. 221.

81. Robert E. Weems, Jr., "Consumerism and the Construction of Black Female Identity in Twentieth-Century America," in *The Gender and Consumer Reader* edited by Jennifer Scanlon (New York: New York University Press, 2000), p. 167.

82. Ibid., pp. 167–168.

83. Ibid., p. 169.

84. I discuss the Protestant background of the early advertising industry in Chapter 1. See Roland Marchand, *Advertising the American Dream: Making Way for Modernity 1920–1940* (Berkeley: University of California Press, 1985), pp. 32–38.

85. All of these statistics are taken from Richard Ohmann's *Selling Culture: Magazines, Markets, and Class at the Turn of the Century* (New York: Verso, 1996), p. 49.

86. Ibid., p. 58.

87. Ibid., p. 83.

88. This is Ohmann's central argument regarding the development of a mass consumer culture in the 20th century. He is not alone in advancing this thesis. For instance, John Philip Jones in *What's in a Name? Advertising and the Concept of Brands* (Lexington, MA: D.C. Heath, 1986), p. 23, states, "the driving force in [early] advertising was . . . the simple and pressing need to sell rapidly the burgeoning output of mechanized production."

89. Sivulka, p. 106.

90. Ibid., p. 49.

91. Ibid., p. 109.

92. Ibid., p. 111.

93. Ibid., p. 168.

94. Jackson Lears, *Fables of Abundance: A Cultural History of Advertising in America* (New York: Basic Books, 1994), p. 10.

95. Ibid., p. 10.

96. Reproduced in Ibid., p. 158.

97. Sivulka, p. 67.

98. Reproduced in Ibid., p. 68.

99. Jeffery Steele, "Reduced to Images: American Indians in Nineteenth-Century Advertising" in *The Gender and Consumer Culture Reader* . . . , p. 113.

100. J. Walter Thompson consistently had the highest dollar billings until it was bypassed by Young & Rubicam in 1975. Information on yearly ad agency billings is provided in the appendix of Stephen Fox's *The Mirror Makers: A History of American Advertising & Its Creators* (Urbana: University of Illinois Press, 1997), pp. 331–333.

101. Ibid., p. 81.

102. Ibid., pp. 81–83.

103. Ibid., p. 84.

104. Quoted in Stuart Even, *PR! A Social History of Spin* (New York: Basic Books, 1996), p. 132.

105. Ibid.

106. Ibid., p. 144.
107. Kerry W. Buckley, *Mechanical Man: John Broadus Watson and the Beginnings of Behaviorism* (New York: Guilford Press, 1989), p. 137.
108. Ibid., p. 119.
109. Ibid., pp. 119–120.
110. Ibid., p. 120.
111. Ibid., p. 139.
112. Ad is reproduced in Sivulka, p. 112.
113. Ad reproduced in Ibid., p. 159.
114. Buckley, p. 141.
115. Ad is reproduced in Sivulka, p. 161.
116. Ad reproduced in Marchand, p. 114.
117. Ad is reproduced in Ibid., p. 202.
118. Jenna Weissman Joselit, *A Perfect Fit: Clothes, Character, and the Promise of America* (New York: Henry Holt & Company, 2001), pp. 7–22.
119. Ibid., p. 25.
120. Quoted in Marchand, p. 51.
121. Joselit, p. 29.
122. Ibid., p. 30.
123. Ibid., p. 30.
124. Ibid., p. 39.
125. Ibid., p. 40.
126. Ibid., p. 40.
127. Marchand, p. 156.
128. Cross, pp. 50–51.
129. Ad reproduced in Sivulka, p. 114.
130. Ad reproduced in Cross, p. 51.
131. Marchand, pp. 160–161.
132. See Gay Wilentz, "Introduction," to Anzia Yezierska, *Salome of the Tenements* (Urbana: University of Illinois Press, 1995), pp. ix–xxiv.
133. Ibid., p. 91.
134. Ibid., p. 27.
135. Ibid., p. 157.
136. Ibid., p. 132.
137. Ibid., p. 33.
138. Ibid., p. 37.
139. Ibid., p. 74.
140. Ibid., p. 74.
141. Ibid., p. 75.
142. Ibid, p. 75.
143. Ibid., p. 75.
144. Ibid., p. 134.
145. Ibid., p. 136.
146. Ewen, p. 240.

CHAPTER 3

1. Gail Bederman, *Manliness & Civilization: A Cultural History of Gender and Race in the United States, 1880–1917* (Chicago: University of Chicago Press, 1995), p. 14.

2. Reproduced in Julie Wosk, *Women and the Machine: Representations from the Spinning Wheel to the Electronic Age* (Baltimore: Johns Hopkins Press, 2001), p. 7.

3. Ibid., p. 4.

4. Steven Gelber, "Do-It-Yourself: Constructing, Repairing, and Maintaining Domestic Masculinity," in *The Gender and Consumer Reader* edited by Jennifer Scanlon (New York: New York University Press, 2000), p. 72.

5. Bederman, p. 12.

6. Ibid., p. 14.

7. Michael Kimmel, *Manhood in America: A Cultural History* (New York: The Free Press, 1997), p. 182.

8. For a summary of these arguments regarding school activities and sexuality, see Joel Spring, *The American School 1642–2000* (New York: McGraw-Hill, 2001), pp. 259–273.

9. Mark A Swiencicki, "Consuming Brotherhood: Men's Culture, Style and Recreation as Consumer Culture, 1880–1930," in *Consumer Society in American History: A Reader* edited by Lawrence B. Glickman (Ithaca: Cornell University Press, 1999), p. 233.

10. Bederman, p. 13.

11. Swienciki, p. 214.

12. Jenna Weissman Joselit, *A Perfect Fit: Clothes, Character, and the Promise of America* (New York: Henry Holt & Company, 2001), p. 77.

13. George Chauncey, *Gay New York: Gender, Urban Culture, and the Making of the Gay Male World 1890–1940* (New York: Basic Books, 1994), p. 13.

14. Ibid., p. 13.

15. My description is based on a photo that I took of the statue.

16. Sivulka, p. 279.

17. This ad is reproduced in Sivulka, p. 105.

18. Bederman, p. 22.

19. Susan Porter Benson, "Living on the Margin: Working-Class Marriages and Family Survival Strategies in the United States, 1919–1941," in *The Sex of Things: Gender and Consumption in Historical Perspective* edited by Victoria de Grazia with Ellen Furlough (Berkeley: University of California Press, 1996), p. 214.

20. Ibid.

21. Ibid., pp. 215–220.

22. The title of Chapter 1 of M. E. Melody and Linda M. Peterson's *Teaching America about Sex: Marriage Guides and Sex Manuals from the Late Victorians to Dr. Ruth* (New York: New York University Press, 1999) is "The Late Victorians and Spermatic Political Economy," pp. 20–49.

23. Quoted in Ibid., p. 30.

24. Quoted in Ibid., p. 31.

25. Ibid., p. 23.

26. See Bederman, pp. 170–217 and Kimmel, pp. 181–188.

27. Kimmel, p. 181.

28. Bederman, pp. 180–181.

29. This quote is transcribed from photos I took inside the Roosevelt rotunda.

30. Ibid.

31. Ibid.

32. Bederman stresses the male orientation of Hall's concept of adolescence. Ibid., pp. 103–105.

33. G. Stanley Hall, *Adolescence*, Vol. 1 (Englewood Cliffs, NJ: Prentice-Hall, 1904), p. xv. Also see G. Stanley Hall, "Childhood and Adolescence" in Charles Strickland and Charles Burgess, eds., *Health, Growth, and Heredity* (New York: Teachers College Press, 1965), p. 108.

34. Bederman, p. 77.

35. G. Stanley Hall, *Adolescence*, Vol. 2 (Englewood Cliffs, NJ: Prentice-Hall, 1904), p. 125.

36. Kimmel, caption on photos between pp. 272–273.

37. Rev. W. J. Hunter, "Manhood Wrecked and Rescued," reproduced in Kimmel in photos between pp. 272–273.

38. Ibid.

39. The cover is reproduced in Ibid.

40. This poster is reproduced in John D'Emilio and Estelle Freedman *Intimate Affairs: A History of Sexuality in America* (New York: Harper & Row, 1988) between pp. 274 and 275.

41. "Tentative Report of the Committee on a System of Teaching Morals in Public Schools," *Proceedings of the National Education Association, 1911*, vol. 49 (Ann Arbor, MI: NEA, 1911), p. 360.

42. Irving King, *The High-School Age* (Indianapolis, IN: Bobbs-Merrill, 1914), p. 80.

43. Michael V. O'Shea, *The Trend of the Teens* (Chicago: Drake, 1920), p. 13.

44. Commission on the Reorganization of Secondary Education, National Education Association, *Cardinal Principles of Secondary Education, Bureau of Education Bulletin* (Washington, DC: U.S. Government Printing Office, 1918), p. 111.

45. V. K. Froula, "Extra-Curricular Activities: Their Relation to the Curricular Work of the School," *National Education Association Proceedings (1915)* (Washington, DC: National Education Association, 1915), pp. 738–739.

46. Quoted by E. Anthony Rotundo, *American Manhood: Transformations in Masculinity from the Revolution to the Modern Era* (New York: Basic Books, 1993), p. 240.

47. Ibid., p. 241.

48. Ibid., p. 243.

49. Margaret Lamberts Bendroth, *Fundamentalism and Gender: 1875 to the Present* (New Haven: Yale University Press, 1993), p. 65.

50. D'Emilio and Freedman, pp. 203–208.

51. "Report of the Committee on Character Education of the National Education Association," *Department of the Interior Bureau of Education Bulletin, 1926, no. 7 Character Education* (Washington, DC: U.S. Government Printing Office, 1926), p. 15.

52. Thomas W. Galloway, *Sex and Social Health: A Manual for the Study of Social Hygiene* (New York: Social Hygiene Association, 1924), pp. i–vii.

53. Ibid., p. 51.

54. Ibid., pp. 33–34.

55. Ibid., p. 65.

56. Ibid., pp. 286–287.

57. Ibid., p. 71.

58. Ibid., p. 51.

59. Ibid., p. 134.

60. Ibid., p. 96.

61. Kathy Peiss, *Cheap Amusements: Working Women and Leisure in Turn-of-the Century New York* (Philadelphia: Temple University Press, 1986), p. 88.

62. Ibid., p. 101.

63. Ibid., p. 102.

64. Quoted in Ibid., p. 99.

65. Quoted in Ibid., p. 125.

66. Quoted in Ibid., p. 126.

67. Peiss, pp. 131–132.

68. Ibid., pp. 178–181.

69. John Dewey, "The School As Social Center," *Annual Proceedings of the National Education Association, 1902* (Washington, DC: NEA, 1922), pp. 373–383.

70. T. Bowlker, "Women's Home-Making Function Applied to the Municipality, *American City*, Vol. VI (1912), pp. 863–869.

71. Beth L. Bailey, *From Front Porch to Back Seat: Courtship in Twentieth-Century America* (Baltimore: John Hopkins University Press, 1988), p. 4.

72. Mary McComb, "Rate Your Date: Young Women and the Commodification of Depression Era Courtship," in *Delinquents & Debutantes: Twentieth-Century American Girls' Cultures* (New York: New York University Press, 1998), p. 45.

73. Ibid., p. 45.

74. Quoted in Ibid., p. 45.

75. Ibid., pp. 52–54.

76. Amy L. Best, *Prom Night: Youth, Schools, and Popular Culture* (New York: Routledge, 2000), p. 6.

77. Ibid., p. 10.

78. Ibid., pp. 35–63.

79. Ibid., p. 4.

80. Kelly Schrum, "Teena Means Business: Teenage Girls Culture and Seventeen Magazine, 1944–1950," in *Delinquents & Debutantes: Twentieth-Century American Girls' Cultures* edited by Sherrie A. Inness (New York: New York University Press, 1998), pp. 140–141.

81. "Report of the Committee on Character Education of the National Education Association, *U.S. Department of the Interior Bureau of Education Bulletin, 1926, no. 7: Character Education* (Washington, DC: U.S. Government Printing Office, 1926), p. 6.

82. William Gellerman, *The American Legion as Educator* (New York: Teachers College, Columbia University, 1938), p. 88.

83. Quoted by Stuart Ewen, *PR! A Social History of Spin* (New York: Basic Books, 1996), p. 215.

84. Howard K. Beales, *Are American Teachers Free?* (New York: Scribner's, 1936), pp. 108–109.

85. Ibid., p. 126.

86. Howard K. Beales, *A History of Freedom of Teaching in American School* (New York: Scribner's, 1941), p. 247.

87. Milton Bennion, "Report of the Committee on Citizenship and Character Education," *School and Society*, vol. 14 no. 351 (September 17, 1921), pp. 190–191.

88. "Report of the Committee on Character Education. . . ."

89. Ibid., pp. 5–7.

90. Ibid., p. 6.

91. Gellerman, p. 20.

92. Ibid., pp. 21–39.

93. Russell Cook, "American Legion," *Proceedings of the Annual Meeting of the National Education Association, 1934*, vol. 72 (Washington, DC: NEA, 1934), pp. 111–116.

94. Ibid., p. 111.

95. Gellerman, p. 68.

96. As quoted in Ibid.

97. As quoted in Ibid., pp. 90–91.

98. As quoted in Ibid., pp. 203–204.

99. As quoted in Ibid., p. 206.

100. Mrs. Russell William Magna, "Daughters of the American Revolution," *Proceedings of the NEA, 1934* (Washington, DC: NEA, 1934), pp. 116–121.

101. Gellerman, pp. 206–207.

102. Ibid., pp. 208–214.

103. Beales, *Are American Teachers Free?*, p. 317.

104. These laws are reviewed by Bessie Louise Pierce, *Civic Attitudes in American Schools* (Chicago: University of Chicago Press, 1930), pp. 231–235).

105. Ibid., p. 246.

106. Roland Marchand, *Advertising The American Dream: Making Way for Modernity 1920–1940* (Berkeley: University of California Press, 1985), pp. 188–190.

107. Ibid., p. 190.

108. Richard M. Fried, "Introduction," to Bruce Barton, *The Man Nobody Knows* (Chicago: Ivan R. Dee, 2000), p. vii.

109. Stephen Fox, *The Mirror Makers: A History of American Advertising & Its Creators* (Urbana: University of Illinois Press, 1997), pp. 101–112, 331–333.

110. Barton, p. 23.

111. Ibid., p. 28.

112. Ibid., p. 23.

113. Ibid., p. 77.

114. Ibid., p. 83.

115. Ibid., pp. 61–64.

116. Reproduced in Sivulka, p. 102.

117. Reproduced in Ibid., p. 112.

118. Reproduced in Susan Strasser, *Satisfaction Guaranteed: The Making of the American Mass Market* (Washington, DC: Smithsonian Institution Press, 1989, p. 98.

119. Reproduced in Ibid., p. 99.

120. Ibid.

121. Sivulka, p. 221.

122. Reproduced in Ibid., p. 155.

123. Reproduced in Lendol Calder, *Financing the American Dream: A Cultural History of Consumer Credit* (Princeton: Princeton University Press, 1999), p. 193.

124. Reproduced in Ibid., p. 198.

125. See Ronald L. Davis, *Duke: The Life and Image of John Wayne* (Norman: University of Oklahoma Press, 1998).

126. I have already referenced the major works of Bederman and Kimmel. William Pinar's *The Gender of Racial Politics and Violence in America: Lynching, Prison Rape, & the Crisis of Masculinity* (New York: Peter Lang, 2001) provides the most complete history of these issues from the 19th to the 21st centuries.

127. Alexander Walker, *Rudolph Valentino* (New York: Penguin Books, 1977), p. 47.

128. Ibid., p. 49.

129. Ibid., p. 50.

130. Quoted in Ibid., p. 68.

131. Ibid., p. 69.

132. Photo shown in Ibid., p. 71.

133. Ibid., p. 8.

134. Ibid., p. 113.

135. Ibid., p. 113.

CHAPTER 4

1. Simon N. Patten, *The New Basis of Civilization* edited by Daniel Fox (Cambridge: Harvard University Press, 1907), p. 123.

2. Ibid., p. 123.

3. Ibid., p. 123.

4. Ibid., p. 136.

5. Ibid., p. 137.

6. Herbert Blumer, *Movies and Conduct* (New York: Macmillan, 1933), p. 50.

7. Quoted in Kathy Peiss, *Cheap Amusements: Working Class Women and Leisure in Turn-of-the-Century New York* (Philadelphia: Temple University Press, 1986), p. 153.

8. A standard history of the early development of films is Lewis Jacobs, *The Rise of the American Film: A Critical History* (New York: Teachers College Press, 1967). Figures on movie attendance and description of early audiences can be found in Lary May, *Screening Out the Past: The Birth of Mass Culture and the Motion Picture Industry* (New York: Oxford University Press. 1980), pp. 35–42.

9. "Cheap Theaters," *The Social Evil in Chicago* (Chicago: Chicago Vice Commission, 1911), reprinted in *The Movies in Our Midst*, ed. Gerald Mast (Chicago: University of Chicago Press, 1982), pp. 61–63.

10. May, p. 37.

11. Terry Christensen, *Reel Politics: American Political Movies from Birth of a Nation to Platoon* (New York: Basil Blackwell, 1987), p. 15.

12. Ibid.

13. Richard Randall, *Censorship of the Movies: The Social and Political Control of a Mass Medium* (Madison: University of Wisconsin Press, 1968), pp. 12–13.

14. Will H. Hays, "Motion Pictures and Their Censors, The American Review of Reviews, Vol. 75 (April 1927), pp. 393–398.

15. *Mutual Film Corporation v. Industrial Commission of Ohio* (1915) reprinted in *The Movies in Our Midst*, ed. Gerald Mast (Chicago: University of Chicago Press, 1982), pp. 136–143.

16. Ellis Oberholtzer, "What Are the 'Movies' Making of Our Children?" *World's Work*, vol. 4 (January 1921), pp. 249–263.

17. Ellis Oberholtzer, "The Censor and the Movie 'Menace'," *The North American Review*, vol. 212, no. 780 (November 1920), pp. 641–647.

18. Ibid.

19. May, pp. 53–55.

20. John Collier, "Censorship and the National Board, *The Survey*, vol. 35 (October 1915), pp. 9–14.

21. Ibid., p. 31.

22. John Collier, "A Film Library," *The Survey*, vol. 35 (March 1916), p. 668.

23. "Discussion," *Annual Proceedings of the NEA, 1914*, p. 747.

24. Alfred H. Saunders, "Motion Pictures as an Aid to Education," *Annual Proceedings of the National Education Association, 1914*, vol. 52 (Ann Arbor, MI: NEA, 1914), p. 744.

25. "Discussion," *Annual Proceedings of the NEA, 1914*, p. 746.

26. Ibid.

27. Neal Gabler, *An Empire of Their Own: How the Jews Invented Hollywood* (New York: Crown, 1988).

28. Ibid., p. 277.

29. Norman Zierold, *The Moguls* (New York: Coward-McCann, 1969), p. 287.

30. Ibid., p. 24.

31. May, pp. 169–177.

32. Gabler, pp. 164–165.

33. Raymond Moley, *The Hays Office* (Indianapolis, IN: Bobbs-Merrill, 1945), pp. 135–137.

34. Gabler, pp. 277–278.

35. Ibid.

36. Randall provides a chart categorizing the various censorship laws of state and city governments. See Randall, pp. 88–89.

37. "Film Censors and Other Morons," *The Nation*, vol. 117, no. 3049 (December 12, 1923), pp. 678–679.

38. For surveys of state and municipal censorship boards, see Thomas Leary and J. Roger Noall, "Note: Entertainment: Public Pressures and the Law—Official and Unofficial Control of the Content and Distribution of Motion Pictures and Magazines," Harvard Law Review, vol. 71(1957), pp. 326–367, and Randall, pp. 15–18, 88–89.

39. Lewis Jacobs, *The Rise of the American Film: A Critical History* (New York: Teachers College Press, 1967), p. 23.

40. Will Hays, "Improvement of Moving Pictures," *Annual Proceedings of the National Education Association, 1922*, vol. 60 (Washington, DC: National Education Association, 1922), pp. 252–257.

41. "Education and the Movies," *The Elementary School Journal*, vol. 23 (February 1923), pp. 406–408.

42. This financial support is recounted in Charles Judd, "Report of Committee to Cooperate with the Motion Picture Producers," *Annual Proceedings of the National Education Association, 1923*, vol. 61 (Washington, DC: NEA, 1923), pp. 243–244.

43. Ibid., p. 245.

44. Col. Jason Joy, "Motion Pictures in Their Relation to the School Child," *Proceedings of the National Education Association, 1927*, vol. 65 (Washington, DC: NEA, 1927), pp. 964–969.

45. Ibid., p. 967.

46. Ibid., p. 967.

47. Moley, pp. 77–78.

48. The following is a list of the authors and their research titles. Many of the researchers sponsored by the Payne Fund were in their own disciplines and consequently added to the prestige of the studies.

1. P. W. Holaday, Indianapolis Public Schools, and George Stoddard, Director, Iowa Child Welfare Research Station. "Getting Ideas from the Movies."
2. Ruth C. Peterson and L. L. Thurstone, Department of Psychology, University of Chicago "Motion Pictures and the Social Attitudes of Children."
3. Frank Shuttleworth and Mark May, Institute of Human Relations, Yale University: "The Social Conduct and Attitudes of Movie Fans."
4. W. S. Dysinger and Christian Ruckmick, Department of Psychology, State University of Iowa. "The Emotional Responses of Children to the Motion Picture Situation."
5. Charles Peters, Professor of Education, Pennsylvania State College "Motion Pictures and Standards of Morality."
6. Samuel Renshaw, Vernon L. Miller, and Dorothy Marquis, Department of Psychology, Ohio State University. "Children's Sleep."
7. Herbert Blumer, Department of Sociology. University of Chicago: "Movies and Conduct."
8, 9, and 12. Edgar Dale, Research Associate, Bureau of Educational Research, Ohio State University: "The Content of Motion Pictures," "Children's Attendance at Motion Pictures," and "How to Appreciate Motion Pictures," respectively.
10. Herbert Blumer and Philip Hauser, Department of Sociology, University of Chicago, "Movies, Delinquency, and Crime."
11. Paul Cressey and Frederick Thrasher, New York University "Boys, Movies, and City Streets."

49. Henry James Forman, *Our Movie-Made Children* (New York: Macmillan, 1933).
50. W. W. Charters, *Motion Pictures and Youth: A Summary* (New York: Macmillan, 1933), p. 12.
51. Ibid., p. 13.
52. Ibid., p. 13.
53. Forman, pp. 280–282.
54. John D' Emilio and Estelle Freedman, *Intimate Affairs: A History of Sexuality in America* (New York: Harper & Row, 1988), pp. 256–257.
55. Cited in Lary May, *Screening Out the Past: The Birth of Mass Culture and the Motion Picture Industry* (New York: Oxford University Press, 1980), p. 203.
56. D'Emilio and Freedman, pp. 256, 268.
57. M. E. Melody and Linda M. Peterson, *Teaching America about Sex: Marriage Guides and Sex Manuals from the Late Victorians to Dr. Ruth* (New York: New York University Press, 1999), pp. 59–63.
58. Ibid., pp. 63–65.
59. Ibid., pp. 72–114.
60. Blumer, pp. 45–49.
61. Charles Peters, *Motion Pictures and Standards of Morality* (New York: Macmillan, 1933).
62. The Legion of Decency, *The Commonwealth*, vol. 20 (May 18, 1934), p. 58.
63. The pledge can be found in Ibid.
64. The pledge can be found in Ibid.
65. Moley, pp. 57–58.
66. Martin Quigley, *Decency in Motion Pictures* (New York: Macmillan, 1937).
67. The 1930 movie code can be found in Moley, pp. 241–248, and Mast, pp. 321–333.
68. Ibid.

69. The 1927 Code can be found in Moley, pp. 240–241.

70. The 1930 movie code can be found in Moley, pp. 241–248, and Mast, pp. 321–333.

71. Will H. Hays, "The Motion Picture in Education," *Proceedings of the Annual Meeting of the National Education Association, 1939*, vol. 77 (Washington, DC: NEA, 1939), p. 80.

72. Juliann Sivulka, *Soap, Sex, and Cigarettes: A Cultural History of American Advertising* (Belmont, CA: Wadsworth Publishing, 1998), pp. 211–222.

73. "British vs. American Radio Slant, Debate Theme in 40,000 Schools," *Variety*, vol. 111, no. 12 (August 29, 1933), p. 1.

74. Ibid.

75. See Philip T. Rosen, *The Modern Stentors: Radio Broadcasters and the Federal Government, 1920–1934* (Westport, CT: Greenwood Press, 1980), pp. 128–133, Erik Barnouw, *A Tower in Babel: A History of Broadcasting in the United States to 1933* (New York: Oxford University Press, 1966), pp. 172–179, and E. Frost, *Education's Own Stations: The History of Broadcast Licenses Issued to Educational Institutions* (Chicago: University of Chicago Press, 1937), pp. 1–5.

76. The other members were the National University Extension Association, the Jesuit Educational Association, The Association of Land-Grant Colleges and Universities, and the Association of College and University Broadcasting Stations.

77. "Virtues, Vices of Radio . . . ," pp. 3–10.

78. Joy Elmer Morgan, "A National Culture—By-Product or Objective of National Planning?" Ibid., p. 29.

79. Ibid., p. 30.

80. Merlin H. Aylesworth, "Radio as a Means of Public Enlightenment," *Proceedings of the National Education Association*, 1934, vol. 72, pp. 99–102.

81. William Paley, "Radio as a Cultural Force: These notes on the economic and social philosophy of America's radio industry, as represented by the policies and practices of the Columbia Broadcasting System, Inc., were embodied in a talk on October 17, 1934, before the Federal Communications Commission, in its inquiry into proposals to allot fixed percentages of the nation's radio facilities to non-commercial broadcasting," Located in CBS Reference Library, New York City, pp. 8–9.

82. Ibid., p. 13.

83. Ibid., pp. 13–14.

84. Barnouw, *The Golden Web*, p. 26.

85. Paley, p. 14.

86. Ibid., p. 18.

87. *Variety*, vol. 117, no. 1 (December 18, 1934), p. 34.

88. "St. Paul Meet on Kid Programs Calls Radio Villains Likeable; Suggest Boycott, Probation" *Variety*, vol. 117, no. 2 (December 25, 1934), p. 29.

89. "Air Reformers After Coin," *Variety*, vol. 117, no. 7 (January 29, 1935), pp. 1, 66.

90. Raymond Stedman, *The Serials: Suspense and Drama by Installment* (Norman: University of Oklahoma Press, 1977), pp. 143–191, and Erik Barnouw, *The Golden Web: A History of Broadcasting in the United States, 1933–1953* (New York: Oxford University Press, 1968), pp. 89–108.

91. Stedman, p. 192.

92. Ibid., pp. 194–195.

93. *Radio's Golden Years* (tape recording) (Minneapolis: Cassettes, Inc., 1972).

94. Clara Savage Littledale, "Better Radio Programs for Children," *Parents Magazine*, vol. 18, no. 13 (May 8, 1933).

95. "Boycott MDSE in Air Protest?" *Variety*, vol. 109, no. 12 (February 28, 1933), p. 47.

96. "Cal. Teachers List 'Bad' Programs," *Variety*, vol. 110. no. 8 (May 2, 1933), p. 34.

97. "Mrs. Harold Milligan," *Educational Broadcasting 1937*, ed. C. S. Marsh (Chicago: University of Chicago Press, 1938), pp. 258–261.

98. "Radio: Mothers Chasing the Ether Bogeyman," *Newsweek*, March 11, 1933, p. 30.

99. "Clubwomen Launch Westchester Cowboys," *Variety*, vol. 117, no. 10 (February 20, 1935), p. 39.

100. "Women's Radio Committee Clarifies," *Variety*, vol. 118, no. 10 (May 22, 1935), p. 36.

101. "Mrs. Harold Milligan," p. 259.

102. Ibid., pp. 258–259.

103. Ibid., p. 261.

104. "Squawks Force NBC Move for Less Honor," *Variety*, vol. 109, no. 12 (February 26, 1933), p. 45.

105. "Now Agree Too Much Honor for Kids, Junior Programs Turning to Fantasy, *Variety*, vol. 111, no. 8 (August 1, 1933), p. 41.

106. "Radio Wants Clubwoman Good Will: Offer Transmitters to Gals with Messages—Will Hays Started It," *Variety*, vol. 112, no. 6 (October 17, 1933), p. 37.

107. "Dime Novel Air Stuff Out: Protests Chafe FCC Into Action," *Variety*, vol. 118, no. 3 (April 3, 1935), pp. 1, 58.

108. "Paley in Annual Report Deprecates 'Straightjacket' for Broadcasting; Air Voluntarily Censors Programs," *Variety*, vol. 134, no. 4 (April 5, 1939), p. 23.

109. "NBC Slant on CBS Policy," CBS Reference Library, p. 37.

110. "Sponsor Rights Defined," *Variety*, vol. 134, no. 4 (April 5, 1939), p. 23.

111. Statement by William S. Paley over the Columbia Network, Tuesday, May 14, 1935, CBS Reference Library.

112. Arthur Jersild and Frances Holmes, *Children's Fears* (New York: Teachers College, 1935), pp. 318–335.

113. "New Policies: A Statement to the Public, to Advertisers, and to Advertising Agencies" (May 15, 1935), CBS Reference Library, p. 4.

114. Ibid., p. 5.

115. Ibid., p. 6.

116. "NBC's Tentative Program Code," *Variety*, vol. 134, no. 4 (April 5, 1934), p. 24.

117. Ibid.

118. Ibid.

CHAPTER 5

1. Lendol Calder uses this magazine cover for the cover of his book, *Financing the American Dream: A Cultural History of Consumer Credit* (Princeton: Princeton University Press, 1999). Calder discusses the artist's original intentions on p. 305.

2. Stuart Ewen, *PR! A Social History of Spin* (New York: Basic Books, 1996), p. 147.

3. Edward S. Herman and Noam Chomsky, *Manufacturing Consent: The Political Economy of the Mass Media* (New York: Pantheon, 1988).

4. For a review of these early works on controlling public opinion, including Lippmann's *Public Opinion*, see Ewen, pp. 131–174.

5. Quote by Ewen, p. 149.

6. Ibid., p. 303.

7. Ibid., pp. 322–323.

8. Quoted by Ewen, p. 304.

9. Ibid., p. 167.

10. Ibid., p. 163.

11. Ibid., pp. 297–298.

12. Photos of billboards shown in Ewen, p. 323.

13. Ibid., p. 306.

14. Ibid., p. 314.

15. Ibid., p. 315.

16. Commission on Character Education, Tenth Yearbook, *Character Education* (Washington, DC: Department of Superintendence of the National Education Association, 1932), p. 15.

17. Educational Policies Commission, *Learning the Ways of Democracy: A Case Book of Civic Education* (Washington, DC: NEA, 1940), pp. 63–64.

18. Ibid., p. 65.

19. Ibid., p. 109.

20. Ibid., p. 110.

21. Ibid., p. 171.

22. William Gellerman, *The American Legion as Educator* (New York: Teachers College, Columbia University, 1938), p. 93.

23. Gellerman, p. 122; Harold Hyman, *To Try Men's Souls: Loyalty Tests in American History* (Berkeley and Los Angeles: University of California Press, 1959), pp. 323–326; Edward A. Krug, *The Shaping of the American High School, 1920–1941* (Madison: University of Wisconsin Press, 1972), pp. 231–232.

24. C. A. Bowers, *The Progressive Educator and the Depression: The Radical Years* (New York: Random House, 1969), p. 15.

25. Russell Cook, "American Legion," *Proceedings of the National Education Association, 1934*, vol. 72 (Washington, DC: NEA, 1934), pp. 111–116.

26. As quoted in Mary Anne Raywid, *The Ax-Grinders: Critics of Our Public Schools* (New York: Macmillan, 1963), p. 51.

27. Augustin G. Rudd, *Bending the Twig: The Revolution in Education and Its Effect on Our Children* (New York: New York Chapter of the Sons of the American Revolution, 1957), pp. 26–27.

28. Harold Rugg, *That Men May Understand: An American in the Long Armistice* (New York: Doubleday, Dome, 1941), pp. 36–44.

29. Reprinted in Ibid., pp. 54–69.

30. Ibid., pp. 10–11.

31. Ibid., p. 25.

32. Ibid., pp. 29–30.

33. Quoted by Stephen Fox, *The Mirror Makers: A History of American Advertising & Its Creators* (Urbana: University of Illinois Press, 1997), p. 123.

34. Ibid., pp. 123–124.

35. Quoted by Gary Cross, *An All-Consuming Century: Why Commercialism Won in Modern America* (New York: Columbia University Press, 2000), p. 135.

36. Ibid., p. 135.

37. Rudd, p. 85.

38. "Advertising Groups Pursuing Professor Rugg's Books," *Publishers Weekly*, vol. 138 (September 28, 1940), pp. 1322–1323.

39. Ibid., p. 1323.

40. Rudd, p. 65.

41. "Book Burnings: Rugg Texts," *Time*, vol. 36 (September 9, 1940), pp. 64–65.

42. Rugg, p. 3.

43. Ibid., p. 4.

44. Ibid., p. 12.

45. William Carr, "An Educator Bids for Partners," *Nation's Business* (March 1941), pp. 19–20, 96–97.

46. Walter Fuller, "Industry and the War," *Proceedings of the NEA, 1942*, pp. 111–114.

47. John Studebaker, "Our Country's Training Program," *Proceedings of the National Education Association, 1941*, Vol. 79 (Washington, DC: NEA, 1941), pp. 115–122.

48. As quoted by Elaine Tyler May, *Homeward Bound: American Families in the Cold War Era* (New York: Basic Books, 1999), p. 11.

49. Elaine Tyler May, "The Commodity Gap: Consumerism and the Modern House," in *Consumer Society in American History: A Reader* edited by Lawrence Glickman (Ithaca: Cornell University Press, 1999), pp. 298–299.

50. Ibid., p. 302.

51. Mary Anne Raywid, *The Axe Grinders: Critics of Our Public Schools* (New York: Macmillan, 1963), pp. 35–51.

52. Ibid.

53. Ibid., pp. 59–63.

54. Jack Nelson and Gene Roberts, Jr., *The Censors and the Schools* (Westport, CT: Greenwood Press, 1963), pp. 99–100.

55. Ibid., p. 109.

56. Ibid., pp. 109–110.

57. Joel Spring, *The Sorting Machine Revisited: National Educational Policy Since 1945* (White Plains, NY: Longman, 1989), p. 9.

58. Ibid.

59. Ibid.

60. Kelly Schrum, "Teena Means Business: Teenage Girls' Culture and 'Seventeen Magazine', 1944–1950," in *Delinquents & Debutantes: Twentieth-Century American Girls' Cultures* (New York: New York University Press, 1998), p. 149.

61. Ibid., p. 149.

62. Ibid., p. 156.

63. Ibid., p. 136.

64. Ad reproduced Ibid., p. 143.

65. Ad is reproduced in Juliann Sivulka's *Soap, Sex, and Cigarettes: A Cultural History of American Advertising* (Belmont, CA: Wadsworth Publishing Company, 1998), p. 262.

66. Reproduced in Schrum, p. 148.

67. Ibid., p. 142.

68. Erik Barnouw, *The Golden Web: A History of Broadcasting in the United States, 1933–1953* (New York: Oxford University Press, 1968), pp. 295–296.

69. The code can be found in *Documents of American Broadcasting*, ed. Frank Kahn (Englewood Cliffs, New Jersey: Prentice-Hall, 1973), pp. 340–355.

70. As quoted by Ben Bagdikian, *The Media Monopoly, Second Edition* (Boston: Beacon Press, 1987), p. 137.

71. As quoted in Barnouw, p. 257 (capitalization in original).

72. Ibid., pp. 253–257, 265.

73. As quoted in Ibid., p. 273.

74. Ibid., pp. 273–274.

75. Ibid., p. 88.

76. Ibid., p. 92.

77. Ibid., pp. 168–169.

78. "Comic Book Publishers Promise Reforms," *Christian Century*, vol. 71 (November 10, 1954), p. 1357.

79. *Comic Books and Juvenile Delinquency: A Part of the Investigation of Juvenile Delinquency in the United States: Interim Report of the Subcommittee to investigate Juvenile Delinquency to the Committee on the Judiciary Pursuant to S. Res. 89 and S. Res. 190* (Washington, DC: U.S. Government Printing Office, 1955), p. 3.

80. "Senate Sub-Committee Holds Hearings on 'Comics'," *Publishers Weekly*, vol. 165 (May 1, 1954), p. 1903.

81. *Comic Books and Juvenile Delinquency . . .* , pp. 8–9.

82. "Purified Comics," *Newsweek*, vol. 32 (July 12, 1948), p. 56; "Better Than Censorship," *Christian Century*, vol. 65 (July 28, 1948), p. 750; *Comic Books and Juvenile Delinquency . . .* , p. 31.

83. "Comics' Publishers Institute Code, Appoint 'Czar'," *Publishers' Weekly*, vol. 166 (September 25, 1954), p. 1386; "Progress in Comic Book Cleanup," *America* (October 30, 1954), pp. 1–14; "Code for Comics," *Time* (November 8, 1954), p. 60.

84. "First 'Seal of Approval' Comics Out This Month," *Publishers' Weekly*, vol. 167 (January 15, 1955), p. 211.

85. "Comics' Publishers Institute Code," p. 1386; "Correspondence: Comic-Book Code," *America* (November 13, 1954), p. 196.

86. May, p. 148.

87. Abraham Tannenbaum, "Family Living in Textbook Town," *Progressive Education*, March 1954. Reprinted in *Hearings Before the Ad Hoc Subcommittee on De Facto School Segregation, Committee on Education and Labor, House of Representatives, 89th Congress, 2nd Session, on Books for Schools and the Treatment of Minorities, August 23, 24, 30, 31, and September 1, 1966* (Washington, DC: U.S. Government Printing Office, 1966), pp. 806–816.

88. Ibid., pp. 813–814.

89. Wini Breines, "The Other Fifties: Beats and Bad Girls," in *Not June Cleaver: Women and Gender in Postwar America, 1945–1960* edited by Joanne Meyerowitz (Philadelphia: Temple University Press, 1994), p. 385.

90. As reported by Ronald L. Doris, *Duke: The Life and Image of John Wayne* (Norman: University of Oklahoma Press, 1998), p. xi.

91. Ibid., pp. 15–96.

92. See Clayton R. Koppes and Gregory D. Black, *Hollywood Goes to War: How Politics, Profits and Propaganda Shaped World War II Movies* (Berkeley: University of California Press, 1987).

93. Doris, p. 279.

94. Ibid., p. 119.

95. Larry Ceplair and Steven Englund, *The Inquisition in Hollywood: Politics in the Film Community, 1930–1960* (Berkeley and Los Angeles: University of California Press, 1983), p. 211.

96. John Cogley, *Report on Blacklisting* (Fund for the Republic, 1956), p. 11.

97. Quoted by Doris, p. 118.

98. Quoted by Doris, p. 12.

99. Ibid., p. 5.

100. Ibid., p. 8.

101. Sivulka, p. 279.

102. Molly Haskell, *From Reverence to Rape: The Treatment of Women in the Movies Second Edition* (Chicago: University of Chicago Press, 1987), p. 254.

103. Ibid., p. 243.

104. Ibid., p. 253.

105. Breines, pp. 390–396.

106. Ibid., p. 398.

107. The ad is reproduced in Lynn Spigel's *Make Room for TV: Television and the Family Ideal in Postwar America* (Chicago: The University of Chicago Press, 1992), p. 87.

108. Ibid., p. 83.

109. Ibid., p. 83.

110. Reproduced in Ibid., p. 93.

CHAPTER 6

1. "The Negro in American History Textbooks: A Report of a Study of the Treatment of Negroes in American History Textbooks Used in Grades Five and Eight and in the High Schools of California's Public Schools" (Sacramento: California State Department of Education, 1964), p. 2.

2. "The Negro in American History Textbooks," reprinted in *Hearings Before the Ad Hoc Subcommittee on De Facto School Segregation*, of the Committee on Education and Labor, House of Representatives, 89th Congress, 2nd Session, on Books for Schools and the Treatment of Minorities, August 23, 24, 30, 31, and September 1, 1966 (Washington, DC: U.S. Government Printing Office, 1966).

3. Erik Barnouw, *The Golden Web: A History of Broadcasting in the United States, 1933–1953* (New York: Oxford University Press, 1968), p. 297.

4. "The Negro in American History Textbooks . . . ," p. 770.

5. Ibid., pp. 770–771.

6. Ibid., p. 772.

7. Roy Wilkins, "Books for Schools and Treatment of Minorities: Introduction" (National Association for the Advancement of Colored People, 1966), p. 1.

8. "Statement of Lerone Bennett," *Hearings Before the Ad Hoc Subcommittee . . .*, pp. 214–215.

9. Ibid., pp. 213–214.

10. "Statement of Austin J. McCaffrey, Executive Director, American Textbook Publishers Institute," Hearings Before the Ad Hoc Subcommittee on De Facto School Segregation, of the Committee on Education and Labor, House of Representatives, 89th Congress, 2nd Session, on Books for Schools and the Treatment of Minorities, August 23, 24, 30, 31, and September 1, 1966 (Washington, DC: U.S. Government Printing Office, 1966), p. 107.

11. Joel Roth, "Dick and Jane Make Some New Friends," *Book Production Industry,* June 1965, reprinted in *Hearings Before the Ad Hoc Subcommittee on De Facto School Segregation . . .* , p. 816.

12. "Statement of Austin McCaffrey . . . ," p. 114.

13. "Statement of Robert W. Locke, Senior Vice President, McGraw-Hill Book Co.; Accompanied by Dr. Richard Smith, Senior Editor, Text-Film Division, McGraw-Hill Book Co., *Hearings Before the Ad Hoc Subcommittee on De Facto Segregation . . . ,*" p. 191.

14. "Statement of Darrel E. Peterson, President, Scott, Foresman & Co.," *Hearings Before the Ad Hoc Subcommittee on De Facto Segregation . . .* , pp. 122–123.

15. "Integrating the Texts," *Newsweek,* March 7, 1966, reprinted in *Hearings Before the Ad Hoc Subcommittee on De Facto Segregation . . .* , pp. 826–827.

16. A. Kent MacDougall, "Integrated Books-School Texts Stressing Negroes' Role in United States Arouse the South's Pre-Primers Show Mixed Scenes, Some Publishers Turn Out Special Editions for Dixie," *Wall Street Journal,* March 24, 1966, reprinted in *Hearings Before the Ad Hoc Subcommittee on De Facto School Segregation . . .* , p. 804.

17. "Statement of Darrel E. Peterson . . . ," p. 122.

18. Ibid., pp. 124–125.

19. "Statement of Ross Sackett, Executive Vice President, Holt Rinehart & Winston, Inc.," *Hearings Before the Ad Hoc Subcommittee on De Facto Segregation . . .* , pp. 217–273.

20. "Statement of Craig T. Senft, President, Silver Burdett Co., a Division of General Learning Corporation," *Hearings Before the Ad Hoc Subcommittee on De Facto School Segregation . . .* , pp. 115–117.

21. Statement of Robert W. Locke, Senior Vice President, McGraw-Hill Book Co.; Accompanied by Dr. Richard Smith, Senior Editor, Text-Film Division, McGraw-Hill Book Co., *"Hearings Before the Ad Hoc Subcommittee on De Facto Segregation . . .* , p. 191.

22. "Statement of G.M. Fenollosa, Vice President and Director, Houghton Mifflin Co., Boston, Mass.," *Hearings Before the Ad Hoc Subcommittee on De Facto School Segregation . . .* , p. 129.

23. Robert E. Weems, Jr., "Consumerism and the Construction of Black Female Identity in Twentieth-Century America," in *The Gender and Consumer Culture Reader* edited by Jennifer Scanlon (New York: New York University Press, 2000), p. 167.

24. Ibid., p. 171.

25. Ibid., pp. 171–172.

26. Ibid., p. 173.

27. Ibid., p. 173.

28. Ibid., p. 175.

29. Ibid., p. 175.

30. The ad is reproduced in Juliann Sivulka, *Soap, Sex, and Cigarettes: A Cultural History of American Advertising* (Belmont, CA: Wadsworth Publishing Company, 1998), p. 293.

31. Ibid., p. 264. See Stephen Fox's *The Mirror Makers: A History of American Advertising and Its Creators* (Urbana: University of Illinois Press, 1997), pp. 272–314 on the racial integration of advertising agencies and ad content.

32. Bernice Kanner, *The 100 Best TV Commercials . . . and Why They Worked* (New York: Random House, 1999), p. 137.

33. Ibid., p. 137.

34. Ibid., p. 139.

35. Ibid., p. 139.

36. Ibid., p. 141.

37. Elissa Moses, *The $100 Billion Allowance: Accessing the Global Teen Market* (New York: John Wiley & Sons, Inc. 2000), p. 10.

38. Ibid., p. 36.

39. Leslie Savan, *The Sponsored Life: Ads, TV, and American Culture* (Philadelphia: Temple University Press, 1994), p. 55.

40. Gail Bedesman, *Manliness & Civilization: A Cultural History of Gender and Race in the United States, 1880–1917* (Chicago: University of Chicago Press, 1995), p. 3.

41. Quoted by Kenon Breazeale, "In Spite of Women: Esquire and the Male Consumer," *The Gender and Consumer Culture Reader* . . . , p. 229.

42. Ibid., p. 233.

43. Ibid., p. 235.

44. Ibid., p. 235.

45. Ibid., p. 239.

46. "National Organization for Women's 1966 Statement of Purpose" (Adopted at the Organizing Conference in Washington, DC, October 29, 1966), http://www.now.org.

47. For a survey of accomplishments in changing female images in public schools see "Opening Doors in Education," http://www.feminist.org.

48. Savan, p. 225.

49. Ibid., pp. 226–227.

50. Sivulka, p. 303.

51. Reproduced in Ibid., p. 374.

52. Reproduced in Savan, p. 205.

53. Ibid., p. 205.

54. Ibid., p. 198.

55. Ibid., p. 198.

56. Ibid., p. 199.

57. Kanner, p. 41.

58. Eric Johnston, *America Unlimited: The Case for a People's Capitalism* (Garden City, NY: Doubleday, Doran, 1944), p. 13.

59. Ibid., p. 6.

60. Ibid., p. 343.

61. Eric Johnston, *Intolerance* (New York: U.S. Chamber of Commerce, 1945), pp. 3–7.

62. Edward De Grazia and Roger Newman, *Banned Films: Movies, Censors & The First Amendment* (New York: Bowker, 1982), pp. 70–71.

63. Ibid.

64. Ibid., pp. 230–231.

65. Ibid., pp. 238–240.

66. William S. Paley, *As It Happened: A Memoir* (Garden City, NY: Doubleday, 1979), p. 232.

67. Thomas Cripps, "Amos 'n' Andy and the Debate over American Racial Integration," in *American History/American Television: Interpreting the Video Past*, ed. John E. O'Conner (New York: Frederick Ungar, 1983), pp. 33–54.

68. Ibid., p. 41.

69. Ibid., p. 49.

70. J. Fred MacDonald, *Blacks and White TV: Afro-Americans in Television since 1948* (Chicago: Nelson-Hall, 1983), pp. 68–69, 72–73.

71. As quoted in Ibid., p. 16.

72. Ibid., pp. 81–82; quote from p. 101.

73. Ibid., pp. 93–95.

74. *Office of Communication of the United Church of Christ v. Federal Communications Commission*, reprinted in *Documents of American Broadcasting*, ed. Frank J. Kahn (Englewood Cliffs, NJ: Prentice-Hall, 1973), pp. 639–681.

75. As quoted in Kathryn C. Montgomery, *Target: Prime Time Advocacy Groups and the Struggle over Entertainment Television* (New York: Oxford University Press, 1989), pp. 23–24.

76. Ibid., pp. 24–26.

77. Ibid., p. 58.

78. Ibid., pp. 51–58.

79. Ibid., p. 73.

80. Ibid., pp. 75–80.

81. Ibid., pp. 28–30.

82. MacDonald, pp. 108–111.

83. Angela M. S. Nelson, "Black Situation Comedies and the Politics of Television Art," in *Cultural Diversity and the U.S. Media* edited by Yahya R. Kamalipour and Theresa Carilli (Albany: State University of New York Press, 1998), p. 80.

84. Ibid., pp. 81–86.

85. See Richard Morris and Mary E. Stuckey, "Destroying the Past to Save the Present: Pastoral Voice and Native Identity," in *Cultural Diversity and the U.S. Media . . .* , pp. 137–147.

86. Kanner, p. 222.

87. Ibid., p. 223.

88. Ibid., p. 222.

89. Ellen Condliffe Lagemann, *The Politics of Knowledge: The Carnegie Corporation, Philanthropy, and Public Policy* (Middletown, CT: Wesleyan University Press, 1989), pp. 222–223.

90. As quoted in James L. Baughman, *Television's Guardians: The FCC and the Politics of Programming, 1958–1967* (Knoxville: University of Tennessee Press, 1985), pp. 34–35.

91. Ibid., p. 33.

92. Ibid., p. 33.

93. As quoted in Lagemann, p. 220.

94. Alan Pifer, "When Fashionable Rhetoric Fails," *Education Week*, vol. 23 (February 1983), p. 24.

95. Carnegie Commission on Educational Television, *Public Television: A Program for Action* (New York: Harper & Row, 1967), p. 95.

96. Ibid., p. 95.

97. Lloyd Morrisett, "Introduction" in Gerald S. Lesser, *Children and Television: Lessons from "Sesame Street"* (New York: Vintage, 1975), p. xxi.

98. Ibid., p. xxvi.

99. Lesser, p. 7.

100. Ibid., pp. 8–9.

101. Ibid., p. 23.

102. Ibid., pp. 24–25.

103. Ibid., pp. 254–255.

104. Ibid., p. 95.

105. Ibid., p. 200.

106. Ibid., p. 80.

107. Ibid., pp. 80–81.

108. Ibid., p. 47.

109. Ibid., p. 204.

110. Ibid., pp. 208–211.

111. "PBSKids: Sesame Street-Caregivers," *http://pbskids.org/sesame/caregivers/index.html.*

112. Ibid.

113. I found these product names and associated icons on the Amazon Web site, *www. amazon.com.*

114. Ibid.

CHAPTER 7

1. Anzia Yezierska, *Salome of the Tenements* (Urbana: University of Illinois Press, 1995), p. 27.

2. Amy L. Best, *Prom Night: Youth, Schools, and Popular Culture* (New York: Routledge, 2000), p. 46.

3. Kurt M. Landgraf, "Testing, Accountability, and Funding: Key to Education Reform," Paid advertisement in *The New York Times* (June 25, 2001), p. A9.

4. Ibid.

5. Alex Molnar, *Giving Kids the Business: The Commercialization of America's Schools* (Boulder: Westview Press, 1996).

6. Constance L. Hays, "New Report Examines Commercialism in U.S. Schools," *New York Times on the Web* (September 14, 2000).

7. Ibid.

8. Lynne Schrum, "Education and Commercialization: Raising Awareness and Making Decisions" (Athens: University of Georgia, College of Education, 2002), p. 5.

9. Alexandra Stille, "Textbook Publishers Learn to Avoid Messing with Texas," *The New York Times on the Web* (June 29, 2002).

10. Ibid.

11. Ibid.

12. Ibid.

13. Ibid.

14. Coby B. Simerly, Penny A. Ralston, Lydia Harriman, and Barbara Taylor, "The Scottsdale Initiative: Positioning the Progression for the 21st Century" in *Themes in Family and Consumer Sciences: A Book of Readings 2001, Volume Two* edited by Coby B. Simerly, Sharon Y. Nickols, and Jan M. Shane (Alexandria, VA: American Association of Family and Consumer Sciences, 2001), p. 15.

15. "Our Mission," *www.cwu.edu/~fandcs/fcsea.*

16. Marilyn R. DeLong, "Apparel Shopping on the Web," in *Themes in Family and Consumer Sciences . . .* , pp. 109–113.

17. "AACS: Who We Are," *www.aafcs.org.*

18. Ibid.

19. "About FCSEA," *www.cwu.edu/~fandcs/fcsea.*

20. "National Standards for Family and Consumer Sciences Education," *www.isbe.net/ secondaryed/FCS/fcs.htm.*

21. Ibid.

22. Ibid.

23. Ibid.

24. Ibid.

25. Elissa Moses, *The $100 Billion Allowance: Accessing the Global Teen Market* (New York: John Wiley & Sons, Inc. 2000), pp. 4, 10–11.

26. Moses, Back cover copy.

27. Back cover copy, Ibid.

28. Back cover copy, Ibid.

29. Ibid., pp. 35–60.

30. Ibid., pp. 168–170.

31. Ibid., pp. 86–87.

32. Ibid., p. 90.

33. Ibid., p. 91.

34. Juliann Sivulka, *Soap, Sex, and Cigarettes: A Cultural History of American Advertising* (Belmont, CA: Wadsworth Publishing Company, 1998), p. 421.

35. Ibid., p. 421.

36. Moses, p. 84.

37. Ibid., p. 86.

38. Ibid., p. 98.

39. Moses, p. 101.

40. Ibid., p. 82.

41. Ibid., p. 155.

42. Ibid., p. 120.

43. Quoted by Ellen Gruber Harvey, *The Adman in the Parlor: Magazines and the Gendering of Consumer Culture, 1880s to 1910s* (New York: Oxford University Press, 1996), p. 54.

44. Ad reproduced in Ibid., p. 63.

45. Ad reproduced in Ibid., p. 56.

46. Susan Strasser, *Satisfaction Guaranteed: The Making of the American Mass Market* (Washington, DC: Smithsonian Institution Press, 1989), pp. 115–119.

47. For a chronological list of Walt Disney's films see Leonard Mosley, *Disney's World* (Lanham, MD: Scarborough House, 1990), pp. 309–315.

48. Quoted by Bob Thomas in *Building A Company: Roy O. Disney and the Creation of an Entertainment Empire* (Hew York: Hyperion, 1998), pp. 67–68.

49. Ibid., p. 68.

50. Quoted in Ibid., p. 69.

51. Quoted in Ibid., p. 70.

52. Ibid., p. 198.

53. Ibid., pp. 187–188, 198.

54. http://www.sixflags.com/intl/intl_movieworldgermany.html.

55. Bob Thomas, *An American Original: Walt Disney* (New York: Disney Editions, 1994), p. 11.

56. Thomas, *Building A Company* . . . , p. 197.

57. http://disneyland.disney.go.com/disneylandresort/ResortInfo/Tickets/TicketPrices/index?id=6072&Grouping=TG.

58. Http://dlr.reservations.disney.go.com.

59. Thomas, *An American Original* . . . , pp. 251–262.

60. Ibid., p. 251.

61. Http://disneyland.disney.go.com.
62. Ibid.
63. Ibid.
64. Ibid.
65. Gottdiener, p. 127.
66. Http:dollywood.com.
67. Http://www.wholesaleeverday.com.
68. Henry A. Giroux, *The Mouse that Roared: Disney and the End of Innocence* (New York: Rowman & Littlefield Publishers, Inc., 1999).
69. Eric Schlosser, *Fast Food Nation: The Dark Side of the All-American Meal* (Boston: Houghton Mifflin Company, 2001), p. 48.
70. "McDonald's USA–Happy Meal Featuring the Many Adventures of Winnie the Pooh," *http://www.mcdonalds.com*.
71. Schlosser, p. 41.
72. Ibid., p. 48.
73. Ibid., p. 47.
74. "Little Known Black History Facts," *http://www.mcdonalds.com*.
75. "Little Known Black History Facts: Scope and Sequence," *http://www.mcdonalds.com*, Ibid., p. 1.
76. Ibid., pp. 2–3.
77. Schlosser, p. 22.
78. "Burger King Big Kids," http://www.burgerking.com.
79. "BK Academies," http:www.burgerking.com.
80. Ibid.
81. "BKScholars," http:www.burgerking.com.
82. "Welfare Reform," http:www.burgerking.com.
83. "Welcome to yum!," http://www.yum.com/home.asp.
84. "America's Original Fast Food Chain" and "History," *http://www.a-wroobeer.com*.
85. "Long John Silver's," *http://www.ljsilvers.com/about/history.htm*.
86. "The Pizza Hut Story," *http://www.pizzahut.com*, p. 6.
87. "Taco Bell History," http://www.tacobell.com.
88. "Discovery Science Center," *http://www.discoverycube.org*.
89. "TEEN SUPREME," http://www.teensupreme.org/main.html.
90. "Pizza Hut Story . . . ," p. 4.
91. Ibid., p. 3.
92. "Pizza Hut News: Facts about Book It and Book It! Beginners," *http://www.pizzahut.com*.
93. "About KFC: The Story of Colonel Harland Sanders," http://www.kfc.com.
94. "Nation's First Colonel's Kids Child Care Center Opens August 4, 2001!," http://www.colonelskids.com.
95. "Colonel's Kids charity–The Child Care Issue," http://www.colonelskids.com.
96. Schlosser . . . , pp. 52–53.
97. Ibid., p. 53.
98. Ibid., p. 53.
99. Ibid., p. 57.

Author Index

Numbers in parentheses are footnote numbers and indicate that an author's work is referred to, although his or her name may not be cited in the text. Numbers in italic show the page where the complete reference is given.

A

Apple, R. D., 31(8), *213*
Aylesworth, M. H., 116(80), *224*

B

Bagdikian, B., 142(70), *228*
Bailey, B. L., 77(71), *219*
Barnouw, E., 115(75), 117(84), 119(90), 141(68), 142(71, 72, 73), 143(74, 75, 76, 77), 155(3), *224, 227, 229*
Barton, B., 85(110, 111), 86(112, 113, 114), 87(115)
Baughman, J. L., 175(90, 91, 92), *232*
Beales, H. K., 81(86), 84(103), *219*
Bederman, G., 29(3), 63(1, 5, 6), 64(10), 65(18), 67(26, 28), 69(32), 70(34), 163(40), *212, 217, 231*
Bendroth, E. A., 73(49), *218*
Bennion, M., 81(87), *219*
Benson, S. P., 65(19, 20), 66(21), *217*
Best, A. L., 78(76), 79(77, 78, 79, 80), 183(2), *219, 233*
Black, G. D., 148(92), *228*
Blumer, H., 96(6), 107(48), 109(60), *221*

Bowers, C. A., 131(24), *226*
Bowlker, T., 77(70), *219*
Breazeale, K., 163(41, 42), 164(43, 44, 45), *231*
Breines, W., 147(89), 150(105, 106), *228*
Buckley, K. W., 51(107, 108, 109, 110), 52(111), 53(114), *216*

C

Calder, L., 89(123, 124), 125(1), *220, 225*
Carnegie Commission on Educational Television, 176(95, 96), *232*
Carr, W., 135(45), *227*
Ceplair, L., 148(95), *229*
Charters, W. W., 107(50, 51), 108(52), *223*
Chauncey, G., 64(13, 14), *217*
Chomsky, N., 125(3), *225*
Christensen, T., 98(11, 12), *221*
Cogley, J., 149(96), *229*
Collier, J., 101(20, 21, 22), 121(22), *222*
Commission of Character Education, 129(16), *226*
Cook, R., 82(93, 94), 131(25), *220, 226*
Cowan, R. S., 36(31), *213*
Cressey, P., 107(48), *223*

236

Subject Index

FISHING ONLINE:

1,000
BEST
WEB SITES

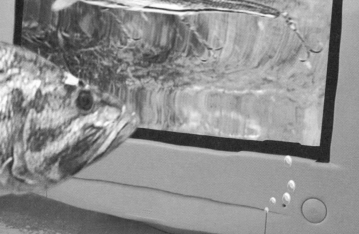

BY CRAIG BUDDE

STOEGER PUBLISHING COMPANY, ACCOKEEK, MARYLAND

STOEGER PUBLISHING COMPANY
is a division of Benelli U.S.A.

BENELLI U.S.A.
Vice President and General Manager:
Stephen Otway
Vice President of Marketing and
Communications: Stephen McKelvain

STOEGER PUBLISHING COMPANY
President: Jeffrey Reh
Publisher: Jay Langston
Managing Editor: Harris J. Andrews
Design & Production Director:
Cynthia T. Richardson
Photography Director: Alex Bowers
Imaging Specialist: William Graves
National Sales Manager: Jennifer Thomas
Special Accounts Manager: Julie Brownlee
Editorial Assistant: Christine Lawton
Administrative Assistant:
Shannon McWilliams

Published by Stoeger Publishing Company
17603 Indian Head Highway, Suite 200
Accokeek, Maryland 20607

BK0307
ISBN: 0-88317-251-8

Library of Congress Control Number:
2002110068

Manufactured in
the United States of America.

Distributed to the book trade and
to the sporting goods trade by:
Stoeger Industries
17603 Indian Head Highway, Suite 200
Accokeek, Maryland 20607
301-283-6300 Fax: 301-283-6986
www.stoegerindustries.com

Cover:
Photo Illustration by William Graves with
photos by Larry Larsen and Alex Bowers;
8, 21, 110, 222: Alex Bowers;
22: George Gentry/USFWS;
142: Jay T. Langston

OTHER PUBLICATIONS:
Shooter's Bible 2004 - 95th Edition
 The World's Standard Firearms Reference Book
Gun Trader's Guide - 26th Edition
 Complete Fully Illustrated Guide to Modern
 Firearms with Current Market Values
Elk Hunter's Bible
Shotgunning for Deer
Trailing the Hunter's Moon
Hunt Club Management Guide
The Turkey Hunter's Tool Kit: Shooting Savvy
Hunting Whitetails East & West
Archer's Bible
The Truth About Spring Turkey Hunting
 According to "Cuz"
The Whole Truth About Spring Turkey
 Hunting According to "Cuz"
Complete Book of Whitetail Hunting
Hunting and Shooting with the Modern Bow
The Ultimate in Rifle Accuracy
Advanced Black Powder Hunting
Hounds of the World
Labrador Retrievers
Hunting America's Wild Turkey
Taxidermy Guide
Cowboy Action Shooting
Great Shooters of the World
Sporting Collectibles
The Working Folding Knife
The Lore of Spices
Antique Guns
P-38 Automatic Pistol
The Walther Handgun Story
America's Great Gunmakers
Firearms Disassembly with Exploded Views
Rifle Guide
Gunsmithing at Home
Complete Guide to Modern Rifles
Complete Guide to Classic Rifles
FN Browning Armorer to the World
Modern Beretta Firearms
How to Buy & Sell Used Guns
Heckler & Koch: Armorers of the Free World
Spanish Handguns
The Handloader's Manual of Cartridge Conversions
Modern Sporting Rifle Cartridges
Complete Reloading Guide
Ultimate Bass Boats
Bassing Bible - 2004 Edition
The Flytier's Companion
Deceiving Trout
The Complete Book of Trout Fishing
The Complete Book of Flyfishing
Peter Dean's Guide to Fly-Tying
The Flytier's Manual
Flytier's Master Class
Handbook of Fly Tying
The Fly Fisherman's Entomological Pattern Book
The Legend of Harley-Davidson
The Legend of the Indian
Best of Harley-Davidson
Classic Bikes
Great Trucks
4X4 Vehicles
Fish & Shellfish Care & Cookery
Game Cookbook
Dress 'Em Out
Wild About Venison
Wild About Game Birds
Wild About Freshwater Fish
Wild About Waterfowl
The World's Best Catfish Cookbook

online code: SPBK0307AC

Acknowledgements

For allowing me a first glimpse into the world of outdoor writing and publishing, I'd like to thank Nick and Frank Amato of Amato Publications, Inc. in Portland, Oregon. For their many encouraging words and generous screenshot permissions, I'd like to thank the hundreds of webmasters I contacted in the course of researching this book. For uncountable taxi trips to Nayland and Wivenhoe and for generally being the best parents one could wish for, I'd like to thank George and Mary Buddo of Colchester, Essex, England.

Dedication

This book is dedicated to Rachel A. Fusco and Scout A. Fusco— my two favorite Americans.

FISHING ONLINE: 1,000 BEST WEB SITES
TABLE OF CONTENTS

CHAPTER 1
HOW TO FIND FISHING INFORMATION ON THE INTERNET

This book is the best available tool for finding fishing information on the Internet. I've spent thousands of hours over the last two years surfing links, clicking through directories, typing keywords into search engines, scanning forums and following up on recommendations, to select the best web sites for every type of fishing interest.

I undertook the project because I saw there was a strong need for someone who loves and understands the sport to carve away all the dull, badly designed, broken-down fishing sites clogging up the Web, obscuring the hundreds of worthwhile sites out there.

For every web site included, and there are more than 1,000 individual sites referenced within these pages, at least a dozen were rejected. The ones left, whether they come from corporate publishers, individual enthusiasts, fishing groups, or government agencies, were overwhelmingly selected for usefulness and quality content. To me that means a combination of any of the following: good numbers of general articles or coverage of specialist topics; up-to-date fishing reports and news stories; the best online tools and resources for trip planning; popular community centers; pleasing design and regular maintenance.

A Word About Organization

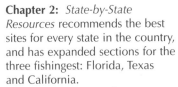

Chapter 2: *State-by-State Resources* recommends the best sites for every state in the country, and has expanded sections for the three fishingest: Florida, Texas and California.
Chapter 3: *Know Before You Go* complements those sites with national trip-planning resources such as weather forecasts, tide tables, streamflows, maps, and solunar tables, all of which can be searched and applied on a local basis.
Chapter 4: *Fishing the Web* separates the sport into its different branches, listing the best sites for bass fishing, freshwater fishing, saltwater fishing and fly fishing.
Chapter 5: *Media* singles out print magazines and other media providers that have migrated to the Web, as well as purely online fishing magazines.
Chapter 6: *Groups* recommends web sites giving a voice to the sport's underrepresented members: women, youth and disabled anglers and has listings for conservation groups and fishing clubs.
Chapter 7: *Tackle and Boats* is divided into sites for making and collecting tackle, how to find bargains online, and the best boating magazines and resources.
Chapter 8: *International* explores the true worldwide fishing Web by pointing to, among other countries, the best Canadian, Australian and British sites, and some of the specialist travel companies catering to globe-trotting fishermen.

Sites are listed in alphabetical order, though occasionally a review will go on to mention a closely related site. The URL List at the back of the book (Appendix III) gives the full title and address of every site referenced in the text. It's important to browse all the chapters, especially if you're trying to find local information, because many of the best sites are strong in two or three areas. **Florida Sportsman Online, http://www.floridasportsman. com** or **Reel-Time, http:// www.reeltime.com** for example, could fit seamlessly into three different chapters. As a reminder, some of these multitasking sites are crossreferenced in different chapters.

TOP RATED

There are things of value in every one of these sites but the ones that really stand out in terms of design and content have been given a **TOP RATED** designation. Each of the the more than 310 sites that made the cut is listed for quick reference in Appendix I.

For the sake of consistency, what different web sites variously label message boards, chat boards, discussion forums or discussion boards are collectively referred to in the text as "forums," whether the site uses the term or not. To acknowledge the special importance of these community areas, as sites were reviewed a quick assessment was made of the health and responsiveness of each site's forum. Appendix II lists more than 250 of the best.

For the sake of technical accuracy, all URLs are listed with the http:// prefix, but the only time you might want to actually type it out is for those rare sites that forego the traditional "www." at the beginning of the address, such as **MuskieFIRST** at **http://muskie. outdoorsfirst.com**. If you have a newer version of either Internet Explorer or Netscape, it isn't strictly necessary to include either the www. or the http:// as long as you type in the rest of the address: muskie.outdoorsfirst.com gets you there just the same.

Warning: Contents May Shift

The reviews in this book highlight a few of the best features of each site and often suggest a pathway through the site to find them. Because good web sites are constantly developing and because webmasters just seem to enjoy tinkering with their creations, features are often shifted, renamed or archived. But it's unusual for good content to disappear completely because web sites aren't hedged in by the space limitations of traditional media. If a feature or section isn't where it's supposed to be, scout around and for larger sites, use the site map or search function.

Here Today, Here Tomorrow

Though the Web is a good deal more stable than it's usually given credit for, sites do come and go, especially those that rely on e-commerce or advertising revenue. Few of the sites in the book fall into that category, but it will still happen that an occassional site seems to have disappeared. They may be unavailable rather than dead and gone, so try this four-part resurrection plan before dismissing them.

1. Check spelling.
As obvious as that sounds, it's one of the primary reasons sites appear to be missing. URLs can be long and convoluted, especially those for homepages, government sites and university departments, and they have to be entered exactly as written. The URLs in this book have been checked and re-checked, but as a general search rule try substituting different top-level domains (if it's written as .com try .net or .org; if it's a Canadian site try .ca, for a British site, .co.uk, and so on), or for sites that end in .html try .htm and vice versa.

2. Enter the title keywords or URL into a favorite search engine. If you take this book's advice and become a fan of Google, you'll see it stores or "caches" a copy of the pages in its search results. If the site is unavailable, the cache feature at least confirms it was alive not too long ago and shows you what the page looks like so you can decide if it's worth coming back to.

3. A "Not Found 404" error message indicates the URL you're looking for can't be found on its host server. It may mean the site has changed address or is no longer online, but in the case of addresses such as **http://www. epa.gov/adopt/resources/ toprelated.html**, which is pointing to a single page within a web site, it's possible the page may have moved or been deleted but the larger site is still available. Find out by starting at the end of the address and deleting the directory paths separated by the forward slashes. In this example, delete /toprelated.html and press Enter.

If that doesn't open the page you're looking for, delete /resources and press Enter, or /adopt/resources to go straight to the homepage.

4. Sites may be unavailable because of issues to do with your Internet Service Provider (ISP), the web site's server, or heavy traffic to the site or on the Internet as a whole. In which case the best answer is to just wait an hour or try again in a few days. If you're consistently having problems accessing the Web, it might be time to consider upgrading your computer or switching to a different ISP. For sites that seem to be available but aren't loading properly, use the browser's Stop button and then click Refresh or Reload. It may be necessary to update your browser to access some of the newer, graphically advanced sites. The latest browsers can easily be downloaded from either **Netscape** at **http:/www. netscape.com** (Browser Central) or **Microsoft** at **http://www. microsoft.com** (Downloads).

Links

Many of the best sites in this book were discovered by trawling through the links recommended by similar sites. Quality sites usually recognize and want to be associated with other good content providers, so as you read through the chapters make a habit of exploring each site's links section. If your favorite site merely links to advertisers or one-dimensional tackle company web sites, encourage them to start publishing readers' link recommendations: the ability to surf to other sites of interest is one of the founding principals of the Web and there's no better judge of what's worthwhile to fishermen than their web-surfing brethren.

The Directories section of Chapter 5 Media reviews some of the best sites set up as pure fishing link directories.

Search Engines —
A Very Short Guide

Search engines are an essential tool for finding anything on the Web and they couldn't be more straightforward to use: type your chosen keywords into a little box and click on Search or press Enter. But getting the results you want is a different matter. That's to be expected when you consider the information you're looking for might only be contained on a single document out of billions of pages on the Web.

Most of the better-known search engines work by releasing a software program called a "spider" or "crawler" to move across and record what's on the Web. They then feed the information back to the search engine's computers to form a huge index of current web pages. When you put a term into a search engine the search doesn't go out onto the Web, it goes to the search engine's index. For the most part then, the bigger the index the better the chance it has of finding what you're looking for. As of this writing, some of the biggest search indexes are **Google** at **http://www.google.com** (4 billion web pages and the industry leader by a hefty margin), **AltaVista** at **http://www.altavista.com**, and **AlltheWeb** at **http://www.alltheweb.com**.

There are many other good search engines available, some with added features that can help you find material others can't. While not one of the biggest, **Ask Jeeves** at **http://www.askjeeves.com**, for example, is set up for users

to pose questions—"Who caught world's biggest bass?"—in natural language, as they would conversationally. **Search Engine Colossus** at **http://www.searchengine colossus.com** is a directory of homegrown search engines for every major country in the world. Many have searches and directories drawn from a far greater number of national web sites than U.S.-based search engines. Click on South Africa, for example, for links to nine English language search engines including the promising **Ananzi** site at **http://www.ananzi.co.za**, offering thousands of options for fishing guides, outfitters, lodges, clubs and magazines.

It's good practice not to get too attached to one engine: try out several, bookmark two or three favorites and run difficult searches through each one. Whichever you choose, follow these tips to make your searches more accurate:

1. The golden rule is to choose your words carefully. Always keep in mind the words you type into the search box are all that the search engine has to work with. Think before you type.

2. Keywords should be nouns, and the more specific the noun the better. Multiple keywords: "fishing reel levelwind saltwater," not "fishing reel" allows the search engine to narrow in on what you're looking for.

3. If you're getting poor results, try as many permutations of your search phrase as possible.
We know that bass, largemouths, and black bass are all the same thing, but your search engine needs some help making the connection.

4. Words are weighted according to order, so put the defining terms first.

5. Use capitalization to indicate proper names, but otherwise always use lowercase letters.
"Salmon River" should take you to New York; "salmon river" will probably land you in Alaska.

6. Don't forget to read the search engine FAQ or instructions for advanced searches to get the most from the available technology.

7. Various commands can be incorporated alongside your keywords instructing the search engine to include or exclude terms or otherwise refine its search. The names given to them might remind you of being in math class, but modifiers and Boolean operators are simple to use and can cut down on fruitless searches. Simply type in the command next to or between your normal keywords to see if they improve the quality of your results.

Non-Boolean Modifiers
• To specify that another word must be included use the plus sign, as in: bass + boat.
• To exclude a word use the minus sign, as in: bass - guitar.
• To search for an exact phrase use quotation marks, as in "Bass Professor."

Boolean Operators
• To include both words type AND, as in: bass AND boat.
• To include at least one word use OR, as in: bass OR walleye boat.
• To exclude pages that contain a word, use NOT or AND NOT, as in: bass NOT guitar or bass AND NOT guitar.

To wade much deeper into how to get the most from search engines, try the excellent industry review site **Search Engine Showdown** at **http://www. searchengine showdown.com**. A good source for researching the specialist terms and acronyms associated with search engines, the Web and the Internet is **NetLingo – The Internet Dictionary** at **http://www.netlingo.com**.

FREEBIES FOR FISHERMEN ON THE WEB

Along with information and online communities, many fishing web sites offer useful free features as promotional tools. These are just a few highlights from sites reviewed in this book:

Free Fishing Logs
Register at **NJ Striper** at **http://www.njstriper.com** or go to **Fly Fishing NC** at **http://www.flyfishingnc.com** to create your own catch log and hatch chart.

Free Software
Eli Robillard's SuperFly Fishing Machine at **http://www.ofifc.org/Eli/ SuperFly/default.asp** is a downloadable program for recording fly patterns and hatches.

(continued on page 15)

Online Communication

As useful and entertaining as many fishing web sites are, it's the unprecedented ability to connect with other fishermen within forums, mailing lists, chat rooms and newsgroups that's the real revolution offered by the Internet. Fishing "talk"—with all the opinion and arguments, wise words and B.S. that goes along with it—has gone global. No matter where you fish, what you fish for, or what type of tackle you prefer, you can find a community out there somewhere chatting about it.

Rules of Conduct

The relative anonymity of being online can cause people to say things they never would in person. Anyone who regularly uses forums or other forms of online communication has probably witnessed discussions heating up into arguments and arguments into tirades, even threats. These standard rules of behavior, which can be broadly applied to all forms of online communication, won't help you avoid someone who's deliberately provocative, but they will prove to everyone else you're a responsible participant. Communities that require detailed registration or that are overseen by a moderator are less appealing to rogues and dingbats.

1. Be polite. Unless you're logged onto **http://www.jackass.com**, don't be one. Write as if you were talking face-to-face and treat others as you would wish to be treated yourself.

2. Read the FAQ or rules of conduct before posting. As well as information about what's permitted and maintaining privacy, you'll sometimes find a statement about the aims of the community, and answers to questions that are repeatedly posted to the group and everyone is bored of answering.

3. If you're new to a community "lurk" for a while and read over old posts to get a feel for the group dynamic.

4. Don't write in CAPS: it's the online equivalent of shouting.

5. Don't advertise, beyond what's permitted by the rules.

6. Be specific with subject headers to help others decide if it's something they're likely to be interested in.

7. It's about fishing and subjects related to fishing: keep on topic. Wise webmasters will create a separate forum for that all-time number one argument starter: politics.

8. Cross-posting or posting the same message in multiple forums or on several newsgroups is considered bad manners. It suggests you're trying to mine the group for information, rather than engage it in a real discussion.

9. Be community minded. Occasionally people use forums and mailing lists as if they were making a telephone call.

Exchanges such as:

Big Dog: You out there, Fish Boy?
Fish Boy: Hey
Big Dog: Git any?
Fish Boy: Couple
Big Dog: Any size?
Fish Boy: Couple
Big Dog: Out at the usual spot?
Fish Boy: Yeah
Big Dog: Going this weekend?
Fish Boy: Nah

...aren't doing the community much of a service. Keep your audience in mind by posting topics that are likely to interest most of the members.

Forums

Forums are areas for posting and reading messages from other visitors to the site. They are usually split into topics: as well as a forum for general discussion, there might be ones for different fisheries, different species or styles of fishing. Most require some form of registration before you can contribute. Though they can be set up in different ways—watch out for those that don't display the most recent post at the top of the forum where you expect to find it—they all show the subject line of posted comments and the number of

replies it generated. Click on the subject line to read the full comment then go on to read the replies or "discussion thread" it generated. Many forum templates give statistics for the number of registered users, how many posts or threads have been generated over a period of time, and offer keyword searches into the archive of old messages.

The biggest fishing forums have thousands of users, but they don't need a huge audience to be worthwhile. Forum quality is measured more by how responsive members are, how polite and community minded, and how well the flow of messages is organized.

The list of fishing forums in Appendix II has suggestions for finding every type of fishing community from bamboo rod makers to Northeast striper fanatics, plus a few international options, but there are a couple of other ways to track down likely communities. Most of the sites referenced in this book offer forums of some kind: occasionally a site reorganization can kickstart a community so be sure to check them all out, even if they aren't otherwise mentioned. A promising new search engine

FREEBIES FOR FISHERMEN ON THE WEB:

Free Packing Lists
Free Travel Tips at http://www.freetraveltips.com has print-ready packing lists for general travel. **Fish Alaska** at http://www.fishalaskamagazine.com lists everything you should take on a fishing trip to the Great Land.

Free Books
Go to the **Wisconsin Sea Grant** web site at http://www.seagrant.wisc.edu/greatlakesfish to download a copy of *Fishes of Wisconsin* by George C. Becker, or to **All-About Fly Fishing** at http://www.about-flyfishing.com for a copy of *The Complete Angler* by Izaac Walton.

(continued on page 17)

developed at the University of Michigan hunts for keywords just within forums. Enter your query at **BoardReader, http://www. boardreader.com** and potentially you'll not only lock onto a discussion about your subject of interest, but the larger forum and web site may turn out to be a winner.

The forum software provider **ezboard** at **http://www.ez board.com** pubishes a directory of all the sites using their forum template. Put "fishing" into the Find a Community Search Box to find details of nearly 500 fishing ezboards. The first few pages list the most popular examples.

Mailing Lists
Mailing lists follow the same principal of posting and replying to messages, but they're delivered to your e-mail account rather than published on a central web site. Some mailing lists maintain a web page for explaining list rules, introducing members, or organizing conclaves and fishing get-togethers.

Rules for subscribing to mailing lists vary slightly but the usual routine is to put "Subscribe" into the subject field of an e-mail and then "Subscribe me to [mailing list name] [your first name] [your last name]" in the body of the message and then send it to the list moderator. Just as with forums, moderators oversee the direction and content of discussions on the list. The moderator will add you to the list and you'll begin receiving messages according to your preference— as they come, once a day, or in some other form of digest mode where multiple messages are grouped into a single e-mail. Some

lists generate more than 100 messages a day, so it's worth giving your delivery options some real thought. To contribute to the list e-mail your comments and questions to the list moderator.

The challenge with fishing mailing lists is finding them in the first place. There doesn't seem to be a single comprehensive list of them on any web site and the general mailing list directories don't have fishing categories worth bothering with. The upside of that is because they're much harder to find than forums, they often attract serious enthusiasts and produce insightful, detailed comments.

Some established lists can be found at these homepages:

CANFF: **http://www.sfu. ca/~epoole/canff.htm**

Flyfish@: **http://www.uky.edu/ ~agrdanny/flyfish/main.htm**

Eur-flyfish@: **http://www. shconnect.de/eur-flyfish**

Fishwest Mailing List: **http://www.fishwest.net/utah**

International Muskie Home Page: **http://www.trentu.ca/muskie/ muskie.html**

Missouri Flyfishing List: **http://www.agron.missouri.edu/ flyfishing/inet_resources.html**

Rodmakers: **http://www. canerod.com/rodmakers**

Virtual Flybox: **http://www.virtualflybox.com**

The Walleye List:
http://www.walleyelist.com

Walleye News:
http://www.walleyenews.com

Mailing lists are one of the features offered within the online communities of **Yahoo! Groups** (see the Clubs section of Chapter 6 Groups for a review). Hundreds of these groups are devoted to fishing but a few of the most popular ones offering mailing lists include:

Carp Angler's Group:
http://groups.yahoo.com/group/CarpAnglersGroup

Flyfishing the West:
http://groups.yahoo.com/group/flyfishingthewest

Texas Warmwater Fly Fishers:
http://groups.yahoo.com/group/txwwff

Warmwater Angler:
http://groups.yahoo.com/group/WarmwaterAngler

Finding other mailing lists is a matter of asking for recommendations from knowledgeable forum users or scouting individual web sites, though make sure what you're signing up for is a mailing list and not the sometimes similarly worded e-mail list for the site's newsletter or press releases.

Start Your Own List
If you can't find a list devoted to your fishing interest, it's easy to start your own. Lists can be created using list management software, but the simplest option is to use the free web site and mailing list service at Yahoo! Groups. Register at Yahoo!, then go to the Groups page at **http://groups.yahoo.com** and click on Start a New Group. Over the next few pages choose a group name, decide how you'd like it organized, if the list is to be moderated and what category it falls into. You can then enter a welcome message and the e-mail addresses of up to 50 initial members. The last page confirms the details of the group. Click on View Your Group Page to see how

FREEBIES FOR FISHERMEN ON THE WEB:

Free Maps
The **Florida Fish and Wildlife Conservation Commission** at http://marine fisheries.org/guide.htm gives out free Boating and Angling Guides to the Florida coastline. **MapServer** at http://mapserver.maptech.com can create a customized map for sections of any fishery in the country.

Free Postage
Subscribe to fishing magazines, send an e-postcard, or renew a fishing license from **LandBigFish** at http://www.landbigfish.com or **Big Fish Tackle** at http://www.bigfishtackle.com.

Free Fly Patterns
Copy hundreds of fly patterns from **Ultimate Fly Tying** at http://www.ultimateflytying.com or **The Flyfishing Resource Guide** at http://www.flyfish.com.

(continued on page 19)

the finished page is laid out. You are now the proud owner of a fishing mailing list and a home on the Web for your own personal fishing community.

Newsgroups

Newsgroups are the Internet's original community meeting places. Like forums and mailing lists, they offer a place to connect with other people interested in a particular topic by reading and replying to posted comments or by starting new discussions. Newsgroups are not technically housed on the Web but on the Internet, which is the overarching system of connected computers that makes the Web possible. They can be viewed in a couple of ways. The old way is to download a software program called a "newsreader" from your ISP to your proprietary e-mail service such as Outlook Express or Netscape Messenger (AOL users can find instructions at AOL keyword: newsreaders). For tutorials on how to do this and sources for newsreaders go to **http://www. newsreaders.com**. The newer, simpler option is to use Google's unique web-based newsgroup directory at **http://groups. google.com**.

The first page of the Google Groups directory lists subject categories. The abbreviation for the category—alt. for alternative, can. for Canada, rec. for recreation —forms the first part of the newsgroup name and is followed by successively narrower subject descriptions, so the full name of the newsgroup, "rec.outdoors. fishing.fly.tying," for example, spells out its category exactly.

The Google Groups directory lets you read, contribute to, or search the newsgroup archive across tens of thousands of subject areas. Newsgroup discussions are often unmoderated, uncensored and sometimes wildly off topic, but they can also be great fun to wander around and several of the fishing-themed newsgroups attract a hardcore of regulars, some of whom meet up offline for fishing outings and to put faces to comically optimistic nicknames.

Newsgroups of interest to fishermen include:
alt.fishing
alt.fishing.catfish
alt.fishing.minnesota
alt.fishing.muskellunge
alt.fishing.walleyes
alt.test.fishing.spin
can.rec.fishing
can.rec.boating
rec.autos.4x4
rec.outdoors.fishing
rec.outdoors.marketplace
rec.outdoors.fishing.bass
rec.outdoors.fishing.fly
rec.outdoors.fishing.fly.tying
rec.outdoors.fishing.saltwater
rec.boats
rec.boats.marketplace
rec.boats.electronics
rec.boats.paddle
sci.bio.entomology
sci.bio.fisheries
sci.geo.satellite-nav
uk.rec.fishing.coarse
uk.rec.fishing.game
uk.rec.fishing.sea

Chat Rooms

Chat rooms allow people to get together and communicate in

real-time by typing back and forth conversationally. First-time users will be asked to download a software chat program, register and choose a username. The chat room page indicates who else is in the room and records their messages in a scrolling list in the center of the chat window.

If several people are in the room and chatting freely, conversation threads will be piling on top of each other. Hang back a little to decipher where the different conversations are going. If you have something to add, jump in by typing your comment into the message box and sending.

Chat rooms aren't for everyone. They sometimes reflect the awkwardness of any conversation between strangers, and it helps if you're a reasonably fast typist, but in the right circumstances its effect is not so far removed from chatting with other fishermen over coffee or around the counter at your local tacklestore.

Many fishing web sites offer chat rooms. Some of the best are hosted by experts who post a schedule of when they'll be in the room to answer questions and moderate

discussions. Try out these established chat rooms, then venture into ones offered at your favorite web sites:

Brotherhood of Catfishermen: http://www.brotherhood-of-catfishermen.com

Capt. Mel Berman's Fishing Florida Online Magazine: http://www.capmel.com

Fish & Fly: http://www.fishandfly.co.uk

Fly Anglers Online: http://www.flyanglersonline.com (Has eight hosted chat rooms devoted to different fly-fishing topics)

Fly Fisherman: http://www.flyfisherman.com

Fly Fishing in Maine: http://www.flyfishinginmaine.com

Flyfish Saltwaters.com: http://www.flyfishsaltwaters.com

IceFishingFIRST: http://icefishing.outdoorsfirst.com

Lake-Link.com: http://www.lake-link.com

FREEBIES FOR FISHERMEN ON THE WEB:

Free Art
Fancy up your desktop with screensavers from **Walker's Cay Chronicles** at http://www.walkerscay.tv, or decorate anything you care to with clip art from **@Streamside: Journal** at http://www.helmintoller.com/streamside.

Free Plans
Build your own fishing craft with the free boat plans listed at **Duckworks Magazine**, http://www.duckworksmagazine.com. Print out float plans before heading off for the day at **SportFishingFlorida.net**, http://www.sportfishingflorida.net.

MuskieFIRST:
http://muskie.outdoorsfirst.com

New York Bass:
http://www.nybass.com

Noreast.com:
http://www.noreast.com

North Georgia Trout Online:
http://www.georgia-outdoors.com/ngto/index.html

Outdoors Network:
http://www.outdoors.net

ProBass:
http://www.probass.com

Walleye Central:
http://www.walleyecentral.com

WalleyeFIRST:
http://walleye.outdoorsfirst.com

WesternBass.com:
http://www.westernbass.com

I'll Take Another

The majority of sites listed in this book weren't set up or developed as profit-making ventures: they run on the enthusiasm, hard work and community-mindedness of fishermen who understand the Web's potential to bring us all together and enrich the sport. If a good web site covers your type of fishing, help them out by buying a t-shirt or book or other merchandise, make a donation or send in some content. We're all in this together.

A few people have been surprised that I found over 1,000 fishing web sites within a "best of" book. My answer is that, quite literally, no one has ever looked so hard across so many fishing categories. Wander the chapters, dip in here and there: the range and quality of sites are their own best advertisement. I'm more concerned with the sites that were inevitably overlooked. To put that right and to keep track of those that change focus or fall off the Internet altogether, I'll be maintaining a dedicated area for this book within Stoeger Publishing's web site at **http://www.stoegerpublishing.com.** There you'll find free articles, web site updates, and a place to recommend sites for future editions of the book. See you there.

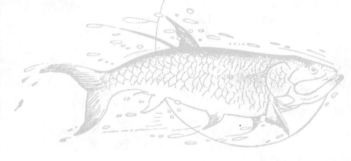

CHAPTER 2
STATE-BY-STATE RESOURCES

Fifty states, fifty ways to fish, from drifting egg patterns for leg-sized rainbows in Alaska to tossing livebait to tarpon in the Keys, from Great Lakes steelhead to Rocky Mountain trout streams to yellowfin tuna off the coast of Southern California. These sites, made up from a great assortment of community magazines, online newspapers and pages created by clubs, guides and individuals, have given a permanent home to the flow of information and camaraderie that has always existed in fishing: they are the best places on the Web to find local information and to connect with local fishermen.

Web sites with a strong regional bias reviewed in other sections of the book are crossreferenced in sidebars within each region.

New England

For many New Englanders, whatever method of fishing they prefer, there's no fish like the striped bass. But the region has much more to offer than "just" linesiders. These sites cover the fishy spectrum from pond-dwelling brookies to shad to mako shark.

Capt. Tom's Guide to New England Sharks
http://www.newenglandsharks.com

TOP RATED

Capt. Tom's Guide to New England Sharks

http://www.newenglandsharks.com

TOP RATED

Tom says it best himself: "Most fishermen...usually only have two questions. 1. Where do I go to catch them? 2. What do I use for equipment? Well, I think it's about time you learned something about the species themselves for a change."

What follows are pages of shark natural history, some stunning photographs, and tips for identifying every shark species you're likely to encounter within 50 miles of coastal New England. For the unreconstructed shark fishing nuts in the audience, articles cover essential topics from assembling tackle to "How to Battle that Trophy Mako."

New England Shad Association

http://www.newenglandshad.com

TOP RATED

In season, the forum on this site is probably humming with excited fishermen trying to get a jump on the shoals moving into the Connecticut River and other New England shad highways.

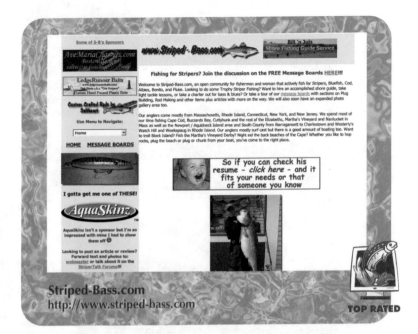

Striped-Bass.com
http://www.striped-bass.com

Early summer sees regular fishing reports and fish counts for the Connecticut River. Shad tournaments and derbies are part of the New England fishing scene: there's advice on how to fish them, plus listings of a few individual events.

New England Sportsman Network

http://www.nesportsman.com

The New England Sportsman Network covers Maine, New Hampshire, Massachusetts, Rhode Island, Vermont and Connecticut. Choose your state from links on the homepage to find regulations, news stories, articles and shortcuts to state fish and wildlife departments. Features relevant to all the states include funny fishing tales, video articles and forums for general fishing, bass fishing and fly fishing.

Northeast Bass.com

http://www.northeastbass.com

Mouse over the headings at this newly remodeled site to find forums, articles and fishery profiles. Look out in particular for links to the lake and pond-finding resources provided by the Connecticut Department of Environmental Protection and the Massachusetts Department of Fisheries, Wildlife, and Environ-mental Law Enforcement.

Striped-Bass.com

http://www.striped-bass.com

TOP RATED

Wrapped around popular forums for New England striper discussion, boats and boat fishing, fly fishing and lure making, this site has Massachusetts resource links, conservation updates and club listings. The bragging board is full of site regulars posing with huge rockfish.

CONNECTICUT
CT Fisherman.com
http://www.ctfisherman.com

TOP RATED

The creators of CT Fisherman.com have pruned anything from the site that doesn't strictly relate to the interests of Connecticut anglers. They've achieved it by encouraging visitors to submit as much of the site's content as possible: there are hundreds of neatly organized catch shots, much-used forums, a chat room and reader reports, articles and recipes. To supplement visitor fishing reports they reference the **Connecticut Department of Environmental Protection at http://dep.state.ct.us/rec-nat.htm** for its weekly fishing roundup and 70-page guide to species and fisheries.

MAINE
Fly Fishing in Maine
http://www.flyfishinginmaine.com

TOP RATED

The established home on the Web for Maine fly fishermen. Every path here leads to rewarding material. The heading Destinations splits the state into 12 regions and gives a basic outline of where each fishery is and how to fish it (covers both freshwater and saltwater). The Community option leads to a large pattern library and friendly forums. If it's being caught anywhere in the state you'll probably be able to read about it in the Reports area, which links to online fishing reports from guides, outfitters, fly shops and other sources.

State-by-State Resources

AND DON'T FORGET...

Flyfish Saltwaters.com
http://www.flyfishsaltwaters.com
An attractive magazine with a New England slant. See Chapter 4 Fishing the Web, Best Fly-Fishing Sites for a review.

**Global FlyFisher –
Raske's New England Streamers**
http://www.globalflyfisher.com/streamers
Traditional and new fly patterns for trophy trout. See Chapter 4 Fishing The Web, Best Fly-Fishing Sites for a review of the Global FlyFisher parent site.

Ken Abrames' Striper Moon
http://www.stripermoon.com
Rhode Island guide, artist, author, and fly tier plays host to multiple

forums and provides thoughtful articles. See Chapter 4 Fishing the Web, Best Fly-Fishing Sites, Personal Pages for a review.

Reel-Time
http://www.reel-time.com
A popular saltwater fly-fishing site with particularly good forums and catch reports for the Northeast. See Chapter 4 Fishing the Web, Best Fly-Fishing Sites for a review.

Surfcaster.com
http://www.surfcaster.com
New England surf fishing community site. See Chapter 4 Fishing The Web, Best Saltwater Fishing Sites for a review.

WATER WORKS WONDERS
http://www.waterworks
wonders.org

TOP RATED

This whale of a resource from the Recreational Boating and Fishing Foundation is a grandly ambitious database of every significant body of water in the country used for fishing and boating.

Choose the Fishing option then look for where-to-fish information by progressively clicking on the U.S. map. The first click takes you to the state, the next click to the region, then the county. Once there, scroll down the page to view listed bodies of water. Descriptions include available facilities, a topographical map link, fishing advice, and species information. Links on the lefthand side of the page offer shortcuts to useful information from the relevant state fish and wildlife department, such as how to buy a fishing license online, dates of free fishing days, and programs for junior fishermen. The boating channel of the site offers the same broad service for boating venues, facilities and education.

The scale of this project—they hope to eventually have complete descriptions for an incredible 400,000 venues—means the database is being built over a long period of time, so be patient if your local waters aren't yet covered.

MaineToday.com –
Outdoors
http://outdoors.mainetoday.com/
fishing

TOP RATED

Pooling the resources of three state newspapers means MaineToday.com can take a team approach to outdoor coverage. In season, Dick Pinney and Bruce Joule provide weekly freshwater and saltwater reports. Throughout the year, Dwayne Rioux and Ken Allen weigh in with news stories and articles. Secondary attractions include charter boat listings, current ocean conditions, species information, saltwater records and tournament details.

MASSACHUSETTS
The Lower Forty
http://www.thelowerforty.com

A handsome Worcester fly-shop site offering a little bit about flies, a little bit about tackle, dates of seminars and fishing clinics, and frequent river and saltwater reports.

Massachusetts Striped
Bass Association
http://www.msba.net

Clubs offer a place to share information and connect with local fishermen. A web site meshes perfectly with those goals, but it's surprising how few clubs make the effort to develop them properly. This one does. As well as a history of the organization, tournament details and event notices, they publish the Association's newsletter directly to the site and offer a mailing list. The section Access Points splits the coast into five areas listing the best boat ramps and beach access.

NEW HAMPSHIRE
NH Outdoors

http://www.nhoutdoors.com

A useful collection of links to outdoor sports information and services. Choose fishing from the activity list to find options for where to go, a weekly fishing report from the **New Hampshire Fish and Game Department** at **http://www.wildlife.state.nh.us**, species profiles and a few lodge and guide listings. Check other channels of the site for information about hunting, camping and outdoor survival.

RHODE ISLAND
Rhode Island Saltwater Anglers Association (RISAA)

http://www.risaa.org

RISAA was formed to give the state's saltwater fishermen a coordinated voice on conservation and sportfishing issues. And if that allows everyone to get together, swap fishing notes and generally have a good time, so much the better. Three thousand members belong to the group and many of them have contributed to the site. The archives section features member-authored articles, boat ramp reviews, recipes and profiles of local captains. Find club news within the Events, Seminars and Tournaments headings in the lefthand navigation.

See also **The Rhode Island Mobile Sportfisherman** web site at **http://www.rhodeislandmobile sportfishermen.org** for tournament and conservation news and a forum for connecting with fellow dune-buggy surf fishermen. The link they give to Tom Meade's weekly fishing report published in *The Providence Journal* requires registration at **http://www.projo. com/fishing**.

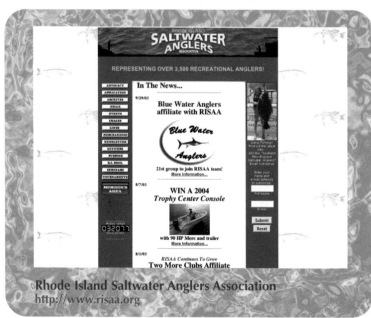

Rhode Island Saltwater Anglers Association
http://www.risaa.org

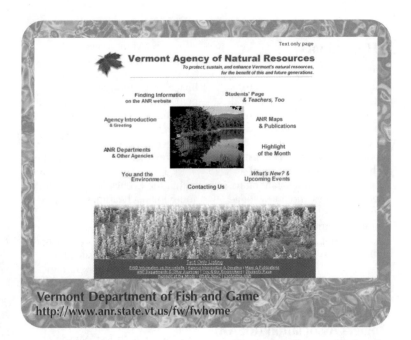

Vermont Department of Fish and Game
http://www.anr.state.vt.us/fw/fwhome

VERMONT
Vermont Department of Fish and Game

http://www.anr.state.vt.us/fw/fwhome

Fishing and hunting are blended together without a great deal of organization, but dip into the central list of headings to find some useful offerings: stocking schedules by species, fishery, numbers and sizes of fish; the date and locations of kids' fishing days; fish consumption advisories; and an invaluable resource for Batten Kill river regulars—downloadable archives of the *Batten Kill Newsletter*, focused on conservation initiatives and habitat analysis of the river.

Trout Streams of Vermont

http://www.caddis.middlebury.edu/trout

Trout Streams of Vermont only offers a couple of features but carries them off with aplomb. If your computer has Netscape 4, IE 4 or later, choose the Enchanced Atlas version to explore 70 streams. Mouse over a text link to see it highlighted on the state map. Clicking on it reveals the stream name, its length and drainage area and a link to a topographic map.

Mid Atlantic

Mid Atlantic trout rivers are the cradle of American fly fishing, but thousands fish for bass with the same commitment. And don't forget the party boats out to fill freezers with wreck fish, or the sportfishers streaming from Montauk with shark and tuna tackle in the rod holders. This may be the most populous part of the country, but its fishing landscape is big enough to accomodate everybody.

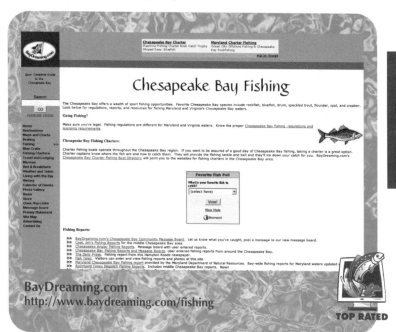

BayDreaming.com
http://www.baydreaming.com/fishing

DELAWARE AND MARYLAND
At The Beach
http://www.atbeach.com/fishing

This tourist guide recognizes and caters to its large base of visiting and permanent DelMar fishermen. Much of the fishing material comes courtesy of Oyster Bay Tackle. Owner Sue Foster provides a regular fishing report, a shore fishing guide, dozens of articles and links to local fishing sites. She's on the

TOP RATED

Web at **http://www.oysterbay tackle.com**. At The Beach's general visitors' guide runs to hundreds of pages and covers everything necessary for planning a vacation.

BayDreaming.com
http://www.baydreaming.
com/fishing

The fishing channel of this Chesapeake travel and recreation site links to 10 fishing reports from

TOP RATED

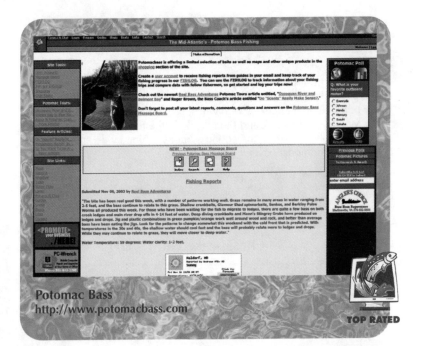

Potomac Bass
http://www.potomacbass.com

TOP RATED

area web sites and newspapers, and has full listing for Bay hotspots, tournaments and charters.

Beach-Net!
http://www.beach-net.com/ Fishinghome.html

Fishing content at this comprehensive beach resort guide includes business listings, tide charts, a popular forum and a few reports from charter captains in both Maryland and Delaware.

The Chesapeake Angler
http://www.chesapeake-angler.com

The Chesapeake Angler is a free monthly distributed in tacklestores and marinas in Delaware, Maryland and Virginia. It links to fishing reports from each state's fish and wildlife department and

posts a selection of articles from the magazine. The charter boat directory offers plenty of options for a day on the water.

Potomac Bass
http://www.potomacbass.com

TOP RATED

The designers at Potomac Bass have included every feature to make this an outstanding community site. Sign up for a group mailing list under the heading Join our E-Group on the homepage, or pick from the chat room, the forum or the FISHLOG for recording recent catches. The FISHLOG can be used as a private online fishing diary, but most users let others benefit from their experiences (or lack of them). All the background information for planning a Potomac trip—river flows, weather forecasts, navigation and contour maps, tips for different sections of the river—is organized and easily accessible.

See also the **Maryland BASS Federation** at **http://www.mdbass. com** for lists of Maryland bass clubs, an event calendar and forum.

Woods and Waters Magazine

http://www.woodsandwaters

magazine.com

Click on Waters in the lefthand navigation to read overviews of 13 lakes in Maryland and 12 in Virginia. Go through the articles, destination pieces and readers' reports for advice on how to fish them.

NEW JERSEY
ACFishing.com

http://www.acfishing.com

TOP RATED

The AC stands for Atlantic Coast but the weight of this site's forums and resources for fishing piers, beaches, charter boats, reefs and wrecks is centered on New Jersey. Weather and tide forecasts, species information and galleries of visitors' catch shots are all nicely presented.

Atlantic Saltwater Fly Rodders (ASWF)

http://www.aswf.org

The ASWF began its most recent incarnation in a Tuesday night fly-tying get-together at Bob Popovic's home in New Jersey. It now has 250 members, a permanent clubhouse and looks worth joining if only for the stellar line-up of fly-fishing authors that often address the group. Check out nine of Popovic's original patterns in the Saltwater Flies section or read through the Getting Started guide to essential tackle and tactics.

FISHBOX.TV

http://www.fishbox.tv

TOP RATED

One of the best features of this saltwater site is its table of species information. It profiles 40 different fish within a large calendar of what's peaking in what month. Click on the fish name to view photographs, descriptions, fishing articles and regulations. Once you know what can be caught, check the reports forum for the latest word from tackleshops and charter captains. Other features worth the visit include business listings, Jersey weather links and fishing tips from Julius Ruehle.

BORN TO FLY FISH

New Jersey is unlikely to ever be featured on one of those celebrity fly-fishing shows, and that's probably fine with the locals. They get to keep their low-key stream fisheries—and even the occasional shot at anadromous brown trout from the Atlantic—all to themselves. **NJ Trout** at **http://www.njtrout.com** and **North Eastern Fly Fishing Forums** at **http://www.njflyfishing.com** are two stops for sleuthing likely streams and connecting with those in the know.

TheBassBarn.com
http://www.thebassbarn.com

TOP RATED

NJ Striper.com
http://www.njstriper.com

TOP RATED

They do talk about other saltwater species at this busy community site—there are 18 forums in all—but all fish make way for *Morone Saxatilis*. Outside the forums you'll find twice weekly chat room sessions and a Q & A for stubborn technique and tackle questions. Register to take advantage of the site's free personal fishing logs.

TheBassBarn.com (TBB)
http://www.thebassbarn.com

TOP RATED

Regulars at the 'Barn demonstrated the strength of their online community by raising $10,000 to sponsor the sinking of an artificial reef 23 miles out from Ocean City. Coordinates for the TBB reef and more than 100 others sunk off the Jersey coast and Delaware Bay by the Artificial Reef Foundation are listed under the heading GPS Numbers. Site goers meet within busy forums discussing stripers, tackle, offshore fishing, the Delaware Bay, fly fishing and surf fishing. Beach access information, a business directory, tournament listings and links to weather and regulations takes care of the rest.

NEW YORK
Black Lake, New York
http://www.blacklakeny.com

TOP RATED

Few lakes can have inspired such definitive web sites. The contents menu at the bottom of the homepage directs visitors to, among other things, fishing articles and tips, dozens of resource links and an event calendar. To find statewide bass clubs, fishing forums and resource pages, look for the heading New York Fishing Links.

The Black Lake web site is also host to a national listing of bass clubs and recommended forums. Both are found on the homepage under Lake Internet Fishing.

FishSalmonRiver.com
http://www.fishsalmonriver.com

TOP RATED

A skillfully presented guide to salmon, steel-head and brown trout fishing in the Salmon River and eastern Lake Ontario. Unusually clear access maps divide the Salmon and two of its tributaries into eight sections and are accompanied by descriptions of hotspots and best methods. For current conditions check the sections for fishing reports, forums, weather and streamflows.

The advice found within the Anglers Library is relevant to many Great Lakes feeder rivers.

Another New York river to get a custom fishing web site, albeit a simpler production, is the Niagara. **Rick Dubas' Niagara Fishing Net** at **http://www.niagarafishing.net** features articles, a weekly fishing report, a forum and web cams.

The Fishing Line
http://www.thefishingline.com

TOP RATED

Rich Johnson uses his television show, two weekly radio slots and now this large informative web site to report on the New York and tri-state fishing scene. The Fishing Line Fishing Report covers Long Island from Montauk to the New York Bight, including the whole of Long Island Sound, and is broadcast on the

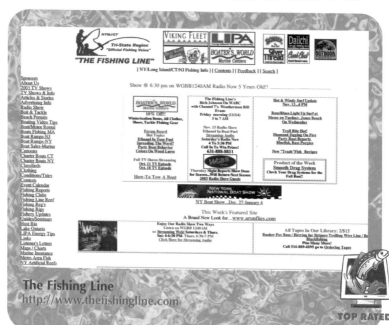

New York Bass
http://www.nybass.com

TOP RATED

radio every Saturday evening, then updated for the following day's show. Look for the link "Enjoy our Radio Show Two Ways" in the main body of the homepage to read the report online or listen to it as a web broadcast. Other tasty features include video clips and articles, lists of regional fishing clubs and a comprehensive directory of boat ramps for New York, the Hudson River and New Jersey.

The Fishing Line has a separate forum site at **http://www.the fishingline.org**.

Montauk Sportfishing
http://www.montauksport fishing.com

Captain Gene Kelly's guide to the famous fishing port on the tip of Long Island features a regular fishing and tournament roundup and the complete online archive of the annual magazine *Montauk Sportfishing*, devoted to the big-

game pursuit of sharks, marlin and tuna. The rest of the site is meant to move you from spectator to participant, with charter boat and business listings, tide tables, tournament schedules and regulations.

New York Bass (NYB)
http://www.nybass.com

TOP RATED

New York Bass eschews the NASCAR stylings of the commercial bass scene and goes for humor and cool web design. The Bass Illustrated section has videos, a bragging board and photomontages of unlikely bass scenarios, such as largemouths plucked from the icy flows of the Antarctic and the NYB web development team taking advantage of cheap office space in the former Enron building. Polite and busy forums include Places to Fish, Tackle, Fishing Tactics and Fishing Reports.

Rob J's Western New York Bass Fishing Pages

http://home.adelphia.net/
~thewavzone

Rob J. charts his bass fishing adventures with passion and technical skill. If you're inspired to build your own site, the About **TOP RATED** this Website article discusses how he assembled the computer and selected all the necessary software that allowed him to build it. The tackle and equipment choices of experienced anglers are always enlightening: within articles and captioned photo guides, he catalogs his entire set up from favorite lures to favorite fishing truck.

PENNSYLVANIA
FishErie.com

http://www.fisherie.com

Pennsylvania may only have a sliver of Great Lakes real estate, but the 11 feeder creeks **TOP RATED** that flow into Lake Erie provide quality fishing for steelhead, salmon and trout. The site takes the town of Erie as its base camp and uses headings in the lefthand navigation from Anglers Maps down to Angler Library to introduce the full potential of the local fishing. Each creek gets a large map, a seasonal overview and fishing tips. Read what the locals have to say in the forums and fishing reports.

State-by-State Resources

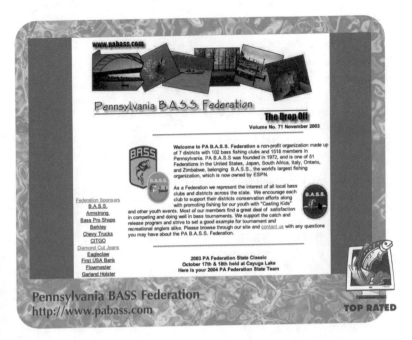

Pennsylvania BASS Federation
http://www.pabass.com

TOP RATED

Pennsylvania BASS Federation

http://www.pabass.com

TOP RATED The Bass Anglers Sportsmans Society, universally known as BASS, commissioned a team of judges to pick the organization's five best Federation web sites based on design and service to members. Pabass.com took top honors. Its most impressive feature is the way it stays up-to-date with all the tournament and event news generated by its more than 100 affiliated clubs. Other highlights include an active forum and departments for conservation news and youth fishing.

Pennsylvania Fly Fishing

http://www.paflyfish.com

Pennsylvania Fly Fishing covers all the Keystone fly-fishing bases: they list which streams are stocked and which are designated as wild trout water; they post current regulations and contact information for local fly shops; there's a popular forum and plenty of hatch information.

At several points, the site references the **Pennsylvania Fish and Boat Commission** at **http://www.fish.state.pa.us.** A longer look at the Commission web site shows they've really thought about the information needs of their fishing constituents. Click on Fishing in the lefthand navigation for a full index of material, including a special area for junior fishermen from the Pennsylvania League of Angling Youth (go to Education in the top navigation) and content from the Commission's fishing and outdoor magazine, *The Pennsylvania Angler & Boater.*

VIRGINIA
The Fishin' Musician
http://www.thefishinmusician.com

Aside from singling out useful information from the **Virginia Department of Game and Inland Fisheries** at **http://www.dgif.state.va.us/fishing** and linking to assorted fishing reports, weather web sites and other Virginia resources, webmaster John Stanley contributes thoughtful articles about smallwater fishing and provides a forum for sharing tips and fishery reports.

VAflyfish.com
http://www.vaflyfish.com

TOP RATED Over its eight years on the Web, VAflyfish.com has refined itself into a model of what a good regional fishing site should be.

The reports section is one of the most impressive features. It's a list of waters matched to trip reports from site regulars and access maps from the Virginia Department of Game and Inland Fisheries. If you find yourself heading straight to the same reports or directly to the forums or to any of half a dozen other dynamic areas, use the My VAflyfish link to customize the layout of the homepage.

Virginia Beach Sport Fishing (VBSF)
http://www.virginiabeach
sportfishing.com

The combination of the fish-magnet Chesapeake Bay Bridge Tunnel Complex and accessibility to the Gulf Stream makes **TOP RATED** Virginia Beach one of the sportfishing capitals of the East Coast. This sparkling trip-planning site has charter boat and tackleshop listings, a local weather center and shortcuts to regional fishery agencies. Look under Angling at the bottom of the lefthand navigation to sign up for the VBSF mailing list.

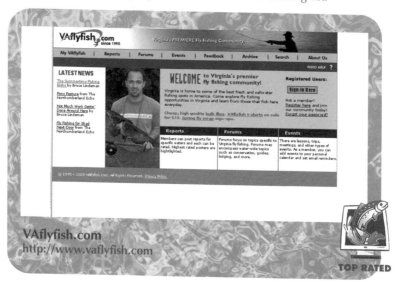

VAflyfish.com
http://www.vaflyfish.com

TOP RATED

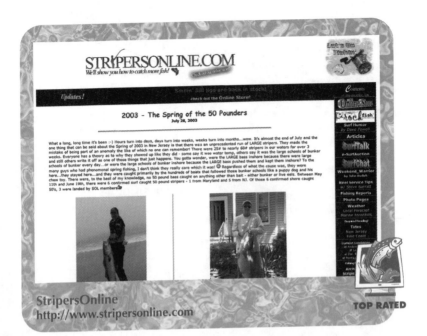

STRIPERSONLINE.COM
We'll show you how to catch more fish!

Updates!

check out the Online Store!

Contents

2003 - The Spring of the 50 Pounders
July 28, 2003

What a long, long time it's been :-) Hours turn into days, days turn into weeks, weeks turn into months...wow. It's almost the end of July and the one thing that can be said about the Spring of 2003 in New Jersey is that there was an unprecedented run of LARGE stripers. They made the mistake of being part of an anomaly the like of which no one can remember! There were 25# to nearly 60# stripers in our waters for over 3 weeks. Everyone has a theory as to why they showed up like they did - some say it was water temp, others say it was the large schools of bunker and still others write it off as one of those things that just happens. You gotta wonder, were the LARGE bass inshore because there were large schools of bunker every day...or were the large schools of bunker inshore because the LARGE bass pushed them and kept them inshore? To the many guys who had phenomenal spring fishing, I don't think they really care which it was! Regardless of what the cause was, they were here...they stayed here...and they were caught primarily by the hundreds of boats that followed those bunker schools like a puppy dog and his chew toy. There were, to the best of my knowledge, no 50 pound bass caught on anything other than bait - either bunker or live eels. Between May 11th and June 19th, there were 6 confirmed surf caught 50 pound stripers - 1 from Maryland and 5 from NJ. Of those 6 confirmed shore caught 50's, 3 were landed by SOL members

StripersOnline
http://www.stripersonline.com

TOP RATED

AND DON'T FORGET ...

Noreast.com
http://www.noreast.com
The region's biggest saltwater fishing magazine. See Chapter 4 Fishing The Web, Best Saltwater Fishing Sites for a review.

Pennsylvania Aquatic Flies Are Us
http://paaquaticfliesrus.
bd.psu.edu
Match the Hatch in the Keystone State. See Chapter 4 Fishing The Web, Best Fly-Fishing Sites, Entomology for more buggy references.

Pierandsurf.com
http://www.pierandsurf.com
East Coast forums, interactive maps and resources for those who prefer to foot it. See Chapter 4 Fishing the Web, Best Saltwater Fishing Sites for a review.

StripersOnline
http://www.stripersonline.com
Plenty of articles and forums for Delaware, Maryland and the Chesapeake Bay. See Chapter 4 Fishing the Web, Best Saltwater Fishing Sites for a review.

StriperSurf.com
http://www.stripersurf.com
Gear guides, technique articles and many other features for East Coast saltwater fishermen. See Chapter 4 Fishing the Web, Best Saltwater Fishing Sites for a review.

Tidal Fish
http://www.tidalfish.com
Strong forums, especially for the Chesapeake Bay. See Chapter 4 Fishing the Web, Best Saltwater Fishing Sites for a review.

The Roanoke Times – Outdoors

http:/www2.roanoke.com/
outdoors

The Roanoke Times has a triple-header of writers covering the Virginia fishing scene. Columnists Bill Cochran (saltwater), Harry Slone (fly fishing) and Mark Taylor (outdoors) supply news stories, catch reports and articles.

See also Lee Tolliver's nicely presented fishing forecast and map reference at *The Virginian-Pilot*, **http://www.pilotonline.com/sports/fishing.**

WEST VIRGINIA
West Virginia BASS Federation

http://www.wvbass.com

This 30-year-old club has kept up with the times by migrating much of their club business to the Web, but you don't have to be a member to benefit from the site's Q & A forum or its exceptional collection of resource links. You'll find: shortcuts to fishing reports from *The Charleston Daily Mail, The Dominion Post* and the West Virginia Division of Natural Resources, a directory of state bass clubs, links to streamflows and Ohio River navigation charts. In other words, much of everything you need to get dialed in to the West Virginia fishing scene.

WVSportsman

http://www.wvsportsman.com

Go to Trout Stocking Locations to find out exactly which parts of which streams are being stocked on which days. Elsewhere, there's advice about the best state fishing maps and, within the forums, tips on where to head for trout, bass and catfish.

South

Southern fishermen have choices: Tailwaters and mountain streams, ponds and impoundments, barrier islands and offshore hotspots. And, of course, the species that call these places home: double-digit trout, catfish as long as your leg, bass, speckled trout, redfish, Spanish mackerel … One more piece of good fortune: warm temperatures year-round mean that many Southern seasons never have to end.

Night Hawk Publications
http://www.nighthawkpublications.com

TOP RATED

ALABAMA
Fishing Lake Guntersville
http://www.fishinglake
guntersville.com

TOP RATED Jason Fleming lives right on the banks of Lake Guntersville and passes on some very specific advice for chasing down its resident bass. As well as providing large annotated maps of the lake he even illustrates the most productive contour breaks and underwater features. Regular reports of the lake's water clarity, temperature and "mood" come unfiltered, direct from personal observation. A link on the home-page titled Step By Step Bass Fishing Strategies describes the skills you need to successfully tackle such large waters.

Night Hawk Publications
http://www.nighthawk
publications.com

Outdoor communicator and publisher John E. Phillips showcases his writing and photography talents in more than 200 articles, many specific to Alabama. Click on John's Journals or Free Fishing Tips to view the selection.

If traveling around, photographing and writing about fishing sounds like your kind of nine to five, John devotes a portion of the site to the craft and graft of outdoor journalism. It's full of advice about writing, marketing and business practices, and includes interviews with 10 established professionals.

North Alabama Fishing Forum
http://hiwaay.net/~ksgrisse/
wwwboard
Webmaster Kerry Grissett moderates a large, polite forum, and suggests other sources for Alabama fishing reports and discussions.

Combined with a few articles, links to weather web sites and fishery information from the Tennessee Valley Authority, it adds up to a hardworking state reference.

ARKANSAS
The Ozark Angler
http://www.ozarkangler.com

This fly-shop web site offers an impressive guide to three Arkansas trout fisheries. Go to River Reports for current conditions, a 14-day forecast, hatch information, fly recommendations and maps for the White River, the Little Red River and the North Fork River. The maps are exceptional, showing river features, access points, beats and pool names, even marking where the fish usually hold. Local anglers can take advantage of the many

The Ozark Angler
http://www.ozarkangler.com

TOP RATED

The Ozark Mountains Travel & Recreation Directory
http://www.ozarkmtns.com

TOP RATED

seminars and events organized by the shop.

See also **Scott Branyan's Ozark Fly Flinger** at **http://www.fly flinger.com** for White River fishing reports and pattern suggestions.

The Ozark Mountains Travel & Recreation Directory
http://www.ozarkmtns.com

TOP RATED
Appropriately for an area that boasts the all-tackle world record brown trout, Bull Shoals Lake and Norfolk Lake, a great deal of fishing information is sprinkled though this visitors guide to north central Arkansas and south central Missouri. The pages for the White River offer the best fishing material. Sign up for the Shad Kill Alert and you'll receive an e-mail as soon as the shad begin to die off in Bull

Shoals Lake. This is a matter of some celebration because the little forage fish are then sucked into dam turbines feeding the White River tailwater, creating a chummy good time for the river's huge predatory trout and an Arkansas Mardi Gras for local fishermen.

Click on the name of individual fisheries in the lefthand navigation or choose the Fishing option to access a group of articles, maps and links titled Fishing the Arkansas Ozarks.

GEORGIA
Coastal Outdoors
http://www.coastaloutdoors.com

It isn't immediately obvious, but this is the online edition of a Georgia saltwater fishing magazine. It provides a few helpful links, articles and resources, but its best feature is its popular forum. See also Captain Judy Helmey's charter boat report at **http://www. missjudycharters.com.**

Georgia Outdoors.com
http://www.georgiaoutdoors.com

This general outdoors site draws its trip-planning information from dozens of Georgia web sites. Fishing content ranges from trout stream maps and pond descriptions, to tournament and charter boat listings.

Georgia River Fishing
http://www.georgiariverfishing.com

TOP RATED

Fishing can get awfully complicated if you let it. Anyone interested in simplifying their approach should bookmark Sam

Wilson's guide to fishing small rivers. He sets the tone in his introduction: "About five years ago, a small group of friends and I gave up reservoir fishing for the simpler, less expensive and far more rewarding experience of fishing Georgia's rivers and streams. We have left behind not only the hassles of waterskiers, boat ramp lines, and overdeveloped shorelines, but we catch more fish than we used to as well!"

What follows is a guide to fishing and floating small rivers for bass, especially useful to someone making the transition from the impoundments and huge lakes so often pushed in the bass fishing media. Overviews or "River Quicktakes" of 14 rivers describe hotspots, hazards and available species. Use the forum to connect with other reservoir refugees.

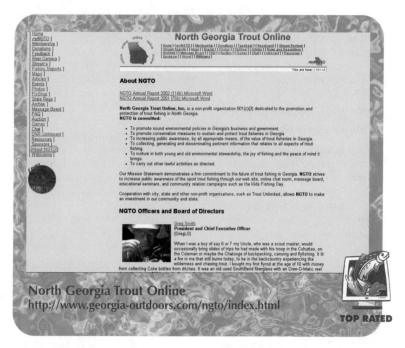

North Georgia Trout Online
http://www.georgia-outdoors.com/ngto/index.html

TOP RATED

North Georgia Trout Online (NGTO)

http://www.georgia-outdoors.com/ngto/index.html

TOP RATED

The NGTO is a nonprofit organization concerned with the conservation and management of Georgia trout streams. The site is obviously meeting a need: according to figures on the homepage there are 40,000 registered users and the site receives 9,000 visitors a day. Busy forums for warmwater, the Chattahoochee River, fishing partners, fly-tying, ask the experts and general discussion are the engines that drive the popularity of the site. Members also get involved by supplying hundreds of stream reports, as well as articles and reviews.

NGTO, Georgia River Fishing, and a regularly updated bass fishing report from Ken Sturdivant are all accessible from the **Georgia Outdoors** landing page at http://www.georgia-outdoors.com.

KENTUCKY Fishin.com

http://www.fishin.com

A bit of a mixed bag at this Southern-flavored general fishing magazine. There are fishing reports and forums for several states but they vary in freshness and popularity. The Kentucky forum, for example, was much visited but reports were patchy. Reports for Georgia were solid but the forum had hardly been used. So, mix and match between the states, or settle for reading dozens of articles about Kentucky fisheries.

See also **The Creek Bank** at
http://www.creekbank.com for
stream fishing forums and links.

Stewart's Cumberland River Guide Service

http://www.stewartsguide
service.com

TOP RATED

These fly-fishing guides
on the Cumberland River
are unusually generous
in passing on informa-
tion about their home
water (which in itself should
recommend their services).
John Stewart and Brandon Wade
describe the river section by
section in terms of fishing
approach, recent conditions and
recommended patterns. Weather
links and dam operating schedules give an updated picture of
what's waiting on the bankside.
The links section points to several
sites worth investigating, including
the club page for the **Northern
Kentucky Fly Fishers** at
http://www.nkyflyfishers.org.

LOUISIANA
Mike Lane's RodnReel.com

http://www.rodnreel.com

TOP RATED

Mike Lane's
RodnReel.com offers a
huge amount of informa-
tion tightly focused on
the practical needs of
Gulf fishermen. Everything here
posts big numbers. Thousands of
visitors a week look through the
site's catalog of articles and current
fishing reports. There are 1,800
catch photos up on the bragging
board. Classifieds and business
listings are both comprehensive.

But the most impressive site features are all focused on tracking
down the best places to fish in the
Gulf. The weather center has
coastal and offshore forecasts,
buoy reports, and satellite and
radar images. Pull-down menus let
you select daily, weekly or monthly tide charts for dozens of points
along the coast and display a host
of related information, such as

Stewart's Cumberland River Guide Service
http://www.stewartsguideservice.com

TOP RATED

nautical and civil twilight times, high tide, low tide and tidal ranges, and color graphs for interpreting it all visually. The GPS section contains more than 100,000 waypoints, including the daily coordinates of the mobile oilrigs that move around the Gulf concentrating gamefish into temporary hotspots.

Louisiana Fly Fishing
http://www.laflyfish.com

A solid and well-designed resource site listing clubs, fly shops, guides, fly patterns and other useful stuff. Each of the forums—for reports, for classifieds and announcements, and the Puddlers Forum for coastal paddlecraft fishermen—responded well to posted questions.

One nice touch is that they encourage members to post their favorite links. There are recommendations for maps, weather sites, club pages and the outdoors coverage of several state newspapers.

Louisiana Sportsman
http://www.louisiana sportsman.com

TOP RATED

The online edition of this popular print magazine features Q & A's with GPS and mapping experts, articles from pro staffers and news stories. Areas for fishing reports and classifieds had seen plenty of recent activity.

Jerry LaBella – Saltwater Fishing Articles
http://www.jerrylabella.com

Outdoor writer and Louisiana saltwater specialist Jerry LaBella explores the bounty of his local

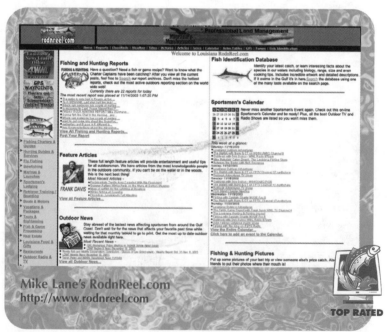

waters within illustrated articles and video clips, and helps you do the same by posting dozens of large navigation maps, reports from charter captains and business listings.

MISSISSIPPI
Doc's Best Bets for Fishing the Mississippi Gulf Coast
http://www.datasync.com/~dbb

TOP RATED

Doctor Fred Deegen recommends casting into the Gulf twice daily for whatever ails Mississippi saltwater fishermen. To make the cure as swift as possible, he provides advice on everything from the proper way to fish a popping cork, to the questions to ask yourself before hiring a guide, to how to better your chances with

cobia, seatrout and flounder. The lively homepage links to a few other departments worth exploring, such as directions to boat launches, fishing piers and offshore wrecks, and a calendar of prime times for different species.

We've all experienced a cornering maneuver by some old fella keen to remind us this is a pale shadow of the sport he knew as a young man, now *that* was fishing. Doc isn't that kind of Doc. He's Deputy Director of Mississippi's Department of Marine Resources, so listen up.

His employer doesn't post much fishing information on its site, but what they do have is essential. The Gulf Coast Fishing page at **http://www.dmr.state.ms.us/ Fisheries/Reefs/reefs.htm** lists the

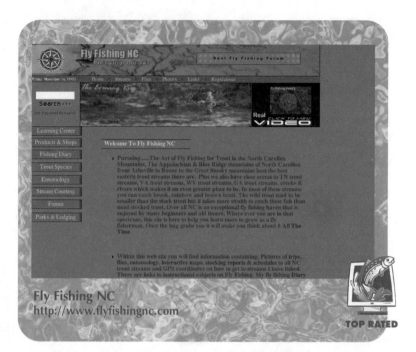

Fly Fishing NC
http://www.flyfishingnc.com

locations of inshore and offshore reefs, a link for finding marinas and boat ramps in Hancock, Harrison and Jackson counties, and updated regulations.

NORTH CAROLINA Blue Ridge Trout – Fly Fishing North Carolina
http://www.kbrcomm.com/trout

Several noteworthy features are tucked away within this personal site, including a well-used forum, where-to-fish suggestions, a hatch guide and the author's illustrated fishing diary going back to 1997. 2000 was a good year (43 trips), but there was a lamentable tailing off in 2002 (26 trips). Perhaps he was busy selling fishing books from his Amazon bookstore, prominently advertised around the site.

Fly Fishing NC
http://www.flyfishingnc.com

TOP RATED

One of the best regional fly-fishing sites in the country. What does it do so well? Pages of recommended flies match to big bright photographs of every important local insect. You can record your own hatch observations within the custom template found in the Flies section. The Streams heading leads to a set of pull-down menus for zeroing in on hundreds of small rivers, each linked to maps and directions from MapQuest. The Learning Center shows just how useful a really discriminating links section can be. Clicking on the banner at the top of the homepage leads to some gorgeous photography and instructional videos.

The forum side of things is taken care of by a link to **High Country Outdoors Guide Service TOP RATED** at **http://www.highcountry outdoors.net.** Aside from the forum, they provide their own excellent guide to North Carolina hatches and hot streams.

North Carolina Sportsman

http://www.northcarolina sportsman.com

The online edition of *North Carolina Sportsman* has Q & A's and contributions from a team of

TOP RATED regular writers, including David Fritts on bass, Capt. Jerry

Dilsaver on saltwater fishing and Captain Paul Titus answering readers' GPS queries. Sections for fishing reports, news stories and classifieds are all worth visiting.

North Carolina Waterman

http://www.ncwaterman.com

Perhaps it's just me but I consistently missed this site because of typing "Waterman" rather than

TOP RATED "Watermen." I'm glad I eventually got it right. The Waterman site covers the whole coast and is topped up daily with readers' catch reports, news stories, and even live weather and

THE OUTER BANKS

The Outer Banks are a true fisherman's playground. Around these barrier islands you can try every popular method of saltwater fishing there is: surfcasting, wreck fishing, fly fishing, wade and pier fishing and offshore big game.

Fish Mojo

http://www.fishmojo.com

Fish Mojo will hook you up with what's biting and where (The Mowire); put you in touch with other resource-minded fishermen (Conservation Corner); and help you locate secondhand tackle (Beachcombers Billboard). Hook them up (with a few bucks) and you'll be able to access the Hatteras Explorer forum for catch reports, tips and features.

If you only follow one of Fish Mojo's links it should be to the **NC Onshore & Inshore Fishing Page** at **http:// www.ncoif.com.**

NC CoastalFishing.com

http://www.nccoastalfishing.com

Of several sites that have raided

the Web to create directories of OBX fishing information this one has the edge in thoroughness and presentation. The

TOP RATED Fishing Reports and Message Boards area, for example, recommends 14 forums and more than 30 sites that post regular fishing reports. Browsing these leads to such worthwhile stops as **Dwayne Creech's Saltwater Surf Fisherman** at **http://saltwatersurf fisherman.com,** and **Joe Malat's Outer Banks Surf Fishing Adventures** at **http:// www.joemalat.com.**

For Outer Banks travel information mixed with fishing content, try **The Insiders' Guide to North Carolina's Outer Banks** at **http://www.insiders. com/outerbanks.**

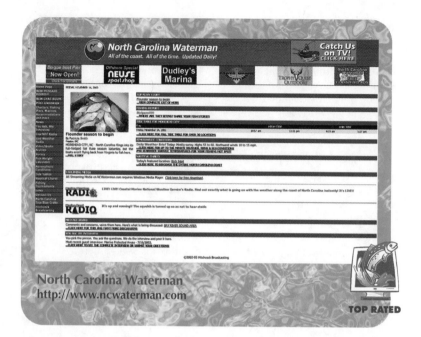

North Carolina Waterman
http://www.ncwaterman.com

fishing updates radioed in from charter captains still out on the water. Video and audio clips, business listings and a popular forum make it a complete resource for NC saltwater anglers.

See also the **Reel Buzz** at http://www.reelbuzz.com for Outer Banks and Morehead City/Wilmington fishing reports.

WNC Trout

http://www.wnctrout.com

Scott Cunningham has been publishing this stream fishing guide to western North Carolina for eight years. It covers stocked and wild rivers in more than 25 counties. Directions and access points for many of the streams are listed within the Trails to NC Trout Streams feature, which is a directory of forest service trails. No-nonsense fly selections and the standard set of regulations and

business listings make up the rest.

See also **Wilson Creek Outfitters** at **http://www.wilsoncreekout fitters.com.**

SOUTH CAROLINA
CharlestonFishing.com

http://www.charlestonfishing.com

TOP RATED

Not only do Charleston residents get to live in one of the most charming cities, they have great saltwater fishing right in their backyard and this feature-filled web site to bring the local fishing community together. Highlights: popular forums for catch reports and a match-up area for finding a charter boat or fishing partner; a fish identification page with large photographs and links to 10 other sites offering species profiles; a weekly newsletter; GPS coordinates and how-to articles.

Low Country Boating
http://www.lowcountryboating.com

This new-looking site does a good job of providing a community platform for low country fishermen within areas for reports and catch shots, forums and free classifieds.

See also **Captain Ben Alderman's Superfly Fishing** site at **http://www.superflyfishing.com** for a table of what species are hottest in what months, a fishing report and equipment guides.

South Carolina Lakes
http://www.geocities.com/
norwood_dr

A tremendous service from lake enthusiast Danny Norwood profiling more than 60 state waters. Lakes are

TOP RATED

categorized as large, small, state or public. Every lake is photographed, given a paragraph-long description and linked to water levels, fishing reports and local guides. Though it's predominantly a lake guide, Danny doesn't pass up an opportunity to suggest a book, lake map or web site for further fishing information.

TENNESSEE
Tennessee Wildlife Resources Agency (TWRA)
http://www.state.tn.us/twra/
index.html

In a state not exactly overflowing with good fishing web sites the TWRA admirably plugs the information gap with this multipurpose resource guide. Click on Fishing, then choose from dozens of options, including downloadable

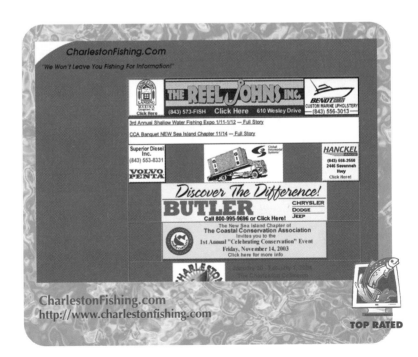

reservoir maps, guides to the state's wild trout and tailwater fisheries, sections for beginners and lists of family fishing lakes. Lucky Tennesseans have 195,000 small ponds and lakes scattered around their state. Go to Forms & Publications in the lefthand navigation to find an online booklet about managing small ponds as fisheries and an introduction to bank fishing techniques and locations.

TN Angler.com
http://www.tnangler.com

Freshwater fishermen in Tennessee hardly ever need leave the state ...

Reelfoot Lake, the Mississippi River, the Cumberland River, Old Hickory, Dale Hollow ... Webmaster Bill Glenn takes on the challenge of introducing all that prime water by splitting the state into West, Middle, and East Tennessee. Each area includes guides to individual waters and lists of businesses and facilities. A small but essential collection of links rounds it off.

See also **Paris Landing.com** at **http://www.parislanding.com** for Kentucky Lake and Lake Barkley fishing information.

AND DON'T FORGET ...

Fly Fisherman
http://www.flyfisherman.com
A Southern States forum, fishing reports, articles and guide listings. See Chapter 5 Media, Print Magazines Online for a review.

Game & Fish Magazines
http://www.gameand fish.about.com
Features content from

magazines covering Alabama, Georgia, Kentucky, South Carolina, and Tennessee. See Chapter 5 Media, Print Magazines Online for a review.

Harold Well's Gulf Coast Fisherman
http://www.gulffishing.com
Gulf Coast articles, tips, resources and fishing forecasts. See Chapter 4 Fishing the Web, Best Saltwater Fishing Sites for a review.

Florida

"The Greatest Saltwater Fishing on Earth" may sound like a line for the tourists, but hit the right day on the Keys or any number of places along the east and west coasts, and you'll be casting into a supercharged fishery, an environment where it seems every resident is either feeding on its neighbor or desperately trying not to get eaten. And from that carnage happy fishermen emerge.

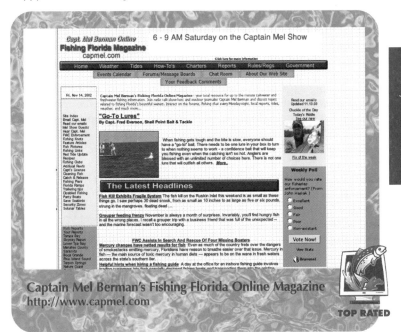

Captain Mel Berman's Fishing Florida Online Magazine
http://www.capmel.com

TOP RATED

Bite Tracker
http://www.bitetracker.com

It's easier to find up-to-date fishing reports in Florida than in any other state, but before you pass over this subscription-based service for the coast between Bayport and Charlotte Harbor, take the Demo Fish Tracker tour. It's a cool-looking, map-based tool that describes and pinpoints what's been caught by area captains and guides within the last 24 hours.

Captain Mel Berman's Fishing Florida Online Magazine
http://www.capmel.com

TOP RATED Captain Mel's magazine is an outstanding attempt to report on the entire Florida saltwater scene. To choose a couple of features from many that stand out, the site is known for the quality and reliability of its fishing reports. These come from guides and captains in twenty parts of the state and includes Mel's own radio report replayed on the web site. For advice about species and tactics read through hundreds of essays within the sections How-To's and Feature Articles, or get instant feedback from the forums and chat room. The Artificial Reef link lists the coordinates, depth and materials of these fish-magnetizing hotspots off the coast of 35 counties.

Central Florida East Coast Fishing
http://home.cfl.rr.com/
floridafishing

TOP RATED

Webmaster Gary Craig keeps everything shipshape and weed-free within this guide to the waters around Port Canaveral and the Indian and Banana Rivers. Among the 10 topic areas are weekly fishing reports, maps and GPS coordi-

nates, a fishing calendar and lists of marinas and boat ramps. Articles are borrowed from other sites and cover boating, flats, surf and offshore techniques.

CyberAngler
http://www.cyberangler.com

TOP RATED

CyberAngler dips its toe into the national fishing scene but its roots and best content are all for Florida saltwater. There are 280 Florida guides listed in the directory and a good number of them contribute regular fishing reports to the site. Tournament listings and coordinates for artificial reefs are both comprehensive. The site was undergoing a major re-styling so expect some new and updated features. New forums for seven areas of the state were just beginning to find an audience at review time.

Central Florida East Coast Fishing

On the Net since 1997

Bringing you the best in Port Canaveral, Indian and Banana River Fishing
Report marine resource violations, call 1- (800) DIAL-FMP (342-5367)

This site has been brought to Brevard County, Florida anglers as a community service since 1997

This web site is optimized for viewing at 800x600 screen resolution

Enter

[PREV 5 SITES | RANDOM SITE | SITELIST | NEXT 5 SITES]
FishHoo! — MEMBER —
Team FishHoo!
TeamFishHoo WebRing

International Angler Ring
Member   Current Global Rank #4
previous cast | random | poll |tackle|search| next cast

Central Florida East Coast Fishing
http://home.cfl.rr.com/floridafishing

TOP RATED

Florida Fish and Wildlife Conservation Commission
http://www.floridafisheries.com

Florida Fish and Wildlife Conservation Commission (FFWCC)

http://www.floridafisheries.com

Florida has three million acres of freshwater lakes and 12,000 miles of river, in addition to its embarrassment of saltwater riches. The FFWCC does a heroic job of organizing all that opportunity into a single reference. Click almost anywhere on the homepage block of graphics to find information tailored to the needs of Florida fishermen. The Fishing Sites & Forecasts link opens a mass of regional information, highlighted by profiles of the best catfish, panfish and bass lakes. The Publications link leads to PDF (Portable Document Format) brochures and guides, including a special section introducing Florida's unique peacock bass fishery.

Saltwater content is just as good. Sections for Boat Ramps and Fishing Piers map hundreds of facilities. Go to Publications for excellent species identifiers and free Boating and Angling Guides produced by the Florida Marine Research Institute. These are detailed mini-guides to 14 areas and feature large maps and fishing notes. They can be viewed online, but they're so detailed and useful you're probably better off ordering a paper copy instead.

Florida Keys.net

http://www.floridakeys.net

This tourist page has a few noteworthy fishing resources, most obviously the Keys Fishing Reports section. Eleven guides provide monthly fishing summaries and forecasts. There's also an up-to-date tournament calendar and a link to species and regulation information.

One report that isn't included but that's well worth seeking out is

Islamorada Sport Fishing Online
http://www.islamoradasportfishing.com

TOP RATED

Captain Jack Backus' **Fishme.com** at **http://www.fishme.com.** It features a backcountry and off-shore report, species overviews and a nicely self-deprecating attitude. Modest maybe, but reliable: the backcountry report has been posted to the site every Monday for the last seven years.

Fly Fishing the Southeast
http://www.sefly.com

Sefly.com has a solid collection of articles about saltwater fly fishing, many written by Florida guides. As is often the way when you begin to follow down a subject path on the Web, two of those authors turn out to publish pretty good sites in their own right. Rick Grassett's **http://www.snookfin-addict.com** offers a fishing report and several colorfully presented introductions to Florida target species. Tom Rowland's **Big Blue Flyfishing** at **http://www.bigblue flyfishing.com/newhome.htm** has tournament updates and tutorials.

Islamorada Sport Fishing Online
http://www.islamorada sportfishing.com

TOP RATED

Islamorada is a fishing fantasy island halfway down the Keys. Islamorada.com is an attractive and highly organized guide to the island and the whole Keys fishing experience. Links in the lefthand navigation lead to species, tournaments, fishing reports and weather resources. There's some great how-to information within the articles section, and comprehensive tide and current tables. The Florida Keys directory offers listings for offshore and backcountry guides, tacklestores and all those subsidiary things necessary to fully sample paradise: food, accommodation, nightlife.

See also the official tourist site for the Florida Keys at **http://www.fla-keys.com.** Choose Fishing from the text links in the top navigation, then pick from Key Largo, Islamorada, Marathon, Lower Keys or Key West, to find guide listings and a definitive list of fishing tournaments.

Jim Porter's Guide to Bass Fishing
http://www.jimporter.org

TOP RATED

Stick Marsh/Farm 13 bass guide and writer Jim Porter uses his colorful web site to help visitors find success on his home water. His catch reports bear no resemblance to the "took a few fish on spinnerbaits near the dam" variety often served up on fishing web sites, but are instead detailed

essays discussing seasonal patterns and the changing tactics needed to keep up with the bass.

For a general overview of how to fish the lake, the About Stick Marsh link leads to four articles outlining a seasonal game plan. The section Lake Guides in the top navigation does the same for 12 other Florida bass lakes. The Articles Archive runs to more than 100 features from Jim and guests and pushes the site beyond its Florida borders into the category of a national bass fishing magazine.

South Florida Sport Fishing
http://www.southflorida sportfishing.com

TOP RATED

A sharp-looking companion site to *South Florida Sport Fishing Magazine*. The site's fishing reports stay on top of the action in seven localities; there are piles of how-to articles and reviews, plus a species guide and South Florida fishing events calendar.

FLORIDA NEWSPAPERS

Sportfishing is such a part of the way of life in Florida that most state newspapers have an outdoors section with local fishing coverage. To take two examples, *The Miami Herald* at http://www.miami.com/mld/miamiherald/sports/outdoors publishes an annual *South Florida Outdoor Guide* offering tips on how to catch all the major saltwater species and a directory of piers and parks with fishing access in Broward County. Weekly coverage includes a Best Bets fishing forecast, news stories and articles.

The Florida Keys Keynoter puts out a free fishing supplement every quarter, the whole of which can be read online at http://www.keynoter.com/ffk/index.htm.

See the Newspaper sidebar within Chapter 5 Media for directory sites that link to every major and minor newspaper in the country.

BASS REPORTS

For a state that's the genetic home to the quickest growing, smartest bass in the country, there aren't many quality sites about Florida bass fishing. Fill in the gaps at **ProBass, http://www.pro bass.com**, which reports on 13 Florida lakes, or the **Bass Fishing Home Page, http://www.bassfishinghome page.com,** which has a well-used Florida report forum.

Southern Charm Sportfishing

http://www.floridasaltwater.com

This above-average charter boat web site features a library of technique articles, profiles of the most important gamefish and baitfish,

and fishing reports from Tampa Bay, Tarpon Springs and Sarasota.

SportFishingFlorida.net

http://www.sportfishingflorida.net

TOP RATED

For days when the weather or the fish aren't playing along, spend some pleasant hours reading through the big article archive, researching hotspots or following discussion threads on the 900-member forum. Greg Hatcher's project restoring an old sportfishing boat is a good read, but perhaps now's the time to find the site's Float Plan templates and print out a few dozen copies. Similar to a pilot's flight plan, they list essential information about the boat and its crew, giving rescue services a head start should anything go awry.

AND DON'T FORGET ...

FishnBottom.com
http://www.fishnbottom.com
For the Florida fish that don't jump. See Chapter 4 Fishing the Web, Best Saltwater Fishing Sites for a review.

Flats Hunter
http://www.flatshunter.com
A gorgeous resource for sneaking up on 'em in shallow water. See Chapter 4 Fishing the Web, Best Saltwater Fishing Sites for a review.

Florida Sportsman Online
http://www.floridasportsman.com
A huge companion site to the state's most popular fishing magazine, with 13,000 registered forum users, a statewide weekly fishing forecast, and many other features. See Chapter 5 Media, Print Magazines Online for a review.

Snook Angler.com
http://www.snookangler.com
Cool-looking site about the terror of the mangroves. See Chapter 4 Fishing the Web, Best Saltwater Fishing Sites for a review.

Midwest

There's hardly a truck big enough to haul all the fishing tackle a true Midwestern all-rounder would need. There would be a mountain of gear for smallmouth bass, largemouth bass, walleye, muskie, pike, catfish and panfish. In the winter, you'd have to pull all the ice-fishing equipment to the front—the portable shanty, the augers and tip-ups and boxes of jigs. And don't bury that old fishing vest, stained with last season's secret egg cure. You'll need it to hand when the salmon and steelhead and giant browns start their exodus from the Big Water.

Midwest Bass Tournaments Internet Magazine
http://www.midwestbasstournaments.com

TOP RATED

Midwest Bass Tournaments Internet Magazine (MBTIM)
http://www.midwestbass
tournaments.com

TOP RATED

MBTIM was developed to be the web site of record for the bass tournament scene in Missouri and Illinois. It succeeds admirably with a homepage full of fishing reports, tournament news and results. Background on the tournament waters, trip-planning information and fishing tips are covered within articles and lake guides for each state, and in the lively exchange of advice and opinions within the forum.

They're a bit free and easy with font sizes and colors, but don't let it distract you from the underlying service.

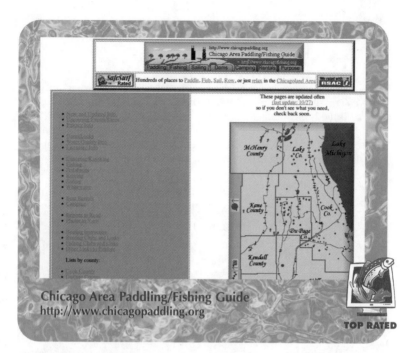

Chicago Area Paddling/Fishing Guide
http://www.chicagopaddling.org

TOP RATED

Midwest Fly Fishing Online
http://www.mwfly.com

The online teaser for *Midwest Fly Fishing* magazine has fly-tying and entomology articles, Midwestern fly-fishing links, events, and news stories.

Midwest Trout Fishing
http://www.midwest
troutfishing.com

Pick from Indiana, Iowa, Michigan, Minnesota and Wisconsin to find the name and county of prime fly-fishing rivers, local fly shops, current weather conditions and directions from MapQuest. What about poor old Illinois? The author suggests giving up the search for IL trout water but reminds residents they're only "a Johnny Cash CD listening-length" away from good water over the state lines.

ILLINOIS
Chicago Area Paddling/Fishing Guide
http://www.chicagopaddling.org

TOP RATED

This veteran community site was set up to publicize opportunities for fishing and boating on all the smaller rivers and lakes in the region. Click on Fishing to view a long menu of waters. An accompanying key indicates if regulations allow fishing, paddling, sailing, motor boating or camping, or if there are potential water hazards. Click on the name of each river or lake to come to maps, directions, species information and descriptions. The same format is followed within sections for paddling, sailing and camping.

ChicagolandFishing.com
http://www.chicagolandfishing.com

ChicagolandFishing.com grew out of an online fishing report for the Fox River. Webmaster Angler Al now oversees 15 forums for Chicago-area lakes and rivers, as well as areas for general discussion, fly fishing, ice fishing and other topics. Though the forums are the heart of the site, other useful features include lists of Chicago fishing clubs, conservation links and the telephone numbers of fishing report hotlines.

TOP RATED

Lake Online's Fishin' Hole
http://www.lake-online.com/fishinhole

This fishing supplement to a tourist web site introduces Illinois' Chain-O-Lakes system, listing available species, access points and amenities. The homepage offers a couple of unexpected treats. Click on Bait Recipes to find one of the better carp, catfish and general bait concoction pages on the Web, or on Solunar Tables for a detailed explanation of solunar theory and a yearlong forecast.

Will on the Web's Fishing
Will County, Illinois
http://www.willontheweb.com/fishing/index.html

A mini fishing magazine hitched to a trip-planning site for Will County, Illinois. It describes 13 fisheries, and includes a forum and two major recipe sections: one for preparing fish and one for preparing stink bait.

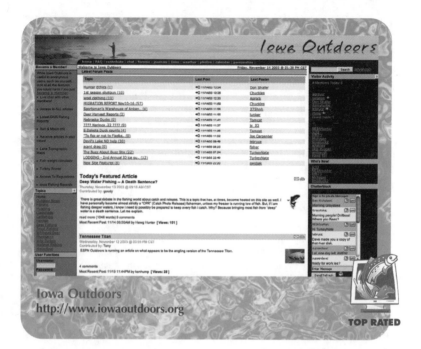

Iowa Outdoors
http://www.iowaoutdoors.org

TOP RATED

Indiana Division of Fish and Wildlife

http://www.state.in.us/dnr/fishwild

TOP RATED All the usual good stuff—regular fishing reports, county-by-county descriptions of major fisheries, stocking schedules and regulations—mixed in with mini-guides for ice fishing and how to target the state's muskie, pike, bass and walleye. Those without a boat will appreciate the eight-part guide to fishing the tributaries and shoreline of Lake Michigan.

INDIANA
Steelhead Shangra-La

http://www.geocities.com/steeldredge

Shangra-La to webmaster "Dredge" means steelheading on Indiana's St. Joseph River, Trail Creek, Little Calumet and Salt Creek. To help you find this happy place, he describes local tactics and fly patterns and draws maps of the four main rivers. There are other productive streams there-abouts, "but they need to be discovered on your own." Spoken like a true fisherman.

IOWA
Iowa Outdoors

http://www.iowaoutdoors.org

TOP RATED Go through the simple registration to find a sophisticated looking site for Iowa fishing and hunting. It depends on forum posts and news items for most of its content, but there's no shortage of either flowing to the site. Other features include state fishing records, topographic maps and a chat room.

Many of the news items originate from the **Iowa Department of Natural Resources** at **http://www.iowadnr.com**, which has where-to-fish information and reports for every region of the state, ice thickness updates, a species identifier and many other resources.

See also **Fishing in Iowa** at **http://omega.grad.uiowa.edu**, a personal site from Andy Jenkins, offering descriptive snapshots and a few photographs of 12 trout streams.

MICHIGAN
Michigan Fishing Information
http://www.trophyspecialists.com/mifishinfo/index.html

TOP RATED

How can one person develop a site that does justice to Michigan's fishing riches? By carefully linking to all the best material from other sites. Outdoor writer Michael Vein links to sea surface temperature maps from the **CoastWatch** web site at **http://www.coastwatch.msu.edu**, suggests dozens of forum and classified pages and picks out the choicest parts of the **Michigan Department of Natural Resources** web site at **http://www.michigan.gov/dnr**. Add recommended articles, more than 30 fishing reports and a directory of fishing businesses and clubs, and you really begin to see a full outline.

Michigan Fishing Information
http://www.trophyspecialists.com/mifishinfo/index.html

TOP RATED

THE GREAT LAKES

You can't begin to effectively fish the Great Lakes without planning and preparation. These sites not only give advice within articles and forums, they're resource centers for checking the latest lake levels, sea surface temperatures, weather forecasts and tides.

Great Lakes Information Network

http://www.great-lakes.net

The health of the Great Lakes has seesawed over the decades. This site is a directory of Great Lakes environmental information and links to every state agency and research group with a stake in the management of the Lakes. Go to Economy, then Fish and Fisheries for a content list.

Great Lakes Sport Fishing Council (GLSFC)

http://www.great-lakes.org

TOP RATED

The GLSFC is a nonprofit conservation and sport-fishing advocacy group with branches in all the states bordering the Lakes, and one in the province of Ontario. Its huge web site serves more than 300,000 members and is the first place to turn for state-by-state Great Lakes information and community connections. Fishing information and resources for each state are organized into as many as 40 topic areas, including business listings, species guides, consumption advisories, fishing reports, forums and fish and wildlife department links. Use the site index or State Fishing Pages link to display complete lists of topics and departments.

Lake Michigan Angler (LMA)

http://www.lakemichigan angler.com

TOP RATED

If they're guided by a discriminating eye, a site that points to the best features of other web sites is often more useful than one that struggles to supply original content. Lake Michigan Angler takes this approach and presents its findings in an attractive, orderly way. The Fishing Reports section, for example, links to 10 report pages for Michigan, and has tips on where to look in Illinois, Indiana and Wisconsin. Shore-bound fishermen will welcome the information LMA has ferreted out from the **Great Lakes Fishery Trust** web site at **http://www.glft.org**, consisting of maps and descriptions of more than 20 shore hotspots. A link to the **Wisconsin Sea Grant** web site at **http://www.seagrant.wisc.edu/greatlakesfish,** offers a free online edition of George C. Becker's definitive guide, *Fishes of Wisconsin*. Set some time aside for this—it's more than 1,000 pages long.

The people behind LMA don't quite surrender the whole dance to external web sites. Go to Techniques and Tips for dozens of original boat fishing tips.

Michigan Interactive
http://www.fishweb.com

TOP RATED

For exceptional lake maps try the fishing and boating departments of Michigan Interactive. Fish, Tips & Tackle on the Fishing start page leads to pull-down menus for species, rigging and tactical information. Lake Michigan fishing adventures are skillfully captured within the Photo Stories archive.

The Michigan Sportsman
http://www.michigan-sportsman.com

TOP RATED

This outdoor magazine hosts established forums for talking over coldwater and warmwater species, ice fishing, fly fishing, fly tying and trout streams. The section Logs and Locations introduces 13

of the state's most famous rivers. A few articles, a fly-pattern archive and more than 2,000 member catch shots are the best of the rest of the fishing content.

Trails to Trout
http://www.trailstotrout.com

TOP RATED

A combination fly-fishing and trail-finding directory for Michigan and Montana. The fly-fishing report pages, which link to more than 80 sources of online reports, are especially worth lingering over. To single out just a couple from the list: the **Great Lakes Fishing Station** report at **http://greatmich.com** is updated every day by a community of site regulars; the fun and readable **http://www.troutbums.com**, web site of The Fly Factory in Grayling, is usually worth dropping in on; and, in a true sign of how impor-

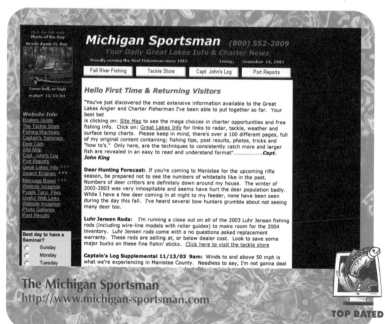

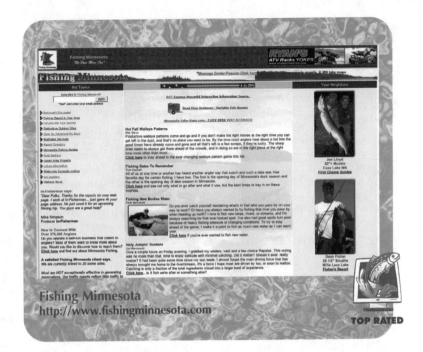

Fishing Minnesota
http://www.fishingminnesota.com

TOP RATED

tant fishing is in this part of the world, the Michigan AAA even gets in on the act at **http://www. autoclubgroup.com/michigan/ fishing.asp.**

The trails section follows a similar format, linking to route information from a host of contributing sites.

MINNESSOTA
Fishing Minnesota
http://www.fishingminnesota.com

TOP RATED

The place for Minnesota fishing discussion, with individual forums for more than 30 fisheries and some of the busiest ice-fishing discussion areas on the Web. But the site is more than a simple forum host: there are fishing reports from several lodges, dozens of articles and a business directory for guides, lodges, resorts

and campgrounds. Don't leave the site without following the link to the awesome Lake Finder Feature offered by the **Minnesota Department of Natural Resources** at **http://www.dnr.state.mn.us/lake find/index.html**. It has maps and data for more than 4,500 lakes.

Fishing Minnesota is the home of a popular walleye mailing list, the Walleye News. Sign up from the homepage.

In-Depth Angling
http://www.in-depthangling.com

TOP RATED

Fans of the defunct sites Fishtheriver.com and Fishthelake.com will be happy to know webmaster James Holst and team have essentially grafted the contents of both sites onto a new creation for Midwestern fishermen, In-Depth Angling.com. The site still revolves around a great lineup of active forums, with especially useful and frequent reports of Minnesota fisheries and the Mississippi River. The homepage serves as a directory of recently posted reports and forum threads.

SE Minnesota Trout Flies
http://users.myexcel.com/dolfnlvr/

TOP RATED The 200 insect and fly-pattern photographs displayed here could probably be referenced by fly fishermen across the whole Midwest. Click on the section "Local Natural Flies" to view photographs of each insect in different stages of development. Patterns to imitate them are divided into eight categories: local, new, dry flies, nymphs, subsurface, emergers, streamers and terrestrials.

Up North Outdoors.com
http://www.upnorthoutdoors.com

TOP RATED A colorful portal to hunting, fishing and ice-fishing opportunities in six Northern states, with the most information for Minnesota. The fishing channel includes business listings and articles from pro fishermen on the North Country's favorite species—walleye, pike, muskie, perch and smallmouth. The Fishing Reports section houses 12 forums for Minnesota lakes and a weekly statewide report from the Minnesota Office of Tourism. A couple of other highlights: go to The Newsstand for links to the outdoors sections of newspapers all over the country, and to BWCA for a guide to the Boundary Waters Canoe Area.

Up North Outdoors.com
http://www.upnorthoutdoors.com

TOP RATED

If that's where you're headed, don't neglect to visit **Canoe Country.com** at **http://www.canoecountry.com**, a top-rate planning site to the area, and the **Boundary Waters Canoe Area Wilderness** page at **http://www.bwcaw.org** for reserving permits.

MISSOURI
Go Fishing Missouri.com
http://www.gofishingmissouri.com

Gofishingmissouri.com links to fishing content from the **Missouri Department of Conservation** at **http://www.conservation.state.mo.us** (a statewide fishing report and fishery maps), and to tourist sites for such famous waters as the Lake of the Ozarks, Table Rock Lake and Bull Shoals Lake. A 1,000-entry business directory and lists of Missouri fishing clubs earn it a solid bookmark.

OzarkAnglers.com
http://www.ozarkanglers.com

Though Phil Lilley owns a marina and resort on the banks of Lake Taneycomo, this guide to the lake and other fisheries in the region—Table Rock Lake, Bull Shoals Lake and the White River—has the unmistakable tenor of someone who's a fishermen first and a businessman second. Phil's regular Taneycomo report and those for other fisheries are presented with links to lake levels and dam discharges. The White River Journal link on the homepage leads to a bimonthly fishing newsletter.

Trout Talk
http://www.trouttalk.net

The Lebanon Daily Record publishes a worthwhile fishing supplement offering news, articles, a visitor's guide to Bennett Spring State Park and the Niangua River and access information for the disabled. The links section has sourced dozens of fishing reports from Missouri fly shops and general fishing sites.

See also **Fishing the Missouri Trout Parks** at **http://www.missouritrout.com** for its descriptions of four public spring creeks.

AND DON'T FORGET ...

Game & Fish Magazines
http://www.gameandfish.about.com
A hub of state-by-state freshwater fishing information with good coverage of the whole Midwest. See Chapter 5 Media, Print Magazines Online for a review.

Great Lakes Angler
http://www.glangler.com
Great Lakes articles, forums and links. See Chapter 5 Media, Print Magazines Online for a review.

The Ice Fishing Home Page
http://hickorytech.net/~jbusby/iceangler.html
Jump to all the best ice-fishing pages on the Web. See Chapter 4 Fishing the Web, Best Freshwater Fishing Sites for a review.

The Steelhead Site
http://www.steelheadsite.com
The number one option for Great Lakes steelhead information. See Chapter 4 Fishing the Web, Best Fly-Fishing Sites for a review.

OHIO
GoFishOhio.com
http://www.gofishohio.com

TOP RATED

Buckeye fishermen can tilt the odds in their favor by going through the excellent lake profiles at GoFishOhio.com. Every lake has a clickable topographic map that can be expanded to show hotspots, depth contours and access points. Below each map there are tables describing the fishery, how to get there and what you might catch. Lake profiles are found under the heading Ohio Fishing Information. Fishing reports for many of the lakes come courtesy of the site's 3,700 registered forum users.

GoFishOhio.com is part of a network of sites, including ones for the Great Lakes, New York and Pennsylvania. Find links for all the sites at **http://www.gofish greatlakes.com**.

Ohio Fishermen.com
http://www.ohiofishermen.com

TOP RATED

It must have taken years for Mark Boyette to single-handedly assemble this guide to Ohio angling. You'll find driving directions and maps to some of the most productive lakes and rivers, and tactical advice for salmon, steelhead, catfish and muskie. Mark's editorials handle prickly issues such as stream overcrowding and selective harvest with calm good sense. The site is updated regularly and links to all the most useful bits of the **Ohio Department of Natural Resources** web site at **http://www.dnr.state. oh.us**.

State-by-State Resources

Lake-Link.com
http://www.lake-link.com

TOP RATED

WISCONSIN
Lake Chippewa Flowage
http://www.chippewaflowage.com

The name Chippewa Flowage is embedded in the minds of muskie fanatics as the place where Louie Spray caught his near-70 lb. world record in 1949. The Big Chip is still a premier muskie destination, as they make clear at this fish-focused tourist site. Click on Fishing in the top navigation to find articles, notable catches and fishery research. Trip planning is taken care of with a large map, lodge and business listings and details of the annual Muskie Hunt competition.

Lake-Link.com
http://www.lake-link.com

TOP RATED

There are so many avenues to go down at Steve and Darin Novak's Lake-Link.com, including forums, field editor reports, fish identification pages and maps and articles, that you could visit for hours without exploring the site's main feature which is a huge database of Wisconsin and Midwestern lake fishing information.

There are channels for Illinois, Indiana, Iowa, Michigan, Minnesota, North Dakota and

South Dakota, but the Wisconsin entry posts the biggest numbers. Go to Lake Finder, then Wisconsin, then pick a county for a table of lakes. Each lake is profiled with a map, facts about the lake, a list of species and comments from people who've recently fished the water. This feature has really been embraced by site users: it's effectively a mini-report forum for every major lake in the state.

See also **Fish-Wisconsin** at **http://www.fishwis.com** for lake guides and hundreds of topographic maps.

SW Wisconsin Stream Locator
http://www.swwisconsin.com

A lean, functional fly-fishing guide to six counties. Click on a county for a stream list, its categorization according to the **Wisconsin Department of Natural Resources** at **http://www.dnr.state.wi.us**, a TerraServer map and a list of what fish have fallen to author Todd Templen while conducting his "research." Discussions of Wisconsin's most reliable bugs and the patterns that imitate them give a few ideas of what to tie on once you've found your stream.

Central

The Dakotas, Oklahoma, Nebraska and Kansas don't feature in many fishing magazines but there's some beautiful country here with over-looked trout streams and healthy lake fisheries for bass, walleye, pike, catfish and panfish. Keep repeating the words "beautiful," "overlooked" and "healthy" to yourself, and you'll soon stop worrying about what magazines think.

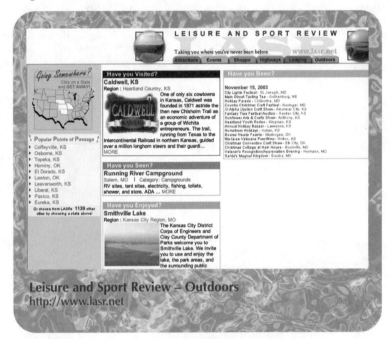

Leisure and Sport Review – Outdoors
http://www.lasr.net

KANSAS
Flatland Fly Fishers
http://www.flatlandflyfishers.org

This Wichita club has an informative site balanced between club news, advice for outwitting the mostly warmwater species available to Kansas fly fishers, and useful links. The most important of these is the **Kansas Department of Wildlife and Parks** at **http://www. kdwp.state.ks.us/fishing/fishing. html** for its statewide fishing report and urban fishing program.

Leisure and Sport Review (LASR) – Outdoors
http://www.lasr.net

Select Kansas from the U.S. map then look for the Into the Outdoors heading on the righthand side of the page. Fishing information is mostly borrowed from the Kansas Department of Wildlife and Parks, but the Area Lakes heading in the lefthand navigation leads to original profiles of 26 fisheries.

The Bass Zone
http://www.basszone.com

Fishermen in Kansas City should bookmark the **U.S. Army Corp of Engineers, Kansas City District** web site at **http://www.nwk. usace.army.mil**. Within the section Lake Pages are photographs, maps, trail guides, lists of facilities and fishing overviews for 17 reservoirs.

OKLAHOMA
The Bass Zone
http://www.basszone.com

The Zone has some national coverage but its bass boat is firmly docked in Oklahoma. The forums for tournament chat and reader's catch reports were both well used. State tournament reports and news from the national trails makes up the rest. Aspiring bass writers take note: they sometimes offer tournament-reporting internships.

See also **Oklahoma Bass Fishing** at **http://www.oklahomabass fishing.com** for Greg Myers' weekly fishing report, a collection of articles from some nationally known bass writers and links to Oklahoma tournaments.

THE ULTIMATE BASS FISHING RESOURCE GUIDE
http://www.bassresource.com

Glenn May's brilliant guide to bass behavior and fishing techniques also points to the best bass fishing web sites in every state. From the homepage go to Links then State for listings. Recommendations range from magazine sites to club and guide pages to forums.

The Fishing Notebook
http://www.fishingnotebook.com

TOP RATED

The Fishing Notebook
http://www.fishingnotebook.com

TOP RATED This bright-looking freshwater fishing magazine has impressive Oklahoma features including brush pile and hotspot maps for 100 waters, and a page of links for stream-flows, lake levels and weather conditions. Articles, species information and The Great American Fish Story, an area for posting tall fishing tales, offer something for non-Okies.

Oklahoma Fly Fishing
http://home.att.net/~brockrut/

Provides most of everything you need to explore nine of Oklahoma's best trout streams: maps, fishing descriptions, articles, fly patterns and streamflows.

It doesn't have a forum, but links to a good one hosted by the **Beavers Bend Fly Shop** at **http://www.beaversbend flyshop.com**.

Though fly fishing is gaining in popularity in Oklahoma, some habits die hard. One post on the forum lamented the sight of a local angler taking a five-pound trout for the pot: "He couldn't understand my dismay at why he would be grilling such a fine fish. He looked at me like I was crazy when I answered 'catch and release' when he asked me what I would do with it. I think his question 'What would you do with it?' was meant 'How would you cook it?'"

NEBRASKA
Nebraska Game and Parks Commission
http://www.ngpc.state.ne.us/homepage.html

The Nebraska Game and Parks Commission makes up for the absence of Nebraska fishing content on the Web by taking its two outdoor publications online. *NEBRASKAland* at **http://www.ngpc.state.ne.us/nebland**, covers camping, fishing, canoeing and outdoor skills. Go to Outdoor Ed on the Commission's homepage to find articles from the *Outdoor Nebraska* newspaper, as well as details of youth fishing programs and trail guides. Regular fishing resources include maps, stocking schedules, fishing reports and details of the agency's urban fishing program.

Nebraska Lake Guide
http://www.lakeguide.com

Part visitor's guide, part fishing site, the *Nebraska Lake Guide* is an annual print magazine re-published on the Web. Choose one of the six regions from the state silhouette to find large maps, fishing overviews and contact numbers. Links at the bottom of the page lead to articles, clubs and tournaments.

NORTH DAKOTA
Fishing Buddy Outdoors (FBO)
http://www.fishingbuddy.com

TOP RATED

One way to judge if it's worth subscribing to a site that charges for premium content is to assess the quality of

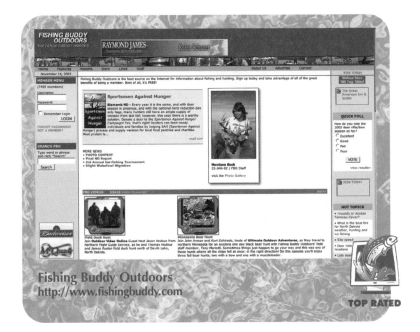

Fishing Buddy Outdoors
http://www.fishingbuddy.com

TOP RATED

what they give away for nothing. Here, that would be fishing reports for nearly 30 North Dakota waters—with particularly thorough coverage of Devil's Lake—a busy forum and classifieds area and general resource links. For cast and blasters, the site offers a comprehensive hunting channel.

At several points FBO links to the **North Dakota Game and Fish Department** at **http://www.state. nd.us/gnf**. Click on the Fishing in ND tab to find guides to the state's best waters, including the Red River and the Missouri River, contour maps for hundreds of smaller fisheries and links to the department's official outdoor magazine, television and radio show.

SOUTH DAKOTA
Black Hills Fishing
http://www.rapidnet.com/~ jtuxford/welcome2.htm

As webmaster John Tuxford points out "you can only take so many pictures of Mt. Rushmore and Wall Drug." What you should do after that is head to the Black Hills streams or load the truck for bass

and panfish. The Black Hills menu leads mostly to lake descriptions, but Al Campbell's Fly Fishing Pages is a mini-guide to hatches, flies and small stream tactics. Links at the bottom of the page lead to general travel and tourism sites, water levels and the latest news from the **South Dakota Department of Game, Fish, and Parks** at **http://www.state. sd.us/gfp**.

South Dakota BASS Federation
http://www.sdbassfederation.com

An obvious cause for celebration if you're a Dakota bass chaser, but there's much to commend this site to any freshwater fisherman in the region. Tournament followers can research results, standings and the competition histories of different entrants. The Lakes link supplies general information about Lake Oahe, Lake Sharpe, Lake Francis Case, Lake Lewis & Clarke and Angostura Reservoir. Each is presented with a large map, scene-setting photos and links to the most useful information from the U.S. Army Corp of Engineers and other sites.

AND DON'T FORGET ...

Game & Fish Magazines
http://www.gameandfish. about.com
Choose Great Plains from the menu of state-by-state information for professionally reported freshwater fishing articles. See Chapter 5 Media, Print Magazines Online for a review.

Walleye Central
http://www.walleyecentral.com
The 'eyes have it. See Chapter 4 Fishing the Web, Best Freshwater Fishing Sites for a review.

The Ice Fishing Home Page
http://hickorytech.net/~jbusby/ iceangler.html
A man only needs one ice-fishing directory. This is it. See Chapter 4 Fishing the Web, Best Freshwater Fishing Sites for a review.

Texas

Texas has more fishermen within its borders than any other state. They're fanatical bass fishermen, of course, but they take to the salt with equal enthusiasm, wade fishing for specks and redfish or prowling offshore for big game. And there's a growing number that wouldn't dream of fishing either freshwater or saltwater without a fly rod in their hand.

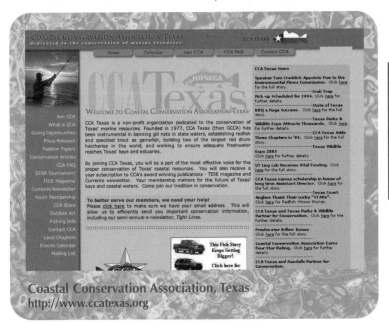

Coastal Conservation Association, Texas
http://www.ccatexas.org

Bass Fishing in North Texas
http://www.bassfishing.org

TOP RATED Bass guide Richie White must spend a lot of time on the water judging by the shoulder-to-shoulder "hawgs" in his inspiring clients' photo album, but it hasn't stopped him putting together this impressive bass site. Original material comes in the form of profiles of seven North Texas lakes, with his home water of Lake Fork getting the most in-depth treatment. The rest of it is built around the most useful information he could patch in from sources such as the **Texas Parks and Wildlife Department** (TPWD) at **http://www.tpwd.state. tx.us**, the U.S. Corps of Engineers and sources for prime times, moon phases and local weather.

Coastal Conservation Association, Texas
http://www.ccatexas.org

The national Coastal Conservation Association grew out of the success and determination of this group of Texas coastal anglers. As you'd expect, the site is a center for

Corpusfishing.com
http://www.corpusfishing.com

TOP RATED

Gulf conservation news, but it can also be used to search for CCA-sponsoring fishing guides and has all the details of the State of Texas Anglers Rodeo (STAR), a popular saltwater trophy tournament offering nearly a million dollars in boat, tackle and scholarship prizes.

Corpus Christi Caller Times – Outdoors
http://www.caller.com

TOP RATED

They take saltwater fishing seriously in the historic port town of Corpus Christi: the Outdoors column has a privileged place in the first level of navigation at the top of the homepage. David Sikes' fishing page for the Coastal Bend area of Corpus, Aransas Pass and Rockport proves itself worthy of the distinction, and must be up there with the best fishing

coverage from a city newspaper anywhere in the country.

His fishing report is a weekly roundup of 10 areas (a couple of them freshwater); there are vector tables for predicting hot fishing periods, a big directory of local fishing guides and links to marine forecasts. The Anglers' Guide is a broad introduction to local opportunities matched to large clear maps. All of Sikes' fishing articles are available back to 1999.

Corpusfishing.com
http://www.corpusfishing.com

TOP RATED

Sites that consistently post decent fishing reports should be cherished, and on review day five of Corpusfishing.com's six reports were usably up-to-date. Reports, which are often illustrated with catch shots, come from fishing stations between Padre Island and Port Aransas, and are usually three or four paragraphs long. Weather and tide links and an active forum make it one for a permanent bookmark.

Dallas Fly Fishers
http://www.dallas-flyfishers.org

The best of the Texas fly-fishing club pages. A nice bright design lays out all the benefits of joining and upcoming events. Download PDF copies of the group's newsletter *The Leader* for more information.

Texas' premier river fly fishing is in the beautiful Hill Country streams in the north central part of the state. **Texas Flyfishing** at **http://www.texasflyfishing.com** has some decent maps and a trip planner for six rivers in the region.

SPORTSMAN'S RESOURCE
The directory site **Sportsman's Resource** at **http://www. sportsmansresource.com** has a useful collection of state-by-state fishing information, as well as recommendations for Canada and other countries. From the homepage, mouse over the heading Local and Regional, then choose the country or state. Each entry begins with an overview of the fishing potential then lists associations and clubs, government agencies, lodges and guides, marinas, tacklestores and magazine web sites.

Honey Hole
http://www.honeyhole magazine.com

The state's leading bass publication bills itself as a trophy magazine, but there's something here for all bass fans. The Main Menu leads to sections for the *Honey Hole* print magazine, television show and tournament series. Go to Lakes, Guides & Gear for more than 25 lake profiles and links to external fishing reports. Those thinking about a subscription can download a complete 60-page sample issue of the magazine.

Houston Chronicle – Outdoors
http://www.chron.com

The Houston Chronicle has the good sense to employ a trio of professional outdoor writers to cover the state's huge fishing and hunting opportunities. Go to Sports then Outdoors to read current and archived columns from Doug Pike, Joe Doggett and Shannon Tompkins. Toward the bottom of the Outdoors page there's a brief daily fishing report and tide tables.

Lake Fork, Texas – ETS Systems
http://www.ets-systems.com

TOP RATED

Lake Fork is arguably the best lake in the country for 10-pound-plus largemouths. If you're determined to break that golden-green barrier, this web site does everything but put you in the boat and tie on the lure. The Lake Fork Directory has all the trip-planning information you'll need, including maps, contact information for guides and lodges and the locations of boat ramps, RV parks and campgrounds. Two must-see features are the guide reports and the collection of more than 50 Lake Fork Pro Tips.

Texas Gulf Coast Fishing

http://www.texasgulfcoast fishing.com

TOP RATED

You might be surprised to learn how many different species are available to Texas saltwater fishermen. Do your homework within the fish identification pages of Texas Gulf Coast Fishing. Elsewhere there are useful and entertaining features within How-to/Tips, Articles, and the "Liars Ring," as well as links to tides, regulations, accommodation, party boats and weather forecasts. The navigation links at the bottom of each page offer the most complete list of everything here. Kids get their own special section.

Texas Saltwater

http://www.texassaltwater fishing.com

Texas has more than 600 miles of coastline, including the longest bar-

rier island in the world. This simple directory splits the coast into upper, middle and lower sections. Click on each for links to guides, charters, accommodation, tacklestores and trip-planning information.

See also **Louis Rodgers' Texas Fishing 2004** at **http://www.austin resource.com/texasfishing.htm**, for web site recommendations and links to coastal maps and weather resources.

TexasMojo.com

http://www.texasmojo.com

TOP RATED

A popular forum leads the homepage, but perhaps even more useful are the neatly organized saltwater fishing links below it. Scroll down for links to recipes, guide listings, fishing maps, web cams, fishing reports and many other categories. Mike Lane's RodnReel.com provides thousands of GPS coordinates for Gulf hotspots.

Tom Nix's Salty Angler

http://www.saltyangler.com

Tom Nix offers a subscription fish-

TOP RATED

ing report covering the Coastal Bend, but there's enough free information at the Salty Angler to justify a regular visit whether you sign up or not. Tabs in the top navigation lead to tips, news and fishery updates from six guides. The section Coastal Bend Top 7 Hot Spots ranks areas according to the most positive recent fishing reports.

To confirm that Tom and friends know their way around the Texas coast, check the Big Girls of Baffin Bay link for a gallery of some huge speckled trout.

TX Fishing.com

http://www.txfishing.com

TOP RATED

TX Fishing.com makes itself the state's most useful fishing site by offering three distinct

services. The first is J. P. Greeson's Weekly Fishing Report, dividing the state into central, northwest, south, panhandle, west and coastal regions. Each water in each region is summarized in terms of water clarity, temperature, what species are being caught and successful baits and lures. The second pillar of the site is the very popular Texas Fishing Forum, a gathering point for thousands of Texas fishermen to talk bass, stripers, catfish and saltwater topics. To seal the deal, from the homepage find links to the fishiest features of the Texas Parks and Wildlife Department web site, the United States Geological Service, and the U.S. Army Corps of Engineers. The top navigation has links to clubs, guides, readers' catch photos and that rarest of features, an events calendar that's not only filled in but up-to-date.

West

As any number of TV advertisements for SUV's and brokerage firms prove, fly fishing and the West (and stylish living) are now bound in the popular imagination. It's always been this way for fly fishermen. The West of their imagination spreads from the high country of New Mexico and Colorado along the spine of the Rockies to the promised land of Wyoming, Idaho and Montana. No dress code or portfolio required.

WaynesWords – Lake Powell Fishing Information
http://www.wayneswords.com

TOP RATED

ARIZONA
The Arizona Republic – Outdoors

http://www.azcentral.com

The state's biggest newspaper has outdoor news and articles, a weekly fishing report, travel guides to Arizona lakes and national parks and links to the **Arizona Game and Fish Department** at **http://www.gf. state.az.us**.

WaynesWords – Lake Powell Fishing Information

http://www.wayneswords.com

TOP RATED

The word from wildlife biologist Wayne Gustaveson is that if you want to be successful on huge Western waters like Lake Powell, you need a very clear understanding of the dynamics of the fishery through the seasons. He and his web site regulars are here to help. Between articles and tips and the detailed Fish Report, you'll find plenty of advice on how to target the lake's bass, bluegill, crappie, catfish, walleye, and the real star of the show, landlocked stripers. Wayne's professional background comes through in every section as he discusses the interrelation of predatory fish, forage fish and the aquatic environment.

The site's forum is a good place for tracking down the nomadic striper shoals. Come across one of those in a feeding blitz and what other word describes it but, Schwinnggg!

COLORADO
Blue Quill Angler
http://www.bluequillangler.com

You could spend a season duct-taped to your computer before finding a better fly-shop web site than bluequillangler.com. An obvious highlight is guide

TOP RATED

director Pat Dorsey's Fly Fishing Stream Report. This weekly information sheet begins with The Pro's Picks, recommending the best fly patterns based on developing conditions and the stage of the season. The main body of the report details 11 of Colorado's best-known rivers in terms of water clarity, temperature, major food organisms, hatches, effective patterns and a 14-day fishing forecast. Sign up for e-mail delivery and you'll never miss an installment.

If you're not distracted by several other features on the site, you'll see they place special emphasis on introducing newcomers to the sport: along with a busy schedule of in-store events, classes and schools, they've assembled a stellar beginner's guide titled Keep On Learning. To find it, click on Colorado Fly Fishing Schools from the homepage.

The Blue Quill Angler

Blue Quill Angler
http://www.bluequillangler.com

TOP RATED

Colorado Fishing Network
http://www.coloradofishing.net

TOP RATED

The Information and Reports Page at this fishing directory site links to fly-shop reports and hatch charts for more than a dozen rivers. Stories and articles from readers provide the inspiration to get you pawing through the Network's guide and lodge listings. Where-to-fish information is found within sections titled Regions, Wild Trout, Gold Medal and Merit Water. The first of these is a summary table of fisheries, fly shops and guides in nine areas; the other three refer to stream quality assessments from the **Colorado Division of Wildlife** at **http://wildlife.state.co.us/index.asp**.

Colorado Fly Fishing – Stream Information
http://www.pdsdata.net/flyfish.htm

You have a local river. It may not be the best in the state or even the best in your area, but it's home water and you care for it. Orv Petersen probably feels this way about the Eagle River near Vail. He's written about it and other local fisheries in his online fishing journal every month for the last six years. For anyone who'd like to give it a try, he includes access information, a hatch chart, stream-flows and recommended patterns. He even rates some of the local guides and outfitters working the river, including a few that make a "Wall of Shame" for questionable practices.

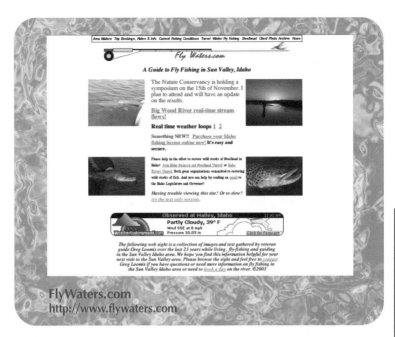

FlyWaters.com
http://www.flywaters.com

IDAHO
FlyWaters.com
http://www.flywaters.com

Greg Loomis has 20 years experience fly fishing and guiding the waters around Sun Valley, Idaho, so you ought to be able to trust his assessment of local fisheries. Look for either of the sections Current Conditions or Area Waters to read hatch information and updates for Silver Creek, Wood River, Lost River, Little Wood River, area lakes and Snake River steelhead. The steelhead report links to three web sites that publish fish counts for the Snake River dams.

Greg books through **Silver Creek Outfitters** at **http://www.silvercreek.com**, which posts its own fishing report for many of the same rivers.

Idaho Fish 'n' Hunt
http://www.idfishnhunt.com

Idaho has 22 state parks, 15 national forests, over 16,000 miles of river and more than 200 reservoirs and natural lakes. The northern third of the state has the greatest concentration of lakes in the West. That's a lot of lonesome fishing potential. This outdoor site discusses regions according to the major target species—trout, warmwater, steelhead, salmon and sturgeon. The Magazine link opens the archive of a quarterly fishing magazine going back to 1996. Fishing reports cover six areas and, combined with a steelhead report and stocking information, give a good idea where to point the truck come the weekend.

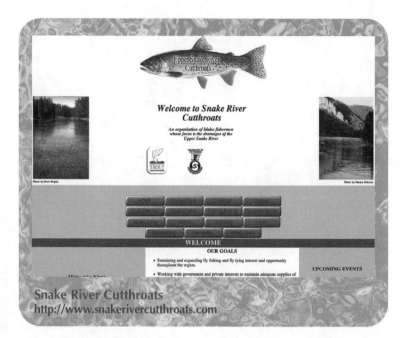

Snake River Cutthroats
http://www.snakerivercutthroats.com

Snake River Cutthroats
http://www.snakeriver
cutthroats.com

The conservation group Snake
River Cutthroats publishes a site
nicely balanced between conservation initiatives for protecting and
enhancing the upper Snake River
and its drainages, and straight
fishing talk. Fly of the Month features more than 20 local patterns,
there's a fishing report from
Jimmy's All Seasons Angler and
archives of the club newsletter.

The site's links section is really
worth delving into: you'll find a
directory of all the Idaho chapters
of Trout Unlimited and the Federation of Fly Fishermen, shortcuts
to famous local fly shops such
as **Henry's Fork Anglers** in Last
Chance at **http://www.henrysfork
anglers.com**, and odd bonuses like
details of the new outdoor maga-

zine published by **Idaho Fish and
Game** at **http://www2.state.
id.us/fishgame/fishgame.html**.

Twin River Anglers
http://www.traflyfish.com

Go to Fishing Reports at this
Lewiston fly-shop web site, then
click on Idaho within the Western
map. Mousing over the links clev-
erly highlights the river on the map
and pops up a brief description.
You can then click on the fishery
name for a more detailed map, a
fishing report and useful links.
Reports contained some valuable
information but a few were old
enough to be curling at the edges.

Perhaps the most impressive feature
of the site isn't strictly to do with
Idaho. Click on The Tying Bench for
photographs and basic recipes for
hundreds of salmon, steelhead, saltwater and warmwater patterns.

MONTANA
Big Sky Fishing.com
http://www.bigskyfishing.com

TOP RATED

An accomplished solo effort introducing 35 of Montana's best rivers, and at least as many lakes. Click on the name of a river or lake to bring up a main body introduction, then read through the Details section in the lefthand navigation for more about the fishing and how to organize a float.

Sections for Glacier National Park, Yellowstone National Park and Gear and Techniques are equally well done. This last section includes guides to small fishing craft and digital photography for

FLY SHOPS

The informal over-the-counter fishing report that's a feature of every decent fly shop—yours for the price of a few Woolly Buggers—is now often available as a regular report on the shop's web site. With business reputations on the line, most fly shops have a stake in providing accurate and timely information, but it's probably best to steer clear of any report that uses more than a couple of exclamation points per week. These four shops are all in Montana, but their services are typical of what's offered at hundreds of fly-shop web sites across the U.S. and Canada.

Dan Bailey's
Online Fly Fishing Shop
http://www.dan-bailey.com
Dan Bailey's in Livingston, one of the best-known fly shops in the country, has a well-organized fishing report section. Within entries for the Gallatin, the Madison, Yellowstone River, Yellowstone Park and local spring creeks, you'll find river conditions, hatches, patterns, comments, maps and a four-day weather forecast. Go to Fly Patterns for examples of essential Western flies.

George Anderson's
Yellowstone Angler
http://www.yellowstone
angler.com
This Paradise Valley shop covers the famous local spring creeks, the Yellowstone River, Yellowstone

Park and the Bighorn. Fishery profiles and links to weather, streamflows and snow pack information round it out. They encourage calls to the shop for late updates.

The Grizzly Hackle
http://www.grizzlyhackle.com
Over in the western part of the state in Missoula, The Grizzly Hackle fly shop has brief but specific reports on Rock Creek, the Bitterroot, the Clark Fork and the Blackfoot.

Madison River Fishing Company
http://www.mrfc.com
The Madison River Fishing Company in Ennis reports on the Madison, the Beaverhead and the Big Hole.

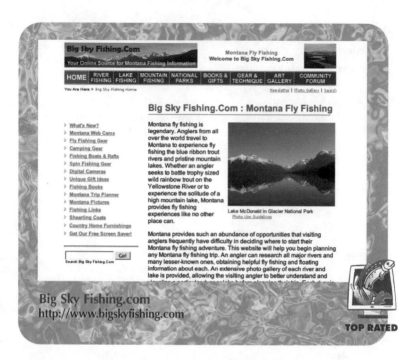

Big Sky Fishing.com
http://www.bigskyfishing.com

TOP RATED

the outdoorsman. Good design and lots of sharp landscape photography makes the site a pleasure to browse around.

Montana Fish, Wildlife and Parks (MFWP)
http://www.fwp.state.mt.us/default.asp

In states that don't inspire many fishing web sites, and for some reason most of the West falls into this category, fish and wildlife department sites are even more critical resources. Montana has an especially good one.

Go to Fishing in the lefthand navigation to find regulations, fishing records, stocking schedules for hundreds of waters, streamflow conditions and road and weather links. The Planning a Trip link lets you search for stream and lake access points on every water managed by the department. The heading Montana Fisheries Information System in the Hot Topics box leads to a huge custom database for locating waters according to species, region, and "value" (on a scale of 1–5, with 5 being outstanding). Even allowing for a little hometown pride, the 900 fisheries awarded the highest rating could wear out even the most dedicated fishing bum.

Montana Fly Fishing
http://www.glacierto yellowstone.com

The route leading from Yellowstone National Park to Glacier National Park would score high on any Western angler's fantasy fishing itinerary. Author David Archer has removed any excuse for not making the trip by writing a fishing and camping trail guide to the region, backed up by this planning web site. The core of the site divides the route between the Parks into five regions. There's enough fishing, camping and service information in each section to plan an entire trip. The book can be ordered from the site.

NEVADA

With the exception of the Eastern Sierra web sites profiled in the California section of this chapter, it's probably best to abandon the search for independent Nevada fishing sites and head straight for the **Nevada Department of Wildlife** (NDOW) at **http://www. ndow.org.** As they write in the introduction to their fishing pages, there are plenty of places to go fishing in Nevada, you've just got to know where to look. Go through the stocking schedules, the fishing report and table of Fishable Waters for ideas. The leads you'll find at the NDOW site combine well with park information from the **Nevada Division of State Parks** at **http://www.parks.nv.gov**, and the brilliant guide to exploring the state offered by **Camping Guide Nevada** at **http://www.herronweb.com/ campgroundguide.html**.

AND DON'T FORGET ...

Fly Fisherman
http://www.flyfisherman.com
Many Western fly-fishing sites know a quality resource when they see one and simply link to this site's Rocky Mountain and Southwest reports and forums. See Chapter 5 Media, Print Magazines Online for a review.

The Flyfishing Connection
http://www.flyfishing
connection.com
A national fly-fishing magazine with strong Western coverage. River information includes hatches, driving directions, basic maps and business listings. See Chapter 4 Fishing the Web, Best Fly-Fishing Sites for a review.

The Fish Sniffer Online
http://www.fishsniffer.com
Covers the breadth of Western and West Coast fishing from bass to fly fishing to saltwater. See Chapter 5 Media, Print Magazines Online for a review.

Flyfishing the West
http://groups.yahoo.com/
group/flyfishingthewest
Register to join this active, friendly community.

WesternBass.com
http://www.westernbass.com
The meeting place for Western bass anglers. See Chapter 4 Fishing the Web, Best Bass Fishing Sites for a review.

Westfly
http://www.westfly.com
Home to several Western forums and full of articles, entomology and fly-tying resources. See Chapter 4, Fishing the Web, Best Fly-Fishing Sites for a review.

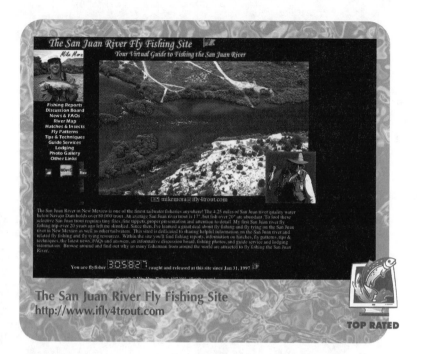

The San Juan River Fly Fishing Site
Your Virtual Guide to Fishing the San Juan River

Mike Mora

Fishing Reports
Discussion Board
News & FAQs
River Map
Hatches & Insects
Fly Patterns
Tips & Techniques
Guide Services
Lodging
Photo Gallery
Other Links

mikemora@ifly4trout.com

The San Juan River in New Mexico is one of the finest tailwater fisheries anywhere! The 4.25 miles of San Juan river quality water below Navajo Dam holds over 80,000 trout. An average San Juan river trout is 17", but fish over 20" are abundant. To fool these selective San Juan trout requires tiny flies, fine tippets, proper presentation and attention to detail. My first San Juan river fly fishing trip over 20 years ago left me skunked. Since then, I've learned a great deal about fly fishing and fly tying on the San Juan river in New Mexico as well as other tailwaters. This sited is dedicated to sharing helpful information on the San Juan river and related fly fishing and fly tying resources. Within the site you'll find fishing reports, information on hatches, fly patterns, tips & techniques, the latest news, FAQs and answers, an informative discussion board, fishing photos, and guide service and lodging information. Browse around and find out why so many fishermen from around the world are attracted to fly fishing the San Juan River.

You are flyfisher caught and released at this site since Jan 31, 1997

The San Juan River Fly Fishing Site
http://www.ifly4trout.com

TOP RATED

NEW MEXICO
FlyFishNM
http://www.flyfishnm.com

Phil Springer introduces New Mexico fly fishing from several perspectives. Most obviously, there are basic outlines and maps of eight major watersheds. For a more personal take on the area he has posted his online fishing diary going back to 1998. Finally, he doesn't ignore what's useful from outside sources, such as Mike Mora's web site for the San Juan River or the statewide fishing report compiled by the **New Mexico Department of Game and Fish** at **http://www.gmfsh. state.nm.us**.

The San Juan River
Fly Fishing Site
http://www.ifly4trout.com

TOP RATED If you fish the four miles of tailwater below the San Juan Dam and don't catch anything, try not to torture yourself thinking of the 80,000 trout that have just outsmarted you. No, go to Mike Mora's micro-level guide to the river and arm yourself with all the tools necessary for a big payback. The entomology section describes important river bugs and the best patterns for imitating them. A monthly tips area deals with tail-water techniques and hotspots. Regular reports and decent maps for the upper and lower half of the tailwater will give you an idea where to stage your comeback.

UTAH
Fly Fishing Utah
http://www.fishwest.net/utah

TOP RATED

Courtesy of the Fishwest fly shop in Salt Lake City, you'll find an organized set of river reports, hatch charts, regulations and weather links. Sign up for the mailing list, post a question to the forum or copy some winning local patterns from The Fly Box. A link to the **Utah Division of Wildlife Resources** at **http://www.wildlife.utah.gov** leads to its statewide fishing report.

Go Fly Fishing
The Green River
http://quickbyte.com/greenriver

TOP RATED

A super guide to the Green River as it passes through the Flaming Gorge National Recreation Area. The Maps link at the bottom of the homepage summarizes how to approach each section of the river and lists current conditions, access points and campsites. Webmaster Curt Brogren wants you to use the right fly. Every week he recommends six patterns based on developing conditions, and he's drawn up a calendar showing what flies are usually best in what months.

Utah Fish Finder
http://www.utahfishfinder.com

Search by Fly Fishing, Bass, Walleye or South/North of I-70 to read summaries of hotspots in the last month. A forum, stocking histories and fishery descriptions add some depth and context to the reports. Whirling Disease is a factor on some of these waters and those affected are clearly labeled.

Fly Fishing Utah
http://www.fishwest.net/utah

TOP RATED

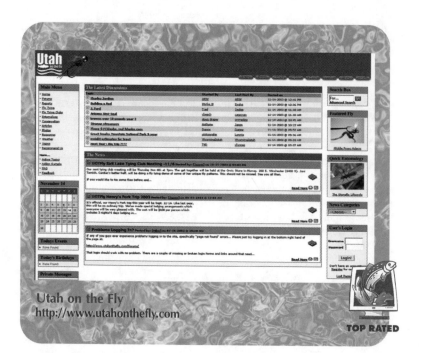

Utah on the Fly
http://www.utahonthefly.com

TOP RATED

Utah on the Fly
http://www.utahonthefly.com

TOP RATED

Utah on the Fly understands how thoughtfully conceived web sites can become a focal point for people with the same interest. Connect online with other Utah fly fishers within the 1,000-member forum or find out about the four regional (and real world) fly-tying clubs organized by the site. Shared information and inspiration comes in the form of hatch charts for seven major rivers, large galleries of member catch shots and an exceptional collection of resource links.

WYOMING
High Country Flies
http://www.highcountryflies.com

TOP RATED

Use this Jackson Hole fly shop site to quickly get up to speed on local opportunities. The section Fly Fishing in Jackson Hole contains large maps and no-nonsense advice about hatches, patterns and techniques. Click on the Fly Fishing Library to find streamflows, regulations and essays, or assess recent catches within fishing reports for the Snake, Yellowstone and Green Rivers.

Jack Dennis Sports
http://www.jackdennis.com

Pioneering Western fly tier Jack Dennis owns a fly shop in Jackson Hole and publishes an online newsletter describing many local fisheries. In season, his guides contribute to a weekly fishing report for the Snake River, Jackson Hole lakes, the Pinedale area, Yellowstone Park and Western Idaho.

JacksonHole.Net
http://www.jacksonholenet.com

TOP RATED

With mirror sites for Yellowstone, West Yellowstone, Big Sky, Bozeman and Cody, this network of regional travel guides should be bookmarked by anyone putting together a Western

fly-fishing road trip. Aside from all the general visitor information, each sub-site has an efficient search function for tracking down guides, lodges, fly shops, and in some cases, articles and fishing reports.

Wyoming Fishing Network
http://www.wyomingfishing.net

Wyomingfishing.net has effectively picked around on the Web to present this digest of state fishing information. Fly shops and guides supply local patterns, river reports and hatch charts. Fish and wildlife departments and other government agencies are the source for Yellowstone Park information and where-to-fish profiles of lakes, reservoirs and rivers. Site visitors chip in with fishing stories and articles.

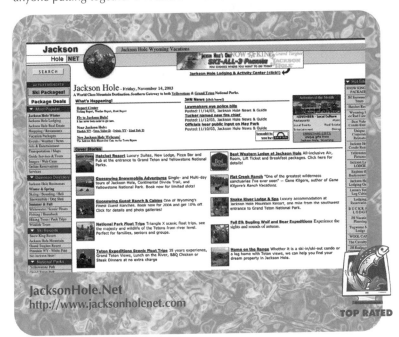

Northwest

Salmon country, steelhead country, trout country, on a fly rod or more often on conventional gear, many Northwest fishermen arrange their whole fishing lives around run timings—what's staging at the mouth, what's moving up river and what's coming next on the curve of a perpetual season.

Alaska Outdoor Journal
http://www.alaskaoutdoorjournal.com

TOP RATED

ALASKA
Alaska Outdoor Journal
http://www.alaskaoutdoor
journal.com

Alaska Flyfishing Online
http://www.alaskaflyfishing
online.com

TOP RATED Search for Alaska fishing web sites and what turns up are uncountable numbers of lodge and guide brochures, but few sources of substantial information. Perhaps they're all too busy actually fishing. Two that break the trend are the Alaska Outdoor Journal and its little sister, Alaska Flyfishing Online.

The Journal covers all outdoors and has a solid fishing section with articles, tips and readers' fishing reports. In the top righthand corner of the homepage the link to Salmon Run Charts displays run counts and river data for some of the most popular fishing regions in the state. The Journal's forum is the place for Alaskan fishing chat.

Alaska Flyfishing Online is a relatively new site with a reasonable spread of articles organized around tackling streams, lakes and saltwater. Alaska's own brand of fly tying (think Hungry Man dinner) and lots of information siphoned from the indispensable **Alaska Department of Fish and**

Game web site at **http://www.state.ak.us/adfg/adfghome.htm** make up the rest.

If you *are* searching for guides and lodges in Alaska, the designers of **Alaska Fishing Online** at **http://www.alaskafishingonline.com** have put some real effort into making their directory uncluttered and easy to browse. Click on the sections for Guides & Chapters, Lodges & Resorts, and Fly-in Services to find a state map divided into five regions. Choose a region to view contact information for each business, including a link to the company's web site. Listings are usably deep in most categories.

The Anchorage Daily News – Outdoors
http://www.adn.com/outdoors

The Anchorage Daily News has a fine fishing section supplemented by feature stories from fly-fishing author Ken Marsh and others. During Alaska's short but intense season they publish a weekly fishing report, and a section titled Outdoors Hotline lists classes, events, meetings and other happenings in the outdoor world. The newspaper's parent company publishes a definitive Alaska visitor's guide with a healthy amount of fishing information tucked away within its regional centers. Go to **http://www.alaska.com** and click on one of the regions of the Alaska map to find all the trip-planning information you could wish for and an outdoors section with fishing articles and resources.

Fish Alaska
http://www.fishalaska magazine.com

The publishers of the print magazine *Fish Alaska* make available two or three articles from each back issue going back to August 2001. When you've read those, go through the species guides or print off copies of an Alaska fishing trip packing list.

Kenai Peninsula Online

http://www.peninsulaclarion.com/
outdoors

There can't be many more fishy
places on the planet than the
Kenai Peninsula. The local newspaper, *The Peninsula Clarion*,
has the recreational fishing scene
well covered within fishing and
conservation articles, run-timing
charts and links to local salmon
and halibut fishing derbies.

Rudy's Alaska Fishing Page

http://www.alaska.net/~guidesak/
rudy/rt.htm

A great personal page from
Ryuichi "Rudy" Tsukada following
his seasonal adventures in the
ultimate fishing playground of
south central Alaska. Full of bright
photographs, his fishing logs go
back to 1995 and give an authentic

look at the life and times of your
average Alaskan fishing nut. He'll
even let you buddy along if you
agree to a few simple rules. See
site for details.

OREGON
BoatEscape.com

http://www.boatescape.com

TOP RATED

BoatEscape.com provides
boaters and fishermen
with well-organized
planning information for
all the major lakes and
rivers in Oregon. Go to Lakes &
Rivers and use either the View
Map option or search by area,
water name, amenity or fish type.
You'll discover driving directions,
fees, boat ramp locations and links
to local facilities. There are 420
lakes and rivers in the database
and 1,000 campgrounds.

Fish Passage Center (FPC)

http://www.fpc.org

Set up by the Northwest Power Planning Council, the FPC monitors salmon survival in the Columbia River Basin and offers technical advice to agencies about managing flow, spilling water over dams and other measures to protect endangered runs of salmon and steelhead. Which means they know a lot about what's going on in the river at any moment in time. They share much of that information on their web site, where you'll find real-time data for flows, spill rates and water temperatures, plus hatchery release figures and fish counts. They'll even e-mail you a weekly report summarizing conditions and fish returns.

Ifish

http://www.ifish.net

TOP RATED

Part diary of webmaster Jennie Logsdon's fishing adventures on the Oregon coast, part resource directory for river data, fishing reports and business listings, the feature that makes Ifish one of the most visited Northwest sites are its very popular forums (5,000 registered users) discussing salmon, steelhead, warmwater and saltwater topics.

Oregon Fishing with The Guide's Forecast

http://www.theguidesforecast.com

For about the price of a steak entrée, The Guide's Forecast will e-mail you a detailed weekly fishing forecast for the state's most popular salmon and steelhead

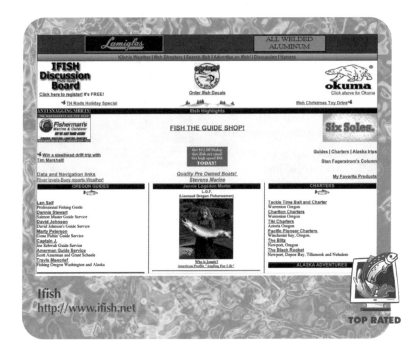

Ifish
http://www.ifish.net

TOP RATED

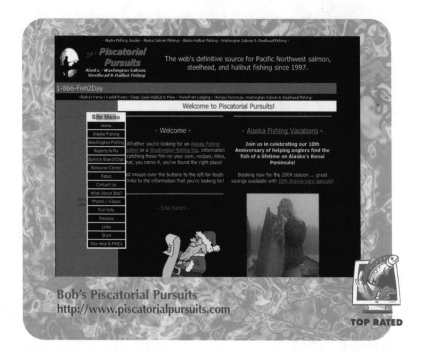

Bob's Piscatorial Pursuits
http://www.piscatorialpursuits.com

TOP RATED

rivers. A free and quite usable fishery report is posted to the site every week. To see what a subscription buys, click on Sample under Weekly Report at the bottom of the homepage.

WASHINGTON
Bob's Piscatorial Pursuits
http://www.piscatorialpursuits.com

TOP RATED

Somehow Bob Ball manages to juggle a guiding business in Washington and Alaska and the maintenance of this exceptional regional fishing site. There's plenty of fishing advice within areas for Washington, Alaska, Fishing Tips and species guides, but the most impressive features are reports for the Olympic Peninsula and Kenai Peninsula, updated every two to three days, and the Piscatorial

Pursuits forum. Three thousand people are registered here, and the yearly archive runs to more than 60,000 messages.

Dickson Flyfishing Steelhead Guides
http://www.flyfishsteelhead.com

TOP RATED

This guide's site goes well beyond the usual service descriptions with a collection of more than 40 stories and articles, hints and tips for this hardest form of fly fishing and regular river reports.

Fishing Northwest
http://www.fishingnorthwest.com

TOP RATED

Gordon Gracey, a fly-fishing guide on the Olympic Peninsula, has developed his business brochure into a content-led fishing resource. Among several noteworthy features are regular river and saltwater roundups, a no-fuss guide to fly tying and a summary table of steelhead rivers on the Peninsula, their peak months and the best sections to concentrate on. To find the table look for the Map link buried within one of the introductory paragraphs on the homepage.

Gamefishin.com
http://www.gamefishin.com

TOP RATED Webmaster Bruce Pearson oversees a handsome and helpful reference for the state's diverse fishing opportunities. Articles deal with freshwater and saltwater topics; there are lake profiles and visitors' fishing reports. The Resources section has basic topographic maps for more than 200 lakes and trout stocking schedules from the **Washington Department of Fish and Wildlife** at **http://www.wa.gov/wdfw.** The Gamefishin' forum is home to a friendly and responsive crew of regulars.

Puget Sound Fly Fishing
http://www.pugetsound flyfishing.com

Only a few features—the fly archive and Northwest baitfish gallery—were online at the time this newly launched site was reviewed, but they were done so well it deserves an early bookmark.

If you fish for sea-run cutthroat or target nearshore structure for any other species, take note. Under the heading Mapping Utility, they link to a huge aerial photo archive from the **Washington Department of Ecology** at **http://apps.ecy.wa. gov/shorephotos/index.html**, which spent five years taking oblique aerial photographs of the whole Washington coastline, all 2,500 miles of it. There are 10,000 photographs in the database, deliberately taken on days of low cloud cover and at low tide to show as much of the underlying beach, rock and manmade structure as possible.

Salmon University
http://www.salmonuniversity.com

Salmon charter captains and seminar hosts John Keizer and Tom Nelson have packed this tightly **TOP RATED** organized web site with

ULTIMATE FLY TYING
The directory site **Ultimate Fly Tying** at **http://www.ultimatefly tying.com** has gathered a huge collection of state fly-fishing links. Go to State/Regional and choose your area to find 30 to 40 general fly-fishing links and information about specific rivers. Refreshingly, they include content from a range of sources rather than just the old faithful fish and wildlife departments. You'll be directed to hatch charts, species information, forums, stream reports, even to Amazon.com for recommended fishing guidebooks.

Gamefishin.com
http://www.gamefishin.com

TOP RATED

maps, tips and resources for Northwest salmon fishermen. Washington is particularly well represented, but there are sections for Oregon and British Columbia. Using links in the lefthand navigation or clicking on the Washington map brings up 25 sub-maps showing hotspots, recommended tackle, tide information and boat ramp locations. Fishing reports from around the region are provided by lodges and charter operators. Mix in a salmon fishing Q & A and salmon derby listings and you begin to believe the claim that hundreds of thousands of fishermen a month stop by the site.

The Seattle Times – Outdoors
http://seattletimes.nwsource. com/html/fishing

Outdoor writer Mark Yuasa passes on the Washington Department of Fish and Game's regular creel census and adds a fishing forecast for what's hot and where to go in the coming week.

Steelheader.net
http://www.steelheader.net

Steelheader.net illustrates the basic techniques for all the noble arts of rigging worms, tying spawn bags, making slinkies, trolling, float fishing and plunking. There are helpful shortcuts to streamflows and the best fishing reports from other web sites. A simple registration lets you into the site's popular steelheading forum.

Washington Fly Fishing
http://www.washington flyfishing.com

The kind of site any fly fisher would be lucky to have covering their home waters. Looking through

TOP RATED

the forum archives is a good way to research the state's hundreds of rivers and lakes. The current forum proves to be visited by a helpful, responsive crowd: a box on the homepage highlights recent discussion threads: "Fishing camera suggestions?" 5 replies; "Shops?" 45 replies; "Browns in the Stilly?" 12 replies. The Resources & Links area is a carefully chosen directory to WA fly-fishing clubs and the best reports and forums from other sites.

WashingtonLakes.com
http://www.washingtonlakes.com

Don't approach this site with a view to reading the latest fishing reports, because they're mostly out-of-date: use it as a trip-preparation tool. Reading through old reports offers tips and a general sense of how regulars fish each lake (most are about lure and bait fishing for trout). The Topo Maps feature shows the basic depths and contours of more than 250 waters: another little piece of the puzzle filled in. Fifty of the lakes are given expanded coverage within the Featured Lakes section. To round off, go through the

Essential Links where you'll find, for example, such excellent resource sites as the **Interagency Committee for Outdoor Recreation and Boating** web site at **http://boat. iac.wa.gov**, which maps every boat launch in the state.

Worley Bugger Fly Co.
http://www.worleybuggerflyco.com

TOP RATED

The best fly shops have always acted as community fishing centers. A few of the most progressive do everything they can to extend that service through their web sites. Fly fishers in Eastern Washington or anyone visiting the Yakima River are lucky to have the Worley Bugger Fly Co. in the neighborhood and online.

Start with Yakima River Information, which houses the Yakima River Journal fishing report, river flows, reservoir levels and a safe-wading guide. The site has excellent hatch-matching coverage within sections for monthly hatches and a gallery of aquatic insects. Go to Fly Fishing Information for a guide to 12 rivers in neighboring Montana.

State-by-State Resources

AND DON'T FORGET ...

BC Adventure – Fish BC
http://www.bcadventure.com
Exceptional coverage of the Northwest's best-loved fishes: salmon, steelhead, trout and bottom fish. See Chapter 8 International, Canada for a review.

FishWithUS.net
http://www.fishwithus.net
A multimedia magazine with

a strong Northwest bias. See Chapter 5 Media, Online Magazines, for a review.

Westfly
http://www.westfly.com
Covers Northwest fly fishing better than any other site. See Chapter 4 Fishing the Web, Best Fly-Fishing Sites, for a review.

California

The Sacramento-San Joaquin Delta, the Eastern Sierra, the kelp beds and blue water of the Pacific, record-shaving bass in the reservoirs near San Diego: California is the golden state of angling opportunity.

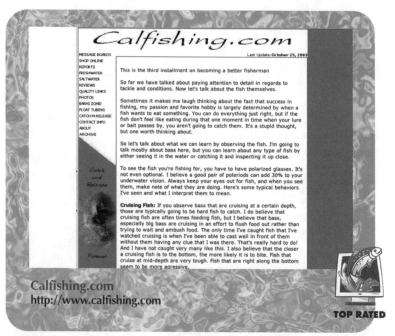

Calfishing.com
http://www.calfishing.com

TOP RATED

Bite's On!
http://www.biteson.com

Bite's On! offers a well-regarded weekly saltwater catch report for Southern California and Baja. They canvass the big charter boats, private boaters, commercial fishermen and area experts for the "late breaking dope" every fishermen wants to be in on. A free report is posted every week covering more than 25 areas, or you can subscribe to a more detailed e-mail version giving GPS coordinates, first-hand reports and other unfair advantages.

USAfishing at **http://www.usa fishing.com** provides a similar combination of free and subscription-based saltwater reports, this time for the Bay Area.

Calfishing.com
http://www.calfishing.com

TOP RATED

Calfishing.com presents its multispecies information with humor and intelligence. Editorial content is divided into freshwater and saltwater articles, reviews, news and "The Barnie Zone," which skewers a few huckstering bass personalities.

The forums, which are all worth a visit, are split into general discussion, freshwater, saltwater, trophy fishing, float tubes and kick boats.

California Delta Chambers & Visitors Bureau
http://www.californiadelta.org

TOP RATED

The Sacramento-San Joaquin Delta is 1,000 miles of interconnected bays and channels spread out in a lowland bowl to the west of Sacramento and Stockton. In the last few years it's become one of the hottest bass fisheries in the country. This chamber of commerce site and its weekly Delta fishing report should be your first stop when planning a trip to the area. The larger tourist site supplies directions, maps, navigation aids, tide tables and marina and accommodation listings: just about everything you

need to exit the real world for a while and become a bass river rat. Now, where did I put those Senkos?

Eastern Sierra Fishing
http://www.easternsierra fishing.com

TOP RATED

The editors of Eastern Sierra Fishing really hold your hand through the steps in planning a trip to this famously scenic and trouty region. They begin with basic guides to fly fishing and bait fishing, then it's on to lake profiles, stocking schedules and topographic maps. Of course, you'll need a place to lay your head and buy a few worms or flies: they finish the tour with service listings for guides, accommodation and tacklestores. For more impromptu advice and the latest catch reports, register at the forum.

California Delta Chambers & Visitors Bureau
http://www.californiadelta.org

TOP RATED

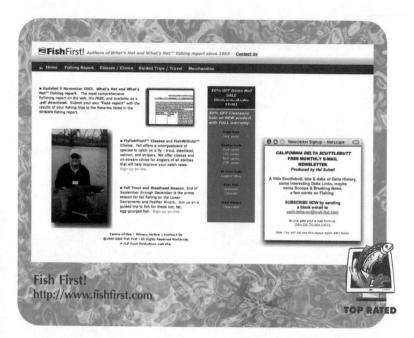

Fish First!
http://www.fishfirst.com

FliFlicker
http://www.fliflicker.com

As Los Angles-area fly fisherman Doug Martin describes it, down where he lives you can either join the crowds in the Eastern Sierra, "like fishing while waiting in line for U2 tickets" or develop new skills and head to the Pacific surf, "a wide open frontier for the fisherman." There's enough here between pattern recipes, articles gathered from other sites and links to surf-condition web sites, to get you started right. Use the forum to connect with other surf-fishing pioneers.

Fish First!
http://www.fishfirst.com

This Albany fly shop publishes a wonderfully detailed biweekly Northern California fly-fishing report. From the homepage click on What's Hot and What's Not – The Northern California Flyfishing Report to find a table of information summarizing 14 rivers and lakes. The table describes current conditions and how each water is fishing, which stretches are receiving the most fishing pressure and which flies are doing the most damage. Register and they'll e-mail you each new report.

To connect with area fly fishermen join the lively discussion at the **Northern California Fly Fishing Board** at **http://www.ncffb.org**.

Gary Bulla's
Fly Fishing Adventures
http://www.garybulla.com

If you fly fish the surf or like to kayak-fish out past the breakers, Gary Bulla's So Cal Surfcast is a monthly dose of advice, reflection and inspiration: he's landed over 65 species using this stealthy combination. The homepage links to fly-tying recipes, equipment talk and trip photos from Baja fishing adventures.

Ichthy.com
http://www.ichthy.com

TOP RATED

This page has morphed from a Bay Area fishing report into one of the best bass fishing personal pages on the Web. Creator Nico Raffo regularly updates his online fishing diary and photo album and, as you'll see, this guy gets out on the water more than is probably decent. Click on Freshwater to read 17 lake reviews or the sections Articles and Fish for tactical hints and location advice.

The Log
http://www.thelog.com

The Log is a free boating paper available at tacklestores, marinas and docks along the Southern California coast. Mixed in with port reviews, news stories and boating columns are fishing and conservation updates, directories of California and Baja charter boats and a guide to trout fishing the Eastern Sierra.

The Orange County Register – Outdoors
http://www.myoc.com/sports/ recreation/fishing_report.shtml

TOP RATED

Outdoor writer Jim Matthews compiles reliable weekly overviews of what's being caught in the major freshwater and saltwater fisheries, plus his top three picks for the week ahead. The Ocean Report has daily sportfishing landing stats from Newport Beach to Oxnard.

AND DON'T FORGET ...

AllCoast Sport Fishing
http://www.sport-fish-info.com
California's sportfishing community site for forums and reports. See Chapter 4 Fishing the Web, Best Saltwater Fishing Sites for a review.

CharkBait!
http://www.charkbait.com
A superior California saltwater magazine. See Chapter 4 Fishing the Web, Best Saltwater Fishing Sites for a review.

Pier Fishing in California
http://www.pierfishing.com
Ken Jones' all-star guide for California pier rats. See Chapter 4 Fishing the Web, Best Saltwater Fishing Sites for a review.

Trophy Bass Only
http://www.trophybassonly.com
Big bass and big bass hunters. See Chapter 4 Fishing the Web, Best Bass Fishing Sites for a review.

WesternBass.com
http://www.westernbass.com
The home of California's most popular bass forums. See Chapter 4 Fishing the Web, Best Bass Fishing Sites for a review.

2003 . . . 22 years of excellence!

In small groups Ralph and Lisa Cutter will lead you through an intense learning experience. Our **on the water instruction** simply can't be duplicated on a city lawn or parking lot. *We guarantee you'll become a better flyfisher.* We are one of the oldest and most respected "fly" schools in the country. We've been profiled in such diverse publications as *National Geographic Adventure, the L.A. Times, Outside, Adventure West, the Wall Street Journal, Sunset,* and *Playboy.*

Every year Ralph spends hundreds of hours underwater observing fish behavior. Combining this perspective with years of guiding experience, he has redefined the flyfishing envelope. His innovative techniques and fly patterns are used by anglers world wide. Ralph has contributed to over a dozen books, writes and photographs for virtually all of the outdoor publications, and his award-winning *Sierra Trout Guide,* has sold over 60,000 copies. He is editor for *California Flyfisher* and *Worldwaters.*

Lisa is one of the best known female flyfishers in the world. Her instructional techniques are on the cutting edge of flyfishing and **an incredible 80% of her clients are referred by previous students.**

Ralph and Lisa flyfish the planet yet remain devoted to their home waters of the Sierra Nevada. In pursuit of trout, they have packed well over 4,000 miles throughout the range.

Lisa and Ralph are members of the NCFFF **Hall of Fame** and Ralph is a recipient of the prestigious **Order of the Mayfly** award. Both Cutters are fully certified FFF casting instructors. They are internationally bonded, licensed by California Department of Fish & Game and sanctioned USFS and Army Corp permittees.

World renowned CLASSES
* Introduction to Flyfishing: gain a rock-solid foundation
* Complete Flyfisher: grow years of experience in 2 days

Sierra Trout Guide
* 50,000 anglers can't be wrong

Flyfishing Report
* honest conditions & hatches

Ralph and Lisa Cutter's California School of Flyfishing
http://www.flyline.com

TOP RATED

Ralph and Lisa Cutter's California School of Flyfishing
http://www.flyline.com

TOP RATED

Fly-fishing instructors Ralph and Lisa Cutter post a comprehensive fishing report for the Truckee, Little Truckee and Martis Creek, plus an Eastern Sierra overview. They aren't guides or retailers so when the report says the fishing is Dead (represented by one ladybug) or Insane (five ladybugs), it's all the more credible. The report recommends the most effective dries, wets and streamers for the season, all of which are photographed and listed with tying instructions.

San Diego Fish Online
http://www.sdfish.com

TOP RATED

A stylish guide to freshwater fishing near San Diego. There's an active forum, a section for reader-submitted reports and a fishing yellow pages, but it's the lake profiles that stand out. Each of 20 lakes gets its own page with a map, directions, regulations, facilities, fishing tips and links.

The San Diego Union-Tribune – Outdoors
http://www.signonsandiego.com
Go to Sports then Outdoors to find a collection of fishing and hunting features from writer Ed Zieralski and a link to a weekly fishing report covering freshwater, saltwater, outdoor events and stocking schedules.

The San Diego reservoirs probably provide the best bass fishing close to a major city anywhere in the country, and there's a helpful link on the *Union-Tribune* outdoors page to **The City of San Diego's Water Department** recreation web site at **http://www.sannet.gov/water/recreation/map.shtml.** It describes 12 reservoirs within the city limits, including how to get there, regulations, current water levels and, on the Bulletin page, stocking schedules for the bass's favorite snack, hatchery rainbows.

The San Francisco Chronicle – Outdoors
http://www.sfgate.com/sports/outdoors
The San Francisco Chronicle features articles from Tom Stienstra, one of the best-known outdoor writers in the country and author of

the definitive *Fishing California*, backed up by a weekly Bay Area fishing report from Brian Hoffman.

It may not have the polish of a newspaper web site but the forums at **http://www.fishingnetwork.net** provide plenty of Eastern Sierra trout fishing advice, among a mass of Southern California resource links. The navigation and layout of the site could be clearer, but it's easy enough to find your way to the forums. Click on Tips n' Bits! to find tips of the week and nuggets of advice culled from old forum threads.

Southern California Marlin Online (SCMO)
http://www.marlinnut.com

TOP RATED

Stan Ecklund Jr.'s SCMO has been on the Web since 1996 and looks to have found that difficult balance between being

San Diego Fish Online
http://www.sdfish.com

Southern California Marlin Online
http://www.marlinnut.com

TOP RATED

commercially sustainable (paid subscriptions) and providing a free community resource (everything else on the site). Explore the links in the lefthand navigation for tournament schedules, coordinates and a guide to billfish catch and release. The Marlin Club forum, found under the heading Interactive, is polite and enthusiastic.

Though the site has a strong regional focus, it attracts a worldwide audience and is beginning to develop its international coverage.

Trout Fishin' – Cali Style!
http://www.alumni.caltech.edu/~naturboy/fishing

One of the few sites to deal exclusively with bait and lure fishing for trout. Webmaster Alfred Wang gives overviews of tackle,

TOP RATED

techniques, lures and baits; there's a fishing diary, lake descriptions and a useful collection of fishing report pages for California and the Eastern Sierras.

West Coast Angler
http://www.westcoastangler.com

West Coast Angler is steadily building its content into one of the strongest California saltwater fishing sites on the Web. It's centered on charter boat fishing with reports from the major boat landings, profiles of boats and captains and articles about offshore tactics. The forum sees a regular turnover of posted questions and answers, and they've put together a links section that's a real West Coast resource center.

TOP RATED

Hawaii

According to the brochures, Hawaii is the only place in the world it's possible to hook up with a 1,000-pound marlin in any month of the year. For the biggest of big game, check these charter boat listings.

Hawaii Fishing Adventures and Charters at **http://www.sportfish hawaii.com** brokers the services of charter boats out of Kauai, Kona, Maui and Oahu. The text link See What's New at Hawaii Fishing Adventures leads to a fishing report, a calendar of fishing tournaments and advice about what to expect from your day on the water. Click on Great Overnight Fishing Trips for destination articles.

See also **Fish Maui** at **http://www. fishmaui.com** and **Fish Kona** at **http://www.fishkona.com**, for guides to both islands' fishing fleets.

For a description of a crew's progress through a round of big money tournaments and the stories behind its clients' captures, have a look at **http://www.aloha zone.com**, the web site of the Kailua-Kona charter boat, The Anxious.

The charter boat **Kuuloa Kai** based in Oahu, **http://www.kuuloa kai.com**, has moved its site beyond a simple brochure by including

fishing reports, identification charts and plenty of trip-preparation material.

It's worth visiting Captain Jeff Rodgers at **http://www.fishin kona.com** just for his straight talk about seasickness remedies and the questions you should be asking yourself before committing to an expensive charter. His monthly fishing report and a calendar of what's biting in what months are other bonuses.

Those interested in breaking records, or at least looking at some very large fish, should check the **Hawaii Fishing News** site at **http://www.hawaiifishingnews. com**. They are the state's official record compiler and as such have photographs and details of dozens of exceptional specimens from tilapia to marlin. The 100-Plus Club is a database of giant trevally (ulau) captures. All those photographed and described in the long list not only break three digits, they were all caught from shore.

CHAPTER 3
KNOW BEFORE YOU GO

You may be marooned in a gray city hours from decent water, but sitting right on your desk is the most sophisticated fish-finding gadget ever invented. Just about every aspect of deciding where and when to go fishing can now be researched from your home computer. Online weather forecasts, streamflows, lake levels, tide times, stocking schedules, and solunar tables are all widely available to help you figure out where the fish are likely to be and in what kind of mood.

But that isn't all. There are hundreds of general travel-planning sites on the Web that are potentially useful to fishermen. Find hotels and check road conditions in the most remote areas of the U.S., or smooth over every bump in the progress of a foreign fishing trip. Research guide services, book a campsite, or get driving directions to Bob's Bait and Tackle. It's enough to make you wonder how we ever got out the door ten years ago.

State Fish and Wildlife Departments

In Alaska it's referred to as the Division of Wildlife and Freshwater Fisheries; in Maryland it's known as the Department of Natural Resources; in Wyoming it's the old school Fish and Game Department, but whatever title they give themselves, as a group these state agencies in charge of fish and wildlife management offer indispensable web sites tailored to the needs of fishermen and hunters. Typically, they publish all current regulations, weekly fishing reports, stocking schedules, guides to all the major fisheries and species, and details of programs to encourage women, kids, and the disabled into fishing and other outdoor sports. Every Internet-using fisherman should bookmark their state's fish and wildlife department web site.

Several of these sites are referenced in different chapters within this book, but just about all of them would qualify for a **TOP RATED** designation. **Texas Parks and Wildlife Department** (TPWD) at **http://www.tpwd.state.tx.us** is a good example of what to expect from the best of them.

Click on Fishing at the top of the encyclopedic TPWD homepage to find channels for freshwater and saltwater. Saltwater content includes weather and tide information, a map of artificial reefs, and the latest conservation news. Freshwater has wonderful interactive maps for all the major lakes and rivers in the state, trout stocking tables, and a link to The Freshwater Fisheries Center.

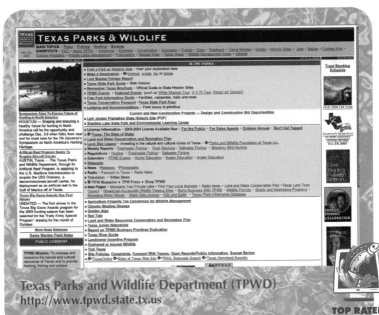

Texas Parks and Wildlife Department (TPWD)
http://www.tpwd.state.tx.us

TOP RATED

TPWD's weekly fishing report for freshwater and saltwater is well regarded and crossreferences with maps and fishery profiles. Other links on the Fishing menu page lead to species information, angler education, and fishing records.

If you regularly fish out of state it makes sense to bookmark a web site that has gathered links to all the state fish and wildlife departments in one place. Literally hundreds of sites offer this service, but a few popular ones are:

Big Fish Tackle
http://www.bigfishtackle.com
Go to Resources then Fishing License Info.

Cabela's
http://www.cabelas.com
Under In the Field go to State-by-State Information.

Fish and Wildlife Management Offices – State, Territorial, and Tribal
http://offices.fws.gov/state links.html
Links to every regional agency managing fish and fisheries.

LandBigFish
http://www.landbigfish.com
Under Free Resources, go to DNR Links.

Weather

Even though they live in a different element, weather affects fish just as much as any land-dwelling creature. Seeing the big picture of current conditions—atmospheric pressure, temperature, light intensity, wind direction, and approaching storm systems—is the first step in deciding where to fish. For fishermen out on the big lakes or saltwater, knowing the weather can be even more important than that.

Intellicast
http://www.intellicast.com

TOP RATED

Intellicast offers "Weather for Active Lives" and they live up to the slogan with tailored forecasts for several types of outdoor recreation, as well as current weather and 10-day predictions. Forecasts scale from general overviews to detailed breakdowns of temperatures, winds, precipitation, thunder, rain, sunniness, and fog.

To find the most relevant information for fishermen and boaters, go to Weather Planners on the homepage. The Boat and Beach option has current temperatures, high- and low-tide times, sunrise and sunset times and wind speed for hundreds of points along both coasts; the

Outdoors heading links to weather forecasts for National Parks and federal recreation areas. If your active fishing life requires knowledge of the shifting course of the Gulf Stream or weather for the Great Lakes, they've got that covered too.

National Weather Service (NWS)
http://www.nws.noaa.gov

TOP RATED

The NWS is the forecasting authority and source of data relied on by all ocean-going commercial and recreational boaters. The organization's home on the Web is full of topic channels, but go to Forecasts then Marine then your local area to find coastal, offshore, and high seas forecasts, and reports from the National Oceanic and Atmospheric Administration's

(NOAA) network of data buoys. About those buoys … The **National Data Buoy Center** at **http://www. ndbc.noaa.gov** is the operational hub for NOAA's automated observing stations or "smart" buoys. They record wind data, wave height, atmospheric pressure, pressure tendency, air and water temperature, and how each has changed over the last 24 hours. That's a complicated set of information, but they manage to make it straightforward to find and interpret. From the homepage, click on the boxes overlapping the U.S. map, then on each buoy for its coordinates and collected data. Each is listed with a telephone number allowing cell phone-equipped boaters to access its information while they're on the water.

The buoy network includes data provided by the **Meteorological Service of Canada** at **http://www.**

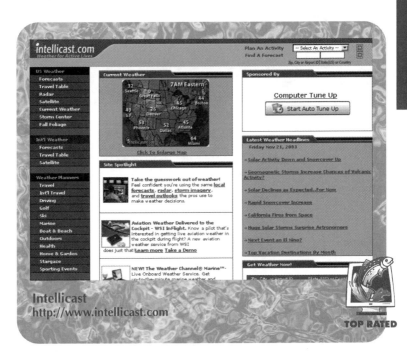

Intellicast
http://www.intellicast.com

TOP RATED

atl.ec.gc.ca/msc/index_e.html, a weather and forecasting center for every province in the country.

The Weather Channel
http://www.weather.com

Very often the best thing about having cable , The Weather Channel duplicates its round-the-clock service television within this multimedia site for breaking weather news, forecasts, and driving advisories. Use the Weather Tools - Stay Connected text link to have alerts and forecasts sent to your mobile phone, PDA or e-mail account. Also offers weather reports tailored to different activities.

The Weather Underground
http://www.wunderground.com

TOP RATED

The Weather Underground has forecasts for major towns and cities including temperatures, humidity, pressure, rain-

fall, and cloud cover. Maps on the homepage give the broad countrywide picture of tempera-tures, fronts, wind direction, the jet stream, and UV intensity (shows minutes to skin damage). Use the Favorites option to quickly isolate local information or click on Marine Forecasts for a clear presentation of NWS forecasts.

Other Options
If those sites don't satisfy your weather craving, explore the links collected by the University of Michigan's **UM Weather TOP RATED** site at **http://yang.sprl. umich.edu/wxnet/**. It lists more than 300 weather web sites, many from the metrological departments of other universities, and includes options for Canadian forecasts, the best weather cams, and sites for NEXRAD and satellite imagery.

Great Lakes Angler at **http:// www.glangler.com** reviewed in Chapter 5 Media, has a weather

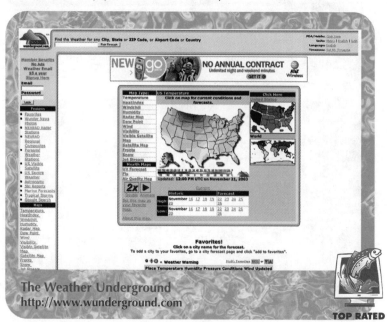

The Weather Underground
http://www.wunderground.com

TOP RATED

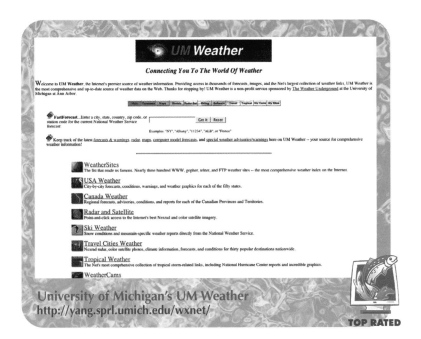

University of Michigan's UM Weather
http://yang.sprl.umich.edu/wxnet/

TOP RATED

section ideal for bookmarking. It links to the NWS's Great Lakes field offices and to sea surface temperature charts from the **CoastWatch** web site at the University of Michigan, **http://www.coastwatch.msu.edu.**

All the biggest saltwater fishing web sites have weather centers,

but two in particular have good coverage of the West Coast for forecasts and sea surface temperature charts. At **Southern California Marlin Online**, **http://www.marlinnut.com**, look for the Weather Center and SST Charts, and at **CharkBait!**, **http://www.charkbait.com**, look under So. Cal Resources then Water Conditions.

Sea Surface Temperatures

Most fish like to be warm. Identifying bands of warmer water that concentrate baitfish and gamefish is a cornerstone of saltwater fishing strategy. So many sites offer sea surface temperature charts it's surprising to learn they all originate from the same raw data—NOAA's four Polar orbiting satellites armed with infrared sensing equipment. Several sites charge for a customized service that picks out the most relevant information from NOAA and overlays it with other data to help predict offshore hotspots. Four prominent examples are:

HotSpots Charts
http://www.sstcharts.com

Jenifer Clark's Gulfstream
http://users.erols.com/
gulfstrm/

SST Online
http://www.sstol.com

Terrafin Software
http://www.terrafin.com

Aside from product and pricing details, each site discusses how to read the charts. The HotSpots, site

in particular provides a useful introduction on incorporating them into a fishing strategy. Click on How to Use Sea Surface Temperature Charts for Saltwater Fishing to find a table of preferred temperatures for different gamefish and a tutorial for understanding the "structure" thrown up by temperature breaks.

Jenifer Clark's site links to university departments offering free charts. The best of these in her opinion, and she's a 25-year veteran of the subject, are from **John Hopkins University's Ocean Remote Sensing TOP RATED** web site at **http://fermi.jhuapl .edu**, and **Rutgers University's Coastal Ocean Observation Lab TOP RATED** at **http://marine. rutgers.edu/mrs/sat.data2.html.** The John Hopkins site offers real-time high-resolution images for the East Coast and a guide to understanding what you're looking at. Visitors to the Rutgers site should include a side trip to the **COOLroom** web site at **http://www.thecoolroom.org**, for an explanation of the technology involved in ocean temperature measurement and ocean condition links useful to New Jersey fishermen.

Tides

United States tide information all derives from data collected by NOAA. It uses its **Center for Operational Oceanographic Products and Services** at **http://www.co-ops.nos.noaa.gov** to explain the principles and terms used when discussing tides. Click on the links to **Tides Online TOP RATED** at **http://www.tidesonline.nos.noaa.gov** and **Great Lakes Online TOP RATED** at **http://www.glakesonline.nos.noaa.gov**, for nationwide tidal heights, ranges, and predictions.

Tides Online
http://www.tidesonline.nos.noaa.gov

TOP RATED

Know Before You Go

WWW Tide and Current Predictor
http://tbone.biol.sc.edu/tide/sitesel.html

An à la carte tide prediction service from Dean Pentcheff, a big brain at the University of South Carolina. It offers choices for different measurements and presentations and can single out, for example, specific time periods or the highest or lowest tides.

Tide Tool 2.1c
http://www.toolworks.com/bilofsky/tidetool.htm

This free software program is designed to be downloaded to a Palm Pilot. The FAQ link explains installation and what it can do. The section How People Use Tide Tool publishes comments from people around the world who've put the software to good use. One multitasking South African wrote: "I like to fish and having the tides helps. Also, I'm a pagan who uses the moon in ceremonies, so having the moon phases is nice too."

Best Fishing Times

In the decades since John Alden Knight published his "solunar" theory—sol for sun, lunar for moon—fishermen have become convinced of the galvanizing influence of certain alignments of the sun, moon, and earth. His original tables and variations on the theory are available for free at several web sites.

ESPN Outdoors at **http://www. espn.com/outdoors** uses Rick Taylor's Astro Tables which take account of "critical solar energies as well as lunar." They give a visual and numeric rating of the fishing potential for every day of the month as well as what cycle the moon will be in. Homepage heading: Solunar Charts.

In-Fisherman magazine at **http:// www.in-fisherman.com** has solunar calendars for the current and following two months. Homepage heading: Solunar Calendar.

Outdoor Life at **http://www.out doorlife.com** uses Maori Charts, "developed over centuries by the ancient Polynesians, whose lives literally depended on their ability to catch fish." Instructions on how to get the most from the charts begins with the recalculations necessary for different timezones. Homepage heading: Maori Charts.

Discover the Outdoors at **http://www.discovertheout doors.com** has a basic explanation of solunar theory and displays

Discover the Outdoors
http://www.discovertheoutdoors.com

TOP RATED

Joe Bucher
http://www.joe-bucher.com

TOP RATED

tables according to zip code, which neatly handles the question of timezones. Homepage heading: Solunar Tables.

Famed muskie hunter **Joe Bucher** has his own take on solunar theory. From the landing page at **http://www.joe-bucher.com** go to fishing, then look for Joe's Bucher's Moon Phase Secrets to find essays and a customizable best fishing times calculator.

Perhaps based on the solid scientific theory that fishermen will probably go fishing anyway, bass expert Doug Hannon's tables on the **FishingWorks** web site at **http://www.fishingworks.com** simply state the best two times of every 24-hour period to be on the water. Click on any topic on the homepage then look for Best Fishing Times in the lefthand navigation.

Maps

Most fishing web sites aren't equipped to offer really detailed maps of the fisheries they discuss, but between bookmarks for the resources available from the USGS and NOAA and the online products offered by different fishing map vendors, it's possible to create an incredible tool for finding, and finding your way around, any water in the country.

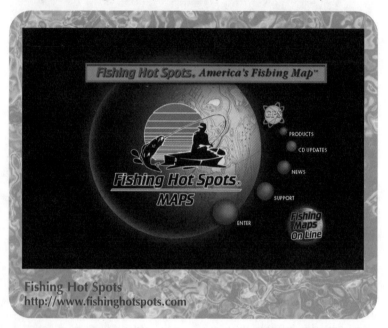

Fishing Hot Spots
http://www.fishinghotspots.com

Fishing Hot Spots
http://www.fishinghotspots.com

Fishing Hot Spots publishes lake maps for more than 500 waters in 33 states. To get an idea of the product go to Fishing Maps Online from the landing page to view free digital maps of 50 lakes. As well as standard features like depth contours, facilities and ocean points, these maps show underwater structure such as stumps and piles and submerged vegetation. Numbered hotspots on the map are discussed within the Fishing

Areas tab. Other tabs offer a profile of the fishery and boat ramp locations.

Topo-Log
http://www.topo-log.com

This company has digitized the whole Fishing Hot Spots map archive and developed software that allows each map to be customized with icons, text notes and options for adjusting the level of detail displayed. This is pretty cool stuff. If you find a brush pile or tire reef, for example, you can punch

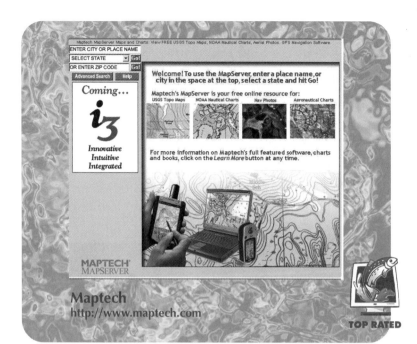

Maptech
http://www.maptech.com

TOP RATED

in its GPS coordinates to mark its exact location on the map. If a certain depth line is crucial to a seasonal pattern, you can temporarily erase the other depth contours or reconfigure the map to show different lake levels. The original maps come on CD-ROMs and the customized version is saved to your hard drive.

To view the whole of fishing maps offered by different companies browse around **Fishingmap.com** at **http://www.fishingmap.com**.

Most people know that the USGS provides real-time streamflow information, but the Service is also the source of the free nationwide topographic maps and aerial photographs featured on several high-profile web sites.

Maptech
http://www.maptech.com

TOP RATED

Maptech has some very attractive products— Contour 3D Charts, for example, simulate the real landscape of the ocean bed off the entire U.S. coastline—but the company gets the nod here for its free MapServer application, allowing customization of standard USGS topo maps. Zero in on a lake or river by using the name, zip code, or longitude and latitude search, then go down to the box of Fun Tools and pick through the icons, including a set specifically for fishing mapmakers. These can be placed on the map to show a hotspot, a campsite, a boat put-in, a text notation, or dozens of other options. Maps can be printed or sent as an e-mail attachment.

MapServer is found by going to the Online Maps Charts and Photos

TerraServer
http://terraserver.usa.com

TOP RATED

heading at the top of the Maptech homepage, or direct at **http://map server.maptech.com**.

Another big reason to love the Maptech site is that it's the only place on the Web that publishes NOAA's nautical charts. These show depths and navigation hazards and aides, and are the standard reference for all mariners. Find the nautical charts by clicking on a tab at the top of each map wherever you're using MapServer.

Tutorials on how to read them are found at the Maptech site and within the FAQs section of the **Office of Coast Survey** at **http://chartmaker.ncd.noaa.gov/m cd/enc**, which also offers a free PDF booklet titled *The Nautical Chart Users Manual*.

Nautical charts on paper can be purchased from the Office of Coast Survey. They also sell bathymetric

fishing maps on paper and CD via the **National Geophysical Data Center** (NGDC) at **http://www. ngdc.noaa.gov**.

It's easy to get turned around on these pages and bob up in the midst of sub-departments or different agencies. From the NGDC homepage put "fishing maps" into the search box and click on the first entry it returns to find a straightforward list of available maps and the checkout.

TerraServer
http://terraserver.usa.com

TOP RATED

TerraServer is the means to explore the USGS's complete archive of satellite photographs, an epic project that has captured an image of every acre of U.S. soil. Search for places by key word, by clicking on a map, or by entering latitude and longitude coordinates. Click around the edges of the black and white photograph it presents to shuffle in different directions, or zoom in using commands to the side of the photograph.

It takes a bit of time to become proficient but this application has enormous benefits for fishermen looking to discover new waters or structural features only visible from the air. A good start would be to scout around places you're already familiar with—that far-bank tributary that's always looked inviting, that chain of ponds you've never quite fished your way down. If you find something worth investigating, click down for a closer look or go over to the box Other Imagery and choose the topographic map option. It replaces the aerial photograph with a topo map of exactly the same coordinates, giving a better idea of the terrain and how to get down to the water.

TerraFly
http://www.terrafly.fiu.edu

TOP RATED

TerraServer isn't the only site that uses the USGS's aerial photographs. TerraFly, a program developed at Florida International University, goes one better by seamlessly linking each individual aerial photograph for an effect like watching video footage from a low-flying aircraft you control. Once you've chosen the area, click towards the edge of the image to start "flying." The image will pan in that direction until you click another edge. To freeze it, click in the middle of the image. The pilot can control resolution and flying speed, and if the image is frozen over a roadway or street it superimposes the name of the thoroughfare onto the photograph. Some of the regions are in color.

TopoZone
http://www.topozone.com

TopoZone has a well-designed interface for navigating the USGS's topographical map collection. There are two million place names in its geographic database —if a name exists on a USGS map, it's in the TopoZone search tool—but you can also hunt by latitude and longitude. Sections for Map Tips, FAQ, and Topo Map Symbols explain how to get the most from the services.

BASS FISHING FROM LOW ORBIT?

For a very helpful article describing how fishermen can use Web-based mapping resources go to the Basslabs web site at **http://www. basslabs.com** and use the search function to find the feature "Bass Fishing From Low Orbit?" Basslabs is a new and promising general fishing magazine that's well worth a click around.

Where to Go

The nation's system of public lands offers tremendous opportunities for fishermen. Use these sites to get directions, buy a permit online, or research access points and facilities at hundreds of lakes and rivers managed by more than half a dozen agencies. Many have recreation pages catering specifically to fishermen.

American Trails
http://www.americantrails.org

American Trails is the only national non-profit organization working on behalf of trail users. And that includes us. Search for information about river trails by using pull-down menus on the U.S. map or by clicking on Trails in the top navigation. Find out, for example, about the Kenai Canoe Trails in the Kenai National Park in Alaska, The Lake of the Ozarks Aquatic Trail in Missouri, or the 75-mile long Florida paddling and trail route known as Paddle Manatee. Content for other trail categories including snowshoeing, hiking, biking, 4-wheeling, and horse-riding, is drawn from a diverse collection of public land management agencies, commercial web sites, and citizen groups.

GORP – Parks
http://www.gorp.com

TOP RATED

GORP, or the Great Outdoors Recreation Pages, earns several references in this book for its exceptional coverage of the outdoor life. Click on the Parks tab in the top navigation to open a comprehensive guide to the nation's public lands. As well as

articles and information covering the whole National Park system, links in the lefthand navigation lead to sections for National Forests, Wilderness Areas, Wildlife Refuges, Trails, Rivers, Lakes and Shores. Rivers puts the spotlight on 160 rivers within the National Wild and Scenic Rivers System. Lakes and Shores does the same for a collection of National Seashores, National Recreation Areas, and National Lakeshores. If you're con-fused by all those categories, there's a nice article within this area titled "National What? A people's guide to public land designation."

The **National Wild and Scenic Rivers System** has its own page at **http://www.nps.gov/rivers**.

ParkNet
http://www.nps.gov

TOP RATED

This is the official web site of the National Park Service, which looks after more than 800 mil-lion acres of public land in 384 different locations. Search by state and then by individual park or go to Visit Your Parks then Search by Interests to pull out all the fishing references on the site. Buy a National Parks Pass direct from the homepage.

Recreation.Gov
http://www.recreation.gov

TOP RATED

Public Lands Information Center (PLIC)
http://www.publiclands.org

TOP RATED The PLIC web site is a one-stop shop for information about public lands in the Western states. Navigate the site by clicking on detailed state maps that expand into sub-pages full of local information.

Recreation.Gov
http://www.recreation.gov

TOP RATED Recreation.Gov is the one essential source for finding out about recreation opportunities on public lands in the U.S. It blends content from eight land management agencies, including the U.S. Forest Service, the National Park Service, and the Bureau of Land Management, and offers searches by activity (including fishing, hunting, camping, and boating), by state and by agency type across more than 500 areas.

Tourism Offices Worldwide Directory
http://www.towd.com

TOP RATED This directory of 1,200 tourist offices, information bureaus, and chambers of commerce is a superb general resource for researching distant fishing locations in the U.S. and internationally. A simple state or country search brings up full contact information including e-mail and web site links. To varying degrees, they all describe local amenities, where to stay, how to get around, and what to do for fun.

U.S. Department of Agriculture (USDA) Forest Service – Fish Your National Forests

http://www.fs.fed.us/fishing

The USDA Forest Service is caretaker of the 150,000 miles of streams and two and a half million acres of lakes found within the country's National Forests and grasslands. Each river and lake within nine regions is mapped and described in terms of what you're likely to catch, driving directions, access points, and campgrounds.

U.S. National Parks

http://www.us-national-parks.net

TOP RATED

An exceptional (non-official) guide to the National Parks. Depending on the area, there are camping guides, background on the social and natural history of the area, bird watching primers, fishing regulations, contact numbers, links, and forums.

Wildernet

http://www.wildernet.com

Wildernet has over 40,000 area and activity descriptions within its database of outdoor recreation opportunities. Choose a state from the map or pull-down options then choose fishing from the activity list. The database keys on the activity word and matches it to basic descriptions of campgrounds and public lands. It's very fast, and for many of the Western states at least, it returns hundreds of options. It would be a good resource for finding out the name of a camp site or recreation area close to potentially good fishing, then investigating it more fully elsewhere on the Web.

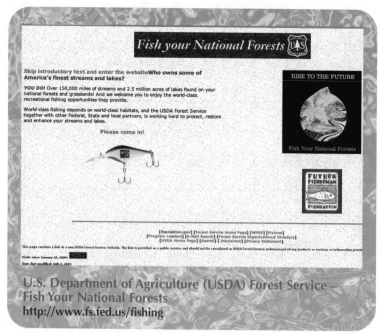

U.S. Department of Agriculture (USDA) Forest Service – Fish Your National Forests
http://www.fs.fed.us/fishing

On the Road

Road trips and fishing are a natural complement, but how much more painful to be stuck in traffic on the way to a hot bite than on the way to a hot office? Avoid this disaster by adopting the services offered at these traffic and road travel web sites.

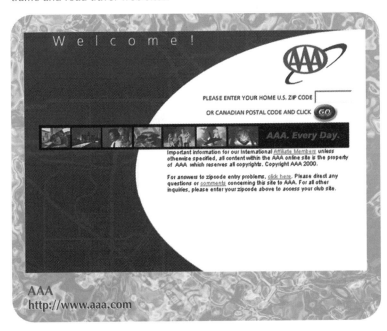

AAA
http://www.aaa.com

AAA
http://www.aaa.com

A simple registration gives AAA members access to a huge travel-planning resource. Enter your zip code to be transferred to your regional AAA web site. Content varies but somewhere on each site you'll find a travel section allowing you to reserve accommodation and rental cars, research toll fees or find out the latest traffic and weather reports. The other perks of membership—breakdown assistance, some of the most complete

trip-planners available, known as Trip Ticks, and discounts on travel services—are all available to read over and take advantage of from the site.

AccuTraffic
http://www.accuweather.com/ www/accutraffic

Choose either the weather or traffic channel for a clickable state map and subsequent links to enough national road condition and weather information to satisfy even the most cautious traveler.

Federal Highway Administration (FHA) – National Traffic and Road Closure Information

http://www.fhwa.dot.gov/trafficinfo

The FHA site is a portal for road safety information across the country. Click on a state to be taken to its Department of Transportation web site. These vary in the amount of information they provide—some have web cams, mileage calculators, incident maps, and other bells and whistles—but as a minimum they all provide weather advisories and updates (hourly or better) on road conditions and construction and accidents delays.

Links on the homepage point to other national weather and traffic condition web sites, such as **http://www.traffic.com** for traffic flows and delays around major cities.

MapQuest

http://www.mapquest.com

MapQuest tells 40 million people where to go every month. Simply put your departure and destination addresses for driving directions anywhere in the U.S. As with other road mapping sites, the service isn't infallible—a good road atlas is still essential—but it's accurate enough to be a very useful tool in most instances. Directions can be customized to include a list of what's near the route such as hotels, RV Parks, and campgrounds. Or choose the map option to view a street map of your destination and its neighborhood. You can even view an aerial photograph of the same location.

See also **Yahoo! Maps** at **http://maps.yahoo.com**, and **MSN Maps and Directions** at **http://mappoint.msn.com**.

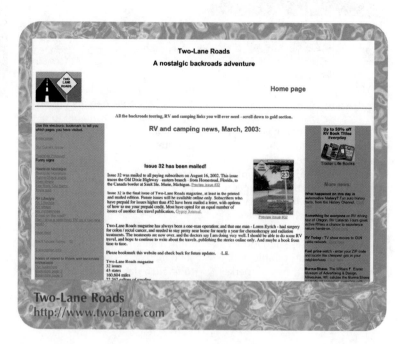

Rand McNally

http://www.randmcnally.com

Choose directions based on the fastest or shortest route and research towns and locations along the way thanks to content from Moon guidebooks. Book a room and find out road conditions and traffic laws for each state you'll be going through. Merge it all together within a feature called Plan a Road Trip. Print and drive.

Two-Lane Roads

http://www.two-lane.com

Most fishermen have idly dreamed of cruising the country from lake to river in an RV or campervan. Check out author Lisa Wetchel's in-depth site devoted to RVing, camping, and two-lane highways. She lists hundreds of RV and travel-planning resources, but to steal two of her recommendations:

The FHA's **http://www.byways. org** provides information about the National Scenic Byways Program. Seventy-two of these recreationally or historically significant roads wind across three-quarters of the country. Choose a state to find maps, directions and points of interest along the way, plus links for digging up further information.

Frugal fisherman should like **http://www.gaspricewatch.com/ USGas.** Compare pump prices countrywide with a simple zip code search. The site displays prices for Regular, Plus, Premium, and Diesel, and notes how fresh the information is. Results are more dependable for towns and cities (they rely on web visitors to report prices), but the search function will at least let you locate gas stations in the tiniest burgs and backwaters.

Where to Stay

The best fishing destinations are, almost by definition, beyond the reach of your normal round. These sites can ring a virtual bell at thousands of hotels, motels, bed and breakfasts and campsite offices in even the most remote backwaters.

All-hotels

http://www.all-hotels.com

All-hotels has 60,000 hotels, motels, and bed and breakfasts in its database. Rooms can be booked online, and many of the hotels link to MapQuest for driving directions. There are plenty of choices and economy rates in even the kind of boony places fishermen are fond of.

Places to Stay.com

http://www.placestostay.com

Take the map route through this site and you can quickly go from a map of the world to a map of any obscure corner of any state. Once there, search the clearly presented hotel listings and book online. There is good coverage even in sparsely populated areas like west Texas (35 listings) or eastern Oregon (27 listings).

See also **Hootle** at **http://www. hootle.com,** and for those who like to bring along their favorite fishing retriever, **Petswelcome.com** at **http://www.petswelcome.com,** which lists 25,000 pet-friendly accommodations.

CAMPING

There are so many camping resources on the Web, retreat to the safe haven of **http://www. camping.about.com** and let subject guide David Sweet filter out all the second-rate sites for you. The section Campgrounds by State lets you search State Parks, National Parks, National Forests and Campgrounds with Web Sites. Go to the A to Z index to find a list of 400 camping web sites and resources.

If you're still stuck for a place to rest your head, try **ReserveUSA TOP RATED** at **http://www. reserveusa.com.** This site is a joint program of the USDA Forest Service and the U.S. Army Corps of Engineers to provide a single online "ticket office" for both agencies. Choose from 1,700 campsites on federal land as well as cabins and day-use areas, or reserve permits for the Boundary Waters Canoe Area in Michigan's Upper Peninsula. Information for each area includes amenities, how to get there, regulations, and contact numbers.

The hundreds of Forest Service cabins in the Chugach and Tongass National Forests are an ideal way to organize a discount Alaskan fishing holiday. Go to Cabins at the top of the ReserveUSA home-page, then click on the map of Alaska to view cabin locations and links to web sites for each area.

Reserve America at **http://www. reserveamerica.com.** is another option. This company processed over three million camping reservations per year and has a database with details of 140,000 campsites in 44 states. Search for reservations with a simple three-step process. Choose the facility type (campsite, cabin, day use area); look for a specific campground or search state listings; then check availability.

International Travel Resources

The opportunities for worldwide fishing travel have never been greater—given the resources you could literally fish your way through an international alphabet from the Azores (marlin and tuna) to Norway (Atlantic salmon) to Zaire (tigerfish)—but the success of any trip still depends on planning and preparation. Somewhere within these best-of-class travel sites is all the information you need to disaster-proof your trip. Specialist fishing travel agencies are reviewed in Chapter 8 International.

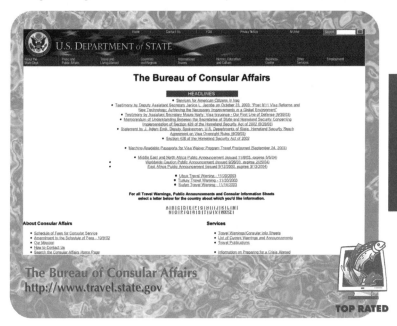

The Bureau of Consular Affairs
http://www.travel.state.gov
TOP RATED

The Bureau of Consular Affairs
http://www.travel.state.gov

TOP RATED

Among many other services, the Bureau of Consular Affairs issues Travel Warnings advising Americans to avoid certain countries based on recent events and ongoing hazards. Consular Information Sheets are a traveler's summary of every country on earth including entry requirements, crime figures, medical facilities, consular and embassy locations, traffic safety and road conditions.

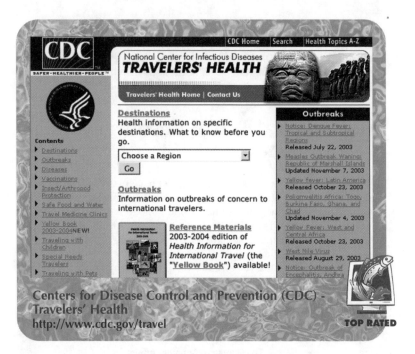

Centers for Disease Control and Prevention (CDC) - Travelers' Health
http://www.cdc.gov/travel

TOP RATED

Other headings and sections lead to foreign visa requirements, passport information, lists of foreign doctors and hospitals and a complete summary of resources for Americans abroad.

Centers for Disease Control and Prevention (CDC) – Travelers' Health
http://www.cdc.gov/travel

TOP RATED The most complete travel health resource on the Web. Going to Destinations then choosing a country or area produces a factsheet outlining potential health hazards, a list of recommended vaccines and tips for staying illness-free. Links within different sections expand on terms and topics, and the truly malady-curious can browse a huge A-Z subject list. Keep out of the reach of hypochondriac fishing companions.

Federal Aviation Administration (FAA) Traveler Briefing
http://www2.faa.gov

From the homepage click on Passengers in the lefthand navigation for links to flight delay information, comparisons between different carriers, weather forecasts, and safety tips.

Fodors
http://www.fodors.com

TOP RATED Fodors condenses the essential stuff from its travel guidebooks into Miniguides for a huge number of places across the U.S. and internationally. They cover sights and activities, restaurants, hotels and nightlife, and offer links for more information. To create your own mini-guide checkmark the most relevant bits

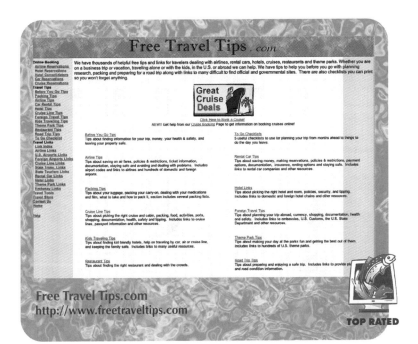

Free Travel Tips .com

Online Booking
Airline Reservations
Hotel Reservations
Hotel Consolidators
Car Reservations
Cruise Reservations
Travel Tips
Before You Go Tips
Packing Tips
Airline Tips
Car Rental Tips
Hotel Tips
Cruise Line Tips
Foreign Travel Tips
Kids Traveling Tips
Theme Park Tips
Restaurant Tips
Road Trip Tips
To Go Checklist
Travel Links
Link Index
Airline Links
U.S. Airports Links
Foreign Airports Links
Cruise Line Links
State Trans. Links
State Tourism Links
Rental Car Links
Hotel Links
Theme Park Links
Embassy Links
Travel Tools
Travel Store
Contact Us
Home

Help

We have thousands of helpful free tips and links for travelers dealing with airlines, rental cars, hotels, cruises, restaurants and theme parks. Whether you are on a business trip or vacation, traveling alone or with the kids, in the U.S. or abroad we can help. We have tips to help you before you go with planning research, packing and preparing for a road trip along with links to many difficult to find official and governmental sites. There are also checklists you can print so you won't forget anything.

Great Cruise Deals

Click Here to Book a Cruise!
NEW!! Get help from our Cruise Booking Page to get information on booking cruises online!

Before You Go Tips
Tips about finding information for your trip, money, your health & safety, and leaving your property safe.

To Go Checklists
5 useful checklists to use for planning your trip from months ahead to things to do the day you leave.

Airline Tips
Tips about saving on air fares, policies & restrictions, ticket information, documentation, staying safe and avoiding and dealing with problems. Includes airport codes and links to airlines and hundreds of domestic and foreign airports.

Rental Car Tips
Tips about saving money, making reservations, policies & restrictions, payment options, documentation, insurance, renting options and staying safe. Includes links to rental car companies and other resources.

Packing Tips
Tips about your luggage, packing your carry-on, dealing with your medications and film, what to take and how to pack it, section includes several packing lists.

Hotel Links
Tips about picking the right hotel and room, policies, security, and tipping. Includes links to domestic and foreign hotel chains and other resources.

Cruise Line Tips
Tips about picking the right cruise and cabin, packing, food, activities, ports, shopping, documentation, health, safety and tipping. Includes links to cruise lines, passport information and other resources.

Foreign Travel Tips
Tips about planning your trip abroad, currency, shopping, documentation, health and safety. Includes links to embassies, U.S. Customs, the U.S. State Department and other resources.

Kids Traveling Tips
Tips about finding kid friendly hotels, help on traveling by car, air or cruise line, and keeping the family safe. Includes links to many useful resources.

Theme Park Tips
Tips about making your day at the parks fun and getting the best out of them. Includes links to hundreds of U.S. theme parks.

Restaurant Tips
Tips about finding the right restaurant and dealing with the crowds.

Road Trip Tips
Tips about preparing and enjoying a safe trip. Includes links to provide pla and road condition information.

Free Travel Tips.com
http://www.freetraveltips.com

TOP RATED

from each topic area and use the Customize My Results feature. Tips for Smart Traveling provides advice about getting around the area and the easiest way to get to and from the airport. A language center lists key phrases in French, German, Italian and Spanish, and will even speak them to you via a sound file and your computer's speakers.

The forums at Fodors are particularly good: there are more than 10, including a Rants and Raves area for applauding or bad mouthing restaurants and hotels.

Free Travel Tips.com
http://www.freetraveltips.com

A mother lode of useful tips and links for smooth travel. Click on any of the topics under Travel

TOP RATED

Tips to bring up a page of common questions and detailed answers. Subjects range from health and safety abroad, rental car tips (with links to the major rental companies), to travel insurance and money issues. Sections titled Packing Tips and To Go Checklist have packing and preparation checklists to print out and use.

How to See the World
http://www.artoftravel.com

In a perfect world, you could follow the advice in this free 100,000 word guide to backpacking and traveling on the cheap and write a sequel titled *How to Fish the World (Without Ever Seeing the Inside of a Lodge)*. A valuable 101 for the budget fishing traveler.

Know Before You Go

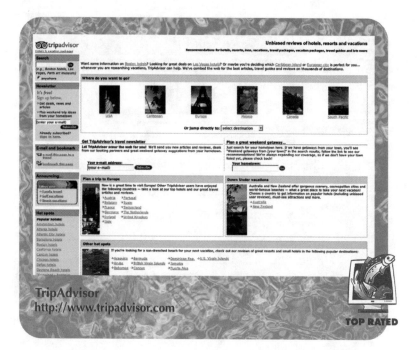

TripAdvisor
http://www.tripadvisor.com

TOP RATED

IgoUgo
http://www.igougo.com

TOP RATED

IgoUgo relies on the experiences of everyday travelers to describe 2,000 destinations around the world. They are free to rejoice or complain as the place strikes them, which they do by filling out Travel Journals organized into reviews of accommodation, restaurants, things to do and general tips. The site offers good forums to connect with other IgoUgo members, booking services, and the usual trip-planning tools.

Time Zone Converter
http://www.timezoneconverter.com

Hopefully at some point in your fishing life it'll be helpful to know the time in the Christmas Islands (on your way to a bonefish flat) or

when passing through Ulan Bator (en route to a taimen river). Print out a personal reference page if you're going to be crossing several time zones.

TripAdvisor
http://www.tripadvisor.com

TOP RATED

If you don't have a lot of time to hunt for information about an area, TripAdvisor grabs the best articles about the destination from other web sites, posts visitors' reviews of the area and provides a good-sized map to get you oriented. The U.S. section is restricted to major cities, but there is good Caribbean and Mexican coverage. Click on Grand Cayman for example, to find instant airfare quotes from booking agents, more than 70 articles drawn from popular travel sites and 20 user-reviews.

Travel Document Systems

http://www.traveldocs.com

Passport Express

http://www.passportexpress.com

Express Visa Service

http://www.expressvisa.com

You're browsing a favorite fishing travel agency site and see a tempting last-minute deal for three days big-game fishing in Cabo San Lucas. You can already see the roiled blue water, the way a big striped marlin will ... your passport expired last month. For disasters of this magnitude, go to a company like Travel Document Systems or Passport Express. They can expedite passports and visa applications for most countries in as little as four days, direct from the web site.

U.S. Department of Homeland Security – U.S. Customs and Border Protection

http://www.cbp.gov

The new division of Customs and Border Protection offers an invaluable Know Before You Go online brochure stating exactly what you can and can't bring into the country. To find it go to Travel in the top navigation, but you might as well know now, puffing a Cuban between sips of absinthe while reclining on your new dog-hair rug, should not be in your plans as you head to the airport after an exotic fishing trip. Something else to read over: they provide a table of waiting times for each port of entry into Canada and Mexico.

U.S. Department of Homeland Security –
U.S. Customs and Border Protection
http://www.cbp.gov

Visa

http://www.international.visa.com

MasterCard

http://www.mastercard.com
(go to Cardholder services)

Discover

http://go.vicinity.com/discoverd

American Express

http://www.americanexpress.com
(go to Travel and Entertainment)

There aren't too many bumps in the fishing traveler's road that can't be smoothed out with a little cash. The Visa, MasterCard and Discover sites allow you to track down ATMs all over the world and list international customer service numbers. American Express offers a location finder for its travel offices and the option to buy travelers checks online.

Guides

Booking a guide is worth every cent if you have a memorable day, but can seem awfully expensive if the service or arrangements aren't as expected. Cut down on the variables by studying guide web sites before you pick up the phone. Apart from pricing and availability details (and often, online reservations), most will describe what to wear and what to bring, what species are available, and the usual itinerary for a day's charter.

So how do you find guides in Dutch Harbor or Apalachicola? One answer is to look in the phonebook.

SuperPages.com

http://www.bigyellow.com

TOP RATED

A complete online yellow pages for the whole U.S. If you need to find a guide, a tacklestore, a bar, a baitshack, or anything else wherever you're headed in the 50 states, this zippy web site displays the appropriate listing from that area's yellow pages in seconds. Most businesses are listed with a web site and e-mail link. Seaches can be done by category, business name, city, or by nearness to your location, and each entry is accompanied by a MapQuest link for maps and driving directions.

SuperPages.com Global Directories

http://www.superpages.com/global

TOP RATED

A worldwide yellow pages from the same company. The Australia directory, to take one example, has two million business listings and includes sections for Fiji, Micronesia, New Zealand, Papua New Guinea, and outer lying islands and countries. If you have an old computer or a slow connection go to the bottom of each country's start page for a text-only option.

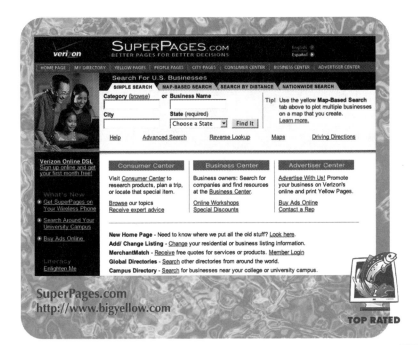

SuperPages.com
http://www.bigyellow.com

TOP RATED

SMARTpages.com
http://www.smartpages.com

TOP RATED

Put "fishing" into the search box and choose Business Type, then the name of the state and town you'll be staying in, and SMARTpages.com will return a list of all fishing-related businesses in the area. Note: for some reason it refers to guides as "fishing parties." See also **http://www.best yellow.com**.

Outdoors Yellow Pages
http://www.outdoorsyp.com

TOP RATED

The Outdoors Yellow Pages has combed yellow page directories across the country and picked out every listing for fishing and hunting (and many other outdoor sports) and rolled them into this online database.

There are more than 35 categories within fishing, the biggest of which is the section for Fishing Guides and Charters. Use the search box in the lefthand navigation to sort by company name, keyword, place name, or zip code.

Many fishing web sites claim they have comprehensive guide directories but with the odd exception such as **LandBigFish** at **http://www .landbigfish.com**, or **FishingWorks** at **http://www.fishingworks.com**, which lists more than 6,000 guides in the U.S.and internationally, there aren't many with listings deep enough to resemble a nationwide resource. These three are partial exceptions:

Charternet.com
http://www.charternet.com

This quick-loading marine recreation directory has a solid fishing

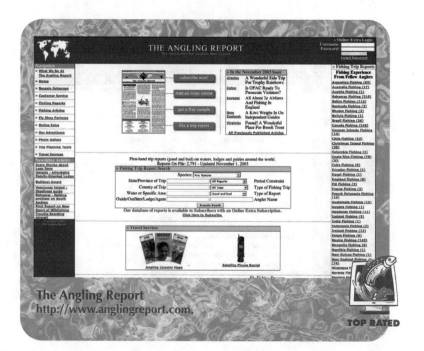

The Angling Report
http://www.anglingreport.com

TOP RATED

charter section. Sponsored listings link to the company web site; regular entries simply state the name of the company, where they are, and their telephone number. The coastal states claim the most entries but there are decent listings in the majority of areas. And that includes internationally: Canada, Australia, and Central America all posted good numbers.

Fishing Guides Home Page
http://www.1fghp.com

The Fishing Guides Home Page is divided into boxes and columns that make it a little hard to tell listings apart, but it gets the main thing right: it links to worthwhile numbers of guides and charters in most states. Restrict searches to ice fishing, saltwater, or the Gulf Coast, or get recommendations from the site's forum.

WorldWideFishing.com
http://www.worldwidefishing.com

A sportfishing company with its own show on the Outdoor Channel, WorldWideFishing.com has hundreds of state and international listing for freshwater and saltwater guides. Click on a heading to bring up a brochure page about each guide or charter and, in most cases, a link to that company's web site.

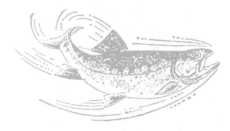

CAN I GET A WITNESS?

Whether you're looking to spend $300 on a guide or $6,000 on a lodge in Alaska, a nice looking web site is, of course, no guarantee you'll have a memorable trip. That's a hard thing to be sure of however you plan your fishing, but the Internet has made it far easier to hedge your bets than for previous generations of traveling fishermen. There is no better way to find out what a guide, a lodge, or a fishing package is really like than by asking someone who has paid for the service and has no financial interest in gilding the truth.

A first step could be to ask the person you're booking with for the e-mail addresses of a few past clients. Send them a brief message asking their opinion of the trip and fishing arrangements. You're unlikely to be sent to the in-boxes of disgruntled customers, but their opinions will still be more plainly stated than an agency's or guide's. E-mail is so much less intrusive than a phone call: it's hard to imagine many fishermen objecting to a polite request to relive a happy trip, or a bad one.

The other option is to ask for recommendations by using a forum, mailing list, or newsgroup. See the forums list at the back of the book, or explore the web sites covering the type of fishing you want to do elsewhere in these chapters. The best sites discussed in Chapter 2 State-by-State Resources will probably have home waters covered better than anyone in terms of forums and guide advertisements.

Whatever format you use, it's important to ask specific, detailed questions if you want specific, detailed answers. If you go the forum route and someone replies with a lead, contact them off the forum with thanks and a request for more information.

The value of tapping into un-biased views and reviews of lodges, outfitters, and destinations is the unique niche occupied by **The Angling Report TOP RATED** at **http://www.anglingreport.com**. Sign up to receive a bi-monthly newsletter and access to a huge online database of subscribers' own trip reports. Most of the reports deal with the Rocky Mountains, the East Coast, Alaska, Canada, the Caribbean, and Latin America. Because subscribers understand everyone benefits from the fullest disclosure, trip reports are usually complete. As well as naming the outfitter and when and where the trip took place, there are sections for target species and what was actually caught, contact information for the report writer, and service ratings in several categories.

General Resources

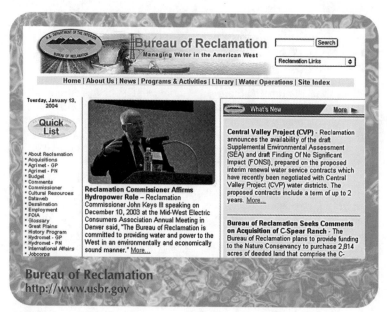

Bureau of Reclamation
http://www.usbr.gov

Bureau of Reclamation
http://www.usbr.gov

The 101-year old Bureau of
Reclamation is responsible for the
construction of more than 600
dams and reservoirs in 17 Western
states. Go to Water Supply in the
lefthand navigation to access pages
for the Bureau's five regions. They
offer differing levels of information,
but each is at least good for finding
out the latest lake and reservoir levels, with comparison figures showing if the water is above or below
average for the year. Some regions
post spill rates, discharges, streamflows, and estimates of the amount
of snowmelt in the water.

U.S. Army Corps of Engineers
http://www.usace.army.mil

The U.S. Army Corps of Engineers
has broad responsibilities to do
with the nation's water supply:
management of hydro-electric
dams, navigation authority for
12,000 miles of inland waterway,
and oversight for thousands of
recreation areas, including some
of the best known fisheries in the
country. And that adds up to a
significant amount of fish-finding
information held within each district's web site. From the central
homepage click on Where We
Are, then What Districts Are in My
State? to find local pages. Most
districts have an entry somewhere
for Recreation or Public Services.
Depending on the area, you might

find fishing reports, fish counts, lake-level information, maps, fishing regulations and lists of boat ramps.

U.S. Fish and Wildlife Service

http://www.fws.gov

TOP RATED

The U.S. Fish and Wildlife Service has a huge web site for describing its role as manager of the nation's wildlife resources. Choose Fishing from the portal list to find a guide to the National Wildlife Refuge System and a subset of pages for the National Fish Hatchery System. One unique site feature is the option to read or download the *2001 National Survey of Fishing, Hunting, and Wildlife-Associated Recreation*. This survey is carried out every five years in cooperation with the U.S. Census Bureau and is a definitive guide to the habits and preferences of the nation's millions of fishermen.

The direct URL for the **National Wildlife Refuge System** is **http://refuges.fws.gov.**

United States Geological Service (USGS) Real-Time Daily Streamflow Conditions

http://water.usgs.gov/realtime.html

TOP RATED

You can't browse many fishing web sites without finding links to the USGS. Founded in 1879 it describes itself as "an independent fact finding agency that collects, monitors, analyzes and provides scientific understanding about natural resource conditions, issues and problems." Fishermen have most directly benefited from the Service's development of real-time streamflow information for thousands of rivers across the country.

Choose a state USGS office from the map or text options on the homepage. Once at the state page, click on the dots representing individual stream gauges or use the pull-down menu titled Predefined Displays for a complete list of rivers. Data is recorded at 15-60 minute intervals and published on the web site between one and four hours later. So you can find out exactly what shape the river will be in and what's been happening the last few days—both determining factors for knowing where and how to fish—all while sitting in the comfort of your home office, or just your office.

Streamflow graphs are easy to read, but for an article on how to get the most from them have a look at "Stream Gauging for Angling Success" posted on the fishing page of the **USGS Recreation** web site at **http://recreation.usgs.gov/fishing.html.** Other features here include links to Great Lakes forecasts and to weather and water data provided by the **Chesapeake Bay Observing System** at **http://www.cbos.org/index.php.** Use the rest of the recreation homepage to find boating and camping information.

CHAPTER 4
FISHING THE WEB

To the unconverted it must seem that fishing is fishing, and not much more than a PowerWorm at one end and a harmless fool at the other. But fishermen are tribal, with different cultures, different dreams and different waters wetting their boots. This chapter looks at the many good web sites devoted to different species and styles of fishing. And to acknowledge that we do have a few common concerns, there are also recommendations in four categories important to all fishermen—records, knots, cookery and fish identification.

Best Bass Fishing Sites

Bass are America's favorite sportfish because they offer something for everyone. They are tournament fish and trophy fish. You can take them on surface lures in Florida and lead-head jigs in Maine. Somewhere within the sites that follow you're guaranteed to find your bass brethren.

Bass Anglers Sportsmans Society
http://www.bassmaster.com

TOP RATED

Bass Anglers Sportsmans Society (BASS)
http://www.bassmaster.com

TOP RATED The Bass Anglers Sportsmans Society, or BASS, is the 600,000-member church of bass fishing in the U.S. Founded by Ray Scott in 1968 and recently sold to ESPN, it runs the most prestigious tournaments, publishes *Bassmaster* magazine and oversees 2,800 regional clubs. Bassmaster.com is a huge site full of meaty material for tournament

followers, Federation members and regular bass fishermen. The homepage leads with tournament headlines but click on sections for Features, Destinations or Departments to find hundreds of articles and columns about general tactics, conservation, bass biology, boating and tackle. Links in the left-hand navigation point to member-ship services, fishing resources and the site's forum center. Questions posted here were thoroughly and politely answered.

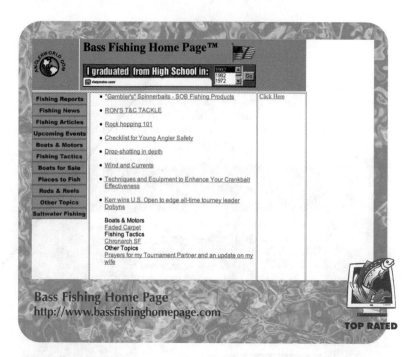

Bass Fishing Home Page™

I graduated from High School in: 1992 ▾ Go

- "Gambler's" Spinnerbaits - SOB Fishing Products
- RON'S T&C TACKLE
- Rock hopping 101
- Checklist for Young Angler Safety
- Drop-shotting in depth
- Wind and Currents
- Techniques and Equipment to Enhance Your Crankbait Effectiveness
- Kerr wins U.S. Open to edge all-time tourney leader Dobyns

Boats & Motors
Faded Carpet
Fishing Tactics
Chronarch SF
Other Topics
Prayers for my Tournament Partner and an update on my wife

Fishing Reports
Fishing News
Fishing Articles
Upcoming Events
Boats & Motors
Fishing Tactics
Boats for Sale
Places to Fish
Rods & Reels
Other Topics
Saltwater Fishing

Click Here

Bass Fishing Home Page
http://www.bassfishinghomepage.com

TOP RATED

Bass Champs
http://www.basschamps.com

TOP RATED Bass fishing is as much a part of the fabric of life in Texas as Willie Nelson or BBQ. Bass Champs organizes tournaments in northern and central Texas, and publishes this web site to keep track of results and schedules. There are tips from some famous names under Pro Articles, and forums for fishing reports, general chat and classifieds.

Bass Fishing Home Page
http://www.bassfishing
homepage.com

TOP RATED On review day the Bass Fishing Home Page was making a clean sweep of those Top 100 rankings often displayed on fishing web sites. It has achieved this elevated state solely on the back of its popular forums. These include areas for fishing reports (very busy—157 reports for the two days I looked at the site), tactics, boat and places to fish. Founders Jerry Lebing and Mark Kutsko were pioneers in the fishing web site world and have related sites at **http://www.anglerworld. com** and **http://www.wmi. org/saltfish**.

Bassdozer
http://www.bassdozer.com

TOP RATED There's no shortage of confidence in the Bassdozer camp: they claim to be "the best bass fishing resource, not just on the web, but in the entire world." Bassdozer is indeed a big piece of equipment—a kind of bass Yahoo! with a central directory of links to articles, equipment and boats, tournament reports, clubs and fisheries. The links section has a helpful page recommending the best bass forums on the Web.

BassFan

http://www.bassfan.com

TOP RATED

BassFan provides the kind of journalistic coverage of tournament fishing that should be in the sports pages of national newspapers. Never mind, it can be done better on the Web. Lots of fishing tips and a pro Q & A supplement all the tournament news. They've also developed a statistical method for merging the FLW Outdoors and BASS rankings, resulting in a top 100 list of the undisputed best professional bass anglers. Look under Interact, then BassFan Feedback in the top navigation to find the site forums. Forum threads were polite and detailed.

Bassin' USA

http://www.bassinusa.com

TOP RATED

Bassin' USA is "designed by fishermen for fishermen." Luckily these fishermen know a few things about attractive web sites. It's split evenly between tournament and general bass fishing; there are articles, tips, forums and a selection of useful resources such as best fishing times, a tournament and marina finder and the option to buy your fishing license online.

Bronzeback.com

http://www.bronzeback.com

A good effort from smallmouth enthusiast Warren Witkowski. The site covers tactics for rivers and streams, for the six calendar periods, and for jerk bait fishing. I liked the product reviews which range from *one smallmouth* awarded for ok if you get it for free in a cereal

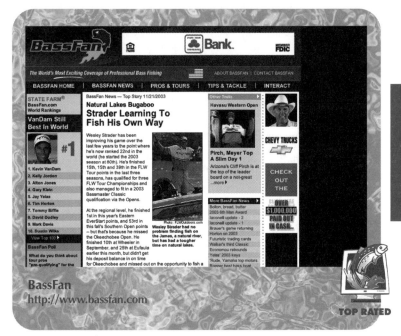

BassFan
http://www.bassfan.com

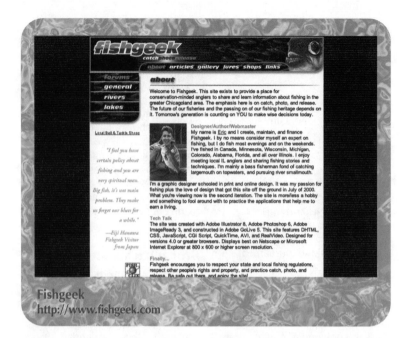

Fishgeek
http://www.fishgeek.com

box, to *five smallmouth* awarded for just owning this product will let you to kick Van Dam's ass (Kevin, that is), to one *carp* awarded for tackle best recommended to "competitors" or people who keep asking you "Whatdya catch 'em on?"

A shame there weren't more reviews. That could be a general comment applied to the rest of the site, but there's more to come as the author promises on the Sneak Preview Page. See also **The Smallmouth Alliance** at **http://www.smallmouth.org** reviewed in Chapter 6 Groups.

Fishgeek
http://www.fishgeek.com

A personal web site done right. Eric Schaaf's Fishgeek focuses on small river and pond fishing in the Chicago and Illinois area. Apart from profiles of Eric's favorite lures

and a gallery of fishing photos there are a handful of interesting articles, the most profound of which is certainly "The Shrine of Dance's Eel." This chronicles a lure endorsed by the great Bill Dance that was so stunningly ineffective it had to be enshrined in the author's loft. Its promotional mojo could not be silenced however, and the grinning image of Dance began to appear on the "shroud" that the lure rests on. It's all here, documented by the Smithsonian Institute.

FLW Outdoors
http://www.flwoutdoors.com

FLW Outdoors is the organizing body behind the other major professional bass tour. This news-focused web site keeps FLW tournament followers up-to-date on their fishing heroes. Click on the logos at the very top

KNOTS AND RIGS

Knots

The Australian site **Marinews** at **http://www.marinews.com** describes the function and uses of 22 fishing knots and seven boating knots. From the homepage click on Fishing Knots to see step-by-step illustrations and an animation of it all coming together.

Some sophisticated animation is on display at the **Discover the Outdoors** web site at **http://www.dto.com.** From the homepage, click on the Learn to Tie this Knot box in the lefthand navigation, then choose between 10 standard knots. Steps can be repeated by using the controls at the bottom of the box. The East Coast saltwater fishing site **Noreast.com** at **http://www.Noreast.com** offers similar large, high-quality animations for six essential saltwater knots.

Fishnet at **http://www.fishnet.com .au** doesn't offer animated knots, but they do have exceptionally clear knot and rig diagrams taken from Geoff Wilson's book *The Complete Book of Fishing Knots and Rigs.* There are 33 fishing knots and 28 fishing rigs in the section: to find it look for Library then Related Info then Knots and Rigs. It's another Australian site, so some knots familiar to U.S. fishermen may have different names.

For a directory of other fishing knot resources (some illustrated, some animated and some shown on Internet video) try **Knots on the Web** at **http://www.earlham.edu/ ~peters/knotlink.htm.** This is Peter Suber's exhaustive reference site to all things knotty. As he advises, don't just scroll down the page and spend all your time going through the fishing and boating references, check out the other sections on general knots, knot art and knot theory: "You just might become happily entangled."

Rigs

One must-see site for saltwater fishermen is **Rigs for Fishing from the Beach or at Sea**, **http://home. wanadoo.nl/escort/introuk.htm** which is a Netherlands page devoted to surfcasting and general saltwater fishing rigs. Rigs are shown in exceptionally clear diagrams and though the majority are explained in Dutch, it isn't difficult to understand what they're meant to do. The Rigs webmaster promises everything will be translated to English eventually.

Most tackle company web sites offer few details about how their products are used in actual fishing situations. Three that understand the benefit in educating customers are Water Gremlin, Lindy Little Joe and Luhr Jensen.

Water Gremlin has made sinkers for the U.S. market for more than 50 years. The Gremlin site at **http:// www.watergremlin.com** is full of rigging diagrams and suggestions for how to use their sinkers, split shot and worm weights. **Lindy Little Joe** produces the Mick Thill range of slim line European bobbers or "floats," and at **http://www. lindylittlejoe.com** you can view or print out a 12-page instructional PDF on how to rig and deploy each bobber. **Luhr Jensen** at **http://www. luhrjensen.com** publishes very helpful Tech Reports on freshwater and saltwater trolling, lure fishing and bait fishing.

of the homepage for news from each tournament, or on the sections Columns and Tips and Techniques for articles about competitive fishing. Links on the righthand side let you join the organization, which you'll need to do if you want to post a question to one of the forums.

Kevin's Bass Fishing Site
http://www.bassfishin.com

This accomplished solo effort from the doggedly one-named "Kevin," has a good selection of articles **TOP RATED** from Bass Coach Roger Lee Brown and other high-profile guides and writers (Kevin also welcomes submissions from readers), as well as links to tackle companies and several active forums. One other notable feature is the large page of lure, line and tackle reviews submit-

ted by readers. Reviews are not much more than two or three sentences, but they get right to the point.

ProBass
http://www.probass.com

This site for fans of tournament fishing is one of the most visited bass sites on the web. Read **TOP RATED** through the mix of technique articles and tournament news on the homepage, or explore the menu of options in the lefthand navigation for events, lake reports, weather information, secondhand boats and pro tips. For those who dream of making the move from fan to pro fisherman, there's a link to Tim Tucker's site at **http://www.tim tuckeroutdoors.com.** Tim publishes a newsletter that deals with the business side of becoming a professional bass angler. You can order *Tim*

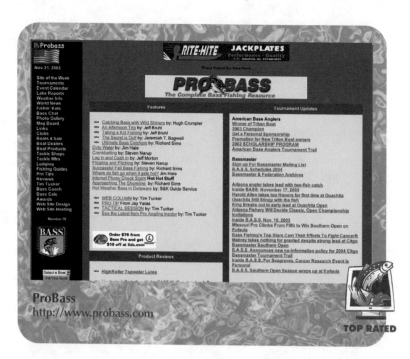

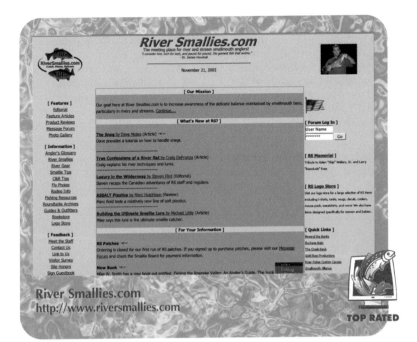

River Smallies.com
The meeting place for river and stream smallmouth anglers!
"I consider him, inch for inch, and pound for pound, the gamest fish that swims." – Dr. James Henshall

November 21, 2003

[Our Mission]

Our goal here at River Smallies.com is to increase awareness of the delicate balance maintained by smallmouth bass, particularly in rivers and streams. Continue...

[Features]
Editorial
Feature Articles
Product Reviews
Message Forum
Photo Gallery

[Information]
Angler's Glossary
River Smallies
River Gear
Smallie Tips
C&R Tips
Fly Photos
Rodeo Info
Fishing Resources
Roundtable Archives
Guides & Outfitters
Bookstore
Logo Store

[Feedback]
Meet the Staff
Contact Us
Link to Us
Visitor Survey
Site Honors
Sign Guestbook

[What's New at RS?]

The Snag by Dave Motes (Article) NEW!
Dave provides a tutorial on how to handle snags.

True Confessions of a River Rat by Craig DeFronzo (Article)
Craig explains his river techniques and lures.

Luxury in the Wilderness by Steven Flint (Editorial)
Steven recaps the Canadian adventures of RS staff and regulars.

ASSALT Plastics by Marc Hutchinson (Review)
Marc field tests a relatively new line of soft plastics.

Building the Ultimate Smallie Lure by Michael Little (Article)
Mike says this lure is the ultimate smallie catcher.

[For Your Information]

RS Patches NEW!
Ordering is closed for our first run of RS patches. If you signed up to purchase patches, please visit our Message Forum and check the Smallie Board for payment information.

New Book NEW!
Mike W. Smith has a new book out entitled, Fishing the Roanoke Valley: An Angler's Guide. The book

[Forum Log In]
User Name
•••••••• Go

[RS Memorial]
Tribute to Galen "Skip" Walters, Sr. and Larry "Bassdude" Rose

[RS Logo Store]
Visit our logo store for a large selection of RS items including t-shirts, tanks, mugs, decals, coolers, mouse pads, sweatshirts, and more! We also have items designed specifically for women and babies.

[Quick Links]
Beyond the Banks
Buchoos Baits
The Crash Bank
Gold Bass Productions
River Valise Custom Canvas
Smallmouth Alliance

River Smallies.com
http://www.riversmallies.com

TOP RATED

Tucker's Pro Angling Insider at the site; his tournament and session notes, tackle reviews and pro interviews are posted online for free.

River Smallies.com
http://www.riversmallies.com

TOP RATED

Sites like River Smallies. com demonstrate many of the strengths of web publishing. It's an attractive production with thoughtful articles and reviews, tips and reader resources, all aimed at a narrow specialization that's unlikely to ever support a print magazine but which a lot of people are nonetheless interested in. The site is flourishing, as is obvious if you drop into the forums. Really, fishermen have never had it so good.

Trophy Bass Only
http://www.trophybassonly.com

TOP RATED

There aren't too many good resources for trophy bass fishing on the Web, but this small site from "Fish" Chris Wolfgram has thoughtful articles and a 20-page gallery of whopping bass (choose the Top Ten option to display the real über-hawgs). Sign up from the site to join the Trophy Bass Only mailing list.

The Ultimate Bass Fishing Resource Guide
http://www.bassresource.com

TOP RATED

A well-tended green monster of bass fishing tips, articles and forums. Graphics are kept to a minimum in favor of quick-loading pages, which is smart because there's a lot to read through here. The articles link in the lefthand navigation lists seasonal tactics, lures, equipment, techniques and tournaments. Beginners get their own section, and there's a page of information and links on bass biology and natural history.

Western Outdoor News (WON) Bass

http://www.wonbass.com

WON Bass is the tournament division of the country's largest weekly outdoor newspaper. Contestants can fish on either the PRO, the AAA or Team Tournament circuits. The site gives full schedules and standings for the three circuits, and there are some active forums for talking it all over and finding a fishing partner.

WesternBass.com

http://www.westernbass.com

Without argument, the leading web site for Western bass anglers. Travel around by clicking **TOP RATED** one of the 11 states in the top navigation. At each you'll find articles, lake information, fishing

reports and forums. The sections for Northern and Southern California lead the way in terms of articles and resources, and are host to the most popular California bass forums you'll find anywhere. General services include Find A Partner, club listings, a video library and news center.

WorldRecordBass.com

http://www.worldrecordbass.com

The best option on the Web for trophy bass information. Among its offerings are profiles and **TOP RATED** interviews with some of the country's most successful record chasers, big bass lake reports, club listings and a popular forum. Look under Teleclass on the homepage for details of monthly phone conferences with big bass experts.

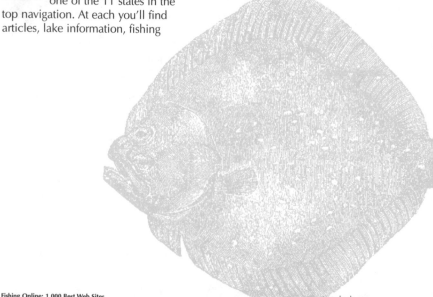

Best Freshwater Fishing Sites

What describes you? Catman? Crappie fan? Walleye hunter? Muskie nut? Carp dude? Sneak a look at what the other guy finds so appealing: you might be missing out on a lot of fun.

Carp Anglers Group
http://www.carpanglersgroup.com

TOP RATED

Carp Anglers Group (CAG)
http://www.carpanglersgroup.com

TOP RATED

The 1,000 members of the Carp Anglers Group make no apologies for thinking that carp are America's best gamefish. After you've read the introductory essays about location, baits, rigs and tackle, move on to the CAG forum for more confirmation of how much thought and effort they put into their fishing. The Fishins section has details of the friendly tournaments and get-togethers they hold around the country.

See also **Carp Net** at **http://www. carp.net**.

Carp.com
http://www.carp.com

TOP RATED

A new and promising magazine site covering the sport in both Europe and North America. Vote on the quality of featured articles, post queries to the forum or download carpy wallpaper and screensavers. World's greatest gamefish or ol' bugle lips? You be the judge.

Catfish Ed.com
http://www.catfished.com

Perhaps its because catfish have such a dingy reputation that the people who love them react defensively by dressing their sites in crazed patterns of fonts, colors and flashing graphics—not to mention appeals to the almighty. One of the more useful, and sedate, offerings comes from Catfish Ed.

Catfish Ed is a lucky man: he can fish from his deck into Clear Lake, California. His web site is a good basic guide to lake fishing for channel cats. Baits, rigs, tackle and seasons are all well covered, and there's plenty of Clear Lake-specific information such as catch reports and guide listings. Catfish Ed has an alter ego—Carphead Ed—and he maintains a parallel site about Clear Lake "golden drum."

Brotherhood of Catfishermen (BOC)
http://www.brotherhood-of-catfishermen.com

The largest catfish community on the Web with more than 3,500 members talking it over **TOP RATED** in well-organized forums for tactics, tales, regional hotspots, tackle evaluation and general chat. The homepage has shortcuts to the most interesting recent posts, and there's a chat room for those who prefer it real-time.

Game & Fish Magazines – Catfish
http://www.gameandfish.about.com/cs/catfish

Housed within the subdivisions of About.com, *Game & Fish* magazines online have sections for **TOP RATED** all the most popular

Over 5,550 **CATFISH** Members and 15,500,000 hits
47 States and 32 Countries.

ENTER THE LARGEST CATFISHING WEBSITE IN THE WORLD, PERIOD!

PAST CATFISHING MEMBER ARTICLES AND CATFISH TALK

CATFISH MEMBER ARTICLE

The Flathead Catfish: Pylodictis Oliveris, is probably the most elusive of all catfish, even the most knowledgeable catfisherman can go days, or even weeks without a fish.

It takes extreme patience & determination to successfully pursue these whiskered giants. I'm going to try and explain some of the information required to attempt to track and catch these elusive catfish. There are many variables to factor in when tracking flatheads but I'm going to start with the basic information about the flathead.

The Flathead Catfish, unlike other catfish, is a predator, therefore it prefers its food to be alive. Flathead feeding activity peaks at night. They have well-defined territories, & relate heavily to cover. If you remember nothing else in this article, those four rules should put you on a flathead or two. But, understanding the seasonal patterns can make those encounters a little more frequent.

When flatheads emerge from their winter haunts in early spring they have two things on their mind, eating & spawning. This is one of the best times to catch a Trophy Flathead, after winter they eat very heavily regaining their energy and feeding up for the spawn, reaching their biggest size of the year right before spawn. The water is very cool at this time so fishing can be good day or night, although flathead activity usually peaks at night, cool water coupled with Spring weather such as heavy winds & rain can make

CATFISH MESSAGES

CHANNEL CATFISH CATFISHING

FLATHEAD CATFISH CATFISHING

BLUE CATFISH CATFISHING

CATFISH CATFISHING SECRETS

CATFISH CATFISHING BAITS

WEL CATFISH WELLS CATFISHING

GENERAL CATFISH MEMBER TALK

Brotherhood of Catfishermen
http://www.brotherhood-of-catfishermen.com

TOP RATED

freshwater fish, including plenty of information about regional catfishing.

The Professional Catfishing Association
http://www.procats.com

A good cyberhole to rest up in while you digest a meal of trophy cat photos, articles, forums and a neat North American Catfish Family Tree. Now you can put that freckled madtom firmly in its place.

Wells catfish aren't available in this country, but no cat man, no fisherman period, could fail to be awed by the whiskery monsters on display at **Siluris Glanis - Wells Catfish, http://xvella.free.fr/photos-eng.php**. These things could swallow a German shepard. Or a German.

Crappie USA – The American Crappie Association
http://www.crappieusa.com

Crappie are the lovely fish with a crappy name, and one of the country's most pursued species. For those with a competitive gene, this site has lots of information about Crappie USA tournaments across the Southern states. For those just wanting to improve their game, there's a large digest of articles from three esteemed crappie publications: *The Crappie Journal, The Crappie 2000 Newsletter*, and *Crappie World*. Part of the appeal of the little predators is culinary: go to the Cook's Corner for seven ways to prepare them or to one of the two forums to connect with the crappie fishing and crappie eating community.

See also **Crappie.com** at **http://www.crappie.com** for articles, recipes and a few active forums.

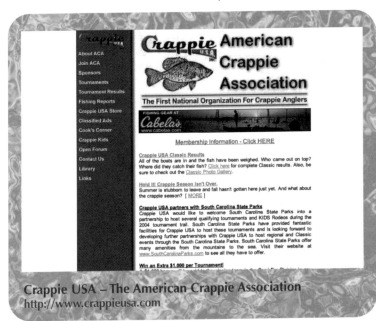

Crappie USA – The American Crappie Association
http://www.crappieusa.com

Gar Fishing!
With the Gar Anglers' Sporting Society
http://www.garfishing.com

TOP RATED

For a good illustrated guide to filleting crappie, plus a selection of technique articles follow the blood trail to **The Crappie Killer** at **http://www.thecrappiekiller.com**.

Gar Fishing! With the Gar Anglers' Sporting Society (G.A.S.S.)

http://www.garfishing.com

TOP RATED

I strongly suspect the folks behind this e-zine delight in being known by the acronym G.A.S.S., and are undeterred by people who have called them "sick in the head" for cheering this half-fish, half-crocodile. As the photos on these neatly layed out pages show, gar varieties are actually quite striking. The site has notes on identification and techniques, a digest of gar articles and a forum. There's a photo of someone's gar tattoo on one page. From such love could flower a whole G.A.S.S empire, with metal-flake jon boats, flurocarbon trot lines and designer chum buckets.

International Muskie Home Page

http://www.trentu.ca/
muskie/muskie.html

TOP RATED

This Canadian-flavored site stresses catch and release and resource protection as much as fishing techniques and stories. For links to recommended sites in the U.S. and Canada go to the carefully indexed Muskie Hotlist. Muskie inspiration is supplied by a section called Big Release Tales, which is a collection of trophy stories that always end with a photograph and a tail disappearing into the depths rather than a dead fish on the bank. No forum, but there's an active mailing list.

MuskieFIRST

http://muskie.outdoorsfirst.com

TOP RATED

You may or may not consciously care about good web design, but when pages such as Muskie-FIRST and the company's mirror site **WalleyeFIRST TOP RATED** at http://walleye.outdoors first.com load onto the screen, you'll see well-proportioned pages, clear navigation, easily readable text and an attractively muted color scheme. It all inspires confidence the site is there for the long term. Content highlights include a long menu of articles, popular forums, video interviews with well-known muskiers, an archive of chatroom Q & A sessions and a tournament calendar.

FISH IDENTIFICATION

FishBase

http://www.fishbase.org/search.cfm

TOP RATED

FishBase is surely unparalleled as an online fish identification and natural history resource. It's an amazing team effort from more than 700 contributors and academics across the globe. Organized by the International Center for Living Aquatic Resources Management (ICLARM), it catalogs 26,700 fish species worldwide. There are over 30,000 photographs and illustrations on the site and the whole database is searchable by an array of parameters—by common name, by country, by ecosystem, by "inclination" (Dangerous, Deepwater, Reef-associated), and several other options. Information given for each fish includes preferred environment, distribution, common names and links to other Web resources about the species.

North American Native Fishes Association (NANFA)

http://www.nanfa.org

If FishBase is too broad a resource, visit NANFA for an index and health assessment of all the true North American species, plus links to every agency in Canada and the U.S. concerned with fisheries.

For thumbnail field guides to more than 300 species of American fish, plus thousands more for birds, mammals, native plants, trees and wildflowers, the photo-rich **http://www.enature.com** is a brilliant service provided by the National Wildlife Federation.

Fish seem to excite both scientists and artists. Superb portraits of native trout and other salmonids can be found at artist and author James Prosek's elegant **http://www.troutsite.com.** The Trout Lookup and Art Gallery sections feature paintings used to illustrate the author's books and some original works. Each is generously reproduced one per page.

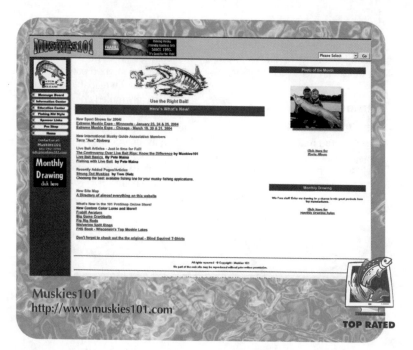

Muskies101
http://www.muskies101.com

Muskies101
http://www.muskies101.com

TOP RATED

Muskies101 is a service to anyone taking up the sport that might be intimidated by the perceived difficulty of the fishing, or the challenge of handling these big toothy creatures. The Education Center has plenty of illustrated articles for figuring out seasonal patterns, how to efficiently catch and release and what tackle to purchase. The forum attracts a regular group of experienced muskie anglers and would be a great place to pose beginners' questions. Among other features, the Information Center links to members of the International Musky Guide Association and has state-by-state record lists.

If the folks at Muskies101 convince you to give it a go, you couldn't do better than outfitting yourself at **Helen and Rollie's Musky Shop, http://www.muskyshop.com.** It's the best kind of independent online tacklestore. They only sell muskie and pike tackle. They have a lot of it. Every item from bucktails and jerk baits to planer boards and unhooking tools is easy to find, clearly photographed and listed with a word about its function. Shop regulars get together in the forum to talk over tackle and tactics.

Roughfish.com
http://www.roughfish.com

TOP RATED

Think that suckers, gar, bowfin, drum, mooneye, codfish and eels are beneath your fishing dignity? As they argue in the Roughfish FAQ, you're giving up the opportunity to make your own fishing discoveries, to fish un-crowded waters and study new species rather than new tackle catalogs. Curious? Start with the species profiles. Among lots of good reading you'll find a "world exclusive" Sucker Spawning Chart and some pretty atypical location advice: "Where to fish for them? Once again, only the eels know. If you find a dark, evil-looking place, full of mud and slime and half rotten logs, you might as well try there. Preferably at night."

Striper Chaser
http://www.striperchaser.com

Striped bass have the decency to live in cool water lakes and rivers as well as saltwater, and this site concentrates mostly on inland stripering in the Carolinas and Virginia. Click on the multicolored balls on the homepage to read 50 technique and destination articles, or go to sections for regional clubs, tackle retailers and lake information.

See also **Striper Strategies** at **http://community-2.webtr.net/ RockandReel/StriperStrategies** for essays on freshwater striper tackle and tactics, and guides to fishing Cherokee Lake and Norris Lake in Tennessee.

Trophy Trout
The biggest brown trout in the world was caught from the Little Red River, Arkansas in 1992. For a fascinating discussion of why rivers like the Little Red and the White River, also in Arkansas, are capable of producing such monster trout, plus several articles about how to fish for them through the seasons see **http://www.whiteriver.net**.

The other option for trophy trout information is to explore web sites covering the Great Lakes, which are consistent producers of jumbo browns. See the recommendations in Chapter 2 State-by-State Resources, or the magazine sites **http://www.glangler.com** and **http://www.fishontario.com.**

Walleye Central
http://www.walleyecentral.com

TOP RATED

A big resource for walleye fans that understands the primary rule of good web sites: content is king. The homepage has a menu of articles from pros such as Rick Olson, Norb Wallock and John Kolinski. To access all the pro-authored stories on the site, go to Pro Pages in the top navigation (on any page past the homepage).

CARPE CARPIO FISH DESIGNS
http://www.carpecarpio.com
Just because you cut bait or take a few fish home for the freezer doesn't mean you have to sacrifice personal style. The cool fish designs of Carpe Carpio celebrate the carp chaser, the flathead wrangler, the lovers of stalking walleye and fat bass. The company's caps, t-shirts, sweatshirts and pins are all nicely showcased. If you don't feel like shopping, articles from unusual corners of the fishing universe such as snakehead fishing in Thailand or profiles of the U.S. match fishing team, complement galleries of fish photos and links to international fishing sites.

A Fantasy Angler Challenge lets you pick three tournament anglers per month (March through October) from the various tours, then accumulate points for prizes based on their catches. Like many web sites, they organize chat room Q & A's with expert anglers. Unlike many, they have the good sense to keep a record of each one for those who missed it.

When the walleye have done a disappearing act, what else is there to do but go out for muskie? If that describes your kind of mindset, drop in on the company's equally impressive **Muskie Central TOP RATED** at **http://www.muskie central.com**.

Walleye Hunter
http://www.walleyehunter.com

TOP RATED

Don't you love to see the yo-yo motion of vertical scroll bars loading pages of free material? That's exactly what happens when you go to the articles section of Walleye Hunter. Webmaster Chris Lehner also links to fish and wildlife departments for the U.S. and Canada, and to the outdoor pages of several Northern state newspapers. Among several other departments worth visiting, there's a whole section devoted to "hard water fishing."

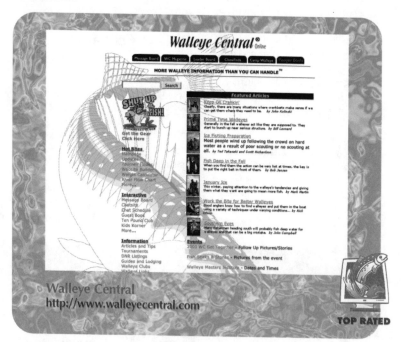

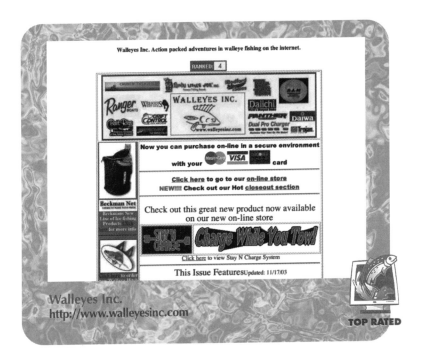

Walleyes Inc.
http://www.walleyesinc.com

TOP RATED

Walleyes Inc.
http://www.walleyesinc.com

TOP RATED

A huge reservoir of articles, news stories and resources is squeezed within Walleye Inc.'s boxy page design. The homepage doesn't really hint at the encyclopedic article archives from many of the top pros—including some by Randy Tyler the webmaster of the site and a competitor on several tournament trails. The forum looks a popular place for walleye chat, and there's a useful collection of fishing reports from web sites in the upper Midwest and Northern states.

See also **The Next Bite** at **http://www.thenextbite.com** for articles, tips and pro angler Q & A's.

ICE FISHING
The Ice Fishing Home Page
http://hickorytech.net/~jbusby/iceangler.html

The "Gateway to all Ice Fishing" is a directory of the best ice-fishing links on the Web. Its recommendations range from tackle sellers and magazine sites to sources for solunar tables, weather links and ice-thickness updates. The best of its recommendations both earn **TOP RATED** status: **IceFishing-FIRST** at **http://icefishing.outdoorsfirst.com**, is a complete hardwater magazine, and **IceShanty.com** at **http://www.iceshanty.com**, is home to some of the most popular ice-fishing forums on the Web.

Fishing the Web

Ice Team Web Report
http://www.iceteam.com

There's talk of leading an "ice-fishing revolution" on this homepage. Perhaps the invasion plans are hidden in the members-only section of this general and tournament ice-fishing site. Articles covering the specialized world of ice tackle and tactics are posted on the free side of the site, as is a reprint of the 2000-2001 Ice Team Annual, where you'll find more articles and Dave Genz's Q & A column.

Judging by the site, is it worth paying to join the team? If I lived in one of the ice-belt states, I'd be wearing my Ice Team hat with revolutionary pride.

On Ice Tour
http://www.onicetour.com

Ice-fishing boosters Chip Leer and Tommy Skarlis are behind this nice little ice-fishing site, with articles going back two years and details of their teach-ins, presentations and annual ice-fishing magazine.

IceShanty.com
http://www.iceshanty.com

TOP RATED

Best Saltwater Fishing Sites

With sophisticated weather and tide information freely available online and forums to keep track of who's catching what and where, the Web can give saltwater fishermen a real edge, whether they hunt the Gulf Stream or sit on an upturned bucket at the pier.

AllCoast Sport Fishing
http://www.sport-fish-info.com

TOP RATED

AllCoast Sport Fishing
http://www.sport-fish-info.com

TOP RATED

AllCoast is forum-central for U.S. saltwater anglers and a great way to join in a countrywide discussion about saltwater fishing, boating and resource issues. Just some of the topics covered include long-range fishing, tackle, tuna fishing, surf fishing, charter reports and boat reviews. There are other forums for international destinations—Canada, Mexico, Australia and Venezuela—and an area on the homepage reporting the catch-es of 16 Southern California charter boats. Tap into the archives of all that fish chatter by keyword, date or author searches.

BC Adventure – Saltwater Fishing
http://bcadventure.com/adventure/angling/saltwater

For a look at how it's done in the Northwest, try the saltwater pages at BC Adventure. The page leads with maps and profiles of BC hotspots, but there's a great deal of broadly applicable information about saltwater salmon fishing and

bottom fishing for halibut and lingcod. Two sections devote themselves to saltwater fly fishing, Northwest-style.

The saltwater pages are but one path through this exemplary site, which covers every type of fishing in the province.

Big Marine Fish

http://www.chambers associates.org

TOP RATED

A celebration of big-game fishing for tuna, billfish and sharks, mixed with salutary reports about the health of these apex sportfish. Chambers and Associates are a marine science consultancy led by a keen big-game fisherman, and the site blends lengthy fishing and conservation articles with photo galleries of some record-breaking fish.

Billfish Tournament Network

http://www.billfishnetwork.com

TOP RATED

A portal for billfish tournaments worldwide. The Top 100 Worldwide Tournaments judges events based on numbers of fish caught, competitiveness (number of boats and anglers), and the amount of prize money on offer. Take a bow, Ocean City White Marlin Open. Click on a tournament title to bring up a page of information, including contact addresses, the rules and history of the tournament and a link to its web site. The Billfish Tournament Network takes conservation very seriously and there are several links and prompts encouraging readers to click through to various conservation groups.

For billfish charter information, articles and a couple of places to chat about the billfish circuit try: **InTheBite**.com at **http://www. inthebite.com**; the **World Billfish Series** at **http://www.worldbill fishseries.com**; and **Billfish International** at **http://www.bill fishintl.com**.

CharkBait!
http://www.charkbait.com

TOP RATED

Mark Smith calls California-focused CharkBait! "a perpetual work in progress," which is exactly what you want to hear when you discover a new and promising web magazine. Start by looking through the articles submitted by friends and regular readers touching on everything from light-tackle halibut fishing and trolling for albacore, to buying used boats and dealing with sea sickness. Detailed trip reports, multiple forums ("CharkBoards") and a reader's gallery make this a particularly communal site. And in that spirit of giving, the owner even directs readers to some of his favorite Huntington Beach-area fishing marks.

The Coalition of Confused Coastal Fishermen (CCCF)
http://www.coastalfishing.org

Headline: "Confused Fishermen Unite and as a Result Become Less Confused." This isn't really a site to find hard information about the popular coastal fish it features on the homepage (speckled trout, redfish and flounder), though there are useful tips and recipes posted by members and excellent links to other sites that provide just that. Rather, it's an example of a bunch of guys using the Web to get something more from their sport and to put a little back at the same time.

The Texas-based CCCF began with 12 members in 1999 and now has

RECORDS

LandBigFish at **http://www.land bigfish.com** has the clearest and most detailed presentation of state fishing records I could find. Go to Research then Fishing Records then choose a state for a table showing the species, the weight, the name of the captor and where and when it was caught. Many of the species and locations are hyperlinked so you can find out a bit more about the life cycle of the fish and where it came from. See also **Hot Spot Fishing** at **http://www.hotspotfishing.com**.

State Fish Records at **http://www. statefishingrecords.com** lets you research the biggest fish caught around the country via links to state fish and wildlife web sites. Format and content varies a little from page to page, but listings are complete.

Disappointly, the governing body of fishing records, the **International Game Fish Association (IGFA)** doesn't publish current world record lists on the organization's web site, **http://www.igfa.org**: they want you to buy an annual record book. You can at least learn how to qualify for record submission and download an application from the homepage.

Coastal Shark Fishing
http://www.coast-shark.com

over 1,000 registered users. They organize friendly fishing tournaments and clean-up days, and sponsor a fishing derby in conjunction with Big Brothers and Sisters of Houston. The site has active forums for fishing reports and general chat, and briefly profiles most of the members.

Coastal Shark Fishing
http://www.coast-shark.com

A regularly updated newsletter for those interested in nearshore shark fishing. Tales from the Deep offers bimonthly feature articles and news stories archived for the last two years. The Shark Guide gives life cycle and identification details for 11 types of shallow water shark. Webmaster Beach Bum stresses the need to protect these fish by learning how to

properly release them and by taking part in tagging programs. Go to the Gallery to view some cautionary photos of shark bites (the kind they inflict on other fish rather than tasty shore fishermen), or connect with other shark fans in the forum.

FishnBottom
http://www.fishnbottom.com

For "bottom-fishing junkies" this site provides a colorful showcase for grouper, cobia, jacks and snappers. There are brief profiles of each fish and some decent-length articles. Links to bottom-fishing charters, Florida fishing reports and conservation groups make up the rest. The site is still developing its content, but has the framework to become a really good magazine.

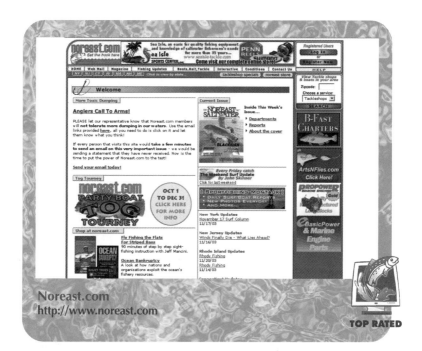

Noreast.com
http://www.noreast.com

TOP RATED

Flats Hunter
http://www.flatshunter.com

TOP RATED

The lovingly designed Flats Hunter looks like a page from a custom car magazine. Fortunately, there's some substance within its Tequila Sunrise borders. Mouse over one of the species (bonefish, permit, tarpon, snook, redfish and seatrout) in the curving top navigation to bring up a four-part guide covering Tackle, Finding, Casting to and Fighting. The sections for Flats 101, Knots/Leaders and Boating were all worth visiting, but the forums had hardly been used. Webmaster Tony Lauro deserves a wider audience for his cool-looking baby.

Noreast.com
http://www.noreast.com

TOP RATED

Just like a print publication each issue of this monthly magazine for Northeastern saltwater fishing has a "front cover" with teasers about what's inside. Complete issue archives going back to 1998 (that's something you won't get from a traditional publisher) are found under Magazine in the left-hand navigation. Each issue has articles, news, columnists and fishing reports.

Among many other features to look out for here are state resources, a wreck finder, animated knot illustrations and a section that allows you to superimpose a favorite fishing photograph on to the cover of the magazine. Go to Cover Shots within Interactive to view 700 readers who have done just that.

COOKING

Dan Hernandez, bon vivant and host of his own sportfishing show, has a good page for fishermen within the **Big Fish Tackle** site at **http://www.bigfishtackle.com/ cooking.** Some of the large collection of saltwater, trout, salmon and catfish recipes are described in terms of fat content and protein percentages, and all are given estimated preparation and cooking times (reassuringly brief). There are also sections for butters, sauces and salsas, and a chart showing which types of fish can be successfully substituted for others.

If your fish dishes have become as predictable as the tides, sort through the hundreds of recipes listed in the fishing directory at **http://www.fishingworks.com/sea food_recipes**. From the start page of this section browse recipes by either of 10 cooking methods, or use the search function to sort recipes by fish type.

Black Lake, New York has a wonderful fishing web site, and unluckily for its many freshwater gamefish, that extends to providing shore lunch instructions. The cooking section at **http://www. black lakeny.com/fishrecipes.html** has tips for preparing your catch, including how long different fish should be stored in your freezer,

how long they take to thaw, and recipes for bass, pike, walleye, panfish, salmon, trout and catfish.

Among the many reasons to visit **LandBigFish** at **http://www.land bigfish.com** is the site's superior cooking section. Go to Resources then Fish Recipes to find 300 dishes searchable by fish type and meal type. There are recipes for the full line-up of saltwater and freshwater species: they tell you 17 ways to prepare bass, for example, from wrapped in bacon to striper cocktails. Site-goers can submit their own dishes or vote on the merits of those already posted.

Sadly, the initial step to a memorable fish dinner isn't preparing it, or even how to catch it, it's learning whether you should bring it home in the first place. The **U.S. Environmental Protection Agency's Fish Advisories** page at **http:// www.epa.gov/waterscience/fish** has state listings for every fish identified as a health risk. Go to National Listings of Advisories in the lefthand navigation to come to a map and search function. I found filling in the search fields easier than using the map. In the box marked Map Query Functions, type the name of the water and the state to get the advisory list.

Pier Fishing in California
http://www.pierfishing.com

TOP RATED

Author Ken Jones has put together an awesome resource in support of his book of the same title. Choose Pier of the Month or Fish of the Month to bring up profiles and archives. This last feature stands as an introduction to nearshore possibilities along the whole West Coast. Each species is pictured and described in terms of habitat, identification, bait, tackle, food value and pier suggestion.

Pierandsurf.com
http://www.pierandsurf.com

TOP RATED

The guts of the site are nine lively forums covering general topics, distance casting, boating and regional fishing from Florida to New Jersey. The large section devoted to knots has clear diagrams and instructions, and there are several links to tackle-stores catering to shore anglers. Send them your trophy shots and they'll pin them up on the site braggin' board.

Saltwater Fishing Home Page
http://www.wmi.org/saltfish

A saltwater fishing warehouse: not much to look at, save for a few news stories and tackle tinkering articles on the homepage, but potentially full of useful stuff. And that's a product of the site's multiple forums covering East and West Coast catch reports, surf fishing, fly fishing, striped bass, boats for sale and several other categories.

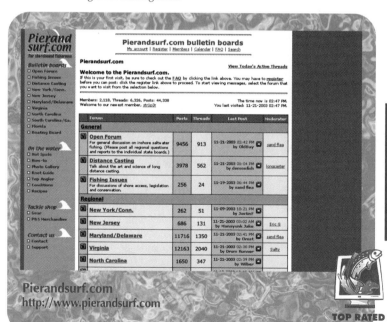

StripersOnline
http://www.stripersonline.com

 TOP RATED

Snookangler.com
http://www.snookangler.com

As webmaster John McLean notes, other people's fishing diaries often make interesting reading. To that end he not only describes his own trips, but he's designed a fishing log template for readers to print out and create their own catch records. Elsewhere, this spacious, clean-looking site has articles and tips, a snook store, and links to weather resources and conservation web sites.

StripersOnline
http://www.stripersonline.com

 TOP RATED

A big striper hooked in the pounding surf is about as iconic as American fishing can get. If you agree, StripersOnline has plenty to offer.

Chiefly, it's host to some of the busiest striper forums on the net. Skip around the links to find articles, fishing reports and photo pages or use the tide and weather resources to plan your weekend.

StriperSurf.com
http://www.stripersurf.com

TOP RATED

Start with the articles at this great gathering spot for surf fanatics to read a long account of Al Raychard's 78 lb. 8 oz. world striper record. Then move on to Frank Daignault's own little corner of the site or "Fly Guy" Ed Zaun's primer on adapting the long rod to beaches and saltwater. Good forums.

Surfcaster.com
http://www.surfcaster.com

TOP RATED

Surfcaster.com
http://www.surfcaster.com

TOP RATED

An attractive, useful community resource for New England surf fishermen. Their site logo incorporates a striped bass but the membership are fans of all the Northeastern gamefish as you discover by wandering the forums, articles, recipes and fishing reports. The Resource guide links to surf-casting clubs and guides in several states, but the strongest listings are in Massachusetts. Surfcaster.com has been on the web for several years and has more than 300 registered forum users.

Tidal Fish
http://www.tidalfish.com

TOP RATED

Popular forums for the Chesapeake Bay, Virginia, Florida and "BS," are the lure at this site. The links directory recommends fishing sites in multiple categories.

Best Fly-Fishing Sites

There are more quality web sites about fly fishing than any other branch of the sport. Beginners can find advice on every aspect of getting started, and experienced fly fishers can choose between dozens of quality sites offering advanced articles, planning resources and online communities.

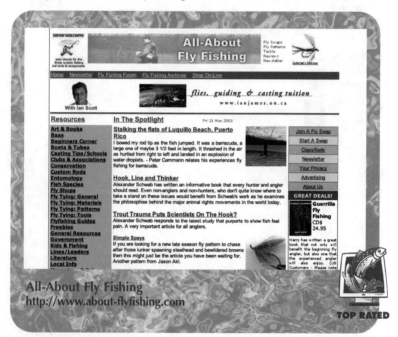

All-About Fly Fishing
http://www.about-flyfishing.com

TOP RATED

All-About Fly Fishing
http://www.about-flyfishing.com

TOP RATED

If the name and look of this site seem familiar, you were probably a visitor to the fly-fishing section of About.com before January 2002 when a corporate shakeup forced the original guide to transfer all the contents and link recommendations to this new site. Ian Scott recommends the best fly-fishing content on the Web within more than 30 topics areas, from techniques, species and tackle, to less obvious categories such as personal pages, literature, freebies and software. Click on a topic title to open a digest of links to articles within other sites, or whole web sites on the subject.

The site has especially good fly-tying links, and within the literature section, the entire text of *The Complete Angler*. Now you have no excuse.

Beginner's Netguide To Flyfishing

The main purpose of this page is to help people discover the sport of flyfishing. I have put together the resources needed for anyone to begin their endeavor, and hope you enjoy reading them as much as I've enjoyed writing them. Good luck and good fishing!

Join **Fly Fishing Loop** Member sponsored by flydepot.com

The Fly Fishing Loop is sponsored by flydepot.com
[Home Waters I Next I Random I List I Search]

HOME

OVERVIEW | EQUIPMENT | KNOTS | CASTING | LINKS | BOOKS

Copyright © 1997-2002 Robert Yacullo. All Rights Reserved.
Last Updated June 16, 2002.

Beginner's Netguide to Fly Fishing
http://www.associatedinternet.com/flyfishing101

Beginner's Netguide to Fly Fishing
http://www.associatedinternet.com/flyfishing101

FlyFishing Tools.com
http://www.flyfishtools.com

Two sites clearly outlining the fundamentals of taking up the sport. The Netguide begins by stressing the simplicity of fly fishing, then discusses equipment, assembly, knots and casting, all in language stripped of the jargon that sometimes creeps into fly-fishing writing. Continue your education by studying the recommended books and links.

Fly Fishing Tools.com is a compact introduction to the basics of fly tying and fishing, courtesy of an online fly shop. Go to Tying Technique from the company homepage to find areas for equipment, materials, tying your first fly and using a whip finisher. Fishing Your Own Flies illustrates what to do with your creations, and Practice makes Perfect teaches the finer points such as curve casts and etiquette.

BC Adventure – Stillwater Fly Fishing
http://www.bcadventure.com/adventure/angling/stillwater

One of the best introductions to lake fly fishing on the Web. There's lots of British Columbia information, including a profile of the famous Kamloops strain of rainbow, but much of the content could be applied to the rest of North America. Go down the lefthand navigation for advice about patterns, lake structure, sight fishing and tackle. A detailed entomology corner complements the tactical side of things with profiles and illustrations of the most important lake bugs.

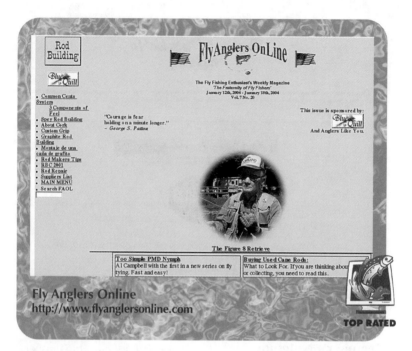

Fly Anglers Online
http://www.flyanglersonline.com

TOP RATED

Derrick's Pike Pages
http://members.shaw.ca/mrpike

Derrick's Pike Pages has everything you probably need to know about *esox* on the fly, from the outsized fly patterns to constructing wire leaders and what you need in the way of unhooking tools. Much of the technique information supplied by Derrick comes from interviews with pike aficionado Clive Schaupmeyer. Go to **http://www.members.shaw.ca/clives/pikeflyfish.html** to view Clive's own colorful and helpful site, **Fly-Fishing for Northern Pike**.

Fish & Fly
http://www.fishandfly.co.uk

TOP RATED A first stop for anyone interested in U.K. and European fly fishing. The guys behind this site take their fishing seri-

ously, but they aren't too stuffy to publish a travel article about good fly water adjacent to the best rural pubs (author: John Beer). Fish & Fly has all the features that distinguish the very best sites: active forums and several other ways for readers to get involved, unusually well-written articles and reviews, attractive design and the cohesive voice of a true magazine. The travel section is recommended for articles about European destinations rarely covered in U.S. fishing publications.

Fly Anglers Online (FAO)
http://www.flyanglersonline.com

TOP RATED The unassuming FAO homepage is a gateway to one of the biggest and best fly-fishing sites on the Web. Click on FEATURES in the main menu or use the bottom navigation to dis-

PERSONAL SITES

The Web is the most democratic of publishing media. It allows anyone with something to say (or sell) have a universal forum. This has resulted in thousands of enthusiastically conceived web sites that the creator's own mother would have a hard time praising. But wander the Net long enough and you'll come across personal pages that are well designed and worthwhile. Fly fishing has more than its fair share.

Ken Abrame's Striper Moon
http://www.stripermoon.com

TOP RATED Striper Moon is author and artist Ken Abrame's saltwater fly-fishing site. There are articles, tying instructions for Ken's original creations, a large baitfish gallery for matching the saltwater hatch and more forums than you can shake The Stick at. "The Stick" being Ken's own design of saltwater fly rod. Look for The Stick link on the homepage to find specifications and an absorbing essay about its development. Ken even leads occasional free fishing clinics/poking around sessions along the Rhode Island shore. Check the forums or e-mail Ken for details.

Angling Matters
http://www.anglingmatters.com

Pioneering outfitter, fly-casting expert and author Jim Chapralis uses his personal web site as part soap box, part aide to traveling fishermen (see the English-Spanish fishing phrase guide), part promotional tool for his recent book and part forum for passing on his decades of fishing experience.

Dan Blanton
http://www.danblanton.com

Dan Blanton is a well known West Coast fly-fishing author, photographer and speaker. His colorful site has a generous catalog of articles (some by Dan, some by friends of Dan) and descriptions of his professional slide presentations, tackle tips and fly creations.

While you're in the fly section, follow the link to **John McKim Illustrations TOP RATED** at http://www.johnmckim.com to see fly-tying illustrations turned into art. Each print expands to full screen size, but the idea isn't really to follow the recipe from the web site. For patterns and instructions you can use immediately, go to Fly Ideas.

Sidney Du Broff's Fishing and Shooting Journal
http://www.sidsjournal.com

TOP RATED Probably less than half of Sid Du Broff's Journal is about fly fishing, but the site's volumes of essays, reviews and reflections on the sporting life are such an exceptional example of personal web site publishing, it's an easy

Continued on page 175

The Fly Fishing FORUM
http://www.flyfishingforum.com

---

cover thousands of pages on rod making, warmwater fly fishing, fly tying, fishing stillwaters, entomology, book reviews and fishing destinations in the U.S. and internationally. The site is updated every week and hosts exceptionally popular forums.

The Fly Fishing FORUM
http://www.flyfishingforum.com

Dana Sturn's Spey Pages
http://www.speypages.com

TOP RATED

Quality fishing sites still sneak under the radar of many search engines and stumbling across them is one of the chief pleasures of browsing the fishing Internet. Such was my experience with The Fly Fishing FORUM and Dana Sturn's Spey Pages.

The Forum is a fully developed magazine with freshwater and saltwater articles by established fly-fishing writers and regular readers (look for the Writer's Guild link on the homepage for submission details). Forums are divided into four topics: Pacific Northwest steelhead, gear talk, stripers and coastal gamefish.

Dana Sturn's Spey Pages is affiliated with the FORUM site and covers the specialized tackle and techniques involved in learning to Spey cast. Test reports for rods, reels and line will point you in the direction of the right equipment. Video clips and articles will show you how to put it to use, including advice about one of the toughest forms of fly fishing—winter steelheading.

recommendation. Du Broff is a transplanted American living the life of an English sporting gentleman, and his journals record his outdoor adventures in flavorful and opinionated articles on everything from fly fishing the English chalkstreams and shotgunning in Ireland, to sporting travels in such diverse places as Israel, Russia and Texas.

Of special note is the series of articles teaching children how to fly fish in lakes and ponds. It begins in Issue 3 and covers all the major points by its conclusion in Issue 10.

Jack Gartside's Home Page
http://www.jackgartside.com

Jack Gartside is a renowned fly tier and angling author and his homepage shows off his off-kilter approach to fishing and tying. The author self-publishes fishing books and booklets, all of which are available from the site. Articles, patterns, a forum, risqué postcards and Jack on a giraffe: what more do you want from a fishing web site?

@Streamside: Journal
http://www.helmintoller.com/streamside/journal

A lovely little site from artist Stuart Helmintoller demonstrating how suited personal web sites are as fishing diaries. Occasional trip descriptions from the last three years are illustrated with sketches and photographs, and the Gallery shows off the best trout and salmon clip art on the Web.

Trout Ball
http://www.troutball.com

Musician, artist and fishing poet Gary Keller offers a delightfully crooked tributary to the mainstream of fly-fishing representation at this personal web site. To give a taste, track 11 of the Trout Ball CD is described as "Greg explores the sociological differences between trout and suckers in an industrialized society;" track 2, Neoprene Waders, is about "sex, rubber, and fishing." Listen to snatches of other songs from the CD via an audio file, or read through Greg's anti-pastoral fishing poetry.

Dave and Emily Whitlock – The Art and Science of Fly Fishing
http://www.davewhitlock.com

Fly fishing renaissance man Dave Whitlock writes, draws, teaches and creates flies, and does it all to a high standard. With davewhitlock.com, add publishes a pretty good fishing web site to the list. There are tips and articles and a good deal of information about the Dave and Emily Whitlock Fly Fishing School in Mountain Home, Arkansas. If you have your own site you might want to plunder Dave's fly-fishing clip art: all he asks is that you acknowledge where you got it from.

Fishing the Web

The Flyfishing Connection

http://www.flyfishing
connection.com

TOP RATED

I spent most of my time here looking at the gallery full of readers' shots and the hundreds of patterns in the fly-tying archive, but there are many reasons to give this one a bookmark: technique and destination articles, a multipart section for beginners (under Fly Fishing Basics on the homepage), and large departments describing major rivers in 14 states, as well as fly-fishing opportunites around the Great Lakes and off the Northeast coast.

FlyFish Saltwaters.com

http://www.flyfishsaltwaters.com

TOP RATED

All the material for this attractively presented magazine—the articles, fishing reports, fly patterns and, of course, the forums—is generated by readers. Forums for general discussion, "Ask Tony Stetzko," Boats/Electronics and Offshore/Bluewater receive regular traffic. The Reports stays current with what's being caught in several states, with the best coverage for Massachusetts and the Northeast. Many of the patterns in the fly-tying section are shown in multiple photo sequences.

The Flyfishing Resource Guide

http://www.flyfish.com

This venerable site was recently overhauled and given a new, more advanced design. Most of the sections have yet to properly fill back in with fresh content, but the former site had better-than-average forums, business listings, classifieds and article archives. Hopefully, the new site will recapture its audience and be around for another decade.

Flyfish@ Home Page
http://www.uky.edu/~agrdanny/
flyfish/main.htm

TOP RATED

More than 1,000
members belong to the
Flyfish@ mailing list, and
this is their clubhouse on
the Web. The homepage
has clear joining instructions and
troubleshooting tips, and the
Flyfish@ Archives provides a very
quick way to search the thousands
of old discussion topics by keyword. The archives are maintained
by Joel Dunn: follow the link to
his site to find calculators for esti-
mating fish weights and advice for
making your own tapered leaders.

Services like Joel's—just for the
hell of it and in the interests of the
rest of the membership—inform
the rest of the Flyfish@ site.
Submit stories, articles, opinion

pieces and recipes, or read about
upcoming conclaves.

Canada has its own national fly-
fishing mailing list. The **CANFF**
page (for Canadian fly-fishing
internet discussion list) at **http://
www.sfu.ca/~epoole/canff.htm**
simply explains how to subscribe
and unsubscribe, how to request
the digest version, and what they
hope the list becomes: "a
low-volume 'serious' list … a
first-class source of information
and ideas for academics, writers,
activists as well as professionals
interested in angling and conservation."

To swap notes with European
fly anglers sign up for the
Eur-flyfish@ mailing list found at
**http://www.shconnect.de/
eur-flyfish**.

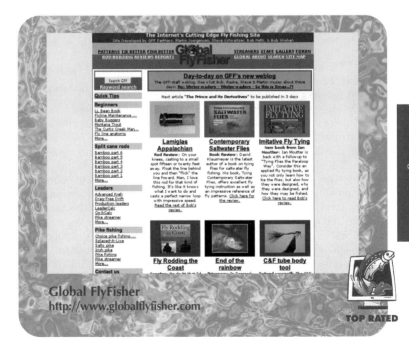

Global FlyFisher
http://www.globalflyfisher.com

TOP RATED

A History of Fly Fishing
http://www.flyfishinghistory.com

Global FlyFisher (GFF)
http://www.globalflyfisher.com

TOP RATED

A holy alliance between three top-quality web sites: Martin Joergensen's Fishing Denmark, Steve Schweitzer's Midwest Fly Tyer, and Bob Skehan's Paske's New England Streamer Page. Along with fly-tying writer Bob Petti, they've joined forces to try and make "the best site there is on flyfishing and flytying. End of story."

The emphasis is on techniques and improving skills, and there are thousands of pages of precisely organized material to investigate. Click on Streamers in the top navigation, or on any of the fly-tying links on the lefthand side to discover exceptional tying coverage, including a thorough beginners guide. Other treats are in-depth book and tackle reviews, a hatch chart applicable to much

of the U.S., and an alarmingly detailed section about making leaders (including a downloadable spreadsheet). GFF has contributors from Europe, the U.S., and around the world.

A History of Fly Fishing
http://www.flyfishinghistory.com

Author Dr. Andrew Herd has posted a very generous chunk of his book *A History of Fly Fishing* on these pages. And it's quite a long history, as he shows in condensed chapters from the book starting with the first mention of fly fishing in the English Language in about 200 A.D., all the way through to the tackle revolutions of the last 50 years. In addition, look for historical inquiries into hooks and fly-tying vices, and the complete text of *Treatyse of Fysshynge with an Angle*, the first fly-fishing book ever published.

Reel-Time
http://www.reel-time.com

TOP RATED

REI - Learn & Share Fly Fishing

http://www.rei.com/rei/learn

What REI wants to teach you are all the smart questions you should be asking yourself before you throw down several hundred dollars on new fly-fishing equipment. They'd like it if you eventually bought that equipment from them, of course, but they don't let that interfere with a useful information service. There are buyer's guides to the whole fly-fishing armory from discussions of the anatomy of fly rods and how to choose a pontoon boat, to what to look for in reels, lines, accessories, sunglasses and clothing. The advice on stocking a fly box includes hatch guides for the Eastern and Western states, and a technique section illustrates all the basic methods. If you're unsure about a major purchase, stop in here first.

Reel-Time

http://www.reel-time.com

TOP RATED

If saltwater fly fishing is your thing, this site should be at the top of your bookmarks. Browsing the Reel-Time pages, it's obvious this is a much-loved and much-used creation. The heart of the site is made up of East Coast fishing reports, with especially strong coverage of New England and the Northeast. Plenty of feature articles, a large Q & A archive from various saltwater guides, a photo gallery and several forums make it a complete resource.

A River Never Sleeps

http://www.ariverneversleeps.com

TOP RATED

A River Never Sleeps uses fishing photography to the best effect of any site on the Web. It focuses on

Entomology

Ernest Schwiebert added "matching the hatch" to the fly-fishing lexicon with the publication of his book of the same title in 1955. It sets out the principles of fly fishing's version of entomology: identifying the aquatic insects that trout feed on in different waters and selecting or tying a fly to mimic them. Aside from the major fly-fishing web sites reviewed in this chapter and in Chapter 5 Media, several regional and specialist sites have entomology and hatch-matching sections worth seeking out.

Wisconsin Fly Fishing
http://www.wisflyfishing.com/
bridge.html

Provides calendars for the emergence of all the major varieties of Mayfly, stonefly and caddisfly important to Midwestern fly fishers. These can either be viewed on the site or as a set of print-ready PDFs. Get a second take on the same general region at **SE Minnesota Trout Flies** at **http://users.myexcel. com/dolfnlvr/.**

Fly Fishing North Carolina
http://www.flyfishingnc.com

Has color photographs of the five major insect orders and common varieties within each order. The Flies department houses a blank hatch chart which can be filled in with personal observations, and an identification page that matches patterns to different stages of the insect's life cycle.

Fly Craft Angling
http://www.flycraftangling.com

TOP RATED

Philip Rowley profiles all the major lake bugs and includes a pie chart showing the relative importance of different insects in the spring, summer and fall. Drop into the pattern and

article archives for an ongoing discussion about stillwater flies and approach.

The biology departments of many universities have entomology sections useful to fly fishermen. Four of the best for information and links to the wider world of aquatic bugs are:

Entomological Research at Florida A & M University
http://www.famu.org/ent/

Mayfly Central at Purdue
http://www.entm.purdue.edu/ entomology/research/mayfly/ mayfly.html

Pennsylvania Flies Are Us
http://paaquaticfliesrus. bd.psu.edu

The Chironomid Home Page
http://www.ouc.bc.ca/fwsc/ iwalker/intpanis

But my favorite page is the **Insect Drawings Gallery** at **http://www. life.uiuc.edu/entomology/insect gifs.html.** These sketches were commissioned as a WPA project during the Depression, and then used as teaching aids at the University of Illinois. Usefully for fishermen, they represent an overview of the major orders

Continued on page 182

British Columbia fly-fishing and has a true magazine feel, complete with an archive of all the old "issues." There are long, well-written articles from the leading lights of Canadian fly fishing, as well as news, commentary and resources. A gem.

SalmonAnglers.com
http://www.salmonanglers.com

TOP RATED

SalmonAnglers.com was started by Luke R. Dyer as a way to celebrate fly fishing for Atlantic salmon along the Canadian seaboard. The site is applying for nonprofit status with a mandate to promote salmon fly fishing to beginners, and several of the features on the site were being revamped in accordance with this. Some good articles, up-to-date river reports and a salmon fly dressing competition are keeping it functional in

the meantime. One to keep an eye on.

Sexyloops
http://www.sexyloops.co.uk

TOP RATED

If Austin Powers was an international man of fly fishing, Sexy Loops would be his favorite bookmark. It really is quite smashing. English fly-casting instructor Paul Arden and co-conspirators have mixed humor, instruction, the diary form and original presentation to create one of the freshest fishing sites on the Web. Two of the many areas worth noting are the great big sections given over to casting and stillwater fishing. Both are comprehensive introductory guides written in a style that'll keep you engaged even if you've done it or read it all before. Updated daily.

rather than a catalog of every winged thing that's ever landed in your camp coffee.

Click on any of the 21 thumbnails to see expanded sketches of each insect, some showing different stages of development or close-ups of identifying features like the wings and head. Apart from the scientific and common name, no text information is given but there is a link beside each sketch to the **Tree of Life Web Project** at the University of Arizona, **http://www.tolweb.org/tree/ phylogeny.html.** Each "Tree" page has identification and distribution details, and links to other sites for more information.

If you'd prefer something less academic, **Bug Bios** at **http:// www.bugbios.com** introduces 14 insect orders with descriptions pitched at the non-scientist, color photographs and extensive links.

The Fisher Monk
http://www.fishermonk.com

Bruce Williams has devised an ingenious match the hatch application to pair fly patterns to the names and descriptions of different Mayflies. Click the pattern name option and choose from a large list of imitations to see a photograph of the fly and tying instructions. Mayflies that are often grouped together under common names can be individually selected to show the nymph, dun and spinner stage, and what fly is used to imitate it. The system is in beta testing, but worked flawlessly.

Paul makes the point that there aren't many good casting resources on the Web, but he does provide a link to the **Fly Casting Forum** at **http://home.att.net/~slowsnap**. It's not much more than a collection of text pages but there's a lot of material here, including casting tournament news, tips, club details and tackle company listing.

Smallstreams.com
http://www.smallstreams.com

TOP RATED

Though this site celebrates the virtues of little no-name rivers and creeks, it was also inspired by the idea "that we are all small streams of information." Which is to say, here's your chance to get published on the Web because readers submit all the material. Recent stories are featured on the homepage: go to Top 10 to read the most popular contributions. Other "streams" of community involvement include the chance to post tackle reviews or contact members through the forum and member directory. Traveling fly fishers can sign up for two mailing lists—one for Mexico and one for South Africa.

The Steelhead Site
http://www.steelheadsite.com

The introduction of steelhead to the Great Lakes must be one of the

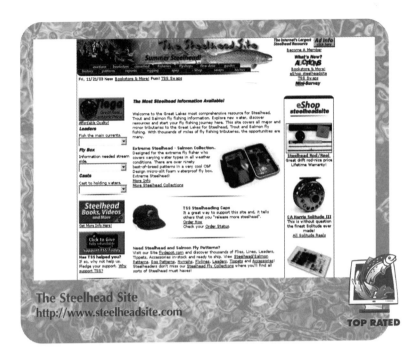

The Steelhead Site
http://www.steelheadsite.com

TOP RATED

TOP RATED

most successful stocking programs of the modern era (Michigan's program began in 1876). Mid-western fly fishers are doubly lucky then, because they also have this superb magazine devoted to their unique branch of the sport. Sections are full of solid regional information, including fishing reports for the eight states with Great Lakes runs, flow data from the USGS, a guide data-base and the history of each state's stocking program. Steelhead fisher-men wherever they live could get something from the Spey Casting and Rigging forums.

The site is partnered with **http://www.flydepot.com**, which looks like it could supply every conceiv-able steelhead pattern, or flies for any other species. Flies can be selected in a number of thoughtful ways. Choose a region, fish species

or insect type and the magic Fly Depot hatch matcher will recom-mend a list of patterns, or you can choose from ready-bundled selec-tions in 31 categories.

For similar selection and pattern picking go to **Umpqua Feather Merchants** at **http://www.umpqua.com** or **Yager's Flies** at **http://www.yagersflies.com**.

The Tropical Angler
http://www.cyberisle.com/
tropical/angler.htm

Don Phillip's valuable guide to tropical fly fishing with special emphasis on Southwest Florida. Go to the bottom of the homepage to read the 12 sequential chapters. It begins with fly-fishing history and illustrated sections for game-fish species and peak fishing times in southwest Florida. Then it's on to clear discussions about rods,

Fishing the WebFishing the Web   183

reels, lines, knots and patterns, where to find them and how to protect them.

Westfly
http://www.westfly.com

TOP RATED

The creation of Oregon author Scott Richmond, and now a nonprofit with a laudable mandate to "advance the quality of Western fly fishing," Westfly beautifully synthesizes a mass of regional fly-fishing information. The site covers California, Idaho, Montana, Oregon and Washington, and for each state there are links to regularly updated fishing reports, weather, river levels, tide reports for the coastal states, events, guides and lodges. There are thoughtful articles, and a clever hatch guide that can be read by calendar month, area and water type. Complementing the hatch informa-

tion are hundreds of pages of tying instructions and photographs.

FLY TYING
Classic Salmon Flies
http://www.classicsalmonflies.com

Webmaster and fly tier Wolfgang Von Malottke has posted more than 80 traditional dressings in the Flies gallery (all tied "freestyle" without a vice). Each fly is clearly photographed and described, and there's advice on how to locate some of the more unusual materials.

The Complete Sportsman
http://www.rareandunusual.com

TOP RATED

You don't know how beautiful fishing flies can look until you've roved the feathery halls of The Complete Sportsman.

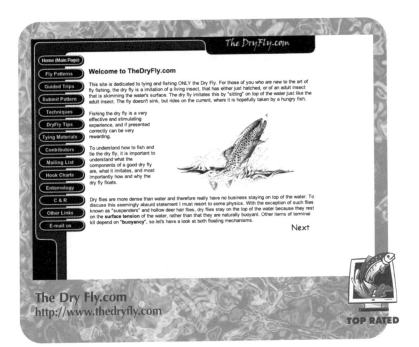

They're the publishing company behind the folio works *Rare and Unusual Fly Tying Materials* and *Forgotten Flies*, and their web site displays the same visual flair and attention to detail. The site navigation is squeezed down into a frame at the bottom of the homepage. Click on any of the links within that frame, especially the Radical Fly Gallery, the Fly Pattern Dictionary and the Classic Fly Gallery, to view hundreds of exquisitely tied and photographed Atlantic salmon flies with full tying instructions. There's a complete bibliography of sources used in their research, and author/publishers Paul Smookler and Ingrid V. Sils will even photocopy difficult-to-find material from their library if you're conducting your own investigations.

The Dry Fly.com
http://www.thedryfly.com

A small, tidily executed site focused on the delights of … you guessed it. Patterns are shown as thumbnails: clicking on them expands the photo and reveals the full recipe. Tips for selecting materials and tying techniques can be applied to all the featured patterns. Hook Charts match descriptions of different hook styles to manufacturer's inventory codes. Get involved by submitting your own creations or by joining the site mailing list. This is a new-looking site that will hopefully pack on weight for the long haul.

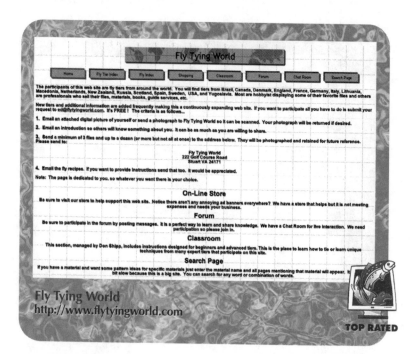

Fly Tying World
http://www.flytyingworld.com

TOP RATED

Killroy's Fly Tying and Fishing
http://www.killroys.com

This site hasn't been updated for a while, but you can still go to the bottom navigation and click your way through perennially useful resources such as charts for tippets and bead to hook size balancing and hatch guides for Arkansas, California, Idaho, Michigan and Alberta's Bow River. Move on to hook comparison data for five brands of commonly used hooks and a knot index. Basic recipes for hundreds of patterns and descriptions of essential fly-tying tools make up the rest.

See also **Wes' Virtual Pattern Book** at **http://www.magiclink.com/web/wesn**. This one is sadly mummified, but you can still copy from its album of original patterns for dries, streamers, stillwater,

nymphs, steelhead, bass bugs and saltwater. Click on the thumbnails for big pictures and detailed notes.

Fly Tying World
http://www.flytyingworld.com

TOP RATED

A truly international site using clear photographs and precise instructions to showcase the work of tiers from 17 countries. Use the Fly Tier Index to see the collected patterns of each contributor.

Flytier's Page
http://www.danica.com/flytier

TOP RATED

Hans Weilenmann's exceptional photo pattern album comes from well-known U.S., European and worldwide tiers. Many of them are briefly profiled: choose a name from the first two columns on the homepage or use the A to Z pattern index. All the patterns are given large close-ups and full tying directions, plus occasional notes about inspiration and development. Hans photographed all the flies, and he's obviously comfortable using a camera as the rest of the site is given over to photo journals of trips to New Zealand, the Western U.S. and Europe.

Philatelic Phly Tying
http://home.att.net/~kholm/
PHLYTYING

Many flies achieve the unusual hat trick of beauty, utility and regional character. Presumably these are the talents that appealed to the postage stamp designers showcased in this unusual site. Stamps of various fly patterns from Africa, the U.S., Canada and New Zealand are reproduced to a good size (click

on the image to enlarge it further), and webmaster Keith Holm has helpfully tracked down the tying recipe for each featured fly.

Salmonfly.net
http://www.angelfire.com/
wa/salmonid

One of the few real fly-tying magazines on the Web, a new salmon and steelhead pattern is **TOP RATED** posted on the site every week. Novices will find tutorials, a Glossary of Modern Tying Materials and advice about essential tools.

Troutflies.com
http://www.troutflies.com

The Tutorial section of this online fly shop features one of the most heavily illustrated step-by-step tying guides you'll find. Once

Ultimate Fly Tying
http://www.ultimateflytying.com

TOP RATED

you've selected a pattern from the main menu of nearly 20 options, a 25-30 step photographic sequence shows exactly what it should look like at each stage of the dressing. Just to confirm he knows what to do with the flies he makes, owner Harry Mason includes a photo diary from a recent trip to Mongolia.

Ultimate Fly Tying
http://www.ultimateflytying.com

TOP RATED

Many fishing sites build content by referencing material from other sources, but few have raided the Web as effectively as the directory Ultimate Fly Tying. The Fly Patterns database offers more than 1,000 recipes within its sections for dries, wets, terrestrials, nymphs and caddisflies. The Fly Indexes department offers dozens of fly selections grouped around a theme: pike flies, bass bugs, BC shrimp patterns, flies for New Zealand trout and so on.

Virtual Flybox
http://www.virtualflybox.com

TOP RATED

The Virtual Flybox is built around the fraternal idea of fly swaps. Sign up for a swap and you'll be asked to tie a particular style pattern for each member of the group. And the other members do the same. All the patterns are sent to the swap moderator who distributes them evenly, so you end up, for example, with 20 caddis interpretations or 12 different Wooly Buggers. There are more than 1,000 swapped flies in the Virtual Fly Box database: all are photographed and the majority have the tying recipe included, or fuller notes about the development and function of the fly. The site welcomes readers to

Virtual Flybox
http://www.virtualflybox.com

TOP RATED

submit original patterns even if they don't want to be involved in a swap. Other areas worth exploring include feature articles and a forum for connecting with other tiers.

For more pattern inspiration try the **Edmonton Chapter of Trout Unlimited Canada** at **http://www. freenet.edmonton.ab.ca/trout/ flytying.html**, which has a great collection of links to pattern pages within other fly-fishing sites.

Vladimir Markov's Fly-Tying Websites
http://www.markov.baikal.ru

TOP RATED

Vladimir displays his considerable talents within pages of beautifully tied and photographed nymphs, wets, emergers, dry flies, salmon flies and original patterns. Each comes with a recipe and tying notes. Go to Keep Tying to find articles and a select list of the best fly-tying web sites.

CHAPTER 5
MEDIA

Did you ever see that television ad for *The Wall Street Journal*? It showed two men, one of whom grew up reading about the financial world in the *Journal* and was now a captain of industry; the other of whom grew up reading fishing magazines and was now a motel chambermaid who lived with his mom. I would usually miss it, of course, because I had my nose buried in *Big Bass Weekly* or *Trout Confidential*. If you want to whittle away precious hours not calculating P/E ratios, there's a huge amount of fishing media out on the Web to do it with: magazines, newspaper columns, television shows, computer games, book stores, and, of course, thousands and thousands of regular web sites. Is living with your mom really so bad?

Print Magazines Online

Many of the best fishing web sites come from print magazines. They know what their readers are interested in and they're skilled at providing fresh, well-designed content. Some of these sites have extra features than the print versions. If you just prefer to get your magazine in the mail, they all offer subscriptions online.

American Angler/Fly Tyer/ Saltwater Fly Fishing
http://www.flyfishingmagazines.com

American Angler/Fly Tyer/ Saltwater Fly Fishing
http://www.flyfishing
magazines.com

Abenaki Publishing puts out these uniformly high-quality fly-fishing magazines. Content is a little thin on the web site, but there are bonus articles for each magazine, and you can search and order back issues from several years past. A regular trivia contest, a fly-fishing bookstore and business directory fill in the gaps.

eBassin'
http://www.ebassin.com

eBassin' isn't much to look at: there are a few articles and departments from *Bassin'* magazine and a couple of resource links, but it does set out all the rules and results of the popular Big Bass World Championship. Now in its 14th year, contestants have from January 1st to August 1st to catch and certify the five largest bass by length in their home state. State winners meet on Table Rock Lake, Missouri, and whoever catches the largest bass over a two-day competition takes home $50,000 and a fully rigged bass boat.

Field & Stream
http://www.fieldandstream.com

TOP RATED

Field & Stream
http://www.fieldandstream.com

TOP RATED

Field & Stream transfers a good deal of content from its venerable, century-old print magazine to its no less high-standard web site. Fishing is divided into Freshwater, Saltwater, Fly Fishing and Q & A. Each section has eight to 10 articles plus a link to The Fish Finder Database, which describes nearly 100 types of gamefish and how to catch them. Gear reviews run to 2,000 fishing, hunting and camping items, searchable by keyword or category, and there is a separate department for SUV and truck reviews.

Fish and Game Finder Magazine
http://www.fishandgame.com

Fish and Game Finder has the rare organizational base to post monthly fishing reports for states in the Midwest, Georgia, Florida, Arkansas, New York and Arizona because they publish free monthly magazines in each region. Reports vary in length and quality, but a few helpful pointers usually turn up in each entry. Articles and news stories are focused on bass, walleye and ice fishing.

The Fish Sniffer Online
http://www.fishsniffer.com

TOP RATED

The Fish Sniffer is a straight-talking Western fishing magazine that's enthusiastically taken its content to the Web. It has good catch reports and busy forums covering freshwater, saltwater, trout, bass and fishery issues. There are plenty of articles, and a fishing map section charts more than 50 lakes. Add in areas for female anglers, conservation, cooking and secondhand boats, and you have a great all-around Western fishing resource.

Fishing Facts
http://www.fishingfacts.com

A small but pioneering freshwater fishing magazine that's making some effort at online publishing. There are a few previously published articles, a forum and a decent links section. It's owned by *MidWest Outdoors*, also on the Web at **http://www.midwest outdoors.com**. The site isn't much more than a brochure for the magazine, but it does have an active freshwater forum.

Florida Sportsman Online
http://www.floridasportsman.com

TOP RATED

Florida's largest fishing magazine is also host to its most popular fishing site. Florida sportsman. com has a real community

feel led by a huge forum (9,000+ registered users) and a comprehensive, statewide Weekend Fishing4Cast written by local guides and journalists. Elsewhere on the site you'll find illustrated articles, links to Florida conservation groups and shortcuts to weather forecasts, best fishing times and state records.

Fly Fish America Online
http://www.flyfishamerica.com

TOP RATED

Fly Fish America is a free magazine available at fly shops all over the country. The entire contents of the magazine is posted on the site and is built around regional articles for the Pacific, Rocky Mountain, Mid Atlantic, Mid America, Northeast and Southeast. There are stellar contributors to sections for entomology (Al Caucci), techniques (Jason Borger), and saltwater (Dan Blanton). A fishing reports section (under Regional Articles in the top navigation) has records for each region from 1996 to 2000. Despite being out of date, they still contain solid information about hatches and hotspots through the seasons—

NEWSPAPERS

Many newspapers have sports sections with at least some fishing coverage. The best of them are great sources for weekly catch reports and staying up-to-date on the local fishing scene. Chapter 2 State-by-State Resources spotlights several examples from around the country, but to check all the papers in your state try a newspaper directory such as **Newspapers.com** at **http://www.newspapers.com** or

News Voyager.com at **http://www.newspaperlinks.com/voyager.cfm**, which link to all the major regional newspapers in the U.S. To mine for fishing information, go to the sports section in each paper and look for the heading Outdoors or Other Sports.

It isn't as comprehensive, but **SportsPages.com** at **http://www.sportspages.com** takes you directly to the sports pages of all the major U.S. newspapers.

a good reference for future trips. A comprehensive Buyer's Guide to rods, reels, lines and accessories is available as a downloadable PDF.

Fly Fisherman
http://www.flyfisherman.com

TOP RATED

The biggest fly-fishing magazine in the country has one of the oldest and best online editions. Exceptional regional coverage divides the country into 11 areas and includes reliable, well-regarded fishing reports and forums, as well as business listings and how-to articles. Other notable features include regularly hosted chat rooms, classifieds and an auction for bidding on second-hand tackle.

Fly Fishing and Fly Tying
http://www.flyfishing-and-flytying.co.uk

The pleasing online edition of a U.K. magazine sometimes sold on U.S. newsstands. Absorbing technique, tying and travel articles are regularly pinched from the pages of old issues and posted to the site. They're kept company by recent news stories and catch reports from the major English trout fishing reservoirs.

Fly Fishing in Saltwaters
http://www.flyfishinsalt.com

TOP RATED

Great photography and design make this one of the "glossiest" fishing sites on the Web. Lengthy articles cover travel, techniques and gear. Fishing Hall of Famer Lefty Krey is on site to answer readers' questions.

Fly Fisherman
http://www.flyfisherman.com

TOP RATED

Fly Rod & Reel
http://www.flyrodandreel.com

Fly Rod & Reel
http://www.flyrodandreel.com

TOP RATED

Apart from contributions by Ted Williams and A.K. Best, *Fly Rod & Reel* takes the welcome approach of using its site to publish original material that can't be fitted into the magazine. So you'll find, for example, stories from runners-up in its annual Robert Traver Fly-Fishing Fiction Award, and the daily progress of teams in its TroutBum Tournament, which challenges six teams to get the most troutbum road trip fishing fun out of $500. There are plenty of other diversions here including trivia questions, a wide-ranging Q & A and a popular, friendly forum.

FlyLife OnLine
http://www.flylife.com.au

TOP RATED

This Australian and New Zealand fly-fishing magazine has stylishly laid out pages, quality photographs and a good range of content. Go to FlyLife Magazine and then click on the FlyLife Library to read more than 30 articles. Contact other Aussie and Kiwi fly fishers by using the forum or Fly Club Directory, or investigate lodges in both countries within the Travel Directory.

Game & Fish Magazines
http://www.gameandfish.
about.com

Game & Fish magazines are published in 30 regional editions. With some of the magazines covering two states, they effectively report on fishing and hunting opportunities in

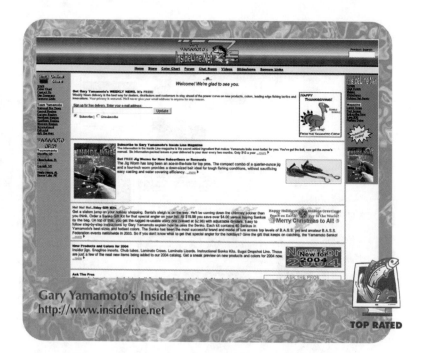

Gary Yamamoto's Inside Line
http://www.insideline.net

TOP RATED

every part of the country once a month. And that mass of timely information is then funneled into a huge central fishing and hunting site on the About network.

Search by region or individual state for the latest technique articles, season forecasts and destination features. Or, if you're just looking for general fishing articles, go to the technique and species headings in the lefthand navigation. There's a designated area for fly fishing, but the magazines are targeted to a more general fishing audience, with some of the best coverage you'll find for bait and lure fishing for trout, steelhead, salmon, inland stripers, catfish, crappie and panfish. Sections for ice fishing and saltwater fishing make it a complete fishing resource.

Gary Yamamoto's Inside Line

http://www.insideline.net

TOP RATED

Gary Yamamoto is best known as a lure designer, but he also publishes a bass magazine, *The Inside Line*. Full of techniques articles, the online edition will even send you weekly bass tips via e-mail. There's a popular bass forum and, as you'd expect, a link to the company's lure offerings. Some of the color choices are web site specials, not available anywhere else.

Gray's Sporting Journal
http://www.grayssporting
journal.com

Gray's has an elegant site that mirrors the look of its literary fishing and hunting magazine. Editorial content is a little sparse, but there are good lodge and guide resources for the traveling angler. See also **Sporting Classics** at **http://www.sportingclassics.net**.

Great Lakes Angler
http://www.glangler.com

TOP RATED

From the homepage of this forum-based site, go to Ask a Pro for a giant (800+) archive of questions and answers about all aspects of fishing and boating the Great Lakes for salmon and walleye. Check other forums for swap meets and general fishing talk or use trip-planning features

such as weather links, lake temperature information and tournament listings.

Harold Wells' Gulf Coast Fisherman
http://www.gulffishing.com

Devoted to nearshore and offshore fishing in the Gulf of Mexico, Harold's web magazine has a catalog of tips and articles from previous issues and plenty of links to Gulf Coast weather, tides, regulations and waypoints.

In-Fisherman
http://www.in-fisherman.com

TOP RATED

In-Fisherman publishes Web Exclusives they weren't able to fit into the street editions of their bass, walleye, catfish and multi-species magazines. Other regular content comes from

In-Fisherman
http://www.in-fisherman.com
TOP RATED

four monthly columns—Ask the Electronics Doc, Ask the Motor Doc, Ask the Science Doc and Ask the Editors. The section "In-Fishermen TV Staff Tested Tough Stuff" recommends products from battery chargers to tackle storage systems. Links in the lefthand navigation lead to the Professional Walleye Trail and schedules for In-Fishermen TV and radio broadcasts.

Marlin
http://www.marlinmag.com

TOP RATED

Lots of features and reviews about the stuff that matters to big-game anglers, including an identification page for each of the seven types of billfish.

They offer some inspiring marlin photography to download as wallpaper or screensavers, and intriguing details about "Marlin University." Like all the best schools, it offers "small class sizes" and "course materials," but unlike your typical State U., students graduate from the bluewater of Costa Rica, the U.S. Virgin Islands or Venezuela.

Musky Hunter
http://www.muskyhunter.com

TOP RATED

Musky anglers are known for their dedication and attention to anything that gives them an edge. They should check out The Ultimate Fishing Log at musky hunter.com. It's a database of 500 catches from popular muskie waters and logs tackle, tactics, weather and water conditions. Anyone with something to report can contribute. Other features on the site include The Classics, which archives important past articles from the magazine, and a directory to muskie businesses, clubs and organizations.

North American Fisherman
http://www.fishingclub.com

TOP RATED

You have to take out a subscription to the magazine to enter this popular freshwater fishing site (subscribe from the landing page). They've made several efforts to bring the magazine's club members together including Trade a Trip where you can advertise for fishing partners or offer trip swaps, free classifieds for selling secondhand tackle, general forums and discounts from guides and businesses. Features on the

Outdoor Canada
http://www.outdoorcanada.ca

horizon include a catch database, personal web pages hosted by the site and daily Q & A's with the club's resident experts.

Outdoor Canada
http://www.outdoorcanada.ca

TOP RATED

Canada's largest outdoor magazine has been very successfully transplanted to the Web. Take advantage of tools such as the Fishing Chart, which mixes sun, moon and tide data to pinpoint the best fishing times in each of five regions—Pacific, Mountain, Central, Eastern and Atlantic—or the Regulations section, which has updated rules for each of the 13 provinces. There's enough editorial material covering fly fishing, freshwater and saltwater fishing to put the brakes on the most degenerate web surfer.

Outdoor Life
http://www.outdoorlife.com

TOP RATED

Outdoor Life comes from the same company that publishes *Field & Stream* and its web site shares some of the same functions and design, but editorial content (articles, views and reviews) are distinct. Mouse over the fishing link on the homepage, then decide between Bass, Trout, Panfish, Pike/Walleye/Muskie or articles from Jerry Gibbs, the magazine's fishing editor. You'll also find regional fishing reports, Maori Fishing Charts, and truck, RV and boat reviews.

Black's Sporting Directories publish an annual business directory for the fly-fishing industry, and visitors to either the *Field & Stream* or *Outdoor Life* web sites can view a complete online edition by going to the *Black's Sporting Directory* link at the bottom of each homepage. Divided into Instruction, Equipment and Destinations, it lists more than 2,000 businesses within its subcategories and state-by-state listings. It's a couple of years old and none of the companies are hyperlinked, but running names through any search engine will soon correct stale information.

Salt Water Sportsman (SWS)
http://www.saltwater
sportsman.com

Salt Water Sportsman online has all the features you'd hope to find in a major fishing magazine. **TOP RATED** There are destination articles, boat and tackle reviews, a weather and tide center and illustrated Fish Files for life cycle information. Bob Stearns' Ultimate

Guide to Fish Temperature Preferences, naming the optimum temperatures for dozens of game-fish, and a search function that also delves into the archives of the magazines *Yachting* and *Motor Boating*, are nice bonuses.

Sport Fishing
http://www.sportfishingmag.com

This national saltwater publication has success-fully cloned itself into one of the best saltwater **TOP RATED** fishing magazines on the Web. There's a special emphasis on U.S. and international destinations, including dozens of articles within four Hot Spots categories, lists of guides and charter boats and an accommodation directory. Gear guides, a newswire for conserva-tion updates, plenty of boating and electronics coverage and an exceptionally thorough links sec-tion could trap you here for hours.

Sport Fishing
http://www.sportfishingmag.com

TOP RATED

Online Magazines

Online magazine publishers range from corporations with millions of dollars to play with, to one man, a modem and a lot of enthusiasm. One of the great things about the Web, of course, is there are no guarantees the first is going to come up with a better site or stick around any longer than the second. These sites are grouped together because they don't concentrate on a single species or region but adopt a more general magazine format.

Big Fish Tackle
http://www.bigfishtackle.com

TOP RATED

Big Fish Tackle
http://www.bigfishtackle.com

TOP RATED

Using the huge inventory of Bass Pro Shops, Big Fish Tackle qualifies as one of the biggest tackle-stores on the Web. But they earn a recommendation here because of the site's magazine section and reader resources, rather than the siren song they aim at your Mastercard. The Fish Species Identifier, culled from the book *Sport Fish of Florida* by Vic Dunaway (with West Coast content by George Van Zant) gives a snapshot of the major freshwater and saltwater species found in North America. Articles are divided into freshwater and saltwater fishing, and there's a special section about getting the most from baits and scents. Go to Big Fish Fun on the homepage for light relief.

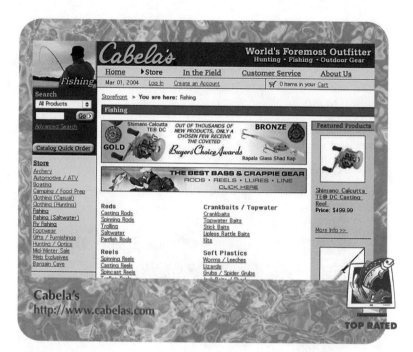

Cabela's
http://www.cabelas.com

TOP RATED

Cabela's
http://www.cabelas.com

TOP RATED

Cabela's is about more than those alluring catalogs: they have a newsstand magazine called *Cabela's Outfitter Journal*, a TV show (find show description and schedules on the site), and a fully featured online magazine. Go to In the Field then search Field Guides for a long list of fishing articles and excellent regional resources. Under General Outdoors you'll find a companion set of articles about cooking, camping, truck accessories, GPS, staying safe outdoors and other topics of interest to the avid fisher-outdoorsman. They also have the odd bit of gear for sale.

Browse around the hundreds of product categories and you'll see they've invested heavily in making the site easy to shop from and packed full of temptation.

Discover the Outdoors
http://www.discoverthe outdoors.com

TOP RATED

You need a recent browser to get the most from this frequently updated outdoor magazine. It repays that small effort with an attractive fishing section featuring news, tips and advice, and special areas for women in the outdoors, camping and cookery. Clips from the show Heartland Adventures are quick-loading and unusually watchable for Internet video.

ESPN Outdoors
http://espn.go.com/outdoors

TOP RATED

You might not guess it from looking at ESPN's homepage full of the latest goings on in the NBA, NFL and MLB, but a bright, fully featured magazine hides behind the diminutive "outdoors" link in the lefthand navigation. Divided into areas for general fishing, fly fishing, hunting, conservation and television listings, this media giant really seems to have done their fishing homework: you'll find expert fly-fishing articles from the editors at *American Angler* and *Saltwater Fly Fishing*, and regional freshwater coverage from the *Fishing & Hunting News* group. Columnists such as Keith Sutton and Curt Gowdry and other professional journalists provide regular feature articles and news stories.

The ESPN homepage also links to **BASS** at **http://www.bassmaster. com**. See Chapter 4 Fishing the Web, Best Bass Fishing Sites for a review.

Fishing-Boating Online
http://www.fishing-boating.com

Fishing-Boating Online doesn't sound too cosmopolitan, but it's one of the few sites to have an international edge. On review day there were news stories and fishing articles from the U.S., Australia, Britain, Italy, Holland and Indonesia, plus links to web sites around the world.

Fishing-Hunting.com
http://www.fishing-hunting.com

Patriotic colors define the look of this outdoor magazine. Content is split between bass tournament news and technique articles,

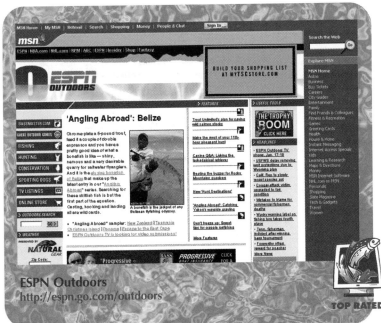

ESPN Outdoors
http://espn.go.com/outdoors

TOP RATED

fly fishing and saltwater fishing, and the site invites readers to have a go at contributing features. Some scattered reports and links to state fish and wildlife departments make up the rest.

FishWithUs.net

http://www.fishwithus.net/ home.html

This multimedia site goes in so many directions it takes a minute to figure out its focus. And that would be freshwater and saltwater fishing in the Northwest. Go to Articles on the homepage for a complete list of features, most of which are about salmon, steelhead and Alaska. Or, if you have a high-speed Internet connection, choose from 60 hours of fishing video footage on FishWithUs TV. When your bloodshot eyes can take no more, use the RealPlayer down-

load to listen to segments from Northwest fishing radio shows.

GORP

http://www.gorp.com

TOP RATED

Presided over by Mark D. Williams, the fly-fishing pages of this huge outdoor recreation site court the beginner with articles, resources, instructional video clips, an Orvis shop and active forums. GORP wants to get you outside and there are extended travel guides to state parks, scenic drives, rivers, lakes and shores. Don't forget to browse the other activity channels. The section on bird and wildlife watching, for example, could be very useful. Being able to say, "Oh Margaret, you should have seen these mottled warblers," sounds so much more convincing than "it's just

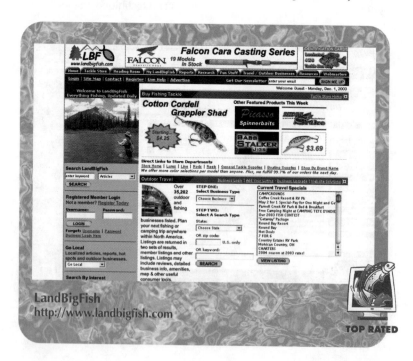

LandBigFish
http://www.landbigfish.com

TOP RATED

good to be on the water" the next time you get skunked. Look for fishing within the Activities directory on the homepage.

LandBigFish
http://www.landbigfish.com

TOP RATED If you're impressed by big numbers as well as by big fish, LandBigFish claims more than 1,200 fishing articles (includes news stories and reviews), and a business directory that has 30,000 listings within categories for guides, lodges, retail shops, fishing clubs and campgrounds. Go to Resources then State Pages to find a table of license requirements and regulations for all 50 states, or to Interactive for a free fishing log.

The site has recently begun to charge a subscription for full access to its features, but there's more than enough free content to warrant a bookmark.

Louis Bignami's Fine Fishing
http://www.finefishing.com

TOP RATED Louis maintains this valuable e-zine for seemingly no other reason than the pleasure of being its publisher. There are no advertisements and nothing for sale other than some unobtrusively listed flies. Instead you'll find hundreds of diverse articles written and photographed by top angling journalists (the Fine Fishing team is responsible for a scary 500 books in print at last count). Click on the Professional Authors link on the homepage to read their biographies or go straight to the lefthand topic lists within each section.

Fine Fishing has a dedicated travel section with more than 200 fishing and general travel articles: Louis promises you won't find "puffs for overrated operators or the mundane." I believe him.

ANTIS
Anti-fishing groups are propagandists, skilled at using the media to exaggerate their popularity and influence. Keep an eye on the opposition at:

People for the Ethical Treatment of Animals (PETA)
http://www.peta.org
PETA clearly recognizes the power of the Web to disseminate information: they publish more than 20 sites in support of their anti-vivisection, anti-fur, anti-circus, anti-meat, anti-aquaculture, pro-Vegan agenda. And they don't much care for fishing or hunting, believe it or not. The central PETA site lays it all out within campaign overviews and action alerts on everything from demanding justice for pond ducks in Florida to getting the Girl Scouts to lay off killing and torturing small animals.

Fishing Hurts.com
http://www.nofishing.net
This is PETA's dedicated anti-fishing page, and it's aimed at children if the pastel colors and fun activity feel are any indication. There are headings and information about Commercial Fishing, Sport Fishing, What You Can Do, Kids' Corner and "Ask the Boy Scouts to De-Merit Fishing." A section called Campaign History gives a good sense of their media and marketing savvy.

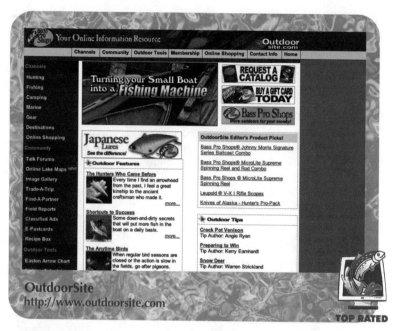

OutdoorSite
http://www.outdoorsite.com

TOP RATED

OutdoorSite
http://www.outdoorsite.com

TOP RATED

The calm, spacious layout of OutdoorSite houses channels for hunting, fishing, camping, marine and gear (and they're well endowed gear-wise thanks to site parents Bass Pro Shops). The fishing section is divided into half

a dozen categories and includes tips from some such luminaries as Kevin VanDam, Jay Yelas and Woo Davis within the bass department. State-by-state listings for trip trades and finding fishing and hunting partners were popular enough to be a real service in several of the more outdoorsy states. Thousands of people regularly stop by for a chat in the forums.

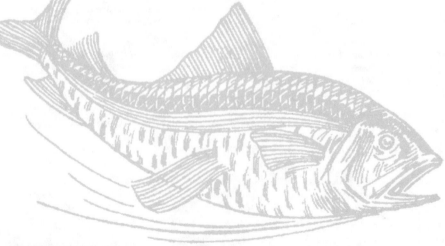

Outdoors Network
http://www.outdoors.net

The Outdoors Network oversees three fishing sites with an "all" prefix: **http://www.allfishing.com**, **http://www.allflyfishing.com**, and **http://www.allbass.com**. From the homepage, choose your preferred site for articles, forums and breaking news. Registering once provides access to every forum on the network.

The Sportsman's Guide
http://www.sportsmansguide.com

TOP RATED

One of the biggest mail-order sellers of fishing, hunting and outdoor gear has a well-rounded online magazine. Scroll past the Amazing and Brand New Deals! to find Your Guide to the Great Outdoors.

A lot is squeezed in here. There's a group of essential resource links to weather sites, maps, road condition updates and fish and wildlife departments. Click on Fishing under Articles and Tips to open a directory of all the editorial content on the site. Fishing coverage is divided into largemouth bass, smallmouth bass, walleye, northern pike/muskie, panfish, saltwater and freshwater fly fishing, and each category is in turn split into Adventures, Gear and Tips. Adventures consists of longer articles and destination pieces; Gear has new product descriptions; Tips are short technique explanations and skill builders. A link on the homepage titled Understanding Fish and Game opens a multipart guide to learning the life cycle, habits and biology of the most popular freshwater species. All the better to catch them with.

FishingWorld.com
http://www.fishingworld.com

TOP RATED

Like a wire service for the whole sport, this site gathers news stories about tournaments, the tackle industry, fishery science and conservation, notable catches and any other event likely to interest U.S. fishermen. Search the archives for thousands of past reports and full-length, illustrated articles.

THE WRITING LIFE
Outdoor Writers Association of America
http://www.owaa.com

For a logical starting point to a career in outdoor writing, go to the web site of this professional development group for outdoor communicators. You have to have published a handful of articles to qualify for membership, but it's well worth joining if you qualify. From the site you can learn the history of the group, how to join and ways that membership will further your career. For members, there's a job market, industry and club news and details about competitions and grants. Download an application from a link on the homepage.

Directories

One of the quickest routes to fishing information on the Web is through online directories. Some of these are by-products of search engines such as Google or Yahoo! and some are dedicated fishing directories such as FishingWorks or FishHoo! Both types sort and display thousands of links to fishing web sites all over the world under subject headings.

Directories which act like online yellow pages and offer free listings to anyone who registers are good places to find companies and products, and often provide articles and resources on the homepage. Search engines and other "human-picked" directories are more likely to list content-led web sites.

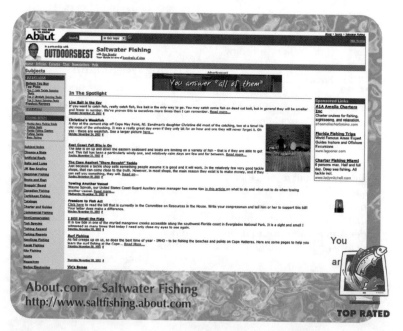

About.com – Saltwater Fishing
http://www.saltfishing.about.com

TOP RATED

About.com

Fly Fisherman
http://www.flyfisherman.com

Freshwater Fishing
http://www.fishing.about.com

Saltwater Fishing
http://www.saltfishing.about.com

Game & Fish Magazines
http://www.gameandfish.
about.com

TOP RATED

This super-sized directory calls itself "the human Internet," the humans being the 700 subject matter guides who personally recommend web sites in each category. Fishing is divided into Freshwater and Saltwater, and is made up of hundreds of organized links, briefly introduced by the subject guide. The About.com guides (Ronnie Garrison for freshwater and Ron Brooks for saltwater) offer their recommendations in a conversational style and occasionally refer to their own fishing adventures, making it a much more personal experience than browsing most directories.

About.com also hosts the web sites for *Fly Fisherman* and *Game & Fish* magazines. Both are highly recommended for content and strong regional reporting.

FishHoo!
http://www.fishhoo.com

FishHoo! lists 4,000 fishing sites. Most are retailers and other businesses, but there are plenty of noncommercial links here too. Everything is organized into clear categories—see the radio, television and software entries for more links within the world of fishing media. You can vote for your favorite site within the directory, and they publish lists of the most popular sites on a regular basis.

100 Top Fishing Sites
http://www.hitsunlimited.com

TOP RATED

100 Top Fishing Sites is a neatly presented ranking, 25 per page, according to which of the registered web sites gets the most individual visitors on a daily basis. There are hit lists for the most popular sites to do

---

SPECIALIST DIRECTORIES

Several sites offer link directories concentrating on a single branch of the sport. For bass fishing try **Bassdozer** at **http://www.bass dozer.com** (also good for striped bass), **ProBass** at **http://www.pro bass.com,** and **The Ultimate Bass Fishing Resource Guide** at **http:// www.bassresource.com. The Sportsman's Resource** at **http:// www.sportsmansresource.com** and **Mr River** at **http://www.mrriver.com** offer well-organized state-by-state listings. **Mel's Place** at **http://www. mels-place.com** lists 2,900 saltwater fishing sites in multiple categories.

There are at least 10 fly-fishing-only link directories, but many of them haven't been updated for years. The following four are all worth bookmarking. **Len Gorney's Fishing Links Notebook** at **http:// www. kings.edu/lsgorney/fishing.**

htm has more than 2,500 links, mostly about fly fishing for trout. **The Global Fly Fishing Links Directory** at **http://www.davis brown.com/ffindex.htm** uses pull-down menus and lists sites alphabetically, by category and by country. **Start4all** at **http://flyfish. start4all.com** is a Dutch directory with an exceptional European and U.S. fly-fishing section.

Another foreigner, this one an all-topics directory from Belgium, gets my vote for best fly-fishing directory on the Web. **Cbel – Fly Fishing TOP RATED** at **http://www.cbel. com/fly_fishing** puts 1,100 hand-picked, categorized links on a single page, offers keyword searches, uses asterisks to indicate new sites and is regularly raked over to find dead links. Despite its parentage, the listings are dominated by sites from the U.S.

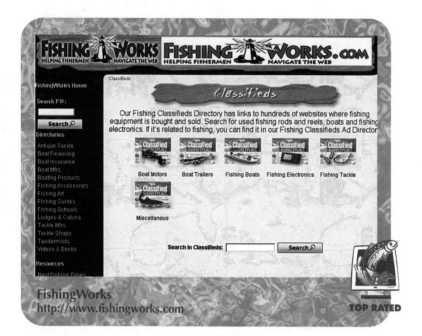

FishingWorks
http://www.fishingworks.com

with bass, bait, boats, captains, catfish, fly fishing, hunting, resorts, saltwater and walleye.

FishingWorks
http://www.fishingworks.com

TOP RATED

FishingWorks is brightly designed and organized into channels for every fishing product and service imaginable, among more than 35,000 listings. But you could spend hours here without even looking at the commercial sites. Among many helpful features are large service directories of weather web sites, conservation groups, recipes and kids' fishing resources.

Google – Directory
http://www.google.com

TOP RATED

It's likely Google's creators didn't have fishing in mind when they gave it life, but it's nonetheless the fisherman's friend on the Internet. It uses a multi-tiered page ranking system to zero in on the most likely sites, sifting billions of web pages in seconds and very often nailing exactly what you're looking for within the first couple of entries. Google has greatly simplified access to Usenet discussion groups (Google Groups), and among many specialized search options, allows you to hunt for images, news stories or only the freshest web content. The fishing directory (go to Directory then Recreation then Outdoors then Fishing) lists and describes 3,500 fishing sites in multiple categories, and is regularly scoured for dead links.

Google lends its services to the **Open Directory Project** (ODP) at **http://www.dmoz.org**, which is a noncommercial effort to build the best and largest subject directory on the Web. It has 3,200 sites within its fishing directory, and each entry displays with extra links to popular search engines and biology web sites.

Fishing World Network
http://www.fishing-world.net

The Fishing World Network is home to the International Fishing Ring, which is a group of hundreds of web sites linked by a common banner. Click on the banner, which is always at the bottom of web sites in the ring, and you're taken to other sites in the community. You can also search for sites from the ring homepage.

Yahoo! – Directory
http://www.yahoo.com

Yahoo! hasn't ignored fishermen in their quest to be "the hottest guide to everything on the web." Go to the Web Site Directory on the homepage and click on Outdoors to bring up hundreds of links searchable by region, by subject, alphabetically or by popularity.

See Chapter 6 Groups for a description of Yahoo!-hosted fishing groups.

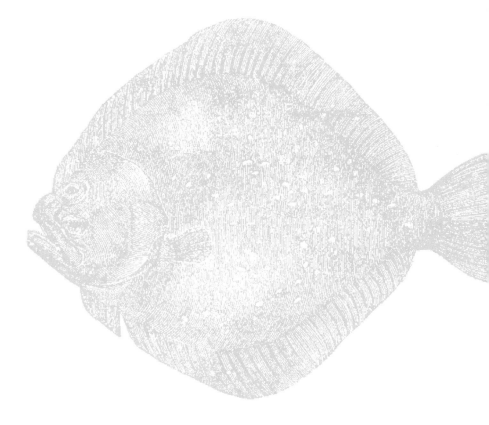

Bookstores

Is there a more literary sport than fishing? Baseball and golf have some great essayists and metaphorical novelists, but they don't come close to fishing if you consider the whole backlist from Walton in the 17th century to people like John Gierach and Nick Lyons writing today. You can find rare, used, out-of-print, or just plain new books on every conceivable aspect of fishing at these bookstores and publishers' web sites. All offer online ordering.

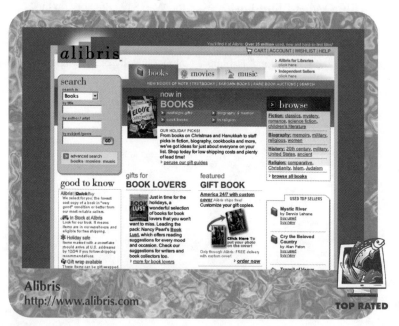

Alibris
http://www.alibris.com

Alibris
http://www.alibris.com

TOP RATED

The company's slogan is "Books You Thought You'd Never Find," and for once it isn't just marketing babble. Alibris gathers and presents the inventories of hundreds of independent booksellers to help you locate out-of-print and otherwise difficult-to-find titles. A quick and accurate search returns more than 500 titles about bass; the same number for

fly fishing and saltwater fishing. A tremendous resource for fishing bibliophiles.

See also
http://www.abebooks.com.

Amazon.com
http://www.amazon.com

TOP RATED

If you want to buy a fishing book, video or computer game or if you just want to find out what's available,

Amazon.com leads the way. Renowned for its customer service and intuitive recommendations, the best feature of the site lets customers post a review online and rate the product based on five stars. The site is searchable every which way, but going to Outdoors & Nature within Books, then Hunting & Fishing will bring up a page of top sellers, plus a list of about-to-be published titles that always contains something to look forward to. You can then browse the fishing book list (4,000 titles about recreational fishing) or hop on over to fishing videos (more than 500) or fishing software (48 on review day). Like a giant time-vacuum for anyone who likes armchair angling.

Barnes & Noble at **http://www.barnesandnoble.com** works from the same inventory: to be competitive they often have matching promotions such as discounts and free shipping.

The Angler's Art
http://www.anglersart.com

The Angler's Art specializes in newer fly-fishing books and videos. They have a basic catalog site that can be searched by topic, keyword, title and author. Deep discounts on select items.

Books of the Black Bass
http://www.hometown.aol.com/bassbks

TOP RATED

As angling writer John Merwin has pointed out: "general fishing books are outnumbered by flyfishing books (mostly about trout) by almost 10 to 1 even though more people fish for bass. By this you may infer that fly-fishermen are either supremely literate or compulsively verbose, depending on your point of view."

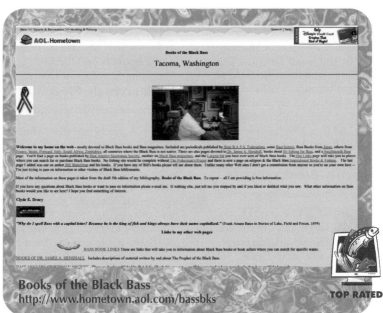

Books of the Black Bass
http://www.hometown.aol.com/bassbks

TOP RATED

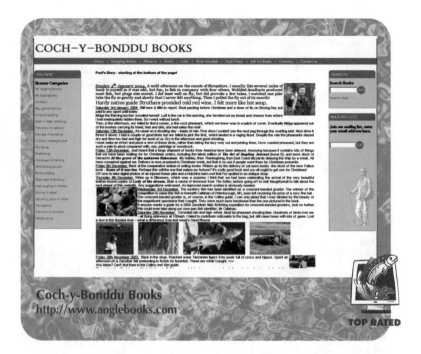

Coch-y-Bonddu Books
http://www.anglebooks.com

TOP RATED

One man determined to reclaim a bit of literariness (or the other) for bass anglers is Clyde Day, creator of Books of the Black Bass. This site describes nearly everything published about bass since 1800, including bass tomes from Japan, Spain and South America. There are links to magazines and bass fishing organizations, and a long essay about the life and times of James A. Henshall. As Clyde says, the site is a tonic for "victims of Black Bass Bibliomania."

Coch-y-Bonddu Books
http://www.anglebooks.com

TOP RATED

Based in the U.K., Paul Morgan's Coch-Y-Bonddu Books offers a huge selection of rare, used and genuinely discounted European and U.S. fishing titles. Choose from eight fishing cate-

gories and as many again for hunting, or search for individual titles by keyword, author or ISBN. The staff is quick to respond with prices and shipping costs in dollars and they provide a currency converter. Gets my vote for best fishing bookstore on the Web.

The Derrydale Press
http://www.derrydalepress.com

The Derrydale Press offers a brief but fine selection of fly-fishing and saltwater game fishing books: some are reissues of out-of-print classics, some are titles from other fishing publishers and some are new and original works. It's a handsome, functional site that also lists books about hunting, food and wine and other diversions popular with outdoor folks.

Fishing Online
http://www.pvisuals.com/
fishing/online/main.html

Amazon.com is such the 800 lb.
gorilla of online book selling, that
most of the bookstores attached to
fishing web sites are simply affiliates of the company (click on a
book and you're taken directly to
the mother site). Fishing Online is
an affiliate site, but they do a better than average job of organizing
and presenting the books. They
offer fly-fishing titles and a good
selection of freshwater books
about bass, catfish, walleye and
other species. Each is given a
page-long description and illustrated with large color photographs
from the book.

The Flyfisher's
Classic Library
http://www.ffcl.com

The Flyfisher's Classic Library has
a smoothly operating site that
offers over 70 reprints of classic
works, stretching back to Izaak
Walton. These are collector's
works: leather bound, gilt-edged,
limited editions. It's an English
company, but they obviously have
an eye to the American market
because they display prices in
dollars and claim four-to-seven
days for transatlantic delivery.

Frank Amato Publications
http://www.amatobooks.com

The online catalog of a prolific
Northwest fishing publisher known
for its heavily illustrated guides
and fly-fishing technique books.
Click on the title of each book
to see a brief description of the
contents. Amato is the home of

the River Journal series (see the Great Rivers link at **http://www.fly anglersonline.com** to get a much better look at these volumes), and a very good range of fly-tying books. They are also one of the few companies to offer books about bait and lure fishing for trout, steelhead and salmon. Amato publishes two fishing magazines, *Flyfishing & Tying Journal* and *Salmon Trout Steelheader,* both of which you can subscribe to from the landing page.

Globe Pequot Press/ The Lyons Press
http://www.globepequot.com

Now an imprint of the general outdoor publisher Globe Pequot Press, The Lyons Press is the leading publisher of fly-fishing titles in the U.S. Mouse over Outdoor Life in the top navigation and choose Fishing from the menu to view hundreds of titles divided into species, locations, tips and techniques, cookbooks and literature.

Meadow Run Press
http://www.meadowrunpress.com

If unusual, lovingly produced fishing books are your thing, take a minute to look at Meadow Run Press' small but tempting web site. Not too many fishing publishers, after all, are going to take a chance on a book described as

"an erotic, fantastic tale of a young woman's first encounter with Atlantic salmon." See also **The Medlar Press** at **http://www. medlar.uk.com.**

Milne Angling Collection
http://www.izaak.unh.edu/milne

To remind yourself of the breadth of fishing literature, and specifically the richness of the American fly-fishing canon, browse the list of 2,000 titles held within the Milne Angling Collection at the University of New Hampshire. The Angling Books and Periodicals link within the fly-fishing resources section has lists of fishing publishers, book dealers and magazines.

Wilderness Adventures Sporting Books
http://www.wildadv.com

TOP RATED

A meaty publisher's bookstore for fly fishing, hunting, cookery and outdoor adventure titles. Fly fishing is divided into 16 categories from introductory to fireside reading and collecting. Some of the books are signed and it's possible to post online reviews, though few people had taken advantage of it. The company is best known for its series of regional fly-fishing guides, and you can look at the complete state-by-state list in its own section of the site.

Television

Oh son, there's some good and there's some bad. The best are beautifully filmed and carefully written: passports to dream venues around the world, or the best kind of teaching distilled from years of experience. The worst are a good deal less entertaining than late night infomercials, or Jay Leno. These sites promote individual shows and whole networks, where you'll find information about the company's complete outdoor programming.

Addictive Fishing
http://www.addictivefishing.com

Addictive Fishing
http://www.addictivefishing.com

For some good use of streaming fishing video, have a look at the web site of this pumped-up Florida sportfishing show. There are clips from many of the episodes and video tips just for site visitors. A poster board full of viewer's catch shots and a forum for comments about the show round it out.

Bill Dance Outdoors
http://www.billdanceoutdoors.com

One of the country's most recognizable bass fishermen through his long-running show and tournament career, the man in the Tennessee hat has his own presence on the Web. Visitors will find brief details about future shows, a few fishing tips and a bibliography. A link to his recently launched magazine at **http://www.billdancefishing.com** extends the content with a Q&A page and popular forum.

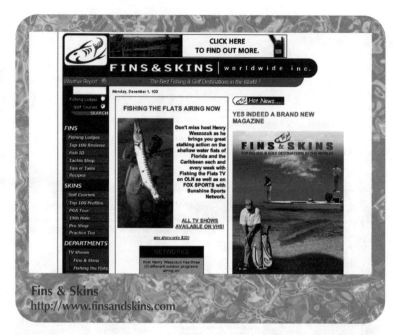

Fins & Skins
http://www.finsandskins.com

Fins & Skins
http://www.finsandskins.com

Not fishing and hunting, but fishing and golf. This slick-looking site is built on the back of a television show called Fins & Skins Classic Adventures, hosted by Henry Waszczuk and shown on the Outdoor Life Network and the Sunshine Network (a Florida sports channel). The premise is to highlight the best destinations in the U.S. and abroad for a fishing and golf combo.

Mark Sosin's Saltwater Journal
http://www.marksosin.com

This long-running show has the standard information set on its web site—details about the presenter and the forthcoming season, a few words of wisdom from the

man—but one handy feature is a contact link for every guide and lodge he fishes with. If you like what see on Saturday morning, a reservation is only a few clicks away. There's also a great portfolio of saltwater fishing scenes to download.

Outdoor Life Network (OLN)
http://www.olntv.com

OLN covers the range of outdoor sports, including some good fishing programming. Click on Field and Stream in the top navigation to get listings for In-Fisherman, The Best of Bill Dance, Fly-Fish Television, Gray's Sporting Journal, and several others. Like an electronic shout down to the basement, if you register they'll send you an e-mail reminder when your favorite show is coming on.

The Outdoor Channel
http://www.outdoorchannel.com

Click on TV Show Information, then the Fishing tab in the top navigation to list shows just about fishing. Scroll down the list to access pages about each show, including schedules, e-mail addresses and a web site link. Under Outdoor Forums on the homepage are several areas for viewer comments.

ESPN at **http://espn.go.com/ outdoors** is the only other cable net work signifigant outdoor programming. See the Online Magazines section of this chapter for a review.

Fishing with Shelly and Courtney
http://www.tvfishing.com

This is an established show covering British Columbia and the Northwest hosted by the affable team of Shelly Todd and Courtney Hatfield. The format is usually fishing—cooking—a bit more fishing—lodge details, and that's about what you get from the web site, with recipes, lodge profiles and descriptions of upcoming shows. One feature worth lingering over is the Top Rod fishing web site awards found within Contests in the top navigation.

Trout Unlimited (TU) TV
www.tutv.org

Hosted by Montana fly-fishing guide Tim Linehan, Trout Unlimited Television mixes fishing travelogue and conservation reports. The site includes trip-planning information for each river featured on the show so you can plan your own excursion. TU's informal motto is "if we take care of the fish, then the fishing will take care of itself." But they want to start you off right: newcomers can get most of what they need from the detailed beginner's section also posted here. It's taken from Tom Meade's book *Essential Fly Fishing*, and covers Casting, Catch and Release, Presenting the Fly, Safe Wading, Trout Behavior, What Trout Eat, Reading the Water and Getting the Right Stuff.

VIDEOS

Fly Fishing Videos
http://www.flyfishing videos.com
The Fly Fishing Videos site run by and starring Jim and Kelly Watt sells 170 destination, technique and fly-tying videos. You can see the high quality of the films they make by watching their Fly Fishing Video Magazine on the Outdoor Life Network.

Bennett Marine – Fishing Videos
http://www.bennett marine.com
Bennett Marine offers a good selection of mostly saltwater fishing titles listed by species from albacore to yellowtail. While at the site, browse the boating video section for titles on maintenance, knots and rope work, GPS and navigation.

The best series of videos for freshwater anglers comes the team at *In-Fisherman* magazine, **http://www.in-fisherman.com**.

Walker's Cay Chronicles
http://www.walkerscay.tv

Flip Pallot's Walker's Cay Chronicles is consistently one of the best fishing shows on television. The site has biographical information about the host, an up-to-date show schedule, and video clip downloads from every episode for the past nine seasons. There are videos and a book for sale, or you can send an e-mail postcard with a Walker's Cay scene on it for nothing.

Software

Computer fishing games have become so sophisticated and realistic that even the most hardcore fishermen have been known to hunch down over a console—big, wind-chapped fingers gripping the little joystick. Plus, if you can stop yourself cursing or punching the air, you could probably sneak a game or two while you're at work. These sites also link to software for real fishing situations such as reading maps, keeping a log or organizing a tournament.

Angler's Assistant
http://home.flash.net/~tvandy

This free program was developed by Tim Vanderwater and is available to anyone with Windows 95 or later. It was specifically designed for lake fisherman and provides a detailed log for catch information, weather conditions, lure data, topographical map references and other records.

Bassdozer
http://www.bassdozer.com/ bass_software.shtml

CyberAngler
http://www.cyberangler.com/ marketplace/software

These two sites have hunted the Web for links to fishing software and games. Bassdozer's dedicated page lists nearly 40 bassy programs and games. CyberAngler recommends 10 software programs useful for fishermen, such as elec-tronic logs for boat maintenance and catch statistics. They also provide a link to **ZDNet** at **http://www.zdnet.com.** Go to Downloads on the homepage and put "fishing" in the search box to find game demos and shareware.

Knots and Fishing Knots
http://www.members.aol.com/ idfrank/knots.html

An e-commerce site offering animated knot-tying software. The program has controls that let you stop, go back and review a step, and front and back views of the finished knot (34 fishing knots and 37 general purpose). For free knot-tying information see the Knots and Rigs sidebar in Chapter 4 Fishing the Web.

The SuperFly Fishing Machine
http://www.ofifc.org/eli/superfly

The SuperFly Fishing Machine
http://www.ofifc.org/eli/superfly

This hatch and fly pattern database was designed by Eli Robillard and is yours for the price of sending the inventor three home-tied flies—which looks like a serious bargain. Detailed anatomy and tying pages have buttons beside each heading to jump you to other sections of the site for more information.

Among other features, the program has a notebook and fishing log so you can add your own material to the database, and a section for cataloging your fishing library. The homepage has clear instructions for downloading the program.

UglyBass.com
http://www.uglybass.com/software.htm

UglyBass.com offers two free software programs. One is described as a "Windows based game that plays somewhat like Defender, with a fishing twist. Good for MINUTES of gaming excitement." The other, UglyBass Utilities, allows you to map favorite fishing spots onto topographic or other maps, and includes a fishing log, sunrise and sunset information and a weight calculator.

The World of Computer Fishing Games
http://www.geocities.com/timessquare/lair/8646

An amateur enthusiast's guide to computer fishing games. There are more than 200 games listed according to platform (Gameboy, Playstation, Windows, Mac), and links to each manufacturer's web site. From there, you can usually download a demo, or the whole program if it's free. A few product reviews mix with discussions about new releases, ways to cheat and other software gossip.

CHAPTER 6
GROUPS

The Web's virtually free publishing space has given a platform to fishing's underrepresented voices. Traditional fishing media hasn't given much attention to the millions of women, junior and disabled anglers who are happy participants in the sport, but there are scores of quality web sites out there for these groups. Add in web sites supporting conservation groups with a special concern for fisheries and specialist fishing clubs of every stripe and speckle, and you can see that somewhere on the Web there are people with the same fishing interests and motivations as you. Use this chapter to find them.

Women

There's a theory that women make better salmon anglers because they respond biologically to the chemical signals given off by the fish as they prepare to reproduce. More likely, women are often successful because their egos don't get in the way of listening to what a guide or experienced companion advises them. It fits with the true equality of the sport: millions of women not only like fishing, they are free to be every bit as good at it—or as bad—as men.

ChicksWhoFish
http://www.chickswhofish.com

Groups

ChicksWhoFish
http://www.chickswhofish.com

Many women are attracted to the finesse and catch and release ethic of fly fishing, but it's reassuring to know there are those whose idea of a good day is to come home smelling of saltwater and tuna blood. Members of the educational sportfishing club ChicksWhoFish don't mind getting a little dirt under their nails. Lead Chick Dara Fry proves the point with lots of photographs of grinning members and seminar-goers hugging various

California gamefish. Go to ChicksTalk or the Guest Book to contact the Chicks or look for a fishing partner.

The Fish Sniffer Online – Angling Women
http://www.fishsniffer.com/women

The Angling Women section of this recommended Western fishing magazine has 30 female-authored or female-focused articles covering all types of fishing, and a gallery of ladies hoisting some enormous trophies. The articles page is

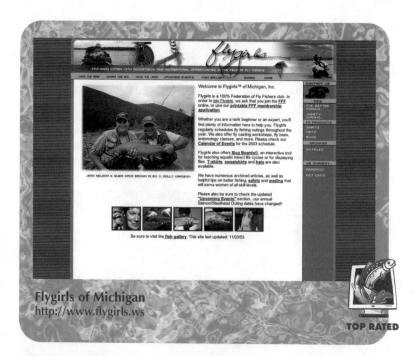

Flygirls of Michigan
http://www.flygirls.ws

sponsored by seven "women-friendly" California charter services.

Flygirls of Michigan
http://www.flygirls.ws

The Flygirls banded together seven years ago and they use this beautiful site to encourage others into the fold with joining details, upcoming events and an impressive fish photo gallery. Members can post fishing stories, there are wading and safety tips and a bibliography of women's fishing books. They belong to the Federation of Fly Fishers, and I'd be surprised if any club in that great organization has a nicer web site.

GORP – Women and Flyfishing
http://www.gorp.com

Go to Activities then Fishing then look for the Women and Flyfishing link to find a series of articles by Amy Becker Williams. She discusses options for learning about the sport, what's available in waders and clothing and essential tackle and gadgets. As with all GORP pages, there are helpful crossreferences to related articles.

International Women Fly Fishers (IWFF)
http://www.intlwomenflyfishers.org
Join this nonprofit aimed at promoting women's fly fishing and you'll receive a quarterly newsletter, a Club Liaison service for help setting up your own local fly-fishing club and an invitation to the annual conference. The IWFF

Festival is in its seventh year and consists of seminars, demonstrations, trade shows and a general fly-fishing good time. The site has full joining details, a conference report and links to 30 women's fly-fishing clubs.

"Ladies, Let's Go Fishing!"
http://www.ladiesletsgofishing.com

According to the team at Florida's "Ladies, Let's Go Fishing!" the number one reason more women don't fish is that husbands, friends, and relatives don't have the patience to teach fishing skills. That's where the Ladies step in by offering fun and crankiness-free saltwater fishing weekends. The program begins with classroom instruction on the essentials of handling rods and reels, tying knots and unhooking, and ends with a fishing charter.

LandBigFish (LBF) – The Woman Angler
http://www.landbigfish.com/women

Cecilia "Pudge" Kleinkauf and Juni Fisher write about fly fishing, and Bonita Staples of Texas' *Honey Hole* magazine is the bass authority for LandBigFish's ladies department. A toolkit of Fishing Resources is boxed off on the righthand side of the page with links to knot tutorials, fish identification pages, recipes and women's fishing clubs. LBF invites article submissions from female anglers.

Ottawa Women Fly Fishers
http://www.owff.org

A simple but nicely done club page featuring online newsletters, joining information and links of interest to fishing ladies. One of the best of those leads to the club's own vice president, Brenda

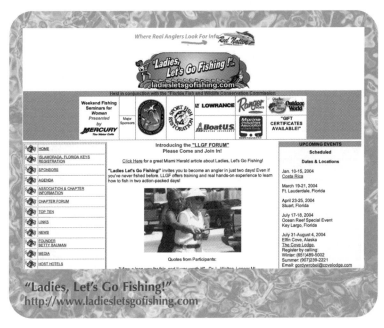

"Ladies, Let's Go Fishing!"
http://www.ladiesletsgofishing.com

Reel Women Fly Fishing Adventures
http://www.reel-women.com

Sharpe, who has written an online guide to finding fishing information on the Web titled *The Wired Angler*. It covers general fly-fishing resources and gateways to the Web, magazine sites, finding local fishing information, mailing lists, discussion groups, chat rooms and what you can get for free.

Reel Women Fly Fishing Adventures
http://www.reel-women.com

Lori-Ann Murphy's Reel Women Fly Fishing Adventures is based in Idaho and is a female-staffed guiding operation (they have a few lucky men on the team as well). They can float you down some of the most famous rivers in the West or teach you the basics at regularly held fishing schools. If you've fallen hard for the fly-fishing life and have some decent skills you might consider one of the two schools offered for women who want to become professional guides. The Reel-Women store has signature hats and clothing.

The Blue Quill Angler at **http://www.bluequillangler.com** also runs a fly-fishing school for women under the expert eye of Dana Rikimaru, author of *A Women's Guide to Fly Fishing*, and sells a range of women's fishing apparel. Women's resources are just one part of this exceptional Colorado fly-shop site. Wander around to find fishing reports, a newsletter and a great beginner's section.

Texas Women Fly Fishers
http://www.twff.net

A better-than-average club page for the warm and saltwater fly fishing ladies of the Lone Star State. As well as the usual club details, joining instructions and event calendars, an editorial section

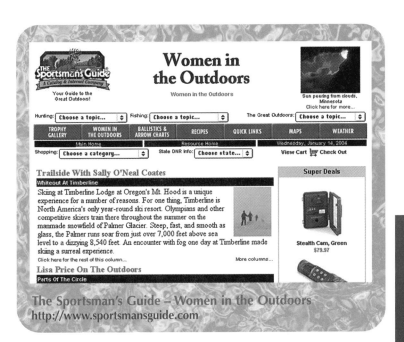

The Sportsman's Guide – Women in the Outdoors
http://www.sportsmansguide.com

provides tips for camping, wade fishing, using a kayak, setting the hook and other essential skills.

The Sportsman's Guide – Women in the Outdoors
http://www.sportsmansguide.com

Online outfitter The Sportsman's Guide has a large corner for Women in the Outdoors. Scroll to the bottom of the homepage and click on the link to find dozens of articles about women and the outdoor life, including traditional sports such as fishing and hunting, as well as hiking, archery, rafting, mountain biking and horse riding.

The Ultimate Bass Fishing Resource Guide
www.bassresource.com/women/women.html

George Kramer's superior bass fishing site has a ladies section with profiles of prominent female bass anglers, articles about equipment and clothing trends, plus links to more than 30 women's fishing sites. If you're new to bass fishing, the beginner's section elsewhere on bassresource.com is one of the best on the Web.

Women's Bass Fishing Association (WBFA)
http://www.wbfatour.com

The WBFA Tour is the only national tournament circuit for professional and amateur lady bass anglers. The site has dates and standings for the six regional events going into the tour championship, and a forum for fans and competitors. The section Member Webpages posts the tournament résumés of six ladies who've made the leap to professional status.

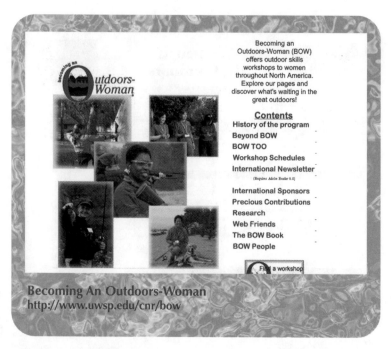

Becoming an Outdoors-Woman (BOW) offers outdoor skills workshops to women throughout North America. Explore our pages and discover what's waiting in the great outdoors!

Contents

History of the program

Beyond BOW

BOW TOO

Workshop Schedules

International Newsletter
(Requires Adobe Reader 5.0)

International Sponsors

Precious Contributions

Research

Web Friends

The BOW Book

BOW People

Find a workshop

Becoming An Outdoors-Woman
http://www.uwsp.edu/cnr/bow

Women's Fly Fishing
http://www.womensflyfishing.net

TOP RATED

Owned by prominent lady fly fisher Cecilia "Pudge" Kleinkauf, Women's Fly Fishing is an Alaska-based women's guide service and information source. The site describes their services in pursuit of trout, salmon, grayling and pike, and several fly-fishing schools they conduct at a women-only lodge. Exceptionally good links to women's clubs and resources lead to these three national programs:

Casting for Recovery at http://www.castingforrecovery.org, arranges for women whose lives have been affected by breast cancer to retreat for a few peaceful days and learn to fly fish. In 2003, 25 retreats were organized in more

than 15 states. Go to Retreat Information for a schedule and application form.

Becoming An Outdoors-Woman (BOW) at http://www.uwsp.edu/cnr/bow consists of two- and three-day workshops that encourage women to participate in outdoor sports. Events are held in nearly every state and provide options for fishing, shooting, mountain biking, camping, outdoor survival and archery. The site has schedules and regional links for upcoming BOW weekends and a history of the program's development.

Step Outside at http://www.stepoutside.org, encourages those already active in the outdoor sports to invite newcomers out for a day's fishing, hunting, shooting or archery.

Kids

Many fishing parents would prefer to see their kids outside having the kind of everyday waterside adventures they once experienced, but it's the Internet age and there are powerful new distractions. One answer is to use the Web to maintain a child's interest and learning curve while they're away from the water. These sites range in target age from small fry to early teens and are a mixture of games, fishing education and community programs. Several of them advise parents and teachers on how to bring their kids into the sport the right way.

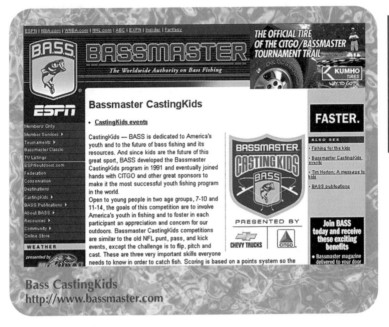

Bass CastingKids
http://www.bassmaster.com

Groups

BASS CastingKids
http://www.bassmaster.com

The BASS CastingKids competition is a fishing version of football's pass, punt and kick challenge, except kids have to flip, pitch and cast. Since 1991 the program has reached more than a million kids and given away two million dollars in prizes. Find out about events in your area at the CastingKids section of bassmaster.com, or at BASS affiliated club pages such as **http://**

www.pabass.com, which has illustrations of the required casts and details about the individual events for 7 to 10 and 11 to 14 year-olds.

BoatSafeKids
http://www.boatsafe.com/kids

A fun, educational site that explains the logic behind safe boating practice rather than just telling them what not to do. It takes the form of boating orientation and safety Q & As, mixed

Boating Safety Sidekicks
http://www.boatingsafetysidekicks.com

TOP RATED

with articles about navigation, nautical flags, and how to use safety equipment.

Boating Safety Sidekicks
http://www.boatingsafety sidekicks.com

TOP RATED Boating Safety Sidekicks is a combination web site and activity book produced by The National Safe Boating Council, aimed at teaching young people how to boat and fish responsibly. They've made a big effort to make the site as fresh and lively as possible by including games, puzzles, animation and interactive features. Choose from the semi-circles of topic headings to find descriptions of flotation devices and survival stories from kids who owe their life to them, advice on how to move around a boat, fish from a dock and avoid sun burn.

The site is designed to be used as part of a formal teaching curriculum. Go to Teach and Learn on the homepage to find activity sheets and companion material to Sidekicks books for younger and older children.

Fascinating Facts About Fish
http://www.nefsc.noaa.gov/ faq.html

TOP RATED A fun look at the top 100 questions asked of the scientists employed by the National Marine Fisheries Service. Haven't we all wanted to know at some point: How do fish sleep? Can fish distinguish color? What is the fish listed as "scrod" in New England restaurants? How do fish know to bite within that precise window of time when you're pouring a cup of coffee, taking your jacket off or glancing at the horizon? The homepage recommends several other sites for learning about fish and oceans.

Fish'n Kids Resources
http://www.fishnkids.com

Hosted and sponsored by the ProBass web site, Fish'n Kids is a place to submit fishing stories, tips and photos or pose a burning question. Descriptions of books and games designed for young anglers and advice on setting up a kid's fishing club makes it one for parents as well as the juniors.

FishingWorks – Kids Fishing
http://www.fishingworks.com

The FishingWorks directory has the best kid-fishing links on the Web. It lists hundreds of sites within 12 main categories, just a few of

which include interactive game sites for the little ones (under Activities for Tadpoles), an excellent series profiling the best family outdoor vacations from *Game & Fish* magazines, and listings for summer fishing camps and kid tournaments and derbies all over the U.S.

GORP – Teaching Kids to Fish
http://www.gorp.com

Among the many useful areas at GORP is a section aimed at parents planning to introduce kids and teenagers to fishing. It's full of sensible advice and tips from fishing expert Mark D. Williams, ably assisted by teenager Sarah Denise Williams, who passes on advice to would-be teachers and encouragement to her peers. GORP, in fact, has a whole channel for outdoor family recreation, where you'll

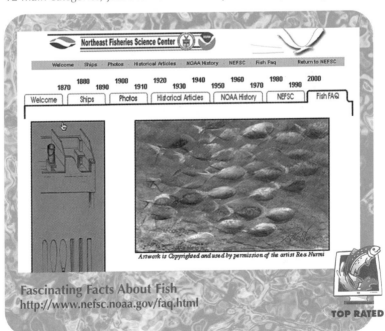

Fascinating Facts About Fish
http://www.nefsc.noaa.gov/faq.html

TOP RATED

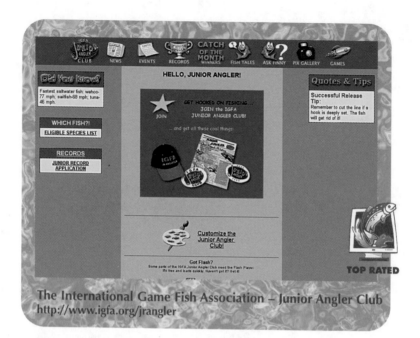

The International Game Fish Association – Junior Angler Club
http://www.igfa.org/jrangler

find advice on traveling with kids, lists of kid-friendly river outings, an outdoor family forum, essays and resources.

To find the kid fishing section, go to Activities then Fishing and look for the heading Teaching Kids to Fish. To find Family, go to the Find it on GORP section of the homepage and look for the heading Interests.

The International Game Fish Association (IGFA) Junior Angler Club
http://www.igfa.org/jrangler

Join the IGFA Junior Angler Club to receive the kind of goodies I would have trampled smaller children to get hold of when I was that age—a cap, a badge, *The International Junior*

Angler magazine, a membership card and free admittance to the newly opened IGFA Fishing Hall of Fame and Museum.

Hop along the top navigation to find an event calendar, a complete Junior Angler World Record List, competition winners, fishing stories and a strangely compelling game called "Fishy's Escape." Don't get caught playing this by anyone who depends on you professionally.

Kidfish – All About Lakes and Fly Fishing Too!
http://kidfish.bc.ca

KidFish is a wonderful Web-based tool for teaching kids about the interconnectedness of freshwater ecology, fly fishing and fly tying. It was inspired by Erich Franz, a British

Columbia teacher and fly fisher, and achieves its goals on two levels: the text is aimed at kids aged between 10 to 17, while links at the bottom of each page suggest lesson plans and activity sheets so teachers can use the pages as a formal curriculum.

The majority of the site explains the dynamics and natural history of lakes and rivers, but the author's love of fly fishing comes through

within areas for Where to Find Fish in a River and a thorough introduction to fly tying which demonstrates in step-by-step photos how to tie 12 imitative patterns. Click on a fly to see the pattern, its importance to fly fishing and how to fish it.

The site builders hope the finished web site will be three times as large as it is currently—let's hope they manage to do it.

PROGRAMS AND SERVICES FOR KIDS

Most state fish and wildlife departments have programs aimed at encouraging kids to take up fishing, ranging from seminars and workshops to tackle loaner sites and web tutorials. The **Alabama Division of Wildlife and Freshwater Fisheries** at **http://www.dcnr.state .al.us/agfd/fishsec.html**, for example, lists kids' free fishing days, the location of public fishing lakes and has help for scouts taking the fishing merit badge. The **Wisconsin Department of Natural Resources** at **http://www.dnr.state.wi.us/ org/water/fhp/fish/** has a dedicated area for kids, parents and educators, in addition to a special where-to-fish guide for youngsters that recommends over 120 lakes, ponds and rivers.

And these two states aren't exceptional in the level of information or programs offered. Parents keen to introduce their kids to the outdoors should make their fish and wildlife department web site a permanent bookmark. See Chapter 3 Know Before You Go for the URLs of sites

that link to all the departments.

Future Fisherman Foundation

http://www.futurefisherman.org

The Future Fisherman Foundation is the group behind the initiatives Hooked on Fishing – Not on Drugs (HOFNOD), and the Fishing Tackle Loaner Program (FTLP). HOFNOD encourages young people away from drugs by introducing them to fishing, conservation and aquatic ecology. Close to a half-million kids and adults have benefited from the Fishing Tackle Loaner Program, which allows anyone who'd like to give fishing a try the chance to borrow tackle at no charge from 550 loaner sites.

For both programs and for a new service, the Camp Fishing Initiative, which assists youth camps in providing fishing as an organized activity, you can search for more information by using the Program Database.

National Fishing Week (NFW)

http://www.national fishingweek.com

Canada's National Fishing Week runs from July 6th to the 14th and its organizers publish a series of colorful, clever web sites for finding local events and promoting fishing to kids, teenagers and parents.

The NFW homepage is aimed at adults and older kids and leads with a description of the program, a fishing contest and a quiz to test boating competency. A section labeled Just4Kids leads to two mini-web sites for fishing games and education. Both have been imaginatively designed, but the version for older kids especially uses sophisticated effects to present fishing summaries for each region of the country, how-to tips and fish identification. A homework help section offers math calculators for dispensing with time-draining homework and getting to the waterside all the sooner.

Back on the homepage, clicking on the NFW Events heading leads to **Catchfishing.com**, another self-contained site with information and contact numbers for taking part in NFW events, plus fishing articles, games and regional links. It can be accessed directly at **http://www.catchfishing.com**.

Ontario Ministry of Natural Resources Fish and Wildlife – Take A Kid Fishing

http://www.mnr.gov.on.ca/ MNR/fishing/aa.html

In the campaign to have your children grow up and become

happy fishermen rather than Frisbee golf players or loan sharks, a fun and relaxed introduction to the sport is your first weapon. This site offers a free 40-page guide titled *Take A Kid Fishing*, aimed specifically at parents. Avoiding any kind of technical talk it covers tackle, baits, lures, fish identification, knots, cookery, clothing and tips for keeping them safe and interested.

Outdoor Canada – Kids
http://www.ockids.ca

OC Kids tests the creativity and knowledge of younger children within areas for games, word searches and quizzes. Fishing Fun has Rapala Fishing Tips and catch photos and the Storytime section publishes jokes and tales from kid contributors.

Recreational Boating and Fishing Foundation – Aquatic Science, Fishing, and Boating Education Web Directory
http://www.rbff-education.org

TOP RATED

This valuable directory of 2,000 educational programs and resources was set up to provide a single place for anyone who wants to create a curriculum or event based on teaching fishing, boating or aquatic science. Because most of the information comes from noncommercial web sites, many of the listings are hidden from traditional search engines. Choose from six categories, then click on the folder icons to search more narrowly.

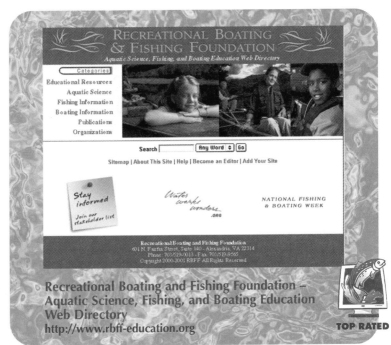

Recreational Boating and Fishing Foundation – Aquatic Science, Fishing, and Boating Education Web Directory
http://www.rbff-education.org

TOP RATED

Groups

StreamNet
http://www.streamnet.org

TOP RATED

Aside from excellent resources for educators and event planners, such as the Publications area which links to free fishing booklets and guides, there are some seriously useful links within the Fishing Information section, including shortcuts to 29 state stocking programs and 40 sites that post regular catch reports.

StreamNet
http://www.streamnet.org

TOP RATED

For kids who show an interest in freshwater biology and conservation, the Public Education section of StreamNet richly illustrates and describes more than 100 types of trout, salmon and other species. Most departments emphasize how

changes in the environment and ocean conditions affect salmonid survival. Go to Especially for Kids for a collection of coloring templates and suggestions for various fishy activity projects.

Take A Kid Fishing
http://www.takeakidfishing.com

Once a year at every Wal-Mart store in the country kids are invited for a free fishing education and activities day featuring casting instruction, scavenger hunts, games and tackle give-aways. Takeakidfishing.com has a general description of the program, but you need to check at your local store for event dates: it traditionally kicks off National Fishing Week, which runs from June 1st to the 8th.

Texas Gulf Coast Fishing – Kids Corner

http://www.texasgulfcoastfishing.com/kids.htm

It's never too early to stress the higher benefits of fishing—an appreciation for the aquatic world and our role as participants and stewards. The Kids Corner discusses what an estuary is and some of the threats facing the Texas coast, then moves on to angling ethics and links to conservation and education sites. The rest of the Corner has tips for parents taking their kids fishing, what to look for in a rod and reel and how to tie a few essential fishing knots.

U.S. Fish and Wildlife Service – Student's Page

http://educators.fws.gov/students.html

Links at the Student's Page are aimed at both kids and educators. The Fish option—you can also choose from Birds, Habitat, Endangered Species, Wildlife, Plants and Refuges—features examples of classroom projects for getting kids interested in fisheries conservation.

Among these links are two sites using interactive features to involve kids in fisheries conservation projects. The **Adopt-a-Trout** web site at **http://www.fwp.state.mt.us/adoptatrout**, allows elementary students in the Blackfoot Valley, Montana to trace the movements of individual trout and suckers in the Blackfoot River. The fish have been fitted with tiny tracking devices in an effort to see how Milltown Dam interferes with normal fish movement and populations. The Montana Fish and Wildlife Service updates the site once a week.

The **Salmon Challenge** at **http://dnr.metrokc.gov/wlr/waterres/salmonch.htm**, is an interactive quiz for learning about salmon survival. Correct answers help the online salmon stocks thrive and move toward the ocean; incorrect answers threaten their health and eventually kill them off.

Wal-Mart Kids All American Fishing Derby
http://www.fishingworld.com/kids-fishing
A quarter-million kids attended one of these events last year, hosted by local parks and recreation departments, civic service clubs and city, state and regional agencies. Organized by the charity Hooked on Fishing International, each derby is a half-day event for kids up to 16 and features casting competitions, a Big Fish Contest, games and activities. Anyone interested in holding a derby can download an application and view the free Derby Kit that's sent to organizers.

See also the **C.A.S.T. for Kids Foundation** at **http://www.castforkids.org**.

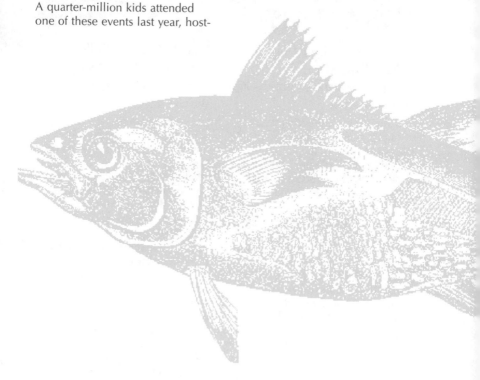

People with Disabilities

For a few seconds, imagine the difficulties of going fishing when confined to a wheelchair, or if you're dependent on a nurse or caregiver. Thousands of anglers continue to get deep satisfaction from the sport despite such hurdles, and they maintain these web sites to let others know about special programs and tournaments, modified tackle and other considerations for safe and enjoyable days on the water.

The British Disabled Angling Association
http://www.bdaa.co.uk

The British Disabled Angling Association
http://www.bdaa.co.uk

Wherever your homewater, this site deserves a bookmark. The Adaptations section describes custom fishing tackle such as automatic reels, rod holders, knot threaders and bite alarms, and the recommended links point to more than 50 disability web sites from fishing clubs, equipment manufacturers and magazines.

For the Brits, there are fishing essays, an event calendar for fundraisers and competitions and a directory of holiday venues with disabled access. Note: a new version of the site is being launched in 2004.

See also Terry Lawton's guide to products for disabled fly fishermen titled "Too Good a Sport ..." within the July 2000 archives of **Fish & Fly** at **http://www.fish andfly.co.uk/tledit0700.html**.

PROGRAMS AND SERVICES FOR PEOPLE WITH DISABILITIES

Unfortunately, no single site links to all the resources for disabled fishermen offered by state fish and wildlife departments. That's a shame, because these sites are easily the best option on the Web for tracking down access-friendly fishing venues. The **Florida Department of Environmental Protection** at **http://www.dep.state.fl.us/parks /information/accessforall.htm,** for example, offers a directory of wheelchair-accessible beaches and piers; the **Maryland Department of Natural Resources'Accessability For All** page at **http://www.dnr. state.md.us/accessforall,** lists accessible fishing piers, campsites, boat ramps and amenities.

As with searching for kids fishing resources, there are a couple of ways to go. Find a fishing web site that has collected all the state links for you, such as **Active Angler** at **http://www.activeangler.com/ resources/agencies**. Or conduct a straightforward Internet search. Google is as good as any, but for variety, **Metacrawler** at **http://www.metacrawler.com** "searches the search engines" to skim off the best listings returned by other engines.

It's always worth trying a few different terms for these searches: "disabled fishing Oregon," for example, gets 62 returns on Metacrawler. "Wheelchair access fishing Oregon" returns the same sites, but a third less of them.

A Disabled Fisherman
http://www.geocities.com/ scosmo451

A personal page from Scott Smothers offering plenty of practical advice and quiet inspiration. Mixed in with his thoughts about safety, equipment, locations and the importance of fishing partners, are reflections on superstitions, diary entries and photographs.

You've got to like a guy who takes the first opportunity he can to go fishing after months of not feeling up to it, even if does coincide with a certain un-missable appointment: "Of course, everybody thought I was an idiot for going fishing before my wedding, but a man has to have some standards, ya know?"

Fishing Has No Boundaries (FHNB)
http://www.fhnbinc.org

People find their calling in unexpected ways. Bobby Cammack had been a guide on the Chippewa Flowage for decades when he broke his foot. Because his livelihood depended on getting out on the water he was forced to confront the logistical problems of going fishing without full mobility. It set off a chain of thinking that eventually resulted in the founding of Fishing Has No Boundaries, which has a mission to open the outdoors to people with disabilities.

Eighty people showed up to the first event: it's now a national organization with 13 chapters in eight states and helps thousands of people every year. The pull-down Events menu has contact information for each chapter and event dates. Go to the Gear link to find an eight-page guide to adaptive fishing reels, rods, rod-holders, boats and accessories.

NJ Striper – Disabled Fishermen

http://www.njstriper.com

A useful collection of links assembled by a character calling himself "Old Spook"—banish all images of peg-legged sea captains from your mind, should you have them—listing disabled fishing resources in 14 states, and a few tips for wheelchair users. Some of the links were stale but don't assume they're dead without putting the titles through a search engine.

Paralyzed Veterans of America (PVA) – National Bass Trail

http://www.pva.org

Founded in 1946 to assist veterans of the armed forces with spinal cord injuries, the PVA organizes the National Bass Trail, the first

true tournament series for disabled anglers. The competition is open to all disabled fishermen whether they're veterans or not and is made up of five regional events. Event winners in boat and bank fishing categories go on to the Grand Championship.

To find the tournament page, go to Sports & Recreation then Boating & Fishing then click on the tournament logo. The site has competition dates, entry forms, and a match report from the two-day championship.

Project Access

http://www.projectaccess.com

Project Access builds switchback paths so that the mobility impaired can get down to productive trout streams in the Catskill Mountains. They helpfully document all the steps and considerations for the project in a seven-part guide. Go to Developing an Access Site for illustrated advice on every phase of the project from selecting a site to long-term care of the finished path.

Conservation

The conservation movement in this country has its roots in sportsmen's organizations, and fishing has continued to be a sport front and center in the fight for clean water and healthy fisheries. These sites include some of the best known individual groups closely aligned with anglers' interests, and directory sites which link to thousands of other groups pledged to protecting rivers and oceans.

American Rivers
http://www.americanrivers.org

TOP RATED

American Rivers
http://www.americanrivers.org

TOP RATED

American Rivers was founded in 1973 with a mandate to increase the number of rivers protected under The National Wild and Scenic Rivers system, and to prevent the construction of new dams on the last wild rivers. It now has 30,000 members and focuses on assisting local campaigns for dam removal, threats to watersheds and getting the message out that healthy rivers and watersheds matter. Go to River Issues in the lefthand navigation to read about individual campaigns.

One of the site's best features is the Gateway to Rivers & Groups directory, which lists hundreds of river conservation organizations. Search by river name, by group name or by state and region. Click through for information and a link to the group's own web site.

Atlantic Salmon Federation (ASF)
http://www.asf.ca

TOP RATED It can be as plainly stated as: without help the Atlantic salmon could become extinct in our lifetime. The Atlantic Salmon Federation's goal is to prevent that from happening. One small part of the effort is this informative site for breaking conservation news and links to member councils and river associations in Canada and the U.S. Editorials and articles from the *Atlantic Salmon Federation Journal*, and descriptions of the group's education and conservation programs offer plenty to read.

The Billfish Foundation
http://www.billfish.org

TOP RATED The Billfish Foundation identifies threats, funds research and seeks to influence worldwide fisheries management policy in the name of these magnificent creatures. At billfish.org you'll find detailed explanations of the group's aims and objectives, the latest conservation and tournament news and a downloadable 11-page newsletter called *Billfish News*. It's a PDF: use the Zoom In function on the Acrobat toolbar (150% should do it) to read this brightly designed publication putting a face to the people behind the group and keeping members up-to-date on campaigns and events.

Groups

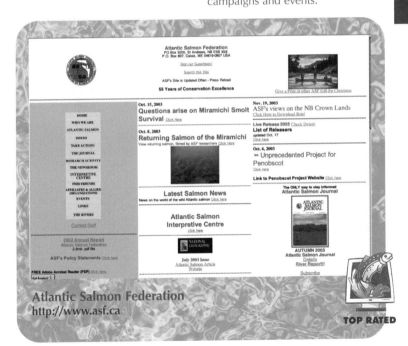

Atlantic Salmon Federation
http://www.asf.ca

TOP RATED

Coastal Conservation Association (CCA)

http://www.joincca.org

TOP RATED

It's reported that at the inaugural meeting of the Gulf Coast Conservation Association, a fisherman pounded the table and swore: "We'll save the redfish if we have to raise $20,000!" It may have cost a bit more than that, but what became the Coastal Conservation Association kept good on their promise and made a huge contribution to the redfish comeback, and subsequent campaigns on behalf of kingfish, billfish and striped bass. With chapters in 15 states and 80,000 members, the CCA has become a guardian and advocate for fisheries along the whole East Coast.

The web site lays out their three-forked approach of education, leg-islation and restoration, and links to each chapter's individual web site. Join the group and you'll receive the award-winning *Tide* magazine.

Columbia and Snake Rivers Campaign

http://www.wildsalmon.org

When Lewis and Clarke encountered the Snake River in 1805 it's estimated that between five and eight-and-a-half million salmon returned to the river that year from the Pacific. The expedition's bicentennial celebration will probably see about 5,000 wild fish make the same journey.

Orchestrated by the Save Our Wild Salmon Coalition, a collective of more than 50 conservation groups and sport and commercial fishery organizations, the Columbia and Snake Rivers Campaign argues

that partially removing four dams on the lower Snake River will massively regenerate the fishery. The heading Find Information leads to a page describing the various stakeholders in this complex issue, and About Campaign fully explains the case for dam removal.

Creekbank
http://www.creekbank.com

TOP RATED

A tremendously good idea, Creekbank is a links directory connecting fishermen to national and local organizations concerned with restoring and preserving coldwater streams. Links in the lefthand navigation lead to groups and resources for Stream Restoration, fish and wildlife departments, Wetlands Banking, Water Education, Watershed Associations and funding sources for stream conservation projects.

The Izaak Walton League of America (IWLA)
http://www.iwla.org

TOP RATED

Chicago, 1922. Fifty-four conservation-minded outdoorsmen meet to discuss the deteriorating condition of America's trout streams. They form the Izaak Walton League of America to do something about it. Eighty years later the League has 50,000 members and has broadened its concerns to include guardianship of soil, air, woods and wildlife, but clean water remains a central focus. Some of its many programs include advocating for sustainable agricultural practices and wetlands preservation, teaching outdoor ethics and Save Our Streams, a countrywide initiative teaching youths and adults how to monitor and protect streams.

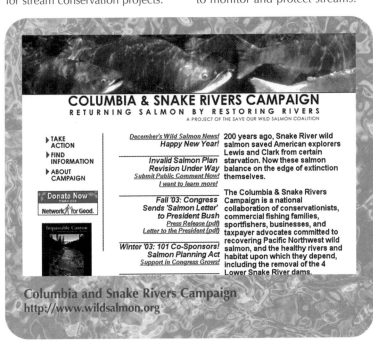

COLUMBIA & SNAKE RIVERS CAMPAIGN
RETURNING SALMON BY RESTORING RIVERS
A PROJECT OF THE SAVE OUR WILD SALMON COALITION

▶ TAKE ACTION
▶ FIND INFORMATION
▶ ABOUT CAMPAIGN

Donate Now
THROUGH
Network for Good.

Impassable Canyon

December's Wild Salmon News!
Happy New Year!

Invalid Salmon Plan
Revision Under Way
Submit Public Comment Now!
I want to learn more!

Fall '03: Congress
Sends 'Salmon Letter'
to President Bush
Press Release (pdf)
Letter to the President (pdf)

Winter '03: 101 Co-Sponsors!
Salmon Planning Act
Support in Congress Grows!

200 years ago, Snake River wild salmon saved American explorers Lewis and Clark from certain starvation. Now these salmon balance on the edge of extinction themselves.

The Columbia & Snake Rivers Campaign is a national collaboration of conservationists, commercial fishing families, sportfishers, businesses, and taxpayer advocates committed to recovering Pacific Northwest wild salmon, and the healthy rivers and habitat upon which they depend, including the removal of the 4 Lower Snake River dams.

Columbia and Snake Rivers Campaign
http://www.wildsalmon.org

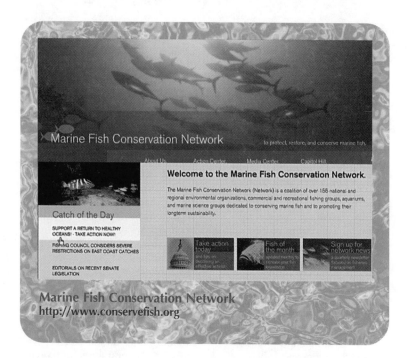

Marine Fish Conservation Network
http://www.conservefish.org

If you want to get involved, find your local branch within the directory of 300 IWLA chapters, or go to News & Publications then Email Lists to sign up for the *Action Alert and Conservation Issue Update,* which are newsletters reporting on conversation legislation and federal agency activities.

Marine Fish Conservation Network (MFCN)

http://www.conservefish.org

The MFCN is a coalition of more than 150 environmental, marine science and fishing organizations, dedicated to conserving marine fish and promoting sustainable development. Go to the links section within About Us for a list of member groups, or to the Action Center to subscribe to the Network newsletter.

National Coalition for Marine Conservation (NCMC)

http://www.savethefish.org

The NCMC's members are a diverse lot—fishermen, scientists, divers, boaters and wildlife enthusiasts—but they have the distinct common goal of conserving marine fish and the healthy ocean environments needed to sustain them. Prospective members can assure themselves the group is helmed by an intelligent and persuasive leader by reading President Ken Hinman's Open Letter to People for the Ethical Treatment of Animals (PETA). Snippets from the Coalition newsletter and an outline of the group's five-pronged conservation strategy make up the rest.

The Recreational Fishing Alliance (RFA)
http://www.savefish.com

The Recreational Fishing Alliance is fishing's political lobbying group, "the only full-time political action organization fighting the important battles in Washington." The column on the left of the homepage introduces the organization's current campaigns and links to state chapters, newsletter archives and the Environmental Extremist Alert, which sounds the alarm about blanket fishery closures and restrictions. The column on the right has updates on legislation and resource issues.

The RFA are sponsors of the Freedom to Fish Act, which is an effort to fight the trend toward total fishing bans within Marine Protected Areas. California has

already lost some of its best offshore fishing: log on to **Freedom to Fish** at **http://www.freedomto fish.org** for ways to get involved.

River Network
http://www.rivernetwork.org

TOP RATED

Like American Rivers, this umbrella organization acts as a service to grassroots organizations, offering workshops, trainings, consultations, grants and publications. In line with its mission to forge alliances, it offers an online directory of 3,600 river and watershed conservation groups, local agencies and government departments. Look for the heading Special Features then click on Directory of River Groups to search by federal agency, state and local groups or lists of national nonprofits.

Trout Unlimited (TU)
http://www.tu.org

TOP RATED

Trout Unlimited began with 16 members and a pledge to "to conserve, protect, and restore North America's trout and salmon fisheries and their watersheds." Forty-four years later they have 125,000 members organized into 500 regional chapters and have become one of the leading fisheries conservation groups in the U.S. The site has the full story of the organization, a chapter-finder (within the Act Now pull-down menu at the top of each page) and plenty of information about ongoing campaigns for small dam removal, acid rain, Atlantic salmon and Western water.

U.S. Environmental Protection Agency (EPA) – Surf Your Watershed
http://www.epa.gov/surf

TOP RATED

Healthy fisheries begin with healthy watersheds. To find out what's being done in your region to protect them, try the EPA's Surf Your Watershed. The Search by Map option within Locate Your Watershed displays a clickable map of the U.S. Click on the state then a sub-region to find local watershed information and resources. Other searches are available using place names, river names, lake names and zip codes. Back on the homepage, the link to Environmental Websites opens a state-by-state directory of agencies and citizen conservation groups acting to protect watersheds, rivers and lakes.

The Wild Salmon Center
http://www.wildsalmoncenter.org

TOP RATED

Founded in 1992, The Wild Salmon Center is dedicated to protecting the stocks and ecosystem of Pacific salmon, steelhead, char and trout. In support of that, they've created an unusually good web site full of articles and resources. One of the center's most innovative projects pairs fee-paying U.S. fly fishers with Russian fishery scientists to monitor salmon and steelhead stocks on the pristine Kamchatka Peninsula, home of possibly the last best salmon and steelhead fishing in the world. It's the ultimate in sneaking off for a good time in the interests of research. You can confirm this for yourself by watching a 12-minute Internet video shot on location.

Find out about the Center's other initiatives by going to Programs, or read through the archives of *The International Journal of Salmon Conservation* booklet in the Publications section.

Whirling Disease Foundation
http://www.whirlingdisease.org

What do you do about a tiny crippling parasite that can survive freezing and desiccation; that can lie dormant in a stream for 20 or 30 years, and that is easily spread by people, animals and birds? The first thing must be to make as many people aware of the problem as possible. At the Foundation web site you'll find a map of the states known to have the disease, most of everything you need to know about *myxobolus cerebralis* within a bibliography of papers and articles, plus a three-page guide to Prevention Methods for Anglers.

The Wild Trout Trust
http://www.wildtrout.org

A pretty and detailed site from an English group dedicated to wild trout and natural rivers. Start in the Library, which has technical articles and papers, an anthology of essays from some of the best British and American fishing writers and links to other conservation groups. Go to Projects then Locations to find out about dozens of Trust-supported river improvement projects.

Groups

Clubs

Joining a fishing club is often the easiest way to make your fishing more productive and enjoyable. Apart from your own experience, nothing's better than the cumulative knowledge of people who've fished local rivers, lakes and seashores for decades. No single web site offers a central directory of all fishing clubs, but there are several that have good coverage of individual branches of the sport. Otherwise, the regional sites listed in Chapter 2 State-by-State Resources are a good first place to begin looking for clubs in your area.

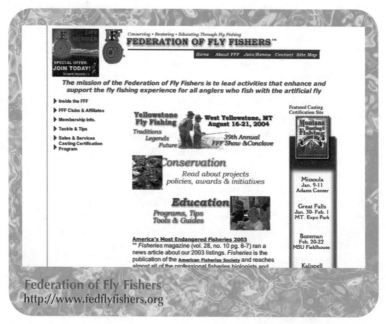

Federation of Fly Fishers
http://www.fedflyfishers.org

American Casting Association

http://www.americancasting assoc.org

In 1906 what became the American Casting Association organized its first tournament for casting distance and accuracy. Other than two years during the Second World War, the group has held the event every year since. Use the site to contact one of the 20 clubs in the Association or for finding out tournament dates.

See also **The International Casting Federation** at **http://www.casting sport.com**.

BASS Federation

http://www.bassmaster.com

Click on Federation on the bassmaster.com homepage to open a corner just for club members. There are more than 2,800 clubs within the organization's state and international federations. The section Federation Stories and Standings puts the spotlight on individual members and clubs, and reports on the National Federation Tournament Trail. Go to Tournament Schedule for the dates and locations of competitions or search for clubs in your area within the links to federation web sites.

Federation of Fly Fishers (FFF)

http://www.fedflyfishers.org

TOP RATED The Federation of Fly Fishers has a multitasking web site for satisfying the group's broad objectives. The FFF is the governing body and national conservation voice of 300 affiliated fly-fishing clubs. Click on Clubs & Affiliates to find contact information and web links for all member clubs. The section Tackle & Tips gets beginners off to the right start and a mini-magazine called *The Salmon Flyer* keeps the fly-tying membership happy.

The FFF also certifies casting instructors, and the site includes a complete directory of certified instructors by state, province and country, plus extracts from the casting newsletter *The Loop.*

FishingWorks – Clubs & Organizations/ Conservation

http://www.fishingworks.com

Among several things Fishing-Works does better than any other directory are its conservation and fishing group listings. Go to Clubs & Organizations and click on the map or text links to find groups of like-minded anglers in the U.S., Canada and abroad. Groups are listed alphabetically by state so

Groups

OTHER CLUB OPTIONS

Try these five sites, all reviewed in Chapter 4 Fishing the Web, for links to bass and walleye clubs countrywide.

Bassdozer

http://www.bassdozer.com

From the homepage click on Bass Fishing Clubs or BASS Federations to find a clearly presented state directory.

ProBass

http://www.probass.com

Go to the Clubs section for links to more than 200 organizations.

The Ultimate Bass Fishing Resource Guide

http://www.bassresource.com

Among the 1,500 sites listed in the links directory are 470 bass clubs.

Walleye Central

http://www.walleyecentral.com

As you'd expect, entries are strongest in the Midwest, but in all, 80 clubs in 24 states.

Walleye Inc.

http://www.walleyesinc.com

Links to more than 30 walleye clubs and organizations and has listings for bass, muskie and general fishing clubs.

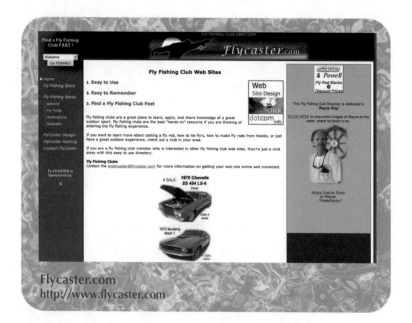

Flycaster.com
http://www.flycaster.com

things can get a bit jumbled, what with your Hog Wild Bass Club practically next door to your Ernest Schwiebert Chapter of Trout Unlimited, but overall it's a valuable service.

The Conservation directory is divided into six branches: Fly Fishing, Government, International, National, Regional and Species, and is one of the few online conservation directories with a real fisheries focus.

Flycaster.com
http://www.flycaster.com

A simple directory site motivated by the idea that "Fly fishing clubs are the 'hands-on' resource if you are thinking of entering the fly fishing experience." Use the little pull-down box to search by state or to list your own club. Listings vary in length and detail, but enough are recorded in each state that you'll probably be able to find a local club.

Great Lakes Sport Fishing Council (GLSFC) – Fishing Clubs
http://www.great-lakes.org/profiles.html

The GLSFC has more than 325,000 members within its affiliated fishing clubs. This corner of their central web site uses a pull-down menu and Go command to display lists of member clubs in eight states and Ontario. Click through to find local club web sites and essential state resources.

Lake Internet – Bass Clubs Online
http://www.blacklakeny.com/links/linksclubs.html

TOP RATED

Lake Internet Bass Clubs Online is an alphabetical and state directory of more than 750 clubs countrywide. Click on a club name to open its web site, where you'll find membership

Yahoo! Fishing Groups
http://www.groups.yahoo.com

TOP RATED

Discovering the hundreds of fishing groups at Yahoo! is like stumbling on a secret meeting hall for all those minority fishing interests that aren't represented anywhere else on the Web. Want to swap Powerbait recipes or discuss tactics for blue pike or meet gay Kentucky bass anglers? You're home. They've congregated here because Yahoo! provides a free web page and mailing list function to anyone who signs up through a simple registration.

Go to the Directory to view 500 fishing groups organized by species, location and style of fishing. The biggest groups within each category are listed first. Click on a group name to find out its focus, how many members there are and whether the mailing list is moderated or archived. They aren't all devoted to narrow topics—some of the fly-fishing and bass groups have 400 members; there are more than 200 saltwater groups—but there really does seem to be something here for every fishing kink and obscurity.

The Join this Group button allows you to select membership options. Some of the mailing lists can get very active, especially when discussions spill over into outright "debates," so unless you can keep up with 50 to 100 e-mails a day, select the digest mode which delivers messages in bundles of 25 or daily, whichever comes first.

MSN – Fishing Groups
http://groups.msn.com

The Microsoft Network offers an online clubhouse similar to Yahoo! Groups. The quickest way to look for a particular fishing group is to type keywords into the search box on the Groups homepage. If you just want to browse the outdoor sports category, go to Sports & Recreation in the lefthand navigation, then Outdoors. Be warned: they throw 1,300 fishing and hunting sites together and once you move past the start page you aren't given another opportunity to do a keyword search. They do, however, tell you how many people belong to each group and how active it is.

However you make your way through the directory, you'll find some big resources here: 180 groups for bass fishing, 126 for fly fishing, more than 40 for saltwater fishing. Group pages display message archives and have areas to post photographs, articles, links and whatever else might be interesting to members. Follow the links on the Groups homepage to create your own club page or join an existing group.

See also **Groups@AOL** at **http://groups.aol.com**, home to an active online fishing club community. AOL keyword Fishing leads to piped-in content from Time4Media outdoor magazines: *Field & Stream*, *Outdoor Life*, and *Salt Water Sportsman*.

Groups

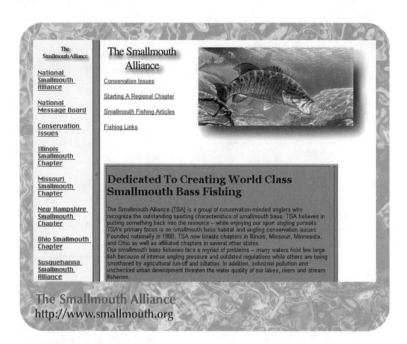

The Smallmouth Alliance
http://www.smallmouth.org

The Smallmouth
Alliance

Conservation Issues

Starting A Regional Chapter

Smallmouth Fishing Articles

Fishing Links

The
Smallmouth Alliance

National
Smallmouth
Alliance

National
Message Board

Conservation
Issues

Illinois
Smallmouth
Chapter

Missouri
Smallmouth
Chapter

New Hampshire
Smallmouth
Chapter

Ohio Smallmouth
Chapter

Susquehanna
Smallmouth
Alliance

**Dedicated To Creating World Class
Smallmouth Bass Fishing**

The Smallmouth Alliance (TSA) is a group of conservation-minded anglers who recognize the outstanding sporting characteristics of smallmouth bass. TSA believes in putting something back into the resource – while enjoying our sport angling pursuits. TSA's primary focus is on smallmouth bass habitat and angling conservation issues. Founded nationally in 1988, TSA now boasts chapters in Illinois, Missouri, Minnesota, and Ohio as well as affiliated chapters in several other states.
Our smallmouth bass fisheries face a myriad of problems – many waters hold few large fish because of intense angling pressure and outdated regulations while others are being smothered by agricultural run-off and siltation. In addition, industrial pollution and unchecked urban development threaten the water quality of our lakes, rivers and stream fisheries.

information, descriptions of local waters and state fishing resources. Search just within BASS Federation club listings from a link on the homepage.

Muskies Inc.
http://www.muskiesinc.com

Native Americans named them the ugly fish; you can't eat them and it takes 10,000 casts to catch one, but few fish have inspired as much devotion as the muskie. Muskies Inc.'s 6,500 members bill themselves as "America's most conservation conscious anglers" for their catch and release ethic and efforts at protecting and developing fisheries. From the homepage go to the heading Main Menu to find chapter links and a long list of members' e-mail addresses for contacts and local muskie advice.

Join the group for access to the password-protected areas of the site containing a forum, a chat room and the Lunge Log, which records the lure, location and weather details behind 140,000 muskie catches.

The Smallmouth Alliance
http://www.smallmouth.org

The Alliance is a growing network of conservation-minded smallmouth anglers with chapters in Illinois, Mississippi and Ohio, and affiliate groups in several other states. Go to Conservation Issues to find out about local campaigns. Alliance members share plenty of smallie fishing advice within articles and extracts from chapter newsletters, and there's a much-used forum.

CHAPTER 7
TACKLE AND BOATS

Tackle and boats are the two great enablers of the angling obsession. Fishermen get a ceremonial thrill out of the annual cycle of cleaning out their gear, stocking up on new items and starting over with fresh hope when the season opens. This chapter not only helps you shop smarter for everything from a packet of hooks to a $30,000 bass boat, it points to the online efforts of those people for whom fishing hardware has become central to their enjoyment of the sport: collectors, tacklemakers, reviewers and boat and paddlecraft enthusiasts.

Tackle

There are those fishermen whose rods and reels are held together by duct tape and fish gunk, and those who think it would be pure folly not to have the latest NASA-inspired fly rod or test pilot-endorsed waders. The rest of us are somewhere in-between, casting an eye over new products, hunting for bargains, swapping notes on what works and what doesn't and constantly adding to that secret wish list all anglers carry in their heads.

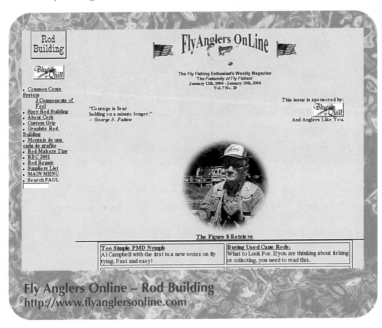

Fly Anglers Online – Rod Building
http://www.flyanglersonline.com

TACKLE MAKING
Fly Anglers Online – Rod Building
http://www.flyanglersonline.com

Fly Anglers Online has an exceptional rod building corner. Al Campbell's 12-part guide to building graphite rods is a standout, but you'll also find a rod repair tutorial, James Castwell's With Bamboo column, rodbulding tips, articles and book extracts. Cane lovers can sit in on a weekly chat room roundtable hosted by Ron Kusse.

The **Global FlyFisher** at **http://www.globalflyfisher.com** also has a rod building section packed with articles and reviews.

Frank's Personal Waste of Time
http://www.fneunemann.com

Photographer and cane rod builder Frank Neunemann probably wasted a good chunk of personal time assembling this precise site for making bamboo fly rods. The Articles section has the bulk of information (continuing pages for

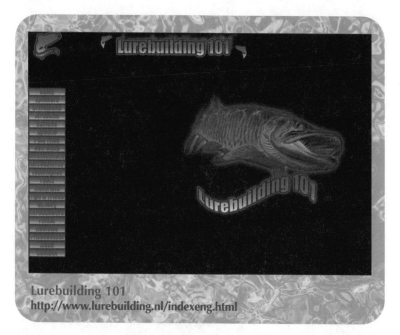

Lurebuilding 101
http://www.lurebuilding.nl/indexeng.html

each article are found at the top
left of the page), but there are also
links to rod makers, suppliers,
reference materials and a set
of downloadable taper charts.

Lurebuilding 101
http://www.lurebuilding.nl/
indexeng.html

If your interest is building pike
and muskie lures, this Netherlands
site is a real treat. In addition to
instructions, photographs and lists
of components for spinners,
crankbaits, spoons and jerkbaits,
there are articles on selecting
materials and accessories, painting
and finishing. The Gallery is a great
source of ideas for pattern and
color combinations, and there are
discussions of how some of the
lures perform "in the field" within
the Reviews section. Join the Lures
101 forum to connect with
European lure fans.

LureMaking.com
http://www.luremaking.com

TOP RATED

LureMaking.com is
the offering of Canada's
leading supplier of lure
making components, but
its web site takes pains
to be an information resource as
well as an online store. The section
Lure Maker's Workshop is a multipart guide to building spinners,
crankbaits and trolling spoons. The
Downloads feature lets you view
and print the company's latest
component and mold catalogs, as
well as seven tip sheets for different lure projects. But the real
bonus is a 64-page manual titled
*The Canadian Guide to Lure
Making*. This normally sells for
$10, but is free to site visitors. It
shows how to make spinners, lake
trolls, spinnerbaits, buzzbaits,
spoons, bait harnesses, crankbaits
and bucktail jigs.

Another online supplier teaching the fundamentals of lure construction is the Australian outfit **Luresonline** at **http://www.luresonline. com.au.** Go to the sections Lure Design and Making Lures for tutorials.

Over My Waders
http://www.overmywaders.com

Reed Curry's web journal promises "serious contemplation" rather than the strings of "errant bubbles from leaky waders" that sometimes passes for fly-fishing writing. That doesn't mean his reflections on silk lines, cane rods and the fly-fishing condition are anything but fun and refreshing. The tech- and spec-hungry will find relief within the Extracts, which is a digest of rod building articles and book chapters, including the entire texts of *Fly Rods and Fly Tackle* (1901) by H.P. Wells and *The Idyl of the Split Bamboo* (1920) by Dr. George Parker Holden. They have both been photographed from the original and at first glance don't seem readable. Set the Zoom-in function on the Acrobat tool bar to 200% and they become quite clear. The Over My Waders links are a good source of cane rod building

web sites. Here you'll find, for example, rod maker Chris Wohlford's encyclopedic guide to bamboo and bamboo-related articles, books, publishers, videos and booksellers. **The Ultimate Bamboo Fly Rod Library** is at **http://www.wohlfordrods.com**.

RodBuilding.org
http://www.rodbuilding.org

TOP RATED

RodBuilding.org only does a couple of things but it does them well. Most importantly, it hosts one of the best forums on the Web for bamboo and graphite rod makers. Before diving in with a query, newcomers should check the FAQ link in the lefthand navigation which answers 22 of the most common questions posted to the forum. The Rod Builder Directory and manufacturer and dealer links are the places to look for components and custom builders.

If the man to make you that special wand isn't listed at RodBuilding.org, try the directory of custom makers and rod and reel

BaitNet
http://www.baitnet.com

BaitNet provides a simple, useful service: it's a directory of bait shops and fishing tacklestores. Though there's an option for a keyword search, the easiest way through the database is to click on a state within the U.S. map. You'll see headings for the major fisheries and subheadings for nearby towns and cities. Click on the pla-

cename for a list of business addresses and telephone numbers. Many of the states have more than 200 listings and some have more than 500.

If you can't find what you're looking for at BaitNet, try the online yellow pages reviewed in Chapter 3 Know Before You Go. Businesses are often listed with driving directions, maps and a link to the store's web site.

repairers at **TackleWorks, http://www.tackleworks.org** or the busy forum at the **Custom Rod Builders Guild, http://www.rodguild.com**.

Rodmakers

http://www.canerod.com/rodmakers

TOP RATED

A web site companion to the popular Rodmakers mailing list for swapping notes about cane rods and rod making. Eight years of archives from the list makes Rodmakers one of the best places on the Web for rod building tips and research. Follow the simple instructions within the section Join/resign RM to begin receiving messages from the list. The rest of the site has handy links to articles, professional rod builders and suppliers. The section Taper Archive has rod blank statistics from 20 well-known makers.

If sorting through the Rodmaker's archive to find useful tips is just too onerous, don't worry, someone has done it for you. **Bamboo Rodmaking Tips** at **http://www.bamboorodmaking.com** has singled out hundreds of building tips from the list's old discussion threads and sorted them into 50 categories.

TackleMaking

http://www.tacklemaking.com

TOP RATED

TackleMaking claims 80,000 unique visitors each month to its multipurpose site aimed at hobby and professional lure makers. It funnels them to four distinct areas: they can browse the large supply shop; they can read through a growing collection of articles, manufacturers' tips and component charts within the Angler's Workshop; they can visit

TackleMaking
http://www.tacklemaking.com

TOP RATED

Antique & Classic
Fishing Reels

Welcome to Antique & Classic Fishing Reels. This site is dedicated to the reel collector as well as people who are just interested in finding out more about their old fishing reels. Contained in these pages you will find information to help you identify your reel, assess the condition, age, and also help you to determine the value of you reel. There are also comprehensive lists of manufacturers, lots of old photos of reels as well as an old photo gallery of wonderful old fishing pictures. Please feel free to contact me if you need more information about your reel, wish to sell your reel or just want to talk about old fishing reels.

"REELS AS BIG AS YOUR HEAD"

For over 15 years I have been researching and collecting big game fishing reels and related big game fishing tackle. In this site you will find a good deal of information about big game reels to help you identify and learn more about your reel. There is also an extensive photo gallery of these monsters of the fishing tackle world showing examples of all of the major manufacturers and many unknown reel makers from many different countries. Don't forget to check out the old photo gallery for some classic pictures of big game fishing. If you need more information or have a reel that you would like to sell please feel free to contact me. Thank you for stopping by and have fun looking around!

Home | About Us | Contact Us
Grading | Valuation | Determining Age | Major Mfgrs | Smaller Mfgrs | Big Game Mfgrs | Vintage Reel Gallery | Classic Fishing Gallery

Antique and Classic Fishing Reels
http://www.antiquefishingreels.com

---

the forums for chatting with other enthusiasts; and they can surf the carefully chosen and summarized web sites in the links directory.

Thomas Penrose's Bamboo Fly Rod Pages
http://www.thomaspenrose.com/bamboo.htm

Thomas Penrose ignores the preamble and Tonkin cane mysticism and heads straight to the workshop. The site is made up of seven densely illustrated guides following the complete gestation of a split-cane fly rod from selecting and preparing the culm in China to making steel planning forms, shaping the handle, deciding where to put ferrules and applying finish.

COLLECTING Antique and Classic Fishing Reels
http://www.antiquefishingreels.com

Nothing finely wrought or decorative here, but "Reels as Big as Your Head"—the kind of monster drums used to tackle marlin, tuna and sharks in the earlier part of the last century. The site is divided between explaining how to grade and evaluate the reels and showcasing owner Ed Pritchard's collection. The gallery of Classic Fishing photographs has shots from the Golden Age of Hemingway and Zane Grey.

Antique Lure Collectibles
http://www.antiquelurecollectibles.com

The place on the Web to gain a lure collecting education, this highly organized site teaches

TOP RATED the practical aspects of

Tackle and Boats

collecting and identifying old lures. The homepage is a contents menu for learning about cleaning, cataloging, displaying, photographing, evaluating and checking for frauds. If you just want to look at some cool old lures, the link to the "list of individual lures" cuts straight to a huge collection of pre-1930 wooden examples from makers such as Heddon, Shakespeare and Pflueger.

The site is complemented by the equally informative **AntiqueLures TOP RATED** at **http://www. antiquelures.com**, which has 500 pages of advice, discussions and photographs of pre-1960 lures.

To learn more about collecting antique reels try Tom Greene's **http://www.antiquereels.com.**

Lure Lore
http://www.lurelore.com

TOP RATED

Antique lure collectors usually restrict themselves to a few companies or types of lure in the hope they'll be able to amass a meaningfully deep collection within their specialty. Tom Jacomet's obsession is with Heddon's River Runt Spooks, and he uses this site to show his collection and publish his crazily detailed research. River Runt fans will find a company history, model descriptions, color codes and "errata"—a list of rare manufacturing anomalies. But there's plenty here for the general collector as well. Each of the 30 archived newsletters (go to Back Issues under Lure Lore Contents) profiles one or two different lures and the section Collector Information has links, show calendars and tips for cleaning and displaying.

THE SPLIT-CANE SUCKER CONNECTION

The last 15 years has seen a blossoming of companies making traditional angling tackle in Britain, and something unusual in the U.S., much of it has been aimed outside the fly-fishing market. So if you're a lure angler or bait soaker and have looked longingly at fly fishing's sweet reeds and magical wheels, explore these sites for split-cane river and stillwater rods, centerpin reels, wicker seat boxes and other accoutrement for the well-outfitted freshwater angler.

The Edward Barder Rod Company
http://www.barder-rod.co.uk

Norman Agutters Online
http://www.norman-agutters.com

Traditional Angling
http://www.traditional-angling.co.uk

Center Pin Fishing Reels
http://www.center-pin-fishing-reels.com

Classic Cane
http://www.interalpha.net/customer/cane-rods

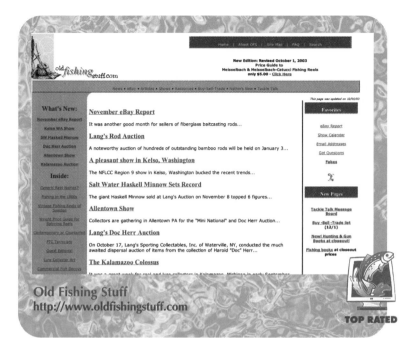

Old Fishing Stuff
http://www.oldfishingstuff.com

TOP RATED

See also Charlie Santangelo's **The Creek Chub Bait Co. Surfster Experience** at **http://home.si.rr. com/ccbcosurfster** for a lure history and portraits of Charlie's collection, some of them impressively chewed.

Mr. Lure Box
http://www.mrlurebox.com

TOP RATED

Outdoor writer and collector Robbie Pavey's wide-ranging site displays antique lures and matching boxes from 180 small companies, and has good holdings from the majors—Heddon, Creek Chub, Pflueger, South Bend, and others. Navigate the collection via a simple alphabetical company list. Click on a company name to view a short profile of the lure and a photograph of it lounging in its little box. All photos are clickable for an expanded view. Good links

and advice for novice collectors make it a site every lure enthusiast should drop in on.

See also **Joe's Old Lures** at **http://www.joeyates.com**, for Joe Yates' Heddon and Florida lure collection, an events calendar for upcoming shows and a very popular collectors' forum.

Old Fishing Stuff
http://www.oldfishingstuff.com

TOP RATED

Author Phil White's magazine takes a less rarefied approach to collecting antique lures and tackle—he actually fishes with some of his babies—and it's made Old Fishing Stuff one of the most popular collecting sites on the Web. Among the many articles, references, company histories and links are two unique features. On the righthand side of

The Sport Fishing Museum
http://www.sportfishingmuseum.ca

---

the homepage is a link to a complete subject index for The National Fishing Lure Collectors Club magazine and newsletter, going back more than 10 years. This is the premier organization for U.S. collectors and has more than 4,000 members. Find them online at **http://www.nflcc.com**.

Back on the homepage and just above the subject index is the eBay Report. This is a monthly look at vintage tackle (and the occasional fraud) up for sale on what's become the world's most popular auction block. It's an entertaining and conversational summary of prices paid, rarities found, bargains and bidding dramas for rods, reels, lures and miscellaneous items.

Phil declares his special collecting interest at **http://www.oldreels.com**.

Richard's Classic Bamboo Fishing Rods, Antique Tackle and Vintage Reels
http://www.antiquetackle.net

Richard Collar sells a tempting inventory of vintage rods, reels and accessories from this simple site. He'll also sell tackle on your behalf for a small fee. Items are clearly photographed and described and the section Bamboo Rod Grading System sets out the standard criteria used when listing vintage bamboo rods.

The Sport Fishing Museum
http://www.sportfishingmuseum.ca

TOP RATED

Developed to preserve the rich history and artifacts of sportfishing in the Pacific Northwest, the museum web site showcases more than 500 antique reels, including unmatched examples from the English maker Hardy, and hundreds of individually mounted classic fly patterns. Go to Collections in the top navigation to view the museum's holdings in 13 other tackle categories. The site doesn't post much information about individual pieces, but every item is clearly photographed. The museum is located in Vancouver, British Columbia.

TACKLE REVIEWS
OutdoorREVIEW.com – Flyfishing
http://www.outdoorreview.com

TOP RATED

One obvious way to ensure reviews aren't compromised by advertising budgets is to get consumers to do the reviewing for you. This is the approach taken by Outdoor-REVIEW.com's fly-fishing center.

New fly-fishing products are posted to the site along with a brief description from the site editor. Anyone who has used the item can click on Write a Review to describe their impressions. Each review page has areas for value ratings, general impressions, strengths, weaknesses and customer service. Reviewers are free to post as much or as little information as they want, but at a minimum all reviewed products are quick rated on a scale of 1 to 5.

The philosophy of getting visitors involved extends to community areas for selling secondhand tackle, posting catch photos and a friendly forum for tackle advice and fly-fishing chat. The fly-fishing center is a small part of the OutdoorREVIEW network, which includes sites for photography, paddling, backpacking and camping.

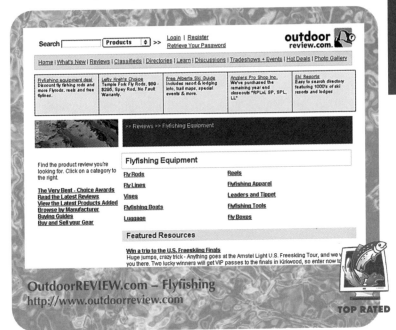

Tackle Tour
http://www.tackletour.com

TOP RATED

Tackle Tour
http://www.tackletour.com

TOP RATED

Tackle obsessives will be throwing their breathable fishing hats into the air on discovering this tackle review site. Editor Alex "Zander" Mei has fattened its content with news feeds from ESPN Outdoors, fishing articles and links, but tackle talk is the unashamed heart of the site with in-depth reviews of the latest reels, rods, lines, basic tackle (lines, hooks, sinkers), tools, storage, watercraft, apparel and fly-fishing equipment.

Reviews offer a level of analysis well beyond what's common in a print magazine. Every review has photographs of the product from several angles, general impressions out of the box, how it performed on the water and complete specifications. Ratings out of 10 for construction, performance, price, features, design and application and a summary of plusses and minuses wrap it up. Though fly-fishing products are reviewed, Tackle Tour is strongest on general lure and bass fishing.

Fishing For Bargains on the Web

"Fishing" really does seem an appropriate metaphor for the process of finding good deals among the thousands of fishing tackle e-tailers. Serious bargain hunters need to run and gun, shoot a few casts into likely holes and move on. A lot still depends on luck and timing, but follow the six stages outlined below and you'll have covered all the most promising water.

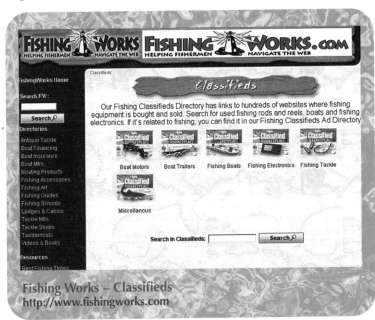

Fishing Works – Classifieds
http://www.fishingworks.com

1. Buy Secondhand

Don't Think Classifieds, Think Forums

The Web is an ideal place for private sellers and buyers to meet. Apart from the potential for a hugely expanded audience, online advertisements can be instantly updated and listed in as much detail as the seller feels like posting.

Despite these advantages, there don't seem to be any really robust national web sites exclusively for buying and selling used tackle. The classifieds directory at **http://www.fishingworks.com** is the best collection of fishing classifieds on the Web. It has some excellent sites listed within its boating categories, but the tackle options are patchy. The best fly-fishing site with a dedicated classifieds area is the online edition of *Fly Fisherman* at **http://www.fly fisherman.com,** with **The Steelhead Site, http://www.steelheadsite.com,** also worth a look. The best way to find secondhand tackle is to give up on "classifieds" and start looking for forums. The biggest regional sites and the biggest sites within fly fishing, bass fishing, freshwater fishing and saltwater fishing all

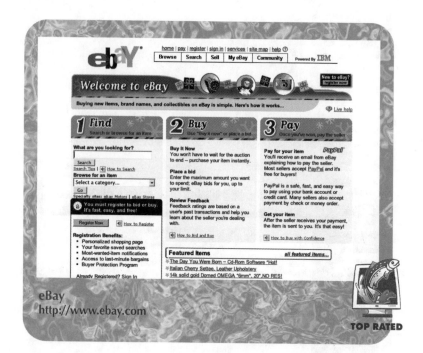

eBay
http://www.ebay.com

TOP RATED

host active forums for selling tackle and boats. To get started try: **Fly Anglers Online**, **http://www.fly anglersonline.com**; **Noreast.com**, **http://www.noreast.com**; **AllCoast Sport Fishing**, **http://www.sport-fish-info.com**; the **Bass Fishing Home Page**, **http://www.bass fishinghomepage. com**; and **Pro Bass**, **http://www.pro bass.com**.

eBay
http://www.ebay.com

TOP RATED

eBay, "the World's online marketplace", is Internet quicksand for fishermen: each step down another tangential path sucks you deeper into a matrix of 30,000 tackle bargains, oddities, rarities and things you never thought you'd get hold of again. To save yourself, search with a purpose. From the homepage, look for the

Sports heading, then click on Sporting Goods then Fishing to find 12 options from Baits & Lures (5,000 items) to Fly Fishing (5,600) to Vintage (9,000). You can then view subcategories (within Baits & Lures, for example, are headings for Crankbaits, Jigs, Soft Plastics, Spoons, and "Spinner-balls"), or perform a keyword search just within the category. To avoid excessive mailing or trans-port fees you might want to search local sellers first. From the home-page go to Browse in the top navi-gation then Regions.

Buyers and sellers have two ways to play. Items are either sold direct or you can bid on them within an auction. If you're prepared to match an asking price, some auction items can be bought directly as well. In practice, it's a remarkably fluid and easy process to both bid and offer items for sale, but check the Help section on the homepage for clear explanations on how to register, bid, buy and sell.

So you could probably use another fly rod … You see a listing for a secondhand St. Croix 6-weight. Clicking on the link opens a description page which has photographs of the rod, details of its condition, how much to add for shipping, a bidding history and how many days and hours are left before the auction closes. There's also a link to see how other users rate the reliability of the seller if they've sold items on eBay before.

The last bid on the rod was $80. So you bid $82 and indicate on the bidding screen your maximum bid is $120. eBay will incrementally increase your bid by $2 if a competing bid comes in, up to your maximum. Bid increments are determined by eBay and vary from item to item, but are displayed on the description page before you're committed to anything. If at the end of the auction competing bids haven't topped your $82 plus $2 raises, you've won the auction and trout should tremble.

Vintage tackle collectors should visit **http://www.antiquelures. com**, and read through the eBay Report at **http://www.oldfishing stuff.com**, for advice about this specialized market.

PHOTOGRAPHY

Many fishermen develop an accompanying interest in photography, spurred perhaps by the understandable desire to crush the weary cynics waiting for them at home. For advice on how to improve your fishing shots, put "photography" into the search box at *Sport Fishing* magazine, **http://www.sportfishingmag.com**. You'll find articles discussing scenic shots, photographing fish and anglers, stopping the action, using point-and-shoot cameras and tips for fishing photojournalists.

Fly tiers and anyone else who wants to advance their fishing photography skills should check these two guides to digital and studio photography. Martin Joergensen's "From Feathers to Bits" series within the **Global FlyFisher** at **http://www.globalfly fisher.com** covers digitizing flies for online publication with typical comprehensiveness and exactitude. Go to Gallery on the homepage for the link. **Fly Anglers Online** at **http://www.flyanglersonline.com** boasts a wonderful set of articles about digital and macro fishing photography. They are both by Al Campbell: look for his archive on the homepage or use the search function.

Outdoor Photographer magazine at **http://www.outdoorphotographer .com** has plenty of tips and articles that can be applied to fishing situations, such as shooting in low light, keeping gear to a minimum and protecting cameras from the elements.

Guidebook publisher **Fodors** has an award-winning site, one small part of which is author Jeff Wignall's travel photography page at **http://www.fodors.com/focus**, covering everything from choosing a travel camera to how to shoot from a plane window.

See also **Yahoo! Auctions** at **http://www.auctions.yahoo.com**.

Newsgroups

The fishing newsgroups listed in Chapter 1 How to Find Fishing Information on the Internet are one more option for finding second-hand tackle. Some members may grumble about commercial solicitations, but "for sale" notices are fairly common in many newsgroups. If you're doing a keyword search within an area such as rec.outdoors.marketplace, don't forget to sort by date for the freshest postings.

2. Try the Big Online Tackle Sellers

These companies all have sale areas and regular promotions, which they'll usually make only too obvious on their homepage. Several sites were recently offering a free rod with the purchase of a Fin-Nor Estima spinning reel (with shipping, about $77), and one company was slicing more than $500 off the recommended retail price of a Mercury Quicksilver Inflatable Boat.

eAngler at **http://www.eangler. com** is a good example of a big, well-run online tackle seller: the sort of fishing megastore anyone with Internet access can walk down the aisles of 24 hours a day. There's a phenomenal amount of tackle on offer here from artwork and gifts to a huge selection of lures, rods, reels, accessories and clothing. To get a visual idea of the site's holdings, click on Shop by Brands to see a three-column list of more than 500 available brands. Navigation is simple and straightforward. Use the menus on the homepage or check out the rotating specials offered every week. Click through the product subcategories to choose colors, sizes and particular models.

eAngler
http://www.eangler.com

The few carefully selected content features include a Florida fishing reports forum, a clever Fish Encyclopedia matching species to habitat, video knot tutorials and a weather and tide center.

Some other of the biggest online tackle sellers include:

Bass Pro Shops
http://www.bassproshops.com

Big Fish Tackle
http://www.bigfishtackle.com

BoatersWorld
http://www.boatersworld.com

Bob Marriot's Flyfishing Store
http://www.bobmarriots.com

Cabelas
http://www.cabelas.com

LandBigFish
http://www.landbigfish.com

Sportfish (UK)
http://www.sportfish.co.uk

The Sportsman's Guide
http://www.sportsmansguide.com

TackleDirect
http://www.tackledirect.com

WorldWaters
http://www.worldwaters.com

(Note: at least three of these companies work from the same inventory, but that doesn't necessarily mean they'll have exactly the same promotions and offers.)

3. Try the Big Sporting Goods Sellers

Dozens of online sporting goods sellers and big-box department stores also carry a full line of fishing tackle. Again, rotating discounts, free shipping and closeout corners are practically mandatory.

Bass Pro Shops
http://www.bassproshops.com

Academy
http://www.academy.com

Dick's Sporting Goods
http://www.dickssporting
goods.com

G.I. Joes
http://www.gijoes.com

Oshmans
http://www.oshmans.com

Overstock.com
http://www.overstock.com

The Sports Authority
http://www.sportsauthority.com

Wal-Mart
http://www.walmart.com

4. Use Shop Bots

Many of the companies listed in steps 2 and 3 can be searched simultaneously by using a "shop bot," which is a specialized search engine that hunts for keywords within the inventories of its partner sites. There are dozens of different bots, but two with good coverage of the sporting goods industry are **BizRate** at **http://www.bizrate. com** and **Shopping.com** at **http:// www.shopping.com**. For both, go to the Sports or Outdoors section and type the product you're looking for into the search box to compare prices across multiple stores. Though they aren't referred to as shop bots, the online shopping malls at **Yahoo! http://www. shopping.yahoo.com**, and **AOL http://www.shop.aol.com** perform the same function in that they host dozens of e-tailers in different categories and provide a simple way to search them all at the same time.

Say a shopper wasn't really interested in the free rod that comes with the Estima reel. They go to

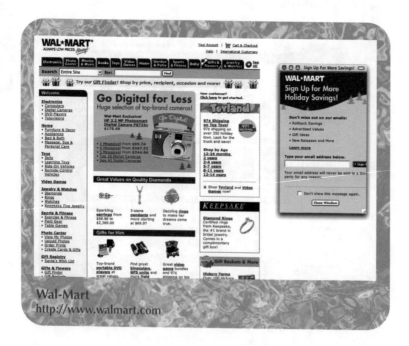

Wal-Mart
http://www.walmart.com

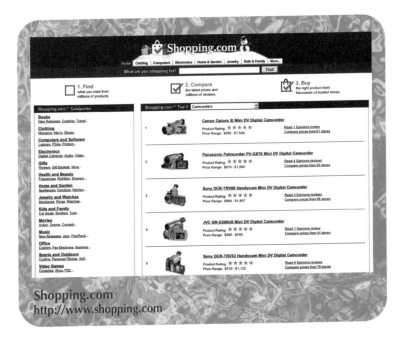

Shopping.com
http://www.shopping.com

the Sports & Outdoors department of Yahoo! Shopping, find the fishing sub-page and type "Fin-Nor Estima" into the search box. It returns 16 products from four different stores, the best of which is Overstock.com offering the same reel without the rod for $39.99, plus a discounted shipping charge for a total of $42.94.

When using a shop bot, always check that you're comparing like with like. Bots aren't so finely tuned that they'll always distinguish between model variations within the same products, such as different capacity reels or rod styles.

5. Look for Coupons
Coupon and discount-finder web sites gather special offers, promotions and deals into a convenient directory. These are not unique offers—they should all be referenced somewhere on the original site—but they're worth scanning to

make sure you aren't missing out on a competitor's offer for free shipping or some other incentive. There are more of these sites on the Web than you'll ever need, but two with reasonable coverage of fishing tackle sellers are **Dealitup.com** at **http://www.dealitup.com** and **eDealFinder.com** at **http://www.edealfinder.com**. The Special Offers section of BizRate also lists promotions going on within its Sports and Outdoors department.

Back to our phantom Fin-Nor shopper. They remember that Dealitup.com has especially thorough listings for each of its companies. It indicates Overstock.com has six current promotions, including one that promises an extra $5 off purchases over $25 for new customers.

In most cases, you're now given a coupon code to enter just before checking out. In this example, a

link takes them to the Over-
stock.com site where they have to
scout around looking for the offer,
but there it is in a little box on the
Sports, Travel & Toys page.

Score. So the reel that several
merchants listed for more than
$75 (with and without the "free"
rod) is in our shopper's hot little
hands for $37.95.

6. Don't Ignore the Specialists

You can find bargains at the online
mega malls and tackle warehouses,
but it's the specialist retailers within
each branch of the sport that really
provide the richness and breadth
of choice. Every tackle item imaginable for every species worldwide
is now within the radius of a few
mouse clicks.

Most fishermen are aware of the
specialist retailers within their
favorite branch of the sport, but
if you just want to browse, try a
categorized business directory
such as the ones offered at Google,
The Ultimate Bass Fishing Resource
Guide, Black's Fly Fishing Directory
or FishingWorks. The online versions of newsstand fishing magazines also very often link to every
advertiser in their print publications. See Chapter 5 Media, Print
Magazines Online for options.

Froogle and Google Catalogs

Google has recently introduced
two features to make online
shopping more efficient. From the
Google homepage at **http://www.
google.com** click on Services and
Tools to find links to **Froogle** and
Google Catalogs or go direct
to **http://froogle.google.com**
and **http://catalogs.google.com.**

Froogle trains the company's
leading-edge search technology
on finding products offered by the
Web's multitude of online sellers.
Go to Fishing and Hunting within
the Sports & Outdoors category
and enter the name of the product
into the search box. Each listing
has a photograph of the item, a
link to the site offering it, its price
and a few words of description.
Froogle was still in the test stage
at the time it was reviewed but
was already drawing from the
largest index of e-commerce sites
on the Web.

Some mail order companies still
list many more products within
their print catalogs than on their
web site. Google Catalogs
overcomes this by offering page-
by-page scanned reproductions
of thousands of popular catalogs.
There are more than 140 to choose
from within the Outdoors section
of the directory. Pages start small
but can be easily expanded to a
comfortable reading size. Use the
link to each company's web site
for online ordering. These pages
are, in effect, one big graphic: you
need a fast computer to get the
most from the service.

Boats

Fishermen have their day on the water in a tremendous variety of crafts: there are kayaks, canoes, sportfishers, skiffs, jet boats, bass boats, drift boats, pontoons, prams, inflatables, float tubes, jon boats—some even fish from surfboards. It seems anglers would float themselves on rafts of tree trunks lashed together with fishing line if it meant they could leave behind the concerns of terra firma and play where the fish are.

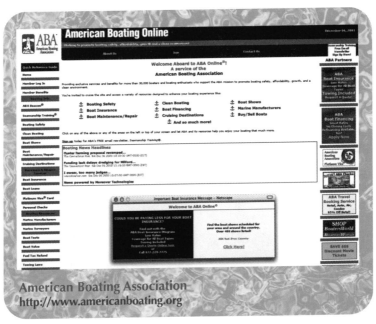

American Boating Association
http://www.americanboating.org

AllKayakFishing.com
http://www.allkayakfishing.com

Kayak Fishing Secrets
http://www.rbbsurf.com

Anyone curious about kayak fishing should cast an eye over these introductory sites. AllKayakFishing.com is a beginner's guide to hardware and buying considerations. Click on Yak Fishing 101 and Rigging Photos for notes and annotated photos of different ways to outfit your yak. The Resources section has a list of better-quality kayak fishing web sites. Kayak Fishing Secrets, a subsection of a New Jersey kayak store and forum center, covers choosing a craft, outfitting it as a fishing machine, transportation options, wetsuit advice and safety considerations.

American Boating Association (ABA)
http://www.americanboating.org

The ABA has all the group services and discounts you'd expect from a professional members organization charging annual dues, but it's actually free to join. Just one part of the benefits package is this resource- and information-packed web site. Some of its highlights include tips for safe and environmentally clean boating, professionally authored articles from the *ABA Beacon* newsletter, destination features, state towing laws, and neatly indexed links to suppliers, boating education and weather resources.

American Canoe Association (ACA)

http://www.acanet.org

TOP RATED

Freshwater and saltwater fishermen have increasingly realized the benefits of fishing from canoes and kayaks: they're comparatively cheap to buy and cost nothing to maintain; they're easily launched by one person; they're unmatched for quietness and

stealth. Convinced? Go through the ACA's Getting Started guide for equipment options, basic techniques and links to clubs all over the U.S.

The Association publishes a group magazine, *Paddler*, for its 45,000 members and a link in the top navigation leads to its own site at **http://www.paddle magazine.com**.

Bass & Walleye Boats Magazine

http://www.bassandwalleye boats.com

TOP RATED

The online edition of the only magazine devoted exclusively to high-performance freshwater fishing boats. If you get excited by sentences like "Merc's prototype 250 features an integral hydraulic steering system that

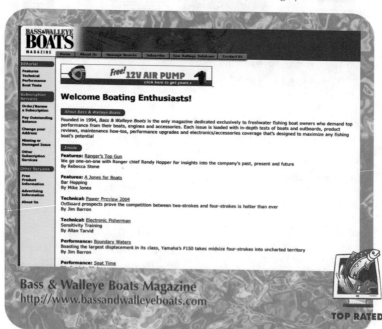

BassBoat Central
http://www.bassboatcentral.com

TOP RATED

does not require a drag link from a hydraulic cylinder back to the tiller arm on the engine," you've found a home. Sections include general boating features, boat tests and performance evaluations of boats, motors, electronics and other equipment. A tow-rating database states the towing capacity for most newer cars and trucks.

BassBoat Central
http://www.bassboatcentral.com

TOP RATED

Could it be that a large reason bass fishing became so popular was the evolutionary development of the bass boat? It's a happy marriage: not only do you get to go fishing, but you're allowed to zoom around in your own personal rocket ship.

The regulars at BassBoat Central certainly seem to love their rigs.

A central feature of the site is the Owner's List, where 2,000 proud parents have posted their boat's vital statistics and the particulars of how they've fine-tuned them. The list is sorted by company name, some are photographed and all provide e-mail addresses for passing on maintenance tips. Other site features include set-up tips from bass boat experts, a Likes & Dislikes area, an active forum, and classifieds for buying and selling boats, motors and props.

See also the forums at the **Bass Fishing Network**, **http://www.bass fishingnetwork.com**, which include popular hangouts for boat buying, selling and note swapping.

BoatersDream
http://www.boatersdream.com

BoatersDream bills itself as the "Ultimate Resource for Great Lakes

Boating Magazines

The boating industry is well served with big glossy magazines, and several of them offer web sites full of articles, product reviews and helpful references. *Boating World*, for example, at **http://www.boatingworldonline.com** offers a sprinkling of product reviews and boat tests from the current issue, as well as articles about tow vehicles, boating skills, classic boats and destinations. *Boating Life* at **http://www.boatinglifemag.com**, and *Motor Boating* at **http://www.motorboating.com**, have comparable web editions with boat and electronics reviews, marine weather centers and travel articles. But the magazine with the most generous online edition is:

Go Boating America
http://www.goboatingamerica.com

TOP RATED

A combi-site for the magazines *Sea and Go Boating*, its departments offer up a whopping 500 boat tests, a massive survey of new boats, gear and electronics, and over 1,000 boat maintenance and travel features. There isn't a separate fishing section but the search function on the homepage shakes out hundreds of articles referencing fishing, from bass boat reviews to port descriptions.

Boating and Great Lakes Fishing." The Marine Weather Center offers daily localized condition reports for every major port on the five lakes, and for the St. Clair, Maumee and Niagara Rivers. The homepage has updated lake levels and links to big areas for fishing articles, boating how-to and advice. Mouse over the heading Boating to find port profiles, GPS coordinates and navigation tips.

The Ultimate? There are better Great Lakes fishing sites on the Web, but a commendable effort.

Boats.com
http://www.boats.com

One of the busiest places on the Web for buying and selling new and secondhand boats (more than 60,000 listings), also provides an array of user services including reviews and valuations, links to manufacturers, and a database for finding boat shows, builders and dealers. On the righthand side of the homepage is a link to a dedicated fishing area containing boat reviews, travel articles, how-to tips and feature articles.

BoatTEST.com
http://www.boattest.com

TOP RATED

Test central for recreational boaters. The homepage lists boats in 14 categories, including bass boats, fish boats and sport boats. Click on a boat type, then scroll down the list of models for a five-page analysis. Two hundred of the tests are available as Internet videos. Engines and electronics get the same thorough review, with tables allowing you to compare dozens of competing products

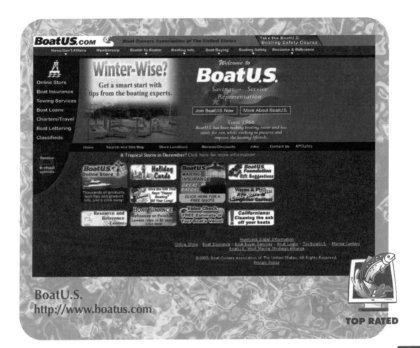

BoatU.S.
http://www.boatus.com

TOP RATED

side by side. If you don't want to browse, the site search lets you plumb the whole archive by manufacturer, size and category. Register to gain full access to the test reviews.

BoatU.S.
http://www.boatus.com

TOP RATED

BoatU.S. provides half a million subscribers with services, discounts, national representation and *BoatU.S.* magazine, but its giant web site is a free community resource. Some of its many noteworthy features include columns by Don Casey and Chuck Husick on boat repairs and marine electronics, links to buyer's guides and friendly forums.

The large Boating Safety section has details of the Sportsman's Forum, which is a project to decrease the number of boating accidents among hunters and fishermen. One of its initiatives is a 37-page safety guide titled *Boating Tips for Hunters and Anglers*, which is downloadable from the site.

Coastal Kayak Fishing
http://www.kayakfishing.com

Kayak fishing is the new rock 'n' roll of inshore saltwater fishing, and two of its pioneers are Dennis Spike and Joe Schuetz of Coastal Kayak Fishing, Inc. They are regularly and happily towed around off the coast of Southern California by white sea bass, halibut, thresher sharks and other nearshore gamefish. Kayakfishing.com is a hub of information and resources for anyone who'd like to give it a go. There are articles, tips, several fishing forums, a store with customized fishing tackle and details of their guide trips and seminars.

Tackle and Boats

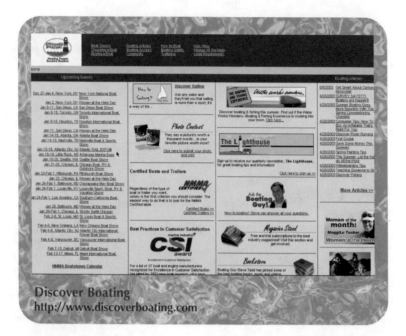

Discover Boating
http://www.discoverboating.com

Canoe and Kayak Magazine
http://www.canoekayak.com

This leading paddle sport magazine has an online edition focused on introducing newcomers to the sport. Get Started Paddling, How to Do It and What to Take have the best beginners advice. There are some in-depth equipment reviews and plenty of links to businesses and other paddling resources, but most of the rest of the site shows off the kind of heavenly backwaters paddlecraft can take you to.

Discover Boating
http://www.discoverboating.com

Discover Boating is a promotional effort from the National Marine Manufacturers Association emphasizing boating education and safety. Under the heading Boating Safety are three navigation simulators, contact information for boating education classes and links to safety quizzes, such as the one provided by http://www.boat-ed.com.

Don't pass on without exploring the article links and in-depth guide to towing from *Trailer Boats Magazine,* which has an above-average site of its own at http://www.trailerboats.com.

Duckworks Magazine
http://www.duckworks
magazine.com

TOP RATED

It must feel pretty self-sufficient and rewarding to float your own boat. The risks are obviously a little higher than when you set out to make, say, your own spinning rod or bait container, but *Duckworks Magazine* "written for and by those wacky homemade boat builders" is there to help. The site is a wonderful resource for building the type of small boat ideal for many fishing situations, like a freshwater pram or drift boat. Full access to the site requires a paid subscription but click on Archives to find dozens of free articles and updates on readers' building projects.

To build a boat you need a plan: the Small Boat listing in the Boat Index links to commercially available fishing boat plans. For freebies, try the Free Boat Plans link at the giant **http://www.boat-links.com**.

iboats
http://www.iboats.com

TOP RATED

That boat with your name on it, whether you want it for floating a brawny Western river or for gliding over inches of water on a bonefish flat, may well be hiding within the thousands of boats for sale at iboats. The majority are secondhand, some are from dealers and some from private sellers. There are strong listings in all the most important categories: 670 fishing boats, 200 aluminum boats and 300 bass boats. iboats has a popular forum for Outboard Engine Troubles & Questions, and links to hundreds of marine product sellers.

If iboats doesn't have the perfect tub, try **Boat Trader Online** at **http://www.boattrader.com**, which has 70,000 boat listings within it's huge classifieds site for all types of vehicles and goods.

FISHING MAGAZINES

Though you can find plenty of fishing material within general boating magazines, don't forget to also approach from the other direction and sort out those fishing magazines with the best boating coverage.

For saltwater fishing start with *Sport Fishing*, **http://www.sport fishingmag.com**, *Fly Fishing in Saltwaters*, **http://www.flyfishin salt.com**, the forums at **Florida Sportsman Online, http://www. floridasportsman.com,** *Marlin*, **http://www.marlinmag.com**, and *Salt Water Sportsman*, **http://www. saltwatersportsman.com**. You'll find boat, electronics and tackle reviews, technique and destination features, boating forums and weather and tide centers tailored to the needs of fishermen.

The boating section at **LandBigFish http://www.landbigfish.com/ boating** has more than 60 articles,

many about freshwater bass and walleye boating. **The Bass Fishing Home Page** and **Saltwater Fishing Home Page**, both accessible from **http://www.anglerworld.com** are excellent places to dip into an informal and determinedly independent dialogue about boats, electronics. props, trailering and towing. Several of the larger bass sites reviewed in Chapter 4 Fishing the Web, in fact, have forums dedicated to reviewing and tinkering with bass boats and outboards.

Though they don't have a specific department named for it, put "drift boat" "pontoon boat" "pram" or "float tube" into the search option at **Fly Angler's Online, http://www. flyanglersonline.com** and it returns hundreds of references. Most come from the regular boating conversations that bubble up on the forums: you might have to browse a few posts to find relevant material, but the forums are so friendly and helpful, wandering around is a pleasure.

Kayak Sportfishing
http://www.kayaksportfishing.com

TOP RATED

Kayak Sportfishing
http://www.kayaksportfishing.com

TOP RATED Kayak Sportfishing uses plenty of illustrative photography to introduce newcomers to this unique branch of salt-water fishing. Sections for Rigged Kayaks and Equipment itemize everything from drift chutes and rod holders to fully tricked-out fishing machines. The site comes out of the kayak fishing stronghold of Southern California and recommends a number of regional fishing sites. For rigging tips or where-to-go information, post a question to the lively forum.

NADA Guides
http://www.nadaguides.com

NADA guides have been advising consumers about used boat prices for 70 years. The company's print guides have to be purchased, but the whole service is available online for nothing. Click the boat tab in the top navigation then choose between newer or older boats, outboard motors or boat trailers. Choose a manufacturer, a year, the model and trim level to discover the low and average retail price and a few summary details.

Ottertooth
http://www.ottertooth.com

Looking at the wilderness canoe routes at Ottertooth as they ribbon through the Canadian bush, it's easy to lose yourself in thoughts of serene Northern lakes and secret brook trout streams. The site describes three wilderness canoe areas in depth: the Sutton River flowing from Hudson Bay to Washagami Lake; the Rupert River in Quebec; and the Temagami River in Ontario. For

Tackle and Boats

Paddle-Fishing.com
http://www.paddle-fishing.com

TOP RATED

each area there are route maps, journals from paddlers who've made the trip and conservation articles. The rest of the site has shorter guides to other regions, camp listings and information about wood and canvass canoes.

See also the **WaterTribe** at **http://www.watertribe.com**, for fishing, paddling and wilderness adventures.

Paddle-Fishing.com
http://www.paddle-fishing.com

TOP RATED

A super resource for Tampa Bay paddlers, with plenty of useful canoe and kayak information for wherever you take to the water. The Articles, Rigging Reviews and Destination areas are meaty

enough for a visitor to settle in for a good read or trip-planning session. The forum's a popular hang-out and it looks like the regulars get together once in a while to put faces to nicknames and harass the local snook and redfish.

Recreational Boating and Fishing Foundation (RBFF) – Aquatic Science, Fishing, and Boating Education Web Directory
http://www.rbff-education.org

The RBFF's web directory, reviewed in the Kids section of Chapter 6 Groups, also has excellent links to boating education resources. Click on the Access folder, for example, to find links to more than 45 regional boating sites listing marinas, ramps and

Water Works Wonders
http://www.waterworkswonders.org

TOP RATED

boat launches. The Foundation is also behind the **Water Works Wonders** campaign at **http://www.waterworkswonders.org,** which has a boating channel centered on a grandly ambitious database for finding boating opportunities and facilities on every major waterway in the country, as well as links to local boating regulations and resources. See Chapter 2 State-by-Sate Resources for a review.

The United States Coast Guard (UCSG)

http://www.uscg.mil/uscg.shtm

The USCG operates on many fronts, but its public face is the nation's marine safety and rescue organization. The Recreational Boating Safety sub-page within the section Maritime Safety (direct at **http://www.uscgboating.org**) has a forest of links to regional and national safety courses and boating laws. For a dedicated navigation page, go to Aides to Navigation under Maritime Mobility for links and information about Loran C, GPS and other navigation programs.

CHAPTER 8
INTERNATIONAL

The Web is so top heavy with U.S. content it can be easy to forget that bit about "World Wide" at the beginning of the phrase, but there are many quality fishing sites out of Canada, Australia, South Africa, Britain, Europe and countries scattered around the world. It's fascinating to look in on a foreign fishing culture for all the peripheral things that are different and all the fundamental things that stay the same, whether you fish for barras in the Northern Territories or follow your fly down an English chalkstream.

Australia and New Zealand

These sites are a mirror of the fishing they report on—big and colorful and full of variety. And for those who can't help thinking of crocodile wranglers and wild-eyed outdoorsmen, it should be said that several of them are among the sharpest-looking, design-led fishing sites on the Web. They're well worth a visit, even if Murray cod are never likely to be in your travel plans.

AusFish.com
http://www.ausfish.com.au

TOP RATED

AUSTRALIA
AusFish.com
http://www.ausfish.com.au

TOP RATED

Based in Queensland, AusFish.com says it's Australia's oldest Internet tacklestore. It's fully stocked with rods, reels, accessories, books, videos and clothing, but the reader resources are what make it so bookmarkable. There's a hugely popular forum center for general chat, Queensland fishing reports and boating discussion. Mouse over Hints & Tips to find mini magazines from fishing writers Dave "Nugget" Downie and Garry Fitzgerald. And lastly, the links section has a directory of resource management agencies and the best Aussie fishing sites.

Australian Fishing Network
http://www.afn.com.au

Go to the Fishing Bookstore for a comprehensive list of freshwater and saltwater technique books, fly-fishing titles from the U.S., videos and artwork. All titles

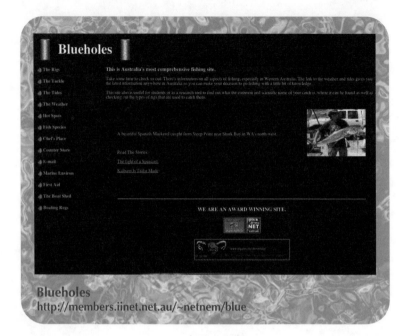

Blueholes
http://members.iinet.net.au/~netnem/blue

are pictured and given a one-sentence description. Order by phone or fax.

Blueholes
http://members.iinet.net.au/~netnem/blue

Blueholes is not, as they boldly state on the homepage, "Australia's most comprehensive fishing site," but rather a good and lean introduction to nearshore saltwater fishing. It's ideal for a newcomer who needs some straight advice on tackle, rigs and boat safety. Site navigation is simple and consistent and will also deliver you to short discussions about the greater marine environment from squid to coral reefs and an overview of shore marks around Western Australia.

The site links to regional weather forecasts and recommends a national tide table resource at **http://www.ntf.flinders.edu.au/**

TEXT/TIDES/tides.html, giving weekly tide predictions for the entire Australian coastline.

Canberra Sweetwater Angler
http://canberrasweetwater angler.com

Fishermen in Australia's capital city have no excuse for doing yardwork or cleaning the car, as this site shows in descriptions of 18 lakes and impoundments and more than 30 rivers. Topographic map references and photos accompany some of the profiles, which are just detailed enough to plan a trip around. The fishing reports section was a little patchy (scroll to the bottom of the page to view the most recent report), but the gallery of successful Canberra anglers should be inspiration enough to set the alarm for Sunday morning.

Fishing Cairns
http://www.fishingcairns.com.au

TOP RATED

Coarse Angling in Australia
http://www.coarsefishing.ws

If you've ever looked at British fishing sites you'll know "coarse fishing" is the misleading term for light-tackle bait fishing. This site applies those methods to Australia's controversial immigrants: carp, tench, roach and perch. It's a high-quality job with explanations and diagrams of the specialized tackle used and links to the best European coarse and competition fishing pages.

For those who aren't keen on European imports, **Native Fish Australia** at **http://www.native fish.asn.au**, has an A to Z Fish Files gallery that pictures and describes all the native species.

Fishing Cairns
http://www.fishingcairns.com.au

TOP RATED

The team at Fishing Cairns says "If you can't catch it in North Queensland, it's probably not worth catching." They back up the claim with reams of information for freshwater and saltwater species running the alphabet from archer fish to yellowfin tuna. As the site describes in sections for Localities, Environments and Trip Reports, many of those species are easily available to Cairns-based anglers.

Visitors will appreciate the lists of local charters, restaurants and places to stay. A good links section provides exit roads to every important fishing region in the country, and all the major Australian sport-fishing organizations.

Fishing Monthly
http://www.fishingmonthly.com.au

TOP RATED

You can see the effort, not to mention the probable expense, which has gone into taking these colorful Queensland and New South Wales magazines to the Web. Weekly fishing reports for both areas have enough depth to be of real value and you can read back through two years of entries to form a "real-time" impression of how the seasons unfold. The Archives section has plenty of boat and truck reviews, destination and how-to articles and there's a forum and tournament list for those who like a bit of company.

Fishing Noosa
http://www.fishingnoosa.com.au

TOP RATED

Fishing Noosa has some of the best catch reports you'll see on any web site—not for the size and quantity of fish they catch in this part of Queensland's Sunshine coast, though these are impressive enough, but for the full descriptions and bright color photographs posted every week. When you've looked at the reports, move on to business listings, technique discussions, or write-ups of the annual Noosa Family Fishing Classic.

A link to national weather resources provided by the **Australian Bureau of Meteorology** at **http://www. bom.gov.au**, should be bookmarked by all Aussie anglers.

Fishing Western Australia
http://www.fishingwa.com

Fishing the Territory
http://www.fishingthe
territory.com.au

The Northern Territory, home of saltwater crocs, large tracts of aboriginal lands and exceptional barramundi fishing, is colorfully mapped in this tourist and traveler's guide. Drop-down menus lead to areas for species, tactics, where to fish, how to get there, guides and lodging. The Fish Planner lets you cruise the site and select the most relevant material to end up with a customized travel guide.

A box at the bottom of the lefthand navigation titled Need the Best Fishing Maps? links to the **North Australian Fish Finder** at **http://www.fishfinderbooks.com**, where you'll find road conditions and fishing regulations for Queensland, Western Australia and the Northern Territories, plus books for sale, articles and business listings.

Fishing Western Australia
http://www.fishingwa.com

A companion site to the *Fishing Western Australia* magazine and television show. To view everything on the site requires a subscription, but while you're deciding they'll let you look at the forums, a few articles and columns from the magazine and a large number of tip sheets. Among other features on the free side of the site, I particularly liked the mad-scientist sound of the "Fish Aggregating Devices" or FADs, they tell you where to find off the Western coast. FADs are like big buoys that provide cover to baitfish and the desirable things that feed on them. Every tacklebox should have one.

Government Fisheries Agencies

As in the U.S., all the regional government fisheries web sites have areas for recreational fishermen, and some have whole sites for angler education and regulations. At the New South Wales site, for example, you can purchase a fishing license online or use the Angler's Info Kit for quick access to regulations, where-to-fish guides and tips for catch and release. Queensland's Fishweb sells regional guides, explains stocking policy and has details of the FishCare Volunteer program.

The major agencies are:

Government of Western Australia Department of Fisheries
http://www.fish.wa.gov.au

New South Wales Fisheries
http://www.fisheries.nsw.gov.au

State of Victoria Department of Sustainability and Environment
http://www.dse.vic.gov.au

State of Queensland Department of Primary Industries and Resources - Fishweb
http://www.dpi.qld.gov.au/fishweb

Government of South Australia Primary Industries and Resources – Fisheries & Aquaculture
http://www.pir.sa.gov.au

Fishnet
http://www.fishnet.com.au

TOP RATED

Australia's leading fishing site is a big colorful portal into the country's big, bright fishing potential. Its content comes from a roster of pro anglers (articles, fishing reports, Q&A's), community involvement (fishing reports, forums, readers' gallery), and editorial resources (fly-tying database, fish species identifier, club listings). Every style of fishing is covered somewhere within these encyclopedic pages, in addition to areas for boating and 4-wheel driving. Requires an updated browser.

FishnTales.com
http://www.fishntales.com

TOP RATED

These tales come from Hervey Bay, "the recreation capital of Queensland and the whale watching capital of the world." Among many well-developed features are maps, fish identification tables and a mini-guide to opportunities on Fraser Island, a World Heritage Site off the Queensland coast. The section GPS Database locates dozens of saltwater hotspots in Queensland and other coastal areas. Use the rest of the FishnTales.com site to research accommodation, fishing guides, restaurants and attractions.

FishOnline
http://www.fishonline.tas.gov.au

Tasmania's fisheries agency publishes a stylish and useful web site just for recreational fishermen. Mouse over the map of Tasmania and outlying islands for short descriptions of fishing opportunities, then click on each grid for maps showing towns, highways and fishing spots. Go to Fish in the top navigation for a special section about trout fishing, including a link to **Trout Guides and Lodges, Tasmania** at **http://www.trout guidestasmania.com.au**, which is the professional standards body for the island's guiding industry.

FishRaider.com
http://www.fishraider.com

TOP RATED

A handy regional resource for Sydney-area anglers with current fishing reports, several long technique articles, GPS coordinates for recommended fishing areas and a local fishing forum. Webmaster Ken Alexander favors quick-loading pages over a lot of photographs and graphics, but he does at least break things up into user-friendly chunks.

FishSA.com
http://www.fishsa.com

TOP RATED

This information-packed site reports on fishing around Adelaide, Yorke, and the Eyre Peninsula. Webmaster Tom Poczman or "Tripod" and co-conspirators Chinook and Coho present engrossing articles within areas for Gone Fishing and Tackle Talk, including a long look at the awesome barramundi. There are attractive profiles of 20 South Australian sportfish, and a whole channel of the site for boating. If you live in the target area you should definitely drop in on the FishSA forums.

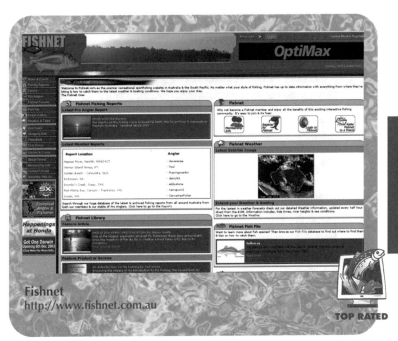

Fishnet
http://www.fishnet.com.au

TOP RATED

FishEP.com TOP RATED at
http://www.fishep.com provides
Eerie Peninsula anglers with a second quality option for local fishing
information. When reviewed the
site was bustling with weekly fishing reports, forum chat and news
stories. Advice on where and when
to fish and a virtual home for the
EP fishing community: what else
can you ask for?

FishVictoria.com
http://www.fishvictoria.com

TOP RATED

The homepage of this
terrific regional site is
a billboard of news
updates, competitions
and pro fishing reports
as well as links to Victoria fishing
clubs, a species identifier and
business directory. Pro reports are
impressively detailed and up-to-
date; the species profiles are full-
page treatments with large illustrations; and the Business Directory

has 4,400 listings under headings
for 4x4, Boats and Marine, Fishing,
Food and Outdoors.

FlyFlickers
http://www.flyflickers.com

The publishing effort of a group
of Melbourne-based guides and
enthusiasts, flyflickers.com exists
to teach others the satisfactions of
fly casting, fly tying and generally
immersing yourself in the culture of
the long rod. They offer fishing software programs, schools, guide trips
and information on local patterns
and hatcheries. The Collectables
section is a rare corner devoted
to collecting fishing books.

Australia's best fly-fishing magazine,
FlyLife, has a carefully designed
web edition with articles, a business directory and an active forum.
Go to **FlyLife Online** at **http://
www.flylife.com.au** to read and
register.

FishVictoria.com
http://www.fishvictoria.com

TOP RATED

Rex's Home Page
http://www.rexhunt.com.au

Harro On Line
http://www.harro.com.au

Rex's Home Page
http://www.rexhunt.com.au

Naturally, Australia's two best-known fishing communicators have brought their brand of experience and enthusiasm to the Web. Rod Harrrison's Harro Online has a good fish photo gallery, tips, opinion pieces and biography. Rex Hunt's lively page has articles, show schedules and areas for kids, cooks and footy fans.

Marinews
http://www.marinews.com

TOP RATED

Articles and resources within marinews.com are split evenly between boating and fishing, with a third category, Exploring, overlapping the two

with GPS coordinates, fishing maps, weather resources and destination features. Articles within each section are summarized on a contents page for quick navigation.

About half of the boating material is only available to subscribers to *Trailerboat Fisherman* magazine, but that still leaves more boating and marine equipment reviews than you'll find on most fishing sites. Weather links point to all the essential information—cloud cover, long-range forecast, tides, and moon phases—necessary for safe and successful boat fishing.

RecFish Australia
http://www.recfishoz.com

A portal into issues of recreational fisheries policy from the Australian Recreational and Sport Fishing Confederation. They are advocates on behalf of sportfishing groups

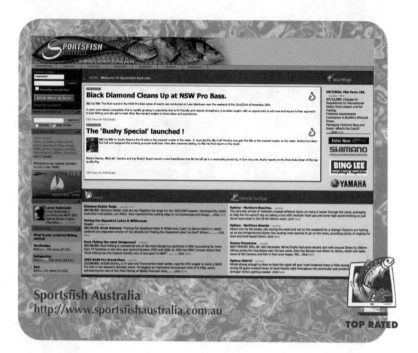

Sportsfish Australia
http://www.sportsfishaustralia.com.au

TOP RATED

at the government level. Use the site to stay current with policy and campaign news, or comb the environmental links for fishery issues in your part of the country. Don't forget to sign the Slimy Mackerel Petition before you leave. Seriously.

Sportsfish Australia
http://www.sportsfish
australia.com.au

Sportsfish Australia is an easy-on-the-eye guide to freshwater and saltwater fishing countrywide.

TOP RATED That's a lot to take on within a place as big as Australia, but the site is well organized and frequently updated. The homepage displays the latest news stories, articles and fishery reports, or you can mouse over headings

in the top navigation for dozens of subsections including forums, species profiles, articles and directory listings for clubs and charter services.

Western Angler
http://www.westernangler.com.au

Articles and commentary on this professional-look-ing companion site to *Western Angler* magazine **TOP RATED** show as much concern for healthy fisheries as for how to put fish in the cooler. Go to the resource center for hundreds of tips sent in by readers or to the Web Magazine for destination and tackle articles. Forums are divided into several regions within Western Australia.

NEW ZEALAND
Fish & Game New Zealand
http://www.fishandgame.org.nz

Fish & Game New Zealand is the
government agency responsible for
managing freshwater fishing and
gamebird hunting. The destination
links in the top navigation take you
from Northland to Southland and
10 areas in between. Coverage
varies from region to region but
can include fishing overviews,
access guides, river flows and catch
reports from Fish & Game officers.
Women and beginners have areas
all to themselves.

Fish with Bish
in New Zealand
http://www.bishfish.co.nz

TOP RATED

Most New Zealand
sites are deeply in the
service of the guiding
and lodging industry. Fair

enough—who wouldn't want to
make a living along those lovely
rivers? But it leads to rather bland
web sites. It takes a site such as
Fish with Bish, the personal page
of all-rounder Tony Bishop, to
remind you what's missing. It's full
of smart and philosophical reflections about the fishing malady, not
to mention lots of original thinking
about strategy and tackle.
Illustrations and animated cartoons
keep up the visual interest.

Fishing.net.nz
http://www.fishing.net.nz

TOP RATED

New Zealand is justly
famous for its edenic
trout fishing, but the
country's best fishing site
concentrates mostly on
the salt. Go to Advice & Info in the
lefthand navigation for tips on how
and where to target popular
species. Reviews of chater boat

Fish with Bish in New Zealand
http://www.bishfish.co.nz

TOP RATED

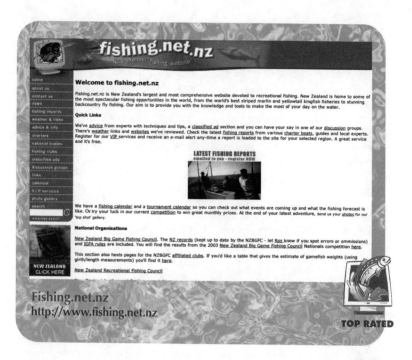

Fishing.net.nz
http://www.fishing.net.nz

TOP RATED

trips are a good idea that isn't seen very often: there are 25 on the site, along with boat, tackle and book reviews. Listings for businesses and fishing clubs and a busy forum make up just some of the rest.

Fishnz.co.nz
http://www.fishnz.co.nz

Web sites don't have to do a lot as long as they do it well. This is simply a page of links to better New Zealand fishing sites from the editors of *New Zealand Fishing News* and *Fish & Game New Zealand*, plus a Fish Species database of more than 40 game-fish. Among their site recommendations I especially liked **Paul's Fishing Kites** at **http://www. fishingkites.co.nz**, promoting an

ingenious system for flying baits and rigs out to the productive water 500 to 1,000 meters off the New Zealand shore.

Frontier Fishing Gazette
http://www.frontierfishing.co.nz

A useful guide to fly fishing Southland. It describes lakes and rivers in the area and has details of the Ring a River program, which has established 19 phone numbers around the region for checking river stages. To get a local's perspective on Kiwi fly-fishing, look through Maurice Rodway's column going back to 1998. The Main Pool site navigation leads to regulations, articles and travel information.

Trout Fishing in New Zealand

New Zealand trout fishing information site, provided courtesy of leading New Zealand trout fishing author Ron Giles.

"Do you want to know **where, when** and **how** to fish for those large New Zealand trout in crystal clear waters?"

If so, this is the site for you, as it offers a "free information service" about any aspect of fly fishing for trout in New Zealand. Unbiased information is provided by Ron Giles, one of New Zealand's leading trout fishing writers.

E-mail your question to Ron, at **rongiles@troutnz.com**

Ron fishes throughout the country and so is able to provide detailed, impartial advice on trout fishing in New Zealand, famous for the quality of its freshwater fishing. He has fished all the major waterways in both islands as well as many backcountry and mountain streams. This knowledge and experience is available free to anyone wanting information on when, how or where to go trout fishing New Zealand.

Below are some references from visitors that have contacted Ron for advice:

"Dear Ron, I'd like to thank you for all the wonderful help you provided my husband and I in planning our first trip to New Zealand. Jeff and I counted ourselves very lucky and blessed to have found such a warm and friendly local that was willing to go out of his way to help a stranger plan their first trip to NZ. The very fact that you stayed in touch with us, answered all our questions, offered your books to us, in addition to any other books

Trout Fishing New Zealand
http://www.trout-fishing-new-zealand.com

New Zealand Professional Fishing Guides Association (NZPFGA)

http://www.nzpfga.com

The NZPFGA site is an obvious place to begin looking for a reputable New Zealand guide. It lists contact information and web sites for member guides in every region. Even the slimmest of these sites will tell you what to bring and what to expect.

Trout Fishing New Zealand

http://www.trout-fishing-new-zealand.com

New Zealand fly fishing is famously demanding: huge wild fish in tiny transparent creeks. Author Ron Giles has years of experience on both islands and welcomes e-mail questions from nervous or frustrated combatants. Advice about the best tackle and techniques comes from his book *Hooked on Trout - How and Where to Catch Large Trout in New Zealand*, and there are brief overviews of the most productive rivers.

International

Britain

For a nation smaller in area than some U.S. states, Britain has an amazing diversity of fishing. England is home to fanatical freshwater anglers and stillwater trout fishermen. The Scottish and Welsh swing flies along beautiful salmon rivers or fish by moonlight for sea trout. And the Irish are the most over-indulged of all with a world-class variety of fishing and an overabundance of those other things close to anglers' hearts—good pubs and spectacular scenery.

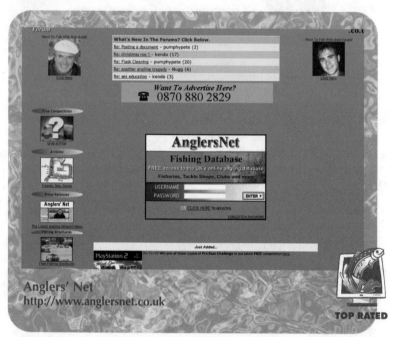

Anglers' Net
http://www.anglersnet.co.uk

TOP RATED

ENGLAND
Anglers' Net
http://www.anglersnet.co.uk

TOP RATED

Anglers' Net has an impressive collection of tackle reviews and article archives for pike and carp fishing, lure fishing and fly fishing. Of the four, carp fishing, which is Europe's most popular form of angling, is most likely to confuse and bemuse U.S. visitors. If you don't know your spod rod from your rod pod, you might try the Anglers' Net Carp Clinic, or you could post a query to one of the active forums.

Instead of a links page, they send you in the direction of a UK fishing web site directory, **http://www. go-fishing.co.uk**, which lists more than 500 sites in 20 categories.

Barbel Fishing World
http://www.barbel.co.uk

Barbel Fishing World
http://www.barbel.co.uk

Barbel are a highly prized river fish known for powerful fights and frequent canniness. The fish's English admirers gather in the forums at the dark and inviting Barbel Fishing World and try to collectively outwit them. Go to the Messages forum to view the most recent postings or the Basics and Archives sections for research into baits, techniques and barbel behavior. Elsewhere on the site are articles, tackle reviews and a league table of members' biggest fish.

Bass Anglers' Sportfishing Society (BASS)
http://www.ukbass.com

Like striped bass fishermen in this country, British saltwater anglers have been engaged in a heroic push to protect the stocks of their own sea bass variety (*dicentrachus labrax*), and the BASS organization is at the forefront of the effort. Ukbass.com is the best place on the Web to study this premier gamefish: use the pull-down menus on the homepage for conservation news, fishing articles, reflection pieces and club happenings.

At the exact opposite end of the aesthetic scale from bass lurks the conger eel. But conger eel fishing has its pleasures, if you can call armwrestling a 100 lb. bicep a pleasure, and its own fan club on the Web. **The British Conger Club** at **http://www.congerclub.org** showcases, and rather nicely, the giant wreck-hugging snakes with fishing tips and articles, photo galleries and charter boat listings. Some of the eels in the gallery are more than seven feet long and as thick as telephone poles.

International

FishingWarehouse.co.uk
http://www.fishingwarehouse.co.uk

TOP RATED

Carpfishing.UK
http://www.carp-uk.net

TOP RATED There are so many carp fishing sites sloshing around England you wouldn't think it would be hard to find a good one. The honors for England's best carp site are equally divided between **Carp.com** reviewed in Chapter 4 Fishing the Web, Best Freshwater Fishing Sites, and this site from Robin Davies. Carpfishing.UK has a more basic presentation but every department is filled out, and there's straightforward advice for beginners within sections for tackle, baits and rigs. The waters guide covers enough counties to be useful, but the biggest draw here are some of the busiest carp forums you'll find for general chat and bait talk.

Diptera.co.uk
http://www.diptera.co.uk

Primarily a fly-tying guide, each of the site's 200 patterns is photographed and can be clicked on for an enlarged view. Learn to tie and fish such English standbys as the Wickham's Fancy and Viva by following the tying recipe and fishing tips.

Fishing4Fun.co.uk
http://www.fishing4fun.co.uk

Fishing4Fun.co.uk holds the attention of newcomers with graphically rich sections for freshwater and saltwater species, baits and techniques. Fishery profiles, club links and weather forecasts should direct you to a good spot.

FishingWarehouse.co.uk
http://www.fishingwarehouse.co.uk

TOP RATED

This huge, bright-looking site is split into three channels: Tackle Shop, Forums and Information. Begin in the Information section. It's organized into magazine pages for Carp Fishing, Coarse Fishing, Game/fly Fishing, Match Fishing, Predator Fishing and Sea Fishing. Each is helmed by a respected angler within that branch of the sport and includes tackle reviews, news and how-to articles.

The site's large links section has an unexpected but welcome Strange Links collection. Some serious bottom fishing has gone on here, with off-kilter ruminations on everything from squirrel fishing to prawnography.

Fishing.co.uk
http://www.fishing.co.uk

TOP RATED

In various incarnations, this has long been one of the premier fishing sites in Europe, and its current one-and-a-half million words of content must make it a contender for biggest fishing site on the Web. Some of its writers have archived more than 100 features (go to the Authors tab in top navigation for a complete scorecard).

The clearest organization of all that material—the majority of which deals with freshwater fishing, with plenty of saltwater and fly fishing mixed in—is under the heading Species in the top navigation. You'll find a welcome blend of topics from technical information to reflections and foreign fishing essays. Among many other well-developed areas are listings for fishing travel companies, a business finder, tackle reviews and forums.

COARSE FISHING

Many of England's most innovative anglers are "coarse fishermen:" bait and lure anglers who fish from the bank for carp, pike, roach, bream and other non-gamefish.

Coarse Fishing UK
http://www.coarse-fishing.org.uk

This instructional site shows how it's done with clear method and rig illustrations. For those nonplussed by terms such as "bodied wagglers" and "stret pegging," there's a glossary. Where-to-fish information takes the lesson outside.

Coarse Fisherman
http://www.coarse-fisherman.co.uk

A sharp-looking introduction to the basics. Click on the Articles heading for more than 40 how-to guides. News stories, a directory of UK waters, tackle reviews and a forum make up the rest.

Floats Gone
http://www.floatsgone.btinternet.co.uk

This site has excellent float- and bottom-fishing diagrams and a guide to the secret world of European groundbait recipes.

International

FISHINGmagic

http://www.fishingmagic.com

TOP RATED Presided over by Graham Marsden, one of Britain's best-known and most versatile fishermen, FISHINGmagic is in the top tier of fishing web sites worldwide. Aside from hundreds of articles and tackle reviews (the majority about freshwater fishing), there's a very strong community vibe with popular forums, daily news updates, reader reviews and links for posting comments about features on the site. Look out for the rolling account of Graham's own fishing season under Digital Diary and pages of diabolical bait fishing ingenuity within the Rig Library. Register to use the forum, find local resources or customize content.

Fly Fishing for Trout and Salmon

http://www.cse.bris.ac.uk/
~cckhrb/kb_fish.html

If the URL trips you up, put "Ken Baron" and "fly fishing" into a favorite search engine to bring up this above-average personal page. You'll find tackle and technique discussions, life cycle tables for Atlantic salmon, sea trout and rainbow trout, and notes on some of the author's favorite fishing places at home and abroad.

Fly Tying and Fly Fishing for Trout – The UK's Premier Guide

http://homepages.enterprise.net/
davefink/index1.html

Dave Fink summarizes how it's done on the stillwaters, rivers and

Lure Fishing UK
http://www.lurefishinguk.com

TOP RATED

fly-tying benches of Britain. Derek Turner chips in with a clear casting tutorial, and there's a good recipe section. Dave is based in Wales and he includes descriptions of a few productive Welsh fly waters.

I hate to contradict a Welshman, but **Fish & Fly** at **http://www. fishandfly.co.uk,** reviewed in Chapter 4 Fishing the Web, Best Fly-Fishing Sites is, in fact, the UK's premier guide to fly fishing and tying.

Hooklinks

http://www.hooklinks.net

A well-organized directory weighted toward freshwater fishing. Hooklinks has more than 1,100 links in 13 categories. Topics are fairly evenly covered: there are listings for 80 regional fishing clubs, 90 fisheries, 177 sites for carp fishermen, and more than 60 for pike fishermen. It was

difficult to tell when the site was last updated, but a random click-around didn't turn up any dead links.

Lure Fishing UK

http://www.lurefishing uk.com

TOP RATED Lure fishing has only really become popular in Britain in the last 10 years, but they're catching up fast if Dave Pugh's excellent Lure Fishing UK is an accurate gauge. Use the Contents and Search page for the clearest picture of what's on the site. And that would include lure descriptions, a frequently used forum and a set of luring articles by Dave and guests. The first article is, helpfully, "An introduction to fishing for predators in the U.K. for visitors from North America," and indeed the site is an expert introduction to lure fishing for pike, something

International

that isn't given a lot of attention in the U.S. fishing press.

British (and worldwide) lure anglers are ably served by the **Harris Angling** online tacklestore. Go to **http://www.harrisangling.com** for pike, bass and saltwater lures and a full array of tackle. Regular specials, accounts of exotic fishing travel and a responsive forum make the site a stopping point for thousands of lure fanatics every month.

MaggotDrowning.com
http://www.maggotdrowning.com

Maggots are a common bait in Europe, where since time immemorial young boy's mothers and recent wives have allowed their fridges to store the pint containers overnight for fishing on Sunday morning. Maggotdrowning.com is a macabre-sounding but quite innocent directory with listings for clubs, fisheries, classifieds, jokes, forums, diary entries and tackle shops. Fish 'n' Tips has species identification and bait fishing advice.

Pike Anglers' Club of Great Britain (PAC)
http://www.pacgb.com

The official web site of Britain's largest predator fishing club has a range of articles and factsheets about pike biology, tackle, tactics and unhooking. A trophy list of fish over 40 lb., a bibliography of the most influential pike books and a gallery of members' best catches provides the inspiration. About the only thing missing is a forum. They make up for it by linking to the busy pike forum hosted by **Predator Publications** at **http://www.pike andpredatorsmagazine.com.**

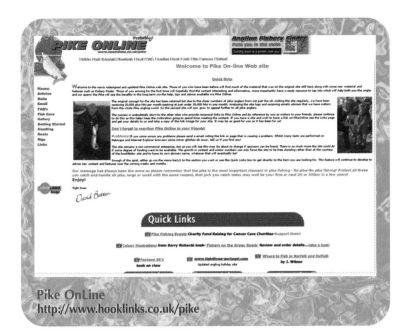

Pike OnLine
http://www.hooklinks.co.uk/pike

Pike OnLine
http://www.hooklinks.co.uk/pike

The presentation of this beginner's guide to pike fishing is first class, quite as good as any printed guide, and covers Getting Started, Fish Care and Handling, Rigs, Baits, Knots and Pike - the Species. If you need that human touch, the people behind Pike Online will answer e-mail questions about taking up the sport, fish care and tactics. The site originates from the pike fishing heart of England, East Anglia, and includes plenty of regional fishing links.

Predator-Fishing.co.uk
http://www.predator-fishing.co.uk

Devoted to all the fish-eating fish, which in Britain includes pike, perch, zander (the Euro-walleye), Wells catfish, eels and chub. The articles archive, with most pieces written in a knowledge sharing, reader's-experience-kind-of-way, is the best feature.

TalkAngling
http://www.talkangling.co.uk

A window into the world of competitive match fishing where anglers fish from the bank using bait and ultralight tackle. It's absent tournament bass fishing's million-dollar payouts, slinky speedboats and stadium weigh-ins, but demands the same intense skill set and ability to fish under pressure. Click on the headings Features and How Do I to find articles, match reports, competition diaries and reports on such things as fishing the chopped-worm and "new approaches to squatt and pinkie fishing." A forum lets match organizers post results.

Where To Fish
http://www.where-to-fish.com

TOP RATED

Where To Fish
http://www.where-to-fish.com

TOP RATED

The *Where to Fish Directory* is something of an institution in Britain, and you can see why from this complete online edition dating from 1998. Though it's few years old, fisheries don't tend to move very much and out-of-date listings can easily be investigated with a quick Internet search. The site's 3,000 pages are divided into England, Scotland, Wales, Ireland, N.Ireland and Abroad, then sectioned into Fishing Stations, Canal Fishing, Sea Fishing Stations and contact numbers for environment agencies and national associations. "Fishing Stations" is just an odd term for all the places and fisheries profiled within each country. Entries are brief summaries of what the fishery is like, who controls it and roughly where it is.

The Abroad section of the directory has fishing snapshots of Africa, Australasia, North America, South America and 15 countries in Europe.

World Sea Fishing
http://www.worldseafishing.com

TOP RATED

Outdoor writer and photographer Mike Thrussell has single-handedly created a complete guide to saltwater fishing around the British Isles. You'll find masses of information and photographs about species, tackle and rigs, surfcasting, pier fishing and boat fishing. Special sections discuss saltwater fishing in Wales, Ireland and internationally. They say you're never more than 70 miles from the sea in Britain—use the World Sea Fishing links to explore what's available along the entire coastline.

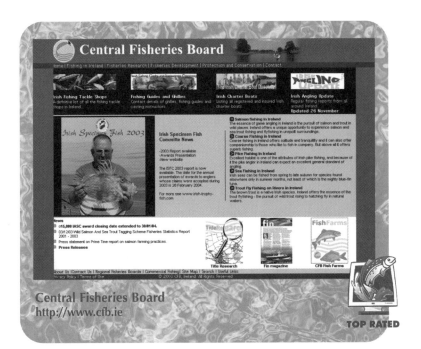

Central Fisheries Board
http://www.cfb.ie

TOP RATED

IRELAND
Central Fisheries Board (CFB)
http://www.cfb.ie

TOP RATED Ireland is spongy with fine fishing water—a great, green angler's playground, and most of it is overseen by the Central Fisheries Board. Stop in to track down opportunities for salmon and trout, freshwater and saltwater fishing all over the country. Within each type of fishing you'll find regulations, a calendar showing the best fishing times for different species and a rundown of effective methods. A Where to Stay link funnels site visitors to the **Irish Tourist Board** at **http://www.ireland.travel.ie/accommodation,** where they can book every level of accommodation from self-catering cottage to everything-catered castle. Visitors can also select the best bits from around the site and gather them into a printable mini-guide.

The most exciting to happen in European saltwater fishing is the return of bluefin tuna to the west coast of Ireland. Go to the Sea Fishing in Ireland section of the Central Fisheries Board site for a detailed report, or to **http://www.tunacharters.ie**, the informative web site of a Donegal tuna boat.

The Great Fishing Houses of Ireland
http://www.irelandflyfishing.com

A simple but beguiling promotional site describing the fishing and accommodations at 21 of the country's best lodges. And Lord, does it look the life for the cultivated angler. Go to Homes then click on either the text links or the map for lodge and fishing descriptions, rates and seasons. Embedded links within each entry take you to fishery profiles from Peter O'Reilly's book *Trout & Salmon*

Rivers of Ireland, so you're privy to an expert's independent assessment of each lodge's water.

Shannon Regional Fisheries Board
http://www.shannon-fishery-board.ie

TOP RATED

This is the largest of the regional boards overseen by the CFB, and they've deliberately tailored their site to the needs of visiting fishermen. The Fishing Services Finder locates useful businesses—guides, tackleshops and hotels that cater specifically to anglers. Where-to-fish information is found within sections for Salmon and Trout, Sea Angling, Coarse Fishing and Pike Fishing. Go to the pull-down menus at the top of each section or use the interactive map to find pages about individual fisheries.

Shore Angling and Charter/Private Boat Fishing in Ireland
http://www.sea-angling-ireland.org

TOP RATED

Webmaster Kieran Hanrahan is to thank for this introduction to Irish saltwater fishing. Use the 80 species profiles to tell your John Dory from your Ballan Wrasse. There are good descriptions of standard tackle from rods and reels to rigs and sinkers, and how to collect, store and fish with commonly used saltwater baits. Where-to-go information is taken care of within a national directory of charterboats and shoremarks.

Shannon Regional Fisheries Board
http://www.shannon-fishery-board.ie

TOP RATED

Fishing in Scotland

Fishing in Scotland

Trout and salmon fishing holidays and vacations, pike fishing trips and a general guide to salmon, trout, coarse angling and sea fishing in Scotland.

For each of the salmon and trout river fishing's and the commercial stooked trout lochs we have tried to include the type of fishing available i.e. fly fishing, bait fishing, bank or boat, together with the type of species i.e. salmon, brown trout, rainbow trout, pike and coarse species such as carp, roach etc.

I would like to thank everyone who has contributed to the information within this site particularly the proprietors and managers of fishing beats and commercial fisheries who have sent me photographs and editorial of their fishings. I hope this site will prove to be a valuable resource not only for anglers in Scotland but for all fisherman who want to visit Scotland from other parts of the UK and abroad.

We are frequently being asked for coarse angling venues in Scotland, so during the course of this season we hope to create listings to cover any venues that have coarse or pike fishing. If anyone is a member of a coarse angling club or association or manages any coarse angling waters anywhere in Scotland please send us the details and we will be more than happy to create a listing for

Fishing in Scotland
http://www.fishing-uk-scotland.com

SCOTLAND
Caithness and Sutherland Trout Angling Group
http://www.fishing-highland.co.uk

Caithness and Sutherland are the most northerly regions of the Scottish Highlands, and this promotional site describes fishing for the area's distinctive wild browns and sea trout. The heart of the site is a collection of large, pretty-looking maps that can be clicked on to display links to accommodation, "ghillies," tuition and permits.

Fishing in Scotland
http://www.fishing-uk-scotland.com

Les Brandie's comprehensive guide is broken down into nine regions (Highlands, Grampian, Tayside, Fife, Central, Lothians, Strathclyde, Dumfries and the Borders). Click on the name of a region to be taken to sections for "The Fishings"

and, depending on the area, accommodations and tackleshops. Les has a special affection for the Tay, home of Britain's most coveted fishing record, Georgina Ballantyne's 64 lb. Atlantic salmon caught in 1922.

Fishing the Fly in Aberdeenshire
http://www.fishingthefly.co.uk

Webmaster Mike Barrio considers the River Don one of the best—and least publicized—brown trout rivers in Europe. He uses this site to describe the river and some of the best Aberdeenshire trout lochs. Trip-planning details are taken care of within mostly up-to-date fishing reports, a forum, local fishing news and where-to-stay recommendations.

The links section has suggestions for other regional fishing sites. Explore author Lesley Crawford's remote northern Highlands at

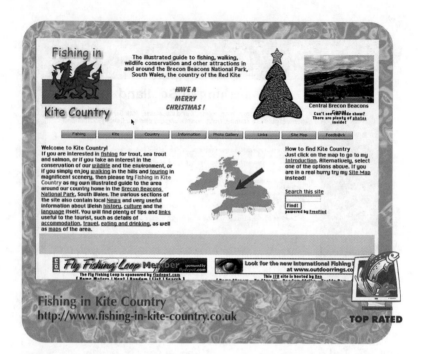

Fishing in Kite Country
http://www.fishing-in-kite-country.co.uk

TOP RATED

http://www.wildtroutfisher.co.uk, for example, or stop by **Speycaster. net** at **http://www.speycaster.net**, which is focused on the Spey and Avon. These salmon and trout rivers are described as being "as clear as Tanqueray," but don't let them divert you from the Spirit of Speyside Whiskey Festival. See Speyside Recreation in the left-hand navigation for more links afore ye go.

Flyfish-Scotland.com
http://www.flyfish-scotland.com

Letsflyfish
http://www.letsflyfish.com

Alastair "Ally" Gowans is a busy fella—he's a professional angling instructor, fly tyer, foreign fishing guide and webmaster of two Scottish angling web sites. Letsflyfish is the more general with technique articles, descriptions of

favorite flies, casting advice and fishing profiles of Scotland, Ireland, Canada, Norway and Spain. Flyfish-Scotland dwells mostly on salmon and trout, and has sections for fly fishing for pike and the Scottish Highlands.

WALES
Fishing in Wales
http://www.fishing-in-wales.com

TOP RATED

A sprawling site that lays out the fishing potential of Britain's least known kingdom. The Valleys Guide is an obvious place to start. Beginning with the Dee and ending in the Wye, the guide describes 12 valley regions in terms of game and freshwater fisheries, accommodations, how to get there, tackle shops and regulations. There are many other areas to explore, so much information in fact, including wildlife and wild-flower guides and sections for youngsters and disabled anglers, that I found it easy to get lost. To get back to the homepage with all its central navigation channels, click on the Fishing in Wales logo at the top of every page.

Fishing in Kite Country
http://www.fishing-in-kite-country.co.uk

 Kite country is the Breacon Beacons National Park in South Wales, home to the rare

TOP RATED bird of prey, the red kite. The fishing part of this carefully constructed site discusses the rivers Tawe, Towy, Wye and Usk, plus park reservoirs and lakes. Links to more general Breacon sites are weaved into the fishing discussions, and along with some fine scene-setting photography, it's practically impossible to make your way through the site without wanting to fish there. If you get hooked, go to the Information section for contact numbers and travel planning.

Simple Flies for Simple Sewin
http://www.simple-flies-for-simple.fishermen.co.uk

"Sewin" or sea trout are tradition-ally fished for by taking up a sta-tion out in the river and fishing through the night, and are revered sport in the healthier wild rivers of Britain and Northern Europe. This simple page from Welsh fly fisher Robert Hatton lists 40 sea trout patterns, picked for the twin virtues of being effective and easy to tie. Each is photographed and given a basic recipe.

Robert is also responsible for a great site devoted to the **Ogmore River**, near Bridgend, South Wales at **http://www.ogmoreriver.com**. It's a complex of visitor's informa-tion, links, fishing tips, reports, maps and fly recommendations.

Canada

It's been estimated Canada has 100,000 lakes and rivers within its 13 provinces. What that means to us is a continent-wide swath of wilderness fishing for everything from smallmouth bass and lake trout to Atlantic salmon and (Pacific) steelhead. These sites have all the information and contacts you need to sample some of that nirvana yourself.

Angling BC
http://www.anglingbc.com

Angling BC
http://www.anglingbc.com

Angling BC is the place to get a feel for the BC fishing scene from a local's perspective. Community services in the shape of forums, fishing reports, a chat room and classifieds were all bustling on review day. BC Info on the homepage points to government resources such as river levels, the *BC Tidal Waters Sport Fishing Guide* and FishWizard, a map-based proagram listing thousands of BC lakes and streams in terms of stocking, salmon escapement and water depths.

Atlantic Salmon Sportfishing by Bob Boudreau
http://members.attcanada.ca/~salmon

Nova Scotian Bob Boudreau provides an enthusiastic introduction to the basics of salmon fly fishing, including necessary tackle, flies, techniques and the no-less-essential considerations of etiquette and conservation awareness. He finishes with some cautionary tales of just how all-consuming the salmon fishing life can become.

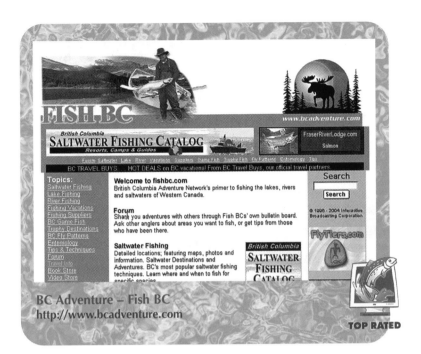

Bass Canada
http://www.basscanada.com

Yawning at the thought of another submarine-sized muskie or walleye, many Canadian anglers prefer the competitiveness of tournament bass fishing. They are nicely serviced by basscanada.com with long technique articles, club listings and tournament calendars for several provinces, especially Ontario.

BC Adventure – Fish BC
http://www.bcadventure.com

The creators of this first-rate BC travel and visitor's guide are either keen fishermen or knew the right people to consult. Either way, the site's FISH BC section is a wonderful guide to freshwater and saltwater opportunities across the province. Choose from Saltwater, Lake Fishing, River Fishing, BC Game Fish, Trophy Destinations, BC Fly Patterns, Entomology and Tips and Techniques. The sections covering saltwater and lake fly fishing are like mini-sites in themselves and earn separate reviews within Chapter 4 Fishing the Web, Best Fly-Fishing Sites and Best Saltwater Fishing Sites.

As good as the fishing material is, it only makes up a quarter of the site's content. Channels on the homepage lead to regional and city guides, route descriptions and recreational options from ATVing to whale watching.

Bob Izumi's Real Fishing
http://www.realfishing.com

Expert angler Bob Izumi has a Real Fishing media empire comprising a television show, a print maga-

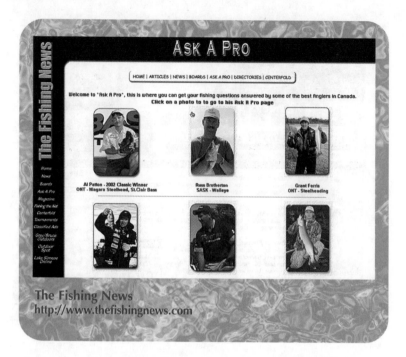

The Fishing News
http://www.thefishingnews.com

zine, a radio show and now real-fishing.com to stitch it all together. Sections for Tips and Fishing Tales have freshwater fishing articles or you can use a species and region finder to search through readers' catch shots. The forum and classifieds receive enough traffic to be worth dropping in on.

Fish Ontario!
http://www.fishontario.com

TOP RATED

Ontarians, with all that Lake frontage and the world-class smallmouth, walleye, salmon and muskie fishing that goes with it, need this excellent multi-species web site to keep track of all their options. Articles about bait, lure and fly fishing, and up-to-date catch reports will help out

when it's time to load the truck. Go to Ontario's Best Fishing Spots or The Backroads for extended where-to-fish information. The Downloads link under Topics has useful booklets from the Canadian government about cooking Ontario sportfish, fishing opportunities around the province and regulations.

The Fishing News
http://www.thefishingnews.com

The Fishing News reports on the latest developments in Canadian and U.S. sportfishing. There are sections for bass tournament news, a magazine area with tackle reviews and articles and some popular forums. The Ask A Pro feature has especially in-depth Q & A archives from six experts.

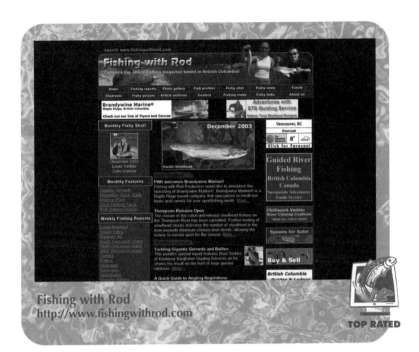

Fishing with Rod
http://www.fishingwithrod.com

TOP RATED

Fishing with Rod (FWR)
http://www.fishingwithrod.com

TOP RATED

British Columbia resident Rod Hsu has built a wonderful site around his enthusiasm for all things fishing and fish-related. He's excited about good web design too from the sharp look of these pages for feature articles, fishing reports and news stories. Every area of the site is well developed and up-to-date. See the link on the homepage for the FWR Youth Fishing School—a commendable-sounding fishing program for seven to 14-year-olds.

Fly Fishing Alberta's Chinook Country
http://www.telusplanet.net/
public/cnangler/html
Alberta's Chinook country is in the southwest corner of the province

and is bordered to the north by the Bow River. This introduction to the region's fly-fishing potential has reports from the Crowsnest Angler fly shop in Bellevue, tying recipes for dozens of local patterns, fishing tips and guides to available species. For the geographically challenged, those species don't include Chinook. It refers here to the westerly winds the region is famous for.

Go Walleye!
http://www.gowalleye.com

TOP RATED

A super page for Alberta walleye anglers with links that would be useful to any Alberta-bound fisherman. General information includes weather forecasts for Alberta and Saskatchewan, real-time snow-pack monitoring for the eastern slopes of the Canadian Rockies, and Alberta

International

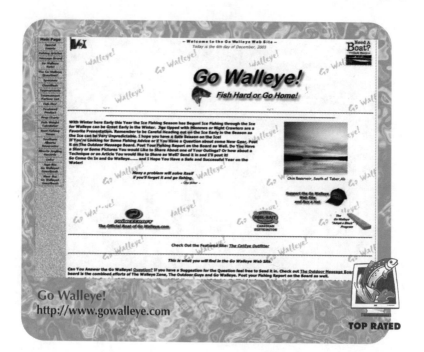

Go Walleye!
http://www.gowalleye.com

TOP RATED

regulations and angling records. The core audience gets together within the lively forum and is well taken care of with walleye articles and tournament news.

HipWader.com
http://www.hipwader.com

A new, friendly BC fly-fishing community site. For a clear menu of all the site features click on Article Categories in the top navigation. A few highlights of the 20-odd departments include Confessions of a Dry Fly Fanatic, River Reports, Hatch Guides and River Stories. They've built in plenty of opportunities for users to get involved, from commenting on site features and submitting articles and fly patterns, to posting to the forum and contributing to fly-swaps.

Inconnu Lodge
http://www.inconnulodge.com

Tincup Wilderness Lodge
http://www.tincup-lodge.com

You can get a good feel for the experience of Yukon backcountry fishing by looking at the brochure sites for these two lodges. The Yukon Fishing section at Inconnu Lodge has tackle advice and a gallery of formidable-looking pike and lake trout. Look within Lodge Facts and Preparing for Your Trip for packing checklists and useful web site links.

As well as the usual service descriptions, Tincup Wilderness Lodge posts a sampling of Yukon articles from national fishing magazines and introduces some of the local residents—super-sized grayling and sheefish.

Newfoundland & Labrador Tourism – Hunting & Fishing
http://www.gov.nf.ca/tourism/welcome

Go to What to Do in the lefthand navigation, then Hunting & Fishing to find lodge and guide listings for both areas. Each business is briefly profiled and you can click through to individual web sites for much more information. The rest of the site answers all those secondary questions, like where to stay and what else you can do for fun if the salmon aren't moving.

Northern Ontario Tourist Outfitters Association (NOTO)
http://www.noto.net

If you're lucky enough to be planning a fishing holiday in Ontario, this large outfitter's directory should give you some leads. From the homepage search for lodges via the headings Regional Destinations and Fishing Pursuits. Click on the name of each resort for a description of amenities and available fishing: most specialize in walleye, trout, bass and pike.

Nova Scotia Fly Fishing, Tying, and Tall Tales
http://users.eastlink.ca/~dryfly/index.html

TOP RATED

Though it's a personal page, Pat Donoghue's site has enough depth to interest anyone wielding a fly rod in Nova Scotia. Its pattern pages follow the author's tying muse from 13 essential brook trout patterns to 30 orange flies and 20 blue ones. A large reference list matches Latin insect names to the flies

Newfoundland & Labrador Tourism – Hunting & Fishing
http://www.gov.nf.ca/tourism/welcome

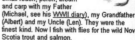

Nova Scotia fly fishing, tying and tall tales

"The secret to fishing is being silly" ... Grandma Hatch, Missouri, 200

Patterns

Truths

Tales

General

Logbook

What's new

Home

Email

Site index

My hook is baited
with a dream,
I fish for Peace.
Robert Service

Frank put his Baycrest slippers on every night after supper, and again in the morning; he didn't take them off until we were ready to go fishing.
The slippers seemed so out of place in the wilderness-who in the world wears plaid slippers on a fishing trip?

Midway through the week, the obvious answer came to me: someone who is at home.

From *The Last Guide* by Ron Corbett

This site received the Best of the Net award for the Personal site and Canadian Local Information categories from Flyfishing.about.com
Pat Donoghue, Canada ©1997-2003

My fishing days began in England, tempting, with maggots and bread paste, small roach, perch, bream and carp with my Father (Michael, see his WWII diary), my Grandfather (Albert) and my Uncle (Len). They were the finest kind. Now I fish with flies for the wild Nova Scotia trout and salmon.

The four flies on this page are taken from *The Tent Dwellers* (Sports fishing in Nova Scotia in 1908) by Albert Bigelow Paine.

You are welcome to copy any of my pages for your own personal use or to share them with fellow fly fishers, but please do not include them on your site, or any other site, nor use them for personal gain.

Nova Scotia Fly Fishing, Tying, and Tall Tales
http://users.eastlink.ca/~dryfly/index.html

TOP RATED

that imitate them, and he includes patterns he ties for "old timers" in his area: "And let me tell ya, they sure do like their old-time favorites." Areas labeled Truths and Tales are a similar mix of usefulness and local color.

Friend and fishing conspirator Bob Lundy has a worthy site of his own at **Bob's Gone Fishin'**, http://www3.sympatico.ca/rlundy.

Nova Scotia Salmon Association (NSSA)

http://www.novascotia
salmon.ns.ca

A conservation group affiliated with the Atlantic Salmon Federation, the NSSA monitors the health of Nova Scotia fisheries and celebrates the silvery (and brown and red-spotted)

rewards of their stewardship with a good deal of straight fishing advice. Plan your fishing trip by species, then piece together the location jigsaw with tide tables, rainfall radar and satellite ocean imaging. Or choose the quick and easy route and hire a guide from the island-wide listings.

Ontario Fishing Net

http://www.ontariofishing.net

This directory calls itself an Ontario fishing search engine and that's about right with its mix of commercial listings and links to personal pages, fishing clubs and organizations. One feature that should be copied by other sites is that they link to recommended forums rather than the usual hap-hazard list of web sites.

Saskatchewan – Fishing & Hunting
http://www.se.gov.sk.ca/fishwild

You can download a colorful 31-page brochure from this government site aimed at anyone planning a fishing trip to the province. From the homepage go to Anglers' Information and then read through the Anglers' Guide for season dates and regulations, fish facts and lists of stocked waters. Buy a Saskatchewan fishing license direct from the site.

Sport Fishing BC
http://www.sportfishingbc.com

TOP RATED

Scroll down the lists of date-stamped articles about salmon, steelhead, bass, halibut and trout, for a green-eyed look

at one of the world's best fishing destinations. Instructional articles cover every style of fishing and there's a decent directory of guide and lodge listings. Fishing reports were up-to-date and detailed, but didn't cover every area. Fill in the gaps at **BC Fishing Reports, http://www.bcfishingreports.com.**

Sport Fishing Canada
http://www.sportfishingcanada.ca

Designed as a "gateway to federal, provincial, and territorial fishing information across Canada," one of the best features of the site bundles together all you need to know about fees, bag limits, season dates and fishing licenses in each province. To find it, go to Angling Publications, then Angling Regulation Summaries to bring up a clickable map of

Sport Fishing BC
http://www.sportfishingbc.com

TOP RATED

FloatFishing.net
http://www.floatfishing.net

TOP RATED

Canada. For more general fishing resources, from the homepage go to the box that asks if you want to search by province or territory. Each area has subsections for events, publications and youth fishing programs.

Travel Manitoba Hunting and Fishing
http://www.travelmanitoba.com/huntfish

They've got their priorities straight up in Manitoba—a large chunk of this general visitor site focuses on sportfishing, and includes angling maps and regulations, a fishing business directory and local fishing links. They also publish a special booklet for fishermen traveling to the region: go to Free Stuff in the top navigation, then click on Information Kits to order a copy.

What's Bitin' in the Toronto Area?
http://zebra.zoo.utoronto.ca/cgi-bin/FBoard/ikonboard.cgi

TOP RATED

It may have one of the more forgettable URLs on the Web but this forum center for keeping up with the Toronto fishing scene is well worth seeking out. Moderators keep the discussions positive and family friendly. The report forums for local fisheries, Lake Ontario and waters outside the immediate area are the most popular stops. The links page offers a discriminating path into the wider world of Ontario fishing for salmon, trout, steelhead and walleye. To single out a couple of the best recommendations:

FloatFishing.net TOP RATED at **http://www.floatfishing.net** is devoted to float fishing for steelhead, trout and salmon in the traditional Canadian style of using long rods and centerpin reels. There are a few tips on selecting tackle, links to suppliers and good fishing maps of Lake Ontario feeder streams, but the center of the site is the lively float forum. You can confirm the effectiveness of the method by going through the 30-page members' gallery of float-caught trophies.

One of Ontario's most prized fisheries is the Credit River, and the **Credit River Anglers Association (CRAA) TOP RATED** at **http://www.craa.on.ca** have built a super little site in praise and protection of it. The CRAA forum is a popular local hangout.

Wolfheart's Fishing Page
http://www.sportfisherman.net

Wolfheart's Fishing Page offers a peek at Alberta's freshwater fishing potential with brief summaries of

the major lakes, rivers and species, and multipart sections for walleye and ice fishing. The site is touchingly dedicated to Frank Boesemeyer, who made the most of what fishing time he had, and who'd probably encourage everyone to do the same.

YukonFishing.com
http://www.yukonfishing.com

Provides a rare and detailed resource for fishing in "Canada's True North"—everything you'd need, in fact, to plan a do-it-yourself adventure. From the homepage look for species information, best fishing times and regulations. The section Where the Fish Are has a long list of what's available in the lakes and streams accessible from different Yukon highways and fly-in lakes. Operator Services provides links to fishing guides, lodges and campgrounds.

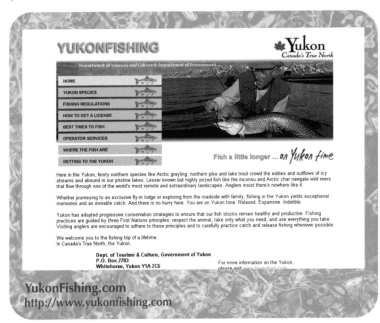

Europe

Though many of the most promising European sites aren't translated into English, enough are for us to glimpse a continent of possibilities from the ice-fed salmon and char rivers of Scandinavia to the languid catfish lagoons of Spain.

Angling Club Lax-a
http://www.lax-a.is

Angling Club Lax-a
http://www.lax-a.is

An above-average outfitter's site describing Icelandic salmon and trout fishing. They have beats on 16 of the best rivers in the country and they tell you why they're the best within descriptions of how and when to fish each river. Clear maps and plenty of photography set the scene.

CyberTrout.com
http://www.cybertrout.com

The aim of CyberTrout.com is to alert U.S. fishermen, tourists, business travelers and military personnel to underreported fly-fishing opportunities in Europe. Introductory pages for Germany, France, Austria and Spain give regulations, license requirements, fishing overviews and scattered fly-shop recommendations. Other links on the homepage lead to brief discussions of fishing in Belgium, Norway, Italy, Slovenia, the Czech Republic, the Balkans, Hungary and Israel.

Fishing Denmark

http://www.globalflyfisher.com/
global/denmark

Martin Joergensen's original web
site is a Danish saltwater fly-fishing
tutorial. Each page leads logically
from the next, so resist the urge to
hop around. From the homepage
you'll progress through beautifully
laid-out pages of instruction and
illustration that could probably be
applied to fishing the coastline of
much of Northern Europe. To see
the subject path you've taken or to
jump to a section, go to Contents
in the lefthand navigation for a
useful site map. Once you've
"done" Denmark, make sure to
visit the Global FlyFisher main
site in the provided link. It's in
the top few percent of fishing sites
on the Web.

Fishing in Finland

http://www.fishingfinland.com

Juha Vainio built this site specifically for visiting anglers, and it's a
fine look at the country's trout and
salmon potential. Browse around
to learn about Finnish fly tactics
or look for specific where-to-fish
advice within Fishing Geography
or How to Plan a Fishing Trip to
Finland. The glossary will at least
let you explain if you katkaista
your vapa and lose a big kojamo.
Oi, what a tunari.

Flugfiskesidan Online

http://www.flugfiskesidan.com

TOP RATED

Flugfiskesidan is Swedish
for fly-fishing pages, and
they originate here from
writers Mikael Båth,
Lasse Mårtensson and
Hans van Klinken, and from the
downloadable *FF Magazine*. Many

MON POISSON EST PLUS GRAND QUE VOS POISSON

Run the following URLs
through a Google search and
click "Translate this," or use the
services of **http://world.
altavista.com,** and what pops
out are wildly mangled but just
decipherable English transla-
tions of these leading Italian,
French and German fishing
magazines. Each site is heavily
illustrated if the text is too
much of a challenge.

Pescare Online

http://www.pescareonline.it

A brightly designed Italian
freshwater magazine with
lots of step-by-step photos.

Pêcheur.com

http://www.pecheur.com

A cool-looking French site with
abundant articles, forums and
tackle purchasing options.
Don't leave without visiting La
Gallerie Des Monstres.

Fliegenfischer-forum

http://www.fliegenfischer-
forum.de

Click on the name of a river
in the Thüringen section of
this German fly-fishing site and
ponder what secrets are hidden
in phrases such as: "The Salle
possesses an almost unbeliev-
able wealth at koecher and
eintagsfliegen, in some summer
evenings one can phaenomi-
nale slips experience." The
fotogaleries are a must-see.

Flugfiskesidan Online
http://www.flugfiskesidan.com

TOP RATED

of the articles have an international flavor, led by van Klinken's travel essays, and there are particularly strong sections on the technical skills of fly tying, entomology and leader assembly. Check the links for a good list of European fishing sites.

Fly Fishing in Bavaria
http://www.users.odn.de/
~odn03061/index.htm

It's a shame this tidy site is no longer being updated but it still offers a rare introduction to fly fishing in Germany. It covers equipment, flies, species (nicely illustrated) and essential advice about Germany's complex license bureaucracy. Tourists are exempt from the apparently quite challenging fishing exam residents have to take.

Medflyfish
http://www.medflyfish.com

This bilingual magazine for fly fishing around the Mediterranean Sea links to two sister sites— MedMag and the Mediterranean Fly Anglers Club. The rewards of browsing all three are colorful pages for destination articles, saltwater fly tying, tackle considerations and species profiles. The site is still building content, but it's off to a good start.

Monster Carps
http://members.rott.chello.nl/
tmarapengopie/wereldrecord.htm

TOP RATED

This Dutch site with a full English translation is devoted to Europe's sumo-sized carp and catfish. Areas for baits, techniques and rigs are illustrated by some spectacular photography and graphics. The galleries of monster carp and catfish are sensational if you like that kind of thing. The galleries of Women and Carp and Women and Catfish are equally sensational, though not exactly typical of the average European carp and catfish angler, who tends to be smelly, over-weight and disheveled, not glistening, pouty and half-dressed.

The Norwegian Flyshop
http://www.flyshop.no

Click on The Guide to explore the delights of fly fishing for cod and pollack (torsk and lyr) or "the mysteries of the eel." There's plenty of regional information matched to other common species and good coverage of salmon and sea trout rivers. Other corners have forums, conservation news and fly-tying articles.

Rackelhanen FlyFishing Magazine
http://www.rackelhanen.se/eng

TOP RATED

The Rackelhanen web site takes its name from a particularly versatile fly pattern. It's an appropriate symbol for a magazine with a broad European focus that also includes plenty of North American content. Swedish web-master Mats Sjöstrand has been overseeing the site since it debuted in 1996, and has steered its content towards rod building, fishing techniques and entomology. A long list gives the Swedish, Danish, Norwegian and English version of all the essential fishing words from Asp to Whitefish.

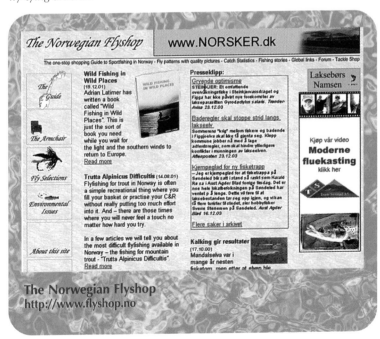

South Africa

Most of Africa is literally unchartered in term of fishing potential, but there are a small group of sites from South Africa that discuss the serious fun to be had with tigerfish and yellowfish, not to mention saltwater fly rodding and big-game fishing. Imagine being able to legitimately work the words "elephant" and "rhinoceros" into your excuse for not catching anything?

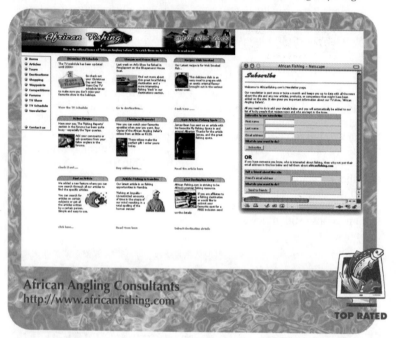

African Angling Consultants
http://www.africanfishing.com

TOP RATED

African Angling Consultants
http://www.africanfishing.com

TOP RATED The logo of this site in support of the television show African Angling Safaris is a golden fish skeleton baring its teeth. It sounds the right note for a fly-fishing trip into the alien waters of tigerfish, sharptooth catfish and African pike. Enthusiastic and well-illustrated feature articles are divided into species, destinations and fly fishing, and there's a nice little beginner's tutorial within the Flycasting section.

The Art link takes you to some special photos combining the site owner's two great loves, and one understanding young lady with no good place to store her tippet material.

Fishing Owl's World
http://www.fishingowl.co.za

Fishing Owl's World is one in which kids learn good fishing and conservation practices. Though I'm

OutdoorPAGES
http://www.outdoorpages.co.za

not 100% sure about the quote on the homepage from James Rennie's *Alphabet of Scientific Fishing* (1883), which forewarns the little ones that angling demands "as much caution as housebreaking." Scroll down the homepage for links to general fishing and fly-fishing articles, a multipart section about boating on inland waterways, and links to fishing clubs, dam levels, tide tables and moon phases.

FlyGuide.co.za
http://www.flyguide.co.za

Trout guide Mario Geldenhuys fishes the Eastern Cape and provides two useful maps of the region within a section called The Area. He recommends basic tackle and flies and shows how they're used in a six-part beginner's tutorial. Choose from the list of seven Eastern Cape rivers and he'll

e-mail you the latest fishery and weather report.

OutdoorPAGES
http://www.outdoorpages.co.za

Some of the articles and tips within this colorful general fishing magazine are in Afrikaans. Look at this as a positive: it means the site is aimed at local fishermen rather than tourists. Channels for Bass, Deep Sea, Fly, Freshwater, Rock, Surf and Tigerfish show off the diversity of what's available, and are made up of articles, resource links, business listings and photo and video galleries. To plan a trip, use the lodge and guide directories or contact a local club.

Nile perch aren't available in South Africa, but to find out more about one of the world's most impressive freshwater fish try **The African Angler** at **http://www. african-angler.co.uk,** a British travel company specializing in trips to Lake Nasser in Egypt.

The site has practical advice about fishing methods, what to bring, lure selection and staying safe on safari.

theflyguide.com
http://www.theflyguide.com

TOP RATED

Do the quick, free registration at this handsome fly-fishing site to view more than 30 articles about species, destinations and saltwater fly fishing. There are business listings and forums and detailed weather information for dozens of locations in South Africa and neighboring countries.

Here and There

Isn't it good to know that someone somewhere in Belize or Korea or Japan is sneaking out of the office or from doing stuff around the house to spend a happy day playing with the fish—just like you?

BAJA, MEXICO
Baja Anglers
http://www.baja-anglers.com

With the Sea of Cortez, "the world's greatest fish trap" on one side and the teeming Pacific on the other, Cabo San Lucas is a sportfishing town like few others. Baja Anglers, a leading Cabo guide service and tackleshop, sets the scene with overviews of what's available, best fishing times and descriptions of the marine wildlife you're likely to see, plus a few restaurant and accommodation suggestions. Sign up to have fishing reports e-mailed to you as soon as they come in.

The Baja Big Fish Company
http://www.bajabigfish.com

Manager Pat Bolles has shaped this Loreto charter site into a model of

TOP RATED

what outfitters can offer clients trying to research a fishing trip. There are excellent species profiles matched to fish season calendars, tackle checklists, condition reports, a beach cam, maps and restaurant guides. The day the site was reviewed the report actually acknowledged poor weather and catches in the Sea of Cortez. Such honesty should be rewarded.

Baja Destinations
http://www.bajadestinations.com

TOP RATED

Gene Kira is the Baja editor for *Western Outdoors* and *Western Outdoor News*, and he's built Baja Destinations with a professional journalist's attention to detail. The links at the top of the homepage lead to reliably updated weekly columns that are a mixture of illustrated

Baja Fishing Reports and Information -- Baja California, Mexico

BajaDestinations.com

--Gene Kira, Baja Editor, *Western Outdoor News* & *Western Outdoors Magazine*

Weekly Baja Fishing Reports ----- Weekly Columns ----- Recommended Tackle

THE MOST TIMELY, UP-TO-DATE FISHING REPORTS & INFORMATION AVAILABLE FOR BAJA CALIFORNIA
Baja fishing reports and information from all over Baja California, Mexico. Fish counts, weather & sea conditions.
Online subscriptions to *Western Outdoor News*. Online store featuring Gene's three Baja books & thoroughly
tested fishing tackle recommended for Baja, including Jointed Rebel Lures, MirrOlure 111MRs, Luhr
Jensen Krocodiles and Stingers, Dr. Slick Pliers and Hook Sharpeners, and Flexx-Rap high tech
finger protection tape. Gene Kira's weekly Baja Fishing Column, Fishing Reports and other
articles from *Western Outdoor News*, America's largest weekly outdoor publication.
Extensive fish identification photo gallery showing real fish actually caught in
Baja California. Complete map set from *The Baja Catch*... and lots more. (IM)

Order Gene's Baja Books Here!

Baja Destinations
http://www.bajadestinations.com

TOP RATED

news stories, advice and reports on what's being caught up and down the peninsula. At the bottom of the page you'll find regulations, lists of Baja businesses useful to traveling anglers and catch shots organized into a fish identification parade. I counted over 100 species from sea robins to blue marlin.

Baja on the Fly
http://www.bajafly.com

Gary and Yvonne Graham's Orvis-endorsed operation guides fly fishermen around the East Cape, La Paz, Magdalena Bay, Loreto and Cabo San Lucas. The site has brief area descriptions and a FAQ section listing hotels, fishing packages, travel tips and recommended tackle. The Condition Report is described as a forum, but it's more commonly used to post catch reports from the

owners, guides, and friends of the company. Reports were detailed and were being posted every couple of days: A great heads-up if you're heading down Mexico way.

OTHER SITES
Anglerstown.com
http://www.anglerstown.com

This colorful and enthusiastic Korean page has photographs and decent-length descriptions of the country's freshwater fisheries. The site's uncOnventional design can make it seem as if you've come to a dead end. In most cases, topics are continued via links at the very bottom of the page. For a clear breakdown of everything on the site find your way to the Introduction page, then look for the site map.

International

Chris and Jeff's Malaysian Angler's Website

http://www.geocities.com/
yosemite/3133

This site has been left in Internet purgatory but it's still functional as a Malaysian angling primer with a few decent articles, where-to-fish information and a gallery of local characters (some of them, fish).

Fishing on Ambergris Caye

http://www.ambergriscaye.com/
pages/town/fishing.html

This guide to Belize's largest island really tries to educate visitors with meaty descriptions of the available fishing for bonefish, permit, snook, tarpon and deep-water species.

An 11-page guide to the basics of saltwater fly fishing, pretty maps, and background on the flora and fauna will have you

PEACOCK BASS

The fierceness and beauty of peacock bass, not to mention the spirit of adventure necessary to tangle with them (they're mostly fished for in the Amazon) has inspired a clutch of worthwhile sites.

For a local's perspective, the Brazilian site **TFW's Peacock Bass Book** at **http://www.fishingworld. com.br/pbb/**, has destination features and a busy fishing and travel forum.

The fishing travel company **X-Treme Angling** has an impressive peacock e-zine at **http://www.pea cockbassonline.com**. Though it's ultimate goal is to lure you to one of their South American peacock lodges, the site is well past being a simple brochure: you'll find a magazine full of photographs and information about the peacock's life cycle and fishing techniques, plus descriptions of the Amazon basin and other South American gamefish.

Larry Larsen is one of the country's best-known peacock anglers and has written several books on the subject. His latest venture is the **Peacock Bass Association**, online at **http://www.peacockbass association.com**. Though it requires paid membership, the site provides free information within articles, an inspiring gallery and a large directory of travel agents offering peacock trips. For more travel and fishing features follow the link at the bottom of the articles page to find **Larsen's Adventure Travel Magazine**, **http://www.larsenoutdoors.com**.

If South America isn't an option, how about Miami? A small section of the Association site tells you how and where to fish for peacocks in Florida's Miami-area canal system. As does a special section of the **Florida Freshwater Fisheries** site at **http://www.floridafisheries.com/ docum/butterfly.html**, reviewed in Chapter 2 State-by-State Resources.

Fishing on Ambergris Caye
http://www.ambergriscaye.com/pages/town/fishing.html

casting an eye over the guide and accommodation listings before you leave. Go to Commons at the bottom of the fishing homepage to find a tourist site that has thought of everything in terms of travel planning and likely questions.

Ken's Fishing Haven
http://home.pacific.net.sg/~kcsk

A photo-rich peek into one man's Singapore fishing diary. Go to the Hall of Fame, The Haven's Archives or Catch of the Month for a look at available species. Beware of crazily alternating font sizes and colors.

Korean Fly-Fishing
http://www.koreanflyfishing.com

A compact guide to what webmaster Young Park states is some of the most demanding fly fishing in the world. The site benefits from above-average fishing pho-

tography within sections for Digital Gallery, Fish of the Day and Reports. The Fish Species link in the top navigation gives the fly-rod lowdown on salmon, trout, bass, chub, mullet and America's most recent fish-villain: the land-crawling snakehead. Use the Are You Coming to Korea? link on the homepage to find out when and where you should plan a trip.

Lure Fishing in Japan Illustrated
http://www002.upp.so-net.ne.jp/Ham

Japanese angler and artist Setsuo Hamanaka was always asked the same thing when he traveled aboard on fishing adventures: "What do you fish for in Japan?" This site is his way of answering the question. Setsuo graphs Japan's diverse fisheries into long species tables for offshore, inshore and coral reef anglers, and for native

International

and transplanted freshwater fish. Each fish is named in English and Japanese and some are photographed. The last column in the table links to the kind of tackle and method usually used to catch it. Visit the Cartoon Updates and Ham's Gallery to view the author's skillful fishing cartoons.

Pescamazon
http://www.pescamazon.com

Pescamazon is a Brazilian sport-fishing company keen to educate visitors about the world's largest river. Go to Amazon Game Fishes for more than 30 profiles discussing habitat and habits, tackle and fishing tips, plus the current IGFA record. When you're up-to-speed on apapá and pintado and pirarara, learn what's meant by the Amazon's clear water, black water, and white water fisheries, or read through tips for safe and comfortable travel in such wild country.

Sport Fishing in Niigata City and Japan
http://www.japan-fishing.com

"Sensei" means teacher in Japanese, and webmaster Sensei has taken on the pleasant task of educating visitors about the fishing scene around Niigata City on the west coast of Japan. Though he prefers fish such as sea bass and trout, Sensei is an all rounder, content with whatever the fish gods send his way: "I often go to Agaro to some of trouts, but I sometimes get no trout but trash fish. And trash fish kindly comfort me."

See also **Tsuribaka Fishing Ltd** at **http://www.tsuribaka.com/jp/fishing,** which is a fun look at hot ticket items from a Japanese tackle manufacturer, including swimming and luminous sinkers, chum tongs and various ingenious devices for turning a cooler into a rod-holding fishing machine.

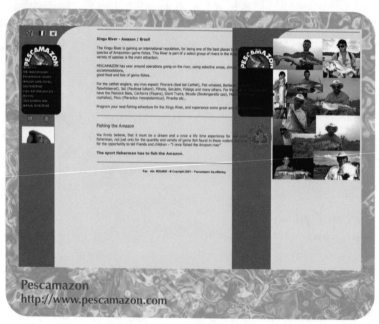

Pescamazon
http://www.pescamazon.com

Trout and Seasons of the Mountain Village
http://www.itow.com/amago/index2.html

TOP RATED

Trout and Seasons of the Mountain Village

http://www.itow.com/amago/index2.html

TOP RATED

A beautiful and unusual site illustrating the seasons of a Japanese highland trout stream, and the "vivid expressions of lovely trouts" that live in it. Author and artist Yoshikazu Fujioka can also use a camera to good effect as we see in photo journals of her favorite Japanese trout streams and the Tenkara fly-fishing style of dapping into pocket water. About her fishing club, "Tsuttenkai" she writes: "One of us is crazy in fishing and forget time. And the other take part only in the party at night." A charming production.

International

Fishing Travel Companies

The likeliest path to a successful fishing vacation is to use the services of a fishing travel company. The ones listed here range from those that send clients all over the world to specialists that concentrate on a couple of countries or species. What they all have in common is in-depth knowledge of what the fishing is like, the best times to go, what tackle to take and the logistical organization to transport and accommodate you in often-remote areas. There are many more fishing travel companies out there on the Web: these were singled out to show the range of options available, and because they offer plenty of online information to go with all that offline temptation.

Acute Angling
http://www.acuteangling.com

TOP RATED

Acute Angling are South American specialists. In addition to lodge and service descriptions they've put together a meaty introduction to fishing for peacock bass, payara, dorado, Amazonian catfish and other fangy exotics. Use the table of contents to find your way through this dense, looping site.

For a collection of articles and resources about South American fly fishing try Bonnie Hamre's recommended fishing links at **http://www.gosouthamerica. about.com/cs/fishsouthamerica**.

Angling Destinations
http://www.anglingdestinations.com

Angling Destinations

http://www.angling
destinations.com

TOP RATED

This fly-fishing agency shows off its worldwide destinations within a sharply designed site, full of exceptional photography and useful trip information. Sections titled Recent Adventures, Tips, and Travel Notes offer articles and recent fishing reports.

B & B Worldwide Fishing Adventures

http://www.wheretofish.com

B & B can send you to Australia for barramundi, to Africa for tigerfish or to five of Mexico's best bass lakes. Go to the bottom of each destination page to find extra pages for itineraries, lodge descriptions, seasons, prices and tackle considerations. Search the rest of this spaciously laid-out site for

other country options.

The Best of New Zealand Fly Fishing

http://www.bestofnzflyfishing.com

All New Zealand, all fly fishing, all the time. The photo board of clients, lit by the reflection of jade rivers and lofting super-sized browns, will provoke feverish clicking through the lodge profiles and fishery descriptions.

Canadian Carp Club

http://www.canadian
carpclub.on.ca

Carp are sometimes referred to as Rocky Mountain bonefish, but the 30 lb. bruisers this company guides anglers to on the St. Lawrence could kick marl in the face of any bone. The river has become North America's most unusual fishing holiday destination, with several companies guiding and

International

Fishing Adventures Thailand
http://www.anglingthailand.com

lodging European anglers after the river's prodigious stocks of big carp.

See also **http://www.canadiancarp in.com**, and **http://www.carp.org**.

Carpentaria Seafaris
http://www.seafaris.com.au

Cruise the Cape York peninsular in Australia's Northern Territories for barramundi, permit, tuna and trevally. Magazine articles about the operation are collected in Seafaris News, or you can download a multimedia brochure. The Fish Species section has a game-fish calendar.

Fishing Adventures Thailand
http://www.anglingthailand.com

For a truly different kettle of fish, browse the fascinating galleries of Thai sportfish at this guide's site. Apart from the circus fish parade,

there isn't a lot of service information here, but it doesn't really matter. Go to the contact area and request more information or ask for the e-mail addresses of some of the company's previous clients. The ones in the photographs definitely look happy.

Fishing International
http://www.fishing international.com

Fishing International has a quarter-century of experience sending fishermen everywhere from Ireland to Australia in search of the foreign bite. It isn't the silkiest-looking web site but offers plenty of information about its worldwide destinations, how to plan and prepare for a trip and what you're likely to catch.

FishQuest!
http://www.fishquest.com

Search FishQuest! for freshwater or saltwater trips by species or destination. Links to pages for peacock bass and payara have tackle and technique tips, what-to-pack checklists and IGFA records.

The Fly Shop – Travel
http://www.flyfishingtravel.com

Kaufmann's Streamborn
http://www.kman.com

These two companies are fly-fishing retailers that also offer a full range of U.S. and international trips. So they can sell you every item of tackle you'll need on a bonefish flat or Atlantic salmon river, and take you someplace to get it wet. Each has a site showing the kind of attention to detail that bodes well for a booking a trip. The Fly Shop produces a great annual travel magazine called

FlyFishing.com and Kaufmann's sends out an equally lavish mail-order catalog. Order both online.

Frontiers
http://www.frontierstrvl.com

Based in Wexford, PA, Frontiers is one of the most respected and high-profile sporting travel agencies in the U.S. They've been around for 30 years and cater primarily to fly fishers and big-game anglers. Every itinerary is described in terms of what the fishing is like, accommodations, what to take and excursions for non-fishing companions.

GourmetFly
http://www.gourmetfly.com

GourmetFly organizes fly-fishing and general fishing holidays all over France and Spain. There are overviews for each region in terms of geography, fishing, accommodation, regulations and

Frontiers
http://www.frontierstrvl.com

Orvis
http://www.orvis.com/travel

"gastronomie." Go to the newsletter archive at the bottom of the left-hand navigation for a section that's equal parts angling report card and reflections on French cuisine.

INSURANCE

Every fishing travel agency recommends you buy trip-cancellation and travel insurance, though only Frontiers names a carrier specifically: **Travelex Insurance** at **http://www.travelex-insurance.com.** One option is to ask your travel company representative to detail exactly what you need, then comparison shop between eight respected companies at **InsureMyTrip.com, http://www.insuremytrip.com.**

For a Spain specialist try **Angling in Spain** at **http://www.angling-in-spain.com**. Among some brief details about regulations and seasons, discover opportunities for zander, largemouth bass, pike, brown trout, sea trout and salmon. The picture gallery has snapshots of rivers in five regions.

To learn about the River Ebro and its monster catfish go to **http://www.eaar.co.uk,** the web site of **Ebro Angling and River-Guiding**.

Orvis

http://www.orvis.com/travel

TOP RATED

Trading on a reputation for high-quality products and service, Orvis had the good idea to begin endorsing lodges, guides and outfitters. Endorsement means the company's services are reviewed on a regular basis and they've taken part in Orvis training seminars. From the travel start page go to Fishing Trips U.S./Canada to find a clickable U.S. map. Each operation is described in some depth, and in all there are links to 51 lodges, more than 80 guides, 54 outfitters and nine fly-fishing schools.

Orvis also lists international trips to the toniest fishing spots world-wide. Click on a country within Fishing Trips Int'l to view drop-down menus for trip planning, clothing, packing and equipment, all tailored to that destination.

Click on Fly Fishing in the top navigation to find quick links to all the company's U.S. and international travel options and a well thought-out resource section with articles, hatch charts, animated knots and tackle tips.

PanAngling
http://www.panangling.com

PanAngling uses a bright, stylish web site to show off the world-wide destinations they've been shuttling clients to for the past 25 years. And they don't discriminate: offshore big game, Canadian fly-in, bonefish flat or salmon river—whatever your preference. Trip-planning resources, links to related Pan-sites for hunting and outdoor adventure and an area for trips under $1,000, make up the rest.

Rod and Reel Adventures
http://www.rodreeladventures.com

A 20-year-old agency providing U.S. and international trips for fly rodders and conventional tackle fishermen. "Join Us" trips are tailored to solo travelers.

PanAngling
http://www.panangling.com

Sportfishing Worldwide
http://www.sportfishingworldwide.com

Roxton Bailey Robinson Worldwide
http://www.rbrww.com

Based in England, Roxton Bailey Robinson has a posh-looking site offering fly fishing, conventional tackle and big-game bluewater trips, plus safaris and other luxury getaways. They send clients to a few destinations not usually offered by U.S. agencies, such as India, Dubai, the Seychelles, the English chalkstreams and the ultimate forbidden fishin' hole, Cuba. Prices are displayed in pounds and dollars.

Sportfishing Worldwide
http://www.sportfishing worldwide.com

Un-syrupy trip descriptions, appealing layout, and checklists of everything included in the price are the best features of this world-ranging company site. A newsletter and specials section offer discounted trips.

Sweetwater Travel Company
http://www.sweetwatertravel.com

Sweet indeed to be able to travel the world as a fishing guide or outfitter. Brothers Jeff, Dan and Pat Vermillion, owners of Sweetwater Travel, have managed to pull it off and they'll not only tempt you with fly-fishing packages to Argentina or Russia or half-a-dozen other countries, they'll teach you how to become a guide yourself in their week-long guide school.

Terry Hollan's Reel Mexican Adventures
http://www.mexican adventures.com

One of the many outfitters specializing in south-of-the-border bass fishing. They send sports to Lake Huites in Sinaloa and use mexicanadventures.com to describe the lodge, the lake and the locality. Read through articles about Huites collected from the outdoor press or the latest catch reports, such as this matter-of-fact entry: "60-80 bass per boat/day. Several between 7-8 lb."

Outfitter Finatic Adventures publishes an overview of six of Mexico's most famous bass lakes. Apart from scene-setting details of each lake—the size and numbers of bass you're likely to catch, lodge and itinerary choices— there's a useful three-part English/ Spanish fishing phrase guide, local weather forecasts and a forum with a little life in its veins for catch reports and tips. **Bass Fishing Mexico** is at **http://www.bass fishingmexico.com.**

Westbank Anglers
http://www.westbank.com

Westbank Anglers has a large site with summaries of their U.S., Caribbean and Central and South American fly-fishing destinations, plus extended coverage of the Bahamas. A check box indicates if the trip is suitable for a non-fishing companion. They also sell pattern selections for the Bahamas, Belize, Christmas Island, Mexico and Alaska. Or you could just use them as a guide for what to tie yourself if you're headed that way, based on the experience of people with a high interest in bent rods and screaming reels.

COARSE FELLOWS

Fly fishermen are unfairly catered to in terms of exotic travel. If you prefer lure fishing or even bait fishing, it can be a struggle to find a worldwide booking agent in the U.S. The fly-fishing cult, ironically, is not so advanced in its ancestral home, so here are two English companies catering to the general fisherman with wanderlust in their wellies. There isn't much of a difference between booking a trip through a foreign company and one based in the U.S., apart from con- verting costs into dollars. See the currency converter at **http://www. oanda.com/converter/classic**.

Angling Travel
http://www.angling-travel.com

Led expedition-style by angling author John Bailey, one of Europe's best known fishermen, Angling Travel specializes in small group trips to seriously wild places, like plunking for mahseer in India, jigging for pike in the Baltic or lure fishing for taimen in Mongolia. Reading the trip descriptions and newsletters leaves a strong impres- sion they're in it for the joy of travel and shared fishing adven- tures as much as turning a profit. If that sounds like your kind of outfit, book online or request a brochure.

Anglers World Holidays
http://www.anglers-world.co.uk

If you're looking for something a little different in a fishing vacation, say, catfishing in Kazakhstan or cod fishing in the fjords of Norway, check the offerings of Anglers World Holidays. Their destinations divide about equally between European fishing pack- ages and more remote adventures. Under the "Polaris" label, they also sell a range of unique tackle items.

International

TOP RATED SITES

CHAPTER 2:
STATE-BY-STATE RESOURCES

NEW ENGLAND

Capt. Tom's Guide to
New England Sharks
http://www.newenglandsharks.com
CT Fisherman.com
http://www.ctfisherman.com
Fly Fishing in Maine
http://www.flyfishinginmaine.com
MainToday.com
http://outdoors.maintoday
.com/fishing
New England Shad Association
http://www.newenglandshad.com
Striped-Bass.com
http://www.striped-bass.com
Water Works Wonders
http://www.waterworkswonders.org

MID ATLANTIC

ACFishing.com
http://www.acfishing.com
At the Beach
http://www.atbeach.com/fishing
BayDreaming.com
http://www.baydreaming.
com/fishing
Black Lake, New York
http://www.blacklakenewyork.com
FISHBOX.TV
http://www.fishbox.tv
FishErie.com
http://www.fishusa.com/fisherie
The Fishing Line
http://www.thefishingline.com
FishSalmonRiver.com
http://www.fishsalmonriver.com
New York Bass
http://www.nybass.com
NJ Striper.com
http://www.njstriper.com
Pennsylvania BASS Federation
http://www.pabass.com

Potomac Bass
http://www.potomacbass.com
Rob J's Western New York
Bass Fishing Pages
http://home.adelphia.net/~
thewavzone
TheBassBarn.com
http://www.thebassbarn.com
VAflyfish.com
http://www.vaflyfish.com
Virginia Beach Sport Fishing
http://www.virginiabeach
sportfishing.com

SOUTH

CharlestonFishing.com
http://www.charlestonfishing.com
Doc's Best Bets for Fishing
the Mississippi Gulf Coast
http://www.datasync.com/~dbb
Fishing Lake Guntersville
http://www.fishinglake
guntersville.com
Fly Fishing NC
http://www.flyfishingnc.com
Georgia River Fishing
http://www.georgiariverfishing.com
High Country Outdoors Guide Service
http://www.highcountry
outdoors.net
Louisiana Sportsman
http://www.louisiana
sportsman.com
Mike Lane's RodnReel.com
http://www.rodnreel.com
NC CoastalFishing.com
http://www.nccoastalfishing.com
Night Hawk Publications
http://www.nighthawk
publications.com
North Carolina Sportsman
http://www.northcarolina
sportsman.com
North Carolina Waterman
http://www.ncwaterman.com

North Georgia Trout Online
http://www.georgia-outdoors.com/ngto/index.html
The Ozark Angler
http://www.ozarkangler.com
The Ozark Mountains Travel
& Recreation Directory
http://www.whiteriver.net
South Carolina Lakes
http://www.geocities.com/norwood_dr
Stewarts's Cumberland River
Guide Service
http://www.stewartsguideservice.com

FLORIDA
Captain Mel Berman's Fishing Florida
Online Magazine
http://www.capmel.com
Central Florida East Coast Fishing
http://home.cfl.rr.com/floridafishing
CyberAngler
http://www.cyberangler.com
Islamorada Sport Fishing Online
http://www.islamoradasportfishing.com
Jim Porter's Guide to Bass Fishing
http://www.jimporter.org
South Florida Sport Fishing
http://www.southfloridasportfishing.com
SportFishingFlorida.net
http://www.sportfishingflorida.net

MIDWEST
Chicago Area Paddling/Fishing Guide
http://www.chicagopaddling.org
ChicagolandFishing.com
http://www.chicagolandfishing.com
Fishing Minnesota
http://www.fishingminnesota.com
GoFishOhio.com
http://www.gofishohio.com
Great Lakes Sport Fishing Council
http://www.great-lakes.org
In-Depth Angling
http://www.in-depthangling.com
Iowa Outdoors
http://www.iowaoutdoors.org

Lake Michigan Angler
http://www.lakemichiganangler.com
Lake-Link.com
http://www.lake-link.com
Michigan Fishing Information
http://www.trophyspecialists.com/mifishinfo/index.html
Michigan Interactive
http://www.fishweb.com
The Michigan Sportsman
http://www.michigan-sportsman.com
Midwest Bass Tournaments
Internet Magazine
http://www.midwestbasstournaments.com
Ohio Fishermen.com
http://www.ohiofishermen.com
SE Minnesota Trout Flies
http://users.myexcel.com/dolfnlvr/
Steelhead Shangra-La
http://www.geocities.com/steeldredge
Trails to Trout
http://www.trailstotrout.com
Up North Outdoors
http://www.upnorthoutdoors.com

CENTRAL
Fishing Buddy Outdoors
http://www.fishingbuddy.com
The Fishing Notebook
http://www.fishingnotebook.com

TEXAS
Bass Fishing in North Texas
http://www.bassfishing.org
Corpus Christi Caller Times – Outdoors
http://www.caller.com
Corpusfishing.com
http://www.corpusfishing.com
Lake Fork, Texas – ETS Systems
http://www.ets-systems.com
Texas Gulf Coast Fishing
http://www.texasgulfcoastfishing.com
TexasMojo.com
http://www.texasmojo.com
Tom Nix's Salty Angler
http://www.saltyangler.com

TX Fishing.com
http://www.txfishing.com

WEST
Big Sky Fishing.com
http://www.bigskyfishing.com
Blue Quill Angler
http://www.bluequillangler.com
Colorado Fishing Network
http://www.coloradofishing.net
Fly Fishing Utah
http://www.fishwest.net/utah
Go Fly Fishing the Green River
http://quickbyte.com/greenriver
High Country Flies
http://www.highcountryflies.com
JacksonHole.Net
http://www.jacksonhole.net
The San Juan River Fly Fishing Site
http://www.ifly4trout.com
Utah on the Fly
http://www.utahonthefly.com
WaynesWords – Lake Powell
Fishing Information
http://www.wayneswords.com

NORTHWEST
Alaska Flyfishing Online
http://www.alaskaflyfishing
online.com
Alaska Outdoor Journal
http://www.alaskaoutdoor
journal.com
BoatEscape.com
http://www.boatescape.com
Bob's Piscatorial Pursuits
http://www.piscatorialpursuits.com
Dickson Flyfishing Steelhead Guides
http://www.flyfishsteelhead.com
Fishing Northwest
http://www.fishingnorthwest.com
Gamefishin.com
http://www.gamefishin.com
Ifish
http://www.ifish.net
Salmon University
http://www.salmonuniversity.com
Washington Fly Fishing
http://www.washington
flyfishing.com

Worley Bugger Fly Co.
http://www.worleybuggerflyco.com

CALIFORNIA
Calfishing.com
http://www.calfishing.com
California Delta Chambers
& Visitors Bureau
http://www.californiadelta.org
Eastern Sierra Fishing
http://www.easternsierra
fishing.com
Ichthy.com
http://www.ichthy.com
Fish First!
http://www.fishfirst.com
The Orange County Register – Outdoors
http://www.myoc.com/sports/
recreation/fishing_report.shtml
Ralph and Lisa Cutter's California
School of Flyfishing
http://www.flyline.com
San Diego Fish Online
http://www.sdfish.com
Southern California Marlin Online
http://www.marlinnut.com
West Coast Angler
http://www.westcoastangler.com

CHAPTER 3:
KNOW BEFORE YOU GO

GENERAL RESOURCES
Outdoors Yellow Pages
http://www.outdoorsyp.com
SMARTpages.com
http://www.smartpages.com
SuperPages.com
http://www.bigyellow.com
SuperPages.com Global Directories
http://www.superpages.com/global
Tourism Offices Worldwide Directory
http://www.towd.com
U.S. Fish and Wildlife Service
http://www.fws.gov
U.S. Geological Service (USGS)
Real-Time Daily Streamflow Conditions
http://water.usgs.gov/realtime.html

WEATHER
Intellicast
http://www.intellicast.com
National Weather Service
http://www.nws.noaa.gov
UM Weather
http://yang.sprl.umich.edu/wxnet/
The Weather Underground
http://www.wunderground.com

SEA SURFACE TEMPERATURES
John Hopkins University's
Ocean Remote Sensing
http://fermi.jhuapl.edu
Rutgers University's Coastal
Ocean Observation Lab
http://marine.rutgers.edu/mrs/
sat.data2.html

TIDES
Great Lakes Online
http://www.glakesonline.
nos.noaa.gov
Tides Online
http://www.tidesonline.
nos.noaa.gov

MAPS/DIRECTIONS
MapQuest
http://mapquest.com
Maptech MapServer
http://mapserver.maptech.com
TerraServer
http://terraserver-usa.com
TerraFly
http://www.terrafly.fiu.edu
TopoZone
http://www.topozone.com

WHERE TO GO
Gorp – Parks
http://www.gorp.com
ParkNet
http://www.nps.gov
Public Lands Information Center
http://www.publiclands.org
Recreation.Gov
http://www.recreation.gov
ReserveUSA
http://www.reserveusa.com

U.S. National Parks
http://www.us-national-parks.net

INTERNATIONAL TRAVEL RESOURCES
The Angling Report
http://www.anglingreport.com
The Bureau of Consular Affairs
http://www.travel.state.gov
Centers for Disease Control
and Prevention – Travelers' Health
http://www.cdc.gov/travel
Fodors
http://www.fodors.com
Free Travel Tips.com
http://www.freetraveltips.com
IgoUgo
http://www.igougo.com
TripAdvisor
http://www.tripadvisor.com

CHAPTER 4:
FISHING THE WEB

BEST BASS FISHING SITES
Bass Anglers Sportsmans Society (BASS)
http://www.bassmaster.com
Bass Champs
http://www.basschamps.com
Bass Fishing Home Page
http://www.bassfishing
homepage.com
Bassdozer
http://www.bassdozer.com
BassFan
http://www.bassfan.com
Bassin' USA
http://www.bassinusa.com
FLW Outdoors
http://www.flwoutdoors.com
Kevin's Bass Fishing Site
http://www.bassfishin.com
ProBass
http://www.probass.com
River Smallies.com
http://www.riversmallies.com
Trophy Bass Only
http://www.trophybassonly.com
The Ultimate Bass Fishing
Resource Guide
http://www.bassresource.com

WesternBass.com
http://www.westernbass.com
WorldRecordBass.com
http://www.worldrecordbass.com

BEST FRESHWATER FISHING SITES
Brotherhood of Catfishermen
http://www.brotherhood-of-catfishermen.com
Carp.com
http://www.carp.com
Carp Anglers Group
http://www.carpanglersgroup.com
Gar Fishing! With the Gar Anglers'
Sporting Society
http://www.garfishing.com
Game & Fish Magazines – Catfish
http://www.gameandfish.about.com/cs/catfish
IcefishingFIRST
http://icefishing.outdoorsfirst.com
International Muskie Home Page
http://www.trentu.ca/muskie/muskie.html
Muskie Central
http://ww.muskiecentral.com
MuskieFIRST
http://muskie.outdoorsfirst.com
Muskies101
http://www.muskies101.com
Roughfish.com
http://www.roughfish.com
Walleye Central
http://www.walleyecentral.com
Walleye Hunter
http://www.walleyehunter.com
WalleyeFIRST
http://walleye.outdoorsfirst.com
Walleyes Inc.
http://www.walleyesinc.com

BEST SALTWATER FISHING SITES
See also Chapter 2 State-by-State Resources
AllCoast Sport Fishing
http://www.sport-fish-info.com
Big Marine Fish
http://www.chambers-associates.org
Billfish Tournament Network
http://www.billfishnetwork.com

CharkBait!
http://www.charkbait.com
Flats Hunter
http://www.flatshunter.com
Noreast.com
http://www.noreast.com
Pierandsurf.com
http://www.pierandsurf.com
Pier Fishing in California
http://www.pierfishing.com
StripersOnline
http://www.stripersonline.com
StriperSurf.com
http://www.stripersurf.com
Surfcaster.com
http://www.surfcaster.com
Tidal Fish
http://www.tidalfish.com

BEST FLY-FISHING SITES
All-About Fly Fishing
http://www.about-flyfishing.com
Dana Sturn's Spey Pages
http://www.speypages.com
Fish & Fly
http://www.fishandfly.co.uk
Fly Anglers Online
http://www.flyanglersonline.com
Fly Craft Angling
http://www.flycraftangling.com
Fly Fishing Connection
http://www.flyfishingconnection.com
The Fly Fishing FORUM
http://www.flyfishingforum.com
Flyfish@ Home Page
http://www.uky.edu/~agrdanny/flyfish/main.htm
FlyFish Saltwaters.com
http://www.flyfishsaltwaters.com
Global FlyFisher
http://www.globalflyfisher.com
Ken Abrames' Striper Moon
http://www.stripermoon.com
Reel-Time
http://www.reel-time.com
A River Never Sleeps
http://www.ariverneversleeps.com
SalmonAnglers.com
http://www.salmonanglers.com

Sexyloops
http://www.sexyloops.co.uk
Sidney Du Broff's Fishing
and Shooting Journal
http://www.sidsjournal.com
Smallstreams.com
http://www.smallstreams.com
The Steelhead Site
http://www.steelheadsite.com
Westfly
http://www.westfly.com

BEST FLY-TYING SITES
The Complete Sportsman
http://www.rareandunusual.com
The Dry Fly.com
http://www.thedryfly.com
Fly Tying World
http://www.flytyingworld.com
Flytier's Page
http://www.danica.com/flytier
John McKim Illustrations
http://www.johnmckim.com
Salmonfly.net
http://www.angelfire.com/
wa/salmonid
Ultimate Fly Tying
http://www.ultimateflytying.com
Virtual Flybox
http://www.virtualflybox.com
Vladimir Markov's Fly-Tying Websites
http://www.markov.baikal.ru/

FISH IDENTIFICATION
FishBase
http://www.fishbase.com

CHAPTER 5:
MEDIA

PRINT MAGAZINES ONLINE
Field & Stream
http://www.fieldandstream.com
The Fish Sniffer Online
http://www.fishsniffer.com
Florida Sportsman Online
http://www.floridasportsman.com
Fly Fish America Online
http://www.flyfishamerica.com

Fly Fisherman
http://www.flyfisherman.com
Fly Fishing in Saltwaters
http://www.flyfishinsalt.com
Fly Rod & Reel
http://www.flyrodandreel.com
FlyLife Online
http://www.flylife.com.au
Game & Fish Magazines
http://www.gameandfish.
about.com
Gary Yamamoto's Inside Line
http://www.insideline.net
Great Lakes Angler
http://www.glangler.com
In-Fisherman
http://www.in-fisherman.com
Marlin
http://www.marlinmag.com
Musky Hunter
http://www.muskyhunter.com
North American Fisherman
http://www.fishingclub.com
Outdoor Canada
http://www.outdoorcanada.ca
Outdoor Life
http://www.outdoorlife.com
Salt Water Sportsman
http://www.saltwater
sportsman.com
Sport Fishing
http://www.sportfishingmag.com

ONLINE MAGAZINES
Big Fish Tackle
http://www.bigfishtackle.com
Cabela's
http://www.cabelas.com
Discover the Outdoors
http://www.discoverthe
outdoors.com
ESPN Outdoors
http://www.espn.go.com/outdoors
GORP
http://www.gorp.com
LandBigFish
http://www.landbigfish.com
Louis Bignami's Fine Fishing
http://www.finefishing.com
OutdoorSite
http://www.outdoorsite.com

The Sportsman's Guide
http://www.sportsmansguide.com
FishingWorld.com
http://www.fishingworld.com

DIRECTORIES
About.com
Saltwater Fishing
http://www.saltfishing.about.com
Freshwater Fishing
http://www.fishing.about.com
100 Top Fishing Sites
http://www.hitsunlimited.com
Cbel – Fly Fishing
http://www.cbel.com/fly_fishing
FishingWorks
http://www.fishingworks.com
Google – Directory
http://www.google.com

BOOKSTORES
Alibris
http://www.alibris.com
Amazon.com
http://www.amazon.com
Books of the Black Bass
http://www.hometown.
aol.com/bassbks
Coch-y-Bonddu Books
http://www.anglebooks.com
Wilderness Adventures
Sporting Books
http://www.wildadv.com

CHAPTER 6: GROUPS

WOMEN
Flygirls of Michigan
http://www.flygirls.com
Women's Fly Fishing
http://www.womensflyfishing.net

KIDS
Boating Safety Sidekicks
http://www.boatingsafety
sidekicks.com
Fascinating Facts About Fish
http://www.nefsc.noaa.
gov/faq.html

The International Game Fish
Association Junior Angler Club
http://www.igfa.org/jrangler
Kidfish – All About Lakes
and Fly Fishing Too!
http://kidfish.bc.ca
National Fishing Week
http://www.nationalfishing
week.com
Recreational Boating and Fishing
Foundation – Aquatic Science, Fishing,
and Boating Education Web Directory
http://www.rbff-education.org
StreamNet
http://www.streamnet.org

CONSERVATION
American Rivers
http://www.americanrivers.org
Atlantic Salmon Federation
http://www.asf.ca
The Billfish Foundation
http://www.billfish.org
Coastal Conservation Association
http://www.joincca.org
Creekbank
http://www.creekbank.com
The Izaak Walton League of America
http://www.iwla.org
River Network
http://www.rivernetwork.org
Trout Unlimited
http://www.tu.org
U.S. Environmental Protection Agency
– Surf Your Watershed
http://www.epa.gov/surf
The Wild Salmon Center
http://wildsalmoncenter.org

CLUBS
Federation of Fly Fishers
http://www.fedflyfishers.org
Lake Internet – Bass Clubs Online
http://www.blacklakeny.com/links/
linksclubs.html
Yahoo! Fishing Groups
http://www.groups.yahoo.com

CHAPTER 7:
TACKLE AND BOATS

TACKLE MAKING
Lurebuilding 101
   http://www.lurebuilding.nl/
   indexeng.html
LureMaking.com
   http://www.luremaking.com
RodBuilding.org
   http://www.rodbuilding.org
Rodmakers
   http://www.canerod.com/
   rodmakers
TackleMaking
   http://www.tacklemaking.com

COLLECTING
Antique Lure Collectibles
   http://www.antiquelure
   collectibles.com
AntiqueLures
   http://www.antiquelures.com
Lure Lore
   http://www.lurelore.com
Mr. Lure Box
   http://www.mrlurebox.com
Old Fishing Stuff
   http://www.oldfishingstuff.com
The Sport Fishing Museum
   http://www.sportfishingmuseum.ca

REVIEWS
OutdoorREVIEW.com – Flyfishing
   http://www.outdoorreview.com
Tackle Tour
   http://www.tackletour.com

BUYING
eBay
   http://www.ebay.com

BOATS
American Canoe Association
   http://www.acanet.org
Bass & Walleye Boats Magazine
   http://www.bassandwalleye
   boats.com
BassBoat Central
   http://www.bassboatcentral.com
BoatTEST.com

http://www.boattest.com
BoatU.S.
   http://www.boatus.com
Duckworks Magazine
   http://www.duckworks
   magazine.com
Go Boating America
   http://goboatingamerica.com
iboats
   http://www.iboats.com
Kayak Sportfishing
   http://www.kayaksportfishing.com
Paddle-Fishing.com
   http://www.paddle-fishing.com

CHAPTER 8:
INTERNATIONAL

AUSTRALIA
AusFish.com
   http://www.ausfish.com.au
FishEP.com
   http://www.fishep.com
Fishing Cairns
   http://www.fishingcairns.com.au
Fishing Monthly
   http://www.fishingmonthly.com.au
Fishnet
   http://www.fishnet.com.au
FishnTales.com
   http://www.fishntales.com
FishRaider.com
   http://www.fishraider.com
FishSA.com
   http://www.fishsa.com
FishVictoria.com
   http://www.fishvictoria.com
Marinews
   http://www.marinews.com
Sportsfish Australia
   http://www.sportsfishaustralia.
   com.au
Western Angler
   http://www.westernangler.com

NEW ZEALAND
Fish with Bish in New Zealand
   http://www.bishfish.co.nz
Fishing.net.nz
   http://www.fishing.net.nz

BRITAIN

England

Anglers' Net
http://www.anglersnet.co.uk

Carp.com
http://www.carp.com

Carpfishing.UK
http://www.carp-uk.net

Fishing.co.uk
http://www.fishing.co.uk

FISHINGmagic
http://www.fishingmagic.com

FishingWarehouse.co.uk
http://www.fishingwarehouse.co.uk

Lure Fishing UK
http://www.lurefishinguk.com

Where To Fish
http://www.where-to-fish.com

World Sea Fishing
http://www.worldseafishing.com

Ireland

Central Fisheries Board
http://www.cfb.ie

Shannon Regional Fisheries Board
http://www.shannon-fishery-board.ie

Shore Angling & Charter/
Private Boat Fishing in Ireland
http://www.sea-angling-ireland.org

Wales

Fishing in Kite Country
http://www.fishing-in-kite-country.co.uk

Fishing in Wales
http://www.fishing-in-wales.com

CANADA

Bass Canada
http://www.basscanada.com

BC Adventure – FishBC
http://www.bcadventure.com

Credit River Anglers Association
http://www.craa.on.ca

Fish Ontario!
http://www.fishontario.com

Fishing With Rod
http://www.fishingwithrod.com

FloatFishing.net
http://www.floatfishing.net

Go Walleye!
http://www.gowalleye.com

Nova Scotia Fly Fishing, Tying,
and Tall Tales
http://users.eastlink.ca/~dryfly/index.html

Sport Fishing BC
http://www.sportfishingbc.com

What's Bitin' in the Toronto Area
http://zebra.zoo.utoronto.ca/cgi-bin/FBoard/ikonboard.cgi

EUROPE

Flugfiskesidan Online
http://www.flugfiskesidan.com

Monster Carps
http://members.rott.chello.nl/tmarapengopie/wereldrecord.htm

Rackelhanen FlyFishing Magazine
http://www.rackelhanen.se/eng

SOUTH AFRICA

African Angling Consultants
http://www.africanfishing.com

OutdoorPAGES
http://www.outdoorpages.co.za

theflyguide.com
http://www.theflyguide.com

HERE AND THERE

The Baja Big Fish Company
http://www.bajabigfish.com

Baja Destinations
http://www.bajadestinations.com

Trouts and Seasons
of the Mountain Village
http://www.itow.com/amago/index2.html

FISHING TRAVEL COMPANIES

Acute Angling
http://www.acuteangling.com

Angling Destinations
http://www.anglingdestinations.com

Orvis
http://www.orvis.com/travel

BETTER FORUMS

Note: saltwater fishing forums are listed according to the region they cover.

NEW ENGLAND
CT River Stripers
http://www.ctriverstripers.com
CT Fisherman.com
http://www.ctfisherman.com
Fly Fishing in Maine
http://www.flyfishinginmaine.com
Flyfish Saltwaters.com
http://www.flyfishsaltwaters.com
Ken Abrames' Striper Moon
http://www.stripermoon.com
New England Sportsman Network
http://www.nesportsman.com
Reel-Time
http://www.reel-time.com
Striped-Bass.com
http://www.striped-bass.com
Surfcaster.com
http://www.surfcaster.com

MID ATLANTIC
Beach-Net!
http://www.beach-net.com/
Fishinghome.html
ACFishing.com
http://www.acfishing.com
The Fishing Line
http://www.thefishingline.org
FishUSA.com
http://www.fishusa.com/Discussion2
New York Bass
http://www.nybass.com
NJ Fishing
http://www.njfishing.com
NJ Striper.com
http://www.njstriper.com
NJ Trout
http://www.njtrout.com
Noreast.com
http://www.noreast.com
North Eastern Fly Fishing Forum
http://www.njflyfishing.com
Pennsylvania Fly Fishing
http://www.paflyfish.com

Pierandsurf.com
http://www.pierandsurf.com
Reel-Time
http://www.reel-time.com
StripersOnline
http://www.stripersonline.com
StriperSurf.com
http://www.stripersurf.com
TheBassBarn.com
http://www.thebassbarn.com
Tidal Fish
http://www.tidalfish.com
VAflyfish.com
http://www.vaflyfish.com
WVSportsman
http://www.wvsportsman.com

SOUTH
CharlestonFishing.com
http://www.charlestonfishing.com
Coastal Outdoors
http://www.coastaloutdoors.com
Fish Mojo
http://fishmojo.com
Fishin.com
http://www.fishin.com
FlyFishSouth.com
http://www.flyfishsouth.com
Georgia River Fishing
http://www.georgiariverfishing.com
High Country Outdoors Guide Service
http://www.highcountryoutdoors.net
Louisiana Fly fishing
http://www.laflyfish.com
Low Country Boating
http://www.lowcountryboating.com
Mike Lane's RodnReel.com
http://www.rodnreel.com
NC CoastalFishing.com
http://www.nccoastalfishing.com
NC Surf Fishing
http://groups.msn.com/ncsurfishing
North Alabama Fishing Forum
http://home.hiwaay.net/~ksgrisse

North Carolina Waterman
http://www.ncwaterman.com
North Georgia Trout Online
http://www.georgia-outdoors.com/ngto/index.html
Red Drum Tackle
http://www.reddrumtackle.com

FLORIDA
Capt. Mel Berman's Fishing Florida
Online Fishing Magazine
http://www.capmel.com
Florida Sportsman Online
http://www.floridasportsman.com
Florida Surf Fishing
http://floridasurffishing.com
Pensacola Bay Fishing Bridge
http://www.fishthebridge.com
SportFishingFlorida.net
http://www.sportfishingflorida.net

Saltwater Fishing Home Page
(East Coast)
http://www.wmi.org/saltfish

MIDWEST
ChicagolandFishing.com
http://www.chicagolandfishing.com
Fishing Minnesota
http://www.fishingminnesota.com
GoFishOhio.com
http://www.gofishohio.com
Great Lakes Angler
http://www.glangler.com
Great Lakes Fishing Station
http://greatmich.com
Great Lakes Sport Fishing Council
http://www.great-lakes.org/boards.html
In-Depth Angling
http://www.in-depthangling.com
Iowa Outdoors
http://www.iowaoutdoors.org
Lake-Link.com
http://www.lake-link.com
The Michigan Sportsman
http://www.michigan-sportsman.com
Midwest Bass Tournaments
Internet Magazine
http://www.midwestbasstournaments.com

CENTRAL
The Bass Zone
http://www.basszone.com
Beavers Bend Fly Shop
http://www.beaversbendflyshop.com
Fishing Buddy Outdoors
http://www.fishingbuddy.com
The Fishing Notebook
http://www.fishingnotebook.com
Nebraska Game and Parks
Commission Outdoor Forum
http://www.ngpc.state.ne.us/homepage.html

TEXAS
Coalition of Confused Coastal
Fisherman
http://www.coastalfishing.org
Coastal Shark Fishing
http://www.coast-shark.com
Corpusfishing.com
http://www.corpusfishing.com
Surf-Masters
http://www.surf-masters.com
Texas Fishing Forum
http://www.texasfishingforum.com
Texas Kayak Fisherman
http://www.texaskayakfisherman.com
Texas Warmwater Fly Fishers
http://groups.yahoo.com/group/txwwff
TexasMojo.com
http://www.texasmojo.com
TotallyTexas Message Board Forums
http://www.2coolfishing.com
WadeFishing.com
http://www.wadefishing.com

WEST
The Fish Sniffer Online
www.fishsniffer.com
Fly Fishing Utah
http://www.fishwest.net/utah
Utah on the Fly
http://www.utahonthefly.com
WaynesWords
http://www.wayneswords.com
Westfly
http://www.westfly.com

NORTHWEST

Alaska Flyfishing Online
http://www.alaskaflyfishing
online.com
Alaska Outdoor Journal
http://www.alaskaoutdoor
journal.com
Bob's Piscatorial Pursuits
http://www.piscatorialpursuits.com
Gamefishin.com
http://www.gamefishin.com
I Boat NorthWest
http://pub56.ezboard.com/biboatnw
Ifish
http://www.ifish.net
Steelheader.net
http://www.steelheader.net
Washington Fly Fishing
http://www.washingtonflyfishing.com

CALIFORNIA

AllCoast Sport Fishing
http://www.sport-fish-info.com
Bat Batsford's Bay Area Tuna Club
http://offshoreanglers.com
Bite's On!
http://www.biteson.com
Calfishing.com
http://www.calfishing.com
California Delta Chambers
& Visitors Bureau
http://www.californiadelta.org
CharkBait!
http://www.charkbait.com
Eastern Sierra Fishing
http://www.easternsierrafishing.com
Northern California
Fly Fishing Board
http://www.ncffb.org
Pier Fishing in California
http://www.pierfishing.com
San Diego Fish Online
http://www.sdfish.com
Southern California Marlin Online
http://www.marlinnut.com
West Coast Angler
http://www.westcoastangler.com

BASS FISHING

Bass Anglers Sportsmans Society (BASS)
http://www.bassmaster.com

Bass Champs
http://www.basschamps.com
Bass Fishing
http://groups.msn.com/BassFishing
Bass Fishing Home Page
http://www.bassfishing
homepage.com
Bass Fishing Network
http://www.bassfishingnetwork.com
Bassdozer (forum directory)
http://www.bassdozer.com
BassFan
http://www.bassfan.com
Bassin' USA
http://www.bassinusa.com
Bill Dance Outdoors
http://www.billdanceoutdoors.com
Gary Yamamoto's Inside Line
http://www.insideline.net
Kevin's Bass Fishing Site
http://www.bassfishin.com
River Smallies.com
http://www.riversmallies.com
The Smallmouth Alliance
http://www.smallmouth.org
Trophy Bass Only
http://www.trophybassonly.com
The Ultimate Bass Fishing
Resource Guide (forum directory)
http://www.bassresource.com
WesternBass.com
http://www.westernbass.com
WorldRecordBass.com
http://www.worldrecordbass.com

FRESHWATER FISHING

Brotherhood of Catfishermen
http://www.brotherhood-of-
catfishermen.com
Carp Anglers Group
http://www.carpanglersgroup.com
Crappie.com
http://www.crappie.com
The Ice Fishing Home Page
(forum directory)
http://hickorytech.net/~jbusby/
iceangler.html
IceShanty.com
http://www.iceshanty.com
Muskie Central
http://www.muskiecentral.com

MuskieFIRST
http://muskie.outdoorsfirst.com
Musky Hunter
http://www.muskyhunter.com
North American Fisherman
http://www.fishingclub.com
Rollie and Helen's Musky Shop
http://www.muskyshop.com
WalleyeFIRST
http://walleye.outdoorsfirst.com
Walleye Central
http://www.walleyecentral.com

FLY FISHING
Dan Blanton
www.danblanton.com
Fly Anglers Online
http://www.flyanglersonline.com
Fly Fisherman
http://www.flyfisherman.com
Fly Rod & Reel
http://www.flyrodandreel.com
Fly Tying World
http://www.flytyingworld.com
The Fly Fishing FORUM
http://www.flyfishingforum.com
SalmonAnglers.com
http://www.salmonanglers.com
Sexyloops
http://www.sexyloops.co.uk
Smallstreams.com
http://www.smallstreams.com
The Steelhead Site
http://www.steelheadsite.com
Virtual Flybox
http://www.virtualflybox.com
Warmwater Angler
http://groups.yahoo.com/group/
WarmwaterAngler

GENERAL
Anglers Chat
http://www.anglerschat.com
Big Fish Tackle
http://www.bigfishtackle.com
FishingWorks (forum directory)
http://www.fishingworks.com
FishingWorld.com
http://www.fishingworld.com
Outdoors Best
http://www.outdoorsbest.com

Outdoors Network
http://www.outdoors.net
OutdoorSite
http://www.outdoorsite.com

TACKLE
Bamboo Fly Rod Forum
http://pub12.ezboard.com/bclarks
classicflyrodforum
The Custom Rod Builder's Guild
http://www.rodguild.com
Joe's Old Lures
http://www.joeyates.com
OutdoorREVIEW.com
http://www.outdoorreview.com
RodBuilding.org
http://www.rodbuilding.org
TackleMaking
http://www.tacklemaking.com
Tackle Tour
http://www.tackletour.com

BOATS
BassBoat Central
http://www.bassboatcentral.com
BoaterEd
http://www.boatered.com
BoatU.S.
http://www.boatus.com
Coastal Kayak Fishing
http://www.kayakfishing.com
Go Boating America
http://www.goboatingamerica.com
The Hull Truth Boating Forum
http://www.thehulltruth.com
Head Turners
http://www.headturners3.com
iboats
http://www.iboats.com
The Kayak Forum
http://www.kayakforum.com
Kayak Sportfishing
http://www.kayaksportfishing.com
Ol' Paw's Fishin' Page
http://pagebiz.com/pawfish.html
Skeeter Owner's Message Board
http://pub30.ezboard.com/
bskeetermessageboard23632frm1
Trailer Boats Magazine
http://www.trailerboats.com

Yak Fishing Forum
http://www.yakfishing.com

INTERNATIONAL
Australia and New Zealand
AusFish.com.au
http://www.ausfish.com.au
Fishing Western Australia
http://www.fishingwa.com
Fishnet
http://www.fishnet.com.au
FishSA.com
http://www.fishsa.com
FishVictoria.com
http://www.fishvictoria.com
FlyLife Online
http://www.flylife.com.au
Sportsfish Australia
http://www.sportsfishaustralia.
com.au
Fishing.net.nz
http://www.fishing.net.nz

Britain
Anglers' Net
http://www.anglersnet.co.uk
Angling Forums
http://www.anglingforums.co.uk
Barbel Fishing World
http://www.barbelfishing
world.co.uk
Carpfishing UK
http://www.carp-uk.net
CarpForum – The UK Carp
Fishing Forums
http://www.carpforum.co.uk
Fish & Fly
http://www.fishandfly.co.uk
FISHINGmagic
http://www.fishingmagic.com
FishingWarehouse.co.uk
http://www.fishingwarehouse.co.uk
Harris Angling
http://www.harrisangling.co.uk
Lure Fishing UK
http://www.lurefishinguk.com
MaggotDrowning.com
http://www.maggotdrowning.com
Predator Publications
http://www.pikandpredators
magazine.com

Talkangling
http://www.talkangling.co.uk
Total-Fishing.com
http://www.total-fishing.com

Canada
Alberta Outdoorsmen
http://www.albertaoutdoorsmen.org
Angling BC
http://www.anglingbc.com
BC Adventure – FishBC
http://www.bcadventure.com
Credit River Anglers Association
http://www.craa.om.ca
The Fishin' Alberta Message Board
http://members.boardhost.com/
fishalberta
FloatFishing.net
http://www.floatfishing.net
Fish Ontario!
http://www.fishontario.com
Go Walleye!
http://www.gowalleye.com
HipWader.com
http://www.hipwader.com
Ontario Fishing Net
http://www.ontariofishing.net
Real Fishing
http://www.realfishing.com
What's Bitin' in the Toronto Area
http://zebra.zoo.utoronto.ca/
cgi-bin/FBoard/ikonboard.cgi

Other
FishingKaki.com
http://www.fishingkaki.com
TFW's Peacock Bass Book
http://www.fishingworld
.com.br/pbb/
theflyguide.com
http://www.theflyguide.com
Wild Bill Skinner's BassMex
http://www.bassmex.com

APPENDIX 3
URL LIST

CHAPTER 1:
HOW TO FIND FISHING INFORMATION ON THE INTERNET
Microsoft
http://www.microsoft.com
Netscape
http://www.netscape.com

SEARCH ENGINES – A VERY SHORT GUIDE
AlltheWeb
http://www.alltheweb.com
AltaVista
http://www.altavista.com
Ananzi
http://www.ananzi.co.za
Ask Jeeves
http://www.askjeeves.com
Google
http://www.google.com
NetLingo – The Internet Dictionary
http://www.netlingo.com
Search Engine Colossus
http://www.searchengine
colossus.com
Search Engine Showdown
http://www.searchengineshow
down.com

FORUMS
BoardReader
http://www.boardreader.com
ezboard
http://www.ezboard.com

MAILING LISTS
CANFF
http://www.sfu.ca/~epoole/
canff.htm
Carp Angler's Group
http://groups.yahoo.com/group/
CarpAnglersGroup
Eur-flyfish@
http://www.shconnect.de/
eur-flyfish

Fishwest Mailing List
http://www.fishwest.net/utah
Flyfish@
http://www.uky.edu/~agrdanny/
flyfish/main.htm
Flyfishing the West
http://groups.yahoo.com/group/
flyfishingthewest
International Muskie Home Page
http://www.trentu.ca/muskie/
muskie.html
Missouri Flyfishing List
http://www.agron.missouri.edu/
flyfishing/inet_resources.html
Rodmakers
http://www.canerod.com/
rodmakers
Texas Warmwater Fly Fishers
http://groups.yahoo.com/group/
txwwff
Virtual Flybox
http://www.virtualflybox.com
The Walleye List
http://www.walleyelist.com
Walleye News
http://www.walleyenews.com
Warmwater Angler
http://groups.yahoo.com/group/
WarmwaterAngler

START YOUR OWN LIST
Yahoo! Groups
http://groups.yahoo.com

NEWSGROUPS
NewsReaders.com
http://www.newsreaders.com
Google Groups
http://groups.google.com
alt.fishing
alt.fishing.catfish
alt.fishing.minnesota
alt.fishing.muskellunge
alt.fishing.walleyes
alt.test.fishing.spin
can.rec.fishing

can.rec.boating
rec.outdoors.fishing
rec.outdoors.marketplace
rec.outdoors.fishing.bass
rec.outdoors.fishing.fly
rec.outdoors.fishing.fly.tying
rec.outdoors.fishing.saltwater
rec.boats
rec.boats.marketplace
rec.boats.electronics
rec.boats.paddle
sci.bio.entomology
sci.bio.fisheries
sci.geo.satellite.nav
uk.rec.fishing.coarse
uk.rec.fishing.game
uk.rec.fishing.sea

CHAT ROOMS

Brotherhood of Catfishermen
http://www.brotherhood-of-catfishermen.com
Capt. Mel Berman's Fishing Florida
Online Magazine
http://www.capmel.com
Fish & Fly
http://www.fishandfly.co.uk
Fly Anglers Online
http://www.flyanglersonline.com
Fly Fisherman
http://www.flyfisherman.com
Fly Fishing in Maine
http://www.flyfishinginmaine.com
Flyfish Saltwaters.com
http://www.flyfishsaltwaters.com
IceFishingFIRST
http://icefishing.outdoorsfirst.com
Lake-Link.com
http://www.lake-link.com
MuskieFIRST
http://muskie.outdoorsfirst.com
New York Bass
http://www.nybass.com
Noreast.com
http://www.noreast.com
North Georgia Trout Online
http://www.georgia-outdoors.com/ngto/index.html
Outdoors Network
http://www.outdoors.net

ProBass
http://www.probass.com
Walleye Central
http://www.walleyecentral.com
WalleyeFIRST
http://walleye.outdoorsfirst.com
WesternBass.com
http://www.westernbass.com

I'll Take Another …

Stoeger Publishing
http://www.stoegerpublishing.com

Freebies for Fishermen on the Web

Free Fishing Logs
NJ Striper
http://www.njstriper.com
Fly Fishing North Carolina
http://www.flyfishingnc.com
Free Software Eli Robillard's SuperFly
Fishing Machine
http://www.ofifc.org/Eli/SuperFly/default.asp

Free Packing Lists
Free Travel Tips
http://www.freetraveltips.com
Fish Alaska
http://www.fishalaska
magazine.com

Free Books
Wisconsin Sea Grant
http://www.seagrant.wisc.edu/greatlakesfish
All-About Fly Fishing
http://www.about-flyfishing.com

Free Maps
Florida Fish and Wildlife Conservation
Commission
http://marinefisheries.org/guide.htm
MapServer
http://mapserver.maptech.com

Free Postage
Big Fish Tackle
http://www.bigfishtackle.com

LandBigFish
http://www.landbigfish.com

Free Fly Patterns
The Flyfishing Resource Guide
http://www.flyfish.com
Ultimate Fly Tying
http://www.ultimateflytying.com

Free Art
@Streamside: Journal
http://www.helmintoller.com/
streamside
Walkers Cay Chronicles
http://www.walkerscay.tv

Free Plans
Duckworks Magazine
http://www.duckworks
magazine.com
SportFishingFlorida.net
http://www.sportfishingflorida.net

CHAPTER 2:
STATE-BY-STATE RESOURCES

NEW ENGLAND
Capt. Tom's Guide
to New England Sharks
http://www.newenglandsharks.com
New England Shad Association
http://www.newenglandshad.com
New England Sportsman Network
http://www.nesportsman.com
Northeast Bass.com
http://www.northeastbass.com
Striped-Bass.com
http://www.striped-bass.com

Connecticut
Connecticut Department of
Environmental Protection
http://dep.state.ct.us/rec-nat.htm
CT Fisherman.com
http://www.ctfisherman.com

Maine
Fly Fishing in Maine
http://www.flyfishinginmaine.com

MaineToday.com
http://outdoors.mainetoday.com/
fishing

Massachusetts
The Lower Forty
http://www.thelowerforty.com
Massachusetts Striped Bass Association
http://www.msba.net

New Hampshire
New Hampshire
Fish and Game Department
http://www.wildlife.state.nh.us
NH Outdoors
http://www.nhoutdoors.com

Rhode Island
The Providence Journal
http://www.projo.com/fishing
The Rhode Island
Mobile Sportfishermen
http://www.rhodeislandmobile
sportfishermen.org
Rhode Island
Saltwater Anglers Association
http://www.risaa.org

Vermont
Trout Streams of Vermont
http://caddis.middlebury.edu/trout
Vermont Department of
Fish and Game
http://www.anr.state.vt.us/
fw/fwhome

And Don't Forget …
Flyfish Saltwaters.com
http://www.flyfishsaltwaters.com
Global FlyFisher – Raske's
New England Streamers
http://www.globalflyfisher.com/
streamers
Ken Abrames' Striper Moon
http://www.stripermoon.com
Reel-Time
http://www.reel-time.com
Surfcaster.com
http://www.surfcaster.com

Water Works Wonders
http://www.waterworks
wonders.org

MID ATLANTIC
Delaware and Maryland
At The Beach
http://www.atbeach.com/fishing
BayDreaming.com
http://www.baydreaming.
com/fishing
Beach-Net!
http://www.beach-net.com/
Fishinghome.html
The Chesapeake Angler
http://www.chesapeake-angler.com
Maryland BASS Federation
http://www.mdbass.com
Oyster Bay Tackle
http://www.oysterbaytackle.com
Potomac Bass
http://www.potomacbass.com
Woods and Waters Magazine
http://www.woodsandwaters
magazine.com

New Jersey
ACFishing.com
http://www.acfishing.com
Atlantic Saltwater Fly Rodders
http://www.aswf.org
FISHBOX.TV
http://www.fishbox.tv
NJ Striper.com
http://www.njstriper.com
NJ Trout
http://www.njtrout.com
North Eastern Fly Fishing Forums
http://www.njflyfishing.com
TheBassBarn.com
http://www.thebassbarn.com

New York
Black Lake, New York
http://www.blacklakeny.com
The Fishing Line
http://www.thefishingline.com
FishSalmonRiver.com
http://www.fishsalmonriver.com
Montauk Sportfishing
http://www.montauk

sportfishing.com
New York Bass
http://www.nybass.com
Rick Dubas' Niagara Fishing Net
http://www.niagarafishing.net
Rob J's Western New York
Bass Fishing Pages
http://home.adelphia.net/
~thewavzone

Pennsylvania
FishErie.com
http://www.fishusa.com/fisherie
Pennsylvania BASS Federation
http://www.pabass.com
Pennsylvania Fish
and Boat Commission
http://www.fish.state.pa.us
Pennsylvania Fly Fishing
http://www.paflyfish.com

Virginia
The Fishin' Musician
http://www.thefishinmusician.com
The Roanoke Times
http:/www2.roanoke.com/outdoors
VAflyfish.com
http://www.vaflyfish.com
Virginia Beach Sport Fishing
http://www.virginiabeach
sportfishing.com
Virginia Department of Game
and Inland Fisheries
http://www.dgif.state.va.us/fishing
The Virginian-Pilot
http://www.pilotonline.com/
sports/fishing

West Virginia
West Virginia BASS Federation
http://www.wvbass.com
WVSportsman
http://www.wvsportsman.com

And Don't Forget ...
Noreast.com
http://www.noreast.com
Pennsylvania Aquatic Flies Are Us
http://paaquaticfliesrus.bd.psu.edu
Pierandsurf.com
http://www.pierandsurf.com

StripersOnline
http://www.stripersonline.com
StriperSurf.com
http://www.stripersurf.com
Tidal Fish
http://www.tidalfish.com

SOUTH

Alabama
Fishing Lake Guntersville
http://www.fishinglake
guntersville.com
Night Hawk Publications
http://www.nighthawk
publications.com
North Alabama Fishing Forum
http://hiwaay.net/~ksgrisse/
wwwboard

Arkansas
The Ozark Angler
http://www.ozarkangler.com
Ozark Fly Flinger
http://www.flyflinger.com
The Ozark Mountains Travel
& Recreation Directory
http://www.ozarkmtns.com

Georgia
Coastal Outdoors
http://www.coastaloutdoors.com
Georgia Outdoors.com
http://www.georgiaoutdoors.com
Georgia River Fishing
http://www.georgiariverfishing.com
Miss Judy Charters
http://www.missjudycharters.com
North Georgia Bass Network
http://www.georgia-outdoors.com/
ngbn/index.html
North Georgia Trout Online
http://www.georgia-outdoors
.com/ngto/index.html

Kentucky
The Creek Bank
http://www.thecreekbank.com
Fishin.com
http://www.fishin.com
Northern Kentucky Fly Fishers
http://www.nkyflyfishers.org

Stewart's Cumberland River
Guide Service
http://www.stewartsguide
service.com

Louisiana
Jerry LaBella –
Saltwater Fishing Articles
http://www.jerrylabella.com
Louisiana Fly Fishing
http://www.laflyfish.com
Louisiana Sportsman
http://www.louisiana
sportsman.com
Mike Lane's RodnReel.com
http://www.rodnreel.com

Mississippi
Doc's Best Bets for Fishing
the Mississippi Gulf Coast
http://www.datasync.com/~dbb
Mississippi Department
of Marine Resources
http://www.dmr.state.ms.us/
Fisheries/Reefs/reefs.htm

North Carolina
Blue Ridge Trout –
Fly Fishing North Carolina
http://www.kbrcomm.com/trout
Fly Fishing NC
http://www.flyfishingnc.com
High Country Outdoors
Guide Service
http://www.highcountry
outdoors.net
North Carolina Sportsman
http://www.northcarolina
sportsman.com
North Carolina Waterman
http://www.ncwaterman.com
Wilson Creek Outfitters
http://www.wilsoncreek
outfitters.com
WNC Trout
http://www.wnctrout.com

The Outer Banks
Dwayne Creech's
Saltwater Surf Fisherman
http://saltwatersurffisherman.com

Fish Mojo
http://www.fishmojo.com
Insiders' Guide to
North Carolina's Outer Banks
http://www.insiders.com/
outerbanks
Joe Malat's Outer Banks
Surf Fishing Adventures
http://www.joemalat.com
NC CoastalFishing.com
http://www.nccoastalfishing.com
NC Onshore & Inshore Fishing Page
http://www.ncoif.com
Reel Buzz
http://www.reelbuzz.com

South Carolina
CharlestonFishing.com
http://www.charlestonfishing.com
Low Country Boating
http://www.lowcountryboating.com
South Carolina Lakes
http://www.geocities.com/
norwood_dr
Superfly Fishing with
Captain Ben Alderman
http://www.superflyfishing.com

Tennessee
Paris Landing.com
http://www.parislanding.com
Tennessee Wildlife Resources Agency
http://www.state.tn.us/twra/
index.html
TNAngler.com
http://www.tnangler.com

And Don't Forget …
Fly Fisherman
http://www.flyfisherman.com
Game & Fish Magazines
http://www.gameandfish.about.com
Harold Well's Gulf Coast Fisherman
http://www.gulffishing.com

FLORIDA
Big Blue Flyfishing
http://www.bigblueflyfishing.com/
newhome.htm
Bite Tracker
http://www.bitetracker.com

Captain Mel Berman's Fishing Florida
Online Magazine
http://www.capmel.com
Central Florida East Coast Fishing
http://home.cfl.rr.com/
floridafishing
CyberAngler
http://www.cyberangler.com
Fishme.com
http://www.fishme.com
Florida Fish and Wildlife
Conservation Commission
http://www.floridafisheries.com
The Florida Keys & Key West
http://www.fla-keys.com
Florida Keys.net
http://www.floridakeys.net
Fly Fishing the Southeast
http://www.sefly.com
Islamorada Sport Fishing Online
http://www.islamoradasport
fishing.com
Jim Porter's Guide to Bass Fishing
http://www.jimporter.org
Snook Fin-addict
http://www.snookfin-addict.com
Southern Charm Sportfishing
http://www.floridasaltwater.com
South Florida Sport Fishing
http://www.southfloridasport
fishing.com
SportFishingFlorida.net
http://www.sportfishingflorida.net

And Don't Forget …
FishnBottom
http://www.fishnbottom.com
Flats Hunter
http://www.flatshunter.com
Florida Sportsman Online
http://www.floridasportsman.com
Snook Angler.com
http://www.snookangler.com

Bass Reports
Bass Fishing Home Page
http://www.bassfishing
homepage.com
ProBass
http://www.probass.com

Florida Newspapers

The Florida Keys Keynoter
http://www.keynoter.com/ffk/index.htm

The Miami Herald
http://www.miami.com/mld/miamiherald/sports/outdoors

MIDWEST

Midwest Bass Tournaments Internet Magazine
http://www.midwestbasstournaments.com

Midwest Fly Fishing Online
http://www.mwfly.com

Midwest Trout Fishing
http://www.midwesttroutfishing.com

Illinois

Chicago Area Paddling/Fishing Guide
http://www.chicagopaddling.org

ChicagolandFishing.com
http://www.chicagolandfishing.com

Lake Online's Fishin' Hole
http://www.lake-online.com/fishinhole

Will on the Web's Fishing Will County, Illinois
http://www.willontheweb.com/fishing/index.html

Indiana

Indiana Division of Fish and Wildlife
http://www.state.in.us/dnr/fishwild

Steelhead Shangra-La
http://www.geocities.com/steeldredge

Iowa

Fishing in Iowa
http://omega.grad.uiowa.edu

Iowa Department of Natural Resources
http://www.iowadnr.com

Iowa Outdoors
http://www.iowaoutdoors.org

Michigan

AAA Michigan
http://www.autoclubgroup.com/michigan/fishing.asp

CoastWatch
http://www.coastwatch.msu.edu

Michigan Department of Natural Resources
http://www.michigan.gov/dnr

Michigan Fishing Information
http://www.trophyspecialists.com/mifishinfo/index.html

Michigan Interactive
http://www.fishweb.com

The Michigan Sportsman
http://www.michigan-sportsman.com

Trails to Trout
http://www.trailstotrout.com

TroutBums
http://www.troutbums.com

Minnesota

Boundary Waters Canoe Area Wilderness
http://www.bwcaw.org

CanoeCountry.com
http://www.canoecountry.com

Fishing Minnesota
http://www.fishingminnesota.com

In-Depth Angling
http://www.in-depthangling.com

Minnesota Department of Natural Resources
http://www.dnr.state.mn.us/lakefind/index.html

SE Minnesota Trout Flies
http://users.myexcel.com/dolfnlvr/

Up North Outdoors.com
http://www.upnorthoutdoors.com

Missouri

Fishing the Missouri Trout Parks
http://www.missouritrout.com

Go Fishing Missouri.com
http://www.gofishingmissouri.com

Missouri Department of Conservation
http://www.conservation.state.mo.us

OzarkAnglers.com
http://www.ozarkanglers.com
Trout Talk
http://www.trouttalk.net

Ohio
GoFishGreatLakes.com
http://www.gofishgreatlakes.com
GoFishOhio.com
http://www.gofishohio.com
Ohio Fishermen.com
http://www.ohiofishermen.com
Ohio Department
of Natural Resources
http://www.dnr.state.oh.us

Wisconsin
Fish-Wisconsin
http://www.fishwis.com
Lake Chippewa Flowage
http://www.chippewaflowage.com
Lake-Link.com
http://www.lake-link.com
SW Wisconsin Stream Locator
http://www.swwisconsin.com
Wisconsin Department
of Natural Resources
http://www.dnr.state.wi.us

The Great Lakes
Great Lakes Fishery Trust
http://www.glft.org
Great Lakes Fishing Station
http://greatmich.com
Great Lakes Information Network
http://www.great-lakes.net
Great Lakes Sport Fishing Council
http://www.great-lakes.org
Lake Michigan Angler
http://www.lakemichigan
angler.com
Wisconsin Sea Grant
http://www.seagrant.wisc.edu/
greatlakesfish

And Don't Forget ...
Game & Fish Magazines
http://www.gameandfish.about.com
Great Lakes Angler
http://www.glangler.com

The Ice Fishing Home Page
http://hickorytech.net/~jbusby/
iceangler.html
The Steelhead Site
http://www.steelheadsite.com

CENTRAL
Kansas
Flatland Fly Fishers
http://www.flatlandflyfishers.org
Kansas Department
of Wildlife and Parks
http://www.kdwp.state.ks.us/
fishing/fishing.html
Leisure and Sport Review
http://www.lasr.net
U.S. Army Corp of Engineers,
Kansas City District
http://www.nwk.usace.army.mil

Oklahoma
The Bass Zone
http://www.basszone.com
Beavers Bend Fly Shop
http://www.beaversbend
flyshop.com
The Fishing Notebook
http://www.fishingnotebook.com
Oklahoma Bass Fishing
http://www.oklahoma
bassfishing.com
Oklahoma Fly Fishing
http://home.att.net/~brockrut/

Nebraska
Nebraska Game
and Parks Commission
http://www.ngpc.state.ne.us/
homepage.html
Nebraska Lake Guide
http://www.lakeguide.com
NEBRASKAland
http://www.ngpc.state.ne.
us/nebland

North Dakota
Fishing Buddy Outdoors
http://www.fishingbuddy.com

North Dakota Game
and Fish Department
http://www.state.nd.us/gnf

South Dakota
Black Hills Fishing
http://www.rapidnet.com/
~jtuxford/welcome2.htm
South Dakota BASS Federation
http://www.sdbassfederation.com
South Dakota Department
of Game, Fish, and Parks
http://www.state.sd.us/gfp

And Don't Forget ...
Game & Fish Magazines
http://www.gameandfish.
about.com
The Ice Fishing Home Page
http://hickorytech.net/~jbusby/
iceangler.html
Walleye Central
http://www.walleyecentral.com

The Ultimate Bass Fishing Resource Guide
http://www.bassresource.com

TEXAS
Bass Fishing in North Texas
http://www.bassfishing.org
Corpus Christi Caller Times
http://www.caller.com
Coastal Conservation
Association, Texas
http://www.ccatexas.org
Corpusfishing.com
http://www.corpusfishing.com
Dallas Fly Fishers
http://www.dallas-flyfishers.org
Honey Hole
http://www.honeyhole
magazine.com
Houston Chronicle
http://www.chron.com
Lake Fork, Texas – ETS Systems
http://www.ets-systems.com
Louis Rodgers' Texas Fishing 2004
http://www.austinresource.com/
texasfishing.htm

Texas Flyfishing
http://www.texasflyfishing.com
Texas Gulf Coast Fishing
http://www.texasgulf
coastfishing.com
Texas Parks and Wildlife Department
http://www.tpwd.state.tx.us
Texas Saltwater
http://www.texassaltwater
fishing.com
TexasMojo.com
http://www.texasmojo.com
Tom Nix's Salty Angler
http://www.saltyangler.com
TX Fishing.com
http://www.txfishing.com

And Don't Forget ...
Bass Champs
http://www.basschamps.com
Coalition of Confused Coastal
Fishermen
http://www.coastalfishing.org
Mike Lane's Texas Fishing and Hunting
http://www.tx.rodngun.com
Texas Warmwater Fly Fishers
http://groups.yahoo.com/
group/txwwff

Sportsman's Resource
http://www.sportsmans
resource.com

WEST
Arizona
Arizona Game and Fish Department
http://www.gf.state.az.us
The Arizona Republic
http://www.azcentral.com
WaynesWords – Lake Powell
Fishing Information
http://www.wayneswords.com

Colorado
Blue Quill Angler
http://www.bluequillangler.com
Colorado Division of Wildlife
http://wildlife.state.co.us/index.asp
Colorado Fishing Network
http://www.coloradofishing.net

Colorado Fly Fishing –
Stream Information
http://www.pdsdata.net/flyfish.htm

Idaho
FlyWaters.com
http://www.flywaters.com
Henry's Fork Anglers
http://www.henrysforkanglers.com
Idaho Fish and Game
http://www2.state.id.us/fishgame/
fishgame.html
Idaho Fish 'n' Hunt
http://www.idfishnhunt.com
Silver Creek Outfitters
http://www.silver-creek.com
Snake River Cutthroats
http://www.snakeriver
cutthroats.com
Twin River Anglers
http://www.traflyfish.com

Montana
Big Sky Fishing.com
http://www.bigskyfishing.com
Montana Fish, Wildlife and Parks
http://www.fwp.state.mt.us/
default.asp
Montana Fly Fishing
http://www.glacierto
yellowstone.com

Fly Shops
Dan Bailey's Online Fly Fishing Shop
http://www.dan-bailey.com
George Anderson's Yellowstone Angler
http://www.yellowstoneangler.com
The Grizzly Hackle
http://www.grizzlyhackle.com
The Madison River Fishing Company
http://www.mrfc.com

Nevada
Camping Guide Nevada
http://www.herronweb.com/camp
groundguide.html
Nevada Department of Wildlife
http://www.ndow.org
Nevada Division of State Parks
http://www.parks.nv.gov

New Mexico
FlyFishNM
http://www.flyfishnm.com
New Mexico Department
of Game and Fish
http://www.gmfsh.state.nm.us
The San Juan River
Fly Fishing Site
http://www.ifly4trout.com

Utah
Fly Fishing Utah
http://www.fishwest.net/utah
Go Fly Fishing The Green River
http://quickbyte.com/greenriver
Utah Division of Wildlife Resources
http://www.wildlife.utah.gov
Utah Fish Finder
http://www.utahfishfinder.com
Utah on the Fly
http://www.utahonthefly.com

Wyoming
High Country Flies
http://www.highcountryflies.com
Jack Dennis Sports
http://www.jackdennis.com
JacksonHole.Net
http://www.jacksonholenet.com
Wyoming Fishing Network
http://www.wyomingfishing.net

And Don't Forget …
The Fish Sniffer Online
http://www.fishsniffer.com
Fly Fisherman
http://www.flyfisherman.com
The Flyfishing Connection
http://www.flyfishing
connection.com
Flyfishing the West
http://groups.yahoo.com/
group/flyfishingthewest
WesternBass.com
http://www.westernbass.com
Westfly
http://www.westfly.com

NORTHWEST

Alaska

Alaska.com
http://www.alaska.com

Alaska Department of Fish and Game
http://www.state.ak.us/adfg/
adfghome.htm

Alaska Fishing Online
http://www.alaskafishingonline.com

Alaska Flyfishing Online
http://www.alaskaflyfishing
online.com

Alaska Outdoor Journal
http://www.alaskaoutdoor
journal.com

The Anchorage Daily News
http://www.adn.com/outdoors

Fish Alaska
http://www.fishalaska
magazine.com

Kenai Peninsula Online
http://www.peninsulaclarion.
com/outdoors

Rudy's Alaska Fishing Page
http://www.alaska.net/~guidesak/
rudy/rt.htm

Oregon

BoatEscape.com
http://www.boatescape.com

Fish Passage Center (FPC)
http://www.fpc.org

Ifish
http://www.ifish.net

Oregon Fishing With The Guide's
Forecast
http://www.theguidesforecast.com

Washington

Bob's Piscatorial Pursuits
http://www.piscatorialpursuits.com

Dennis Dickson's Flyfishing
Steelhead Guides
http://www.flyfishsteelhead.com

Fishing Northwest
http://www.fishingnorthwest.com

Gamefishin.com
http://www.gamefishin.com

Interagency Committee for Outdoor
Recreation Boating Web Site
http://boat.iac.wa.gov

Puget Sound Fly Fishing
http://www.pugetsoundfly
fishing.com

Salmon University
http://www.salmonuniversity.com

The Seattle Times
http://seattletimes.nwsource.com/
html/fishing

Steelheader.net
http://www.steelheader.net

Washington Department of Ecology
http://apps.ecy.wa.gov/
shorephotos/index.html

Washington Department of Fish
and Wildlife
http://www.wa.gov/wdfw

Washington Fly Fishing
http://www.washington
flyfishing.com

WashingtonLakes.com
http://www.washingtonlakes.com

Worley Bugger Fly Co.
http://www.worleybuggerflyco.com

And Don't Forget ...

BC Adventure - Fish BC
http://www.bcadventure.com

FishWithUS.net
http://www.fishwithus.net

Westfly
http://www.westfly.com

Ultimate Fly Tying
http://www.ultimateflytying.com

CALIFORNIA

Bite's On!
http://www.biteson.com

Calfishing.com
http://www.calfishing.com

California Delta Chambers
& Visitors Bureau
http://www.californiadelta.org

City of San Diego's Water Department
http://www.sannet.gov/water/
recreation/map.shtml

Eastern Sierra Fishing
http://www.easternsierra
fishing.com

Fish First!
http://www.fishfirst.com

Fishing Network.net
http://www.fishingnetwork.net
FliFlicker
http://www.fliflicker.com
Gary Bulla's Fly Fishing Adventures
http://www.garybulla.com
Ichthy.com
http://www.ichthy.com
The Log
http://www.thelog.com
Northern California Fly Fishing Board
http://www.ncffb.org
The Orange County Register
http://www.myoc.com/sports/
recreation/fishing_report.shtml
Ralph and Lisa Cutter's California
School of Flyfishing
http://www.flyline.com
San Diego Fish Online
http://www.sdfish.com
The San Diego Union-Tribune
http://www.signonsandiego.com
The San Francisco Chronicle
http://www.sfgate.com/sports/
outdoors
Southern California Marlin Online
http://www.marlinnut.com
Trout Fishin' – Cali Style
http://www.alumni.caltech.edu/
~naturboy/fishing
USAfishing
http://www.usafishing.com
West Coast Angler
http://www.westcoastangler.com

And Don't Forget ...
AllCoast Sport Fishing
http://www.sport-fish-info.com
CharkBait!
http://www.charkbait.com
Pier Fishing in California
http://www.pierfishing.com
Trophy Bass Only
http://www.trophybassonly.com
WesternBass.com
http://www.westernbass.com

Hawaii
Anxious Fishing Charters
http://www.alohazone.com

Fish Kona
http://www.fishkona.com
Fish Maui
http://www.fishmaui.com
Hawaii Fishing Adventures & Charters
http://www.sportfishhawaii.com
Hawaii Fishing News
http://www.hawaiifishingnews.com
Kona Hawaii Fishing with
Captain Jeff Rogers
http://www.fishinkona.com
Kuuloa Kai Big Game Fishing
http://www.kuuloakai.com

CHAPTER 3:
KNOW BEFORE YOU GO

STATE FISH AND WILDLIFE DEPARTMENTS
Texas Parks and Wildlife Department
http://www.tpwd.state.tx.us
Big Fish Tackle
http://www.bigfishtackle.com
Cabela's
http://www.cabelas.com
Fish and Wildlife Management Offices
State, Territorial, and Tribal
http://offices.fws.gov/
statelinks.html
LandBigFish
http://www.landbigfish.com

WEATHER
Intellicast
http://www.intellicast.com
Meteorological Service of Canada
http://www.atl.ec.gc.ca/msc/
index_e.html
National Data Buoy Center
http://www.ndbc.noaa.gov
National Weather Service
http://www.nws.noaa.gov
The Weather Channel
http://www.weather.com
The Weather Underground
http://www.wunderground.com

Other Options
CharkBait!
http://www.charkbait.com

CoastWatch
http://www.coastwatch.msu.edu
Great Lakes Angler
http://www.glangler.com
Southern California Marlin Online
http://www.marlinnut.com
UM Weather
http://yang.sprl.umich.edu/
wxnet/

SEA SURFACE TEMPERATURES
COOLroom
http://www.thecoolroom.org
HotSpots Charts
http://www.sstcharts.com
Jenifer Clark's Gulfstream
http://users.erols.com/gulfstrm/
John Hopkins University's Ocean
Remote Sensing
http://fermi.jhuapl.edu
Rutgers University's Coastal Ocean
Observation Lab
http://marine.rutgers.edu/mrs/
sat.data2.html
SST Online
http://www.sstol.com
Terrafin Software
http://www.terrafin.com

TIDES
Center for Operational
Oceanographic Products
and Services
http://www.co-ops.nos.noaa.gov
Great Lakes Online
http://www.glakesonline.nos
.noaa.gov
HarborTides.com
http://www.harbortides.com
Saltwater Tides.com
http://www.saltwatertides.com
Tides Online
http://www.tidesonline.nos
.noaa.gov
Tide Tool 2.1c
http://www.toolworks.com/
bilofsky/tidetool.htm
WWW Tide and Current Predictor
http://tbone.biol.sc.edu/tide/
sitesel.html

BEST FISHING TIMES
Discover the Outdoors
http://www.discoverthe
outdoors.com
ESPN Outdoors
http://www.espn.go.com/outdoors
FishingWorks
http://www.fishingworks.com
In-Fisherman
http://www.in-fisherman.com
Joe Bucher.com
http://www.joe-bucher.com
Outdoor Life
http://www.outdoorlife.com

MAPS
Basslabs.com
http://www.basslabs.com
Fishing Hot Spots
http://www.fishinghotspots.com
Fishingmap.com
http://www.fishingmap.com
MapServer
http://mapserver.maptech.com
Maptech
http://www.maptech.com
National Geophysical Data Center
http://www.ngdc.noaa.gov
Office of Coast Survey
http://chartmaker.ncd.noaa.gov/
mcd/enc
TerraFly
http://www.terrafly.fiu.edu
TerraServer
http://terraserver-usa.com
Topo-Log
http://www.topo-log.com
TopoZone
http://www.topozone.com

WHERE TO GO
American Trails
http://www.americantrails.org
GORP – Parks
http://www.gorp.com
The National Wild and Scenic
Rivers System
http://www.nps.gov/rivers
ParkNet
http://www.nps.gov

Public Lands Information Center
http://www.publiclands.org
Recreation.Gov
http://www.recreation.gov
Tourism Offices Worldwide Directory
http://www.towd.com
U.S. Department of Agriculture Forest
Service – Fish Your National Forests
http://www.fs.fed.us/fishing
U.S. National Parks
http://www.us-national-parks.net
Wildernet
http://www.wildernet.com

ON THE ROAD
AAA
http://www.aaa.com
AccuTraffic
http://www.accuweather.com/
www/accutraffic
Federal Highway Administration –
National Traffic and Road Closure
Information
http://www.fhwa.dot.gov/trafficinfo
MapQuest
http://www.mapquest.com
MSN Maps and Directories
http://mappoint.msn.com
National Scenic Byways Online
http://www.byways.org
Rand McNally
http://www.randmcnally.com
Traffic.com
http://www.traffic.com
Two-Lane Roads
http://www.two-lane.com
USGasPriceWatch
http://www.gaspricewatch
.com/USGas

WHERE TO STAY
All-hotels
http://www.all-hotels.com
Hootle
http://www.hootle.com
Petswelcome.com
http://www.petswelcome.com
Places to Stay.com
http://www.placestostay.com

Camping
About.com – Camping
http://www.camping.about.com
Reserve America
http://www.reserveamerica.com
ReserveUSA
http://www.reserveusa.com

INTERNATIONAL TRAVEL RESOURCES
American Express
http://www.americanexpress.com
The Bureau of Consular Affairs
http://www.travel.state.gov
Centers for Disease Control and
Prevention – Travelers' Health
http://www.cdc.gov/travel
Discover
http://go.vicinity.com/discoverd
Express Visa Service
http://www.expressvisa.com
Federal Aviation Administration
http://www2.faa.gov
Fodors
http://www.fodors.com
Free Travel Tips.com
http://www.freetraveltips.com
How to See the World
http://www.artoftravel.com
IgoUgo
http://www.igougo.com
MasterCard
http://www.mastercard.com
Passport Express
http://www.passportexpress.com
Travel Document Systems
http://www.traveldocs.com
Time Zone Converter
http://www.timezoneconverter.com
TripAdvisor
http://www.tripadvisor.com
U.S. Department of
Homeland Security –
U.S. Customs and Border Protection
http://www.cbp.gov
Visa
http://www.international.visa.com

GUIDES
The Angling Report
http://www.anglingreport.com

Charternet.com
http://www.charternet.com
Fishing Guides Home Page
http://www.1fghp.com
FishingWorks
http://www.fishingworks.com
LandBigFish
http://www.landbigfish.com
Outdoors Yellow Pages
http://www.outdoorsyp.com
SMARTpages.com
http://www.smartpages.com
SuperPages.com
http://www.bigyellow.com
SuperPages.com Global Directories
http://www.superpages.com/global
The Yellow Pages Superhighway
http://www.bestyellow.com
WorldWideFishing.com
http://www.worldwidefishing.com

GENERAL RESOURCES
Bureau of Reclamation
http://www.usbr.gov
Chesapeake Bay Observing System
http://www.cbos.org/index.php
National Wildlife Refuge System
http://refuges.fws.gov
U.S. Army Corps of Engineers
http://www.usace.army.mil
U.S. Fish and Wildlife Service
http://www.fws.gov
U.S. Geological Service (USGS)
Real-Time Daily Streamflow
Conditions
http://water.usgs.gov/realtime.html
USGS Recreation
http://recreation.usgs.gov/
fishing.html

CHAPTER 4:
FISHING THE WEB

BEST BASS FISHING SITES
AnglerWorld.com
http://www.anglerworld.com
Bass Anglers
Sportsmans Society (BASS)
http://www.bassmaster.com

Bass Champs
http://www.basschamps.com
Bass Fishing Home Page
http://www.bassfishinghome
page.com
Bassdozer
http://www.bassdozer.com
BassFan
http://www.bassfan.com
Bassin' USA
http://www.bassinusa.com
Bronzeback.com
http://www.bronzeback.com
Fishgeek
http://www.fishgeek.com
FLW Outdoors
http://www.flwoutdoors.com
Kevin's Bass Fishing Site
http://www.bassfishin.com
ProBass
http://www.probass.com
River Smallies.com
http://www.riversmallies.com
The Smallmouth Alliance
http://www.smallmouth.org
Tim Tucker's Bass Sessions
http://www.timtuckeroutdoors.com
Trophy Bass Only
http://www.trophybassonly.com
The Ultimate Bass Fishing
Resource Guide
http://www.bassresource.com
WesternBass.com
http://www.westernbass.com
WON Bass
http://www.wonbass.com
WorldRecordBass.com
http://www.worldrecordbass.com

BEST FRESHWATER FISHING SITES
Carp Anglers Group
http://www.carpanglersgroup.com
Carp Net
http://www.carp.net
Carp.com
http://www.carp.com

Catfish

Brotherhood of Catfishermen
  http://www.brotherhood-of-
  catfishermen.com
CatfishED.com
  http://www.catfished.com
Game & Fish Magazines
  http://www.gameandfish.
  about.com/cs/catfish
The Professional Catfishing Association
  http://www.procats.com
Siluris Glanis – Wells Catfish
  http://xvella.free.fr/photos-eng.php

The Crappie Killer
  http://www.thecrappiekiller.com
Crappie USA – The American Crappie
Association
  http://www.crappieusa.com
Crappie.com
  http://www.crappie.com
Gar Fishing! With the Gar Anglers'
Sporting Society
  http://www.garfishing.com

Ice Fishing

The Ice Fishing Home Page
  http://hickorytech.net/~jbusby/
  iceangler.html
IceFishingFIRST
  http://icefishing.outdoorsfirst.com
IceShanty.com
  http://www.iceshanty.com
Ice Team Web Report
  http://www.iceteam.com
On Ice Tour
  http://www.onicetour.com

International Muskie Home Page
  http://www.trentu.ca/muskie/
  muskie.html
Muskie Central
  http://www.muskiecentral.com
MuskieFIRST
  http://muskie.outdoorsfirst.com
Muskies101
  http://www.muskies101.com
The Next Bite
  http://www.thenextbite.com
Rollie and Helen's Musky Shop

  http://www.muskyshop.com
Roughfish.com
  http://www.roughfish.com
Striper Chaser
  http://www.striperchaser.com
Striper Strategies
  http://community-2.webtv.net/
  RockandReel/StriperStrategies/

Trophy Trout

Fish Ontario!
  http://www.fishontario.com
Great Lakes Angler
  http://www.glangler.com
The Ozark Mountains Travel &
Recreation Directory – White River
  http://www.whiteriver.net

Walleye Central
  http://www.walleyecentral.com
WalleyeFIRST
  http://walleye.outdoorsfirst.com
Walleye Hunter
  http://www.walleyehunter.com
Walleyes Inc.
  http://www.walleyesinc.com

Carpe Carpio Fish Designs
  http://www.carpecarpio.com

BEST SALTWATER FISHING SITES

AllCoast Sport Fishing
  http://www.sport-fish-info.com
BC Adventure – Saltwater Fishing
  http://www.bcadventure.com/
  adventure/angling/saltwater
Big Marine Fish
  http://www.chambers-
  associates.org
Billfish International
  http://www.billfishintl.com
Billfish Tournament Network
  http://www.billfishnetwork.com
CharkBait!
  http://www.charkbait.com
The Coalition of
Confused Coastal Fishermen
  http://www.coastalfishing.org
Coastal Shark Fishing
  http://www.coast-shark.com

FishnBottom
http://www.fishnbottom.com
Flats Hunter
http://www.flatshunter.com
InTheBite.com
http://www.inthebite.com
Noreast.com
http://www.noreast.com
Pier Fishing in California
http://www.pierfishing.com
Pierandsurf.com
http://www.pierandsurf.com
Saltwater Fishing Home Page
http://www.wmi.org/saltfish
Snookangler.com
http://www.snookangler.com
StripersOnline
http://www.stripersonline.com
StriperSurf.com
http://www.stripersurf.com
Surfcaster.com
http://www.surfcaster.com
Tidal Fish
http://www.tidalfish.com
World Billfish Series
http://www.worldbillfishseries.com

BEST FLY-FISHING SITES
All-About Fly Fishing
http://www.about-flyfishing.com
Beginner's Netguide to Fly Fishing
http://www.associatedinternet.
com/flyfishing101
BC Adventure – Stillwater Fly Fishing
http://www.bcadventure.com/
adventure/angling/stillwater
CANFF
http://www.sfu.ca/~epoole/
canff.htm
Dana Sturn's Spey Pages
http://www.speypages.com
Derrick's Pike Pages
http://members.shaw.ca/mrpike/
Eur-flyfish@
http://www.shconnect.de/
eur-flyfish
Fish & Fly
http://www.fishandfly.co.uk
Fishing Line.net
http://www.fishingline.net

Fly Anglers Online
http://www.flyanglersonline.com
Fly Casting Forum
http://home.att.net/~slowsnap
The Fly Fishing FORUM
http://www.flyfishingforum.com
Fly-Fishing for Northern Pike
http://www.members.shaw.ca/
clives/pikeflyfish.html
FlyFish Saltwaters.com
http://www.flyfishsaltwaters.com
Flyfish@ Home Page
http://www.uky.edu/~agrdanny/
flyfish/main.htm
The Flyfishing Connection
http://www.flyfishingconnection
.com
The Flyfishing Resource Guide
http://www.flyfish.com
FlyFishing Tools.com
http://www.flyfishtools.com
Global FlyFisher
http://www.globalflyfisher.com
A History of Fly Fishing
http://www.flyfishinghistory.com
Reel-Time
http://www.reel-time.com
REI – Learn & Share Fly Fishing
http://www.rei.com/rei/learn
A River Never Sleeps
http://www.ariverneversleeps.com
SalmonAnglers.com
http://www.salmonanglers.com
Sexyloops
http://www.sexyloops.co.uk
Smallstreams.com
http://www.smallstreams.com
The Steelhead Site
http://www.steelheadsite.com
The Tropical Angler
http://www.cyberisle.com/tropical/
angler.htm
Westfly
http://www.westfly.com

FLY TYING
Classic Salmon Flies
http://www.classicsalmonflies.com
The Complete Sportsman
http://www.rareandunusual.com

The Dry Fly.com
http://www.thedryfly.com
Edmonton Chapter
of Trout Unlimited Canada
http://www.freenet.edmonton.
ab.ca/trout/flytying.html
Fly Tying World
http://www.flytyingworld.com
Flydepot.com
http://www.flydepot.com
Flytier's Page
http://www.danica.com/flytier
Killroy's Fly Tying and Fishing
http://www.killroys.com
Philatelic Phly Tying
http://home.att.net/~kholm/
PHLYTYING
Salmonfly.net
http://www.angelfire.com/
wa/salmonid
Troutflies.com
http://www.troutflies.com
Ultimate Fly Tying
http://www.ultimateflytying.com
Umpqua Feather Merchants
http://www.umpqua.com
Virtual Flybox
http://www.virtualflybox.com
Vladimir Markov's Fly-Tying Websites
http://www.markov.baikal.ru
Wes' Virtual Pattern Book
http://www.magiclink.com/
web/wesn
Yager's Flies
http://www.yagersflies.com

Personal Sites
Angling Matters
http://www.anglingmatters.com
@Streamside: Journal
http://www.helmintoller.com/
streamside/journal
Dan Blanton
http://www.danblanton.com
Dave & Emily Whitlock –
The Art and Science of Fly Fishing
http://www.davewhitlock.com
Ken Abrames' Striper Moon
http://www.stripermoon.com

Jack Gartside's Home Page
http://www.jackgartside.com
John McKim Illustrations
http://www.johnmckim.com
Sidney Du Broff's Fishing
and Shooting Journal
http://www.sidsjournal.com
Trout Ball
http://www.troutball.com

Entomology
Bug Bios
http://www.bugbios.com
The Chironomid Home Page
http://www.ouc.bc.ca/fwsc/
iwalker/intpanis
Entomological Research
at Florida A & M University
http://www.famu.org/ent/
The Fisher Monk
http://www.fishermonk.com
Fly Craft Angling
http://www.flycraftangling.com
Fly Fishing North Carolina
http://www.flyfishingnc.com
Insect Drawings Gallery
http://www.life.uiuc.edu/
entomology/insectgifs.html
Mayfly Central at Purdue
http://www.entm.purdue.edu/
entomology/research/mayfly/
mayfly.html
Pennsylvania Flies Are Us
http://paaquaticfliesrus.bd.psu.edu
Tree of Life Web Project
http://www.tolweb.org/tree/
phylogeny.html
SE Minnesota Trout Flies
http://users.myexcel.com/dolfnlvr/
Wisconsin Fly Fishing
http://www.wisflyfishing.com/
bridge.html

Cooking
Big Fish Tackle
http://www.bigfishtackle
.com/cooking
Black Lake, New York
http://www.blacklakeny.com/fish
recipes.html

FishingWorks
http://www.fishingworks.com/
seafood_recipes
LandBigFish
http://www.landbigfish.com
U.S. Environmental Protection
Agency's Fish Advisories
http://www.epa.gov/water
science/fish

Fish Identification
eNature.com
http://www.enature.com
FishBase
http://www.fishbase.org/search.cfm
North American Native
Fishes Association
http://www.nanfa.org
Troutsite
http://www.troutsite.com

Knots and Rigs
Discover the Outdoors
http://www.discoverthe
outdoors.com
Fishnet
http://www.fishnet.com.au
Knots on the Web
http://www.earlham.edu/~
peters/knotlink.htm
Lindy Little Joe
http://www.lindylittlejoe.com
Luhr Jensen Tech Reports
http://www.luhrjensen.com
Marinews
http://www.marinews.com
Noreast.com
http://www.noreast.com
Rigs for Fishing
from the Beach or at Sea
http://home.wanadoo.nl/escort/
introuk.htm
Water Gremlin
http://www.watergremlin.com

Records
Hot Spot Fishing
http://www.hotspotfishing.com
International Game Fish Association
http://www.igfa.org

LandBigFish
http://www.landbigfish.com
State Fish Records
http://www.statefishingrecords.com

CHAPTER 5: MEDIA

PRINT MAGAZINES ONLINE
American Angler/Fly Tyer/
Saltwater Fly Fishing
http://www.flyfishingmagazines.
com
eBassin'
http://www.ebassin.com
Field & Stream
http://www.fieldandstream.com
Fish and Game Finder Magazine
http://www.fishandgame.com
The Fish Sniffer Online
http://www.fishsniffer.com
Fishing Facts
http://www.fishingfacts.com
Florida Sportsman Online
http://www.floridasportsman.com
Fly Fish America Online
http://www.flyfishamerica.com
Fly Fisherman
http://www.flyfisherman.com
Fly Fishing and Fly Tying
http://www.flyfishing-and-
flytying.co.uk
Fly Fishing in Saltwaters
http://www.flyfishinsalt.com
Fly Rod & Reel
http://www.flyrodandreel.com
FlyLife OnLine
http://www.flylife.com.au
Game & Fish Magazines
http://www.gameandfish.about.com
Gary Yamamoto's Inside Line
http://www.insideline.net
Gray's Sporting Journal
http://www.grayssporting
journal.com
Great Lakes Angler
http://www.glangler.com
Harold Wells' Gulf Coast Fisherman
http://www.gulffishing.com
In-Fisherman
http://www.in-fisherman.com

Marlin
http://www.marlinmag.com
MidWest Outdoors
http://www.midwestoutdoors.com
Musky Hunter
http://www.muskyhunter.com
North American Fisherman
http://www.fishingclub.com
Outdoor Canada
http://www.outdoorcanada.ca
Outdoor Life
http://www.outdoorlife.com
Salt Water Sportsman
http://www.saltwatersports
man.com
Sport Fishing
http://www.sportfishingmag.com
Sporting Classics
http://www.sportingclassics.net

ONLINE MAGAZINES
AllBass.com
http://www.allbass.com
AllFishing.com
http://www.allfishing.com
AllFlyFishing.com
http://www.allflyfishing.com
Big Fish Tackle
http://www.bigfishtackle.com
Cabela's
http://www.cabelas.com
Discover the Outdoors
http://www.discovertheoutdoors.com
ESPN Outdoors
http://espn.go.com/outdoors
Fishing-Boating Online
http://www.fishing-boating.com
Fishing-Hunting.com
http://www.fishing-hunting.com
FishingWorld.com
http://www.fishingworld.com
FishWithUs.net
http://www.fishwithus.net/
home.html
GORP
http://www.gorp.com
LandBigFish
http://www.landbigfish.com
Louis Bignami's Fine Fishing
http://www.finefishing.com

OutdoorSite
http://www.outdoorsite.com
Outdoors Network
http://www.outdoors.net
The Sportsman's Guide
http://www.sportsmansguide.com

DIRECTORIES
About.com
Freshwater Fishing
http://www.fishing.about.com
Saltwater Fishing
http://www.saltfishing.about.com
100 Top Fishing Sites
http://www.hitsunlimited.com
FishHoo!
http://www.fishhoo.com
Fishing World Network
http://www.fishing-world.net
FishingWorks
http://www.fishingworks.com
Google – Directory
http://www.google.com
Len Gorney's Fishing
Links Notebook
http://www.kings.edu/lsgorney/
fishing.htm
Open Directory Project
http://www.dmoz.org
Yahoo!
http://www.yahoo.com

Specialist Directories
Bassdozer
http://www.bassdozer.com
Cbel – Fly Fishing
http://www.cbel.com/fly_fishing
The Global Fly Fishing
Links Directory
http://www.davisbrown.com/
ffindex.htm
Mel's Place
http://www.mels-place.com
Mr River
http://www.mrriver.com
ProBass
http://www.probass.com
Sportsman's Resource
http://www.sportsmans
resource.com

Start4All.com – Fly Fishing
http://flyfish.start4all.com
The Ultimate Bass
Fishing Resource Guide
http://www.bassresource.com

BOOKSTORES
Abebooks
http://www.abebooks.com
Alibris
http://www.alibris.com
Amazon.com
http://www.amazon.com
The Angler's Art
http://www.anglersart.com
Barnes & Noble.com
http://www.barnesandnoble.com
Books of the Black Bass
http://www.hometown.aol.com/
bassbks
Coch-y-Bonddu Books
http://www.anglebooks.com
The Derrydale Press
http://www.derrydalepress.com
Fishing Online
http://www.pvisuals.com/fishing/
online/main.html
The Flyfisher's Classic Library
http://www.ffcl.com
Frank Amato Publications
http://www.amatobooks.com
Globe Pequot Press/The Lyons Press
http://www.globepequot.com
Meadow Run Press
http://www.meadowrunpress.com
The Medlar Press
http://www.medlar.uk.com
Milne Angling Collection
http://www.izaak.unh.edu/milne
Wilderness Adventures
Sporting Books
http://www.wildadv.com

TELEVISION
Addictive Fishing
http://www.addictivefishing.com
Bill Dance Outdoors
http://www.billdanceoutdoors.com
Bill Dance's Fishing Illustrated
http://www.billdancefishing.com

ESPN Outdoors
http://espn.go.com/outdoors
Fins & Skins
http://www.finsandskins.com
Mark Sosin's Saltwater Journal
http://www.marksosin.com
Outdoor Life Network
http://www.olntv.com
The Outdoor Channel
http://www.outdoorchannel.com
Fishing with Shelly and Courtney
http://www.tvfishing.com
Trout Unlimited TV
http://www.tutv.org
Walker's Cay Chronicles
http://www.walkerscay.tv

SOFTWARE
Angler's Assistant
http://home.flash.net/~tvandy
Bassdozer
http://www.bassdozer.com/
bass_software.shtml
CyberAngler
http://www.cyberangler.com/
marketplace/software
Knots and Fishing Knots
http://www.members.aol.com/
idfrank/knots.html
The SuperFly Fishing Machine
http://www.ofifc.org/eli/superfly
UglyBass.com
http://www.uglybass.com/
software.htm
The World of Computer
Fishing Games
http://www.geocities.com/timess
quare/lair/8646
ZDNet
http://www.zdnet.com

Antis
Fishing Hurts.com
http://www.nofishing.net
People for the Ethical Treatment
of Animals
http://www.peta.org

Newspapers

Newspapers.com
http://www.newspapers.com
NewsVoyager
http://www.newspaperlinks.com/
voyager.cfm
SportsPages.com
http://www.sportspages.com

Small Magazines

Art of Angling Journal
http://www.artofangling.com
The Canadian Fly Fisher
http://www.canflyfish.com
The Drake
http://www.drakemag.com
Fish & Fly
http://www.fishandfly
magazine.com
Northwest Fly Fishing
http://www.nwflyfishing.net
Southwest Fly Fishing
http://www.swflyfishing.net
Waterlog
http://www.waterlogmagazine.co.uk
Wild on the Fly
http://www.wildonthefly.com
Yale Anglers' Journal
http://www.yaleanglersjournal.com

Videos

Bennett Marine – Fishing Videos
http://www.bennettmarine.com
Fly Fishing Videos
http://www.flyfishingvideos.com
In-Fisherman
http://www.in-fisherman.com

The Writing Life

Outdoor Writers Association
of America
http://www.owaa.com

CHAPTER 6: GROUPS

WOMEN

Becoming An Outdoors-Woman
(BOW)
http://www.uwsp.edu/cnr/bow

The Blue Quill Angler
http://www.bluequillangler.com
Casting for Recovery
http://www.castingforrecovery.org
ChicksWhoFish
http://www.chickswhofish.com
The Fish Sniffer Online –
Angling Women
http://www.fishsniffer.com/women
Flygirls of Michigan
http://www.flygirls.ws
GORP – Women and Flyfishing
http://www.gorp.com
International Women Fly Fishers
http://www.intlwomenflyfishers.org
"Ladies, Let's Go Fishing!"
http://www.ladiesletsgofishing.com
LandBigFish – The Woman Angler
http://www.landbigfish
.com/women
Ottawa Women Fly Fishers
http://www.owff.org
Reel Women Fly Fishing Adventures
http://www.reel-women.com
The Sportsman's Guide –
Women in the Outdoors
http://www.sportsmansguide.com
Step Outside
http://www.stepoutside.org
Texas Women Fly Fishers
http://www.twff.net
The Ultimate Bass Fishing Resource
Guide – For Her Only
http://www.bassresource.com/
women/women.html
Women's Bass Fishing Association
http://www.wbfatour.com
Women's Fly Fishing
http://www.womensflyfishing.net

KIDS

Adopt-a-Trout
http://www.fwp.state.mt.us/adopt
atrout
BASS CastingKids
http://www.bassmaster.com
Boating Safety Sidekicks
http://www.boatingsafety
sidekicks.com

BoatSafeKids
http://www.boatsafe.com/kids
C.A.S.T. for Kids Foundation
http://www.castforkids.org
Catchfishing.com
http://www.catchfishing.com
Fascinating Facts About Fish
http://www.nefsc.noaa.gov/
faq.html
Fish'n Kids Resources
http://www.fishnkids.com
FishingWorks – Kids Fishing
http://www.fishingworks.com
GORP – Teaching Kids to Fish
http://www.gorp.com
The International Game Fish
Association Junior Angler Club
http://www.igfa.org/jrangler
Kidfish – All About Lakes
and Fly Fishing Too!
http://kidfish.bc.ca
National Fishing Week
http://www.nationalfishingweek.com
Ontario Ministry of Natural Resources
Fish and Wildlife – Take A Kid Fishing
http://www.mnr.gov.on.ca/MNR/
fishing/aa.html
Outdoor Canada – Kids
http://www.ockids.ca
Pennsylvania BASS Federation
http://www.pabass.com
Recreational Boating and Fishing
Foundation (RBFF) Aquatic Science,
Fishing, and Boating Education
Web Directory
http://www.rbff-education.org
The Salmon Challenge
http://dnr.metrokc.gov/wlr/
waterres/salmonch.htm
Salmon & Trout Topics
http://dnr.metrokc.gov/topics/
salmon/SALtopic.htm
StreamNet
http://www.streamnet.org
Take A Kid Fishing
http://www.takeakidfishing.com
Texas Gulf Coast Fishing –
Kids Corner
http://www.texasgulfcoastfishing.
com/kids.htm

U.S. Fish and Wildlife Service –
Student's Page
http://educators.fws.gov/
students.html
Wal-Mart Kids All American
Fishing Derby
http://www.fishingworld.com/
kids-fishing

Programs and Services for Kids
Alabama Division of Wildlife and
Freshwater Fisheries
http://www.dcnr.state.al.us/
agfd/fishsec.html
Future Fisherman Foundation
http://www.futurefisherman.org
Wisconsin Department
of Natural Resources
http://www.dnr.state.wi.us/org/
water/fhp/fish/

PEOPLE WITH DISABILITIES
The British Disabled Angling
Association
http://www.bdaa.co.uk
A Disabled Fisherman
http://www.geocities.com/scosmo451
Fish & Fly
http://www.fishandfly.co.uk/
tledit0700.html
Fishing Has No Boundaries
http://www.fhnbinc.org
NJ Striper – Disabled Fishermen
http://www.njstriper.com
Paralyzed Veterans of America –
National Bass Trail
http://www.pva.org
Project Access
http://www.projectaccess.com

Programs and Services for
People with Disabilities
Active Angler
http://www.activeangler.com/
resources/agencies
Florida Department of
Environmental Protection
http://www.dep.state.fl.us/parks/
information/accessforall.htm

Maryland Department of Natural
Resources'Accessability For All
http://www.dnr.state.md.us/
accessforall
MetaCrawler
http://www.metacrawler.com

Conservation
American Rivers
http://www.americanrivers.org
Atlantic Salmon Federation
http://www.asf.ca
The Billfish Foundation
http://www.billfish.org
Coastal Conservation Association
http://www.joincca.org
Columbia and Snake Rivers Campaign
http://www.wildsalmon.org
Creekbank
http://www.creekbank.com
Freedom to Fish
http://www.freedomtofish.org
The Izaak Walton League of America
http://www.iwla.org
Marine Fish
Conservation Network
http://www.conservefish.org
National Coalition
for Marine Conservation
http://www.savethefish.org
The Recreational Fishing Alliance
http://www.savefish.com
River Network
http://www.rivernetwork.org
Trout Unlimited
http://www.tu.org
U.S. Environmental Protection Agency
– Surf Your Watershed
http://www.epa.gov/surf
Whirling Disease Foundation
http://www.whirling-disease.org
The Wild Salmon Center
http://www.wildsalmoncenter.org
The Wild Trout Trust
http://www.wildtrout.org

Clubs
American Casting Association
http://www.americancasting
assoc.org

BASS Federation
http://www.bassmaster.com
The International Casting Federation
http://www.castingsport.com
Federation of Fly Fishers
http://www.fedflyfishers.org
FishingWorks
http://www.fishingworks.com
Flycaster.com
http://www.flycaster.com
Great Lakes Sport Fishing Council
http://www.great-lakes.org/
profiles.html
Lake Internet – Bass Clubs Online
http://www.blacklakeny.com/links/
linksclubs.html
Muskies Inc.
http://www.muskiesinc.com
The Smallmouth Alliance
http://www.smallmouth.org

Other Club Options
Bassdozer
http://www.bassdozer.com
ProBass
http://www.probass.com
The Ultimate Bass Fishing Resource
Guide
http://www.bassresource.com
Walleye Central
http://www.walleyecentral.com
Walleyes Inc.
http://www.walleyesinc.com

Virtual Fishing Clubs
Groups@AOL
http://groups.aol.com
MSN – Fishing Groups
http://groups.msn.com
Yahoo! Fishing Groups
http://www.groups.yahoo.com

CHAPTER 7: TACKLE AND BOATS

Tackle
Tackle Making
Bamboo Rodmaking Tips
http://www.bamboorodmaking.com

Custom Rod Builders Guild
http://www.rodguild.com
Fly Anglers Online
http://www.flyanglersonline.com
Frank's Personal Waste of Time
http://www.fneunemann.com
Global FlyFisher
http://www.globalflyfisher.com
Lurebuilding 101
http://www.lurebuilding.nl/
indexeng.html
LureMaking.com
http://www.luremaking.com
Luresonline
http://www.luresonline.com.au
Over My Waders
http://www.overmywaders.com
RodBuilding.org
http://www.rodbuilding.org
Rodmakers
http://www.canerod.com/
rodmakers
TackleMaking
http://www.tacklemaking.com
TackleWorks
http://www.tackleworks.org
Thomas Penrose's Bamboo Fly
Rod Pages
http://www.thomaspenrose.com/
bamboo.htm
The Ultimate Bamboo Fly Rod Library
http://www.wohlfordrods.com

BaitNet.com
http://www.baitnet.com

Collecting
Antique and Classic Fishing Reels
http://www.antiquefishingreels.com
Antique Lure Collectibles
http://www.antiquelure
collectibles.com
Antique Reels
http://www.antiquereels.com
AntiqueLures
http://www.antiquelures.com
The Creek Chub Bait Co. Surfster
Experience
http://home.si.rr.com/ccbcosurfster

Joe's Old Lures
http://www.joeyates.com
Lure Lore
http://www.lurelore.com
Mr. Lure Box
http://www.mrlurebox.com
The National Fishing Lure
Collectors Club
http://www.nflcc.com
Old Fishing Stuff
http://www.oldfishingstuff.com
Old Reels.com
http://www.oldreels.com
Richard's Classic Bamboo Fishing
Rods, Antique Tackle and Vintage Reels
http://www.antiquetackle.net
The Sport Fishing Museum
http://www.sportfishingmuseum.ca

The Split-Cane Sucker Connection
Center Pin Fishing Reels
http://www.center-pin-fishing-
reels.com
Classic Cane
http://www.interalpha.net/
customer/cane-rods
The Edward Barder Rod Company
http://www.barder-rod.co.uk
Norman Agutters Online
http://www.norman-agutters.com
Traditional Angling
http://www.traditional
angling.co.uk

Tackle Reviews
OutdoorREVIEW.com – Flyfishing
http://www.outdoorreview.com
Tackle Tour
http://www.tackletour.com

FISHING FOR BARGAINS ON THE WEB
Shopping Sites
Academy
http://www.academy.com
AOL Shopping
http://www.shop.aol.com
Bass Pro Shops
http://www.bassproshops.com

Big Fish Tackle
http://www.bigfishtackle.com
BizRate
http://www.bizrate.com
BoatersWorld
http://www.boatersworld.com
Bob Marriot's Flyfishing Store
http://www.bobmarriotts.com
Cabela's
http://www.cabelas.com
Dealitup.com
http://www.dealitup.com
Dick's Sporting Goods
http://www.dickssportinggoods.com
eAngler
http://www.eangler.com
eBay
http://www.ebay.com
eDealFinder.com
http://www.edealfinder.com
FishingWorks
http://www.fishingworks.com
G.I. Joes
http://www.gijoes.com
Google – Froogle and Catalogs
http://froogle.google.com
http://catalogs.google.com
LandBigFish
http://www.landbigfish.com
Oshmans
http://www.oshmans.com
Overstock.com
http://www.overstock.com
Shopping.com
http://www.shopping.com
Sportfish (UK)
http://www.sportfish.co.uk
The Sports Authority
http://www.sportsauthority.com
The Sportsman's Guide
http://www.sportsmansguide.com
TackleDirect
http://www.tackledirect.com
Wal-Mart
http://www.walmart.com
Worldwaters.com
http://www.worldwaters.com
Yahoo! Auctions
http://www.auctions.yahoo.com
Yahoo! Shopping
http://www.shopping.yahoo.comm

Forums and Information
AllCoast Sport Fishing
http://www.sport-fish-info.com
AntiqueLures
http://www.antiquelures.com
Bass Fishing Home Page
http://www.bassfishinghome
page.com
Fly Anglers Online
http://www.flyanglersonline.com
Fly Fisherman
http://www.flyfisherman.com
Noreast.com
http://www.noreast.com
ProBass
http://www.probass.com
Old Fishing Stuff
http://www.oldfishingstuff.com
The Steelhead Site
http://www.steelheadsite.com
The Ultimate Bass Fishing Resource
Guide
http://www.bassresource.com

Photography
Fly Anglers Online
http://www.flyanglersonline.com
Fodors – Focus on Photography
http://www.fodors.com/focus
Global FlyFisher
http://www.globalflyfisher.com
Outdoor Photographer
http://www.outdoorphotographer
.com
Sport Fishing
http://www.sportfishingmag.com

BOATS
AllKayakFishing.com
http://www.allkayakfishing.com
American Boating Association
http://www.americanboating.org
American Canoe Association
http://www.acanet.org
Bass & Walleye Boats Magazine
http://www.bassandwalleye
boats.com
Bass Fishing Network
http://www.bassfishingnetwork.com
BassBoat Central
http://www.bassboatcentral.com

Boat Trader Online
http://www.boattrader.com
Boats.com
http://www.boats.com
Boat Ed
http://www.boat-ed.com
BoatersDream
http://www.boatersdream.com
BoatTEST.com
http://www.boattest.com
BoatU.S.
http://www.boatus.com
Canoe and Kayak Magazine
http://www.canoekayak.com
Coastal Kayak Fishing
http://www.kayakfishing.com
Discover Boating
http://www.discoverboating.com
Duckworks Magazine
http://www.duckworks
magazine.com
iboats
http://www.iboats.com
John's Nautical and Boatbuilding Page
http://www.boat-links.com
Kayak Fishing Secrets
http://www.rbbsurf.com
Kayak Sportfishing
http://www.kayaksportfishing.com
NADA Guides
http://www.nadaguides.com
Ottertooth
http://www.ottertooth.com
Paddle-Fishing.com
http://www.paddle-fishing.com
Paddler
http://www.paddlermagazine.com
Recreational Boating and Fishing
Foundation (RBFF) – Aquatic Science,
Fishing, and Boating Education Web
Directory
http://www.rbff-education.org
Trailer Boats Magazine
http://www.trailerboats.com
United States Coast Guard
http://www.uscg.mil/uscg.shtm
Water Works Wonders – Boating
http://www.waterworks
wonders.org

WaterTribe
http://www.watertribe.com

Boating Magazines
Boating Life
http://www.boatinglifemag.com
Boating World
http://www.boatingworld
online.com
Go Boating America
http://www.goboatingamerica.com
Motor Boating
http://www.motorboating.com

Fishing Magazines
AnglerWorld.com
http://www.anglerworld.com
Fly Anglers Online
http://www.flyanglersonline.com
Fly Fishing in Saltwaters
http://www.flyfishinsalt.com
Florida Sportsman Online
http://www.floridasportsman.com
LandBigFish
http://www.landbigfish.com/
boating
Marlin
http://www.marlinmag.com
Salt Water Sportsman
http://www.saltwater
sportsman.com
Sport Fishing
http://www.sportfishingmag.com

CHAPTER 8:
INTERNATIONAL

AUSTRALIA AND NEW ZEALAND
Australia
AusFish.com
http://www.ausfish.com.au
Australian Bureau of Meteorology
http://www.bom.gov.au
Australian Fishing Network
http://www.afn.com.au
Blueholes
http://members.iinet.net.au/~net
nem/blue

Canberra Sweetwater Angler
http://canberrasweetwater
angler.com
Coarse Angling in Australia
http://www.coarsefishing.ws
FishEP.com
http://www.fishep.com
Fishing Cairns
http://www.fishingcairns.com.au
Fishing Monthly
http://www.fishingmonthly.com.au
Fishing Noosa
http://www.fishingnoosa.com.au
Fishing the Territory
http://www.fishingtheterritory
.com.au
Fishing Western Australia
http://www.fishingwa.com
Fishnet
http://www.fishnet.com.au
FishnTales.com
http://www.fishntales.com
FishOnline
http://www.fishonline.tas.gov.au
FishRaider.com
http://www.fishraider.com
FishSA.com
http://www.fishsa.com
FishVictoria.com
http://www.fishvictoria.com
The FlyFlickers
http://www.flyflickers.com
FlyLife Online
http://www.flylife.com.au
Harro On Line
http://www.harro.com.au
Marinews
http://www.marinews.com
Native Fish Australia
http://www.nativefish.asn.au
North Australian Fish Finder
http://www.fishfinderbooks.com
RecFish Australia
http://www.recfishoz.com
Rex's Home Page
http://www.rexhunt.com.au
Sportsfish Australia
http://www.sportsfishaustralia
.com.au

Tide Predictions for Australia
and the Pacific
http://www.ntf.flinders.edu
.au/TEXT/TIDES/tides.html
Trout Guides and Lodges, Tasmania
http://www.troutguidestasmania
.com.au
Western Angler
http://www.westernangler.com

Government Fisheries Agencies
Government of South Australia
Primary Industries and Resources –
Fisheries & Aquaculture
http://www.pir.sa.gov.au
Government of Western Australia
Department of Fisheries
http://www.fish.wa.gov.au
New South Wales Fisheries
http://www.fisheries.nsw.gov.au
State of Queensland Department of
Primary Industries and Resources –
Fishweb
http://www.dpi.qld.gov.au/fishweb
State of Victoria Department of
Sustainability and Environment
http://www.dse.vic.gov.au

New Zealand
Fish & Game New Zealand
http://www.fishandgame.org.nz
Fish with Bish in New Zealand
http://www.bishfish.co.nz
Fishing.net.nz
http://www.fishing.net.nz
Fishnz.co.nz
http://www.fishnz.co.nz
Frontier Fishing Gazette
http://www.frontierfishing.co.nz
New Zealand Professional Fishing
Guides Association
http://www.nzpfga.com
Paul's Fishing Kites
http://www.fishingkites.co.nz
Trout Fishing New Zealand
http://www.trout-fishing-new-
zealand.com

BRITAIN

England

Anglers' Net
http://www.anglersnet.co.uk

Barbel Fishing World
http://www.barbel.co.uk

Bass Anglers' Sportfishing Society
http://www.ukbass.com

Carp.com
http://www.carp.com

Carpfishing.UK
http://www.carp-uk.net

The British Conger Club
http://www.congerclub.org

Diptera.co.uk
http://www.diptera.co.uk

Fish & Fly
http://www.fishandfly.co.uk

Fishing.co.uk
http://www.fishing.co.uk

Fishing4Fun.co.uk
http://www.fishing4fun.co.uk

FISHINGmagic
http://www.fishingmagic.com

FishingWarehouse.co.uk
http://www.fishingwarehouse.co.uk

Fly Fishing for Trout and Salmon
http://www.cse.bris.ac.uk/~cckhrb/
kb_fish.html

Fly Tying and Fly Fishing for Trout –
The UK's Premier Guide
http://homepages.enterprise.net/
davefink/index1.html

Go-Fishing.co.uk
http://www.go-fishing.co.uk

Harris Angling
http://www.harrisangling.com

Hooklinks
http://www.hooklinks.net

Lure Fishing UK
http://www.lurefishinguk.com

MaggotDrowning.com
http://www.maggotdrowning.com

Pike Anglers' Club of Great Britain
http://www.pacgb.com

Pike OnLine
http://www.hooklinks.co.uk/pike

Predator Publications
http://www.pikeandpredators
magazine.com

Predator-Fishing.co.uk
http://www.predator-fishing.co.uk

TalkAngling
http://www.talkangling.co.uk

Where To Fish
http://www.where-to-fish.com

World Sea Fishing
http://www.worldseafishing.com

Coarse Fishing

Coarse Fisherman
http://www.coarse-fisherman.co.uk

Coarse Fishing UK
http://www.coarse-fishing.org.uk

Floats Gone
http://www.floatsgone.btinternet.co.uk

Ireland

Central Fisheries Board
http://www.cfb.ie

Irish Tourist Board
http://www.ireland.travel.ie/
accommodation

The Great Fishing Houses of Ireland
http://www.irelandflyfishing.com

Shannon Regional Fisheries Board
http://www.shannon-fishery-
board.ie

Shore Angling & Charter/Private Boat
Fishing in Ireland
http://www.sea-angling-ireland.org

Tuna Charters Ireland
http://www.tunacharters.ie

Scotland

Caithness and Sutherland Trout
Angling Group
http://www.fishing-highland.co.uk

Fishing in Scotland
http://www.fishing-uk-scotland.com

Fishing the Fly in Aberdeenshire
http://www.fishingthefly.co.uk

Flyfish-Scotland.com
http://www.flyfish-scotland.com

Highland Wild Trout Angling
http://www.wildtroutfisher.co.uk

Letsflyfish
http://www.letsflyfish.com

Speyaster.net
http://www.speycaster.net

Wales
Fishing in Kite Country
http://www.fishing-in-kite-country.co.uk
Fishing in Wales
http://www.fishing-in-wales.com
OgmoreRiver.com
http://www.ogmoreriver.com
Simple Flies for Simple Sewin
http://www.simple-flies-for-simple.fishermen.co.uk

CANADA
Angling BC
http://www.anglingbc.com
Atlantic Salmon Sportfishing
http://members.attcanada.ca/~salmon
Bass Canada
http://www.basscanada.com
BC Adventure – Fish BC
http://www.bcadventure.com
BC Fishing Reports
http://www.bcfishingreports.com
Bob Izumi's Real Fishing
http://www.realfishing.com
Bob's Gone Fishin'
http://www3.sympatico.ca/rlundy
Credit River Anglers Association
http://www.craa.on.ca
Fish Ontario!
http://www.fishontario.com
The Fishing News
http://www.thefishingnews.com
Fishing with Rod
http://www.fishingwithrod.com
FloatFishing.net
http://www.floatfishing.net
Fly Fishing Alberta's Chinook Country
http://www.telusplanet.net/public/cnangler/html
Go Walleye!
http://www.gowalleye.com
HipWader.com
http://www.hipwader.com
Inconnu Lodge
http://www.inconnulodge.com
Newfoundland & Labrador Tourism – Hunting & Fishing
http://www.gov.nf.ca/tourism/welcome

Northern Ontario Tourist Outfitters Association
http://www.noto.net
Nova Scotia Fly Fishing, Tying, and Tall Tales
http://users.eastlink.ca/~dryfly/index.html
Nova Scotia Salmon Association
http://www.novascotiasalmon.ns.ca
Ontario Fishing Net
http://www.ontariofishing.net
Saskatchewan – Fishing & Hunting
http://www.se.gov.sk.ca/fishwild
Sport Fishing BC
http://www.sportfishingbc.com
Sport Fishing Canada
http://www.sportfishingcanada.ca
Tincup Wilderness Lodge
http://www.tincup-lodge.com
Travel Manitoba Hunting and Fishing
http://www.travelmanitoba.com/huntfish
What's Bitin' in the Toronto Area
http://zebra.zoo.utoronto.ca/cgi-bin/FBoard/ikonboard.cgi
Wolfheart's Fishing Page
http://www.sportfisherman.net
YukonFishing.com
http://www.yukonfishing.com

EUROPE
Angling Club Lax-a
http://www.lax-a.is
CyberTrout.com
http://www.cybertrout.com
Fishing Denmark
http://www.globalflyfisher.com/global/denmark
Fishing in Finland
http://www.fishingfinland.com
Flugfiskesidan Online
http://www.flugfiskesidan.com
Fly Fishing in Bavaria
http://www.users.odn.de/~odn03061/index.htm
Medflyfish
http://www.medflyfish.com
Monster Carps
http://members.rott.chello.nl/tmarapengopie/wereldrecord.htm

The Norwegian Flyshop
http://www.flyshop.no
Rackelhanen FlyFishing Magazine
http://www.rackelhanen.se/eng

Mon poisson est plus grand que vos poisson

AltaVista's Babel Fish Translation
http://world.altavista.com
Fliegenfischer-forum
http://www.fliegenfischer-forum.de
Pescare Online
http://www.pescareonline.it
Pêcheur.com
http://www.pecheur.com

South Africa
The African Angler
http://www.african-angler.co.uk
African Angling Consultants
http://www.africanfishing.com
Fishing Owl's World
http://www.fishingowl.co.za
FlyGuide.co.za
http://www.flyguide.co.za
OutdoorPAGES
http://www.outdoorpages.co.za
theflyguide.com
http://www.theflyguide.com

Here and There
Baja, Mexico
Baja Anglers
http://www.baja-anglers.com
The Baja Big Fish Company
http://www.bajabigfish.com
Baja Destinations
http://www.bajadestinations.com
Baja on the Fly
http://www.bajafly.com

Other Sites
Anglerstown.com
http://www.anglerstown.com
Chris and Jeff's Malaysian Angler's
Website
http://www.geocities.com/
yosemite/3133
Fishing on Ambergris Caye
http://www.ambergriscaye.com/
pages/town/fishing.html

Ken's Fishing Haven
http://home.pacific.net.sg/~kcsk
Korean Fly-Fishing
http://www.koreanflyfishing.com
Lure Fishing in Japan Illustrated
http://www002.upp.so-net.ne
.jp/Ham
Pescamazon
http://www.pescamazon.com
Sport Fishing in Niigata City and Japan
http://www.japan-fishing.com
Tsuribaka Fishing Ltd
http://www.tsuribaka.com/
jp/fishing
Trouts and Seasons
of the Mountain Village
http://www.itow.com/amago/
index2.html

Peacock Bass
Florida Freshwater Fisheries
http://www.floridafisheries.com/
docum/butterfly.html
Larsen's Outdoor Publishing
http://www.larsenoutdoors.com
Peacock Bass Association
http://www.peacockbassassociation
.com
PeacockBassOnline.com
http://www.peacockbassonline.com
TFW's Peacock Bass Book
http://www.fishingworld.com
.br/pbb/

Fishing Travel Companies
Acute Angling
http://www.acuteangling.com
Angling Destinations
http://www.anglingdestinations
.com
Angling in Spain
http://www.angling-in-spain.com
B & B Worldwide Fishing Adventures
http://www.wheretofish.com
Bass Fishing Mexico
http://www.bassfishingmexico.com
The Best of New Zealand Fly Fishing
http://www.bestofnzflyfishing.com
Canadian Carp Club
http://www.canadiancarpclub.on.ca

Canadian Carpin'
http://www.canadiancarpin.com
Carpentaria Seafaris
http://www.seafaris.com.au
The Complete Angler
http://www.carp.org
Ebro Angling and River-Guiding
http://www.eaar.co.uk
Fishing Adventures Thailand
http://www.anglingthailand.com
Fishing International
http://www.fishinginternational
.com
FishQuest!
http://www.fishquest.com
The Fly Shop
http://www.flyfishingtravel.com
Frontiers
http://www.frontierstrvl.com
GourmetFly
http://www.gourmetfly.com
Kaufmann's Streamborn
http://www.kman.com
Orvis
http://www.orvis.com/travel
PanAngling
http://www.panangling.com
Rod and Reel Adventures
http://www.rodreeladventures.com

Roxton Bailey Robinson Worldwide
http://www.rbrww.com
South America for Visitors
http://www.gosouthamerica
.about.com/cs/fishsouthamerica
Sportfishing Worldwide
http://www.sportfishingworldwide
.com
Sweetwater Travel Company
http://www.sweetwatertravel.com
Terry Hollan's Reel Mexican Adventures
http://www.mexicanadventures
.com
Westbank Anglers
http://www.westbank.com

Coarse Fellows
Angling Travel
http://www.angling-travel.com
Anglers World Holidays
http://www.anglers-world.co.uk
Oanda.com
http://www.oanda.com/converter/
classic

Travel Insurance
Insure My Trip
http://www.insuremytrip.com
Travelex Insurance
http://www.travelex-insurance.com

Index

Index

Index